4/21

The**Green**Guide
Tuscany

© jenifoto/iStock

D0768013

The Green Guide **TUSCANY**

Editorial Director	Cynthia Clayton Ochterbeck
Editor	Sophie Friedman
Updating and Layout	Malerba Editorial & Partners, Milan Francesca Malerba, Laura Magda Barazza, Raffaella Esposito
Contributing Writers	Judy Edelhoff, Martha Burley
Production Manager	Natasha George
Cartography	Peter Wrenn
Interior Design	Chris Bell
Layout	Natasha George

Contact Us	Michelin Travel and Lifestyle North America One Parkway South Greenville, SC 29615 USA travel.lifestyle@us.michelin.com
	Michelin Travel Partner Hannay House 39 Clarendon Road Watford, Herts WD17 1JA UK ✆01923 205240 travelpubsales@uk.michelin.com www.viamichelin.co.uk
Special Sales	For information regarding bulk sales, customized editions and premium sales, please contact us at: travel.lifestyle@us.michelin.com

HOW TO USE THIS GUIDE

PLANNING YOUR TRIP

The blue-tabbed PLANNING YOUR TRIP section at the front of the guide gives you **ideas for your trip** and **practical information** to help you organise it. You'll find tours, practical information, a host of outdoor activities, a calendar of events, information on shopping, sightseeing, kids' activities and more.

INTRODUCTION

The orange-tabbed INTRODUCTION explores Tuscany's **Nature** and geology. The **History** section spans from the Etruscans to the modern day. The **Art and Culture** section covers architecture, art, literature and music, while the **Region Today** delves into modern Tuscany.

DISCOVERING

The green-tabbed DISCOVERING section features Principal Sights by region, featuring the most interesting local **Sights**, **Walking Tours**, nearby **Excursions**, and detailed **Driving Tours**. Admission prices shown are normally for a single adult.

ADDRESSES

We've selected the best hotels, restaurants, cafes shops, nightlife and entertainment to fit all budgets. See the Legend on the cover flap for an explanation of the price categories. See the back of the guide for an index of where to find hotel and restaurant listings

Sidebars

Throughout the guide you will find blue, peach and green-colored text boxes with lively anecdotes, detailed history and background information.

A Bit of Advice 😊

Green advice boxes found in this guide contain practical tips and handy information relevant to your visit or a sight in the Discovering section.

STAR RATINGS★★★

Michelin has given star ratings for more than 100 years. If you're pressed for time, we recommend you visit the ★★★, or ★★ sights first:

★★★   **Worth a special journey**
★★   **Worth a detour**
★   **Interesting**

MAPS

😊   Principal Sights map.
😊   Region maps.
😊   Maps for major cities and villages.
😊   Local tour maps.

All maps in this guide are oriented north, unless otherwise indicated by a directional arrow. The term "Local Map" refers to a map within the chapter or Tourism Region. A complete list of the maps found in the guide appears at the back of this book.

© ViktorCap/iStock

© J. Arnold Images/hemis.fr

PLANNING YOUR TRIP

INTRODUCTION TO TUSCANY

CONTENTS

© StevanZZ/iStock

DISCOVERING TUSCANY

Welcome to Tuscany

With its hilly countryside and high concentration of art, Tuscany is a region that inspires awe at every turn. Alpine peaks in the north feed rich river valleys where rows of vines and grains and pockets of olive trees add texture and order to the land. Tuscany's extensive coastline features major ports, idyllic beach coves and several islands. Meanwhile, breathtakingly beautiful cities – such as Renaissance Florence and medieval Siena – combine with bucolic villages to make Tuscany one of Italy's most appealing destinations.

FLORENCE *(pp92–184)*

Cradle of the Renaissance and former headquarters of one of Italy's most powerful families – the Medici – Florence is the capital of the region. Within its city limits are majestic buildings (Santa Maria del Fiore cathedral); troves of artistic treasures, both in the Uffizi Gallery and modest churches; vibrant markets and grand public squares. It merits a visit in one's lifetime.

San Michele in Foro, Lucca

© O. Forir/Michelin

Mosaics, Battistero, Florence

© Y. Kanazawa/Michelin

AROUND FLORENCE *(pp185–216)*

Outside the busy centre of Florence, Renaissance artists and architects graced the landscape with beautiful art and buildings. The Medici villas, the Valombrosa Abbey, natural hot springs and the town of Fiesole are all situated in the rolling pastoral countryside. The area is also one of central Italy's major manufacturing areas and this is evidenced in Pistoia, a highly industrial town with a breathtaking medieval square. Take a measure of the land with a break from the sightseeing dash.

LUCCA, THE VERSILIA AND THE ALPI APUANE *(pp217–242)*

Enveloped by 16C walls, pretty Lucca boasts a pedestrian-friendly centre, unique religious architecture and the boyhood home of composer Giacomo Puccini. The town lies at the threshold of northern Tuscany, known for its Garfagnana woodlands and the Alpi Apuane, where marble, especially at Carrara, has been quarried since Roman times. The gently rolling hills give way to a lush coastal plain at Le Versilia, dominated by a backdrop of the Alps.

PISA, ETRUSCAN COAST AND METALLIFEROUS HILLS
(pp243–286)

The marvel that is the Leaning Tower makes up one piece of the Campo dei Miracoli, the "miraculous" set of religious buildings that is the centrepiece of Pisa. Lesser-known treasures abound in both the city and the surrounding area; from the "Venetian" canals in Livorno,

Campo dei Miracoli, Pisa

© RomanBabakin/iStock

to a coastal wildlife refuge on the Etruscan coastline. The ports and villages along the shore have their own personalities, ranging from stylish beach resorts at Forte dei Marmi and Punta Ala to historic stretches along the Riviera degli Etruschi. The Tuscan Archipelago, which includes Elba, popular for its natural vistas as well as its historical link to Napoleon, makes up another 200km/124mi of coast. South of San Gimignano, verdant pastures devolve into mineral-rich mining territory, an area known as the Metalliferous Hills.

THE MAREMMA *(pp287–302)*

Etruscan ruins at Murlo, medieval fortifications in Montalcino and Renaissance perfection in Pienza speak of the long history of civilisations in the land south of Siena. Yet nature rules much of southern Tuscany, with the vast Maremma plain covering a wide swath that includes diverse flora and fauna and endless farmland.

SIENA AND CHIANTI
(pp303–361)

The heart of Humanist Tuscany lies in Siena, where the cityscape is little changed since medieval times. The compact centre consists of the elegant Palazzo Pubblico and the Piazza del Campo, site of the twice-yearly Palio horse race, a spectacle that breeds civic pride and attracts tourists in the thousands. An art city, Siena's Cathedral Precinct includes the Duomo, with its beautiful marble pavements, and multiple galleries showcasing early Sienese painting.

The fertile subregion between Florence and Siena is the Chianti, which attracts visitors not only for its proximity to the famous cities, but for its eponymous wine, farmhouse inns and vivid green and blonde landscapes. San Gimignano, at once charming and austere, is a medieval "mini Manhattan" and lies in the rolling hills west of Chianti.

AREZZO AND CASENTINO
(pp362–385)

An illustrious artistic centre as early as Etruscan times, Arezzo is known primarily as the home of Piero della Francesca's astounding "Legend of the True Cross" fresco cycle, which is located in San Francesco church. Recently, Arezzo's fame has been eclipsed by Cortona, a lovely hilltown inhabited by numerous expats from Britain and North America. Beyond Arezzo lies the Casentino Forest, a quiet corner long favoured by the pious, including Saint Francis.

Piazza Grande, Arezzo

© FCerez/iStock

Aerial view of San Gimignano
© ViktorCap/iStock

PLANNING YOUR TRIP

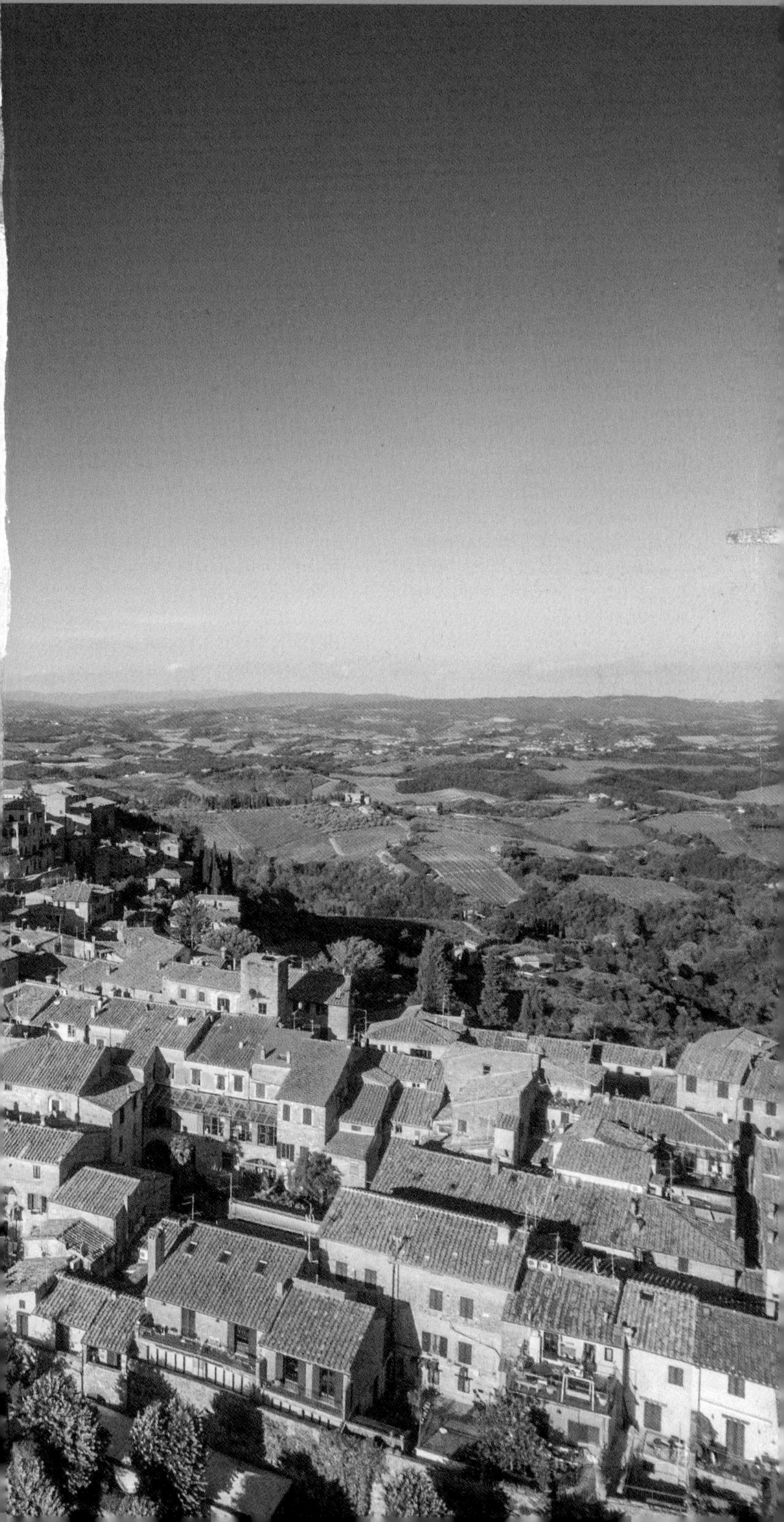

Michelin Driving Tours

1 THE GREAT CITIES

This itinerary takes in the major artistic centres of Tuscany, starting with **Florence**, where at least four days should be allowed to take in the sights. The Duomo, San Marco, the Palazzo Vecchio, the Uffizi, the Accademia, the Bargello, the Galleria Palatina in the Palazzo Pitti, the Boboli Gardens, the Cappelle Mediciee in the Church of San Lorenzo and the view from Piazzale Michelangelo are particularly noteworthy.

Heading towards the coast, the old centres of **Prato** and **Pistoia** merit a stop, prior to visiting **Lucca** with its fine city walls, and of course **Pisa** for the unforgettable sight of the Campo dei Miracoli.

Turning back inland, the itinerary leads to the heartland of Tuscany and **San Gimignano**, famous for its many tower-houses. Moving on, the next stop is **Siena**, pausing at **Monteriggioni**, as mentioned by Dante in the *Divine Comedy*. Return to Florence through the **Chianti** district.

2 ART AND NATURE AROUND THE MARBLE MOUNTAINS

The **Lunigiana** is celebrated for its castles and and Etruscan artefacts. Its rugged valleys open out as they drop down to the coast and the district of **Versilia**, dominated by the marble mountains that rise behind it. The route continues towards **Pisa** and then **Lucca**, from where the **Garfagnana**, on the threshold of the **Parco delle Alpi Apuane**, is readily accessible. The famous Devil's Bridge at **Borgo a Mozzano** is built of legend; continue to head north to return to the Lunigiana.

3 NORTH OF FLORENCE

This route covers the Apennine mountains on Tuscany's border with Emilia. Starting from **Florence**, the first stop is **Fiesole**, a favourite location for Renaissance artists and modern-day travellers alike. The route then enters the uplands of the **Mugello** district, once the favoured rural retreat of the Florentine merchant classes. Returning towards Florence the itinerary takes in the **Villa Demidoff**, where Giambologna's huge statue, the *Appennino*, may be seen in the gardens.

4 NATURE AND RELIGION: CASENTINO, PRATOMAGNO

From **Arezzo**, the itinerary heads into the district of the Casentino, its mountain seclusion long favoured by monks and hermits. In **La Verna**, St Francis spent time in retreat with his followers, and at **Camaldoli**, a Benedictine community and monasticism still exist.

Heading towards **Poppi**, a small detour leads to the charming church at **Romena**. From **Poppi**, its castle visible from some distance, the route takes in **San Giovanni Valdarno** and **Gropina**, concluding a tour through some of Tuscany's most ruggedly beautiful landscapes, where spiritual devotion and fine craftsmen still occupy the landscape.

5 UPPER TIBER VALLEY TO THE CHIANA VALLEY

This route begins in **Arezzo** before proceeding to **Sansepolcro**, birthplace of Piero della Francesca. Following the border with Umbria leads you to **Monterchi** and Piero della Francesca's enigmatic **Madonna del Parto**. The final stop is trendy **Cortona**, perched on a hill and offering fine views of the Chiana Valley and Lake Trasimeno.

A little to the south is the **Abbazia di Farneta** on the way to **Chiusi** and then on to **Chianciano Terme** and **Montepulciano**, a panoramic wine hill overlooking the countryside. Return to Arezzo along the Chiana Valley.

Pieve di San Pietro di Romena near Poppi

© F. Tomasinelli/AGF Foto/Photononstop

6 SIENA AND ITS LANDSCAPE

Situated in the heart of Tuscany, **Siena** is a masterpiece in its own right with a history of splendour and bloodshed.

From Siena step back further in time in **Murlo** with its Etruscan heritage, before reaching the medieval town of **Montalcino** and the nearby **Abbazia di S Antimo**. The route then follows the **Val d'Orcia**, and the path of the Via Francigena, to reach **Pienza**, the planned "Ideal City of the Renaissance".

Continue to **Montepulciano** (*See TOUR 5*), taste wine and visit the Benedictine abbey of **Monte Oliveto Maggiore**. Then on to **Asciano**, before returning to Siena.

7 METALLIFEROUS HILLS TO THE ISLE OF ELBA

Discover beautiful contrasts of scenery, from classic Tuscan rolling hills to the lunar landscape of the Metalliferous Hills, and fine coast. Leaving **San Gimignano**, the route takes in **Volterra**, famous for its alabaster, and **Larderello**, where sulphur rises from the underworld and the roadside becomes lined by huge pipes and tubes.

Towards the sea through countryside rich in Etruscan remains, join the coast at **Piombino**, the port of embarkation for the **Isola d'Elba**. Return to the mainland, then proceed to **Massa Marittima**, which despite its name, sits on a hill. The town has a fine Romanesque cathedral. The SP441 then leads to **San Galgano** with its delightful ruined abbey. The last leg of the trip takes in the fortified town of **Colle Alta Val d'Elsa** prior to returning to San Gimignano.

8 SOUTHERN TUSCANY

The **Maremma** district borders Lazio and is a rugged and unspoiled land famed for its *butteri* (cowboys). Along the coast are **Punta Ala**, **Castiglione della Pescaia** and the **Argentario**, with **Monte Amiata** rising behind. Lovers of archaeology will enjoy visiting **Vetulonia**, **Roselle**, **Ansedonia** (formerly Cosa), **Sovana** and the Archaeological Museum at **Grosseto**. The tufa valleys nearby host the towns of **Pitigliano** and **Sorano**, seemingly untouched by the passage of time; finally the chic ancient spa of **Saturnia** is the ideal place to restore mind and body.

When and Where to Go

WHEN TO GO

Tuscany is beautiful whatever the season, but spring brings flowers and autumn the harvest. March to June sees temperatures ranging from lows of 9°C (49°F) to highs of 19°C (67°F). The mild weather is ideal for touring, as well as more vigorous activities like biking and trekking. These are peak seasons in Florence and Siena, but avoid the mass tourism and hot humidity of high summer. Late June days can be glorious, with lows at 15°C (58°F) and highs at 26°C (78°F). In summer many towns and villages stage festivals, fairs, concerts and other traditions.

Autumn, which enjoys mild temperatures well into late October, brings fewer tourists than summer. The harvest season is joyous, celebrating wine, olive oil and the return of truffles and mushrooms. Winter is Tuscany's quiet time. The weather is unpredictable and many country lodgings close during the colder months. But the landscapes are revealed among the trees, crowds are absent from the art cities, crisp weather beckons for hearty Tuscan food and travel discounts abound.

WHERE TO GO
SHORT BREAKS
Florence, Siena and the Chianti

First-time travellers to Tuscany who wish to combine an art itinerary with fresh air should stay in Florence and Siena, leaving time for a tour of the Chianti countryside. In Florence, visitors should not miss the **Galleria degli Uffizi**, which requires almost a full day to appreciate its artistic treasures. Michelangelo's *David* in the **Accademia** is another must-see and, of course, a visit to **Santa Maria del Fiore** and the **Piazza della Signoria** is essential.

Siena merits a dedicated visit. Famed for the **Palio** horse race, this towered city shows off the heart of medieval Tuscany, retaining its traditions and civic pride. A stroll around the shell-shaped **Piazza del Campo** and tour of the city's Duomo with its exquisite **pavements** welcomes the traveller back in time.

Embracing these two art cities is the **Chianti** countryside, lined with vineyards and olive groves, an ideal getaway for nature lovers and gastronomes. From Florence and Siena's major sights, follow with a day trip or stay in Chianti. From Florence, the road to Chianti passes through **Badia a Passignano**, **Castellina in Chianti** and **Greve in Chianti**, which

Siena

© jenifoto/iStock

Abbazia di Sant'Antimo, Val d'Orcia

is dotted with farms, wineries and castles. From Siena, the route passes through **Radda in Chianti**, **Badia Coltibuono** and **Brolio** (♿*See CHIANTI*).

Spiritual Tuscany

The itinerary starts high in the Casentino forest, at the **monastery** and **hermitage** of Camaldoli. Slightly to the south is the Santuario della **Verna**, where St Francis received the stigmata.

Continuing south to Arezzo and the Chiana Valley, is the **Abbazia di Farneta**, a charming Romanesque church where major archaeological work took place in the 20C. Heading towards Siena, the route passes the **Abbazia di Monte Oliveto Maggiore**, the mother-house of the Olivetian order, with fine frescoes by Luca Signorelli (1498) and Sodoma (1505–08) chronicling the life of St Benedict. 30km/19mi south of Siena are the striking ruins of the **Abbazia di S Galgano**, the earliest Gothic church in Tuscany.

Close to Montalcino, the delightful **Abbazia di Sant'Antimo** stands in a quintessentially beautiful Tuscan landscape. Linger to hear the Gregorian chant within this most elegant and harmonious interior, then taste Brunello in Montalcino.

Florence's "Minor Sights" and Lucchesia's Villas

Any attempt to tackle the Uffizi in limited time can never do justice to the great masterpieces it displays. This itinerary offers an alternative for those already familiar with the major monuments of Florence, focusing instead on some of the smaller jewels which the city has to offer.

Close to Piazza della Signoria is the **Oratorio dei Buonomini**, bedecked in frescoes by the studio of Ghirlandaio. Not far from the Duomo, the **Palazzo Medici Riccardi** also has fine frescoes by Benozzo Gozzoli. The **Opificio delle Pietre Dure** near Via Alfani houses a rich collection of intricately carved precious stones. On the other side of the Arno, the church of S Maria del Carmine includes the **Cappella Brancacci**, which is decorated with frescoes by Masaccio.

Leaving Florence and heading towards Lucca, the route takes in **Collodi**, the "birthplace" of *Pinocchio*. From Collodi, superb villas grace the Lucchesia district that leads to the lively historic city of Lucca.

The Coast for History Lovers

♿*See ETRUSCAN COAST.*

From Versilia to the Maremma, the Tuscan coast offers panoramic views, great swimming and a wealth of sites of artistic, historical and literary interest.

Castagneto Carducci

The **Versilia** hinterland is formed by the marble rich **Apuan Alps**. Heading south, Pisa has the stunning Campo dei Miracoli, which includes the Leaning Tower.

Livorno marks the beginning of the **Etruscan Riviera**. Before heading on to **Populonia**, admire landscapes described by Nobel winner Giosuè Carducci at **Bolgheri** and **Castagneto**.

The choice of resorts between Marina di Carrara and the Promontorio dell'Argentario is vast, both for campers and those in search of more comfortable accommodation.

The Medici Villa Trail

The Medici family, who ruled Florence and much of Tuscany during the Renaissance era, built lavish mansions and estates in the city and countryside, all of which were designed by the top artists and architects of the day.

Beyond the **Palazzo Pitti** in Florence, the Medici commissioned Giuliano da Sangallo to build the Villa Medicea in **Poggio a Caiano** and Buontalenti to construct La Ferdinanda in **Artimino**. **Fiesole**, the hill town that rises above Florence, is home to the Villa Medici, realised by Michelozzo.

A LONGER BREAK

Arezzo, Siena and the Maremma

The landscape between Arezzo, Siena and the Maremma is the ideal backdrop for walking, cycling or riding. Make the most of the countryside by staying in an *agriturismo*; alternatively use Arezzo or Siena as a base from which to tour the area.

Siena's major sights are easily toured in a couple of days, but the city and its province merit further exploration. In addition to being a good base from which to visit Chianti, Siena is near **San Gimignano** with striking medieval towers, and **Pienza**, a Renaissance jewel.

In **Arezzo** are the peerless frescoes by Piero della Francesca in the Church of San Francesco, and the fine Piazza Grande. Nearby lie the towns of **Monte San Savino** and **Lucignano**, known for their splendid medieval centres. Heading towards the sea is the medieval town of **Massa Marittima**. Then join the Via Aurelia and turn south towards the Parco Naturale della Maremma. Further south still, on the border with Lazio, **Pitigliano**, **Sorano** and **Sovana** are towns which appear to belong in another age.

HISTORIC ROUTES

Via Francigena

www.viefrancigene.org.

Pilgrimage routes were principally popular at the beginning of the 11C, driven by a devotion to see the holy sites of Christianity. Pilgrims carried the emblems of the routes they travelled; here on the Via Francigena, which ran from Canterbury to Rome, they bore St Peter's key. The Via Francigena logo depicts a pilgrim resembling a Roman statue, a little squat, with a cane in his hand and a bundle on his shoulder. With stops in the Tuscan towns of Lucca, San Gimignano, Siena and San Quirico d'Orcia, the route was used by medieval pilgrims who managed to cover 20km/12.5mi a day on foot.

Via Aurelia

Construction began in 241 BC of ancient Roman Via Aurelia (SS1), which has linked Rome to Genoa since 109 BC, running along the Tuscan coast, from Marina di Carrara to Capalbio Stazione.

Via Cassia

Laid in the 2C BC, this road through Etruria links Rome to Arezzo and on to Florence. The SS2 bears the same name, linking Rome and Florence.

TUSCAN WINE ROUTES

Viva Bacchus! What could be better than wandering Tuscany's hills and vineyards, tasting prime vintages and savouring hearty meals along the way? Tuscany has 14 dedicated wine routes, known as *Le Strade del Vino*. Each route has its own name and speciality, easily accessible from the region's main tourist hubs (⊙*See CHIANTI and ETRUSCAN COAST*). Enjoy tastings in *enoteche* and in wineries. Some routes for these wines are:

Province of Arezzo: Terre di Arezzo.
Province of Florence: Chianti Colli Fiorentini; Montespertoli; Chianti Rufina e Pomino.
Province of Grosseto: Morellino di Scansano; Monteregio di Massa Marittima, Colli di Maremma; Montecucco.
Province of Livorno: Costa degli Etruschi.
Province of Lucca: Colline Lucchesi e Montecarlo.
Province of Massa Carrara: Colli di Candia e di Lunigiana.
Province of Prato: Strada Medicea dei Vini di Carmignano.
Province of Pisa: Colline Pisane.
Province of Siena: Vernaccia di San Gimignano; Vino Nobile di Montepulciano.

© J. Arnold Images/hemis.fr

Val d'Orcia

What to See and Do

OUTDOOR FUN

BEACHES

See ETRUSCAN COAST.
From Marina di Carrara to the Argentario, Tuscany's coastline offers wide variety, from sandy beaches to more rugged settings.
Sandy beaches: Tuscany's most popular shore is the Riviera Versilia (*www.inversilia.com*), which stretches from Marina di Carrara to Livorno. The sandy beaches at Forte dei Marmi attract jet-setters. Viareggio has nightlife and the Carnevale. More sandy beaches are south of Livorno to Piombino, along the Gulf of Follonica and from Castiglione della Pescaia to Argentario.
Rocky coastline: The area just south of Livorno, from Baratti to Piombino, and the Argentario is known as the Etruscan Riviera (*Riviera degli Etruschi*). Maritime pine groves define the coast. Towns and ruins are of Etruscan origin; Ansedonia (formerly Cosa) is especially notable.
Islands: The Tuscan Archipelago includes the islands of Elba, Capraia and Giglio. Ports and harbours suitable for sailing craft are numerous. More information can be obtained from the Arcipelago Toscano website at www.visitelba.info.

BALLOONING

* **Associazione Aerostatica Toscana** – Strada del Cerro 3, 50028 Tavarnelle Val di Pesa (FI) ℘055 09 88 293. www.flyballoon.it.
* **Ballooning in Tuscany** – Several locations between Montisi, Cortona and Siena. ℘338 146 29 94 (*mobile*). www.ballooningintuscany.com.

CYCLING

Tuscany is a region well suited to touring by bicycle, with a new cycle route, Sentiero della Bonifica, which links Arezzo with Chiusi. See www.discovertuscany.com/tuscany-by-bike. See also www.visittuscany.com/en/theme/cycling for routes in Florence, between medieval villages in Chianti, for routes between Chianti and Siena, on the wonderful hills around Florence, and for a tour through vineyards and wineries. Several tour operators (**Cicloposse**, ℘0578 74 99 83, www.cicloposse.com; **Ciclismo Classico**, ℘1 800 86 67 314 from US and Canada, ℘1 781 64 63 377 from other countries, www.ciclismoclassico.com) plan biking tours throughout Tuscany. In Florence, **Florence by bike** offers interesting tours of the city (℘055 48 89 92, www.florencebybike.it).

GOLF

Tuscany has numerous good-quality courses, from 18-hole courses to practice greens, most of which are open all year. A few popular golf clubs are listed below. More information can be obtained from www.visittuscany.com.

* **Golf Club Punta Ala**, Punta Ala, Grosseto (*near Piombino*), ℘0564 92 21 21; www.golfpuntaala.it.
* **Golf and Country Club Poggio dei Medici**, Scarperia (*25km/15.5mi from Florence*), ℘055 84 35 562; www.golfpoggiodeimedici.com.
* **Golf Club Ugolino**, Impruneta (*15km/9.3mi from Florence*), ℘055 23 01 009; www.golfugolino.it.

RIDING

Every province in Tuscany has farms or parks equipped for professional or casual horseback riding. Some well known horse centres are below.
See also the *Addresses* in each section of this guide.

* **Centro Equestre Ambasciador Arcidosso** (*Grosseto-near Monte Amiata*), ℘339 18 36 923 (*mobile*); www.cavalloamiata.it

Sant'Andrea, Isola d'Elba

© MasterLu/iStock

- **Tenuta San Rossore (horse trekking, carriage rides)**, Centro visite (*near Pisa*): ℘050 53 91 11 or 050 53 37 55 www.parcosanrossore.org. For carriage rides: ℘050 53 19 10 or ℘335 71 13 793 (*mobile*); www.sanrossoreincarrozza.it.
- **Club Ippico Fioralice (riding school and pony trekking)**, Fauglia (*near Pisa*): ℘050 65 91 01; www.fioralice.it.
- **Centro Ippico della Berardenga, Castelnuovo Berardenga**, Siena: ℘0577 35 50 71 or ℘339 831 8519 (*mobile*); www.chiantiriding.it or Facebook @centroippicodellaberardenga

WALKING/HIKING
Walkers can obtain information from the main tourist offices.

🚶 Monte Amiata
One of Tuscany's most distinctive geographical features, Monte Amiata is a dormant volcano in Tuscany's southeast. Its slopes offer skiing and hiking, while the surrounding valleys enjoy a wealth of diverse flora and fauna, including thousands of hectares of nature reserves.

- **Informazioni Turistiche I.A.T. Abbadia San Salvatore**, Via Adua 25, ℘0577 24 17 60; www.terresiena.it.

🚶 Parco Nazionale delle Foreste Casentinesi Monte Falterona e Campigna
This national park with Tuscany's largest woodlands has nine marked nature trails suitable for easy hikes. The La Verna and Camaldoli monasteries are also located here.

- **Sede dell'Ente Parco** Palazzo Vigiani, Via Brocchi 7, Pratovecchio (Arezzo) ℘0575 50 301; www.parcoforestecasentinesi.it.

🚶 Isola d'Elba
The island offers several hiking opportunities, from challenging treks along the northwest coast and up Monte Capanne, to rambles that explore Elba's rich mineral heritage. Hikes that follow a route near Volterraio lead to eagle nesting grounds. Many routes start in Marciana or Rio Elba. Maps of walking trails are available at newspaper kiosks on the island.

- **Ufficio Informazioni e Accoglienza Turistisca dell'Arcipelago Toscano** Calata Italia 44, Portoferraio, (Livorno); www.visitelba.info.

🚶 Parco Regionale della Maremma
Encompassing approximately 100 sq km/39 sq mi, the Maremma parkland in southern Tuscany

Outdoor Contacts

AIGAE – Associazione Italiana Guide Ambientali Escursionistiche
AIGAE Toscana, Via Alessandro Giorgioni 25, Grosseto,
℘327 45 70 748 (mobile),
toscana@aigae.org, www.aigae.eu.

CAI – Club Alpino Italiano
Gruppo Regionale Toscana
Vai Del Mezzetta 2/M, Firenze,
℘0556 12 31 26, www.cai.it/gruppo_regionale/gr-toscana.

Parco Artistico Naturale e Culturale della Val d'Orcia
Via Dante Alighieri 31, San Quirico d'Orcia (Siena), ℘0577 89 83 03, www.parcodellavaldorcia.com.

WWF
www.wwf.it/toscana.

stretches from Principina a Mare to Talamone and from the coast to the Via Aurelia (SS1) route. Its features include the Uccellina Mountains and a variety of ecosystems, including sandy shores, woodlands, marshes and even desert-like conditions. The park has mapped out 10 nature treks ranging from easy to difficult that pass by crumbled towers, caves and beautiful seaside panoramas. Some treks require guides and a few trails are closed during the humid summer months.

Contact:
♦ **Ente Parco Regionale della Maremma, Alberese (Grosseto)**
Via del Bersagliere 7/9
Centro Visite: ℘0564 39 32 38;
www.parco-maremma.it.

Parco di Migliarino, San Rossore, Massaciuccoli

This park occupies undeveloped coast between Livorno and Viareggio, the estates of Migliarino and San Rossore and the area around Lake Massaciuccoli. Its main features are its wetlands, however, several guided walks are possible.

Contact:
♦ **Centro visite La Brilla**
(*near Lucca*), via di Piaggetta, Quiesa (Lucca)
℘0584 17 80 676 or 342 61 87 476

♦ **Centro visite San Rossore**
(*near Pisa*), Località Cascine Vecchie, Tenuta di San Rossore (Pisa)
℘050 53 91 11 or 050 53 37 55
www.parcosanrossore.org.

♦ **Oasi Birdwatching Lipu Massaciuccoli** (*near Lucca*), via del Porto 6, loc. Massaciuccoli, Massarosa (Lucca)
℘0584 97 55 67
www.oasilipumassaciuccoli.org

Mountains of Pistoia

The Montagne Pistoiese, the heart of the Apennines range in Tuscany,

Parco San Rossore

© Panama7/iStock

are easily discovered following the trails of the Ecomuseum, an open-air museum of six itineraries that explore the area's cultural and natural history. The Botanical Garden in Abetone is a highlight.

Contact:
🏔 800 97 41 02, www.ecomuseopt.it.

🏃 Prato and Surrounding Area

Easy and difficult treks are possible around the province of Prato, which includes the hilly terrain of Montalbano and Monteferrato and the mountainous Val di Bisenzio. Flora in the parks and protected areas include olive groves, chestnut trees and wild orchids.

Contact:
- **Club Alpino Italiano Prato**
  Via Banchelli 11, Prato.
  🏔 0574 22 004 (Tue 9–10.30 pm)
  www.caiprato.it.

🏃 Siena and Surrounding Area

Siena's province contains 11 nature reserves with well-marked routes where one can encounter rare flora and fauna and medieval ruins among the dense vegetation. The Provincial Tourist Board has also devised several easy and medium itineraries that explore the area's artistic heritage, from a 4km/2.5mi ramble around Monte Oliveto to a 9km/4.5mi hike in the San Gimignano countryside.

Contact:
- **Terre di Siena**
  Tourist Information
  🏔 0577 28 05 51.
  www.terresiena.it/it/trekking.

SPAS (TERME)

Tuscany has more spa towns than any other region of Italy. The springs have attracted visitors since time immemorial. Some are in the open air like the hot waterfall outside Terme di Saturnia; others have been channelled into elegant buildings offering hosts of medical treatments. The charm and elegance of Saturnia (*east of Grosseto*) and Montecatini are known beyond the borders of Italy.

These spas, like Chianciano, were at the height of their fame in the 19C and early 20C, when people took holidays in the elegant surroundings of fine architecture and landscaped gardens. The Italian Tourist Office (🛈*See Know Before You Go*) provides a complete list with supplementary information about the type of facilities available (drinking water, hot baths, mud baths, underground or surface baths, accommodation). In most centres a medical examination is necessary before embarking on certain types of treatment.

More information can be obtained from the website: www.visittuscany.com and from:

- **Terme di San Filippo**
  (⚬̶ Closed for renovation at the time of going to press).
  Via San Filippo,
  Bagni San Filippo (Siena)
  🏔 0577 87 29 82,
  www.termesanfilippo.com.
- **Terme di Chianciano**
  Via delle Rose 12,
  Chianciano Terme (Siena),
  🏔 0578 68 501,
  www.termechianciano.it,
  www.termesensoriali.it.
- **Sorgente Sant'Elena**
  Viale della Libertà 112,
  Chianciano Terme (Siena),
  🏔 0578 32 17 28,
  www.termesantelena.it.
- **Bagni di Petriolo**
  Loc. Petriolo, Monticiano (Siena),
  🏔 0577 75 71 04,
  www.termepetriolo.it.
- **Terme di Montepulciano Spa**
  Via delle Terme 46,
  Montepulciano (Siena)
  🏔 0578 79 11,
  www.termedimontepulciano.it.
- **Terme Antica Querciolaia**
  Via Trieste 22,
  Rapolano Terme (Siena),
  🏔 0577 72 40 91, www.termeaq.it.
- **Terme San Giovanni Rapolano**
  Via Terme San Giovanni 52,
  Rapolano Terme (Siena).
  🏔 0577 72 40 39,
  www.termesangiovanni.it

Bagno Vignoni

© antoniotruzzi/iStock

- **Centro Termale Fonteverde**
  Loc. Terme 1, San Casciano
  dei Bagni (Siena), 📞0578 57 241,
  www.fonteverdespa.com.
- **Terme di Bagno Vignoni**
  Piazza delle Sorgenti 13, Bagno
  Vignoni (Siena), 📞0577 88 71 50,
  www.termedibagnovignoni.it.

ACTIVITIES FOR KIDS

In this guide, sights of particular
interest to children are indicated with
a KIDS symbol (👫). Some attractions
may offer discount fees for children.
Collodi – The **Parco di Pinocchio**
delights with oversize renderings of
characters from the children's tale.
Florence – The **Giardino di Boboli**
provides a formal garden, fresh air
and lots of space to move; Museo
Archeological has an Egyptian section
with mummies; **Museo Stibbert**
features a stunning collection
of armour (www.museostibbert.it).
Pisa – The **Leaning Tower** will
stir their imagination; a boat ride
on the river.

SHOPPING

Tuscany's craft industry is one of
which it is justifiably proud. Traditional
wares and souvenirs are widely
available. In Florence, look for fine
leather, especially at the Santa Croce
Leather Workshop; discount leather
accessories are in the San Lorenzo

Market, although quality has
declined. Florence gold jewellery is
scenically situated in shops on the
Ponte Vecchio that specialise in gold,
but may not offer the best prices.
Many craft items are also sold in the
region's various monthly markets;
Arezzo is particularly renowned for
its antiques fair, which happens the
last Sunday of each month and the
preceding Saturday.
Elsewhere in Tuscany, look for
Casentino wool, fine textiles,
ceramics, marble souvenirs, wooden
toys and hand-made paper.

- **Alabaster** – Crafted in
  Volterra and Pisa.
- **Paper and papier mâché** –
  Hand-crafted stationery can be
  found in many shops around
  Florence. Viareggio has several
  papier mâché workshops.
- **Ceramics and porcelain** –
  Ceramics are produced in
  Montelupo Fiorentino and
  Cafaggiolo (*to the west and
  north of Florence*). Porcelain can
  be found in Sesto Fiorentino.
  Imprunetta makes terracotta.
  Val d'Elsa is famous for glass
  (including wine goblets).Don't
  forget the vast array of Tuscan
  food products that make ideal
  souvenirs: **pasta, olive oil,
  artisanal vinegars, mushrooms,
  truffles, cheese** and **wine (Vino**

Nobile di Montepulciano, **Brunello di Montalcino, Chianti Classico**, to name just a few). Most shops open from 8.30/9am to 12.30/1pm and 3.30/4pm to 7.30/8pm, although in the centre of large towns and cities, shops usually remain open at lunchtime. Credit cards are accepted in most stores, with the exception of small food shops.

ANTIQUES FAIRS

Tuscany has many regular antiques fairs. Arezzo's monthly fair is one of Italy's best known. All manner of items, from furniture to books and ceramics, are available. Bartering is expected.

- **Arezzo** – Not to be missed, this fair is held on the first Sunday and preceding Saturday of each month (*www.fieraantiquaria.org*).
- **CortonaAntiquaria** – Since 1963, it one of Italy's oldest antiques fair. End Aug–Sep (*www.cortonantiquaria.it*)
- **Florence** – last Sunday each month in Piazza dei Ciompi. A local biennial fair occurs in odd-numbered years end Sep–Oct (*www.biaf.it*).
- **Marina di Grosseto** – This bargain hunters' fair is held on the third weekend of each month.
- **Montelupo** – Annual event, third Sunday of October.
- **Montepulciano** – Second Saturday and following Sunday of each month in Piazza Grande.
- **Orbetello** – August, this antiques fair in the public gardens offers a wide range of collectors' items.
- **Poggio a Caiano** – A monthly fair (*precise date varies, not held in Jul, Aug and Jan*) for antiques and collectibles held at the former Medici stables.
- **San Miniato** – Antiques fair held on the first Sunday of each month except July and August.
- **Siena** – Collectors' fair features stamps and coins, held third Sunday of the month in Piazza del Mercato.

BOOKS

So much has been written about Tuscany, its history, culture, landscape and art that it is impossible to provide a concise list. The following has been compiled for readers who do not have unlimited time. The list focuses on works of easy reference, ample illustration, and classics that have captured the spirit of the region.

HISTORY

The Prince. Niccolò Machiavelli (1532, 1996).
Written during the reign of Lorenzo the Magnificent, this treatise on political thought is still relevant today.
The Merchant of Prato. Iris Origo (1957). This biography of Francesco di Marco Datini provides compelling details of middle-class life in medieval Tuscany.
The House of Medici: Its Rise and Fall. Christopher Hibbert (1982). A definitive guide to Tuscany's most powerful family, Hibbert's book chronicles the Medici influence in the 15C.
War in Val D'Orcia: An Italian War Diary, 1943–1944. Iris Origo (1947). Origo's first-hand account of life at her Tuscan villa during World War II is a classic.

ART

Art and Architecture in Italy 1250–1400. John White (1966; 1993). This hefty book is an excellent primer on the artworks of the Middle Ages and the Renaissance era.
The Agony and the Ecstasy. Irving Stone (1961; 2004). Stone attempts to relate the life, work and emotions of Michelangelo in this biographical novel.
Autobiography of Benvenuto Cellini. Benvenuto Cellini (1728; 2006). One of the most celebrated autobiographies written by an artist, this book is a fascinating look at the goldsmith and sculptor's wild life during 16C Italy.

Brunelleschi's Dome. Ross King (2001). King's look at the politics, rivalries and logistics behind the building of Florence's iconic dome is a quick and satisfying read.

Lives of the Artists. Giorgio Vasari (1550, 1991). This Renaissance bestseller is still in print and still entertaining almost 500 years later.

GENERAL

The Stones of Florence. Mary McCarthy (1956). This personal study of Florence is filled with insightful and often witty observations.

Under the Tuscan Sun. Frances Mayes (1997). This memoir set in Cortona contains recipes and anecdotes about expat life in small-town Tuscany.

Walking and Eating in Tuscany and Umbria. James Lasdun and Pia Davis (1997). Sybaritic travellers will savour this book, which contains 40 gourmet rambles through the central Italian countryside.

COOKERY

Italian Food. Elizabeth David (1954). The legendary British gourmet writes about the pleasures of Italian food and ingredients in a lively style.

Carluccio's Complete A–Z of Italian Food. Antonio Carluccio, Priscilla Carluccio (2007). The popular London-based cook's guide to Italian cuisine features colourful illustrations and regional fare.

NOVELS

The Divine Comedy. Dante Alighieri (1321). This epic poem about *Paradiso*, *Purgatorio* and *Inferno* is Italy's most famous literary work.

The Decameron. Giovanni Boccaccio (1353). The "100 stories" in this medieval Italian classic are set in Tuscany during the plague.

The Adventures of Pinocchio. Carlo Collodi (1883). The original popular children's book is much darker than subsequent versions.

A Room with a View. EM Forster (1908). A young English girl on holiday in Florence confronts the pleasures of travel and society's expectations in this satire.

Summer's Lease. John Mortimer (1988). This novel details the story of an English family who let a Tuscan villa for the summer.

The Tuscan Secret. Angela Petch (2019). Inspired by true events, a World War II historical novel with vivid accounts.

Dante and the Divine Comedy *(1465) by Domenico di Michelino, Duomo, Florence*

© Lexan/iStock

FILMS

The best films made in Tuscany are usually the work of Tuscan film-makers such as Mauro Bolognini, who was born in Pistoia in 1922, and the Taviani brothers, who were born in 1929 and 1931 in San Miniato.

The region is also a popular location for film-makers of other nationalities, and in recent years Tuscany has been the setting for a number of films.

La Provinciale (1953). This story, adapted from a novel by Moravia, is set in provincial Tuscany near Lucca.

8 1/2 (1963). Directed by Federico Fellini. An early scene with Claudia Cardinale as *terme* attendant is in Chianciano Terme.

Lo Spadaccino di Siena (1962). This Franco-Italian production by Baccio Bandini is set in 17C Siena.

Vaghe Stelle dell'Orsa (1965). Luchino Visconti directed this film about Volterra and the balze.

Il Prato (1979). Despite the name, this Taviani brothers' film is about San Gimignano and its towers.

La Notte di San Lorenzo (1982). Directed by the Taviani brothers, this film is about an episode in World War II set in San Miniato (renamed San Lorenzo in the film), and which records the rural and agricultural life of the 1940s.

A Room with a View (1985). The adaptation by James Ivory of the novel by EM Forster is an exploration of Florence and the surrounding countryside by young English men and women early in the 20C.

Con Gli Occhi Chiusi (With Closed Eyes) (1994). Directed by Francesca Archibugi, this film is set in the Sienese countryside in the early 20C.

The English Patient (1996). Directed by Anthony Mingella, this film includes scenes set in Pienza and also the monastery of Sant'Anna in Camprena, in which the dying patient is nursed by Juliette Binoche.

La Vita è Bella (Life is Beautiful) (1997). Roberto Benigni's film is set initially around Arezzo and portrays a father struggling to convince his son (by inventing fanciful and humorous interpretations of events) that the concentration camp to which they are deported, is a holiday camp and that each atrocity is make-believe.

Tea with Mussolini (1999). Directed by Franco Zeffirelli and starring Maggie Smith, Judi Dench, Cher and Joan Plowright, this film is based on Zeffirelli's childhood in Florence before and during World War II with a group of elderly British ladies and a boy coming of age.

Up at the Villa (1999). Set in Florence just prior to World War II, this adaptation of a W Somerset Maugham novella features Kristin Scott Thomas and Sean Penn.

Under the Tuscan Sun (2003). Starring Diane Lane and based on the bestselling novel of the same name, this film is set in Cortona.

La Meglio Gioventù (The Best of Youth) (2003). An Italian family chronicled over four decades, this mini-series is set in Florence, Rome and other parts of Italy.

Miracle at Sant'Anna (2008). Spike Lee. Set in the province of Lucca.

Quantum of Solace (2008). Marc Forster. Set in Siena, Carrara and Talamone.

New Moon (2009). Chris Weitz. Called "Volterra", the set actually was Montepulciano and its town hall, with plenty of vampires.

Letters to Juliet (2010). Directed by Gary Winick. Filmed in Siena and province.

Wondrous Boccaccio (2015). By the Taviani brothers and loosely based on stories from *The Decameron* by Boccaccio, this film is set in Certaldo, Florence, San Quirico d'Orcia, Castello Romitorio and Montepulciano

Calendar of Events

FEBRUARY–APRIL–MAY
Carnival (Shrove Tuesday)
Viareggio and **Santa Croce sull'Arno** – Procession of floats

Easter Sunday
Florence – Scoppio del Carro (♿See FLORENCE)
Prato – Presentation of the Holy Girdle (♿See PRATO)

2nd Sunday after Easter
San Miniato – Festa degli aquiloni (Kite festival): kites are flown from the fortress esplanade, followed by a historic pageant and the launch of a hot-air balloon. www.festadegliaquiloni.it.

1 May
Prato – Presentation of the Holy Girdle (♿See PRATO)

4th Sunday in May
Massa Marittima – Balestro del Girifalco (♿See MASSA MARITTIMA)

Ascension
Florence – Festa del grillo (♿See FLORENCE)

MAY–JUNE
May
Florence – Maggio Musicale Fiorentino: month-long music festival. www.operadifirenze.it.

17 Jun
Pisa – Historic regatta in honour of St Ranieri

3rd Sunday in Jun
San Quirico d'Orcia – Festa del Barbarossa www.festadelbarba rossa.it. (♿See PIENZA)

Penultimate Sunday in Jun
Arezzo – Giostra del Saracino (♿See AREZZO)

23 Jun, evening
San Miniato – St John's Day bonfires (♿See SAN MINIATO)

24 Jun
Florence – Calcio Storico Fiorentino: legendary football tournament in the city's four main squares (♿See FLORENCE).

Last Sunday in Jun
Pisa – Gioco del Ponte (♿See PISA)

JULY–AUGUST
1st half of Jul
Pistoia – Pistoia Blues Festival: this festival draws international blues artists who perform in the city's main square. (♿See PISTOIA)

2 Jul
Siena – Palio delle Contrade: The Palio is a colourful, bareback horse race round the dirt-packed Piazza del Campo, Siena's main square. www.comune.siena.it. (♿See SIENA)

25 Jul
Pistoia – Giostra dell'Orso (♿See PISTOIA)

2nd Sunday in Aug
Massa Marittima – Balestro del Girifalco (♿See MASSA MARITTIMA)

15 Aug
Prato – Presentation of the Holy Girdle (♿See PRATO)

16 Aug
Siena – Palio delle Contrade: historic horse race www.comune. siena.it and www.ilpalio.org. (♿See SIENA)

Last Sunday in Aug
Montepulciano – Bravìo delle botti: two men from each district of the town push a heavy barrel uphill to the cathedral. The *bravìo*, a banner representing Montepulciano's patron, is offered to the winners. www.braviodellebotti.com.

Viareggio carnival

© S. Cella/Sime/Photononstop

SEPTEMBER

1st Sunday in Sept
Arezzo – Giostra del Saracino
(☚ *See AREZZO*)

7 Sept
Florence – Festa della Rificolona
(☚ *See FLORENCE*)

8 Sept
Prato – Presentation of the Holy
Girdle to the congregation to
celebrate the nativity of the Virgin
Mary: large procession in costume
(☚ *See PRATO*)

13 Sept
Lucca – Luminara di Santa Croce
(☚ *See LUCCA*)

2nd Sunday in Sept
Sansepolcro – Palio della Balestra
(Crossbow tournament)
(☚ *See SANSEPOLCRO*)

Last Sunday in Sept
Impruneta – Festa dell'Uva: grape
festival with procession of floats.
festadelluvaimpruneta.it.

OCTOBER

3rd week in Oct
Impruneta – Fiera di San Luca
(☚ *See CHIANTI*)

Last weekend in Oct
Montalcino – Sagra del Tordo
(Thrush festival): historic pageant,
costume ball, archery, tournament

and evening banquet at the
fortress. www.sagradeltordo.it.

NOVEMBER

Last 3 weekends in Nov
San Miniato – Grand white truffle
fair (☚ *See SAN MINIATO*)

DECEMBER

Weekend closest to 8 Dec
San Quirico d'Orcia – Olive oil
Fair. www.lafestadellolio.com.

25 Dec
Prato – Presentation of the Holy
Girdle (☚ *See PRATO*)

Longer Music Festivals

June–August – Lucca Summer
Festival: Since 1998 it is one of the
most prestigious music festivals
in Italy, involving national and
international performers.
www.summer-festival.com

July–August – Chigiana
International Festival & Summer
Academy (Siena): opera and
chamber music. www.chigiana.it.

Mid September – Festival Barocco
di San Gimignano: two weeks of
baroque music concerts in Teatro
Leggieri and Palazzo Comunale.
www.accademiadeileggieri.org

Autumn–Winter (even-numbered
years) – Ferruccio Busoni
International Piano Festival in
Empoli. www.concorsobusoni.it

Events in Florence

Scoppio del Carro

The Explosion of the Cart is held each Easter Sunday in Piazza del Duomo. It dates from 1101, the year in which a crusader returned from Jerusalem with three stones from Christ's tomb. The stones produced sparks that were used to re-light the lamps extinguished on Good Friday. From the 16C onwards the sparks began to light larger and larger "lamps" until the event acquired its present form.

A wooden cart (6m/20ft high), known as *Il Brindellone*, is drawn through the streets by four oxen with gilded horns and hooves; it is accompanied by a procession of people dressed in Renaissance costume, comprising a standard-bearer, representatives of the four districts of the city and the teams participating in the historic football match *(Calcio Storico, see below)*. On arrival in the square in front of the cathedral, the cart is unhitched; from the high altar in the cathedral a dove "flies" along a wire to the cart and sets off a cascade of fireworks *(scoppio del carro)*. Then a young child draws lots to determine the order of play for the semi-finals of the football *(calcio)*.

Calcio Storico Fiorentino

Calcio is football (soccer), here played in 16C style and costume – the first match is on the Feast of St John the Baptist (24 June) and the two others on the following days. The matches are played by teams from the four districts of the city. The Greens represent San Giovanni (the Baptistery and Duomo), the Reds Santa Maria Novella, the Blues Santa Croce and the Whites Santo Spirito. The game has no precise rules and is a combination of football, rugby and wrestling. It is descended from the ball games played by the Romans in Florentia, in which the objective was to carry the ball into the goal of the opposing team.

The tradition was perpetuated into the Middle Ages when the town council was obliged to impose restrictions on the unruly players and their fans who invaded the streets and squares, disturbing the other citizens well into the night. The present game commemorates a match played on 17 February 1530 when the city, which was under siege by the Holy Roman Emperor, Charles V, dared to demonstrate its defiance despite its privations, celebrating Carnival with

Calcio Storico Fiorentino parade

© fotonio/iStock

Calcio Storico Fiorentino teams

© Juergen Richter/age fotostock

much noise and clamour. Charles V was eventually victorious but the match went down in history. At the end of the 18C the game went out of fashion but, on the occasion of the fourth centenary in 1930, the festivities were revived and the tradition has continued unbroken except during World War II.

The event begins with a huge procession of 530 players dressed in period costume, representing every sector of 16C Florentine society. To the sound of trumpets and drums and with standards flying in the wind, the procession sets off from Santa Maria Novella to the square in front of Santa Croce, which is covered with sand for the occasion of the match. The kick-off is given by a blast on a *culverin*, which is also sounded each time a goal is scored.

Play lasts for 50 minutes. The teams each have 27 players – four goalkeepers, three backs, five half-backs and 15 forwards. The winning team receives a white calf which used to be cut up on the spot for the ensuing banquet. Nowadays the calf is sold but the banquet still takes place.

Rificolona

This festival takes place on the evening of 7 September, the eve of the Feast of the Birth of the Virgin. The tradition probably dates from the days when peasants from outlying country and mountain districts used to travel to Florence for the festival, hoping to sell their produce at the fair which was held at that time. The long distances travelled by some of these visitors meant they spent several days on the road and had to carry lanterns when it was dark. The Florentines may have been thinking of these old-fashioned lights when they created the first paper lanterns (*rificolone*). The lights, which were originally in the shape of dolls, consisted of a candle shaded by the doll's skirt, carried high in the air on the top of a long pole. Later the shape of the lanterns changed and people began to hang them in the windows of their houses.

Among the other traditional festivals are the **May Music Festival** (Maggio Musicale) consisting of concerts, operas and ballets in the Teatro Comunale, and the **Trofeo Marzocco** (www.trofeomarzocco.it) when groups perform in Piazza Santa Croce in May in a standard or pennant competition.

Know Before You Go

USEFUL WEBSITES

TUSCANY REGION

www.visittuscany.com/en
This is the official website of the Tuscany Tourism Board, a very good resource for events, itineraries, sport and adventure, attractions, etc.

www.regione.toscana.it
Official website of the government of Tuscany with travel ideas and links for visiting the region.

FLORENCE

www.firenzeturismo.it
Official Florence Tourism website, with information on history and culture. ✆055.055.

www.musefirenze.it
This is the website of the Florentine Civic Museums (Museo di Palazzo Vecchio, Santa Maria Novella, Cappella Brancacci, Museo Stefano Bardini, Museo Novecento, Forte Belvedere, Fondazione Salvatore Romano, Museo del Bigallo, Museo del Ciclismo Gino Bartali, Galleria Rinaldo Carnielo). For all museums, tickets are available online.

OTHER CITIES AND PROVINCES

- **Arezzo**
  www.comune.arezzo.it
- **Florence**
  www.comune.fi.it
- **Grosseto**
  www.comune.grosseto.it
  quimaremmatoscana.it
  Official website of the Maremma region with tips about visiting and exploring Southern Tuscany.
- **Livorno**
  www.comune.livorno.it/portaleturismo
- **Lucca**
  www.turismo.lucca.it
  www.comune.lucca.it
- **Massa e Carrara**
  www.aptmassacarrara.it
- **Pisa**
  www.turismo.pisa.it
  www.comune.pisa.it
- **Pistoia**
  www.comune.pistoia.it
- **Prato**
  www.pratoturismo.it
  www.comune.prato.it
- **Siena**
  www.terresiena.it
  www.comune.siena.it

TOURIST OFFICES

The **Uffici informazioni turistiche** provide brochures, maps and lists of hotels, youth hostels and campsites free of charge.
Details of local information bureaux can be found at the beginning of each entry, indicated by the 🚩 symbol.
In each of Tuscany's provincial capitals and in the main towns of interest there is an **info point** (called **APT** or **IAT**) or a **Proloco** office providing local information.

FLORENCE

The four city centre tourist offices are located near the railway station in piazza Stazione, close to Palazzo Medici Riccardi (via Cavour), in Piazza del Duomo (Bigallo), and at Vespucci airport (arrivals hall). ✆055.000.

INTERNATIONAL

For information, brochures, maps and assistance in planning a trip to Italy, apply to the **Ente Nazionale Italiano per il Turismo** (ENIT), which has offices abroad and in Italy. Contact your country's ENIT bureau or visit ww.enit.it, www.italia.it, www.italiantourism.com

Australia
Level 2, 140 William Street, East Sydney NSW 2011, sydney@enit.it

Canada
365 Bay Street, Suite 503, Toronto M5H 2V1, toronto@enit.it

UK

1 Princes Street, London W1B 2AY,
info.london@enit.it

US

New York
686 Park Avenue, 3rd floor, New
York, NY, 10065, newyork@enit.it

Los Angeles
(1085)0 Wilshire Blvd., Suite
575, Los Angeles, CA 90024,
losangeles@enit.it

INTERNATIONAL VISITORS

ITALIAN EMBASSIES ABROAD

For entry requirements and visas,
ask the nearest Italian outpost.

Australia

12 Grey Street, Deakin,
A.C.T. 2600, Canberra,
✆ 262 73 33 33
www.ambcanberra.esteri.it

Canada

275 Slater Street, 21st Floor,
Ottawa, Ontario K1P 5H9
✆ 613 23 22 401
ambasciata.ottawa@esteri.it
www.ambottawa.esteri.it

Ireland

63/65 Northumberland Road,
Dublin 4, D04 VA89,
✆ 01 66 01 744
ambasciata.dublino@esteri.it
www.ambdublino.esteri.it

UK

14 Three Kings Yard, London W1K
4EH, ✆ 0207 31 22 200
ambasciata.londra@esteri.it
www.amblondra.esteri.it

US

(3000) Whitehaven Street,
NW Washington, DC 20008
✆ 202 61 24 400
amb.washington@cert.esteri.it
www.ambwashingtondc.esteri.it

FOREIGN EMBASSIES AND CONSULATES IN ITALY

Australia

Via Antonio Bosio 5,
00161 Rome ✆ 06 85 27 21;
www.italy.embassy.gov.au

Canada

Via Zara 30, 00198 Rome
✆ 06 85 44 41; www.canada.it

Ireland

Villa Spada, Via Giacomo Medici 1,
00153 Rome, ✆ 06 58 52 381,
www.ambasciata-irlanda.it

UK

Via XX Settembre 80A, 00187
Rome, ✆ 06 42 20 00 01;
www.gov.uk/contact-consulate-
rome

US (Florence)

Lungarno Vespucci, 38,
✆ 055 26 69 51
it.usembassy.gov

US (Rome)

Via Vittorio Veneto 121,
00187 Rome, ✆ 06 46 741
it.usembassy.gov/it

ITALIAN CONSULATES ABROAD

Australia

Melbourne, ✆ 03 98 67 57 44,
congen.melbourne@esteri.it;
Sydney, ✆ 02 93 92 79 00,
info.sydney@esteri.it.

Canada

Montréal, ✆ 514 84 98 351/2/3/4,
www.consmontreal.esteri.it;
Toronto, ✆ 416 97 71 566,
www.constoronto.esteri.it;
Vancouver, ✆ 604 68 47 288,
consvancouver.esteri.it

UK and Ireland

Edinburgh, ✆ 0131 22 63 631
www.consedimburgo.esteri.it;
London, ✆ 020 79 36 59 00
www.conslondra.esteri.it

US

Boston, ℰ617 72 29 201/02/03
www.consboston.esteri.it;
Chicago, ℰ312 46 71 550,
www.conschicago.esteri.it);
Detroit, ℰ313 96 38 560,
www.consdetroit.esteri.it;
Philadelphia, ℰ215 59 27 329,
www.consfiladelfia.esteri.it;
Houston, ℰ713 850-75 20,
www.conshouston.esteri.it;
Los Angeles, ℰ310 82 00 622,
www.conslosangeles.esteri.it;
Miami, ℰ305 37 46 322,
www.consmiami.esteri.it;
New York, ℰ212 73 79 100,
www.consnewyork.esteri.it;
San Francisco, ℰ415 29 29 200,
www.conssanfrancisco.esteri.it.

ENTRY REQUIREMENTS
PASSPORTS

People from outside of the EU must
carry a valid passport (valid at least
six months after the intended date
of departure from Schengen Area).
EU citizens only need a national
identity card. In case of loss or theft,
report to the embassy or consulate
and the police.

VISAS

Entry visas are required for Australian,
New Zealand, Canadian and US
citizens for a visit of more than three
months. Apply to the Italian Consulate.

CUSTOMS REGULATIONS

Since 1999, those travelling between
European Union countries can no
longer purchase "duty-free" goods.
Visitors arriving from another EU
country may import unlimited duty-
paid goods for personal use (see
chart). If a customs officer thinks you
may be bringing in goods to sell, they
may stop you to make checks. For
more detailed information, visit www.
gov.uk/browse/abroad/travel-abroad.
The US Customs Service offers a free
publication **Know Before You Go** for
US citizens: www.cbp.gov/travel.
The Italian Agenzia Dogane Monopoli

DUTY-FREE ALLOWANCES WITHIN EU	
Spirits (whisky, gin, vodka, etc.)	10 l
Fortified wines (sherry, vermouth, port, etc.)	20 l
Wine	90 l (not more than 60 l sparkling)
Beer	110 l
Cigarettes	800
Cigarillos	400
Cigars	200
Smoking tobacco	1kg

also regularly releases a free practical
Traveller's customs charter which
clearly reports on the regulation for
travelling within the European Union,
or from/to non-EU countries, visit
www.adm.gov.it/portale/en/web/
guest/home-english.

HEALTH

Most medical facilities have English-
speaking doctors. Pharmacists can
sometimes supply oral contraception
and medicines for straightforward
ailments. More serious complaints
and injuries may be treated at local
hospital casualty departments (pronto
soccorso).
European citizens should obtain an
**EHIC (European Health Insurance
Card)** before leaving home: www.
gov.uk/european-health-insurance-
card. This entitles the bearer to free
or reduced-cost medical treatment
in the state healthcare system when
temporarily visiting an EU country.
**Separate travel and medical
insurance** is highly recommended.
North Americans can contact the
**International Association for Medical
Assistance to Travelers (IAMAT)**
ℰ716 75 44 883 or, in Canada, ℰ416
65 20 137; www.iamat.org for tips
on travel and lists of local, English-
speaking doctors.

ACCESSIBILITY ♿

Sights in this guide marked with the ♿ symbol have full or near full access for wheelchairs. For information prior to departure contact the following organisations.

In the UK
Tourism for All ☎0845 12 49 971 www.tourismforall.org.uk
Disability Rights UK ☎0330 99 50 400; www.disabilityrightsuk.org

In Italy
Accessible Italy ☎(+378) 94 11 11; www.accessibleitaly.com
Handy Superabile ☎(+39) 349 850 5727; www.handysuperabile.org

In the US
SATH (Society for the Advancement of Travel for the Handicapped), ☎(212) 447 72 84; www.sath.org
Alternative Leisure Co, ☎(781) 275 00 23; www.alctrips.com.

Getting There and Getting Around

BY AIR

AIRPORTS

Tuscany has two international airports, the Amerigo Vespucci airport (FLR), also known as Firenze–Peretola, in Florence and the Galileo Galilei airport in Pisa (PSA).

- **Florence – Aeroporto Amerigo Vespucci (Peretola)**
  Via del Termine 11. ☎055 30 61 5, www.aeroporto.firenze.it.
  Bus service to Florence city centre every 30min.
- **Pisa – Aeroporto Internazionale Galileo Galilei**
  Via dell'Aeroporto. ☎050 84 91 11 (☎050 84 93 00 *Fri after 5pm and weekends*), www.pisa-airport.com.
  Regular rail link to Florence and direct access to A12 (Pisa–Genova) and A11 (Pisa–Florence) motorways, and the Florence-Pisa–Livorno dual carriageway. Bus service to Pisa centre.

ALITALIA

Alitalia is Italy's national airline. It operates services to many different domestic destinations, including Florence and Pisa, and international destinations, including the UK, US and Canada (with stopover). www.alitalia.com
- ◆ **UK**
  ☎0333 56 65 544;
- ◆ **Canada**
  ☎1 800 36 18 336;
- ◆ **US**
  ☎1 800 22 35 730 *(toll-free from US)*;
- ◆ **Italy**
  Viale Marchetti 111, Rome;
  ☎89 20 10 *(from Italy)*,
  ☎+39 06 65649 *(from Abroad)*;

OTHER CARRIERS

Florence and Pisa are served by dozens of international and domestic flights. Connections are more frequent in summer. Besides London, major UK regional airports have direct flights to and from the Italy.
- ◆ **British Airways:**
  ☎02 69 63 36 02 *(from Italy)*,
  ☎0844 49 30 787 *(from UK)*;
  ☎1 800 24 79 297 *(from US)*;
  www.britishairways.com
- ◆ **EasyJet:**
  ☎199 20 18 40 *(from Italy)*,
  ☎0330 36 55 000 *(from UK)*,
  ☎+44 330 36 55 454 *(from other countries)*; www.easyjet.com
- ◆ **Jet2com:**
  ☎0199 40 40 23 *(from Italy)*,
  ☎0333 30 00 042 *(from UK)*,
  ☎+44 203 05 98 336 *(from other countries)*; www.jet2.com

- **Ryanair**
  - ☎ 02 899 80 500 *(from Italy)*,
  - ☎ 0818 30 30 30 *(from Ireland)*,
  - ☎ 0871 24 60 000 *(from UK)*,
  - ☎ +44 871 50 05 050 *(from other countries)*; www.ryanair.com
- **Vueling**
  - ☎ 199 20 66 21 *(from Italy)*,
  - ☎ 020 35 14 39 71 *(from UK)*,
  - ☎ +34 93 15 18 158 *(from other countries)*; www.vueling.com

FROM THE US

- **Alitalia** www.alitalia.com/us_en
- **American Airlines** www.aa.com
- **British Airways** britishairways.com
- **Delta Airlines** www.delta.com
- **United Airlines** www.united.com

FROM AUSTRALIA

- **Emirates**
  www.emirates.com
- **Etihad**
  www.etihad.com
- **Qatar Airlines**
  www.qatarairways.com

CHARTER FLIGHTS/PACKAGES

- **Citalia**
  ☎ 012 93 82 22 41 *(from UK)*;
  www.citalia.com
- **Italian Journeys**
  ☎ 020 74 34 74 92 *(from UK)*;
  ☎ 1 646 74 79 704 *(from US)*;
  www.italianjourneys.com
- **Horizon & Co.**
  ☎ 888 903 20 01 *(from US)*
  www.kensingtontours.com
- **Maupintour**
  ☎ 800 255 42 66 *(toll-free from US)*
  www.maupintour.com
- **Perillo Tours**
  ☎ 866 594 30 32 *(toll-free from US)*
  www.perillotours.com

BY TRAIN

Travelling by rail is a particularly good way to reach the larger towns in Tuscany, especially Florence, as the rail stations there are within easy reach of the city centres.

From London and the Channel ports there is rail service to many Italian towns, including high-speed passenger trains and motorail services. Rail passes offer unlimited travel and group travel tickets offer savings for parties on the Italian Railways network. Take the Eurostar to Paris (2h16min) to catch a sleeper train onwards.

Tickets are also available from principal British and American rail travel centres and travel agencies.

- **Trenitalia** – ☎ 89 20 21 *(from Italy)*, ☎ +39 06 68 47 54 75 *(from Abroad)*; www.trenitalia.com.
- **Rail Europe** – ☎ 800 622 8600 *(toll-free from US)*, ☎ 0844 84 85 848 *(from UK)*; raileurope.com
- **Eurostar** – ☎ 03432 18 61 86 *(from UK)*; www.eurostar.com

🛈 Information and the assistance-request service for persons with reduced mobility (PRM) travelling on the Italian State **Trenitalia** railways are available at the number ☎ 02 32 32 32 (Mon–Sun 6.45am–9.30pm; from landline or a mobile phone) or free number ☎ 800 90 60 60 (from landlines only). You can also consult the site www.trenitalia.com.

BY CAR

You can hire a car in Italy or take your vehicle from UK and cross the channel in 1h30min with the Dover– Calais ferry (DFDS Seaways, www.dfds.com; P&O Ferries, www.poferries.com) or board your car on the Folkestone–Calais train (www.eurotunnel.com) and reach the continent in 35min.

MAIN ROADS

Italian roads are excellent, and there is a wide network of motorways (*autostrade*); information on the Italian highway network is available at www.autostrade.it. Tuscany is served by three highways (*A1, A11 and A12*).

FORMALITIES

Nationals of the European Union require a valid **national driving licence**. Nationals of non-EU countries should get an **international driving licence**, obtainable in the US from the American Automobile Association

(AAA, www.aaa.com) and in Canada from the Canadian Automobile Association (CAA, www.caa.ca). Other documents required include the vehicle's **registration document** and a **green card** for insurance.

MAPS

Use Michelin maps 719, 721 and 735 or the Michelin Atlas Europe to help you plan your route. In addition, the Touring Club Italiano (TCI, www.touringclub.it*)* publishes a regional map series at 1:200 000.

DRIVING TO ITALY

Via France – Roads from France into Italy, with the exception of the Menton/Ventimiglia coast road, are dependent on Alpine passes and tunnels. The main roads go through the Montgenèvre Pass, the Fréjus Tunnel and Mont-Cenis Pass, the Petit-Saint-Bernard Pass and the Mont-Blanc Tunnel.

Via Switzerland – Via Switzerland, three main routes are possible: through the tunnel or pass at Grand-

😊 Michelin 😊
GPS and Route Planning

Try Via Michelin's Sat Nav system, loaded with points of interest like hotels, restaurants and things to do and see from our guides.
Or, use the journey planner on **www.viamichelin.com** for all of the above and more.

Saint-Bernard, through the Simplon Pass and through the St Gottard Pass. If you're planning to drive through Switzerland, budget for the Swiss road tax sticker (*vignette*). The *vignette* costs 40 Swiss francs and can be purchased at the border crossings, post offices, petrol stations, garages and cantonal motor registries, or in advance from the Switzerland Travel Centre (📞+41 43 210 55 00; www.switzerlandtravelcentre.com).

Via Germany and Austria – For those visitors driving through Germany and Austria, there is the Brenner Pass south of Innsbruck. Remember that most of these tunnels or passes levy a toll.

Highway Code

- In Italy vehicles drive on the **right-hand side** of the road.
- The **minimum driving age** is 18 years.
- **Seat belts** must be worn in the front and back of the vehicle. Drivers must wear **shoes**, carry **spare lights** and have a **reflective jacket** and a **red triangle** to be displayed in the event of a breakdown or accident.
- Emergency **road-rescue services** are offered by the **Automobile Club Italiano (ACI)**, 📞803 116, 📞339 99 43 116 (by SMS for the deaf); www.aci.it.
- **Motorways** (*autostrade* – subject to tolls) and dual carriageways (*superstrade*) are indicated by green signs, ordinary roads by blue signs, and tourist sights by yellow or brown signs.
- Italian **motorway tolls** can be paid for with cash, credit or with the **Viacard**, a magnetic card that is sold in Italy at the entrances and exits of motorways, in Autogrill restaurants and in the offices of the ACI (Automobile Club Italiano).
- The following **speed restrictions** are enforced:
  - 50kph/31mph in built-up areas.
  - 90–110kph/56–69mph on open country roads.
  - 90kph/56mph (600cc) to 130kph/81mph (excess of 1 000cc) on motorways, depending on engine capacity.
- **Fuel** is sold as *super* (4 star), *senza piombo* (unleaded 95 octane), *super plus* or *Euro plus* (unleaded 98 octane) and *gasolio* (diesel). Petrol (US: Gas) stations are usually open from 7am to 7pm. Manned petrol stations usually close noon–4pm and at night, automatic petrol pumps are open 24/7.

Where to Stay and Eat

WHERE TO STAY

FOR EVERY BUDGET

The hotels and restaurants appearing in the Addresses sections in this guide were selected to suit all budgets (♨ *See the Legend on the cover flap for a key to the price categories*).

Budget accommodations (♨) include campsites, youth hostels and modest but decent and well-located hotels and *pensioni*. Restaurants in this category, without sacrificing quality, will charge less than €20 for a three-course meal (including drinks). Those on a larger budget will find hotels of greater comfort and charm and better-quality restaurants in the moderate range (♨♨ and ♨♨♨). Rooms in this category will cost from €60 to €100 for a double (€70 to €130 in large cities) and expect to pay between €14 and €40 for a meal (€16 to €50 in large cities). For those in search of a truly memorable stay, luxury accommodations (♨♨♨♨, more than €100; in large cities, more than €130) include elegant hotels, B&Bs, villas, castles, and guest farmhouses with a wide range of facilities, as well as enormous charm and atmosphere. Restaurants in this category will satisfy the most demanding taste buds with prices to match (♨♨♨♨, more than €40; in large cities, more than €50).

BOOKING YOUR LODGINGS

Tuscany's popularity with tourists from all over the world makes booking in advance a sensible precaution, especially between April and October. Generally speaking, hotel prices are lower between November and March and many establishments offer discounted rates for weekend visits and short breaks. Breakfast is usually included in the price but not in the case of some smaller establishments. For more information on accommodation in Tuscany, consult the websites listed in the *Know Before You Go* section of this guide.

Furthermore, the red Michelin Guide Italia, updated on a yearly basis, provides a detailed list of recommended hotels and restaurants in Tuscany.

HOTELS AND GUESTHOUSES

The distinction between hotel and guesthouse is not always apparent, but traditionally guesthouses are small family-run establishments, often forming part of a residential dwelling, offering simple standards of comfort and rooms without en suite bathrooms. Country guesthouses are

Agriturismo in Tuscany.

© Graememo/iStock

usually rustic in feel, with terracotta floors and beamed or vaulted ceilings. Furnishings are usually a mix of antique pieces and country furniture in wood and wrought iron. Seaside establishments are more likely to be modern in style, simple and functional.

In all cases, it is important to check prices by telephone or Internet before making a reservation, as rates may fluctuate depending on season and availability.

RURAL ACCOMMODATION

Rural guesthouses were originally conceived as an opportunity to combine accommodation and the chance to taste the products made on the farm (among them olive oil, wine, honey, vegetables and meat). In the last few years some regions of Italy have witnessed a huge growth in popularity of such guesthouses, some of which are as elegant as the best hotels, with prices to match. As a result, in some you will find a menu that makes use of the farm's own produce while in others you may be provided with a kitchenette in an apartment that offers complete independence; others still may only offer breakfast. The guesthouses included in the guide usually accept bookings for a single night, but in high season the majority prefer weekly stays or offer half or full board as well as requiring a minimum stay. Prices for the latter are only given when this formula is compulsory. Bear in mind that the majority of these rural guest-houses only have double rooms and prices shown here are based on two people sharing a double room. People travelling alone will usually find single rates. The ever-increasing popularity of this type of accommodation makes it advisable to book well in advance.

To get an idea of what is on offer, consult www.agriturismo.it, which has contact information for several farm holiday associations. Some offer horseback excursions.

BED AND BREAKFAST

A varied category, where often the difference between a hotel and a bed and breakfast is indistinguishable. The house or apartment is also often the home of the hosts, who let out a few of their rooms (usually between one and three). Guests are usually required to stay for a minimum period and credit cards are not as widely accepted. Generally speaking a bed and breakfast offers a cosier atmosphere than a hotel at competitive prices.

Although the notion of "rooms to let" (affittacamere) does not have an entirely positive image in the collective imagination, Tuscany offers some delightful accommodation often, though not necessarily always, at very reasonable prices.

For more information, consult the Italian bed and breakfast website: www.bbitalia.it.

CAMPSITES

Campsites offer a value-for-money solution to accommodation near the most important cities, as well as the pleasures of fresh air and country living. They generally have a restaurant, bar and food shop and some have swimming pools. For less spartan travellers some sites have bungalows and caravans. Prices shown in the guide are daily rates for two people, one tent and one car.

An International Camping Carnet for caravans is useful, but not compulsory; it can be obtained from the motoring organisations or the **Camping and Caravanning Club**, Greenfields House, Westwood Way, Coventry CV4 8JH; ✆02 476 422 024; www.campingandcaravanningclub.co.uk. For more information contact the **Confederazione Italiana Campeggiatori**, Via Vittorio Emanuele 11, 50041 Calenzano (Firenze); ✆055 88 23 91; www.federcampeggio.it. The organisation publishes a map of campsites and a list of those offering special rates to holders of the international camping card.

YOUTH HOSTELS AND BUDGET ACCOMMODATION

Hostel accommodation is available only to members of the Youth Hostel Association. Any of the YHA hostels offer membership that provides access to the many YHA hostels located around the world. There is no age limit for membership, which must be renewed annually. Apart from official youth hostels, there are many establishments, mainly frequented by young people, with dormitories or rooms with several beds, all of which have very reasonable prices.
Visit the websites: www.aighostels. it, www.ostellionline.net and www. hostelbookers.com.

CONVENTS AND MONASTERIES

A number of religious orders provide rooms for visitors in the major cities. Accommodation is simple, but clean and reasonably priced. The only disadvantage is the curfew; visitors are usually expected to be in by around 11pm. For information, contact tourist offices or the archdioceses. For a selection of monasteries to stay in, try www.monasterystays.com.

SPA (TERME) HOTELS

These can offer very good rates off season (*not August or spring holidays*) and can be a good base. Treatments generally are available in the day only. Enquire about package rates, which can be economical for meals, too.

WHERE TO EAT

For more information on Tuscan food and wine, see the Introduction.
The region's finest restaurants are listed in the Michelin Guide Italy, which is updated annually
Tuscan cuisine is based on peasant fare and seasonal specialities typical of an agricultural society – ingredients include olive oil, garlic and aromatic herbs. All dishes start with extra virgin olive oil, which in Tuscany is flavourful and of a particularly high standard. Traditional starters include *bruschette*, garlic toast, *crostini di fegato di pollo*,

chicken liver croutons, *finocchiona*, a fennel-flavoured salami, *prosciutto toscano*, a cured ham, and *lardo di Colonnata*, a pork meat cured in marble caves. Among popular first course dishes are *minestra di farro*, a spelt soup, *pappardelle alla lepre o al cinghiale*, wide pasta with hare or wild boar sauce, and *zuppa di crostacei alla versigliese*, a seafood broth, while second courses include *cacciucco alla livornese*, a rich fish stew, *scottiglia*, a meat casserole with slices of garlic bread, *bistecca alla fiorentina*, T-bone steak, *arista di maiale*, roast pork, *pollo* or *coniglio alla cacciatora,* chicken or rabbit with herbs, *fritto dell'aia*, mixed grill, and *misto di pesce*, seafood platter. To finish the meal, try *cantucci di Prato,* almond biscuits, *panforte* and *ricciarelli di Siena*, classic Sienese confectionery, *castagnaccio* and *necci con ricotta*, chestnut specialities. Traditional cuisine is the dominant cuisine of the region, however alternatives are not scarce. Especially in major cities, ethnic (Chinese, Indian, Japanese and Mexican) restaurants are very popular with locals and standards can be quite high. Restaurant opening times vary, but generally they are open for lunch from 12.30pm to 2.30pm and for dinner from 7.30pm to 11pm. Service is usually included, but it is customary to leave a tip in proportion to customer satisfaction. Restaurants where service is not included, a rarity, are brought to the reader's attention; after the price of the meal an appropriate percentage for a tip is suggested. By law bread and the cover charge should be included in the price, but in some *trattorie* and especially in *pizzerie*, they are calculated separately.

RESTAURANTS, TRATTORIE OSTERIE AND PIZZERIE

The distinction between these different types of restaurants is not as obvious as it once was. Formerly, a **ristorante** implied elegant cuisine and service, while a **trattoria**

Panini on the go, Volterra

or **osteria** implied a family-run establishment serving home-made dishes in a more relaxed, informal atmosphere. In typical *trattorie*, the waiter or owner will often tell you what dishes of the day are on offer; while this is usually a good choice, make sure that you know how much you are paying ahead of time to avoid any unpleasant shocks when the bill arrives! A list (*elenco, menu*) is usually available; if in doubt, ask to see it. Be wary of choosing the tourist menu, which usually has very limited choice. *Trattorie* usually have house wine on offer (served by the carafe), as well as a proper wine list which often has a good selection of local (and beyond) wines.

A **pizzeria** is an establishment with a pizza oven (look for woodburning), and some specialise only in pizzas.

WINE BARS (ENOTECHE)

An *enoteca's* (pl. *enotèche*) purpose is to sell wine, but because generally Italians do not drink wine unless they also eat something, you can count on at least some snacks, simple platters, or a hot dish to accompany the wines. Like *osterie*, they often have a kitchen and serve daily specials and light starters, as well as a choice of wines by the glass or bottle. Given the region's heritage of viticulture, it is not surprising that *enoteche* are becoming increasingly popular in Tuscany.

Given the significance of viticulture in the region, reference must be made to Tuscany's most famous wines: Chianti (part of the region), Chianti Classico (nine designated communes), Carmignano (from the Prato Hills), Brunello and Rosso from Montalcino, Vino Nobile and Rosso from Montepulciano and, from the Grosseto, Morellino di Scansano and the small yet prestigious vineyards that produce Bolgheri. Among the few memorable whites, Vernaccia di San Gimignano is noteworthy.

TAKING A BREAK

Cafés and bars are ideal for a quick break in between sightseeing. In Italy, bars are used more as a pit stop for a morning espresso and *cornetto* (custard, jam or chocolate croissant) or a quick lunch, than a place to sit all afternoon. *Panini* and *tramezzini* do a good job of banishing the midday hunger pangs. Italian creativity can be seen in fillings such as prosciutto crudo with artichoke hearts, or *mortadella*, anchovies and cheeses. Also, don't forget that a *pizza al taglio* (pizza slice) makes an excellent snack. 🙂 A bit of advice – Pay at the cash desk first, then present your receipt to the barman. (Some items like *pizza al taglio* or cured meats must first be weighed.) You can then go to the counter to collect your purchase in exchange for the receipt.

Basic Information

COMMUNICATIONS

All forms of communication are widely available in Tuscany, so you'll have no trouble keeping in touch. Italy has fully embraced the internet and you will find **Wi-Fi connections** in many cafés and in the rooms of the majority of hotels.

When making a call within Italy, the area code (e.g. 055 for Florence) is always used, both from outside and within the city you are calling. If calling from outside the country, the international code for Italy is +39. Dial the full area code, even when making an international call; for example, when calling Florence from the UK, dial +39 055 followed by the correspondent's number.

INTERNATIONAL CALLS

For international calls, enter + (or 00) followed by the country code:

- ✆61 for Australia
- ✆1 for Canada
- ✆353 for Ireland
- ✆44 for the UK
- ✆1 for the USA
- ✆64 for New Zealand.

MOBILE PHONES

Since June 2017, all roaming fees have been removed throughout the European Union. This means that any phone user with an EU SIM card travelling in another country of the Union is thus not charged additionally for phone calls, SMS and data connection. Prepaid SIM cards can be purchased from €10.

PHONECARDS

Phonecards *(schede telefoniche)* are sold in denominations of 3€ and 5€ and are supplied by CIT offices and post offices as well as tobacconists (signs bearing a white "T" on a black background). Also useful for foreigners are Welcome cards, available in denominations of 5€ and 10€.

Public phones

Practically everyone in Italy owns a *telefonino* (mobile, cell phone), their use is making telephone boxes a rarity; they may be operated by telephone cards *(sold in post offices and tobacconists)* and by telephone credit cards. To make a call: lift the receiver, insert payment, await dialling signal, punch in the required number and wait for a response.

DISCOUNTS

ACCOMMODATION

♿Visitors trying to keep costs down will find information on budget accommodation (*pensioni*, youth hostels, campsites, convents and monasteries) in the *WHERE TO STAY* section.

TRAVEL

By Train

Various options are indicated on www.trenitalia.com.

The **Carta Verde Railplus** (*€40, valid for a year*) gives a 25% discount for people aged 12–25 on first- or second-class international ticket prices on routes connecting any two of the countries taking part in the RAILPLUS scheme. The ticket is non-transferable. For travellers over 60 years of age, the **Carta d'Argento** (*€30, valid for a year*) offers the same discounts and conditions as the Carta Verde (♿*See above*). Carta d'Argento is free for travellers over 75 years of age.

Families and small groups: Children aged 4–12 travel half-price. Those younger travel free, but must share a seat with a family member. Easter, Christmas and summer holidays may invalidate these offers. Limited availability.

By Air

Some airlines offer discounts for families as long as they meet certain criteria. Check with your airline before booking flights in order not to miss out on any potential discount.

Youths (under-26) – Discounted rates exist for young people aged between 12 and 26 (*under 26 on the day of departure*).

Senior Citizens – Senior citizens aged 60 or over are also eligible for discounts on some airlines, consult individual websites.

Families and small groups: Offers change periodically, consult the airline website.

ELECTRICITY

The voltage is 220v, 50Hz; the sockets are for two-pin plugs. Most laptops and cameras chargers have built-in **convertors** and only require an **adaptor**. Check carefully before trying hair dryers or shavers, however. US visitors may need a **transformer** for some appliances. Seek out an electrical or hardware store (*ferramenta*).

EMERGENCIES

- ☏ **112** **European emergency number**, whose operators will direct you to the relevant services.
- ☏ **113** **State Police** (*Polizia di Stato*).
- ☏ **115** **Fire Brigade** (*Vigili del Fuoco*).
- ☏ **118** **Medical Emergency** (*Emergenza Sanitaria*).
- ☏ **1515** **Forest Fire Service**. Environmental emergencies.
- ☏ **1530** **Coast Guard** (*Guardia Costiera*).
- ☏ **80 31 16** **Automobile Club d'Italia** Emergency Breakdown Service.

All calls are free.

MAIL/POST

Post offices are open 8am–1pm on weekdays and 8.30am–noon on Saturday. In cities and large towns opening hours may extend to 6 or 7pm. The Italian postal service is notoriously slow and unreliable, so if a letter is urgent consider sending it by express service. Stamps cost €0.95 for postage POSTA4 (4 days max) and €2.80 for postage POSTA1 (1 day max) within the EU, Outside EU stamps cost from €1 for postage Postamail Internazionale and from €2.80 for the faster postage Postapriority Internazionale. www.poste.it.

MONEY

The unit of currency is the euro, which is issued in notes (*€5, €10, €20, €50, €100, €200 and €500*) and in coins (*1 cent, 2 cents, 5 cents, 10 cents, 20 cents, 50 cents, €1 and €2*). Many bars, are unable to break a €20 or €50 note. Keep a supply of small notes.

Banks

Banks usually operate Monday to Friday, 8.30am–1.30pm and 3–4pm. Some are open downtown and in shopping centres on Saturday mornings; almost all close on Saturday afternoons, Sundays and holidays. Exchange bureaux include post offices (*except traveller's cheques*), money-changers at railway stations and airports, and some hotel receptions (always on a rather stinging commission).

CREDIT CARDS

Payment by credit card is widespread in shops, hotels and restaurants (although some smaller *trattoria* may not accept plastic – check before ordering) and in petrol stations. Money may also be withdrawn from a bank or from ATM, but may incur interest pending repayment.

TAXES

Like every EU country, Italy imposes a sales tax on most goods and services. The Imposta sul Valore Aggiunto (**IVA**), currently 22 percent – with some reductions up to 10 percent –, lurks unseen, part and parcel of the bill. EU non-resident travellers can get a VAT refund for goods purchased for personal use. For information on how to claim a refund, go to www.adm.gov.it/portale/en/web/guest/home-english.

NEWSPAPERS

The Florentine daily **La Nazione** is the most widely read paper in Tuscany. Foreign newspapers are available in major cities and large towns.

PHARMACIES/CHEMISTS

These are identified by a red and white or green neon cross. When closed, each will advertises on-duty competitors and a list of doctors on call.

PUBLIC HOLIDAYS

A working day is *un giorno feriale*; *giorni festivi* is public holidays and these include Saturdays, Sundays and the following holidays. Each town celebrates the feast day of its patron saint *(details at tourist offices)*.

1 January	New Year
6 January	Epiphany
Easter Sunday and Monday	*Domenica di Pasqua and lunedì dell'Angelo*
25 April	Liberation in 1945
1 May	Labour Day – *Festa dei Lavoratori*
2 June	Anniversary of the Republic
15 August	The Assumption – *Ferragosto*
1 November	All Saints – *Tutti i Santi*
8 December	Immaculate Conception
25 and 26 December	Christmas and St Stephen's Day

SIGHTSEEING

See the *Discovering* section of the guide for information on admission times and charges for museums and monuments. Due to fluctuations in the cost of living and the constant change in opening times as well as possible closures for restoration work, admission times and charges listed in this guide are subject to change without prior notice. Visitors are advised to phone ahead or, where applicable, to check the websites to confirm opening times. Most sites will not allow admission 30min–1hr before closing time.

The admission prices indicated are for single adults; discounts for children, students, persons over 60 or large groups should be requested on site

and be verified by proper identification; generally they do not apply to non-EU citizens. For nationals of EU member countries many institutions provide reduced admission to visitors under 18 and over 65 with proof of identification, and a 50 percent discount for visitors under 25 years of age. Many museums require visitors to leave bags and backpacks in a luggage deposit area at the museum entrance.

Churches and chapels are usually open from 8am to noon and from 2pm to dusk. Visitors should dress in a manner deemed appropriate when entering a place of worship – sleeveless or low-cut tops, miniskirts or skimpy shorts and bare feet are not appropriate. Visitors are not admitted during services. It's best to visit churches in the morning, when the natural light provides better illumination of the works of art; also churches are occasionally forced to close in the afternoons due to lack of staff. When visits to museums, churches or other sites are accompanied by a custodian, it is customary to leave a donation.

SMOKING

In line with the rest of Europe there is a ban on smoking in all public places, though some bars and cafes may have areas where it is possible to smoke.

TIME

In winter, standard time is Greenwich Mean Time + 1 hour (*ora solare*). In summer, the clocks go forward an hour to give Italian Summer Time (*ora legale*, GMT + 2 hours) from the last weekend in March to the last weekend in October.

TIPPING

A 12% service charge and *coperto* (cover charge for bread, pretzels etc) is generally included on restaurant bills, but it is customary to round up the total. Guides and taxi drivers will expect a 10% tip (though this is by no means compulsory); porters, hotel maids and toilet attendants should be tipped a few coins.

Useful Words and Phrases

Useful Phrases

Do you speak English?
Parla inglese?

I don't understand
Non capisco

Please speak slowly
Parli piano per favore

Where are the toilets?
Dove sono i bagni?

At what time does the train/bus/plane leave?
A che ora parte il treno/l'autobus/l'aereo?

At what time does the train/bus/plane arrive?
A che ora arriva il treno/l'autobus/l'aereo…?

How much does it cost?
Quanto costa?

Where is the post office?
Dove è l'ufficio postale?

Where can I buy an English newspaper?
Dove posso comprare un giornale inglese?

Where can I change my money?
Dove posso cambiare i miei soldi?

May I pay with a credit card?
Posso pagare con carta di credito?

The road to…?
La direzione per…?

What time is it?
Che ora è?

I would like…
Vorrei/Desidero…

Common Words

sì/no	yes/no
per favore	please
grazie	thank you
buongiorno	good morning
buona sera	good afternoon/evening
buona notte	goodnight
arrivederci	goodbye
scusi	excuse me
signora	madam
signore	mister
signorina	miss
piccolo/un po'	small/a little
grande	large/big
meno	less
molto	much/very

più	more
basta!	enough!
perché?	why?
perché…	because…
con/senza	with/without
quando?	when?
quanto?	how much?
dove?	where?
dov'è?	where is?
l'aeroporto	the airport
la stazione	the station
un biglietto	a ticket
una scheda per il telefono	a telephone card for the mobile/cell phone

Numbers

1	uno
2	due
3	tre
4	quattro
5	cinque
6	sei
7	sette
8	otto
9	nove
10	dieci
11	undici
12	dodici
13	tredici
14	quattordici
15	quindici
16	sedici
17	diciassette
18	diciotto
19	diciannove
20	venti
30	trenta
40	quaranta
50	cinquanta
60	sessanta
70	settanta
80	ottanta
90	novanta
100	cento
1 000	mille
2 000	duemila
10 000	diecimila

Time

l'una	1.00
l'una e un quarto	1.15
l'una e mezzo	1.30
l'una e quaranta cinque	1.45
mattina	morning
pomeriggio	afternoon
sera	evening

ieri/oggi/domani	yesterday/today/tomorrow
una settimana	a week
lunedì	Monday
martedì	Tuesday
mercoledì	Wednesday
giovedì	Thursday
venerdì	Friday
sabato	Saturday
domenica	Sunday
inverno	winter
primavera	spring
estate	summer
autunno	autumn/fall

Food & Drink

un piatto	a plate
un coltello	a knife
una forchetta	a fork
un cucchiaio	a spoon
un piatto vegetariano	a vegetarian dish
un bicchiere	a glass
acqua minerale (gassata)	mineral water (fizzy)
vino bianco	white wine
vino rosso	red wine
una birra (alla spina)	a beer (draught)
carne	meat
manzo/vitello	beef/veal
maiale	pork
agnello	lamb
prosciutto cotto (cured)	cooked ham (crudo)
pollo	chicken
pesce	fish (pesca – peach)
uova	eggs (uva – grapes)
verdura	vegetables
burro	butter
formaggio	cheese
un dolce	a dessert
frutta	fruit
zucchero	sugar
sale/pepe	salt/pepper
olio/aceto	oil/vinegar

On the Road

il fiume	the river
un lago	a lake
un belvedere	a viewpoint
un bosco	a wood
l'autostrada	motorway
la patente	driving licence
un garage	repair garage
nel parcheggio	in the car park
benzina	petrol/gas
una gomma	a tyre
le luci	headlights
il parabrezza	the windscreen
il motore	the engine

Sightseeing

si può visitare?	can one visit?
chiuso/aperto	closed/open
destra/sinistra	right/left
nord/sud	north/south
est/ovest	east/west
al primo piano	on the first floor
tirare	pull
spingere	push
suonare	ring (the bell)
le scale	stairs
l'ascensore	lift
i bagni per uomo/per donna	WC facilities men's/ladies'
una camera singola/	a single room
una camera doppia	a room with twin bed
una camera matrimoniale	a room with double bed
con doccia/con bagno	with shower/bath
un giorno/una notte	one day/night

Urban Sites

la città	the town
una chiesa	a church
il duomo	the cathedral
una cappella	a chapel
il chiostro	the cloisters
la navata	the nave
il coro	the choir or chancel
il transetto	the transept
la cripta	the crypt
un castello	a castle
un monastero/convento	an abbey/monastery
un cortile	a courtyard
un museo	a museum
una torre	a tower
un campanile	a belfry
una piazza	a square
un giardino	a garden
un parco	a park
una via/strada	a street/road
un ponte	a bridge
un cimitero	a cemetery
la barca	boat
la spiaggia	the beach
il mare	the sea
pericolo	danger
vietato	prohibited or forbidden

CONVERSION TABLES

Weights and Measures

1 kilogram (kg) 6.35 kilograms 0.45 kilograms	**2.2 pounds (lb)** 14 pounds 16 ounces (oz)	**2.2 pounds** 1 stone (st) 16 ounces	*To convert kilograms to pounds, multiply by 2.2*
1 metric ton (tn)	**1.1 tons**	**1.1 tons**	
1 litre (l) 3.79 litres 4.55 litres	**2.11 pints (pt)** 1 gallon (gal) 1.20 gallon	**1.76 pints** 0.83 gallon 1 gallon	*To convert litres to gallons, multiply by 0.26 (US) or 0.22 (UK)*
1 hectare (ha) **1 sq kilometre (km²)**	**2.47 acres** 0.38 sq. miles (sq mi)	**2.47 acres** 0.38 sq. miles	*To convert hectares to acres, multiply by 2.4*
1 centimetre (cm) **1 metre (m)**	**0.39 inches (in)** 3.28 feet (ft) or 39.37 inches or 1.09 yards (yd)	**0.39 inches**	*To convert metres to feet, multiply by 3.28; for kilometres to miles, multiply by 0.6*
1 kilometre (km)	**0.62 miles (mi)**	**0.62 miles**	

Clothing

Women				Men			
	35	4	2½		40	7½	7
	36	5	3½		41	8½	8
	37	6	4½		42	9½	9
Shoes	38	7	5½	Shoes	43	10½	10
	39	8	6½		44	11½	11
	40	9	7½		45	12½	12
	41	10	8½		46	13½	13
	36	6	8		46	36	36
	38	8	10		48	38	38
Dresses	40	10	12	Suits	50	40	40
& suits	42	12	14		52	42	42
	44	14	16		54	44	44
	46	16	18		56	46	48
	36	6	30		37	14½	14½
	38	8	32		38	15	15
Blouses &	40	10	34	Shirts	39	15½	15½
sweaters	42	12	36		40	15¾	15¾
	44	14	38		41	16	16
	46	16	40		42	16½	16½

Sizes often vary depending on the designer. These equivalents are given for guidance only.

Speed

KPH	10	30	50	70	80	90	100	110	120	130
MPH	6	19	31	43	50	56	62	68	75	81

Temperature

Celsius (°C)	0°	5°	10°	15°	20°	25°	30°	40°	60°	80°	100°
Fahrenheit (°F)	32°	41°	50°	59°	68°	77°	86°	104°	140°	176°	212°

To convert Celsius into Fahrenheit, multiply °C by 9, divide by 5, and add 32.
To convert Fahrenheit into Celsius, subtract 32 from °F, multiply by 5, and divide by 9.
NB: Conversion factors on this page are approximate.

Vineyards in Badia a Passignano, Chianti
© J. Arnold Images/hemis.fr

INTRODUCTION TO TUSCANY

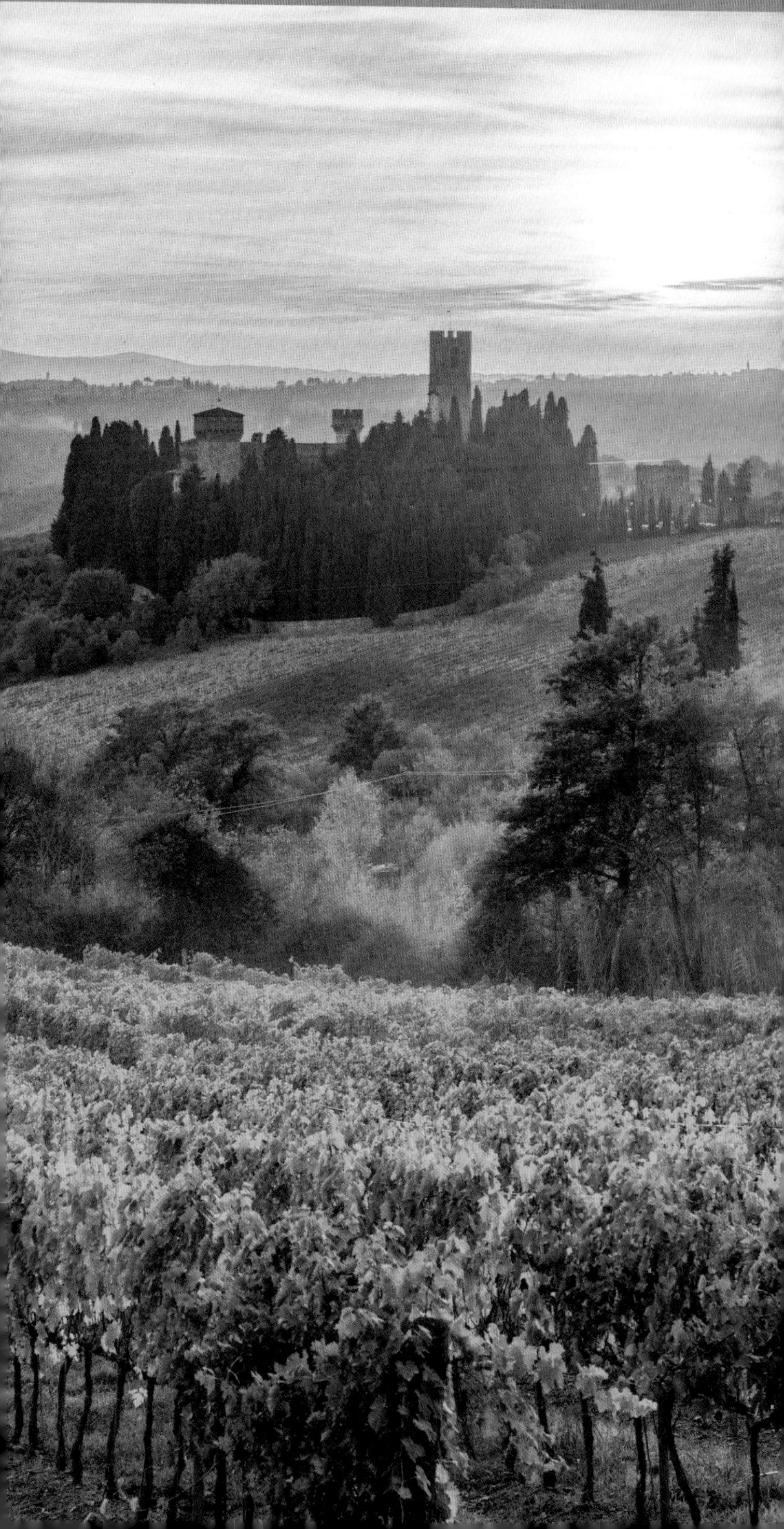

Tuscany Today

Though much of Tuscany still appears to be firmly rooted in the 15C, the region suffers from many modern maladies. Overcrowding, from tourists and the accompanying industry, plus an influx of immigrants looking for work, has led to increased traffic and housing shortages in and around the cities. Light, air and noise pollution are also threatening the distinctive landscape, historic buildings and quiet idylls that drive the Tuscan tourist trade. But, as one of the most prosperous and organised regions in the country, Tuscany is well positioned to address and overcome the challenges that the 21st century has presented.

POPULATION

Tuscany's population is approximately 3.8 million, with about 38 percent of inhabitants concentrated in the Province of Florence. Tuscany is Italy's fifth-largest region, but currently ranks eleventh (out of twenty) in terms of population density. Within the region, the tiny Province of Prato has the highest population density, with approximately 684 inhabitants per square kilometre. Conversely, the Province of Grosseto, Tuscany's largest, claims about 51 inhabitants per square kilometre. Foreign residents, more than half of which come from Romania, Albania and China, account for about nine percent of the population.

Like the rest of Italy, Tuscany has an ageing population, with death rates outpacing birth rates.

LIFESTYLE

The Tuscan way of life has long been admired by visitors. Not only do Tuscans enjoy a per capita income higher than most other Italians, but also a lifestyle that cannot be measured by money and goods. Much of the Tuscan way of life depends on taking the time to enjoy simple pleasures, such as spending time with family, preparing and eating a meal, savouring a glass of wine or taking an evening stroll (*passegiata*). Most elements of a Tuscan's everyday life can still be sourced locally. But factors such as traffic, pollution, globalisation – which is nudging out small family-run businesses – and an ever-growing expat population, are reshaping Tuscan demographics, and as a result, the region's way of life.

RELIGION

Tuscany's religious makeup reflects national trends; about 90 percent of the population is Catholic. Only about one third of Tuscan Catholics attend mass regularly.

There are long-standing Jewish communities in Florence, Livorno, Pisa and Siena and its province, but their numbers are dwindling. Protestant, Muslim and Buddhist communities are prevalent in cities, which have higher immigrant and expat populations.

SPORT

Football (*calcio*) reigns supreme throughout Italy, and Tuscany is no exception. Every city and most large towns have a local squad, some of which are successful enough to play in the Serie A, Italy's premier football league. Regular contenders include Fiorentina and Empoli.

Each year in Florence, rival neighbourhoods gather to play Calcio Storico, a historic form of the sport dating back to the 16C (*See pp. 26-27*). Jousting and archery are two other traditional sports that are celebrated each year in festivals in the region (*See PLANNING YOUR TRIP*).

MEDIA

Behind Rome and Milan, Florence is a major media hub for Italy. The national newspaper *La Nazione* is headquartered here and several English language periodicals are produced in Florence. The region is also a popular film location (*See PLANNING YOUR TRIP*).

ECONOMY

Endowed with a wondrous landscape and a dizzying cultural and artistic patrimony, Tuscany is at the heart of Italy's

Springtime in the Boboli Gardens, Florence

© TT/iStock

giant tourism industry. Tuscany is one of Italy's largest regions and one of Europe's wealthiest.

The region accounts for approximately seven percent of Italy's GDP and its unemployment rate is below the national average. Italy's national economy has stagnated in recent years, due in part to the lack of labour and pension reforms necessary to address high unemployment in one of the world's most rapidly ageing societies. Tuscany, however, maintains a highly diverse, competitive economy, centred on textiles, leather, apparel, jewellery, footwear, petrochemicals, agriculture and, of course, tourism.

While Milan is the centre of Italy's world-renowned fashion industry, Florence is a fashion mecca in its own right.

The venerable houses of Salvatore Ferragamo and Emilio Pucci, along with numerous up-and-coming designers like Save the Queen and Opificio JM, are headquartered here and depend on the region's vast network of small, artisinal producers for both inspiration and supply. In addition to design, petrochemical plants and auto and steel factories employ thousands near the coastal towns of Livorno and Piombino. Expertise in emerging sectors, such as biotechnology and nanotechnology, increasingly contributes to the region's economic growth and the development of its universities, in Florence and Pisa. The region continues to be a leading centre of agricultural production – notably of fine wines and olive oil – which commands almost limitless demand on world markets.

GOVERNMENT

Tuscany is divided into ten provinces: Arezzo, Florence, Grosseto, Livorno, Lucca, Massa-Carrara, Pisa, Pistoia, Prato and Siena. Each province (*provincia*) provides centralised governance to cities and towns (*comuni*), while the regional capital is Florence.

Politically, citizens of Tuscany lean towards the left. The region is perpetually a stronghold of the centre-left Democratic Party, which since February 2014 has been represented by Prime Minister Matteo Renzi (already mayor of Florence).

FOOD AND DRINK

Typified by its simplicity, Tuscan cooking gives pride of place to the fine quality of the abundant local produce.

Catherine de' Medici introduced the pleasures of the table to France upon her marriage to Henri II, the beginning of modern European cookery and gastronomic culture. She also introduced the fork and table napkin to court life, so

"FIASCO"

The traditional Chianti bottle was the *fiasco*, a bulbous shaped flask; it was originally made by glass blowing, with a long neck and a spherical bottom, like a large glass globe. A straw container enveloped the bottle, made it stable, and protected it in shipping. Today, it still exists but has mostly been replaced by Bordeaux-style bottles.

that the behaviour of the guests would be as refined as the dishes they ate.

Like the Tuscan landscape, the specialities of the Tuscan table exhibit a serene sense of harmony. The opportunity to taste them in situ, accompanied by Tuscan wines, is an experience that cannot be reproduced elsewhere.

Traditionally, a Tuscan meal begins by tasting savoury **crostini**, crusty slices of bread topped with large white haricot beans, or, more commonly, spread with poultry liver paté or one of the numerous local variations made from game or mushrooms.

Tuscany's forests yield an abundance of wild mushrooms like *funghi porcini*, of many different species and all of excellent quality. The great variety of vegetables provides a wide range of interesting dishes such as fried artichokes, vegetable flans and soups (*minestrone* and *aquacotta*). Empoli is famous for its artichokes, San Miniato for white truffles, and Bagnone has its onion, *cipolla di Treschietto*. Pork products include the strongly flavoured uncooked Tuscan ham, which is traditionally sliced by hand with a knife, and **finocchiona**, a salami flavoured with wild fennel. Among the cheeses are **Pecorino Toscano** (sometimes called *cacio*) which is made solely from the milk of a ewe (*pecora* in Italian), the soft mild style aged 20 days to harder piquant cheese aged 4 or more months.

Traditional first courses (*primi*) are **pappa al pomodoro** and **ribollita**. The former consists of croutons cooked in herb-flavoured stock to which are added sieved tomatoes; the croutons are left to cook until the bread becomes soft, hence the name *pappa*. The latter is a bean and black cabbage stew which derives its name from the fact that it used to be reboiled and served on several successive days.

Other *primi* are fish soups, such as the famous Livorno-style **cacciucco**.

In Tuscany, as elsewhere in Italy, pasta is cooked in a variety of ways and makes a good start to a meal; typical is *pappardelle* with hare, wild boar or duck sauce. In La Lunigiana pasta is served with olive oil and *pecorino* or with pesto (*testaroli*).

The queen of regional fare is Florentine-steak (*bistecca alla Fiorentina*) or **La Fiorentina**, which consists of a thick slice of tender Chianina beef cut from the sirloin and fillet (about 400g/14oz per person) and usually grilled. Among typical Tuscan main courses (*secondi*) are cinta Senese pig, **tripe** (also **lampredotto style**) and **fried lamb**, **chicken** and **eel**.

Sweets tend to be homespun – from simple **cantucci**, almond-flavoured biscuits that are traditionally accompanied by Vin Santo, to the **castagnaccio**, a flat cake made with chestnut flour, and **brigidini** from Pistoia, small waffles cooked in moulds heated over a flame.

The famous **panforte** of Siena, traditionally consumed only at Christmas, dates to the 13C, made with walnuts, hazelnuts, almonds, spices and crystallised fruit; a later variation adds cocoa.

WINE

Wine has been made in Tuscany for millennia: the Etruscans introduced wine into Gaul. Throughout the region the seasons of the year are marked by the activities and rituals involved in wine production.

Tuscany made early attempts to standardise the criteria for granting a title to good quality wine produced in a specific region (DOC – *denominazione di origine controllata*). Edicts promulgated in the 18C expressed the intention of controlling production in the Chianti and

Carmignano areas. The region is covered in vineyards whose names appear in the registers of the various regions; the map names the main *denominazione di origine*. The characteristics of the soil and other conditions vary considerably from one sector to another and the wine produced in them varies accordingly.

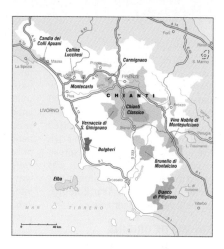

Chianti

Chianti is a red wine produced in the districts around Arezzo, Florence, Pisa, Pistoia and Siena. Chianti is the largest in Tuscany as regards acreage and production.

Chianti must be a minimum 80 percent (up to 100 percent) Sangiovese grapes; if a blend, the remainder must be red grapes as approved by regulations. This deep ruby red wine with a heady bouquet is an ideal accompaniment for Tuscan cooking.

The word *Classico* is reserved for wine produced in the nine designated communes in the provinces of Florence and Siena. The famous Chianti League dates to the Middle Ages. (ⓒ *See CHIANTI*). The **Chianti Classico** consortium, which was set up in 1924 to control production, took over the League's emblem, the black rooster (*gallo nero*) and began to reproduce it on the wine labels, now restricted to *Classico* wines.

An alternative consortium to Chianti Classico was founded under the name of **Vino Chianti**, to include other Chianti *denominazione* – Montalbano, Rufina, Colli Fiorentini, Colli Senesi, Colli Aretini and Colline Pisane; wines produced with grapes harvested and wine bottled within the respective areas.

Heady Reds

Even more prestigious is **Brunello di Montalcino** made from Sangiovese grapes from the commune of Montalcino. Brunello di Montalcino is available also as Riserva. Rosso di Montalcino, also made from Sangiovese, is released for sale on 1 September of the year following the harvest (and is more economical). Brunello, like Chianti, is a DOCG (*denominazione di origine controllata e garantita*).

The famous **Vino Nobile di Montepulciano**, also DOCG, may have acquired its name not only because of its elegance but also because it was produced locally by noble families. Vino Nobile must be made from at least 70 percent Sangiovese (locally called Prugnolo Gentile) grapes, with the remaining 30 percent being grapes authorised by the Tuscany region. The wine is produced in the commune of Montepulciano in southeast Siena province, close to Umbria. **Tignanello**, **Ornellaia** and **Sassicaia** are other prestigious red Tuscan wines.

White Wines

Although most Tuscan wines are red, a pleasant surprise is white **Vernaccia di San Gimignano**, which is documented in the 13C. Vernaccia di San Gimignano obtained its DOC status in 1966 and DOCG in 1993. Modern regulations require the wine contain at least 90 percent Vernaccia di San Gimignano grapes (many winemakers prefer to use 100 percent); it has a characteristic mineral taste with hints of citrus.

Vin Santo is an excellent white. It is traditionally drunk with biscuits called *cantucci*, and is usually made with white Malvasia or Trebbiano grapes, but there is also a red Vin Santo.

History

THE ETRUSCANS

In c. 1000 BC, Indo-European-speaking peoples from the North settled in what corresponds approximately to Tuscany today, as well as Latium, Umbria and Campania. These new arrivals were skilled in the use of iron, and practised ritual cremation of their dead. This civilization, which seems to have spread northwards as far as the Po Plain, was called the **Villanovan** culture and was named after a town near Bologna, where it was first identified.

ENIGMATIC ORIGINS

It was long believed that the Etruscans came from Asia Minor. This at least was the view expressed by Herodotus, who described them as Lydians fleeing from their famine-stricken country in a mass exodus led by the King's son, Tyrrhenos, after whom the Tyrrhenian Sea was named. This hypothesis is born out by the Orientalising character of their art throughout the 8–7C BC; their divination-based religion; and their language, which bore no resemblance to any of the other Indo-European languages spoken in the region at the time, but which had some similarities with Aegean dialects. However, other experts have found evidence of the presence of this Mediterranean tribe in the Italian peninsula long before the Indo–European invasions.

Even if the reason for the development of the Etruscan civilization remains unclear, the explanation of a sudden mass influx of people has been dismissed. Nowadays it is thought that Etruscan trends in art and philosophy spread as a result of trade, especially with the East and also with the arrival of various ethnic groups.

ETRUSCAN ECONOMY

The spread of the Etruscan civilization was based largely on the success of its traders who distributed the products made by its many craftsmen and farmers to destinations near and far. Etruria was not only rich in metal deposits, but also a fertile land, abundantly watered by the numerous streams and rivers rising in the Apennines. The mining of ore – iron, lead, copper and tin – and the related craftworks, were based mostly in northern Etruria. The southern part of the country developed an agrarian economy and the Maremma was extensively drained during this period. The two main products, much prized by the Mediterranean people, were olive oil and wine; the latter was a luxury beverage introduced into Gaul by the Etruscans during the 7–6C BC. This agrarian economy made possible the accumulation of surplus wealth, permitting the introduction of Hellenistic art, traded in return for ceramics and other crafts. This probably paved the way for the arrival of Greek artists who introduced monumental painting, evidence of which can be seen in the magnificent painted tombs situated in present-day Lazio (Roman Latium).

HISTORY AND CULTURE

Etruscan Expansion

The Etruscans appeared in central Italy in the 8C BC. Their power and civilization reached a peak in the 6C but began to fall into decline during the following century, until they were eventually absorbed by Rome.

Etruria, or as it is sometimes called, Tyrrhenian Etruria, covered the area bounded to the east by the Apennines, to the south by the Tiber and to the north by the Arno. With their powerful fleet of ships, the Etruscans soon established commercial links with the East (Greece, Cyprus, Syria), Gaul, Spain and Africa (Carthage), exporting Tuscan iron and copper, and importing fabrics, jewellery, ivory and ceramics.

The Etruscans sought to extend their domination southwards where, during the second half of the 7C BC, they occupied the Latin country, settling on the site of Rome which, for over a century, was governed by the Tarquinian dynasty of Etruscan kings. Early in the 6C they ventured into Campania, making Capua one of their main strongholds, but clashing with the Greeks who had settled in southern Italy (known as Magna Graecia) and from whom they were unable to capture Cumae. In the late 6C BC they spread north throughout much of the Po Plain, founding Bologna (then known as Felsina) and the port of Spina, from where they could control trade in the Adriatic. Their 'empire' stretched as far as Corsica, where they occupied the east coast after winning the Battle of Alalia (now Aleria) c. 540 BC.

During the 6C Etruria reached the height of its influence and power as regards territorial expansion, trading relations, the quality of its artistic expression and the spread of its civilization. Etruria formed a federation of City States, in which each state was called a *lucumonia* (from *lucumon* meaning a person exercising a priestly or regal function). Their fall was in fact hastened by their failure to combine their military might against their enemies. In theory there were 12 cities but it is difficult to know which were part of the federation since the list seems to have varied.

In the late 6C BC Tarquinius Superbus, the last Etruscan King of Rome, was driven from power and in the early 7C BC the Etruscans were cut off from Campania. They made a vain attempt to reach the region by sea but suffered a crushing defeat at the hands of the Greeks off Cumae. Threatened by the Celts in the North, who invaded the Po Valley in the early 4C BC, and in almost constant conflict with Rome, the Etruscans saw their cities fall one by one during the 3C BC in the face of the growing power of Rome. The fall of their religious capital Volsinii (now Orvieto in Umbria) in 265 BC marked the end of their independence. After submitting to the new masters of the peninsula, Etruria shared the fortunes of Rome and was granted official recognition in 90 BC.

Archaeological finds and Greek and Latin texts in which the Etruscan civilization is mentioned, have enabled modern specialists to define the boundaries of Etruria with some accuracy. However, there is no known Etruscan literature. The Etruscan language can be read without difficulty, as the Etruscans adopted the Greek alphabet in the 7C in order to facilitate trading relations, but its structure and the meaning of certain terms remain obscure.

Life on Earth and After Death

The Etruscan civilization was characterised by extreme refinement and great cruelty. The people delighted in luxury, adorning themselves with jewellery and rich clothing and surrounding themselves with beautiful furniture and precious objects. They enjoyed dancing and music so much that many activities were carried out to the sound of a musical instrument. On the other hand it is known that funerals were occasionally accompanied by human sacrifices, and it seems that some of the bloody spectacles which later became popular in Rome, such as gladiatorial combat, were inherited from Etruscan funeral rites.

The Etruscan gods bore a strong resemblance to those of the Greeks. They displayed great faith in divination, through the study of animal entrails (*haruspices*) and the flight of birds (*auspices*) and practised cremation or burial according to time and place. Like most ancient peoples, they believed in life after death for which sacrifices and offerings were required.

ETRUSCAN ART

Most of the remains that have been found are related to funerary art.

In its early phase (8C) the art form seems to have been strongly influenced by the Orient, from which it borrowed its decorative motifs.

Etruscan art reached the peak of its creative excellence from the 7C to the mid-5C BC. This period saw the arrival of Greek pottery in Etruria, the construction of most of the temples, the execution of the famous paintings in Tarquinia in Lazio, and the production of the most highly-accomplished bronzeware and the finest sarcophagi.

During the troubled period of the Roman conquest, Etruscan art lost its strength and character; from the 3C BC onwards it entered its Hellenistic phase. Once Etruscan art had been assimilated by the Romans in the 1C BC, it appeared to lose all individuality.

Town Planning and Architecture

Etruscans usually founded their urban communities on a hill near a plain watered by a river or stream so that they could farm the land. They protected their towns with huge walls such as those at Roselle, and were remarkable technicians, excelling in bridge building and in the provision of water to towns and field irrigation.

Few Etruscan buildings have withstood the passage of time. The materials used in their construction were relatively fragile, but a few arches and monumental gateways, bonded with huge blocks of stone, have survived.

The Etruscans knew how to build semicircular arches and passed on their knowledge to the Romans. Their temples were rectangular in shape and raised above ground level. A flight of steps led up to the entrance which was preceded by a colonnade.

On the outskirts of the towns were vast graveyards, forming veritable cities of the dead, including streets and, in some places, squares. The graves were shaped like temples, houses or simple barrows. In volcanic areas they were hollowed out of the tufa cliffs.

Etruscan styles of housing were reflected in the funerary architecture, which has survived in greater quantity, and most of the available information comes from excavations on the sites of aristocratic residences, as in Murlo. Apparently the mansions were built around an atrium flanked by colonnaded porticoes, a style that was later used in Roman houses.

Sculpture and Bronzework

Etruscan sculptors did not use marble but preferred clay, often painting it in vivid colours or adorning it with gold leaf. The great period of Etruscan sculpture was the 6C BC when statuary was an important element in the decoration of temples and even aristocratic residences. Decorative plaques and friezes, ornamented with animals, banqueting scenes and processions, were made for the same purpose, as were countless antefixes. Figurative sculpture gave rise to votive statues that were smaller than life-size but represented the deceased in their earthly lives (a warrior in battle, a woman washing...). Busts of people are more unusual but, despite the stylised features, they are strikingly realistic owing to the intensity of the facial expressions. Large protruding eyes and enigmatic smiles are characteristic of Etruscan art, as are the famous figures on the sarcophagi, reclining in the manner of guests at a banquet.

The Etruscans excelled in bronzework. Owing to the extensive copper deposits in Tuscany, bronzeware was a major part of the trading economy from the late 7C BC onwards. Etruscan bronzes, both utilitarian and merely decorative, were highly prized by the Greeks and Romans. The bronze was rolled for dishes, mirrors and fibulae, but cast for votive statuettes and statues. The decorative elements were engraved or raised in relief using the *repoussé* technique.

Under the influence of the Orientals and Greeks, Etruscan bronzes reached perfection during the second half of the 6C BC and the first third of the 5C BC, but retained some of their own specific characteristics, such as the marked elongation of the outlines. The end of the 5C BC, when the Hellenistic influence was particularly strong, is the date of the masterpiece of animal statuary, the Chimera of Arezzo (*now in the Museo Archeologico in Florence*). Thereafter, bronze sculptors turned their attention more to the production of monumental statues. During the Hellenistic period there was no longer an authentically Etruscan art form. The famous Arringatore (*also in the*

Museo Archeologico in Florence) has a somewhat dramatic realism that foreshadows Roman art.

Painting

The splendid remains of Etruscan painting were all found in the graveyards of southern Etruria, which is now in Lazio. The paintings were reserved for the wealthiest members of society. They underline the economic schism between the mining area of the North, where people enjoyed an average standard of living, and the richer, agricultural South.

Although no examples of Etruscan art have been found in Tuscany, the paintings prove that Etruscan artists knew and mastered all the various forms of art. The paintings are a precious record of the everyday life and beliefs of the Etruscan people.

In the burial chambers within the graveyards, the paintings were designed to remind the deceased of earthly pleasures. These included games, music, dancing, hunting and, more importantly, banqueting, which was traditionally the main subject. Artists used the fresco technique, applying colours (ochre, a red made with iron oxides; white, produced from lime; coal black; and lapis lazuli blue) on a wet limewash that "fixed" the colours. The so-called "archaic" style (6C BC) covered a wide range of topics. During the "classical" period (first half of the 5C BC), an austere Attic style predominated. Its main features were banqueting scenes, almost to the exclusion of any other subject, less obvious shading, very sophisticated drawing techniques and extreme attention to detail. In the second half of the 5C BC and during the 4C BC, outlines were gradually replaced by spots of colour. Here again, Etruscan artists showed a heightened sense of movement.

Pottery and Jewellery

The Etruscans made pottery in **bucchero**, a terracotta produced from black paste. Their products, most of them linked to the consumption of wine, included amphorae, wine pitchers, two-handled drinking cups and goblets. Buccheroware first appeared in about 670 BC in Cerveteri and was initially characterised by its pure lines and total lack of decoration. Later it was decorated with motifs picked out in dotted lines. Eventually the pottery became more complex in both form and ornamentation and consisted of two types – lightly embossed (*bucchero sottile*) and heavily embossed (*bucchero pesante*). The former was decorated with friezes of repetitive motifs inspired by Greek bronze vases with a similar sheen. The second group, which appeared after the 7C BC, had more sophisticated shapes and was heavier. Some have a beautiful silvery sheen. Pieces were decorated with a single figurative scene in relief. Greek pottery was enormously popular in Etruria. It was imported in huge quantities and reproduced so that today, it is sometimes difficult to tell which of the many kraters, drinking-cups and pitchers in graves were Greek and which were produced locally.

In the 5C BC the artists produced superb cinerary chests (built to contain the ashes of the deceased). Some of them were shaped like animals (zoomorphic); others were shaped like human figures (anthropomorphic). All were decorated with geometric motifs.

R. Corbel/Michelin

Funerary urn, Museo Archeologico, Chiusi

ANTIQUITY – ETRURIA

753 BC   Legendary date of the founding of Rome by Romulus.

Late 8C   Emergence of **Etruscans** in central Italy.

2nd half of 7C   Occupation of the Latin country by Etruscans.

Late 7C–late 6C   Rome governed by sovereigns from Etruria (Tarquin dynasty), whose reign marked the height of Etruscan expansion.

509   Fall of Tarquinius Superbus. Beginning of the decline of Etruscan power. Founding of the Roman Republic.

3C   Etruscan submission to Roman rule. Volterra conquered in 295 BC. Perugia and Arezzo rallied to the Roman camp in 294 BC. Fall of Etruria's religious capital, Volsinii (now Orvieto in Umbria) in 265 BC and the end of Etruscan independence.

AD 330   Byzantium chosen by Constantine the Great as the capital of the Roman Empire and renamed Constantinople in his honour.

395   Division of the Roman Empire into the Eastern and Western Empires with Constantinople and Rome as their respective capitals.

476   Fall of the Western Roman Empire.

DARK AGES AND FOREIGN INVASIONS

568   Occupation by Lombards (from Northern Europe) of the Po Plain (Lombardy is named after them) and of Tuscany, Umbria and Puglia and Campania in the south. Foundation of duchies; Tuscany centred on the Duchy of Lucca. Weakening of Byzantine authority over its empire. Beginning of a period of co-operation with the Kingdom of Lombardy.

570–774   Long and violent occupation of Tuscany by the Lombards.

751   Surrender of Ravenna.

752   Rome threatened by the Lombards. Appeal by the Pope to Pepin the Short, King of the Franks.

756   Undertaking by Pepin the Short to restore the States occupied by the Lombards to the Pope, marking the beginning of the Pope's temporal power and the birth of Papal States that were to be of major importance in Italian history until the 19C.

774   Defeat of the Lombards by Charlemagne (son of Pepin the Short). Tuscany

Greek Ceramics and Etruscan Jewellery

Much prized by the Etruscans, Greek vases were decorated with scenes in which mythology and daily life are closely linked; main characteristics vary from one period to another.

Corinthian ceramics, which were usually pale in colour and decorated with exquisite miniatures in the Oriental style constituting either a single subject or a frieze, were replaced in the 7C BC by Attic pottery produced in Athens. The decoration consisted originally of black figures set against a red background and then, from 530 BC onwards, of red figures against a glazed black background; within the figures, the lines and motifs were no longer incised but were painted on with a brush; eyes were shown facing forwards even when the face was shown in profile. By the beginning of the 5C BC this style had made Athens the main centre of pottery production. In the following century, in Athens and Magna Graecia, exuberant floral motifs and scrolls were painted on the glazed black background in white, yellow and dark red, surrounding a single figure.

Heavy jewellery, often made of gold and showing a high level of skill and sophistication, was worn by both men and women. As craftsmen, Etruscan goldsmiths were unrivalled, and they perfected the delicate technique of filigree work and granulation that had been developed at the end of the third millennium in Troy and later in Greece. The tiny grains of gold were several hundredths of a millimetre in diameter; the method used to produce them has been lost.

under Carolingian rule. Lucca the centre of the new Marches of Tuscany.

9C Break-up of the Carolingian Empire, causing anarchy in Italy and the founding of rival states.

951 Intervention in Italy by King Otto I of Saxony at the request of the Pope.

962 Coronation of Otto I as Emperor by the Pope; founding of the **Holy Roman Empire**. Emperor claims exclusive right to appoint the clergy.

THE CHURCH VS. HOLY ROMAN EMPEROR

In the late 11C, in defiance of the Holy Roman Emperor's growing stranglehold on the Papacy, Gregory VII decreed (1075–76) that no member of the clergy could be appointed to a parish or diocese by a layman, and he excommunicated Emperor Henry IV. This gave rise to the **Investiture Controversy**, the source of a lengthy dispute between Papacy and Empire, constituting the background to a whole era of Italian history.

This period saw the rise of the **Communes** (*comune*), whose role was to become a determining factor in the political life of medieval Italy.

THE COMMUNES

The struggle between imperial power and the Papacy, in which both protagonists attempted to foster support from various cities by granting them privileges, was one of the major reasons for the spectacular development of Italian towns in the late 11C. The Crusades and ensuing economic prosperity, especially in Pisa, further accentuated the expansion, creating an unprecedented boom in trade and industry (principally silk and wool), and resulting in the birth of a new merchant class.

The Communes flourished, and their existence, which was finally officially recognised by both Pope and Emperor, considerably altered political life in northern and central medieval Italy, including Tuscany, changing the face of numerous towns.

The Commune, a self-governing association of citizens, was marked by an unarmed takeover of power by the gentry and wealthy middle classes at the expense of the great feudal landowning nobility. As the prosperity of the towns grew, so the merchants and less wealthy classes of society gained power. The nobles meanwhile were gradually excluded from positions of authority.

In the early years, the Communes were governed by **consuls**, elected by an assembly, who held executive and judicial powers. Later, Frederick Barbarossa appointed a magistrate (*podestà*) as the direct representative of imperial power for each town under imperial rule. In principal, this magistrate came from outside the town and acted as the head of the army and an arbitrator in legal matters. However, like the consuls, he had no legislative power.

When the influence acquired by the craft guilds (*arti*) led to an administrative restructuring of towns and cities and the empowerment of the "popular" classes, a **captain of the people** (*capitano del popolo*), monitored by an increasingly influential assembly, was appointed to govern the town jointly with the magistrate. In the end the *podestà* was replaced by the *capitano*.

The Communes took advantage of the struggle between Church and Empire, adding to its complexity, and the Emperor was faced in many instances with violent hostility. All towns took sides in the controversy between the Pope and the Emperor, some fluctuating by choice or by coercion between the factions. In the furious clashes that set Italian towns and cities against one another, economic rivalries and individual enmities accounted for much of the fighting. Despite these upheavals, the country experienced a major economic and artistic boom during the 13C and the first half of the 14C, stimulated by the power of the Communes which had become not only busy trading towns but also important artistic centres. Universities were founded in Siena, Pisa and Florence, and gained fame throughout Europe. Through Dante, Boccaccio and Petrarch, the Italian language acquired a glory that was never to wane.

The break-up of the Communes was provoked by the Black Death (1348), which was followed by sporadic outbreaks of plague during the second half of the 14C, by endemic fighting between neighbouring towns and by internal conflict within the towns.

1115 Death of Countess Matilda, Marchioness of Tuscany. Tuscany bequeathed by her to the Papacy as a final

Leaning Tower and Duomo, Piazza dei Miracoli, Pisa

© Onfilm/iStock

gesture after half a century of supporting the Pope.

1122 Investiture Controversy brought to an end by the Concordat of Worms, which gave the Pope the upper hand.

1125 Annexation of Fiesole by Florence; in Tuscany, Florentine expansion begins.

1152 Crisis of succession in Germany:supporters of the House of Bavaria oppose the supporters of the House of Swabia. Election of Frederick of Hohenstaufen (Frederick Barbarossa) supported by the House of Swabia.

1155 Coronation in Italy by the Pope of Frederick Barbarossa as Emperor. Barbarossa attempts to impose his rule throughout Italy. Renewal of the struggle between the Papacy and the Empire, complicated by the growing hostility of the Communes. Appointment by Frederick of a magistrate (*podestà*) to control the Communes that he had forced into submission.

1227–50 Renewed struggle led by Pope Gregory IX and Pope Innocent IV against Frederick II of Swabia (grandson of Frederick Barbarossa), crowned King of Sicily in 1194 and Holy Roman Emperor in 1220. New victory for the Papacy in 1245; excommunication and dismissal of the Emperor by the Pope.

CRISIS BETWEEN POPE AND EMPIRE

1250 Death of Frederick II, marking the beginning of a period of strife.

1251 Founding of a federation of Tuscan Ghibelline towns, headed by Pisa and Siena.

1260 Attempt by King Manfred of Sicily, the legitimised bastard son of Frederick II, to conquer the peninsula with the support of the Ghibelline towns. After being defeated at **Montaperti**, Florence, traditionally a Guelf city, which had already been Ghibelline for 13 years during the rule of Frederick II, again support the Ghibelline faction for a short period.

1263–66 Appeal by the Pope to Charles of Anjou (brother of Louis IX, King of France) who defeated Manfred at Benevento (Campania) in 1266. Death of Manfred in battle and the establishment of the Anjou dynasty in Sicily and Naples, subjecting Italy to a period of French control.

1284 Defeat of Pisa by Genoa at the **Battle of Meloria:** Pisa lose. It is made of a blend of cocoa, s Sardinia and Corsica and its supremacy over the Mediterranean.

1289 **Battle of Campaldino** near Poppi, quashing Ghibelline hopes.

Late 13C Siena overtaken by Florence as a banking centre and the largest city in Tuscany. The 14C saw a decline in the power of the Communes and in Florence, as elsewhere in Italy, the rise of great families such as the Medici. The collapse of imperial rule was followed by an erosion of the power of the Papacy, which was faced with grave difficulties. Italy was in crisis. Foreign influence began to take hold within the country, first through the French and later through the Aragonese, both of whom were fighting to gain control of the South. Florence exerted huge power and only Pisa, Lucca

	and Siena still managed to retain their independence.
1300	Division in Florence between the **Black Guelfs**, who support foreign intervention, and the **White Guelfs**, who advocate total independence in the name of freedom.
1301	Annexation of Pistoia by Florence.
1309	Removal of the papacy to Avignon to escape the unrest in Rome.
1328	Appeal for support by the Ghibellines to Louis of Bavaria; failure of his intervention marking the end of German claims in Italy.
1348	Death of almost one-half of the urban population from the Black Death, which sweeps through Italy and spread throughout Europe.

Guelfs And Ghibellines

The names Guelf and Ghibelline (Guelfi and Ghibellini in Italian), which came into use in Florence in 1215, are derived from the names of the two great German families who disputed the throne of the Holy Roman Emperor in the 12C. The Ghibellines were the supporters of the lords of Waiblingen, the cradle of the House of Swabia and therefore of the Hohenstaufen dynasty. The Guelfs, who were rivals of the Hohenstaufen family and therefore supporters of the Pope, were members of the Welf dynasty (House of Bavaria). The later division into White Guelfs and Black Guelfs was confined to Florence. In the 13C the Investiture Controversy was replaced by the issue of primacy between Pope and Emperor. The zeal of the Guelf faction was stimulated by the preaching of the new religious orders (Minor Friars of St Francis of Assisi, Dominicans).

1361	Annexation of Volterra by Florence.
1377	Return of the Papacy to Rome at the instigation of Petrarch and Catherine of Siena.
1378	**Revolt of the Ciompi:** The lower classes, among them the *ciompi* (wool carders), suffers increasing economic hardship during the 14C. The rebellion of this section of society, led by the wool carder Michele di Lando, briefly bring to power one of the most democratic governments in Florentine history, in which all classes of society are represented. Within four years, however, the dominance of the major guilds is restored and the more conservative elements in Florentine society are back in power.
1378–1417	**Great Western Schism:** Papal reinstatement in Rome opposed by the antipope resident in Avignon and a second antipope in Pisa (1409).
1384	Annexation of Arezzo by Florence.

15C – TUSCAN-RENAISSANCE

In the 15C Italy experienced a remarkable increase in economic and artistic activity. The medieval era transformed to the Renaissance which blossomed in Florence, the city of the Medici, which became a glittering "rebirth" of a golden age.

1406	Conquest of Pisa by Florence.
1434	Beginning of the Medici oligarchy in Florence, with the arrival in power of Cosimo the Elder (&See *FLORENCE*).
1454	Political stability in Italy between the great rival States of Milan, Florence, Rome and Naples guaranteed by the **Treaty of Lodi**, which is vigilantly

upheld by Lorenzo the Magnificent, ruler of Florence from 1469.

1494 Policy of interference in Italian affairs resumed by Charles VIII of France, thus putting the new stability in jeopardy. After a triumphant welcome in Pisa and benign indifference in Florence, he passes through Siena, marches on Rome and enters Naples but was soon forced to retreat. His campaign marks the beginning of the Italian wars, which are later resumed by Louis XII, with the same lack of success.

1494–98 Republic briefly established in Florence by Savonarola.

GRAND DUCHY OF TUSCANY

The **16C** was marked by the rivalry between France and Spain that turned Italy into a battlefield as the two great powers struggled for overall control of Europe. Florence was overtaken by Rome as a centre of artistic creativity in the reigns of the great Pope, Julius II (1503–13) and the Medici Pope Leo X (1513–21).

1508–26 François I of France at war in northern Italy; victorious at Marignano but forced to renounce his claim to Italy after defeat at Pavia.

1527 Italy attacked by Emperor Charles V. The power of the Holy See diminished by the sack of Rome. Reinstatement of Alessandro Medici, the Emperor's son-in-law, in Florence which became a duchy (1532).

1545–63 Council of Trent leading to the Counter-Reformation (or Catholic Reformation).

1555 French claims in Italy temporarily halted by the failure of the campaign launched by Henri II, whose supporters were defeated

> ### The Marzocco
>
> The heraldic lion, seated, gripping the Florentine lily in its front paw, symbolises the political power of Florence. It can be seen in the main square of every town and village governed by the city of the Medici and is an impressive testimony to the authority of Florentine rule. Probably its name derives from Mars, the god of war, represented by an ancient statue erected at the entrance to the Ponte Vecchio in Florence in the Middle Ages. The statue was destroyed by the floodwaters of the Arno in 1333 and replaced by the townspeople in 1420, in memory of its predecessor, by Donatello's everlasting sculpture of a lion, named *Marzocco* (little Mars). In 1810 it was moved to the Piazza della Signoria. The original is now in the Museo del Bargello.

by the Emperor's forces at the Siege of Siena. Siena forced to submit by Cosimo I, protégé of Charles V. Unification of Tuscany completed, except for Lucca, Piombino and the Garrison State (the five strongholds controlled by the Spanish: Ansedonia, Orbetello, Porto Ercole, Porto Santo Stefano, Porto Longone).

1559 Treaty of Cateau-Cambrésis marking the end of the Italian Campaign and the beginning of Spanish domination. Central Italy sandwiched between territories subject to foreign rule; the Duchy of Milan under France to the north; and southern Italy, Sicily and Sardinia under Spain to the south.

1569 Tuscany made a **grand duchy** under the absolute rule of Cosimo I.

In the **17C** Italy was in decline and ceased to be the object of dispute between Spain and France during the reign of Louis XIV.

In the **18C** the rulers of a number of Italian States instituted a form of "Enlightened Despotism", a concept which was spreading throughout Europe from France. It was best embodied in Italy by Grand Duke Peter Leopold of Tuscany (1765–90), son of Maria Theresa of Austria, who based his style of government on the most innovatory theories of the day.

The **Treaty of Utrecht** (1713) marked the end of Spanish domination and the beginning of Austrian control. In the ensuing years, however, Italy remained a bone of contention between the Habsburgs and the Spanish Bourbons.

1737 End of the Medici line. Grand Duchy of Tuscany granted by the Austrians to François of Lorraine, husband of Maria Theresa and future Emperor of Austria. Under this dynasty, Florence and Tuscany experienced reform and progress.

NAPOLEONIC EMPIRE

1769–99 Napoleonic campaign ending in the Peace of Campo Formio (1797) by which France annexed Italy. Occupation of Florence.

Early 1800s The early 19C saw the annexation of territory by Napoleon and Italians experienced their first period of unity under governmental and military institutions similar to those established in France.

1800–01 Second Napoleonic campaign; founding of an Italian Republic; Tuscany became the Kingdom of Etruria.

1805–06 Napoleon, now Emperor of France, proclaimed himself King of Italy, and appointed his stepson Eugène de Beauharnais as Viceroy, and gave his sister Élisa control over the newly-formed duchies of Lucca and Piombino. The Kingdom of Naples was ruled initially by his brother Joseph and later by Murat.

1809–11 As Grand Duchess of Tuscany, Élisa moved to Florence. France annexes the Isle of Elba.

1814–15 Collapse of the Napoleonic Empire. The **Congress of Vienna** marked the end of the French occupation of Italy and confirmed the hegemony of Austria, which ruled the North and Centre of the country, including the Grand Duchy of Tuscany. When the Duchy was returned to the House of Lorraine, it was expanded to include the Isle of Elba and the Principality of Piombino. The Duchy of Lucca was granted to the Spanish infanta, Maria Luísa of Bourbon.

RISORGIMENTO

Following the Congress of Vienna, Italy was again divided and subject to the rule of absolute monarchs. An ideological movement began to develop based on a policy of liberalism combined with increasing patriotic awareness. The movement known as **Risorgimento** (from *risorgere* meaning to rise again) was originally led by a cultured elite that was greatly influenced by Romantic ideals. It was later taken over by the liberal and moderate middle classes.

An initial phase of brutally quashed revolts reached a climax in the confusion of the 1848 revolution, which ended in failure. This was followed by a period of diplomacy, during which the spiritual leader and driving force was Cavour; Italy was unified in 1870.

1831 onwards After riots throughout Italy, the rebels band together under **Mazzini**; his "Young Italy" movement attracted numerous Freemasons and former members of the Carboneria, a secret society originating in France, which spreads to central and northern Italy from Naples, where it opposes Murat's regime. It is successful in France, where Napoleon III is one of its Carbonari followers.

1848–49 Introduction by a number of sovereigns, including the Grand Duke of Tuscany, of reforms aimed at establishing a degree of liberalism; increase in the number of rebellions.

February 1849 Republics proclaimed by Mazzini's followers in Rome and Tuscany (the latter lasting only six months) after declaring the abolition of the temporal power of the Pope and expelling Grand Duke Leopold from Florence.

From 1850 the inflexibility of Mazzini gave way to more moderate theories advocating political solutions.

1850 Mechanization of the textile industry in Prato.

1852 **Cavour** becomes President of the Council.

1859 Napoleon III launches a military campaign, marked by Franco-Piedmontese victories over the Austrians at Magenta and Solferino.

1860 Decisive year for Italian unification. Unification with Piedmont of the Grand Duchy of Tuscany, the Duchy of Parma and Modena and the Duchy of Emilia and Romagna. In return, Nice and Savoy granted to Napoleon III under the Treaty of Turin. Unification with Piedmont of southern Italy through the Expedition of the Thousand Volunteers (Red-shirts) under the command of **Garibaldi**, who landed in Sicily and Naples. Only the Papal States and Venetia unaffected by the unification process.

14 March 1861 Victor Emmanuel II of Savoy proclaimed King of Italy with the capital in Turin.

1865–70 Capital transferred from Turin to Florence; final transfer to Rome in 1870 after conquest by Piedmontese troops.

TUSCANY WITHIN UNIFIED ITALY

1905 Resumption of draining the Maremma region, initially launched by the Dukes of Lorraine in the 19C; malaria almost eradicted.

1915–18 First World War

1919 Earthquake in Mugello area.

1929 Industrial and mining activity in Tuscany is badly hit by the economic recession.

1940–45 Second World War

1943 Central Italy, particularly Tuscany, becomes a huge battlefield disputed between the Germans in northern Italy and the Allies in southern Italy (they land in Sicily in July). Major bombing raids on

Pisa, Livorno and Grosseto. German bombing raid on Florence, which destroyed all the bridges except the Ponte Vecchio.

July 1944 Pisa comes under artillery attack, setting fire to the Camposanto.

12 August 1944 Florence liberated by the Allies.

2 June 1946 Italy becomes a Republic, with Tuscany voting massively in favour.

1948 Italy divides into 20 self-governing administrative regions, including Tuscany which is sub-divided into nine provinces.

1966 River Arno floods, causing extensive damage, especially in Florence, some works of art damaged beyond repair.

1988 Cars banished from the centre of major cities such as Florence, Siena, Lucca and Volterra.

1992 Establishment of the Apuan Alps Natural Park.

27 May 1993 Bomb attack on the Uffizi Gallery in Florence causes the destruction of three paintings and varying degrees of damage to numerous works of art.

1993 Council of Europe environmental protection award received by the Maremma Nature Reserve.

1994 Addition of the Province of Prato to the nine existing provinces.

2000 Catholic Jubilee brings thousands of pilgrims to Italy and Tuscany.

2001 December Pisa's Leaning Tower reopens after a 12-year renovation.

2002 January Italy officially replaces the lira with the euro.

2004 September 500th anniversary of Michelangelo's *David*, which underwent a controversial two-year cleaning from 2002–2004.

29 October 2004 The Val d'Orcia landscape added to UNESCO's World Heritage Site list.

19 April 2005 Cardinal Joseph Ratzinger elected Pope, choosing the name Pope Benedict XVI.

2006 May, Giorgio Napolitano elected President.

2007 Prime Minister Romano Prodi resigns after a no-confidence vote.

April 2008 Silvio Berlusconi is re-elected as Prime Minister.

November 2011 Berlusconi forced from office. Mario Monti becomes Interim Prime Minister, serving also as Minister of Economy and Finance.

2013 Cardinal Jorge Mario Bergoglio elected Pope, choosing the name Francesco.

February 2014 Matteo Renzi, member of the Democratic Party and Mayor of Florence, becomes Prime Minister. Dario Nardella (Democratic Party) is elected Mayor of Florence.

2014 The Opera di Firenze – Maggio Musicale Fiorentino, or Florence Opera, opens to the public. This multifunctional cultural institution includes an 1800-seat hall for opera performances and a 2,000-seat open-air performance space. The Opera is currently building a 1,200-seat concert auditorium.

January 2015 Giorgio Napolitano, President of the Italian Republic, hands in his resignation on 14 January 2015, at the end of his term as Italian President of the European Union. On 3 February, Sergio Mattarella is named the new President of the Italian Republic.

13 March 2015 Pope Francesco announces the Extraordinary Jubilee of Mercy through the papal bull Misericordiae Vultus, it will be hold from 8 December 2015 to 20 November 2016.

August 2015 A "downburst" (a strong downdraft that causes a sudden outflow of winds in all directions from the point where the current has dropped, producing wind intensities similar to those of a tornado) hits Florence, causing millions of euros in damages, primarily in the southern Bagno and Ripoli neighbourhood.

November 2015 Art historian and cultural manager Cecilie Hollberg is the new director of the Galleria dell'Accademia, while German art historian Eike Schmidt is the new director of Galleria degli Uffizi and Palazzo Pitti (the first time a foreigner has ever held this position). Schmidt and Hollberg are two of seven foreigners selected to run some of Italy's best museums: new directors were named based on reforms put in place by Italian culture minister Dario Franceschini, giving important state-controlled museums greater autonomy.

March 2016 Eike Schmidt proposes divesting the Vasari Corridor (including the picture gallery contained therein), making the famous hallway linking the Uffizi to Palazzo Pitti available again. The Vasari Corridor reopening is planned for 2021.

25 May 2016 A problem in Florence's aqueduct causes a considerable stretch of road in Lungarno Torrigiani to sink, submerging a large number of parked cars.

November Prime Minister Renzi resigns after losing decisively a referendum on a proposed overhaul of the Italian constitution. He is succeeded by his Democratic Party ally Paolo Gentiloni.

2017 July EU regulators approve a state bailout of the world's oldest bank, Monte dei Paschi, which has been at the centre of Italy's banking crisis.

2018 June Western Europe's first populist coalition government – formed by the anti-establishment 5-Star Movement (M5S) and right-wing League – takes office after elections in March, with an agenda to cut taxes, boost welfare spending, and overhaul European Union budgets and immigration rules. Giuseppe Conte is Prime Minister.

August 2019 Right-wing League party leader Matteo Salvini withdraws from the government in the hope of triggering early elections.

5 September 2019 A new pro-European coalition is formed with the 5-Star Movement and centre-left Democratic Party (PD). Prime Minister Giuseppe Conte is sworn in for a second mandate.

22 January 2020 Foreign minister Luigi Di Maio steps down as 5-Star leader to calm the turmoil within the party that menaces the government's parliamentary majority.

Art and Architecture

THREE CITIES, THREE TRENDS

From the 11C onwards in Tuscany, as elsewhere in central and northern Italy, the Communes played an important part in local history. Three of them – Pisa, Siena and Florence – were in conflict until the 15C when Florence, the city of the Medici, succeeded in acquiring a degree of control over the region as a whole. During this period, political rivalries and subdivisions had major repercussions on the Arts. Each city developed its own forms and style, influencing its immediate neighbourhood and nearby towns.

Pisa, fascinated by the oriental splendours brought back by its seafarers and travellers, created unusual architectural forms showing a frenetic desire for ornamentation. Alternating bands of green and white marble were combined with rows of arcading on façades in which almost every feature was carved or inset with marble or ceramic motifs.

Siena, on the other hand, favoured Gothic architecture and continued to prefer the delights of its lyrical gentleness throughout the 15C. Sienese architecture, painting and sculpture show a search for delicate, floral beauty imbued with a great sense of freshness. Sienese art emphasises symbolism, but it is lively. Often tender or petulantly joyful, it makes use of vivid colour, especially gold, even in sculpture.

Although **Florence** also showed a liking for multicoloured marble decoration during the Romanesque period, it was always a city of haughty rigour, of sobriety akin to austerity, and of intellectual perfection. Florence's painters' natural tendencies led to transcriptions of reality, with accurate drawing and definitions of a rigorous form of perspective. The sensual nature of light and voluptuous colours – features that bring warmth to a scene or a landscape – was less evident in some of the artists of Florence, who differed in this respect from the Venetians. Their search for truth, was in part expressed through perfect beauty.

The famous **sfumato** technique (&See Architecture Glossary, p77) of Leonardo da Vinci, muting outlines and colours, manipulated the distance between the artist and his subject, as well as creating atmosphere.

Despite this diversity in the creative arts, Tuscany found a fundamental unity in these three trends – an intellectual view of art that appealed to the intellect, a beauty perfect in its forms and its tangible reality.

MEDIEVAL ARCHITECTURE

The growth of trade in the 11C and 12C brought with it a universal transformation in Tuscany. Economic changes and the relative prosperity that followed led to the building of numerous churches. Most of them were fairly modest affairs; parish churches (*pieve*), often built in isolated settings. Examples of these may be found in the Garfagnana, Lunigiana, Casentino or Pratomagno regions. Modest or grand, all testify to the emerging importance of Romanesque art and architecture in Tuscany; a more ornate and more universally adopted style than elsewhere in Italy.

The Middle Ages, between the 11C and 14C, also saw the establishment of numerous monasteries. These belonged to the traditional orders, such as the Benedictines or Cistercians, as well as the new mendicant (supported through charitable donation) orders, such as the Dominicans and Franciscans. The first Franciscan communities were founded in the neighbouring region of Umbria, and two of their monasteries in Tuscany were set up by St Francis himself: Le Celle near Cortona and La Verna, east of Florence, where he received the stigmata. Several new orders came into being in Tuscany itself during this period – the Vallombrosans and the Hermit Monks of Camaldoli in the 11C, the Servites, an order founded on Monte Senario, in the 13C and the Olivetan Order founded on Monte Oliveto Maggiore in the 14C.

The spate of building in the countryside soon saw Tuscany's hilltops fortified, with small towns encircled by walls, or with

Renaissance Man

It was in Tuscany that the Renaissance man was born; a person who exhibited great genius for working in diverse fields. The talented artist, who also was a multi faceted Humanist, was versed in a variety disciplines of human knowledge. Architect and musician Leon Battista Alberti (1404–72) studied jurisprudence and wrote treatises on architecture and sculpture. The two most important artists were Michelangelo, sculptor, painter, architect, town planner and man of letters, and Leonardo da Vinci,

Leonardo da Vinci statue at the Uffizi

painter, sculptor, engraver, architect, engineer, inventor and also musician and poet. Galileo Galilei studied medicine before making his famous astronomical observations, writing about the nature of planets, and inventing his own telescope. Piero della Francesca, the famous painter, researched perspective and optics, and late in life wrote two treatises on perspective and geometry. Brunelleschi's studies enabled him to solve the problem of how to cover Florence's Duomo. Even in a single profession, painter Masaccio, a friend of Donatello and Brunelleschi, expressed volume with a fullness more usually found in the works of sculptors, and was the first to master the scientific use of perspective, as applied in architecture. Giorgio Vasari, painter and architect, wrote a bestseller that defined him also as the world's first modern art historian.

fortresses or castles, such as Monteriggioni, Montalcino or Radicofani. More fortresses were built in the Orcia Valley (Montecchio, Poppi, etc.).

In the towns, cathedrals and a large number of churches were built (or rebuilt), including new Franciscan friaries and Dominican monasteries. The aristocracy began to build houses with overhanging upper storeys and towerhouses. Street corners were enhanced with loggias used for trading activities and, to counterbalance the religious power of the church, an administrative building was erected in the town centre (*palazzo comunale or palazzo del podestà*).

ROMANESQUE RELIGIOUS ARCHITECTURE

The main feature of Romanesque architecture was its simplicity (except in Pisa, which is a special case, see below). The materials used included brick, timber and often irregular shapes of local stone.

The buildings were modest in size – a *pieve* is, by definition, a small parish church designed for the people. The layout was simple. The basilica design dating from the palaeo-Christian era remained as popular here as elsewhere in Italy and the nave, sometimes flanked by aisles, extended into a single or sometimes a triple apse, often without a projecting transept. The roof was plain, the rafters being visible in most of the churches. The colours provided little contrast; a harmonious blend of brown, pale yellow or grey stonework unbroken by the vivid brilliance of a stained-glass window. In most cases the window openings were screened by a sheet of alabaster or marble which let in a pale, eerie light.

EXTERNAL INFLUENCES

Apart from the traditional **palaeo-Christian** elements that could be seen throughout Italy (basilica-type layout, rafters, a separate bell tower or none at

Putting on a Façade

San Michele in Foro, Lucca

It was in Tuscany that the idea was first mooted of wall decoration that defines the wall itself and consequently the space behind it.

In Europe, the uniform façade – in which the doors, windows and stone bonding are set in static geometric lines – was first employed in Florence. The same may be said of the harmonious courtyards of Florence, designed around the symmetry of the four façades. The staircase was removed to the interior of the building so that it no longer disturbed the unity created by the architect.

This search for symmetry in the façade of a building was soon to spread to urban planning. Monuments were no longer considered in isolation; they had to harmonise with their surroundings within the available space.

As prominent features, street corners required careful decoration. This might be a loggia for trading purposes, a monumental shield, or a niche. A long façade facing the street used the rhythm of repeating features to articulate the perspective. Squares had to be treated so as to incorporate the existing buildings into a harmonious whole; in the case of a new square, such as the central square in Pienza, uniformity was the desired effect. This architectural sensibility has had an enormous impact on European designs ever since.

Façades became an obsession in Florence. Numerous churches are devoid of any decorative features because of a lack of agreement on, or funding for, the final masterpiece; San Lorenzo and Santo Spirito have totally plain façades and Santa Maria del Fiore and Santa Croce are fronted with 19C pastiches.

Interiors were not neglected and in large buildings they were used as decorative space. While Byzantium used mosaics, and the countries to the north used lavish stained-glass windows and tapestries, Tuscany employed the skills of its fresco painters.

Santa Maria del Fiore, Florence

all), Tuscan architecture incorporated elements from Burgundy. Much of this is owed to the influence, from the end of the 10C onwards, of the Benedictine Abbey of Cluny, and from Lombardy, where the large cities had a unique style of architecture.

The **Burgundian influence** saw the inclusion of a crypt; a re-introduction of a custom earlier established in the palaeo-Christian era. Crypts are evident in the Benedictine monasteries of the day; San Salvatore on Mount Amiata, Farneta Abbey or San Miniato in Florence. The use of the Latin Cross design was also common to Benedictine buildings, such as San Salvatore, Farneta and San Bruzio near Magliano. In Sant'Antimo, which was a Cistercian monastery, the influence of Cluny is obvious in the radiating chancel chapels, the marked difference in height between the nave and the aisles, and in some of the carvings like the narrative capitals.

Benedictine monastic life was comparatively limited in Tuscany, owing to the reservations of the region's bishops, and to the founding in Tuscany of austere religious communities – the Vallombrosans and the Congregation of Camaldoli – which required strict obedience to the Rule of St Benedict. The result was a restrained approach to Benedictine architecture.

Evidence of the **Lombard style** may be found in a few architectural works in Tuscany; arched friezes on the upper sections of buildings and on bell towers; pilaster strips; niches (San Piero a Grado, Sant'Antimo, Gropina, Sant'Appiano in the Chianti region, the parish church in Artimino); the use of single, sometimes clustered, pillars (San Donato in Poggio, San Quirico in Orcia, Sovana, Lucca Cathedral porch); pillars alternating with columns (Sant'Antimo, Gropina, Santa Maria della Pieve in Arezzo); splayed entrances (San Quirico in Orcia, Sarteano, Pieve di Corsignano); and even the presence of a lantern-tower above the dome over the transept crossing (Asciano).

The Lombard style used more **trans-Alpine** features, an influence that spread along the Via Francigena and had particular influence in southern Tuscany

Religious Architecture

San Miniato al Monte (12C), Florence

The church of San Miniato is a perfect example of Florentine Romanesque Architecture, reminiscent of the Baptistery probably dating from the 11C.

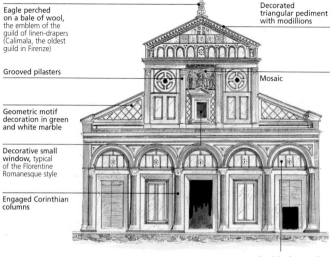

Eagle perched on a bale of wool, the emblem of the guild of linen-drapers (Calimala, the oldest guild in Firenze)

Grooved pilasters

Geometric motif decoration in green and white marble

Decorative small window, typical of the Florentine Romanesque style

Engaged Corinthian columns

Decorated triangular pediment with modillions

Mosaic

Semicircular arcading

R. Corbel/Michelin

Leaning Tower (12C), Pisa

The Leaning Tower, the symbol of Pisa, is universally known for its famous tilt. It is a cylindrical bell tower in the style of the towers in Byzantium and is attributed to Bonanno Pisano.

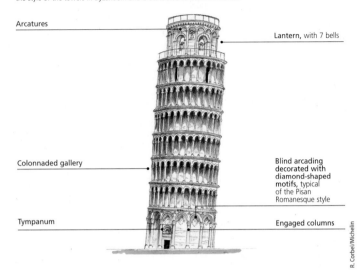

Arcatures

Lantern, with 7 bells

Colonnaded gallery

Blind arcading decorated with diamond-shaped motifs, typical of the Pisan Romanesque style

Tympanum

Engaged columns

R. Corbel/Michelin

– details such as the use of multifoiled oculi, dentil arching, the exceptional use in Sovana Cathedral of quadripartite vaulting (despite the absence of any other Gothic feature), and the appearance of a non load-bearing arch combined with roof rafters in **San Miniato al Monte** in Florence.

From the second half of the 11C onwards these foreign influences began to wane in the face of the increasing popularity of local designs that showed a high degree of inventiveness.

PISAN ROMANESQUE

Through their contacts with Christians in the Middle East and their knowledge of Islamic art forms, the Pisans developed a highly ornate style that reached its peak in Piazza dei Miracoli, where the Baptistery, cathedral, bell tower (the **Leaning Tower**) and Camposanto are laid out like a theatrical stage set.

The Pisan Romanesque style includes; green and white striped marble façades with blind arcading, open-work galleries and inset diamond-shaped decoration on the main façades; a colonnade separating the nave and aisles; and the general use externally and internally of elevated arches.

The Pisan Romanesque style enjoyed enormous success in areas subjected to Pisan influence, but is perhaps best encapsulated in the Campo dei Miracoli in Pisa itself, designed by the architect Buscheto. The features of this style can be seen, to a greater or lesser extent, in the Pistoia and Prato districts, in and around Lucca, in the dioceses of Volterra and Massa Marittima, and as far south as Siena. Siena Cathedral, which is decorated with alternating bands of coloured marble, was begun in the Romanesque period.

FLORENTINE ROMANESQUE

The two main examples of this style, which was prevalent in Florence from the 11C to the 13C, are the Baptistery and the church of San Miniato al Monte in Florence. Both were strongly marked by the palaeo-Christian tradition, and both are outstanding for their classical design, pure volumes and rigorous geometric structure and decoration. Their façades consist of smooth white marble inset with linear motifs in coloured marble. This style was also used in the buildings in the Badia in Fiesole and in the church in Empoli, as well as in the decoration of religious furnishings such as ambos, fonts and pulpits, including the one in San Giovanni Maggiore (near Scarperia). The rational structural geometry of these buildings, which consisted of nothing more than simple volumes, can be seen in churches in areas under Florentine control, such as San Donato in Poggio.

GOTHIC ARCHITECTURE
Religious

The Gothic style came from northern Europe and had little success in Italy where it was seen as a form of political submission to the Holy Roman Emperor and was therefore referred to scathingly as "of the Goths" (*gotico*). The style was introduced by the Cistercians – exemplified in the abbey of San Galgano – adopted by the Franciscans, after the building of the basilica in Assisi, and later used by the Dominicans. During the 13C and 14C, the latter orders built churches in urban centres. Pointed and ogive arches enabled them to erect more spacious buildings, which in many instances had single naves (San Domenico and San Francesco in Siena) so that even the poorest members of the congregation could see everything that was going on in the House of God. In most of the other religious buildings of the time, the Gothic style affected only the decoration and not the structure. In Pisa, the Gothic lancet windows (15C) in the Camposanto are framed by tall semicircular arches, while Santa Maria

della Spina is a gem of stone-cutting, full of gables, pinnacles and niches. It is, however, in Florence and Siena that the major buildings from this period are to be found.

Siena Cathedral was started in the 13C as a Romanesque church with nave and aisles, semicircular arches, black and white striped façades in the Pisan style, and a dome on squinches. In 1284 Giovanni Pisano remodelled the façade in the Gothic style with deep doorways beneath gables, towers with piers and pinnacles, and a plethora of sculptures, mosaics and marble insets. In the 14C, a Baptistery dedicated to John the Baptist (San Giovanni) was built underneath, once the apse had been extended above street level and supported on ogive arches. From 1339 onwards, a project was launched to enlarge the cathedral, in which the older building would have become the transept of the new one, creating the largest Gothic building in Tuscany, had the work been completed (🔖*See SIENA*). The vast size of the project explains the extreme simplicity of the churches belonging to the mendicant orders in Siena; all of the effort and the funding went into the structure of the cathedral, to the detriment of any other work.

In **Florence**, on the other hand, it was the Dominican monastery of Santa Maria Novella that marked the introduction of the Gothic style in the last quarter of the 13C. The vast church, with nave and

Loggia della Signoria (end 14C), Firenze

The loggia is a beautiful example of Gothic architecture, much admired and imitated (most notably in Munich). It was constructed to accommodate the members of the Signoria during official ceremonies.

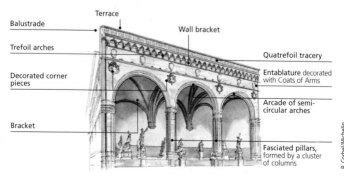

Balustrade

Terrace

Wall bracket

Trefoil arches

Quatrefoil tracery

Decorated corner pieces

Entablature decorated with Coats of Arms

Arcade of semicircular arches

Bracket

Fasciated pillars, formed by a cluster of columns

R. Corbel/Michelin

Duomo or Santa Maria del Fiore (end 13C-15C), Firenze

The commission to build a replacement for the cathedral of Santa Reparata was given to the renowned architect, Arnolfo di Cambio (c 1245-1302) and, although work began in 1296, the cathedral was not consecrated until 1436. Giotto's bell tower was built between 1334 and 1359; Brunelleschi's dome between 1420 and 1434. This grandiose ensemble is a masterpiece of architectural balance.

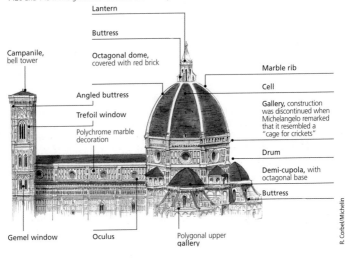

Lantern

Buttress

Campanile, bell tower

Octagonal dome, covered with red brick

Marble rib

Cell

Angled buttress

Trefoil window

Gallery, construction was discontinued when Michelangelo remarked that it resembled a "cage for crickets"

Polychrome marble decoration

Drum

Demi-cupola, with octagonal base

Buttress

Gemel window

Oculus

Polygonal upper gallery

R. Corbel/Michelin

aisles roofed with ogive vaulting, was laid out like a basilica with a flat east end. Shortly afterwards, the Franciscans built a church, Santa Croce, in which the nave was separated from the aisles by great ribbed arches, although the roof was still constructed of traditional palaeo-Christian rafters.

The most unusual building is the Cathedral of Santa Maria del Fiore in which the nave and aisles are almost of the same height. Its main features are its powerful design, its space and its simplicity, and the obvious determination to create a vast interior devoid of luxury. It is the horizontal lines, rather than the vertical, that are emphasised, although verticality was a dominant feature of Gothic architecture. The same principle is at work in the interior of Santa Maria Novella, which is decorated with horizontal bands, and in Santa Croce, where a gallery along the upper section of the wall breaks the vertical lines.

In Florence, therefore, Gothic architecture was revised and adapted to suit a rational and modest feeling that did not easily express itself in a style profuse with slender decorative features.

Secular

Lay architecture was far more open to the Gothic influence than that of Tuscany's places of worship.

The Palazzo Vecchio in **Florence**, which has all the austerity of a fortress in its almost windowless lower section, has an upper section decorated with double windows, machicolations, crenellations and a fine projecting tower. The example of the Palazzo Vecchio was followed by the Bargello, which also has a tower. In **Siena**, the Palazzo del Pubblico consists of a central section flanked by two lower sections. Its many windows give it a lightness echoed in the tall Mangia Tower.

All over Tuscany are other palazzi (del Popolo, or del Podestà) decorated with crenellations and mansions built for wealthy patricians with delightful double or tripartite bays. It was also during this period, the 13C and 14C, that towns such as Siena, San Gimignano, Volterra, Cortona and Arezzo acquired the appearance they have retained to this day.

Palazzo del Podesta e Museo Nazionale del Bargello (13C), Florence

The palazzo was built 50 years before the Palazzo Vecchio and originally housed the Capitano del Popolo, who represented the working classes within the Florentine government, then the Podestà, the first magistrate who held executive and judicial powers. In 1574 the building became the residence of the Chief of Police (called Bargello) and part of it was turned into a prison.

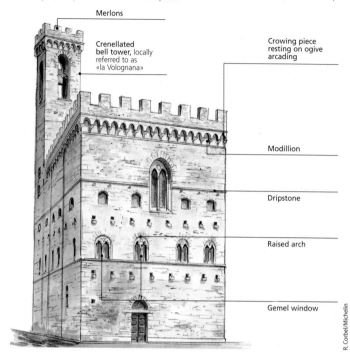

Merlons

Crenellated bell tower, locally referred to as «la Volognana»

Crowing piece resting on ogive arcading

Modillion

Dripstone

Raised arch

Gemel window

R. Corbel/Michelin

MEDIEVAL ART
PAINTING

Tuscan painting had strong links with Greek and Byzantine art. During the 12C a new trend developed in Pisa and Lucca, of displaying a Crucifix in the sanctuary or in the transept crossing. There were two types of Crucifix; one showed Christ in Triumph, a hieratic and serene representation; the other depicted the Passion of Christ, his body twisted and contorted with pain. An example of the former is the Crucifix by **Berlinghieri** painted for Lucca Cathedral c. 1220–30. The latter type was promoted by **Giunta Pisano**, who began to emphasise the pathos of Christ's Passion in the 1240s, and by the success of the sermons preached by the Franciscans, whose founder died in 1226.

Giunta adapted the Greco-Byzantine style to suit the new form of iconography, whereas **Margaritone of Arezzo**

developed a degree of sensitivity and gentleness in his works, especially in the representation of St Francis himself. This trend towards Greek-style icons died out when the artists working on the decoration of the interior of the Baptistery in Florence expressed their skills in mosaics. **Cimabue**, who had worked on the enormous basilica in Assisi at the end of the 13C, showed a new approach within the traditional Byzantine forms. He succeeded in giving his figures an expressiveness that could not fail to move the congregation and induce feelings of tenderness. In addition to several Crucifixes, he painted many *Maestà* – paintings of the Madonna and Child seated on a throne and often surrounded by angels and saints – a tender subject popular in Florence and Siena. **Giotto** also painted Maestà, as did **Duccio di Buoninsegna** in Siena. The Sienese School (*See SIENA*) in

71

The Tower-houses of San Gimignano

In the 12C and 13C, dozens of feudal towers were built in many Italian towns by the powerful families. They were mostly uninhabited but served as a safe place of refuge in times of danger.

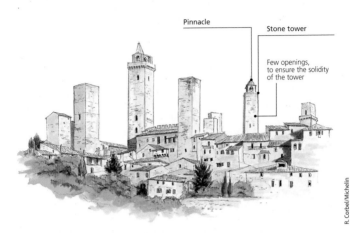

Pinnacle

Stone tower

Few openings, to ensure the solidity of the tower

R. Corbel/Michelin

Palazzo Pubblico (end 13C-14C), Siena

This is one of the finest vernacular buildings in Italy. It is exceptionally elegant and austere and it constitutes a synthesis of all the characteristics of the Sienese Gothic style. It served as a model for most of the other palaces in the city.

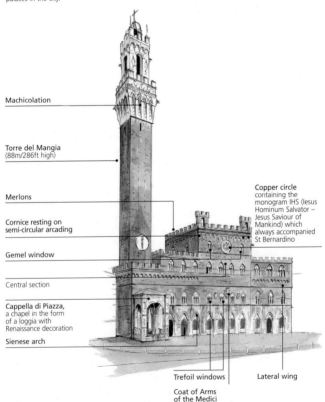

Machicolation

Torre del Mangia
(88m/286ft high)

Merlons

Cornice resting on semi-circular arcading

Gemel window

Central section

Cappella di Piazza,
a chapel in the form
of a loggia with
Renaissance decoration

Sienese arch

Copper circle
containing the
monogram IHS (Iesus
Hominum Salvator –
Jesus Saviour of
Mankind) which
always accompanied
St Bernardino

Trefoil windows

Lateral wing

Coat of Arms
of the Medici

R. Corbel/Michelin

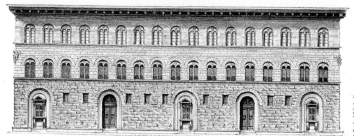

Palazzo Medici-Riccardi

R. Corbel/Michelin

which the leading figures in the 14C were Simone Martini and the Lorenzetti brothers, played a vital role in the **International Gothic** style. This was the most decorative, refined and florid trend of the Late Gothic period, practised by exponents in Paris, Avignon and Prague.

SCULPTURE

A number of works produced in Pisa in the mid-13C had profound importance for medieval sculpture in Tuscany and even in Italy as a whole. There were promising beginnings – the ambo made by **Guglielmo** (12C) for Pisa Cathedral, and works that revealed the Lombard influence such as the figure of St Martin on the west front of Lucca Cathedral (13C). The real trendsetter was **Nicola Pisano**, who carved the pulpit for the Baptistery in Pisa in 1260. His powerful style combined Romanesque lions supporting the columns of the pulpit with Gothic trefoiled arches and low reliefs which were copies of Classical architecture. Pisano turned resolutely towards the Gothic style in the pulpit for Siena Cathedral, which he carved between 1266 and 1268. From the 13C on, this type of furnishing became increasingly commonplace throughout Tuscany. In Pistoia in 1270 **Fra Guglielmo** carved the pulpit set against a wall in San Giovanni Fuorcivitas, and in 1301 **Giovanni Pisano**, Nicola's son, carved the hexagonal pulpit for Sant'Andrea. Giovanni Pisano also worked on Prato Cathedral, on the façade of Siena Cathedral, the chancel of Massa Marittima Cathedral, and carved the huge pulpit (1302–12) – supported on ten columns and a central pillar – for Pisa Cathedral. His pupils included Goro

di Gregorio, who made a name for himself with the sarcophagus of St Cerbone in Massa Marittima Cathedral, but the best known of all was **Tino di Camaino** from Siena who carved the tomb of Henry VII of Luxemburg (*now in the Museo dell'Opera del Duomo in Pisa*). The next generation continued to work in a style that was increasingly detached from architecture: sculptors acquired greater finesse in their use of the chisel and relied less on an impression of strength and force. In Florence **Andrea da Pontedera**, better known as Pisano, created the first of the three bronze doors of the Baptistery (1336) and **Orcagna** carved the Orsanmichele tabernacle (1352–59).

THE RENAISSANCE

During the days of the Communes, the arts flourished in all the politically strong towns and cities in Tuscany. However, in the 15C, the beginning of Florentine domination in the region led to a centralisation of artistic development in the city of the Medici (*See FLORENCE*). The concurrent blossoming of the arts was encouraged by the social climate and economic and financial prosperity. The patronage of its aristocracy and the development of intellectual and philosophical thought, all coincided at a time when ancient ruins were being uncovered in Rome. From then on, the influence of ancient Roman civilization was seen in every field of art and knowledge, leading to what was known as the Renaissance; a rebirth of Classical rather than Gothic aesthetics, a preference for mythology and lay subjects as well as the religious; and for tangi-

Façade of the Holy Trinity Church (1593-1594), Florence

The façade of the Romanesque church built in the 11C can be seen incorporated into the current façade. It was revealed by restoration work carried out at the end of the last century. The Baroque façade by Bernardo Buontalenti (1536-1608) was added in the late 16C. The extremely austere, slender interior is a fine example of the beginnings of Gothic architecture in Florence.

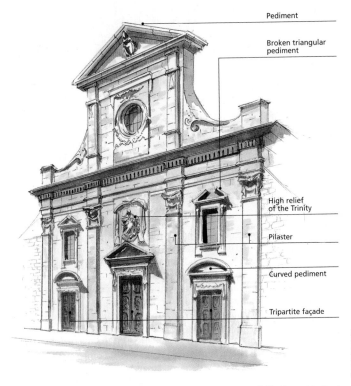

Pediment

Broken triangular pediment

High relief of the Trinity

Pilaster

Curved pediment

Tripartite façade

R. Corbel/Michelin

ble and mathematically-measurable reality rather than only symbolism. This change in aesthetic values in Florence soon embraced the entire region, before spreading to the rest of Italy and Europe.

ARCHITECTURE

Brunelleschi made various trips to Rome to study the ancient Roman remains and to gain an insight into Classical art and architecture. His career was based solely in Florence, where he revolutionised every feature of architecture (◖ *See FLORENCE*). The Old Sacristy in San Lorenzo (designed 1421–28) and the Pazzi Chapel in Santa Croce (designed c. 1430) had a major impact because of their domes. A number of churches followed their example and were laid out like a Greek Cross. Examples include

the Santa Maria delle Carceri in Prato, which was begun in 1485 and designed by Guiliano da Sangallo; the Santa Maria del Calcinaio in Cortona, designed by Francesco di Giorgio Martini from Siena; the San Biagio in Montepulciano (built from 1518 to 1545 by Sangallo the Elder, Guiliano's brother); and Santa Maria Nuova in Cortona, designed by Vasari. In the field of **secular architecture** this period saw the building of **mansions** in towns and cities and **villas** in the country. Michelozzo (1396–1472), who designed the Palazzo Medici in Florence, worked in Pistoia, Montepulciano and Volterra. Guiliano da Sangallo (1443–1516) designed the Medici villa in Poggio a Caiano, which in its day was the only villa to be surrounded by a garden and park. The main entrance was embellished with a central portico

"Fresh" Painting

The fresco technique could be used to cover the entire surface of a wall and also the vaulting or ceiling above. The Tuscan fresco painters used the whole wall as their canvas, rather than as a mere surround for a single, isolated piece of ornamentation.

This technique of wall painting takes its name from the Italian *affresco*, meaning fresh, and involves painting a mural on a fresh coat of plaster, quickly before it dries. As the underlayer dries, it absorbs and fixes the colours, causing the surface to solidify, protecting the wall from water and changes of temperature, and thus from damage over the centuries.

The preparation of the plaster base was very important. The wall was sprinkled with water and covered with a rough base (*arricio*) consisting of one-fifth lime and four-fifths sand. This helped the paint to dry and kept it separate from the wall. It was on this rough base that the preliminary drawing was made.

Detail of the Triumph of Death *fresco, Camposanto, Pisa*

© SaskiaAcht/iStock

As paper was uncommon and very expensive until the 15C, the underdrawing was done on the wall itself using a reddish-brown pigment called sinopia (⟟ *See PISA*). In later years, when paper became more readily available, the drawing was made separately and worked up to scale on a "cartoon" with the outlines of the drawing marked by perforations. The cartoon was held up against the wall, and the outline was transferred to the wall by passing lamp-black across the holes. The drawing could then be recreated on the wall from the black dots.

Small areas of the rough base were then covered with a thin mixture of sand and lime (*intonaco*), in which lime predominated, so that the surface crystallised when drying. This layer was smoothed and polished and remained fresh for just six to seven hours.

There was little room for error and the time limitations, particularly with *buon fresco*, required the detail to be painted in sections before the artist had a working overview. What's more, the fresco had to be painted from top to bottom lest the painting process of one *giornata* ruined the work of previous days.

As the paint dries, the colours are sealed and are preserved so well that even ancient Roman frescoes are fresh and vivid today.

Two Fresco Techniques

There are two fresco painting techniques; *buon fresco* and *fresco a secco*. In *buon fresco*, paint was applied to damp *intonaco*; this was applied in sections known as *giornata* – the amount of surface that the artist could paint in a day. The *giornata*, which can be identified on some frescoes, varied in size according to the difficulty of the work. As the *intonaco* covered the original drawing, the artist had to work using the rest of the composition as a point of reference or he could again make use of the cartoon on the fresh plasterwork. In *fresco a secco*, the paint is applied either on top of dry *buon fresco*, or on dry *intonaco*. Unfortunately *fresco a secco* does not stand the test of time as well as *buon fresco*.

Cappella dei Pazzi (1430–c 1460), Firenze

One of the most exquisite of the designs attributed to Brunelleschi. The artist worked on the chapel until 1445, the year before his death, but it was not completed until c 1460. In this chapel Brunelleschi raised to perfection the architectural ideal that he had already expressed in the old sacristy in San Lorenzo. All the architectural features are emphasised by the grey of the *pietra serena* which stands out against the white pebble-dash in a manner that is strict yet elegant.

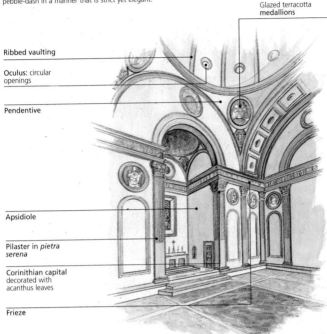

Glazed terracotta medallions

Ribbed vaulting

Oculus: circular openings

Pendentive

Apsidiole

Pilaster in *pietra serena*

Corinithian capital decorated with acanthus leaves

Frieze

R. Corbel/MICHELIN

capped by a pediment, like an ancient Roman temple. This was the first majestic country villa (⟨ *See* PRATO).

During this period some of the towns and cities acquired their own specific character. Florence, of course, owes much to the 15C. Pienza was the setting for the first modern town planning project (1459) designed by **Bernardo Rossellino** (1409–64), who worked with Alberti on the Palazzo Rucellai in Florence; the central square was flanked by the cathedral, the bishop's palace, the patron's palace, the people's palace and a huge well. In Montepulciano the town was renovated and given a Renaissance character by Michelozzo, Antonio da Sangallo and Vignola. The finest buildings in the main street of Monte San Savino are the work of **Sansovino**, a brilliant architect who was born in the town, as his pseudonym suggests.

SCULPTURE AND PAINTING

An impressive number of artists working in these two fields came from Florence (⟨ *See* FLORENCE), but in the 15C the whole Tuscan region became involved in the Renaissance movement. Although Siena followed its own course until the 16C, it was the birthplace of **Jacopo della Quercia** (1374–1438), the inventive sculptor who created, among other works, the tomb of Ilaria del Carretto in Lucca and the Fonte Gaia in Piazza del Campo in Siena. **Francesco di Giorgio Martini** (1439–1502), painter, sculptor and architect, was born in Siena, although his main architectural works are in Urbino and in Pesaro in the Marches; **Baldassare Peruzzi** (1481–1536), who spent most of his career in Rome, was also a native of Siena.

Arezzo and Cortona were the birthplaces of two very great painters – **Piero**

Architecture A–Z

Ambo: small pulpit at the entrance to the chancel from which the Gospel or Epistle was read.

Archivolt: arch moulding over an arcade or upper section of a doorway.

Barrel vaulting: a vault produced by a continuous semicircular arch.

Bucchero: Etruscan pottery; black and shiny.

Cappella: chapel.

Ciborium: a canopy (baldaquin) over an altar.

Cortile: interior courtyard of a palace.

Cupola: dome. *Duomo*: cathedral.

Ecce Homo: Latin for "Behold the Man"; Jesus wearing the crown of thorns

Entablature: The section at the top of a colonnade consisting of: architrave (flat section resting on the capitals of a colonnade), frieze (decorated with carvings) and cornice (top section).

Fresco: mural painting applied over a fresh undercoat of plaster.

Gable: triangular part of an end wall carrying a sloping roof; also applied to the steeply-pitched pediments of Gothic architecture.

Greek cross: a cross floorplan with four arms of equal length.

Lesena (Lombard bands): decorative band of pilasters joined at the top by an arched frieze.

Low relief: bas-relief, carved figures slightly projecting from their background.

Maestà: Madonna in majesty, often enthroned holding Infant Jesus.

Mascaron: medallion carved in the form of a human head.

Mannerism: artistic style, mainly Italian (mid–late 16C), which broke traditional rules, to express powerful emotion.

Merlon: part of a crowning parapet between two crenellations.

Modillion: small console supporting a cornice.

Oculus: round window.

Ogee arch: a pointed arch of double curvature: Cyma Recta (convex lower curve, concave upper curve), Cyma Reversa (vice versa).

Order: system in Classical architecture ensuring a unity of style characterised by its columns (base, shaft, capital) and entablature: Doric (capitals with mouldings – the Tuscan Doric order is a simplified version), Ionic (capitals with volutes), Corinthian (capitals with acanthus leaves) and Composite, derived from Corinthian but more complex.

Pala: Italian term for altarpiece or reredos.

Palazzo: town house usually belonging to the head of a noble family; the word derives from the Palatine Hill in Rome where the Caesars resided and came to mean the residence of a person in authority.

Pediment: ornament in Classical architecture (usually triangular or semicircular) above a door or window.

Piano nobile: the principal floor of a palazzo raised one storey above ground level.

Pietà: Lamenting Virgin with the dead Christ.

Pietra serena: blue-grey stone from the quarries north of Florence.

Pieve: Romanesque parish church.

Polyptych: a painted or carved work consisting of more than three folding leaves or panels (diptych: 2 panels; triptych: 3 panels).

Portico: covered gallery with vaulting supported by columns.

Predella: panelled base of an altarpiece.

Pulpitum: front section of the stage in an antique theatre.

Reredos: ornamental structure on the wall behind and above an altar in a church; French for "behind the back".

Rustication: rough textured dressed stone.

Sfumato: atmospheric impression of perspective (invented by Leonardo da Vinci); outlines and backgrounds are blurred in a light haze.

Squinch: the projecting part of a vault supporting the vertical thrust of an overhanging section in each corner of a square tower; allows the transition from square to octagon.

Stele: a Greek word meaning an upright carved tombstone (1.50m/5ft high) carved in low relief.

Tempera: a painting technique; pigments are ground down and bound usually by means of an egg-based preparation. The technique was replaced by oil.

Tondo: a circular picture, fashionable in Italy in the mid-15C.

Trompe l'œil: two-dimensional painted decoration giving a 3D illusion of relief and perspective.

Tympanum: section above a door (or window) between the lintel and archivolt.

Volute: spiral scroll architectural ornament.

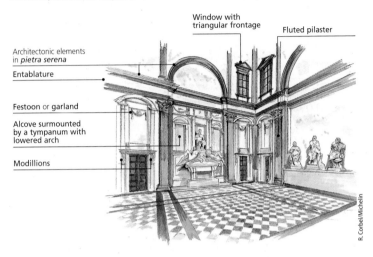

Sagrestia Nuova (1st half of 15C), San Lorenzo, Florence

Michelangelo was commissioned in 1521 by Cardinal Giuliano, the future Pope Clement VII, to build this funeral chapel, which was designed to house the tombs of the Medici family.

Window with triangular frontage

Fluted pilaster

Architectonic elements in *pietra serena*

Entablature

Festoon or garland

Alcove surmounted by a tympanum with lowered arch

Modillions

R. Corbel/Michelin

della Francesca (1416–92), who worked on the fresco cycle in the church of San Francesco (👁*See AREZZO*), and one of his pupils, **Luca Signorelli** (1450–1523), whose drawing techniques were powerful and incisive and who created most of the decoration in the cloisters in Monte Oliveto Maggiore. Filippino Lippi (1457–1504) was born in Prato where his father, Fra Filippo Lippi (1406–69) had painted the frescoes in the cathedral. Lucca was the birthplace of **Matteo Civitali** (1436–1501), sculptor and architect who worked on St Voult's Chapel in Lucca Cathedral, in the manner of Alberti.

MODERN TIMES

In the 15C a few Florentine artists left the city and began to work elsewhere in Tuscany; Benozzo Gozzoli worked on the cathedral in San Gimignano and on the Camposanto in Pisa; others including Donatello and Alberti moved to neighbouring regions such as Umbria and the Marches. In the 16C the movement away from the city gathered pace. Florence had lost its political importance, while the artists she attracted moved to the new artistic centres of the day. Raphael, Michelangelo, Filippino Lippi, Giuliano and Antonio da Sangallo and

others went to Rome; Leonardo da Vinci to Lombardy initially; Sangallo the Younger and Sansovino to Venetia; and Leonardo da Vinci (later), Cellini and Rosso Fiorentino to France.

In the centuries that followed, Tuscany seemed to be exhausted and provided very little in the way of new talent or artistic trends. The end of the 19C, was however marked by the Florentine Verist movement of the **Macchiaioli**, who can be compared with the French Impressionists. The 20C produced **Amadeo Modigliani**, a native of Livorno, famous for his elongated portraits and figure studies, as well as his involvement in the Paris School; and **Marino Marini**, the Florentine painter and sculptor.

In the 19C the golden age of Tuscany was rediscovered and its spontaneity, freshness and search for an ideal were promoted by the German **Nazareans**, a group nick named by the Florentines for their Bohemian lifestyle. There were also the English **Pre-Raphaelites**, such as Rossetti or Burne-Jones, who showed a marked preference for the Italian Primitives dating from the period before Raphael, hence their name. Pietrasanta and Carrara continue to attract the world's foremost sculptors, at least as a temporary base.

Detail of the Galleria degli Uffizi (1560-1580), Florence

The Uffizi Gallery is housed in a building commissioned in 1560 by Cosimo I for the offices (uffizi) of the Medici administration. Giorgio Vasari (1511-74) designed this unusual building in late-Renaissance style on the site of a Romanesque church.

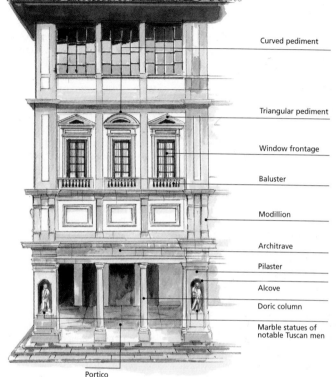

Curved pediment

Triangular pediment

Window frontage

Baluster

Modillion

Architrave

Pilaster

Alcove

Doric column

Marble statues of notable Tuscan men

Portico

R. Corbel/Michelin

The Boboli Gardens, Florence

The gardens were begun in 1549 when Cosimo I commissioned the architect, sculptor and landscape gardener, Nicolo Pericoli alias Tribolo, to convert the hill behind the Pitti Palace into a vast garden. The park is a fine example of an Italian terraced garden with many different perspectives, interspersed with ramps, flights of steps and terraces and dotted with statues and fountains.

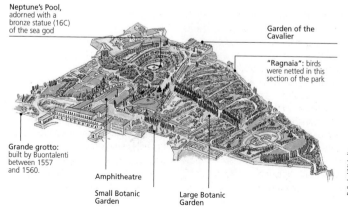

Neptune's Pool, adorned with a bronze statue (16C) of the sea god

Garden of the Cavalier

"Ragnaia": birds were netted in this section of the park

Grande grotto: built by Buontalenti between 1557 and 1560.

Amphitheatre

Small Botanic Garden

Large Botanic Garden

R. Corbel/Michelin

Literature

Tuscany is considered the birthplace of the Italian language. In the early Middle Ages Latin was the only written language – there was no literature in the vernacular. The appearance of poetry written in the Tuscan dialect was the first, and earliest, example of an attempt to preserve one of the many dialects spoken in the Italian peninsula. It was the first step to ensure that it became the language of all of Italy.

EARLY WRITING

From the 13C onwards various literary trends co-existed side by side. St. Francis had set a precedent by writing his poems in the "vulgar" language, rather than Latin. There was the allegorical, didactic style of Dante's teacher, **Brunetto Latini** (c. 1220–95). There were burlesque chronicles like those produced by **Cecco Angiolieri** (c. 1260–c. 1312) from Siena whose sonnets are a celebration of wine, gaming, women and money. There was also lyric verse inspired by the poetry of Sicily and Provence of which the greatest exponent was **Guittone d'Arezzo** (c. 1235–94). The most famous of all the schools of poetry during the 13C was the one that used what Dante called the **gentle new style** (*dolce stil nuovo*). The main poets in this movement, who opposed the earlier tradition by singing of platonic and spiritual love in verse, were **Guido Guinizzelli** (c. 1235–76) and **Guido Caval-**canti (c. 1255–1300) – who was a Guelf and was immortalised in the *Inferno* in the *Divine Comedy* – and Dante himself.

THE WRITINGS OF DANTE

Author of the *Vita Nuova*, chronicling his love for Beatrice, the *Rime*, the *Convivio* and *De Vulgari Eloquentia*, **Dante Alighieri** (1265–1321) is best remembered for his allegorical poem of the afterlife, the *Divine Comedy*. Guided by Virgil in Hell and Purgatory and by Beatrice in Heaven, which consists of nine concentric spheres controlled by God, Dante meets many dead people, some damned and some among the chosen. Their sufferings or joys are proportionate to their behaviour during their time on Earth. It is a racy review of human nature, based on medieval imagery, and also an interesting source of historical detail. Dante, a supporter of the White Guelf faction (See HISTORY), played an active part in the politics of Florence and was appointed prior in 1300. In 1302 he was forced into exile by his opponents, the Black Guelfs, and spent the remainder of his life travelling throughout Italy until he died in Ravenna. Two other Tuscans, **Giovanni Boccaccio** (1313–75) from Certaldo wrote the ribald *Decameron* as well as a major reference work on classical mythology (a standard for 400 years), wrote biographies of 106 famous women, and had a keen interest in the field of archaeology. The poet **Petrarch** (1304–74) is called the "father of Humanism". He, along with Dante and Boccaccio shaped the Italian language for future generations. The letters of **St. Catherine of Siena** (1347–80), of which more than 200 still exist, are considered a major work of Tuscan literature.

15C–20C

The 15C was marked by the preaching of **St Bernardino of Siena** (1380–1444) and **Savonarola** (1452–98), whose campaign against the corruption of the Church was his downfall. **Leonardo da Vinci** (1452–1519) advocated scientific Humanism, laying the foundations for the advances in the sciences in the 16C. **Lorenzo the Magnificent**,

Dante Alighieri

© Michelle7623/iStock

the epitomy of the Renaissance prince, wrote poetry and surrounded himself with philosophers such as Giovanni Pico della Mirandola and poets such as **Poliziano** (1454–94), who was born in Montepulciano. In the 16C, the *Galateo* by **Giovanni della Casa** (1503–56) laid down the etiquette then observed in every court in Europe. Aeneas Silvius Piccolomini (1405-64), who became Pope Pius II, was a lover of the arts and prolific author. Leon Battista Alberti published epic works on painting; *De Pictura* (1435), and *De re aedificatoria* (*Ten Books on Architecture*) (1452) are both still reference works today. Niccolò di Bernardo dei Machiavelli (1469–1527) was historian, playwright, poet, and diplomat (⊙ *See box, right*). His most famous work, *The Prince*, (1498–1512) remains a classic often quoted today. In poetry **Michelangelo** (1475–1564) expressed, with the same vigour that characterises his sculptures and paintings, his torments as a man and an artist, his neo-platonic stirrings of the heart and his later search for God. Poet Vittoria Colonna had a wit sharp enough to captivate the brilliant mind of Michelangelo. In the field of comedy, **Pietro Aretino** (1492–1556), who was born in Arezzo, produced distinguished, elegantly satirical works for numerous patrons. **Benvenuto Cellini** (1500–71), the goldsmith and sculptor wrote a riveting autobiography describing his life as an artist and a passionate and bellicose adventurer. **Francesco Guicciardini** (1483–1540), a Florentine diplomat and friend of Machiavelli, is considered the father of modern history in that he used archival documents in his research to verify his political and historical works. **Giorgio Vasari** was the forerunner of art historians through his valuable work entitled *The Lives of the Most Eminent Italian Painters, Architects and Sculptors*.

The 16C also saw the founding of the **Accademia della Crusca**, which began work on a dictionary of the Italian language in 1591.

The last of the great figures in the most intense period of creativity and

Machiavelli

The works of **Niccolò Machiavelli** (1469–1527) capture our interest today. Some of his plays are regularly performed in English, as well as other languages. His most famous work, *Il Principe* ("The Prince"), with its keen observations and controversial political advice, led him to be called the "father of modern political science". Who was the model for the title character? Historians speculate that most likely it was Roderigo Borgia, who became Pope Alexander VI, or his son Cesare, called "Il Valentino".

inventiveness in the artistic and intellectual history of Tuscany was **Galileo Galilei** (1564–1642), who was born in Pisa, wrote about the world based on scientific observation, rather than a theological or philosophical approach. In the 19C Carlo Lorenzini (1826–90) achieved worldwide fame with **Pinocchio**, which he wrote under the name of Collodi, his birthplace. The first Italian to be awarded the Nobel prize (1906), poet **Giosué Carducci** (1835–1907), also was an outspoken critic of the Catholic Church and spent his youth in Tuscany; in his *Odi Barbare* he attempted to recreate the metre of the ancient poetry which he preferred. **Curzio Malaparte** was the penname of Kurt Suckert (1898–1957) from Prato, author of *The Skin* and a writer who described post-war Italian society in the crudest of terms. Neo-realist **Vasco Pratolini** (1913–91) described everyday life in Florence, his birthplace, depicting the wealthy middle classes and people of more modest means involved in great historic events and in their own private love affairs.

The Tuscan countryside often served as the backdrop to the novels of **Carlo Cassola** (1917–87). **Indro Montanelli** worked as a journalist on *Il Corriere della Sera*, the great national daily, before becoming founder and managing director of *Il Giornale* (until 1994) and later of *La Voce*.

Music

With a few notable exceptions, Tuscany is relatively poor in musical terms compared with other Italian regions and cities.

16C: EARLY COMPOSITIONS AND MELODRAMA

Galileo's father, **Vincenzo Galilei** (c. 1520–91), was one of the first Tuscan musicians. He was a member of the *Crusca* Academy and well versed in the theory of music. He composed madrigals and pieces for the lute, and set the 23 *canti* of Dante's *Inferno* to music, although it has not survived.

Giulio Caccini (c. 1550–1618) devoted himself to *recitar cantando* at the court of the Medici. With the assistance of **Jacopo Peri** (1561–1633), another musician patronised by the Medici, he composed one of the first melodramas, *Eurydice*, which was presented at the Pitti Palace in 1600 for the marriage of Maria de' Medici and Henri IV of France. Melodrama was in fact invented by the **Camerata fiorentina**, also known as the **Camerata de' Bardi**, a group which met at the house of Count Giovanni Bardi del Vernio and included both men of letters and others such as Vincenzo Galilei, Jacopo Peri, Giulio Caccini and Emilio de' Cavalieri, a Roman composer in the service of Cardinal Ferdinand Medici, who was in charge of entertainment at the court of the Grand Duke. The Camerata advocated a return to Greek tragedy. In the same field Antonio Cesti (1623–69), a Franciscan monk, composed grandiose theatrical pieces, much acclaimed abroad.

17C AND 18C: FOREIGN RECOGNITION

Pistoia was the birthplace of **Bernardo Pasquini** (1637–1710), who, although little known as a player of the clavecin, was also an organist and composed many works – toccatas, partitas, suites, concertos and sonatas.

Much better known is **Jean-Baptiste Lully**, who was born in Florence in 1632. At the age of 13 he left Italy for Paris, where he died in 1687. He was composer at the court of Louis XIV and collaborated with Molière to create comedies interspersed with ballet, such as *Le Bourgeois Gentilhomme* and *Psyché*. Lully also composed many lyrical tragedies.

In his wake came the great Tuscan musicians who often worked outside their own country. **Francesco Maria Veracini** (1690–1768), a great violinist from Florence, who composed sonatas for solo violin and base continuo, was also active in Venice, Pisa, Turin, London, Düsseldorf, Dresden, and in Bohemia.

The composer and cellist, **Luigi Boccherini** (1743–1805) was born in Lucca but also worked in Vienna and Madrid. As a composer he favoured string quintets but he also wrote 30 symphonies, which include *La Maison du Diable* in D minor.

19C AND 20C: OPERA TO PIANO

In the 19C Tuscany contributed to the verist trend explored by Verdi through the works of **Giacomo Puccini** (1858–1924) who brought to it his own personal style. Born in Lucca and a resident of Torre del Lago from 1891, Puccini drew inspiration from his turbulent professional and emotional life to compose masterpieces such as the operas *La Bohème*, *Tosca*, *Madame Butterfly* and *Turandot*.

The neighbouring town of Livorno (Leghorn) was the birthplace of **Pietro Mascagni** (1863–1945), who was a teacher of harmony before his major work, *Cavalleria Rusticana*, won the Sonzogno competition, awarded by a publishing house.

Ferruccio Busoni (1866–1924), born in Empoli, was a composer and a pianist of great talent. He gained a certain recognition for his transcriptions of Bach for piano such as *La Ciaccona* taken from the 2nd partita for violin.

Florentine **Mario Castelnuovo-Tedesco** (1895–1968) began his career composing piano pieces and operas. He is renowned, however, for his guitar compositions, which number nearly 100.

Nature

The name Tuscany, first used in the 10C, is derived from the Latin word Tuscia, which was employed from the 3C onwards to describe the region situated between the Tiber and the Arno then known as Etruria, the territory of the Etruscans (who were also known as Tusci). Mountains, hills, inland basins and low coastal plains with varied types of soil are dotted across this mainly highland region, which has some of the largest stretches of woodland in Italy and an abundance of rivers and streams that run down the western slopes of the Apennines and into the Mediterranean.

LANDSCAPE

The northeastern boundary of Tuscany is clearly defined by the curve of the Apennines across the Italian peninsula, from Liguria on the Tyrrhenian coast of the Mediterranean Sea, to the Adriatic coast. This backbone of hills forms a watershed. The geological relief on the northern slopes (where the foothills lie perpendicular to the central ridge) is fairly simple but on the south-facing Tuscan side, there is a series of secondary ranges (low mountains and hills) lying parallel to the main range, creating valleys and inland basins containing the region's major cities such as Florence, Siena and Arezzo.

Like the Apennines, these low mountains are comparatively young, dating only from the Tertiary or Caenozoic eras (65 to 2 million years ago), and consist predominantly of clay and schist, the one exception being the hard and immaculate marble of the **Apuan Alps**. The soil of this region is soft and susceptible to erosion by violent rainstorms, which often lead to the flooding of roads, fields and villages near the river beds, frequently causing dramatic landslides (*frane*) and deep gorges (*calanchi*), which alternate with the crags (*balze*) caused by erosion in the Volterra region. Less extensive landslides have formed jagged peaks among the hills of the Siena region and the Orcia Valley.

Countless rivers and streams rise in the Tuscan Apennines, where the highest peak is **Mount Cimone** (alt 2 165m/ 7 103ft). The range is fringed by small lush valleys – (from north to south) the **Lunigiana** region traversed by the River Magra; the **Garfagnana** region watered by the Serchio; the **Mugello** region containing the Sieve (a tributary of the Arno); the **Casentino** region traversed by the upper reaches of the Arno; the north end of the **Val Tiberina**, where the Tiber River (*Tevere*) rises on the border with Umbria.

Further from the Apennine backbone are folds of soft sandstone and schist forming a series of uplands that vary in appearance from the gently-rolling Florentine countryside to the bare limestone (*crete*) of the Sienese Hills.

A number of rivers – Cecina, Ombrone, Elsa – also rise in these upland regions.

Volterra balze

© hipproductions/iStock

Near the coast the landscape opens out into a wide coastal plain, formed mainly by alluvial deposits from Tuscany's rivers. The Tuscan Archipelago and Monte Argentario peninsula are the last outcrops of the Apennine folds extending into the sea.

The chief delights of the Tuscan countryside are its great variety, its human scale and its abundant vegetation – from the coniferous forests of the high mountains to the olive groves, vineyards and verdant pastures in the valleys.

ARNO BASIN

The Arno River (241km/150mi long), the major Tuscan river, rises on Mount Falterona on the border with Romagna and irrigates the alluvial land on either side of its long course. After flowing through the **Casentino** region, it skirts the south end of the **Pratomagno** range in a deep meander where it is joined, not far from Arezzo, by the fast-flowing Chiana River (one section of which has been canalised – Maestro Canal). The river then flows north through the **Upper Arno Valley** (*Valdarno Superiore*), its course bounded to the west by the Chianti Hills.

When the river reaches Florence, the valley suddenly opens out into the **Lower Arno Valley** (*Valdarno Inferiore*), widening until it reaches the sea. Most of the agricultural and industrial activity is concentrated in this area; it is also the most densely-populated part of the region. The main sectors of employment are intensive and specialised farming (especially around Pistoia, where the maritime climate has favoured the planting of huge nurseries producing fruit trees and house plants), chemical industries and glass-making in Pisa, textiles in Prato and engineering in Florence (where there is still an industrial infrastructure based on old crafts – leather goods, shoes, etc.).

APUAN ALPS

The Apuan Alps north of the Arno glisten with the white marble that made the name "Carrara" so famous.

Blocks and slabs of this marble can be seen piled high on the wharves of Marina di Carrara.

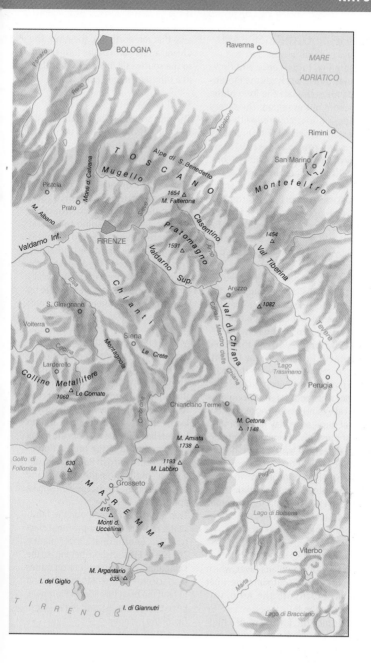

At the foot of the mountains lies the splendid sandy shoreline of **Versilia.** From June to September the packed rows of beach furniture stretch as far as the eye can see. Viareggio is undoubtedly the most popular resort.

The very mild climate is ideal for flower growing.
At the southern end of this flat coastal area lies Livorno (Leghorn), the only real commercial port in Tuscany, with major shipyards and oil refineries.

FLORENTINE COUNTRYSIDE AND CHIANTI DISTRICT

The serenity, irridescence and flowing lines of the works of the Florentine painters emulate the form of the landscapes of this region. The silvery rippling hillsides covered with olive groves, interspersed with mulberry bushes and rows of vineyards, slope gently down to fields of maize or corn. The hilltops, where the dark slender outlines of cypress trees occasionally contrast with clumps of oak or chestnut trees, provide the setting for fortified villages such as Monteriggioni or for majestic old farmhouses (*villas*) dominated by a large central tower used as a dovecot.

A hazy mist often hangs over the region, sometimes persisting throughout the day, softening the distant outlines and drawing a veil of pearly light over the brightly coloured, rolling hills.

South of Florence, on the threshold of southern Tuscany, rise the **Chianti Hills**, extending between the main Siena road and the Autostrada del Sole, the motorway which runs through the Arno Valley. This welcoming region consists of impressive clay hills, home to the famous Chianti vineyards, producers of esteemed wines, some named after the families that own them.

To the west is San Gimignano, which has remained almost unchanged since the Middle Ages. Today it still has numerous medieval towers, identified by some as the forerunners of the skyscraper.

VAL DI CHIANA

The course of the Chiana River, which originally flowed south into the Tiber and not north into the Arno, was reversed in the 16C.

In Antiquity the Etruscans of Chiusi kept a close watch on the river, as it provided an easy link with Rome. When the region was abandoned in the Middle Ages, the river's course gradually blocked with alluvial deposits and stagnated. The Chiana Valley then turned into a vast and unhealthy marshland. In 1551 most of the water was drained off through a canal (Canale Maestro Chiana) that ran north into the Arno. The Chiani, a small arm of the former river to the south, still flows into the Tiber, as a tributary of the Paglia.

SIENESE HILLS

The hills south of Chianti are devoid of vegetation, revealing their pale golden soil which turns to grey beyond Siena. This city is set in the heart of this serene pastoral landscape. Like Florence and Pisa, Siena, the home of the Palio horse race, constitutes a major tourist attraction. The Asciano road leading southwest to Monte Oliveto Maggiore passes through strange limestone landscapes. This is the region of the Sienese *Crete*, of undulating, once barren, chalky hills streaked with deep ravines created by the surface water draining down from the peaks.

METALLIFEROUS HILLS

Between the Florence region and the sea is a zone of low, squat yet forbidding hills. As their name suggests, they are rich in iron ore and also contain deposits of other minerals such as lead, copper, zinc. In the area around Larderello, white steam from the borax (a mineral used in the production of pharmaceuticals) rich hot springs (*soffioni*), is emitted from the bowels of the earth, giving the landscape a dreamlike appearance.

The springs, which colour the landscape red, are used to produce electricity in geothermal power plants. The **Isle of Elba** offshore belongs to the same mountain chain. Its iron mines produce ore that is sent to the mainland to feed the blast furnaces of Piombino. Ferries to the island leave from Piombino harbour.

MAREMMA AND SOUTHERN TUSCANY

On the southern boundary with Lazio are the first volcanic mountains of central Italy, the highest being **Monte Amiata** (1 738m/5 702ft). The mountains are rich in cinnabar, which is used to produce mercury.

Olives and Olive Oil

One of the main features of the countryside in Tuscany is the olive tree. Olive oil is always in abundant supply and of excellent quality; no table is ever without it. Olive oil has been cited in numerous studies for its health benefits. Tuscan olive oil is among the world's best. When olive oil made from less mature olives its colour tends toward

Olives and olive trees

R. Corbel/Micheli

intense green; more mature olives tend toward yellow. An exact ripeness produces the most balanced aroma, between strong and fruity and sweet.

Oil can be negatively affected in smell and taste, too, by worms, soil residue, heat, mould, excessive humidity, acid, a "cooked" taste from heat during grinding, metallic taste from new equipment, too much water on plants, old taste from residue of earlier oil batches, olives picked from the ground, or a rancid smell from oil from excessive contact with air that forms oxidants.

The olive harvest, known locally as the *brucatura*, takes place when the olives are ripe, often the beginning of November. Some farmers pick early for the more piquant taste, others later for the sweeter taste. As olives are gathered from the trees, they are placed on a net (to separate them from olives that have fallen to the ground), then placed into large crates that are stacked onto trucks. The weight alone generates heat and olives are quickly ruined if they are not processed into oil within 48 hours after pressing, as the heat causes the olives to ferment – a nice action for wine or beer but not for olive oil!

The austere landscape provides the backdrop to the **Maremma**, a region of melancholy beauty, erstwhile land of evil spells and dark legends but now an area of quiet rusticity. It has herds of horses and buffalo, once raised there in the wild under the watchful eye of cowboys (*butteri*). Under the agrarian reforms introduced in 1950, these regions, which were formerly the property of a few big city landowners, benefited from land improvement which completely altered their appearance. They were reallocated to farmers from other regions, whose farmsteads are now dotted across the area.

The land is cultivated in a more rational manner (cereal and fodder crops, market-gardening, rice, sunflowers) and modern farming co-operatives have been set up in the region.

Cattle are raised for dairy products, supplying cities such as Florence or Rome, and sheep farming has produced a delicious ewe's milk cheese called *pecorino*.

TUSCAN VILLAS

Tuscany's villas date mainly from the Renaissance period and were once aristocratic residences. They were purchased or built by the members of such prestigious families as the Medici, Rospigliosi, Chigi or Ricasoli. They provided a retreat during hot summer days from the stifling heat of the cities like Florence, Pistoia, Lucca, Siena, where the families spent the rest of the year. Most of them are fairly simply and rigorously designed and all had huge gardens, some of them to magnificent designs. They regained popularity in the 17C when many were extended and lavishly decorated with internal frescoes. The plainest villas are to be found in the countryside around Florence where some still have their medieval structure. Around Lucca on the other hand, the façades were embellished in the 17C with loggias and wide bays, sculptures and balustrades. In the Siena district the villas blend into the countryside, underlining their simple design through the use of natural materials, such as undressed brick and stone.

FLORA AND FAUNA

Tuscany is the most densely wooded region in Italy. The forests (approximately 1,000 000ha/2,471 000 acres) contain an extremely wide variety of vegetation, from subtropical species in certain coastal areas and on the islands to alpine plants on the upper slopes of the Apennines.

TERRACED VEGETATION

Near the sea, pine trees reign supreme, spreading out into expanses of well-protected forests (Versilian and Etruscan Rivieras and the Maremma). Two varieties predominate; the **maritime pine**, which has a conical head and long straight trunk; and the **umbrella pine** with its flattened crown. The umbrella pine has been cultivated since ancient times for its edible oil-bearing pine kernels.

The **cypress** has been widely planted for its ornamental appearance and usage as a windshield for crops. It can be found in the lower regions of the Mugello Valley, the Sienese Hills, the Orcia Valley and, more especially, on the hills of the Chianti region of which it is one of the symbols, together with the grapevine and the olive tree.

For many centuries, the low-altitude areas were covered in coppices, artificially maintained woodlands. Many coppices have now declined after some 30 years of neglect, giving way to *macchia* vegetation consisting of trees and shrubs, mostly evergreens, such as the **holm oak**, or sub-evergreen species, like the **cork oak**. The dark or grey-green foliage and twisted trunks of the trees give the landscape an untamed appearance. The *macchia* vegetation also includes a wide range of thorny and aromatic bushes with tough, glossy leaves such as heather, bramble, butcher's broom (knee-holly), hawthorn, juniper and rosemary. In places where the *macchia* itself peters out, there is a poorer version of the vegetation known as *gariga*, which is generally found in particularly arid areas where plants such as lentiscus, myrtle, cistus and rosemary are able to survive.

Growing near these plants are agaves and prickly pears (common on the Isle of Elba), both of which were imported from the Americas in the 16C.

In the low-lying areas there is a significant amount of natural pastureland and meadow, as well as land devoted to cereal crops, market gardening, vegetable farming and horticulture. Intensive farming extends up to the limit beyond which olive trees will not grow (alt 600–700m/1,970–2,300ft). Together with grapevines, **olive trees** are the main plants on the hillsides. They are grown primarily for the production of oil, with some olives for table.

Chestnut trees, which can grow at altitudes of up to 1,000m/3,280ft, can be found throughout Tuscany, particularly in the woodland on the Isle of Elba, in the Mugello Region and on Monti Pisani and Monte Amiata. The thickest chestnut groves are to be found in the Mugello and Casentino Regions.

Beeches and **fir trees** mark the upper tree line (altitude 1,000–1,700m/3,280–5,580ft) on Monte Amiata and the Apennines. Magnificent coniferous forests cover the area around Camaldoli, Vallombrosa and Abetone. Beeches can be found growing alongside numerous other varieties such as maple, ash, hornbeam, poplar and the Turkey Oak.

Sweet chestnut tree

R. Corbel/Michelin

PADÙLE

In Tuscany, a swamp (*palude*) is called padùle (inversion of the final consonants). Although the swamps have all but disappeared as a result of land improvement in unhealthy areas, the region still includes the Padùle di Raspollino (northwest of Grosseto), the Padùle di Fuccecchio (between Florence and Pisa) and the entire area around the Massaciuccoli Lake, which is considered locally as a padùle.

FAUNA

Tuscany has retained a wide variety of fauna. However, wildlife is under threat from hunting, pollution and technological progress. The creation of nature reserves has been counterbalanced by the recent reclamation of former marshland. Native species like otters and beavers have declined as their natural habitat has been eroded. Among the **large mammals**, wolves can still be found in the Apennines and the upper valley of the Tiber. Stags, imported from Syria during the era of the grand dukes, survive in the Casentino Valley and in the Maremma region along with types of deer. Many deer are in the pine forests of San Rossore, Migliarino, Capalbio and Monte Argentario.

The wild goat, an endangered species in Tuscany, survives only on the island of Montecristo. The wild boar, the emblem of the Maremma, inhabits many areas of scrubland and pine forest, keeping vegetation under control.

Red fox

© stefanocasati/iStock

The most common **small mammals** in the region are the hare and the wild rabbit. The fox, their main predator, adapts to all types of environment. In the dunes of the Maremma are polecats, weasels, martens, stone martens and nocturnal birds of prey. The pine forests are have martens, hedgehogs, porcupines and badgers. Wildcats and polecats can be seen in the shrubby rocky areas of the Maremma region.

Tuscany harbours numerous **species of birds**, including migrants such as passerines (thrushes, swallows, magpies, nightingales, kingfishers), birds of prey (golden eagles, falcons, buzzards, kites, owls), web-footed species (cormorants, mallard ducks, wild geese) and waders (herons, cranes, egrets, storks).

Umbrella pine

Cypress

R. Corbel/Michelin

Portoferraio, Isola d'Elba
© StevanZZ/iStock

Florence has reigned as one of Italy's most prestigious cities since the 15C. Here the first sparks of Humanism and the Renaissance were ignited. Florence is the birthplace of Dante, the cradle of the Italian language and was the proving ground for many of history's most notable painters, sculptors and architects, including Michelangelo and Leonardo da Vinci. Florence's austere beauty and narrow streets can become clogged with visitors. Those who succeed in forgetting the crowds find a rich offering of museums, churches and mansions filled with countless masterpieces and wonderful shops. Although Dante chided Florentines for their pride, some say that the god who created Florence's famous **countryside★★★** – a supremely noble and subtle landscape – must have been a Florentine artist.

The City Today

Florence has long depended on its legacy as the birthplace of the Renaissance for marketing itself, particularly to the millions of foreign tourists who swarm its streets and fill its coffers year after year. But the city's dependence on tourism has also meant a reduction in the native population, who for the last decades have been relocating to the suburbs to escape the crowds and high rents. Florence saw its tourism numbers drop in 2008–9. Although visitors increased again in 2010, the city continues its renewed emphasis on its scientific and manufacturing communities, pushing innovation as part of its riches. The layoffs in the hospitality industry and the shuttering of traditional businesses, from boutiques to butcher's shops, were a warning that its glorious Renaissance heritage cannot weather the economic crisis alone. Elected to the Palazzo Vecchio in 2009, the youthful mayor, Matteo Renzi, had the challenge of leading the city forward. In February 2014 this member of the Democratic Party (left) was appointed Prime Minister of Italy, and his place as mayor of Florence was filled by Dario Nardella, also of the Democratic Party.

In tourism, as in Venice, emphasis is being placed on leading the visitor to treasures away from the main squares. Despite internal opposition, a tram system was launched to ease transport, a good way to connect with some of the sights as well as to explore residential areas.

A BIT OF HISTORY
Roman Origins

The Italiots are said to have settled on the site of Florence between the 10C and 8C BC. They were soon outnumbered by the Etruscans, who preferred the hilltops of Fiesole. In 59 BC Julius Caesar founded a colony on the riverbank to control the Arno crossing

Santa Maria del Fiore and the Palazzo Vecchio viewed from Piazzale Michelangelo

© Tupungato/Shutterstock

and the traffic along the Via Flaminia, the road which ran north from Rome to Gaul. The colony was set up in the spring; its name, Florentia, evokes floral games (*ludi florales*) or flower fields (*arva florentia*).

The Rise of a City

Florence rose to a position of power in Tuscany fairly late in the city's history. For many years Fiesole and later Lucca were predominant. Early in the 11C Count Ugo, Marquess of Tuscany, transferred his residence from Lucca to Florence, where he built an abbey. In the second half of the century, Countess Matilda, who supported Pope Gregory VII in his struggle against the Holy Roman Emperor, ruled this area. During this period Florence began to acquire power and influence. When Matilda died in 1115 the city had already gained a degree of independence which increased during the 12C. Two Romanesque masterpieces, the Church of San Miniato al Monte and the Baptistery, were built. And Florence annihilated its rival, Fiesole (1125). A new, third class of citizen became a phenomenon – the wealthy merchants who enriched the city with an extraordinary level of prosperity, which endured for several centuries.

The Middle Ages

The Power of Money – As trades and crafts developed, their practitioners formed influential **guilds** (*arti*), and formed the basis of legislative power when Florence declared itself a Free Commune in the late 12C.

In the 13C the city enjoyed extraordinary economic development, owing to its wool and, later, its silk industries. Officially it had seven "Major Guilds", five "Medium Guilds" and nine "Minor Guilds" (*See p95*). In the following century the weavers' guild (*Arte della Lana*), whose mansion still stands near the Church of Orsanmichele, and the guild of textile importers (*Arte di Calimala*), employed between them approximately one third of the city's population and exported fine-quality

cloth to all the major trading centres in Europe. Indeed, its reputation spread as far as the Middle East.

In addition to the craftsmen and merchants, Florentine moneylenders greatly increased the wealth of the city. Following in the footsteps of the Lombards and Jews, Florentine **bankers** became influential throughout Europe. In 1269 they instigated the very first bills of exchange, which considerably boosted trade in Florence and Europe. They minted the famous gold florin, bearing the Florentine lily on the obverse and the effigy of the city's patron saint, John the Baptist, on the reverse. This coin became international currency until it was overtaken in the late 15C by the Venetian ducat.

The banking tradition was continued by the Bardi Peruzzi, who advanced enormous sums of money to King Edward III of England at the beginning of the Hundred Years War. They were joined in the world of finance by the Pitti, Strozzi, Pazzi and Medici.

Internal Strife – The economic "miracle" flourished despite the violent feuds that raged not only between Florence and other major towns in Tuscany but also among various factions within the city.

In the 13C the **Guelfs**, supporters of the Pope, and the **Ghibellines**, supporters of the Holy Roman Emperor, first appeared on the scene. At first the Guelfs were victorious. But the Ghibellines set up alliances with other cities that opposed Florence, in particular with Siena, and defeated the Guelfs at Montaperti (⌾ *See CHIANTI*) in 1260. Despite that crushing blow, the Guelfs regained their strength and in 1266 they defeated the Ghibellines and returned to Florence.

Under the Guelfs the city became a republic with a democratic constitution ruled from the Palazzo Vecchio by a government mainly composed of representatives (*priori*) of the guilds.

Divisions then began to appear between Black and White Guelfs, with the latter breaking away from the Papacy. This tragic development led Dante, a member of the White Guelf faction, to be banished for life from his native city in January 1302.

In 1348 the Plague killed more than one-half of the population of Florence, thus putting an end to internal strife.

The Medici

In the 14C several members of the land-owning Medici family moved to Florence. This family of little-known merchants and modest money-changers, was to give the city its leaders for the next three centuries. The Medici also played a vital part in shaping the city's destiny. Several were influential in the world of literature, the arts and the sciences.

The Century of the Medici – Giovanni di Bicci, a prosperous banker and founder of the dynasty, became a leading citizen in his home town by the time he died in 1429. His son, **Cosimo the Elder**, the "Great Merchant of Florence", was then aged 40. He turned the family enterprise into the largest of its kind in Florence, gave the wool and silk industries an "international" dimension and conducted the bank's activities on a European scale. When he came to power, the prosperity of Florence had enabled the city to gain control of several towns in Tuscany. The surrender of Pisa in 1406 made Florence a maritime power. This was a golden era for Florence.

Although Cosimo never held any official position, he acted like a statesman, virtually ruling the city for 30 years. His greatest legacy remains his active patronage of the arts. He encouraged the spread of Humanism by attracting to his circle the very best of Florentine intellectuals and artists, including Brunelleschi, Donatello, the della Robbias, Paolo Uccello, Filippo Lippi, Andrea del Castagno, Benozzo Gozzoli and Fra Angelico. He set up the Platonic Academy and a number of libraries including the famous Laurenziana Library. He had a great love of building and he commissioned numerous major constructions or improvements. When he died in 1464, the Florentines had the inscription *Pater Patriae* (Father of his Country) engraved on his tomb.

His son, Piero I, also known as **Piero il Gottoso** (Peter the Gouty), was a sickly man who had inherited neither his father's political skills nor his business acumen and he survived him for only five years. His marriage to Lucrezia Tornabuoni, however, allied the Medici dynasty to one of the greatest families in Florence.

Piero's eldest son, **Lorenzo the Magnificent** (1449–92), was the most famous of the Medici. Only 20 when his father died, he began to direct the affairs of Florence in accordance with the family tradition. He ruled like a prince, was outstanding for his skilful diplomacy and, like his grandfather, he succeeded in maintaining the dominant position of Florence in Italy and the balance of power between the Papacy and the various States.

As a lover of the arts and a talented writer of verse, he was a supreme example of a Renaissance man. On the other hand, he proved to be less than able in managing the commercial and banking business, and this led to the ruin of the Medici financial empire. The death of Lorenzo the Magnificent in 1492 marked the end of the "century of the Medici"

The "Guilds" in Florence in the Late 13C

The classification of the craft guilds into three categories (major, middle and minor) took place from 1282 to 1293. Initially there was only one guild, for merchants, named after the street where they conducted their business – Calimala. Gradually various crafts set up their own guilds, each with its own coat of arms; the arms below are those of the major craft guilds.

Leading merchants

Wool-workers

Silk-workers

Money-changers

Doctors and apothecaries

Furriers

Magistrates and lawyers

The five middle guilds were swordsmiths and armour-makers; locksmiths; shoemakers; harness-makers and saddlers; tanners and curriers.

The nine minor guilds were linen-drapers and clothiers; blacksmiths; masons and carpenters; joiners; oven-men and bakers; butchers; wine merchants; oil merchants; and hoteliers.

but also the beginning of a new era of discovery.

Savonarola – Girolamo Savonarola (1452–98), a Dominican monk from Ferrara who became prior of St Mark's Monastery, caused the downfall of the Medici by taking advantage of a difficult period when the people of Florence were faced with crumbling republican institutions, and France and Spain were at war for control of Europe. The fanatical, ascetic monk gained power in 1493, when he preached a terrifying and powerful sermon from the pulpit of the cathedral, denouncing the pleasures of the senses and love of the arts. Savonarola was also a critic of the papacy of Alexander VI, and frequently cited it for corruption. In 1497 Savonarola organised a "bonfire of vanities" in Piazza della Signoria. Masks, wigs, musical instruments, books of poetry and major works of art perished in the flames. Soon after, the Pope excommunicated Savonarola and convinced the Florentine government to condemn the monk to death.

In 1498, Savonarola himself was burned at the stake on the very spot where the bonfire had taken place.

The Return of the Medici

After several popular uprisings and several short-lived attempts to govern, the Medici officially returned to power in Florence in 1530, supported by Charles V, the Holy Roman Emperor.

Alessandro, Lorenzo's grandson, took the title of Duke of Florence but he was murdered in 1537 by his cousin Lorenzino, a member of the cadet branch of the Medici family. This branch of

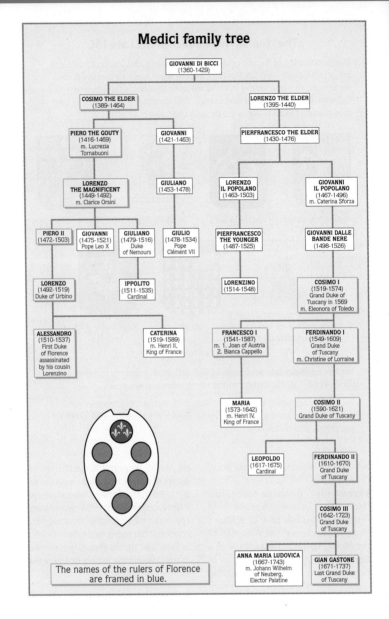

Medici family tree

GIOVANNI DI BICCI
(1360-1429)

COSIMO THE ELDER
(1389-1464)

LORENZO THE ELDER
(1395-1440)

PIERO THE GOUTY
(1416-1469)
m. Lucrezia
Tornabuoni

GIOVANNI
(1421-1463)

PIERFRANCESCO THE ELDER
(1430-1476)

**LORENZO
THE MAGNIFICENT**
(1449-1492)
m. Clarice Orsini

GIULIANO
(1453-1478)

**LORENZO
IL POPOLANO**
(1463-1503)

**GIOVANNI
IL POPOLANO**
(1467-1496)
m. Caterina Sforza

PIERO II
(1472-1503)

GIOVANNI
(1475-1521)
Pope Leo X

GIULIANO
(1479-1516)
Duke
of Nemours

GIULIO
(1478-1534)
Pope
Clément VII

**PIERFRANCESCO
THE YOUNGER**
(1487-1525)

**GIOVANNI DALLE
BANDE NERE**
(1498-1526)

LORENZO
(1492-1519)
Duke of Urbino

IPPOLITO
(1511-1535)
Cardinal

LORENZINO
(1514-1548)

COSIMO I
(1519-1574)
Grand Duke of
Tuscany in 1569
m. Eleonora of Toledo

ALESSANDRO
(1510-1537)
First Duke
of Florence
assassinated
by his cousin
Lorenzino

CATERINA
(1519-1589)
m. Henri II,
King of France

FRANCESCO I
(1541-1587)
m. 1. Joan of Austria
2. Bianca Cappello

FERDINANDO I
(1549-1609)
Grand Duke
of Tuscany
m. Christine of Lorraine

MARIA
(1573-1642)
m. Henri IV,
King of France

COSIMO II
(1590-1621)
Grand Duke of Tuscany

LEOPOLDO
(1617-1675)
Cardinal

FERDINANDO II
(1610-1670)
Grand Duke
of Tuscany

COSIMO III
(1642-1723)
Grand Duke
of Tuscany

ANNA MARIA LUDOVICA
(1667-1743)
m. Johann Wilhelm
of Neuberg.
Elector Palatine

GIAN GASTONE
(1671-1737)
Last Grand Duke
of Tuscany

The names of the rulers of Florence
are framed in blue.

the family, descended from Giovanni de' Bicci, regained power.

Cosimo I (1519–74) was the son of the military leader (*condottiere*), Giovanni dalle Bande Nere (John of the Black Bands, the great-grandson of Cosimo the Elder's brother). He was only 18 years old when he took power but his statesman qualities soon became apparent. His was an authoritarian regime both in administration and policy. Yet he gave Florence back the sparkle that it had lost and brought it renewed prosperity. He created a Tuscan state, keeping the reigns of government firmly in his own hands.

In 1555 he defeated Siena, thus achieving (except for Lucca) the unification of

Tuscany, which became a Grand Duchy in 1569. He also sought to protect his State from external predators such as Charles V, Philip II of Spain and the Papacy. Following in the senior family tradition, he became a patron of the arts and he extended his protection to sculptors such as Giambologna and Benvenuto Cellini and to the painter Bronzino. In 1539 he married the daughter of the Viceroy of Naples, **Eleonora of Toledo**, an intelligent and beautiful woman, whose portrait was painted by Vasari and Bronzino.

The first of their 11 children to reign was **Francesco I** (1541–87) who was more enthusiastic about science and alchemy than political power. He married Joan of Austria, daughter of Emperor Maximilian, and they had one daughter, Maria, the future Queen of France.

His younger brother, **Ferdinando I** (1549–1609), was the last enterprising member of the Medici family. He ensured the prosperity of the State by marrying the French princess, Christine of Lorraine, but his male descendants could not prevent the decline of the Grand Duchy of Tuscany. The last in the female line of this extraordinary family was Anna Maria Ludovica. Upon her death in 1743, she bequeathed the Medici family's vast art collection to Florence with the stipulation that it never leave the city.

The Post-Medici Period

The Grand Duchy passed to the Princes of Lorraine, who maintained possession until the arrival of Napoleon in 1799. He renamed Tuscany the Kingdom of Etruria and made Florence its capital (1801–07) before turning the city into the main town in the French *département* of Arno (1807–09). Finally he restored the Grand Duchy and placed his sister, Elsa, at its head. She was forced to flee from Florence in 1814. Lorraine then regained possession and the Prince of Lorraine remained Grand Duke of Tuscany until 1859.

In 1860 Florence was conquered by the House of Savoy and integrated into the Kingdom of Italy, of which it was the capital from 1865 to 1870.

ART AND ARCHITECTURE
Florentine Painting

From the 13C to the 16C, Florence saw an extraordinary development of the visual arts, which reached its apotheosis during the century of the Medici.

The characteristics of the Florentine School are the search for beauty of form, a preoccupation with evoking an idealised natural environment, a preference for balanced composition and the importance of perspective.

Glimmerings of the Renaissance – The first painter to point Florentine and Tuscan art in this direction was **Cimabue** (1240–1302). He gave his paintings greater humanity through the facial expressions of his figures and by modelling their bodies to give an impression of volume. His pupil and successor was **Giotto** (1266–1337), whose aim was to represent volume in real space and to paint whole scenes (rather than a *Maestà* or a Crucifixion). His figures were draped with grand garments to create a solid mass. The gesture and visual expression in his paintings sought to emphasise the central point in a composition. Among his successors were **Taddeo Gaddi**, **Maso di Banco** (also known as Giottino) and **Bernardo Daddi**.

A Return to Older Values – In the second half of the 14C, every level of society, including art, was affected by the period of crisis which followed the ravages of the Plague in 1348. When **Andrea da Firenze** painted the frescoes in the Spanish Chapel (in the cloisters of Santa Maria Novella) c. 1365, he opted for a style that was less realistic and more dogmatic, typical of preceding century.

Few paintings survive from **Orcagna**, who worked from 1344 to 1368, who painted the reredos in Santa Maria Novella. In the late 14C the narrative style returned, embellished with the beauty of the international Gothic movement which was popular in Siena. **Agnolo Gaddi** (c. 1345–96), Taddeo's son, and **Lorenzo Monaco** (c. 1370–

post-1422) worked in the same style. Monaco, who was a Camaldolite monk in Florence, began by illuminating manuscripts before painting rather static altarpieces, typical of the Gothic period. **Masolino da Panicale** (1383–1447), Masaccio's master, who employed the decorative techniques of the Sienese School, gave greater importance to the representation of volume and space.

Perspective, Volume and Structure: a Design Revolution – A precursor of the technique of foreshortening, **Masaccio** (1401–28) undertook a study of space and the play of light across volume. Assisted by his friend, Brunelleschi, he was the first to define a rigorous, scientific form of architectural perspective. This determination to express the structure of volume reached its height with **Paolo Uccello** (1397–1475) and **Andrea del Castagno** (1423–57). Uccello reduced form to its purest expression, drowning it in light until he achieved an almost abstract use of colour. This is evident in his frescoes in the Chiostro Verde in Santa Maria Novella and his reredos depicting the *Battle of San Romano* in the Uffizi Gallery. These two artists, both draftsmen, created *trompe-l'oeil* sculptures (See THE DUOMO and THE UFFIZI).

Painters of Light and Colour – Some painters who adopted the technique of spatial construction continued to make use of pastel shades, detailed ornamentation or dense composition. The arrival of **Domenico Veneziano** (c. 1400–61) from Venice c. 1435 helped them to find a middle course between the stolid drawings of the early Renaissance and the Gothic-style mannerisms of the heirs of the 14C. He showed the artists of Florence how to use oils and organise space. In this way he reinforced the style of those painters who inclined towards more gentle representations, such as the Dominican monk **Fra Angelico** (1387–1455), who used the new architectural vocabulary to create a very fresh approach to aesthetics.

Narrative Artists – The quietly graceful, descriptive trend led a number of artists to explore the field of narrative painting. From his teacher, Fra Angelico, **Benozzo Gozzoli** (1420–97) inherited a taste for luminous colours, exquisite detail and strong compositions buzzing with activity. Then came **Domenico Ghirlandaio** (1449–94), who excelled in the descriptive style and became a chronicler of Florentine society during the last quarter of the 15C. The arrival in Florence in 1482 of the Portinari triptych by Flemish artist Hugo Van der Goes (*Uffizi Gallery*) had a profound effect on other artists of the day. Apart from the technique of oil painting, of which they had until then seen very few examples, the most outstanding feature of the work was the realism of the figures and the background.

Among those who made even less use of colour than Ghirlandaio were **Antonio Pollaiolo** (1431–98) and his brother, **Piero** (1443–96). Antonio had a vigorous drawing technique, and was interested in conveying a sense of movement and illustrating physical and spiritual contortions. Even the backgrounds of his paintings were filled with sinuous movement, so that his compositions give an impression of great dynamism.

Painters of Grace – The last artistic trend in the 15C focused on ethereal beauty filled with a sense of purity, innocence and delicacy. The artist who was the precursor of this trend was **Filippo Lippi** (1406–69), a monk and pupil of Masaccio, who completed his master's cycle of frescoes in the Brancacci Chapel in Santa Maria del Carmine. His portraits of the Virgin Mary dressed in transparent veils are precursors of works by his pupil, Sandro Botticelli, who taught Lippi's son, **Filippino Lippi** (1459–1504). The apogee (and also the decline) of the early Renaissance was marked by **Botticelli** (1444–1510). The main feature of his work is its sensuality but the artistic experience of the century in which he lived is also evident in his fine, incisive drawing, his sense of background and landscape and the studied poses of his figures draped in filmy garments, with veils fluttering in a gentle breeze.

Masters of the High Renaissance – Although the High Renaissance reached maturity in Rome, it was in the artist studios in Florence that it first took root. **Leonardo da Vinci** (1452–1519) began learning his craft in the studio of the painter and bronze sculptor Verrocchio; **Michelangelo** (1475–1564) was one of Ghirlandaio's pupils; and **Raphael** (1483–1520) came from Urbino to follow his master, **Perugino**.

Leonardo, who came from the nearby town Vinci, was particularly successful in synthesising the art forms developed by his predecessors while enriching the art of painting with his prodigious scientific knowledge. His paintings (*Uffizi Gallery*) are designed to express perfect beauty rendered through technical mastery – perfection in the landscape, the composition, the balance of colours and the architectural and atmospheric perspective (through the use of *sfumato*, which blurs outlines and suffuses backgrounds in a bluish light). Only Michelangelo could rival him, although he took sculpture to be the supreme art. Raphael followed these masters, seeking consummate beauty, first in the manner of Perugino using softness and balance, then using Leonardo's *sfumato* technique, and finally by acquiring Michelangelo's knowledge of anatomy and vigorous creative skills.

Classicism and Mannerism – Although overshadowed by Leonardo da Vinci and Raphael, **Fra Bartolomeo** (1475–1517), a Dominican and follower of Savonarola, and **Andrea del Sarto** (1486–1531), from Florence, represented Florentine Classicism, the final expression of the real Renaissance. Del Sarto was a brilliant colourist and, like Fra Bartolomeo, very fond of *sfumato*. He paved the way for Mannerism by intensifying the expression of feelings (*The Last Supper* in San Salvi). The torments of the soul became more important than the ideal of beauty and the corresponding impression of timelessness.

His pupil, **Pontormo** (1494–1556), gave full vent to his natural anxiety in tormented works. This generation of artists was enormously affected by the paintings of Michelangelo, who painted the ceiling of the Sistine Chapel between 1508 and 1512. The power of his human figures, their sculpture-like positions and his vivid colours were all imitated. The interpretations all varied by artist. **Rosso Fiorentino** (1494–1540) revealed his morbid anxiety in tortured works, elongated figures and strident colours. The second generation of Mannerists moved away from this uncontrolled sensitivity and, conversely, restricted themselves to almost painful solemnity. **Bronzino** (1503–72), instructed by Pontormo, was official portrait painter to the Grand Duchy after 1539. His vigorous, rather cold drawings and vivid colours show the continuing influence of his artistic leader, Michelangelo.

Michelangelo's David, Galleria dell'Accademia

© Philip Coblentz/Brand X Pictures

Vasari, who chronicled Italian art from Cimabue to his own time, was court painter to the Medici and created grand decors in the Palazzo Vecchio, including the allegories and the historical and mythological paintings.

Architecture and Sculpture

The architects of the day created a style based on restrained grandeur. The proportions were harmonious and the decor in religious buildings employed geometric motifs picked out in coloured marble. The mansions had rustication and projecting cornices.

The Middle Ages – The magnificent Baptistery and the Church of San Miniato al Monte are Romanesque. Their simple layouts and harmonious geometric decor of coloured marble made them reference works for the pre-Renaissance movement.

The appearance of the city as it is today owes something to the Gothic style. The blossoming of new religious orders led to several Gothic-style buildings, including Santa Maria Novella for the Dominicans, Santa Croce for the Franciscans, Santa Annunziata for the Servites, Ognissanti for the Humiliati, Santo Spirito for the Augustinians, Holy Trinity for the Vallombrosians and Santa Maria del Carmine for the Carmelites. There were three main architectural designers in the Gothic period. **Arnolfo di Cambio** (c. 1250–1302) created the initial plans for the cathedral and, according to Vasari, for Santa Croce; he was also director of works at the Palazzo Vecchio between 1299 and 1302. **Giotto** built the bell tower (from 1334 onwards). **Orcagna** (1308–68), a pupil of Arnolfo di Cambio and Giotto, designed the Tabernacle in Orsanmichele, a building on which work began in 1336 and which marked the beginnings of an architectural style in which prestige and decoration took precedence over utility. The Loggia della Signoria with its extremely wide arches is a fine example of this style.

Blossoming of the Renaissance – The beginning of this new era in Florence can, for the sake of convenience, be dated to 1401. This was the year in which **Lorenzo Ghiberti** (1378–1455) and Filippo Brunelleschi, among others, took part in the competition to choose the designer of the second doorway to the Baptistery (*See THE DUOMO, p115*). When Ghiberti was chosen, Brunelleschi felt constrained to give up sculpture, although he had trained as a goldsmith. Ghiberti was later chosen to design the third doorway, which Michelangelo called the Gate of Paradise because of its great beauty.

Following his failure to secure the commission, **Brunelleschi** (1377–1446) left for Rome and returned there several times in the following years. He became an enthusiast of classical architecture, for the ruins of ancient Rome and for their gigantic scale. He was the first to understand these structures and to adapt his findings to the needs of his day. The work that revealed his talent and the extent of his knowledge was the dome of Florence Cathedral (*See THE DUOMO, p115*). Nobody else at the beginning of the 15C would have been capable of erecting such a dome without the support of flying buttresses. Brunelleschi, whose building technique was rational and based on calculation and mathematical perspective, is considered the founder of modern architecture.

Leon Battista Alberti (1404–72) was the other great architect of the early 15C. He was a scholar and a Humanist who wrote a number of treatises on painting, sculpture and architecture. Alberti shared with Brunelleschi a love of simple geometric forms, as is evident in his design for the west front of Santa Maria Novella. It is inscribed within a square and its details are structured around this motif. The Rucellai Palace in Florence is also his work.

A friend the two previous artists, especially Brunelleschi with whom he travelled to Rome, was the sculptor **Donatello** (1386–1466). He revolutionised Gothic art by refusing the easy, contemporary stereotypes of draped clothing, gentle movement and serene expressions, and created a great variety of characters, including the young David

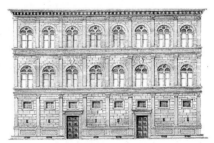

Palazzo Rucellai (1446–51)

Palazzo Davanzati (14C)

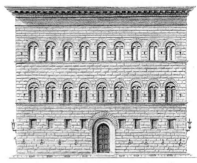

Palazzo Strozzi (1489–1504)

Palazzo Medici-Riccardi (1444–59)

R. Corbel/Michelin

(*in the Bargello*), Judith and Holofernes (*Palazzo Vecchio*) and Mary Magdalen (*Museo dell'Opera del Duomo*).

Golden Age of the Florentine Renaissance – The second half of the century saw the development and blossoming of the forms which had originally been championed by Brunelleschi, Alberti and Donatello. In architecture, **Michelozzo** (1396–1472) made popular in vernacular buildings the forms used by his master, Brunelleschi. He was appointed architect to the Medici and built their mansion in Florence. Mich-

elozzo inspired **Benedetto da Maiano**, another sculptor, who built the Strozzi Palace, and **Giuliano da Sangallo** (1445–1516), who designed the sacristy in Santo Spirito.

Donatello inspired a number of artists, including his contemporaries. **Luca della Robbia** (1400–82) also sought realism in his human figures, but he tended to idealise them, preferring greater flexibility and modesty to the sharpness of his rival. This difference is obvious in the two *cantorie* – one by Donatello, the other by Luca (*now in*

Santa Reparata and the Scoppio del Carro

Although the present cathedral was dedicated to Santa Maria del Fiore, the people of Florence retained a place in their hearts for Reparata, the patron saint of the earlier cathedral. According to legend, when she was beheaded in Palestine at the age of 12, a dove flew out of her body to heaven. Some people claim that this story inspired the metal dove which flies out of the cathedral on Easter Day to set off the cartload of fireworks.

the Museo dell'Opera del Duomo). The popularity of high-reliefs by Luca della Robbia – in azure-blue and white glazed earthenware dotted with yellow and green – established the reputation of his workshop and was perpetuated by his descendants, Andrea (1436–1524) and Giovanni (1446–1527).

Many artists working in or around the middle of the century in emulation of Donatello showed little interest in monumental sculpture. **Desiderio da Settignano** (1428–64) created some magnificent low-reliefs. He died young, leaving the way open for **Mino da Fiesole** (c. 1430–84) and **Benedetto da Maiano** (1422–97), who created the pulpit in Santa Croce; both were famous for their work in marble.

In contrast to this trend in which flexibility was all-important, **Antonio Pollaiuolo** and **Verrocchio** (both of them painters and sculptors) and their pupils were attracted by vigour, energy and muscular strength, which they expressed in bronze.

Michelangelo – At the end of the century, owing to the political upheavals following the death of Lorenzo the Magnificent, Florence entered a period of uncertainty which was perfectly translated by the passionate personality of Michelangelo. Michelangelo's creations exhibited great realism and seem to be throbbing with inner life. Examples of

his genius include his proud *David* (*original in the Galleria dell'Accademia*), his drunken *Bacchus* (*in the Bargello*), his gentle *Virgin Mary and Staircase* (*in the Casa Buonarroti*) and his *Pietà* (*in the Museo dell'Opera del Duomo*).

In architecture also, he breathed life into space by revolutionising the formalism of the classical repertory. He divided up pediments and included empty niches in the new sacristy in San Lorenzo. In the entrance hall to the Laurenziana Library, he treated the internal walls as if they were external and designed the staircase in three parts so that it occupied almost all the floor space. He appropriated Brunelleschi's techniques but used them only to give greater freedom to the dynamics of space.

Florentine Mannerism – Michelangelo had such a strong personality that most artists were influenced by him. The most interesting was **Ammannati** (1511–92) who worked for Cosimo I from 1555 onwards. He designed the courtyard (*cortile*) and the façade of the Pitti Palace; he also designed the Santa Trinita Bridge with its elegant, flattened arches and sculpted the Neptune Fountain in Piazza della Signoria. He often worked with Vasari (1511–74), the architect and painter who supervised work on the Uffizi.

The best of all the late-16C Florentine architects was **Bernardo Buontalenti** (1536–1608) who succeeded Vasari at the Uffizi, designed the west front of Santa Trinita and drew up the project for the Belvedere Fort.

Among the sculptors, **Baccio Bandinelli** (1488–1560) carried over into the 16C a taste for well-balanced, ordered, classical statues. His *Hercules and Cacus* stands opposite Michelangelo's *David* (*copy*) in Piazza della Signoria.

Benvenuto Cellini (1500–71), who wrote a riveting autobiography, was a fervent admirer of Michelangelo. Although principally a goldsmith, he also created bronzes of great impact, in which he managed to combine the many facets of his talent (*Perseus* in the Loggia della Signoria, and a bust of Cosimo I in the Bargello).

Jean Boulogne (1529–1608), known as Giambologna, arrived in Florence from Rome in 1555. His refined talents combined incisive gracefulness with a disciplined academic approach. From this time on, however, Florence began to lose its artists. In the 16C the new beacon was Rome and lucrative papal commissions attracted the finest talents of the day. Over the next few centuries, the Medici city lived in the reflection of its past glories. Never again did it succeed in combining such miraculous rapid economic expansion, financial power, aristocratic patrons and a wealth of talented artists, unequalled since the days of ancient Athens and Rome.

The Florentine House

Towers of the 13C – The economic boom that began in the 13C led to numerous wooden structures being replaced with stone buildings, although **medieval Florentine houses** were still designed to meet the same requirements – the ground commercial floor (workshop or shop) and the family residence in the upper storeys, which could be increased if and when more space was needed. The nobility, who began arriving in the city from their estates in the 11C, habitually commissioned the building of **towers** based, in the early days at least, on the design of their castle keeps. Common interests then brought these nobles and members of the wealthy middle classes from the same district together in "tower communities" which strongly defended each other if they came under attack or fell into dispute with a rival clan. Their towers (up to 70m/230ft high) were interconnected by external wooden galleries. The political upheavals of the 13C led to the destruction of a number of these towers, first those of the Guelfs from 1260 onwards and then, after the victorious return of the Guelfs in 1266, those of their enemy, the Ghibellines. Very few towers – there were said to have been 150 in Florence – have survived to the present day, apart from the bases, which were often used as the

foundations for new buildings. From the 14C onwards, the noblemen abandoned their towers in favour of more elegant mansions.

The 14C/late Middle Ages – The **traditional 14C palazzo** was still capped with battlements and consisted of four main wings surrounding a courtyard (*cortile*) from which an outside staircase led to the upper storeys. On the street front the upper floors were separated by a narrow cornice which, for aesthetic purposes, was set on a level with the window ledges rather than the floors as this gave greater emphasis to the windows. No particular attention, however, was paid to the regularity and symmetry of the façades, nor was any attempt made to conceal the bonding and this gave the residences a fortress-like appearance.

Don't Miss

Florence is so full of art that prioritising a visit will be helpful before succumbing to the Stendhal Syndrome (being overwhelmed by profound beauty). The following sites are highly recommended:

- Piazza del Duomo (*p115–122*)
- Galleria degli Uffizi (*p128–135*)
- Michelangelo's works at the Galleria dell'Accademia (*p158–159*) and in the Museo del Bargello (*p122–126*)
- Palazzo Pitti (*p173–177*)
- Palazzo Vecchio (*p136–141*)
- San Lorenzo and the Tombs (*p150–155*)
- Fra Angelico's works in the Museo di San Marco (*p155–158*)
- Ghirlandaio frescoes in Santa Maria Novella (*p141–147*)
- Frescoes by Masolino, Masaccio and Lippi in Cappella Brancacci (*p180–181*)
- Giotto frescoes in Santa Croce (*p163–165*)
- View from Piazzale Michelangelo (*p183–184*)

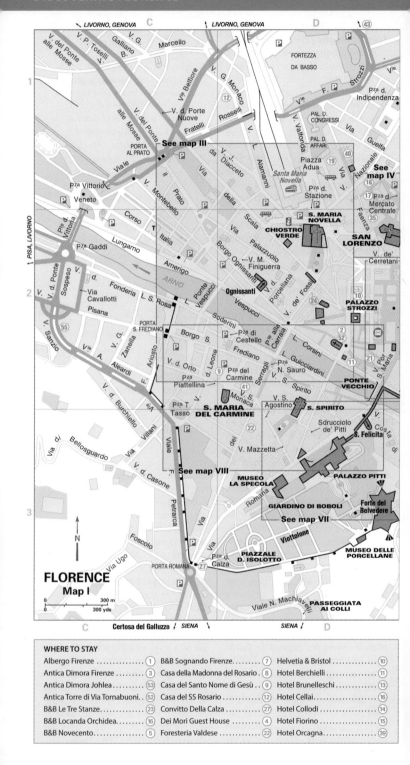

FLORENCE
Map I

WHERE TO STAY

Albergo Firenze . . . . ①	B&B Sognando Firenze. . . . . ⑦	Helvetia & Bristol . . . . ⑩
Antica Dimora Firenze . . . . ③	Casa della Madonna del Rosario . ⑧	Hotel Berchielli . . . . ⑪
Antica Dimora Johlea . . . . ㊾	Casa del Santo Nome di Gesù . . ⑨	Hotel Brunelleschi . . . . ⑬
Antica Torre di Via Tornabuoni. . ㊾	Casa del SS Rosario . . . . ⑫	Hotel Cellai. . . . . ⑯
B&B Le Tre Stanze. . . . . ㉓	Convitto Della Calza . . . . ㉗	Hotel Collodi . . . . ⑭
B&B Locanda Orchidea. . . . . ⑯	Dei Mori Guest House . . . . ④	Hotel Fiorino . . . . ⑮
B&B Novecento. . . . . ⑤	Foresteria Valdese . . . . ㉒	Hotel Orcagna . . . . ㊴

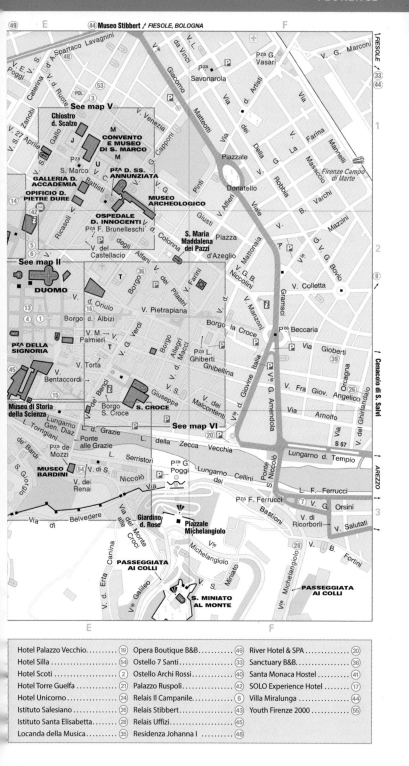

Hotel Palazzo Vecchio........	(19)	Opera Boutique B&B........	(49)
Hotel Silla.............	(54)	Ostello 7 Santi.............	(33)
Hotel Scoti.................	(2)	Ostello Archi Rossi.............	(40)
Hotel Torre Guelfa.........	(21)	Palazzo Ruspoli.............	(42)
Hotel Unicorno.............	(24)	Relais Il Campanile.............	(6)
Istituto Salesiano...........	(26)	Relais Stibbert.............	(43)
Istituto Santa Elisabetta........	(28)	Relais Uffizi.............	(45)
Locanda della Musica........	(35)	Residenza Johanna I..........	(48)

River Hotel & SPA.............	(20)
Sanctuary B&B.............	(36)
Santa Monaca Hostel.............	(41)
SOLO Experience Hotel.........	(17)
Villa Miralunga.............	(44)
Youth Firenze 2000.............	(55)

▶ **Population:** 371,282.

Michelin Map: Atlas p 37, map 563 – K 15 and map 735 Fold 14, 15.

🔲 **Info:** Via Cavour 1. ✆055 29 08 32. www.firenzeturismo.it.

▶ **Location:** Florence's admirable **setting**★★ is on the banks of the Arno in a depression of the Apennines. The city is close to a main junction of two motorways – the A1 and the A11 (*Firenze-mare*).

👪 **Kids:** Museo dei Ragazzi; Giardino di Boboli; medieval armour at Museo Stibbert; mummies at Museo Archeologico; climb the Duomo dome.

🅿 **Parking:** Parking regulations in the town centre are strict – between 7.30am and 6.30pm access is limited to special permits. It is therefore advisable to walk or take the bus and park the car in the Fortezza da Basso or at Santa Maria Novella Railway Station. Contact Firenze Parcheggi, ✆055 50 30 2209. www.firenzeparcheggi.it.

WHEN TO GO

Florence is hot and humid in the summer; the locals flee, but tourists are present. The best times of year to visit Florence are spring and autumn but it is advisable to book accommodation 1–2 months in advance.

USEFUL CONTACTS

TOURIST INFORMATION: Ufficio Informazioni Turistiche
Via Cavour 1r. ✆ *055 29 08 32.*
Piazza Stazione 5. ✆ *055 21 22 45.*
Piazza S. Giovanni. ✆ *055 28 84 96.*
www.firenzeturismo.it.

TRAVEL FOR THE DISABLED: Ufficio Assistenza Disabili, inside Santa Maria Novella train station, ✆ *800 90 60 60.*

24HR PHARMACY: *Comunale n. 13: at Santa Maria Novella railway station,* ✆ *055 21 67 61.*

PHARMACY: *Molteni: Via dei Calzaiuoli 7r,* ✆ *055 21 54 72, 8am–10pm; All'insegna del Moro: Piazza San Giovanni 20r,* ✆ *055 21 13 43, 8am–midnight;*

LOST PROPERTY: *Via Veracini 5/5. Open Mon–Fri 9am–12.30pm, Tue and Thu also 2.30–4pm.* ✆ *055 33 48 02.*

CONSULATES: UK (Milan) – *Via S. Paolo 7.* ✆ *02 72 30 01.* USA – *Lungarno Vespucci 38.* ✆ *055 26 69 51.*

Post and telecommunications Via Pellicceria 3 *(near Piazza della Repubblica)* is the office which deals with *poste restante* mail. At this office there is also a telephone operator service until midnight, although Florence is well supplied with card phones. There is another post office in Via Pietrapiana 53/55.

GETTING ABOUT

Florence is such a rich city that it takes at least four days just to see the main sights. The principal buildings and museums are nearly all in the city centre and fairly close to one another.

BUSES/TRAMS: A transport map, published by the bus company (ATAF), is displayed at Santa Maria Novella railway station. Tickets are sold here, in shops displaying the ATAF sticker, and in tobacconists' (indicated by a sign bearing a "T"). Note that routes can change due to road construction. The ATAF website provides useful information: *www.ataf.net.*
The main routes are: Lines 12 and 13 going to the Colli and the Piazzale Michelanagelo; Line 7 to Fiesole; Line 10 to Settignano; Line 17 to the youth hostel (Ostello dei 7 Santi and Ostello Gallo d'Oro) Tram T1 goes to Scandicci. Most depart from the train station.
Ticket prices – €1.20 (ticket valid for 90 min permitting changes), €2 if purchased on board bus; Carta AGILE pass €10 (10 rides), €20 (21 rides), €30 (35 rides) with each ride valid for 90 min, pass is valid for 12 months.

Buses to Amerigo Vespucci airport are run by private companies, depart from Santa Maria Novella railway station and cost about €5.

FIRENZECARD: The **Firenzecard** is a pass valid for 72 hours from activation and offers entry to more than 75 important museums, churches, villas and historical gardens in the city. Cost €85. The **Firenzecard+** is also valid for all methods of public transport in the city for the 72-hour period (cost+€7). The **Restart** card add 48 extra hours to the Firenzecard when expired (cost+€28). *www.firenzecard.it*

TAXIS: To call a taxi call ℘ *055 42 42, 055 43 90* or *055 47 98*.

CAR HIRE: Cars can be hired at the airport or in town at one of the following agencies: **Avis**, *Borgo Ognissanti 128r;* ℘ *055 21 36 29,* **Budget**, *Borgo Ognissanti 128r;* ℘ *055 21 36 29.* **Europcar**, *Borgo Ognissanti 53r;* ℘ *055 29 04 38.* **Hertz**, *Via Borgo Ognissanti 137r;* ℘ *055 23 98 205,* ℘ *055 30 73 70 (airport).*

BICYCLES: Cycling is a good way to see Florence beyond the centre and to bypass traffic. Bicycles can be rented at some hotels or from **Florence by Bike** (*Via S Zanobi 54, www.florencebybike. it*) which has a range of bicycles and scooters for hire (in summer only) and provides guided cycle tours of the city and the surrounding district. Be sure to lock your bike when parked.

STREET NUMBERS: The street numbering system in Florence seems anarchic, but has a certain logic. There are two entirely independent sequences of street numbers: red indicates a commercial building (noted with an "r"), and blue or black a residential one. To complicate matters further, letters sometimes accompany these numbers (a, b or c).

ADDRESSES

🏨 STAY

🛏 It is strongly advisable to make hotel or apartment reservations before arriving in Florence, one of Italy's most popular tourist cities. Visitors without reservations upon arrival can check with the hotel reservation office, at Santa Maria Novella train station (track 7), with hotels in all price ranges or consult *www.firenzeturismo.it*. See also *www.firenzealbergo.it*. Some accommodations (indicated without descriptive text) are religious in nature and have good rates, but may have curfews (10.30pm or midnight), which exclude the nightlife of Florence. Noise and pollution can be bothersome. The more tranquil pedestrian areas are rare, mostly around Piazza della Signoria. Many hotels have double-glazed windows, but not all are air-conditioned, in summer being hot or noisy or both.

Hotel tax – As of 1 July 2011 the City of Florence has introduced a **tourism tax**, applied for a maximum of 7 consecutive nights. The rate of tax depends on the type of accommodation used (it generally ranges from € 2-5 per person per night in hotels, and is less in hostels).

It does not apply to children (*up to age 12 years*); those who assist patients in hospital (*max 2 per patient*) and patients receiving hospital treatment in day hospitals.

THE DUOMO AND THE MEDIEVAL CENTRE
On the narrow streets in the heart of Florence, this area is certainly the most popular with tourists. It is still full of charm, especially very early in the morning and at dusk.

😋😋 Relais Il Campanile –
Via Ricasoli 10. ℘ *055 21 16 88. www.relais campanile.it. 8 rooms.* Charming B&B, on the first floor of a 17C building, completely restored with lovely rooms.

😋😋💶 B&B Novecento – *Via Ricasoli 10.*
℘ *055 49 31 927. www.lifestyle900.com. 7 rooms.* B&B in the historic centre of Florence. Warm, pleasant atmosphere, well-equipped rooms. Pretty terrace with lovely view of Santa Maria del Fiore.

😋😋💶 Albergo Firenze – *Piazza Donati 4.* ℘ *055 21 83 01. www.albergofirenze.org. 57 rooms.* In the 13C "tower-house" the Donati family offers pleasant common areas and modern, functional rooms. Quite reasonable for the central location.

⊜⊜🛢 **Dei Mori Guest House** – *Via Dante Alighieri 12.* ☏ *055 21 14 38. www.deimori. net. 12 rooms.* Near the house of Dante and the Duomo, this 15C *palazzo* B&B is welcoming. Classic decor with details painted by the beds.

⊜⊜ **Palazzo Ruspoli** – *Via de' Martelli 5.* ☏ *055 26 70 563. www.palazzo-ruspoli.it. 12 rooms.* Elegant rooms, some of which offer a view of the Duomo.

⊜⊜🛢 **Hotel Brunelleschi** – *Piazza Santa Elisabetta 3. www.hotelbrunelleschi. it.* ☏ *055 27 370. 96 rooms.* Opened in 2010, this elegant hotel is situated partly in a Byzantine tower and its own Roman ruins. Furnishings vary from Renaissance-inspired to 19C.

⊜⊜🛢 **B&B Le Tre Stanze** – *Via dell'Oriuolo 43. www.letrestanze.it.* ☏ *329 21 21 28 756 (mobile). 3 rooms.* Close to the cathedral, a small B&B with elegant rooms and bohemian style. The rooms are a mix of contemporary and vintage furnishings.

PIAZZA DELLA SIGNORIA
Centre of the Renaissance and Humanism, this evocative neighbourhood of artistic treasures also bears the brunt of Mass.

⊜⊜🛢 **Hotel Berchielli** – *Lungarno Acciaiuoli 14. www.berchielli.it.* ☏ *055 26 40 61. 76 rooms.* Dating back to 1908, this is set between Ponte Vecchio and Ponte Santa. Classic decor. Lobby lacks pizzazz, but has nice features. Rooms are very large – some with an Arno view. Lavish breakfast.

⊜⊜🛢 **Hotel Torre Guelfa** – *Borgo SS Apostoli 8.* ☏ *055 23 96 338. www.hotel torreguelfa.com. 33 rooms.* Near Ponte Vecchio, this 14C *palazzo* has tastefully decorated rooms with a few retro touches. Breakfast served in guest rooms.

⊜⊜🛢 **Hotel Fiorino** – *Via Osteria del Guanto 6.* ☏ *055 21 05 79. www.hotelfiorino. it. 23 rooms.* This small family-run hotel is in great demand by visitors to the Uffizi. Airy, spacious rooms with sober decor, but comfortable.

⊜⊜🛢 **Antica Torre di Via Tornabuoni 1** – *Via Tornabuoni 1.* ☏ *055 26 58 161. www. tornabuoni1.com. 24 rooms.* Warm beige tones in spacious rooms are inviting. The roof terrace overlooks the Arno river, the hills of Fiesole and Settignano and the Duomo, for buffet breakfast, or hot drinks. A lovely place.

⊜⊜🛢 **Helvetia & Bristol** – *Via dei Pescioni 2.* ☏ *055 266 51. www. starhotelscollezione.com. 64 rooms. Restaurant.* Very elegant, discreet

and attentive. Some rooms that face Palazzo Strozzi are especially impressive.

⊜⊜🛢 **Relais Uffizi** – *Chiasso de' Baroncelli, Chiasso del Buco 16.* ☏ *055 26 76 239. www.relaisuffizi.it. 14 rooms and 5 apartments.* Warm, elegant interior in a medieval *palazzo*, with an outstanding room that faces Piazza della Signoria to relax in at breakfast and begin the day in grand style.

SANTA MARIA NOVELLA DISTRICT
Near the station heading towards the Arno, 10min from the Duomo, very central, a good base near the city, also near parking.

⊜ **Casa del SS Rosario** – *Via Guido Monaco 24.* ☏ *055 32 11 71. Closed Aug. 12 rooms. ospitalitareligiosa.it.*

⊜ **Ostello Archi Rossi** – *Via Faenza 94r.* ☏ *055 29 08 04. 140 beds. www.hostelarchi rossi.com.* Very central location, pleasant ambience. The walls, painted by guests, are contemporary urban art. Youthful, international guests.

⊜⊜ **Hotel Scoti** – *Via de' Tornabuoni 7.* ☏ *055 29 21 28. www.hotelscoti.com. 10 rooms.* Eclectic surroundings, in a recently renovated Renaissance palace; it has a frescoed salon and a slightly decadent aristocratic air.

⊜⊜🛢 **Hotel Palazzo Vecchio** – *Via Cennini 4.* ☏ *055 21 21 82. www.hotelpalaz zovecchio.it. 34 rooms.* Near the conference centre, this hotel has large rooms: nicely decorated, functional but welcoming.

⊜⊜🛢 **Hotel Unicorno** – *Via dei Fossi 27.* ☏ *055 28 73 13. www.hotelunicorno.it. 27 rooms.* On an elegant street with antiquarian shops, in a 17C building; combines antique elegance with comfort.

SAN LORENZO DISTRICT
Near the station, here is the city's main market that spills onto the streets; lively, with small restaurants and close to major sights.

⊜⊜ **Locanda della Musica** – *Via Faenza 85.* ☏ *055 21 38 06. www. locandadellamusica.it. 3 rooms.* Near the San Lorenzo market, on the third floor of a building marked by age, with a comfortable and cosy atmosphere.

⊜⊜🛢 **SOLO Experience Hotel** – *Canto de' Nelli 2.* ☏ *055 29 27 87. soloexperiencehotel. com. 18 rooms.* A comfortable interior made with natural materials facing San Lorenzo.

⊜⊜🛢 **Hotel Collodi** – *Via Taddea 6.* ☏ *055 29 13 17. www.hotelcollodi.com. 12 rooms.*

Situated in the market on a calm street, this ode to Pinocchio has conviviality. Pleasant rooms, terrace and attentive service.

SAN MARCO DISTRICT

A tranquil neighbourhood, near Piazza Santissima Annunziata.

Sanctuary B&B – *Borgo Pinti 15. www.sanctuarybbfirenze.com.* Run by nuns, this BB/holiday home is a jewel in the city's historic centre.

Residenza Johanna I – *Via Bonifacio Lupi 14. 🖉 055 48 18 96. www.antiche dimorefiorentine.it. 10 rooms.* Moderate prices with lovely details (books and magazines for guests to read). Breakfast buffet.

Hotel Cellai – *Via XXVII Aprile 52/R. 🖉 055 48 92 91. www.hotelcellai.it. 72 rooms.* Near San Marco and decorated with great flair, Cellai's gracious hospitality includes splendid lounges and rooms, candlelight breakfast, afternoon tea, free bikes, plus savvy and helpful staff.

Antica Dimora Firenze – *Via San Gallo 72. 🖉 055 46 27 296. www.antichedimorefiorentine.it. 6 rooms.* Small, refined with baldachin beds and antiques.

Antica Dimora Johlea – *Via San Gallo 80. 🖉 055 46 33 292. www.antiche dimorefiorentine.it. 12 rooms.* Small, cosy, elegant and comfortable B&B with lovely touches, yet homelike.

SANTA CROCE DISTRICT

Set around the grand Piazza Santa Croce, colourful with its food markets, many restaurants, ideally situated near the Arno and the Duomo.

Istituto Salesiano – *Via del Ghirlandaio 40. 🖉 055 62 300. 75 rooms. www.salesianifirenze.it.*

B&B Locanda Orchidea – *Via Borgo degli Albizi 11. 🖉 333 52 22 295 (mobile). www.locandaorchidea.it. 10 rooms.* A B&B at the first-floor of a 13C building that creates a tranquil, family atmosphere. High ceilings, simply decorated.

Hotel Orcagna – *Via Orcagna 57/59. 🖉 055 66 99 59. www.hotelorcagnafirenze.it. 17 rooms.* Small, welcoming, family-run hotel. Simple, well-kept. Bike rental and tour guides available.

River Hotel & SPA – *Lungarno della Zecca Vecchia 18. 🖉 055 23 43 529. www.hotelriver.com. 32 rooms.* 19C building faces the Arno. Classic rooms, modern comforts; upper floor rooms have a view of the Arno and Santa Croce. Guided tours.

PITTI PALACE AND GIARDINO DI BOBOLI

In the Oltrarno, without being far away (Piazza della Signoria is only a 10min walk); airy, less bustle and very green.

Convitto Della Calza – *Piazza della Calza 6. 🖉 055 22 22 87. www.calza.it. 41 rooms.*

Istituto Santa Elisabetta – *Viale Michelangelo 46. 🖉 055 68 11 884. 29 rooms.*

B&B Sognando Firenze – *Via Giampaolo Orsini 115. 🖉 055 68 32 78. www.sognandofirenze.it. 11 rooms.* Fully renovated, it is close to Piazza Michelangelo. Warm and cosy decoration.

Hotel Silla – *Via dei Renai 5. 🖉 055 23 42 888. www.hotelsilla.it. 36 rooms.* On the south bank of the Arno, with large terrace, perfect for breakfast.

SANTO SPIRITO DISTRICT

This neighbourhood is more off the tourist path, home to real Florentines.

Foresteria Valdese – *Via dei Serragli 49. 🖉 055 21 25 76. 39 rooms. www.firenze foresteria.it.*

Santa Monaca Hostel – *Via Santa Monaca 6 🖉 055 26 83 38. www.ostellosantamonaca.com. 112 beds.* Between Piazza Santo Spirito and Piazza del Carmine, the 15C convent has become a chic youth hostel. Colourful rooms (2–20 beds each).

Casa del Santo Nome di Gesù – *Piazza del Carmine 21. 🖉 055 21 38 56. www.fmmfirenze.it. 23 rooms.*

OUTSIDE THE HISTORIC CENTRE

Outside the centre is a chance to observe the real life of Florence, away from well-trodden tourist paths.

Ostello 7 Santi – *Viale dei Mille 11. 🖉 055 50 48 452. www.7santi.com. 35 rooms.*

Youth Firenze 2000 – *Viale Raffaello Sanzio 16. 🖉 055 23 35 558. www.cheap-hotel-florence.com. 32 rooms.* Inn/hotel, rooms vary; 1–5 beds with private baths. In the San Frediano neighbourhood, a 15min walk to Ponte Vecchio.

Casa della Madonna del Rosario – *Via Capo di Mondo 44. 🖉 055 67 96 21. www.madonnadelrosario.it. 31 rooms.*

Opera Boutique B&B – *Via Lorenzo il Magnifico 62. 🖉 388 05 85 005. www.operabeb.it. 6 rooms.* Small, discreet bed and breakfast in a Neoclassical building. Nice antique furniture, rooms have high ceilings and parquet. Buffet breakfast.

Relais Stibbert – *Via Lambruschini 39. 🖉 055 46 25 052. www.soggiornostibbert.com. 7 rooms.* Near the Stibbert Museum;

rooms and small apartments, spacious and comfortable. Buffet breakfast with home-made food.

NEAR FLORENCE

😊😊 **Villa Miralunga** – *Via Beato Angelico 37. 9km/5mi E in Fiesole. Bus 7.* ☏ *055 59 593. 4 rooms.* A 19C villa in the hills with wonderful view of Fiesole from every room. Original flooring from 1840.

♟/EAT

Florence is not a city where it is easy to eat well, especially for the quality–price ratio. Best to seek *trattorie*, for traditional Florentine cuisine like tripe (*lampredotto*), soup of beans and black cabbage (*la ribollita*), tomato bread soup (*la pappa al pomodoro*), rigatoni strascicati (pasta), Florentine steak (sold by weight, €40–45/kilo), meatballs in sauce (*polpette in umido*), sausage with white beans and tomatoes (*fagioli all'uccelletto*) and Florentine sweet bread, la *schiacciata*. Restaurants are grouped by neighbourhood.

THE DUOMO AND THE MEDIEVAL CENTRE

😊😊 **Cantinetta dei Verrazzano** – *Via dei Tavolini 18.* ☏ *055 26 85 90. www.verrazzano. com. Closed Sun and evenings, 2 weeks in Aug.* Run by the Castello di Verrazzano winery, an informal place with continuous service and reasonable prices, with a few savoury dishes (salami, *panini*, *bruschette*, cheese) and, of course, wines.

😊😊 **Le Mossacce** – *Via del Proconsolo 55r.* ☏ *055 29 43 61. www.trattorialemossacce.it. Closed Sat and holidays, Aug.* A tiny, authentic, jovial place with tables close together. Tasty Florentine cuisine made with fresh ingredients.

😊😊🍽 **Fishing Lab Alle Murate** – *Via del Proconsolo 16r.* ☏ *055 24 06 18. www. fishinglab.it. Reservations advised.* With rooms stemming from the Renaissance, it's like going back in time. The restaurant in the Palazzo dell'Arte dei Giudici e Notai offers refined cuisine with fish dishes from all over Italy. Interesting lunch menu.

PIAZZA DELLA SIGNORIA

😊 **Trattoria Anita** – *Via del Parlascio 2r.* ☏ *055 21 86 98. Closed Sun. Reservations suggested.* This simple family place attracts local workers for lunch; in the evenings tourists and Florentine families, at moderate prices.

😊 **Vini e Vecchi Sapori** – *Via dei Magazzini 3r.* ☏ *055 29 30 45. Closed Sun, some days in Aug. Reservations suggested.* Behind Palazzo Vecchio, typical Florentine dishes: *la ribollita*, tripe (*lampredotto*), *crostini* and cheeses in a charming ambiance.

😊😊 **Trattoria Nella** – *Via delle Terme 19.* ☏ *055 21 89 25. www.trattorianella.it. Closed Sun, 1 week in Aug.* Good Tuscan cuisine, like *gnocchi* and tripe.

😊😊🍽 **Ristorante Frescobaldi** – *Piazza della Signoria 31.* ☏ *055 28 47 24. www. frescobaldifirenze.it.* This winery restaurant serves good regional cuisine in two small stone and wood rooms. Their wine bar serves simpler fare.

SANTA MARIA NOVELLA DISTRICT

😊 **Osteria delle Belle Donne** – *Via delle Belle Donne 16r.* ☏ *055 23 82 609. www. casatrattoria.com. Reservations advised.* Adorned with 1950–1960s objects and colourful fruits and vegetables, the closely-placed informal tables ensure a neighbourly chat while enjoying classic cuisine.

😊 **I Tre Merli** – *Via de'Fossi 12.* ☏ *055 28 70 62. www.3merli.com.* Traditional Tuscan cuisine, *lampredotto*, *pasta* and *dolce*.

😊😊 **Baldini** – *Via il Prato 96r.* ☏ *055 28 76 63. www.trattoriabaldini.com. Closed Sat, Sun eve (summer also lunch).* Family ambience with both traditional and innovative food. Good choice for a *Fiorentina* steak.

😊😊 **Coco Lezzone** – *Via Parioncino 26r.* ☏ *055 28 71 78. www.cocolezzone.it. Closed Sun, Tue eve and holidays.* In a 15C tower, founded in 19C, cuisine is traditional Florentine, focused on meat.

😊😊🍽 **Il Latini** – *Via dei Palchetti 6r.* ☏ *055 21 09 16. www.illatini.com. Closed Mon, Tue-Fri lunch and 1 week in Aug. Reservations advised.* Florentines and tourists dine together at large wood tables. Convivial, with traditional fare.

SAN LORENZO DISTRICT

Mercato Centrale – *Open 8-00am. First floor (food and beverages). www.mercatocentrale. it.* Main market of Florence; 1874 glass and iron building designed by Mengoni. Fresh produce, fruit, vegetables, fish, meat and poultry, some cheese makers, butchers and bakers for excellent *panini* and pizza.

😊 **Da Nerbone** – *Mercato Centrale di San Lorenzo.* ☏ *339 69 80 251 Closed eve, Sun, 3 weeks Aug. First floor.* Inside the market since 1872, vendors and curious tourists come for legendary *lampredotto* (Tuscan tripe) sandwiches, soups and meat; has a few small tables.

⊖ **Trattoria Mario** – *Via Rosina 2r.* ℰ *055 21 85 50. Closed eve, Sun, Aug.* Informal, noisy, lively trattoria ideal for a quick, traditional lunch. Workers, businessmen and students share tables. No reservations accepted.

⊖⊖ **Trattoria Gozzi** – *Piazza di San Lorenzo 8r.* ℰ *055 28 19 41. Closed eve, Sun, Aug.* The Gozzi brothers run this authentic trattoria spot amidst the San Lorenzo street vendors. Tuscan cuisine.

⊖⊖ **Trattoria Palle d'Oro** – *Via Sant'Antonino 43.* ℰ *055 28 83 83. www. trattoriapalledorofirenze.com. Closed Sun, Aug. Reservations suggested.* Founded in the early 20C, the great-grandsons keep this trattoria going with Tuscan specialities and, if you're in a hurry, *panini* at the bar. A couple of steps from San Lorenzo market.

SAN MARCO DISTRICT

⊖ **Trattoria La Mescita** – *Via degli Alfani 70/r.* ℰ *338 99 22 640. Open 11am–4pm. 3 weeks in Aug, 25–26 Dec.* Lunch of Tuscan specialities: *crostini, panini* and Chianti.

⊖ **Robiglio** – *Via dei Servi 112r.* ℰ *055 21 27 84. Closed Sun in summer.* Pastas, salads, sweets. For lunch or to sip a cappuccino on the terrace. Try also their other restaurant in Via De' Medici 16.

⊖ **Pugi** – *Piazza San Marco 9b.* ℰ *055 28 09 81. www.focacceria-pugi.it. Closed Sun.* Pizza *al taglio, focaccia, panini,* tarts.

⊖⊖ **Accademia** – *Piazza San Marco 7r.* ℰ *055 21 73 43. www.ristoranteaccademia. it.* Across San Marco, art professors, bankers and neighbours come for Aldo's specialities like mushroom strudel with Parmesan sauce, rabbit roll stuffed with artichokes and lasagne with lamb ragout. Good wines.

SANTA CROCE DISTRICT

⊖ **Ruth's** – *Via Luigi Carlo Farini 2.* ℰ *055 248 08 88. www.kosheruth.com. Closed Fri eve–Sat lunch. Reservation advised.* Near the synagogue, this pleasant place follows Kosher rules, has vegetarian cuisine and klezmer music.

⊖ **I' Trippaio di Sant'Ambrogio** – *Piazza Lorenzo Ghiberti.* ℰ *339 37 85 690. facebook. com/ITrippaiodiSantaAmbrogio. Closed dinner and Sun.* Enjoy a tasty, typical *lampredotto* (tripe sandwich), either plain or topped with potatoes and artichokes, as well as a dish of the famous *trippa* here within the historical landmark Sant'Ambrogio market.

⊖⊖ **Boccadama** – *Piazza di S Croce 25–26r.* ℰ *055 24 36 40. facebook.com/ ristoranteboccadama. Closed Wed, Fri, Sat lunch. Reservations recommended for dinner.* Pretty place, courteous service, local cuisine, ample wine selection.

⊖⊖ **Acquacotta** – *Via dei Pilastri 51r.* ℰ *055 24 29 07. Closed Mon, 3 weeks in Jul and 2 weeks in Feb.* Tuscan cuisine, good quality and value, interesting lunch menu.

⊖⊖ **Il Pizzaiuolo** – *Via de' Macci 113r.* ℰ *055 24 11 71. www.ilpizzaiuolo.it. Closed Sun. Reservations advised.* Pizzeria with cuisine from the South including seafood, pizza, pastas.

⊖⊖ **Del Fagioli** – *Corso dei Tintori 47r.* ℰ *055 24 42 85. Closed Sat–Sun, Aug.* Traditional Florentine trattoria with good service and cosy ambiance, for tranquil meals. Great for steaks and grilled meats.

⊖⊖ **Gilda** – *Piazza Ghiberti 40–41r.* ℰ *055 23 43 885. facebook.com/gildabistrot. Closed lunch and Sun, 10 days in Aug.* Near Sant'Ambrogio, market; appetising dishes at reasonable prices.

⊖⊖ **La Corte de 'Pazzi** – *Borgo degli Albizi 54r.* ℰ *055 26 54 094.* Traditional and creative cuisine. Very pleasant service.

⊖⊖ **Trattoria Cibrèo** – *Via de' Macci 122r. www.cibreo.com. Closed Aug, 1 week in Feb.* Near Sant'Ambrogio market, this annexe is a branch of their elegant restaurant. Casual ambiance, delicious traditional dishes. Quality wines.

⊖⊖⊖ **Baccarossa** – *Via Ghibellina 46r.* ℰ *055 24 06 20. www.baccarossa.it. Closed Sun, lunch by reservation.* Contemporary cuisine: carpaccio, gnocchi with seafood, pasta with fresh tuna and citrus pesto.

⊖⊖⊖ **Ristorante Cibrèo** – *Via Andrea del Verrocchio 8r.* ℰ *055 23 41 100. www. cibreo.com. Closed Aug, 1 week in Feb. Reservation advised.* Near Sant'Ambrogio; traditional dishes, lovely presentation, ample wine selection in elegant surroundings. Attentive staff.

⊖⊖⊖ **Osteria Da Que' Ganzi** – *Via Ghibellina 70r.* ℰ *055 22 60 010. www. daqueiganzi.it. Closed Tue. Reservation advised.* Excellent and tranquil restaurant with traditional Tuscan cooking and good meat and fish.

PITTI PALACE AND GIARDINO DI BOBOLI

⊖ **Enoteca Fuori Porta** – *Via Monte alle Croci 10r.* ℰ *055 23 42 483. www.fuoriporta. it. Closed 25–31 Dec. Reservation advised.* One of Florence's first wine bars to serve quality wines by the glass. *Antipasto* menu and cold plates. Traditional Italian cuisine.

🚋 **Trattoria Bordino** – *Via Stracciatella 9r.* 📞 *055 21 30 48. www.trattoriabordino.it. Closed Sun in Summer.* Traditional Tuscan cuisine, including Florentine tripe.

🚋 **La Mangiatoia** – *Piazza San Felice 8–10r.* 📞 *055 22 40 60. trattorialamangiatoia.it. Closed Mon.* Eat in or take out: pizza, rabbit, chicken, pork, *antipasti*, etc.

🚋 **Zeb** – *Via San Miniato 2r.* 📞 *055 234 28 64. www.zebgastronomia.com. Closed Wed and Sun evening.* Gourmet food shop makes salads, soups, Florentine tripe, etc. Very good wines. Excellent for lunch.

🚋🚋 **Osteria Antica Mescita** – *Via di San Niccolò 60r.* 📞 *055 23 42 836. www.osteria sanniccolo.it.* In the ancient crypt of San Niccolò. Traditional cuisine.

SANTO SPIRITO DISTRICT

🚋 **Al Tranvai** – *Piazza T. Tasso 14r.* 📞 *055 22 51 97. www.altranvai.it. Closed Sun, 3 weeks Aug. Reservations advised.* Informal tables and benches. Warm welcome, good traditional Florentine food, and mostly Florentine clientele.

🚋 **La Casalinga** – *Via dei Michelozzi 9r.* 📞 *055 21 86 24. www.trattorialacasalinga. it. Closed Sun. Reservations advised.* Near Piazza Santo Spirito; simple, bustling spot for Florentine food from antipasto to dessert. Courteous, quick service.

🚋 **Del Carmine** – *Piazza del Carmine 18r.* 📞 *055 21 86 01. Closed Sun. Reservations advised.* Tuscan and Italian cuisine, some fish dishes. Terrace.

🚋🚋 **Il Guscio** – *Via dell'Orto 49.* 📞 *055 22 44 21. www.ristorante-ilguscio.it. Closed Sun, Sat lunch, 3 weeks in Aug. Reservations advised.* Between Santo Spirito and San Frediano, gourmets savour Florentine fare and well-chosen wines. Rustic tables, polished service.

🚋🚋 **L'Osteria del Cinghiale Bianco** – *Borgo San Jacopo 43r.* 📞 *055 21 57 06. www. cinghialebianco.com. Closed Mon–Fri lunch.* Warm welcome, typical Tuscan cuisine.

🚋🚋 **l'Brindellone** – *Piazza Piattellina 10 –11r.* 📞 *055 21 78 79. Closed Mon, Tue and Sun lunch.* Near Piazza del Carmine. Very near Palazzo Vecchio, this simple trattoria offers classic cuisine. Excellent *fiorentina*

🚋🚋 **Il Magazzino** – *Piazza della Passera 2–3.* 📞 *055 21 59 69.* The speciality is tripe, abats, also Tuscans fare like rabbit, beef, some vegetarian dishes. Charming.

TAKING A BREAK

THE DUOMO AND THE MEDIEVAL CENTRE

Drogheria Pegna – *Via dello Studio, 26R.* 📞 *055 28 27 01. www.pegna.it.* Since 1860, a true Italian grocery store selling speciality products and premium brands, from coffee in grains to the best Italian delicatessen.

PIAZZA DELLA SIGNORIA

Gucci Garden – *Piazza della Signoria 10.* 📞 *055 75 92 70 10. www.gucci.com/it/it/ store/gucci-garden Open 10am–10pm.* An interesting seasonal organic menu, stylish clientele, well-priced wines, cocktails and view of Piazza Signoria make for a pleasant stop.

Gelateria Vivoli – *Via dell'Isola delle Stinche 9r.* 📞 *055 29 23 34. www.vivoli.it. Closed Mon, holidays, week of 15 Aug.* Artisanal ice-cream since 1932.

Gelateria Perché No – *Via dei Tavolini 19r.* 📞 *055.23 98 969. facebook.com/ GelateriaPercheNo. Closed Tue.* Founded in 1938, Perché No still makes its own ice-cream.

Rivoire – *Via Vacchereccia 4r.* 📞 *055 21 44 12. www.rivoire.it.* On stunning Piazza della Signoria, founded in 1862, even with perhaps the most expensive coffee in Florence, it is still popular.

SAN LORENZO DISTRICT

🚋🚋 **BrewDog Firenze**– *via Faenza 21r.* 📞 *055 70 95 851. facebook.com/BrewDog Fire. Closed Mon lunch.* This just refurbished "Craft Beer Bar with Kitchen" offers burgers, sandwiches, a great choice of beers and a friendly and informal atmosphere.

SAN MARCO DISTRICT

Carabé Gelateria – *Via Ricasoli 60r.* 📞 *055 28 94 76.* Ice cream made by a young Sicilian couple. Pistachio and *crema* are especially good. The speciality is water-ice.

SANTA CROCE DISTRICT

Enoteca Bonatti – *Via Gioberti 66–68r.* 📞 *055 66 00 50. www.enotecabonatti.it. Closed Sun and Mon lunch.* Since 1934, the Bonatti family has been known for its wines: 1,000 from Italy, with a choice of Chianti and Brunello di Montalcino.

Dolci e Dolcezze – *Piazza Beccaria 8r.* 📞 *055 23 45 458. Closed 10 days in Aug.* Coloured marble decor, retro, slightly kitsch, this tiny place makes good pastries.

Note di vino – *Borgo dei Greci 4/6r.* 📞 *334 85 68 706 (mobile). facebook.com/ notedivinotoscana.* Small, pleasant café with tranquil terrace by Piazza di Santa Croce. Tuscan wine, olives, cheeses and salami.

PITTI PALACE AND GIARDINO DI BOBOLI

Caffè Pitti – *Piazza Pitti 9. ℰ 055 23 99 863. www.caffepitti.it.* Elegant bar, chic design. Outside tables have a view of Palazzo Pitti.

Enoteca Bevo Vino – *Via di San Niccolò 59r (corner Porta San Miniato). ℰ 055 20 01 709. facebook.com/enotecabevovino. 11am–12am.* Tuscan wines, cured meats and salamis.

Vip's Bar – *Viale Giuseppe Poggi 21. ℰ 334 34 55 559. Closes when it rains.* Pretty terrace for cocktails or ice cream.

Caffé Bianchi – *Piazza San Felice, 5/r. ℰ 055 22 44 06. bartabacchibianchi.it* Wine bar, coffee bar and pastries, near Palazzo Pitti.

Pitti Gola e Cantina – *Piazza Pitti 16. ℰ 055 21 27 04. Closed Tue and Feb. www. pittigolaecantina.com.* On the portico of Accademia Italiana, a wine cellar and great Tuscan wines. Tastings at the marble counter or on the terrace.

Il Rifrullo – *Via di San Niccolò 55r. ℰ 055 23 42 621. www.ilrifrullo.com.* A Florentine night spot with light fare, plenty of house cocktails, lovely terrace.

GOING OUT

Antico Caffè del Moro "Caffé degli artisti" – *Via del Moro 4r, Santa Maria Novella. ℰ 055 28 76 61. www. anticocaffedelmoro.eu. Closed 3 weeks Aug.* In the 1950s, artists met here and often paid with paintings, which decorate the walls in this cosy bar, now frequented by students.

SPECTACLES

Florence is an art city at night, too, when concerts and shows enliven the theatres. Daily Florentine newspapers *La Nazione* and *Il Corriere Fiorentino* list the programmes. Also, see www.orchestradel-latoscana.it for regional events.

Box Office – *Via delle Vecchie Carceri 1. ℰ 055 21 08 04. www.boxofficetoscana.it.* Reservations for Teatro della Pergola, Teatro Verdi, Teatro Comunale, Teatro Goldoni, Musicus Concentrus and more.

Chiesa di Orsanmichele – ⓒ *See THE DUOMO, p115.* Chamber music concerts.

Teatro della Pergola – *Via della Pergola 12/32. ℰ 055 22 641. www. teatrodellapergola.com.* One of the citiy's oldest opera houses, 17C, declared a national monument in 1925. Year-round theatre, with opera during the May music festival.

Teatro del Maggio Musicale Fiorentino – *Piazzale Vittorio Gui, 1. ℰ 055 20 01 278 www.maggiofiorentino.com.* The pride of Florence for classical music, concerts and operas.

Stazione Leopolda – A former train station, now hosts events regarding fashion, food, music and more.

Teatro Verdi – *Via Ghibellina 99. ℰ 055 21 23 20. www.teatroverdionline.it.* Concerts (classical, pop, jazz), opera, operetta and film premieres, in a red and gold hall with 1,500 seats.

CLUBS

Full Up – *Via della Vigna Vecchia 23r. ℰ 055 21 96 05. fullupclub.com.* One of the longest-lasting discos in the city. There's a piano bar in pub style on the upper floor; downstairs, a dance floor with sofas and music.

Tenax – *Via Pratese 46. ℰ 055 61 37 01. www.tenax.org.* Away from the centre in Cascine Park (*NW*), this club puts on alternative rock concerts, Italian and European.

Jazz Club – *Via Nuova dei Caccini 3. ℰ 333 33 67 242 (mobile). Closed Mon, Jun–Aug.* Every evening a new jazz group, usually Italian.

SHOPPING

Since the Middle Ages, artisans' shops have lined the streets of Florence. Around Santa Croce are **leather goods** (clothes, gloves, objects). Santa Croce houses the craft school for leather.

Borgo Ognissanti has a number of shops for **embroideries** and **antiques**; the latter also are on Via de' Fossi, Via de' Serragli, Via San Jacopo and Via Maggio. Lovely **goldsmiths'** shops are clustered on Via de' Tornabuoni and Ponte Vecchio, with small window displays of jewellery (sometimes being crafted inside) filled with treasures. Via de' Tornabuoni has famous fashion houses (Ferragamo, Prada, Gucci…) and the contemporary lively styles at Save the Queen (*49r*). Florentine **paper** is especially noted for marbled or embossed styles. Heavier, more elaborate designs are made into desk sets. These are sold throughout the city, especially in Piazza della Signoria, Via de' Tornabuoni and Piazza Pitti. Silk, wool and linen textiles are in exclusive shops, especially along Por Santa Maria, Calimala and Roma, as well as Via

Festival del Grillo

The Cricket Festival is held in Parco delle Cascine on the first Sunday after the Ascension. Theories as to its origin are separated by two schools of thought: that crickets symbolise spring and that they were to be honoured, and conversely that there was a need to control numbers for farm-life. Since 1999, crickets are no longer traded in the park, in order to protect their dwindling numbers. The festival today focuses on the joys of spring.

de' Calzaiuoli. Antico Setificio Fiorentino (*Via Bartolini 4, by appointment only. anticosetificiofiorentino.com*) have been mastering silk weavers since 1786, and are often called upon to furnish museums and historic palaces (in 2011, Villa Medici, Rome). Busatti sells their textiles made in Anghiari. **Fashion boutiques**, shoe shops and leather shops are along here, too. Some **bookshops** are near Annunziata and Via Cavour; explore the **flea market** at Piazza dei Ciompi, or by the loggia of Mercato Nuovo, the arcades along Piazzale degli Uffizi and around San Lorenzo, which has become more for souvenirs.

THE DUOMO AND THE MEDIEVAL CENTRE

Borsalino – *Via Porta Rossa 40r.* ⇊ *055 49 32 967. www.borsalino.com. Closed Sun.* Dapper hat shop, priced accordingly for its elegance and fame.

Maestri di Fabbrica – *Borgo degli Albizi 68r.* ⇊ *055 24 23 21. maestridifabbrica.eu.* Every kind of gift, the perfect place for your Italian souvenirs!

SANTA MARIA NOVELLA DISTRICT

Officina Profumo di Santa Maria Novella – *Via della Scala 16.* ⇊ *055 21 62 76. www.smnovella.com.* ☎ *See box p142.* Spices, refined natural beauty products, soaps and teas.

Fratelli Alinari – *Largo Alinari 15.* ⇊ *055 23 951. www.alinari.it.* Catalogue of 3.5 million photos of Tuscany and Italy.

High fashion – Prestigious fashion houses are along Via de' Tornabuoni, the Arno and near Palazzo Strozzi.

Il Bisonte – *Via del Parione 31/33.* ⇊ *055 21 57 22. www.ilbisonte.com.* Wanny di Filippo makes leather accessories – purses, luggage and desk accessories.

SAN LORENZO DISTRICT

Gherardini – *Via della Vigna Nuova 57r,* ⇊ *055 21 56 78.* Leonardo Da Vinci (whose Mona Lisa some identify as Lisa Gherardini) sketched a bag in the late 15C, which Gherardini created as the exclusive La Pretiosa handbag in 2012. Founded as a leather shop in 1885 by Garibaldo Gherardini, their present focus is luxury bags and accessories. They also own the moderately priced Francesco Biasia shops found in Florence and other cities in Italy.

La Norcineria – *Via San Antonino 21r.* ⇊ *055 29 48 59. www.lanorcineria.firenze.it.* A colourful butcher's shop specialising in salamis and hams hanging from the ceiling, pasta, olive oil and other Tuscan specialities.

SANTA CROCE DISTRICT

Mercato Sant'Ambrogio – *Piazza Lorenzo Ghiberti. www.mercatosantambrogio.it. Closed Sun. 7am–2pm.* Butchers, salami and market stalls.

Mercato delle Pulci – *Largo Annigoni. Closed Sun.* Antiquities and every kind of knick-knacks.

Scuola del Cuoio – *Via San Giuseppe 5r.* ⇊ *055 24 45 33. www.scuoladelcuoio.com.* Founded by a family of artisans and Franciscan friars, *Leather School* occupies a hall of Santa Croce with small shops and a range of quality.

Sbigoli Terrecotte – *Via San Egidio 4r.* ⇊ *055 24 79 713. www.sbigoliterrecotte.it. Closed Sun.* Since 1850, one of the most fascinating ceramic artisans' workshops. Complete dinner services, vases and garden objects.

EVENTS

☎ *See also PLANNING YOUR TRIP.*

Cavalcata dei Magi (*Magus parade*) – January 6, Epiphany, a parade in costumes inspired by the Benozzo Gozzoli frescoes in the Palazzo Medici-Riccardi Chapel, from Piazza Pitti to the Duomo.

Trofeo Marzocco – *May.* Contest of standard bearers in historic costume, Piazza della Signoria.

Maggio musicale fiorentino (*Musical Florentine May*) – Founded 1933, prestigious annual series of concerts, operas and ballets. Also lesser-known works of great 19C composers, and contemporary works.

The Duomo★★★
Art and Faith

At the centre of the city stands a remarkable group of buildings in white, green and pink marble: the cathedral, bell tower and Baptistery, which mark the transition from medieval Florentine architecture to the Renaissance period.

SIGHTS

PIAZZA DEL DUOMO★★★
Visit: half day.
The **loggia del Bigallo**, built mid-14C on Piazza San Giovanni and Via dei Calzaiuoli is where abandoned or lost children were left.

A small museum inside shows frescoes (c. 1386) (*reservation* ✆*055 28 84 96*) by Niccolò di Pietro Gerini and d'Ambrogio di Baldese that show women arriving to become their foster mothers. Also 15C paintings on wood: a *tondo* by Iacopo del Sellaio (c.1480), and a Madonna and Child with two angels, Saints Peter and Tobias.

Duomo★★★
🕐*Open Mon–Sat 10am–4.30pm; Sun 1.30pm–4.30pm. Cathedral: free admission. Guided tour available. Crypt:* 🕐*Open 10am–5pm (4.30 Sun).* 🕐*Closed Sun. Hours may vary in case of events.* ✺*€18 combined ticket for: dome, baptistery, bell tower, crypt, museum.* ✆*055 23 02 885. www.opera duomo.firenze.it.*
The **cathedral** is a symbol of the wealth and power of Florence in the 13C and 14C, and is one of the largest Christian buildings in the world. Its dedication to **Santa Maria del Fiore** recalls the golden rose that Pope Eugenius IV presented at the consecration of the cathedral.

The cathedral was built on the site of the Romanesque Cathedral of Santa Reparata, which was deemed too modest a building for such an important city as medieval Florence. Its construction mobilised the resources of the city for almost 150 years. The commission was given to the renowned architect, Arnolfo di Cambio and, although work began

🕐 **Michelin Map:**
pp104–105 E2.
▶ **Don't Miss:** Brunelleschi's dome, Duomo interior, bronze doors on San Giovanni Baptistery, Giotto's Campanile, art treasures in Museo del Duomo.
👥 **Kids:** Climb Brunelleschi's dome and/or the Campanile.
🕐 **Timing:** Two hours, more to climb dome.

in 1296, the cathedral was not consecrated until 1436. During this time modifications to the initial plans were made by Arnolfo's successors, Giotto, Andrea Pisano and particularly Francesco Talenti.

The building, which is mainly Gothic, is a striking example of the original character of this particular style in Florence. A marquetry design of multicoloured marble in typical Florentine style forms the geometrical decoration of the stone courses. The west front designed by Arnolfo di Cambio was demolished in 1588 without ever being completed. It was replaced in the late 19C by the existing front, a complex imitation of the Gothic style.

The huge **dome★★★** (🕐*See p116*), an integral part of the Florentine landscape, is the most beautiful part of the building. It is the work of Filippo Brunelleschi. In 1420 he solved the problem of how to roof the vast sanctuary, by designing a roof made of two flattened domes linked by a complex network of arches and buttresses. The construction of the gigantic dome, erected without any apparent support, aroused enormous admiration and enthusiasm in Florence at the time. For almost 15 years the building site, with its hoists designed by Brunelleschi himself and capable of moving blocks of stone weighing over three tonnes, was an unprecedented sight for the Florentine people.

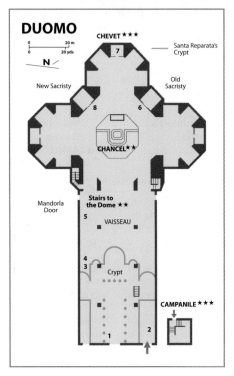

DUOMO

CHEVET ★★★

Santa Reparata's Crypt

New Sacristy

Old Sacristy

CHANCEL ★★

Mandorla Door

Stairs to the Dome ★★

VAISSEAU

Crypt

CAMPANILE ★★★

Exterior

Starting on the south side, walk round the cathedral anticlockwise. From the south side there is a striking view of the building, including its amazing marble marquetry. The **east end★★★** is remarkably extensive, consisting of three polygonal apses radiating from the transept crossing, that, together with the dome, form a complex yet superbly well-balanced composition.

On the north side of the building is the **Mandorla Door**, surmounted by a mandorla containing an early 15C carving of the Virgin Mary of the Assumption by Nanni di Banco. The mosaic on the tympanum (1490) depicting the Annunciation is the work of Domenico Ghirlandaio.

Nave

After the lavish ornamentation of the exterior the nave is surprisingly plain. The stained-glass windows of the west end, especially the central rose window depicting the Assumption of the Vir-

gin Mary, were based on drawings by Lorenzo Ghiberti. The tomb of Bishop Antonio d'Orso, who died in 1321, was carved by the Sienese sculptor, Tino di Camaino, who produced a number of famous monumental tombs during the Gothic period. A fragment of the original work (**1**) (*left of the centre door*) shows the deceased asleep and seated, above a sarcophagus.

In the first bay of the south aisle, just above the place where his tomb was discovered in the crypt (*See p118*) in 1972, is a portrait of Brunelleschi (**2**) (*first medallion on the right on entering*) carved by one of his pupils.

In the north aisle are two frescoes containing equestrian sculptures in honour of two military men (*condottieri*) who hired their services to Florence; the first one (**3**) is of Nicolò da Tolentino by Andrea del Castagno (1456) and the second one (**4**) is of Giovanni Acuto by Paolo Uccello (1436). Another fresco (**5**), painted by Domenico Michelino in 1465, depicts Dante explaining his

Divine Comedy to the city of Florence, which is represented by its cathedral as it was in the 15C; the fresco illustrates the "geography" of the other world as imagined by the poet – the pit of Hell, the mountain of Purgatory and the heavenly ranks of Paradise. The aisles are lit by remarkable 14C stained-glass windows.

Sanctuary★★

It is here that the true grandeur of the building can best be appreciated. The huge octagonal sanctuary is enclosed by an elegant marble screen erected in the mid-16C. From it radiate three vast apses forming a trefoil, each one containing five chapels. Above rises the breathtaking **dome★★★** (50m/162ft in diameter at its base and 91m/296ft high), which is decorated with a huge fresco depicting The Last Judgement; it was begun by Vasari, who worked on it from 1572 to 1574, but it required a further five years' work by Federico Zuccari before it was finished in 1579. Over the high altar hangs a wooden crucifix by Benedetto da Maiano (late 15C).

The tympanum above the door on the right leading to the Old Sacristy (*Sacrestia Vecchia*) (**6**) is decorated with a terracotta Ascension by Luca della Robbia. Beneath the altar (**7**) in the axial chapel lies the tomb of St Zanobi, the first Bishop of Florence. This remarkable work by Lorenzo Ghiberti consists of bronze reliefs depicting scenes from the saint's life. On either side of the altar are two delightful white glazed terracotta angel candle-bearers by Luca della Robbia. Their faces recall those of the adolescents in the famous *Cantoria* by the same artist now in the museum (*See below*).

The door of the New Sacristy (*Sacrestia Nuova*), symmetrically opposite the Old Sacristy, is also surmounted by a tympanum decorated by Luca della Robbia (**8**) depicting the **Resurrection★** in light shades of blue. It was in the New Sacristy that Lorenzo the Magnificent took refuge when attacked by two monks involved in the Pazzi Conspiracy. In this dramatic episode, the Pazzi, great rivals

The Double Pope

It may be a surprise to learn that the Baptistery in Florence contains the tomb of "Pope John XXIII", Baldassare Cossà, who succeeded Alexander V. Pope John XXIII was deposed by the Council of Constance, and succeeded by Martin V who appointed Cossà, the anti-pope, Bishop of Frascati. Cossà died in Florence 1419. His tomb is attributed to Donatello, possibly with Michelozzo. In 1958 when elected, distinguished Angelo Roncalli chose this name (the ordinal was deemed not to have been previously attributed). The "real" John XXIII is buried in St Peter's Basilica, Rome.

of the Medici, mounted a conspiracy in the name of lost freedoms and were supported by the Pope.

The Pazzi attempted to assassinate Lorenzo Medici in the cathedral during the Elevation at the Easter Mass on Sunday 26 April 1478. He was attacked by the monks but was only wounded and took refuge in the New Sacristy; his brother, Giuliano, was killed. Lorenzo then instigated a cruel and merciless repression against the Pazzi.

Skilful lighting shows off (*through a partition*) the **marquetry cabinets★** which reach halfway up the walls of the room and were produced in the second half of the 15C, mainly by Benedetto and Giuliano da Maiano. The splendid bronze door panels depicting figures of the Evangelists and Prophets are also worthy of note.

Dome (Cupola)★★

Access via the north aisle. 463 steps; 45min. ○*Open 8.30am–7pm (5pm Sat); Sun 1–4pm.* ○*Hours may vary in case of events. Reservations required.* ●*€18 (combined ticket: see p115, Duomo).* ℘*055 23 02 885. www.operaduomo.firenze.it.*

The narrow gallery overlooking the chancel provides a breathtaking **view★★** down into the cathedral and also a close-up view of the remarkable **stained-glass windows★** in the oculi of the drum. They were produced in the first half of the 15C and are based on sketches made by the leading figures of the time – Ghiberti, Donatello, Paolo Uccello and Andrea del Sarto. From the staircase leading to the top of the dome, which is constructed between the two vaults, there is an interesting view of the structural features. The final section, which is very steep and close against the wall, is the most spectacular. It leads to the exterior at the foot of the lantern turret which was Brunelleschi's last work and not set in place until after his death.

From here there is a magnificent **panoramic view★★★** of Florence. The view overlooks small private terraces and grand monuments (from right/west turning left/east toward the river): San Lorenzo dome, Santa Maria Novella near the Cascine Park; arch of Piazza della Repubblica, Orsanmichele; across the Arno is Palazzo Pitti and its Boboli Gardens; the Loggia della Signoria and Palazzo Vecchio with the Uffizi; the Church of la Badia; the Bargello Palace; set back, San Miniato and Piazzale Michelangelo; the marble façade of Santa Croce; and in the distance, the hills of Fiesole.

Santa Reparata's Crypt

Staircase by the first pillar on the south side of the nave.

The crypt is all that remains of an earlier Romanesque church (13C–14C), which was discovered during excavation work in 1966. It had itself been created through the conversion of a paleo-Christian basilica (5C–6C) and was demolished during the construction of the present cathedral.

The place where Brunelleschi's tomb was discovered can be seen through an iron grille in an opening overlooking the uncovered section to the left of the staircase.

The structural features so far uncovered have made it possible to reconstitute the layout of the original cathedral (a nave and two aisles and a raised chancel above a crypt). A drawing (*in a showcase*) shows the relevant periods of construction of the different architectural features and the large fragments of mosaic flooring.

Campanile★★★

🕐*Open 8.15am–7.20pm.* 🕐*Hours may vary in case of events.* ⊛€18 (combined ticket: see p115, Duomo). 🖉*055 23 02 885. www.operaduomo. firenze.it.*

The slender **bell tower** (82m/267ft high) by Giotto is no less famous than Brunelleschi's dome. Its straight lines form a harmonious contrast with the curved structure of the dome.

The plans for and decoration of the bell tower were the work of Giotto, who was appointed to supervise work on the cathedral. Construction began in 1334 but only the decorated section of carved panels had been built by the time he died in 1337. Andrea Pisano and Francesco Talenti completed the building work 1349–60 and designed the traceried section of the bays.

Copies have replaced the original low-reliefs in the bottom section of the building. The first register was carved by Andrea Pisano and Luca della Robbia; the second by pupils of Andrea Pisano. The originals, together with the statues of Prophets and Sibyls, which once occupied the niches on the second floor, are in the Museo dell'Opera del Duomo (👆*See p121).*

From the upper terrace (*414 steps to the top*) there is a fine **panoramic view★★** of the cathedral and the city of Florence.

Battistero★★★

🕐*Open 8.30am–10.15 and 11.15am–7.30 pm, Sun 8.30am–1.30pm,* 🕐*Hours may vary in case of events.* ⊛€18 (combined ticket: see p115, Duomo). ♿ 🖉*055 23 02 885. www.operaduomo. firenze.it.*

This elegant octagonal **Baptistery**, clad in white and dark-coloured marble, is highly representative of Florentine architecture. A Romanesque building, probably dating from the 11C, it nonetheless contains a number of Renaissance

Mosaics★★★ of the Baptistery Dome

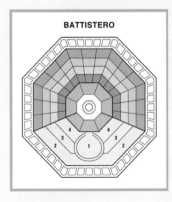

BATTISTERO

Set on a gold background, the mosaics are laid out in concentric registers covering the eight sections of the dome. They depict the following scenes, often in a wonderfully fresh manner.

◆ The Last Judgement (*in yellow on the plan*), consisting of the large Christ in Majesty (**1**), flanked on both sides by the Resurrection of the Dead with Heaven and Hell (**2**), the Virgin Mary with the Saints and Apostles (**3**) and the Angels of the Resurrection (**4**).

◆ Genesis (*pale pink*).
◆ Various choirs of angels or celestial hierarchies (*darker pink*).
◆ The Life of Joseph (*blue*).
◆ The Life of the Virgin Mary and Jesus (*light green*).
◆ The Life of St John the Baptist (*darker green*).

features (pilasters, capitals, triangular pediments, etc) typical of Florentine architecture, which had always drawn on Antiquity for inspiration.

Doors★★★

The bronze doors decorated with magnificent carved panels are famous throughout the world. Begun in 1330 by Andrea Pisano, the Gothic **South Door** (*now the entrance*) is the oldest. The 20 upper panels depict scenes from the life of St John the Baptist, patron saint of Florence. In the eight lower panels, the sculptor represented the Theological and Cardinal Virtues – (*left to right and top to bottom*) Hope, Faith, Fortitude, Temperance, Charity, Humility, Justice and Prudence.

The commission for the **North Door** (1403–24) was given to Lorenzo Ghiberti after a competition in which the city's greatest artists, including Brunelleschi, took part. Although he was working almost 100 years after Pisano, Ghiberti's work achieved a harmony with the other doors, by retaining the quatrefoil composition of Gothic tradition for the medallions.

The eight lower panels depict the Evangelists and the Doctors of the Church. Above are scenes from the Life and Passion of Christ (*from bottom to top*) depicted with remarkable austerity, nobility and harmony of composition. Above the doorway is *St John the Baptist Preaching* (early 16C) by Rustici. The **East Door** (*facing the cathedral*) is the most famous of all, the one which Michelangelo thought worthy to be called the **Gate of Paradise**. Between 1425 and 1452 Ghiberti, then at the peak of his talent, produced a masterpiece of sculpture and metalwork. The ten panels contain highly complex compositions illustrating episodes from the Old Testament executed with an abundance of characters in scenes that are remarkably lively, elegant and poetic.

Interior and Mosaics

The interior of the Baptistery (*25m/82ft in diameter*) comprises marble-clad walls and two orders of granite pilasters and columns, with gilded Corinthian capitals. The most striking feature, however, is the dome covered in sparkling **mosaics★★★** (&See box, above).

Deciphering the Baptistery Doors ★★

Ghiberti's East Door, also known as the Gate of Paradise, depicts scenes from the Old Testament, and is an exceptional work of Renaissance sculpture.

Ghiberti's East Door

Part of Panel 2, depicting the Flood

Part of Panel 3, depicting Jacob and Esau

Each register from top to bottom, including the left and right doors:

1 Creation of Adam and Eve, Original Sin. Adam and Eve expelled. Cain and Abel – Cain the labourer; Abel the shepherd; sacrifices made to God by the two brothers; Abel slain by Cain; the divine curse.

2 Story of Noah – the Flood; the rainbow sent as a sign of God's covenant with Noah; the drunkenness of Noah. Angels appearing to Abraham; his wife Sarah listening at the entrance of the tent; the sacrifice of Isaac.

3 Esau and his brother Jacob – Esau sent hunting by Isaac; Esau gives up his birthright to Jacob; Rebecca advises Jacob; God speaks to Rebecca; Jacob receives Isaac's blessing instead of Esau.
Joseph's life – (*top left*) Joseph sold by his brothers; (*bottom left*) discovery of the cup in Benjamin's sack; storing the corn after Joseph interprets Pharaoh's dream and predicts seven years of famine; Joseph seated on a throne is recognised by his family.

4 Moses receives the Tables of the Law; in his absence the Hebrews at the foot of Mount Sinai fall into despair.
Joshua and the Fall of Jericho; (*above*) the people cross the dry River Jordan and pick up the stones of memory.

5 Saul and David – the battle against the Philistines led by Saul standing in a chariot; David beheads Goliath. Meeting of King Solomon and the Queen of Sheba.

Fine marble mosaics, some with motifs borrowed from oriental designs, form the pavement leading to the Gate of Paradise, which was originally the main entrance to the Baptistery.

To the right of the small apse (*scarsella*) is the tomb of the Antipope John XXIII, friend of Giovanni di Bicci (the father of Cosimo the Elder). It is a remarkable work produced in 1427 by Donatello, assisted by Michelozzo.

Museo dell'Opera del Duomo★★★

Piazza del Duomo 9. ◷*Open 9am–7pm.* ◷*Closed 1st Tue of the month.* ◉*€18 (combined ticket, see p115, Duomo).* ♿ ℘*055 23 02 885. www.operaduomo.firenze.it.*

A tour of the cathedral, bell tower and Baptistery would not be complete without a visit to the **Cathedral Museum**, which houses numerous sculptures and artefacts from the three buildings.

Ground Floor

The great hall situated behind the entrance is devoted to the west front of the cathedral, shown in a 16C drawing as it appeared shortly before it was demolished. The drawing is the work of Arnolfo di Cambio, who produced most of the sculptures decorating the cathedral. Other sculptors carved the monumental statues of the Evangelists (*against the entrance wall*), the most remarkable of which is *St Luke* by Nanni di Banco.

At the far end of the hall (*left*) there is a series of small rooms. The first contains some of the equipment used by Brunelleschi during the construction of the dome. The second room contains scale models of the dome and its lantern, in addition to the death mask of the great architect. The first of the two rooms on the other side of the great hall contains various scale models proposed for the west front of the cathedral – by Buontalenti, Giovanni da Bologna and Giovanni de' Medici – as well as a collection of liturgical chants dating from the 16C. The second room contains part of the cathedral treasure.

Mezzanine Floor

Here is a **Pietà★★** sculpted by Michelangelo at the age of 80. He intended it for his own tomb but left it unfinished because he was dissatisfied with the quality of the marble. He is supposed to have depicted himself as Nicodemus supporting the Virgin Mary and Christ. The figure of Mary Magdalen, added by one of Michelangelo's pupils, attempts to hold up the body as it sinks to the ground.

First Floor

The great hall houses the famous **cantorie★★**, choir galleries that once surmounted the doors of the sacristies in the cathedral. The more famous of the two (*left of the entrance*) is the one by Luca della Robbia (1431–38). These exquisitely carved reliefs are the first known works by the artist.

The gallery (1433–39) by Donatello (*opposite*) was also based on classical low-reliefs. Above the galleries is the famous statue of **Mary Magdalen★** repenting, a late work (1455) by Donatello carved in wood.

In the same room is a group of statues that once adorned the bell tower. They include three more works by Donatello. Along the opposite wall are the prophets Jeremiah and Habakkuk, nicknamed *Zuccone* (pumpkin) because of the shape of his bald head.

The room to the left of the Cantoria room displays the admirable **low-reliefs★★** that once decorated the bell tower. The hexagonal ones, depicting various trades and activities, a number of characters from Antiquity and scenes from the Book of Genesis, were produced by Andrea Pisano and Luca della Robbia.

The room to the right of the Cantoria room contains the magnificent **silver altar★★** from the Baptistery, a splendid example of Florentine gold- and silversmithing from the 14C–15C, which combines Gothic and Renaissance style features and took over a century to produce. The story of John the Baptist was depicted on it by numerous artists, including Michelozzo, Antonio Pollaiolo and Verrocchio. The display cases

THE MEDIEVAL HEART OF FLORENCE
Map II

0 ——— 200 m
0 ——— 200 yds

WHERE TO EAT

Cantinetta dei Verrazzano	②
Fishing Lab Alle Murate	④
Le Mossacce	⑥
Drogheria Pegna	⑤
Ristorante Frescobaldi	⑦
Trattoria Anita	⑧
Trattoria Nella	⑫
Vini e Vecchi Sapori	⑭

Museo della Casa Fiorentina Antica
(Palazzo Davanzati) .... M

on either side of the room contain the panels of the altar **frontal★** from the Baptistery, a splendid silk and filigree embroidery worked with great skill and artistry, which depicts scenes from the life of John the Baptist and Jesus.
In the centre of the room are four original low reliefs from the Gate of Paradise in the Baptistery depicting the Creation, Cain and Abel, David and Goliath and the Story of Joseph.

👣WALKING TOUR

MEDIEVAL HEART OF FLORENCE

A short walk from Santa Maria del Fiore to the Piazza della Signoria can easily fill a whole afternoon. Start from the apse of the cathedral. Before turning into Via del Proconsolo, glance at the 16C **Palazzo Niccolini★** (*15 Via dei Servi*). In Via del Proconsolo make a brief detour into Via del Corso to admire **Palazzo Portinari** (*no 6*, now the Banca Toscana), and its 16C **internal courtyard★**. In Via del Proconsolo, at the corner of Borgo degli Albizzi, stands the late-15C **Palazzo Pazzi★** (*no 10*) with twin windows.

Bargello Palace★★★

1hr 30min. ⏱*Open 8.15am–2pm (1.20pm last admission).* 🎧*English audio guides available (€6).* ⏱*Closed 1st, 3rd, 5th Mon in the month, 2nd and*

4th Sun in the month, 1 Jan, 25 Dec. 🎟*€8. Bookshop.* ♿ ☎*055 06 49 440. www.bargellomusei.beniculturali.it.*
The forbidding **Palazzo della Podestà★** is a fine example of medieval vernacular architecture. The oldest part of the façade was built in the mid-13C and originally housed the Capitano del Popolo, who represented the working classes within the Florentine government, then the *Podestà*. The later part of the building was built in the Gothic style a century later.

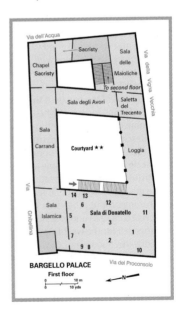

BARGELLO PALACE
First floor

In 1574 the building became the residence of the Chief of Police (called Bargello) and part of it was turned into a prison. Today the building houses the Bargello National Museum, and has some extraordinary Italian Renaissance sculpture and decorative arts.

The severity of the **courtyard★★** is softened by a porch with wide arcades and a loggia reached by a picturesque outside staircase. In fact, this is one of the finest medieval courtyards in Italy. The coats of arms of the magistrates (*podeste*) who lived in the palace from the 14C–16C provide a charming decoration. Condemned prisoners were put to death beside the well.

Works by 16C Tuscan sculptors have been placed along the galleries; the single statues and the impressive group standing against the wall opposite the entrance were once part of a fountain designed by Ammannati, the architect of the Pitti Palace, for the great Hall of the Five Hundred in the Palazzo Vecchio.

▷ Start opposite the entrance at the far end of the gallery.

Saletta del Trecento

This 14C sculpture room contains the museum's few Gothic sculptures, including the Madonna and Child by Tino da Camaino (*against the left-hand wall*).

▷ At the foot of the outside staircase.

Sala di Michelangelo e della Scultura del Cinquecento

The Michelangelo and 16C Sculpture Room is mainly devoted to the two most contrasting artistic figures of the Florentine Renaissance.

There are four splendid Michelangelo sculptures (*left-hand bay*). The **Drunken Bacchus** group accompanied by a laughing satyr (1497–99) is an early work which still bears traces of classical influences. In the famous **Tondo Pitti**, a large roundel representing the Madonna and Child with St John, carved between 1504 and 1506 for one of the members of the Pitti family, the artist seems to have transposed the *sfumato* style of Leonardo da Vinci into sculpture by creating roughly sketched reliefs. The powerful marble bust of **Brutus** (1540) also takes its inspiration from Roman statuary. The unfinished **David-Apollo** (c. 1530) (*further along*) seems captured midway between motion and immobility.

In contrast to the forceful artistry of Michelangelo, the work of **Benvenuto Cellini** is admired for its virtuosity and delicacy. The right-hand bay contains a number of his masterpieces. In the centre of the room stands the marble **Narcissus** with its slender forms and melancholy incurved lines. For many years it was one of the statues in the Boboli Gardens. Around the room are the bronze statuettes of Perseus, Mercury, Danae and her son Perseus, and Minerva and Jupiter, which once filled the niches of the pedestal supporting the famous Perseus in the Loggia della Signoria. On the wall is the original bronze plaque which decorated the base, representing **Perseus Delivering Andromeda**, a work treated with the gusto characteristic of the Mannerist style (graceful drapes, elegant slender bodies, flowing movement). The bronze bust of **Cosimo I** (1546) (*wall to the right of the door*) is an admirable portrait vigorously expressing cruelty, intelligence and energy; the decoration on the armour is worthy of a goldsmith. Also in this room is Danti's *Honour Triumphant over Falsehood*.

▷ Go up to the First floor.

Loggia (Verone)

The **balcony** houses works by Giambologna, including the *Allegory of Architecture* in the centre, and remarkable bronze animals, which once adorned a grotto in the Villa di Castello's gardens (⌖ *See OUTSKIRTS OF FLORENCE, p188*).

▷ Entrance at top of outside staircase.

Sala di Donatello

The vast high-ceilinged **Donatello Room** has the majestic appearance of the nave of a cathedral. Beneath the vaulting there is an outstanding collection of **works★★★** by **Donatello**,

Masterpieces of the Donatello Room★★★

There is a small lively bronze Cupid (**1**). The marble statue of **David** (**2**) is one of the artist's early works (1409), showing a realistic observation far removed from the Gothic tradition. The famous **Marzocco** (**3**), the Florence lion, whose paw rests on the city's shield, stood for many years in front of the Palazzo Vecchio. The bronze **David** (**4**) is a masterpiece dating from Donatello's more mature period. The splendid body, tensed yet carved in gentle relief, is the expression of an artistry that had reached the height of perfection. The imposing **St George** (**5**) (*in the niche in the end wall*) originally stood outside Orsanmichele.

The room also contains a number of other important works from the 15C, such as *St John the Baptist as a Child* (**6**) by **Desiderio da Settignano**, one of Donatello's most illustrious pupils. The touching profile (**7**), also of St John the Baptist as a child, has an exceptionally gentle quality. The artist learned from his master the technique of *schiacciato*: graduated flattened sculpture with slight relief. The delicate relief of the Madonna and Child (**8**) is another charming example of this style. Donatello's pupil, **Agostino di Duccio**, carved the Madonna and Child with Angels placed within a *pietra serena* surround (**9**). The room also contains a number of Madonna and Child interpretations by **Luca della Robbia**. The *Madonna of the Rose Garden* (**10**) and *Madonna with Apple* (**11**) are among his most accomplished, youthful, serene Madonnas.

Along the wall to the right of the doorway to the next room is a painting of St John the Baptist (**12**) by Francesco da Sangallo, and the two quatrefoil panels of the Sacrifice of Isaac, produced in 1401 for the competition to find the architect of the north door of the Baptistery. These panels were made by the winner, Lorenzo Ghiberti (**13**), and by Brunelleschi (**14**).

(*See box above*) whose genius dominated the early Italian Renaissance.

Sala Islamica
The **Islamic Art Room** is a testimony to Florence's trade links with the Middle East. It contains carpets, costumes and weaponry, cloth, ceramics, pewter and bronzeware, and ivories, some of which were collected by the Grand Dukes.

Sala Carrand
The **Carrand Room** houses a large part of the extensive collection bequeathed by Louis Carrand in the late 19C. The collection, mainly consisting of *objets d'art*, is also displayed in other parts of the palace. The room has a remarkable display of enamels including some from Limoges and the Rhineland, dating from the 12C and 13C (*first display case on the left*), 15C–16C Venetian ware (*second group of display cases in the centre*) and

Limoges ware 15C–16C (*fourth display case on the left and last on the right*).

Sala degli Avori
The **Ivories Room** houses one of the most extensive collections of ivories in the world, with works dating from the 5C–17C. Included in the displays are Italian ivories from the 14C–15C and a splendid chess board made by the Burgundy School.

Sala delle Maioliche
The **Majolica Room** contains some spectacular bowls from Urbino (16C) with a highly elaborate combination of shapes, decorative motifs and colours (*display cases in front of the windows*), and some large white and brown Hispano-Moorish dishes (15C–16C) with fine detail made in metallic shades.

▶ Second floor. To the right of the first room is the Sala delle Armi.

Armeria

The **armoury** contains a fine collection of mainly 16C–17C weapons and armour, most of which belonged to the Medici family. The first display case against the left-hand wall contains a series of rifles and pistols decorated with fruit, animals and figures, all beautifully inlaid in ivory and mother-of-pearl. The remainder of the collection consists mainly of the state **armour of the Grand Dukes** of the Medici dynasty, including a number of splendid shields.

Sala di Giovanni della Robbia

This room houses a collection of works by the last of the three great della Robbia sculptors, the great-nephew of Luca. Giovanni della Robbia carried on the technique of glazed terracotta sculpture, extending it to larger and more complex compositions with greater variety of colour. A typical example of this development can be seen (*right of the door*) in the predella depicting Christ and the Saints. The same is true of the large Pietà in bold relief set against a landscape full of rocks, buildings, trees and horsemen, and the huge Nativity surrounded by two Apparitions of Jesus to Mary Magdalen (*Noli me Tangere*).

Giovanni also created simpler and more tranquil compositions such as the tender *Madonna and Child with St John* (*wall opposite the door*).

Sala di Andrea della Robbia

Like his successor, Andrea della Robbia, nephew of Luca and father of Giovanni, also created some delicate and graceful Madonnas. His Madonna and Child interpretations are embellished with heads of cherubs, flowers and foliage and are enlivened with bright colours. No less exquisite masterpieces, if only for the harmony of their composition, are **Our Lady of Architects** (*to the right of the window*), produced for the Guild of Masons and Carpenters, whose tools are depicted in the surrounding frieze, and his **Madonna with Cushion** (*to the left of the door*).

To the left.

Sala del Verrocchio e del secondo Quattrocento

The **Verrocchio Room** contains a collection of several sculptures by the Florentine artist who, as both painter and sculptor, was one of the leading figures of the Italian Renaissance. Near the centre of the room stands the famous bronze **David**, dating from c. 1465 and sculpted for the young Lorenzo the Magnificent and his brother, Giuliano, whom Verrocchio had befriended.

Against the wall opposite the windows, note the bust of a young woman holding a bunch of flowers. Her long hands are admired for their lifelike, aristocratic appearance, and there are very few rivals in the world of sculpture. The identity of the model remains a mystery (it may have been Lucrezia Donti, Lorenzo the Magnificent's mistress). Note also two delightful marble Madonna and Child interpretations, which contrast sharply with the expressionism and dramatic character of works such as the polychrome terracotta *Resurrection* and *Death of Francesca Pitti-Tornabuoni*. Among the works by other sculptors of the late 15C, the most outstanding are: (*left of the door*) Francesco Laurana's bust of Battista Sforza, Duchess of Urbino and (*right of the door*) a number of sculptures by Mino da Fiesole, including a very fine medallion of the Madonna and Child and the remarkable portrait of Rinaldo della Luna.

The rooms at the far end on the left are the **Medals Room**, with an impressive collection of medallions, and the **Room of Baroque Sculpture**, which contains a large bust of Costanza Bonarelli, one of the masterpieces by Gian Lorenzo Bernini (1589–1680).

Sala dei Bronzetti

The **Bronze Statuette Room** (*opposite the Verrocchio Room*) houses a large collection of bronze statuettes which were highly prized items of interior decoration among fashionable society in Renaissance Italy. These bronze statuettes were miniature replicas of either ancient statues (*the Laocoön*), contemporary works by Giambologna or original creations from renowned artists' studios. There are also items in everyday use (mortars, ink-pots, candlesticks).

▶ Opposite the Bargello, entrance in Via del Proconsolo or Via Dante.

Badia

Via del Proconsolo.
This was the church of an ancient and very influential Benedictine abbey (*badia*), founded shortly before the year 1000 by Countess Willa, Marchioness of Tuscany. It was a centre of intense spiritual and intellectual activity throughout the Middle Ages.

It is believed that the building was extensively renovated in the late 13C by Arnolfo di Cambio. The elegant, hexagonal **bell tower★**, rebuilt between 1310 and 1330, is one of the finest bell towers in Florence and can be fully admired only from a distance.

The church underwent further restoration in 1627 and the present interior dates from this period. It is designed in the form of a Greek cross in an austere Baroque style and has a splendid carved wooden coffered **ceiling★★**.

The church contains a number of interesting Renaissance works, including a painting depicting the **Apparition of the Virgin** to St Bernarda by Filippo Lippi, in which the artist is said to have used his mistress and children as models for the Virgin Mary and angels, and an exquisite carved marble **relief★★** by Mino da Fiesole, in which the youth and beauty of the characters (Madonna and Child, St Leonard and St Lawrence) are extremely moving. The church also has two elegant **tombs★** carved by Mino da Fiesole.

The two tombs are those of Bernardo Giugni (*south transept*), an eminent figure of the Florentine Republic and Count Ugo (*north transept*), Marquess of Tuscany, who was a great benefactor of the Church and the son of the founder of the abbey.

▶ Via Dante Alighieri; go to the corner with Via Santa Margherita.

Casa di Dante

Via S Margherita 1 (corner of Via Dante Alighieri). ○Open Apr–Oct Mon–Sun 10am–6pm; Nov–Mar Tue–Sun 10am–5pm (Sat–Sun 6pm). ○Closed 24–25 Dec. Bookshop. ∞€4. Guided tours available. ☎055 21 94 16. www.museocasadidante.it.
The museum retraces the life of the poet from the origins of his family, members of the ancient Florentine aristocracy, to his official positions within the city and his years in exile. It also records Italian history and the position of Florence during Dante's lifetime, which were closely linked to his political preoccupations, as well as his major work, the *Divine Comedy*, and his platonic love for Beatrice Portinari, whose family lived in the same district and who was buried in the Church of Santa Margherita (*further up the street*).
In Via Dante (*corner of Piazza S Martino*) stand the remains of the 12C **Torre della Castagna**, where the representatives (*priori*) of the guilds met before the construction of the Palazzo della Signoria.

▶ Opposite is the Buonomini Oratory.

Oratorio dei Buonomini

Piazza San Martino. ○Open Mon–Sun 10am–noon and 3pm–5pm ○Closed Sun and Fri afternoon.
This chapel belongs to the brotherhood of Buonomini di San Martino, which has looked after the "needy poor" (originally well-off families who had fallen from grace and were too ashamed to ask for charity), since 1441. Requests for help are still posted through the letter box marked *"per le istanze"*. When the Buonomini are unable to help with any more requests, a candle is lit by the door.
The beautiful **frescoes** inside the building date from the end of the 15C. They were painted by the workshop of Domenico Ghirlandaio, and possibly that of Filippino Lippi, and depict the story of St Martin and Works of Mercy.

▶ Continue to Via dei Calzaiuoli.

Orsanmichele★

Via dell'Arte della Lana ⏰*Open 10am–4.50pm;* ☎*055 06 49 450. bargellomusei.beniculturali.it*

This unusually shaped church takes its name from a much older church dedicated to St Michael which was destroyed around 1240. It occupies a building that was initially a loggia used as a grain store. The loggia was partly destroyed by fire in 1304 and was rebuilt in 1337 in a Gothic-Renaissance style. In the late 14C the arcades were walled up and the height of the building was raised so that it could be used as a chapel. The upper storey, however, continued to be used until the 16C for the storage of food in case of famine. In 1569 Cosimo I set up the Deeds Office on the first floor. He also commissioned Buontalenti to construct an arched passage above street level between the rear of the building and the mansion of the Wool Merchants' Guild (*Arte della Lana*), in order to provide an access without having to pass through the chapel.

The **external** niches round the building are occupied by statues of the patron saints of the various guilds (*arti*), which form a veritable museum of 14C–16C Florentine sculpture. On the side in Via dei Calzaiuoli (*from left to right*) are a bronze statue of St John the Baptist cast in 1416 by Lorenzo Ghiberti for the Drapers' Guild; a bronze group for which Verrocchio was commissioned in 1484 by the Merchants' Court depicting the Disbelief of St Thomas (*missing*); and a bronze figure of St Luke made in 1562 by Giovanni da Bologna for the Guild of Judges and Notaries. On the side in Via Orsanmichele were St Peter (*missing*) carved in marble by Donatello in 1413 for the Butchers' Guild; St Philip (1410, *missing*) made for the Shoemakers; a group of four saints (1408) produced by Nanni di Banco for the Master Stoneworkers and Woodworkers; and a copy (*original in the Bargello*) of the famous St George by Donatello, created in 1416 for the Armour Merchants and Sword Cutlers. On the side in Via dell'Arte della Lana are the bronze statues by Ghiberti of St Matthew in 1422 for the Money Changers

Gothic tabernacle, Orsanmichele

© travelview/iStock

and St Stephen for the Wool Merchants in 1426; and **St Eligius** (1416, *missing*) by Nanni di Banco for the Blacksmiths. On the side in Via dei Lamberti are St Mark (1411–13) by Donatello; St James (missing) carved in marble for the Furriers' Guild; a Madonna and Child known as the *Madonna of the Rose* (1399) made for the Physicians and Apothecaries; and a bronze figure of St John the Evangelist cast by Baccio da Montelupo for the Silk Merchants in 1515.

The **interior** is a simple rectangular hall. It contains a splendid Gothic **tabernacle★★**, begun in 1329 by **Andrea Orcagna**.

▷ Go along Via dei Calzaiuoli as far as Via della Condotta.

Mercato Nuovo★

In the 16C Cosimo I ordered the construction of this loggia with elegant Renaissance arcades in a district that had been occupied by traders and merchants since the Middle Ages. Its name, **New Market Loggia**, distinguished it from the old medieval marketplace which was demolished in the late 19C during the construction of Piazza della Repubblica. The loggia now houses a market selling Florentine craftwork including souvenirs, embroidery, lace, leather goods, *pietra dura* ware and gilded and painted wooden items. At the edge of the building, on the side facing the Arno, stands the Porcellino ("piglet") Fountain. The snout has been rubbed shiny for luck; tourists throw coins into the fountain while making the wish to return to Florence.

▷ Turn onto Via Porta Rossa.

Palazzo Torrigiani (Hotel Porta Rossa) is a rare example of a mansion (14C) with well-conserved, corbelled upper storeys. Also in this street is the **Palazzo Davanzati**★ (14C).

Museo della Casa Fiorentina Antica (Palazzo Davanzati)★

Via di Porta Rossa 13. ○*Open Mon–Fri 8.15am–2pm; Sat–Sun 1.15–7pm.* ○*Closed 2nd and 4th Sun and 1st, 3rd and 5th Mon of the month, 1 Jan, 25 Dec.* ○*€6.* ℘*055 06 49 460. bargellomusei.beniculturali.it.*
The **Old Florentine House Museum** (**M**) is housed on the three floors of the **Palazzo Davanzati**★, a narrow, tower-ing residence built in the 14C for a rich wool merchant and purchased in the 16C by the historian and man of letters, Bernardo Davanzati.

The building was superbly restored at the turn of the 20C and it contains a splendid collection of furniture (mainly Florentine or Tuscan from the 14C, 15C and 16C), tapestries, paintings, sculptures, ceramics, everyday objects and fabrics, most of which originate from the Bargello. The museum, part of which dates from medieval times, provides a vivid insight into what a rich Florentine residence would have looked like during the Renaissance period.

The first and second floors each comprise a dining room, bed chamber, lavatory and great hall – the hall on the first floor was used for family gatherings such as weddings, funerals etc, while the room on the second floor was reserved for the mistress of the house and contains a large Davanzati family tree.

▷ Retrace your steps to the corner of Via Pellicceria; turn right and walk as far as Piazza di Parte Guelfa, where the Palazzo di Parte Guelfa (14C) stands.

Piazza della Signoria★★ and The Uffizi★★★

Art and Politics

Set up by Grand Duke Francesco I de' Medici, the Uffizi Gallery contains the world's richest collection of Renaissance paintings and sculpture, including masterpieces by Botticelli, Raphael, Michelangelo and Caravaggio.

THE UFFIZI★★★

Reserve ahead to avoid long queues (○€4). 2hr 30min for all rooms. ○*Open Tue–Sun 8.15am–6.50pm (last entry 5.45pm).* ○*Closed 1 Jan, 25 Dec.* ○*Mar–Oct €20, Nov–Feb €12.* ♿ ℘*055 29 48 83. www.uffizi.it.*

◉ **Michelin Map:** pp104–105 ED2.
▷ **Don't Miss:** Masterpieces in the Uffizi, Palazzo Vecchio Cinquecento Room.
👫 **Kids:** Palazzo Vecchio tours; Galileo Science Museum; chase pigeons in Piazza Signoria; walk along Arno River.
○ **Timing:** Allow half day or more for the Uffizi.

⊛ *The huge project called* **Nuovi Uffizi** *(New Uffizi) will double museum space arranged. Renovation and*

Piazzale degli Uffizi - the courtyard between the two wings of the Uffizi

expansion continues since 2006. Only in 2018 13 rooms were rearranged and 18 redesigned ex novo.

The **Uffizi Gallery** houses one of the world's most important art collections in a building commissioned in 1560 by Cosimo I Medici for the offices (*uffizi*) of the Medici administration. Vasari designed this unusual building in late-Renaissance style on the site of a Romanesque church. It consists of two long parallel wings joined at one end in a curve to form a kind of enclosed square like a courtyard, and extends from Piazza della Signoria to the Arno. An aerial walkway, which is still visible, once linked the Palazzo Vecchio to the gallery and formed the top floor of the latter building.

In 1581 the east section of the gallery was laid out by Francesco I to house the works of art acquired by earlier generations and was opened to the public ten years later. The Medici collections represent a large part of the works of art which now make the Uffizi one of the world's leading art galleries.

The **ground floor** displays relics from the Romanesque church of San Pier Scheraggio, the former occupant of the site. There are a number of fresco portraits by Andrea del Castagno and a fine representation of the Battle of San Martino, painted in oils in 1936 by Corrado Cagli in the style of the famous *Battle of San Romano* by Paolo Uccello. A large portrait of Anna Maria Ludovica shows the last of the Medici who, on her death in 1743, bequeathed to the City of Florence the extraordinary treasures acquired by her ancestors. She also had the vision and wisdom to ensure that they remained for the people of Florence by stipulating that the works must remain in this city.

The monumental staircase built by Vasari leads to the top floor of the building. The lifts (*far right of the foyer*) are reserved for those with special needs.

East Wing – The long corridor displays classical sculptures – sarcophagi, statues (mainly Roman copies of Greek works) and busts from the Imperial era. The ceiling is decorated with grotesque figures.

West Wing – During the era of the Grand Dukes, this wing housed the Medici workshops, where craftsmen worked, producing *pietra dura* artefacts, miniatures and even perfumes, medicines, poisons and antidotes.

Terrace – From the cafeteria terrace, which is situated at the far end of the gallery overlooking the Loggia della Signoria, there is a superb view of the upper storeys of the Palazzo Vecchio. The terrace area used to be a garden with a fountain, where the Medici

129

✿ Sala del Botticelli★★★

The **Botticelli Room (10–14)** in the East Wing is the gallery's crowning glory. Prior to the 2016 renovation, all the Uffizi's paintings by Botticelli were in one room alongside masterpieces by other artists, today they are divided into two sections devoted exclusively to Botticelli. The Botticelli room has been architecturally reconfigured from the ground up, while the technological installations governing climatisation, security and lighting have been brought up to date.

From the peak of the artist's career comes the **Spring** (La Primavera, ⟲ see opposite page) (first section of the room) and the allegorical **Birth of Venus** (La Nascita di Venere, ⟲ see opposite page) (second section of the room), undoubtedly the most representative examples of Botticelli's poetic lyricism and the idealism that characterised the Humanist culture favoured at the court of Lorenzo the Magnificent.

The first section also features the Madonna of the Rose Garden, a tempera on panel painting; the Madonna and Child Enthroned with Saints; the Madonna in Glory with Seraphim; the Cestello Annunciation; and a stupendous, little-known detached **Annunciation** (Annunciazione, ⟲ see p132) fresco by Botticelli formerly located in San Pier Scheraggio after being moved from its original site in San Martino alla Scala.

Sandro Botticelli (1444–1510)

© Vlad333/iStock

Sandro Botticelli was a pupil of Filippo Lippi and later Verrocchio. He was also an admirer of Pollaiolo. All three artists had a great influence on Botticelli, who retained the linearity and contour of Lippi, while showing, in his work, the energy characteristic of the other two. He remained indifferent, however, to the introduction of atmosphere into painting that Verrocchio had begun to explore. By the end of the 15C he was the greatest painter in Florence – he was among the artists called to Rome to paint the walls of the Sistine Chapel – and he mixed with the circle of neo-Platonist scholars, philosophers and writers at the court of Lorenzo the Magnificent. He revived the themes of Antiquity and painted mythological subjects – Venus, Pallas and the Centaur, Primavera (Spring) – bringing to them a tender lyricism that gave them an allegorical quality. He also painted numerous Madonnas and he excelled in introducing a sense of movement and rhythm to fabrics, veils, hair and limbs. The faces of his subjects are tilted rather systematically to one side in a somewhat Mannerist style.

The death of Lorenzo the Magnificent, the preaching of Savonarola and the future development of his artistic style, which through its exaggerated curves bordered on an affectation of the Gothic style, all conspired to push the artist from a state of extreme sensitivity to open doubt, as is shown in his Calumny of Apelles, a work drawn in such an incisive way that it arouses a feeling of distress. Although he embodies all that was best during the finest years of the century of the Medici, Botticelli failed to influence other artists because his originality was difficult to emulate.

In sequence around the *Birth of Venus*, in the second section of the room hang Botticelli's a late work, the *Calumny of Apelles* which shows the development of the artist's skill –; **Pallas and the Centaur** (*Pallade e il Centauro*, ◐ *see p132*) depicting Bestiality tamed by Thought; the *Madonna of the Pomegranate*, a roundel in which the artist displays a skill acquired from his contact with goldsmiths; the *Saint Augustine in His Study*; the *San Barnaba Altarpiece*; the **Madonna of the Magnificat** (*Madonna del Magnificat*, ◐ *see p133*), another roundel including remarkable intricacy of detail and extraordinary harmony; and the *Portrait of a Man with a Medallion of Cosimo the Elder*.

La Primavera

The scene takes place in Venus' garden. The goddess is in the centre of the composition, surrounded by orange trees and myrtle bushes. Above her flies Cupid, his arrow aimed at one of the three Graces, who are dancing with each other and are unaware of his presence.

To the left, Mercury disperses the clouds with his caduceus, while to the right the green-coloured Zephyr pursues the nymph Cloris. (Ovid recounts that after marrying the nymph Zephyr made her queen of the flowers.) Thus transformed, Flora scatters roses over the meadow. There have been many interpretations of this work, which could be seen as a portrayal of the metamorphosis of love. The shy and dreamy young woman about to be hit by the arrow could be Castitas, the girl to the left, Voluptas, and the third figure, Pulchritudo. Venus is a static figure, presiding over these games of love. Mercury, who was thought to accompany souls to the next world, acted as a messenger between men and the gods; here he reaches up to the sky, as Castitas looks on. The harmony of the painting lies in its balanced composition: Mercury's upward motion is balanced by the figure of Zephyr at the opposite side of the painting, who stretches down towards the ground.

La Nascita di Venere

In the **Birth of Venus**, a young woman expressing a melancholy and fragile grace emerges from a background of sea and sky painted in remarkably transparent cold tones; the artist is said to have represented the features of Simonetta Vespucci, mistress of Giuliano, the brother of Lorenzo the Magnificent. Unfortunately, Botticelli

The Birth of Venus *(1485) by Botticelli*

destroyed many of his non-religious works in Savonarola's Bonfire of the Vanities (☾See INTRODUCTION, p97). The composition actually shows the goddess of love and beauty arriving on land, on the island of Cyprus, born of the sea spray and blown there by the winds, Zephyr and, perhaps, Aura. The goddess is standing on a giant scallop shell, as pure and as perfect as a pearl. She is met by a young woman, who is sometimes identified as one of the Graces or as the Hora of spring, and who holds out a cloak covered in flowers. Even the roses, blown in by the wind are a reminder of spring. The subject of the painting, which celebrates Venus as symbol of love and beauty, was perhaps suggested by the poet Agnolo Poliziano.

It is highly probable that the work was commissioned by a member of the Medici family, although there is nothing written about the painting before 1550, when Giorgio Vasari describes it in the Medici's Villa of Castello, owned by the cadet branch of the Medici family since the mid-15C. This hypothesis would seem to be born out by the orange trees in the painting, which are considered an emblem of the Medici dynasty, on account of the assonance between the family name and the name of the orange tree, which at the time was 'mala medica'.

Unlike the *Allegory of Spring*, which is painted on wood, the *Birth of Venus* was painted on canvas, a support that was widely used throughout the 15C for decorative works destined to noble houses.

Botticelli takes his inspiration from classical statues for Venus' modest pose, as she covers her nakedness with long, blond hair, which has reflections of light from the fact that it has been gilded; even the Winds, the pair flying in one another's embrace, is based on an ancient work, a gem from the Hellenistic period, owned by Lorenzo the Magnificent.

Annunciazione

The usual subject of the announcement to the Virgin Mary by archangel Gabriel is set in a renaissance palace, overlooking a garden, closed by a crenellated wall at the end. The portico, through which the archangel Gabriel appears, leads into Mary's room. Behind the Virgin is the tall wooden bed, surrounded by chests and protected by a curtain, shown here moved to one side. The setting therefore offers us some useful information of the fashions in vogue for furnishings in the noble palaces of the Renaissance, including precious carpets, such as the one on which Mary is shown kneeling. The painting is rich with symbolic references to the mother of God, although these are masked behind the everyday appearance of the setting. The walled garden symbolises Mary's purity, while the awning suggests a parallel between Mary, who carries the Christ Child in her womb, and the drape that covered the Ark of the Covenant.

This fresco is usually considered as related to a certified payment to Sandro Botticelli, made in 1481, shortly before the painter departed for Rome, where he worked on the decorations of the Sistine Chapel.

The large mural was originally under a loggia to the front of the church of San Martino in the hospital of Santa Maria della Scala in Florence, but subsequent architectural changes to the building partly concealed the fresco. It was therefore removed from its wall and restored in 1920.

Pallade e il Centauro

Like Botticelli's other paintings with a mythological subject, **Pallas and the Centaur** too, showing the young woman armed with a battle axe, intent on dragging a centaur by the hair, presents many doubts in terms of interpretation. Based on what is written in inventories and literary sources from shortly after the creation of the painting, the attractive, proud feminine figure is thought to be Pallas Athena (Minerva), goddess of knowledge, or Camilla, virgin and warrior, who died in battle defending the country, as well as being a fine example of chastity.

The centaur, a mythical creature, combining man and beast, symbolises the feral instincts of humanity and therefore, the work is to be understood as an allegory to virtues that act as a brake on a bad-tempered, passionate temperament.

A young woman wears a dress with repeat decoration of the three-ring insignia of the Medici family. Her face is surrounded by plant shoots, perhaps the olive that was consecrated to Pallas or the myrtle, a plant associated with Camilla. The painting belonged to the Medici, to Lorenzo di Pierfrancesco, cousin of Lorenzo the Magnificent, and it may have been commissioned on the occasion of his marriage with Semiramide Appiani in 1482.

Pallas and the Centaur (c. 1482) by Botticelli

© DEA/G DAGLI ORTI/De Agostini Editore/age fotostock

Madonna del Magnificat

The Virgin Mary, crowned by two angels, is depicted on a throne. Under the guidance of her son, she is writing the canticle "Magnificat anima mea Dominum" (My soul doth magnify the Lord), which gives the painting its title. Jesus is sitting in his mother's lap. He is touching a pomegranate, a fruit with many symbolic meanings, and whose red seeds recall the blood shed by Jesus to save humankind. The scene takes place before a window that opens out onto a bright, peaceful country landscape; above, the Serena stone frame creates a division between the kingdom of Heaven and the earth. The religious theme becomes almost temporal in the fashionable, elegant hairstyles of Mary and the angels, who, as in various other works by Botticelli, are without wings. The Virgin's blonde hair with bright gold finish is covered by transparent veils under a richly decorated maphorion, while the hairstyles and clothing of the angels are based on the fashions followed by the scions of the rich Florentine families of the late 15C. The originality of the work, together with the sophisticated elegance of the clothing and hair, and the grace of Mary's engrossed expression, have, over the years, brought renown to the invention of Botticelli, whose figures embody an ideal of beauty that was greatly appreciated during the 20C. We don't know the original destination of the painting, which was purchased from a private collection in 1784. Round paintings were usually destined to the secular world in the Renaissance, and above all to noble homes. They were often commissioned on the occasion of marriages or births. However, in the light of the considerable size of the painting, it may have been hung in one of the tribunals of the Florentine Republic, which were often decorated with holy images.

🐾 Hugo van der Goes (Room 15)

In room 15 some of Botticelli's works (such as the monumental *Coronation of the Virgin*) and late 15C Florentine artworks are juxtaposed with the imposing *Adoration of the Shepherds with Angels and Saints* (*Adorazione dei pastori con angeli e i santi*), also known as *Portinari Triptych* (👆*see below*), oil on wood painting by Hugo van der Goes realized for the Portinari family in Bruges. This masterpiece of Flemish art, which graced the altar of the church in the Hospital of Santa Maria Nuova from 1483, played a crucial role in the stylistic development of numerous Florentine artists in the end of the 15C. Perhaps the most important of those artists was Domenico Ghirlandaio, whose *Madonna and Child with Angels and Saints* from the church of San Giusto is on display in this room.

Adorazione dei pastori con angeli e i santi

This skilfully structured work, painted in deep colours, reflects an Italian influence in the taste for huge compositions and life-sized characters. The infant Jesus lies on the ground surrounded by rays of light to signify him as the Light of the world. His mother Mary, father Joseph, various angels and the shepherds stand around him in adoration. In the background, the previous moment in the narrative sequence, when the angel announces the birth of the Saviour, is depicted in the surrounding scenery. The continuity of the background landscape erases the division between the central image and the side panels, where the family who commissioned the work is shown in prayer under the protection of four saints. To the left, Thomas the Apostle and Saint Anthony the Great preside over the head of family Tommaso Portinari and his two sons, while to the right Saint Margaret, victorious on the dragon which had swallowed her, and Mary Magdalen, holding a vial of unguent, stand watch over Maria Baroncelli Portinari and her daughter. The different proportions of the saints and the members of the family reflect their position in social and religious hierarchy.

The Adoration of the Shepherds *(c. 1478) by Hugo van der Goes*

© Fine Art Images/Heritage Image/age fotostock

© Givaga/iStock

Piazza della Signoria

would come to listen to the musicians playing in the square.

The **rotunda** in front of the staircase contains a marble statue of a boar (Hellenistic, 3C BC) given to Cosimo I by Pope Paul IV. A bronze copy of the work, known as *Porcellino*, adorns the fountain in the Mercato Nuovo.

Corridoio Vasariano – (⊶*The Vasari Corridor is open only by reservation several weeks in advance. New opening to the public planned in 2021*) This gallery (1km/0.5mi long) was commissioned by Cosimo I so that he could pass unseen and apart from the crowds from the Palazzo Vecchio to the Pitti Palace. It was built by Vasari in 1565 and runs from the Uffizi, through the top storey of the buildings on the Ponte Vecchio, before penetrating the maze of houses on the south bank of the Arno.

The charm and beauty of this unusual location is enhanced by the view through the windows of Florence, the Arno and the surrounding hills.

The corridor forms a coda to the Uffizi galleries and is hung with 17C–18C works and famous self-portraits. The first paintings are from the school of Caravaggio (*Adoration of the Christ Child* by Gherardo delle Notti), followed by works from other Italian schools – Bologna (Guido Reni, Albani, Guercino), Venice (Liss), Rome (Bamboccio), Tuscany (Lorenzo Lippi) and Naples (Sal-

vator Rosa). The 17C Lombardy artists are represented by Giovanni Battista Crespi, and 18C Venetians by Bellotto and Rosalba Carriera. The French School is represented by La Tour, La Hyre and Boucher. The section of the corridor above the Ponte Vecchio is lined by about a hundred self-portraits by Titian, Veronese, Rosalba Carriera and Correggio. The remaining section of the corridor is hung with portraits by Velázquez, Rubens, Élisabeth Vigée-Lebrun, Ingres, Delacroix and Chagall. It provides a view of the interior of the church of **Santa Felicità** and ends at the Pitti Palace, where Boboli Gardens begin.

⬤⬤ WALKING TOUR

PIAZZA DELLA SIGNORIA
Piazza della Signoria★★

This was, and still is, the political centre of Florence set against the backdrop of the magnificent Palazzo Vecchio, the Loggia della Signoria and, in the wings, the Uffizi Gallery. It was created in the 13C when the victorious Guelfs razed to the ground the tower-houses belonging to the Ghibellines in the city centre.

The numerous statues along the outside of the Palazzo Vecchio and the loggia make this a veritable open-air museum. In the middle of the square is an equestrian statue of Cosimo I – Duke of Florence

1537–74 and a lavish patron of the arts – made in 1594 by Giambologna. At the corner of the Palazzo Vecchio, the Neptune Fountain, whose local nickname is Il Biancone, is more impressive for its maritime gods, its elongated Mannerist-style nymphs and its bronze fawns than for its enormous marble statue of the sea-god Neptune.

The fountain was made by **Bartolomeo Ammannati**, assisted by Giambologna, for the wedding in 1565 of Cosimo I's elder son to Joan of Austria. It was to some extent a rebuttal of the rigorous morality preached by the Dominican friar, Savonarola, who had constantly criticised the Medici style of government, as it was erected on the very spot where he was burned at the stake on 23 May 1498. In front of the fountain is a round slab marking the place of execution. Savonarola's death is commemorated every year in a ceremony known as the Fiorita.

Beside the steps up to the building (*left*) is the Marzocco, the lion of Florence, gripping a heraldic lily, executed by Donatello (*original in the Bargello*). Beside it is an admirable copy of the famous group by the same artist representing **Judith and Holofernes★** (*original in the Palazzo Vecchio*). Near the entrance is a huge marble statue of David, a copy of Michelangelo's famous work (*original in the Galleria dell'Accademia*).

Loggia della Signoria★★

The loggia was constructed at the end of the 14C to accommodate the members of the *Signoria* (◔*See below*) during official ceremonies. When later it was used as a guard room by Cosimo I's lancers (16C), it became known as the **Loggia dei Lanzi**. Although Gothic in design, it has wide semicircular arches built in the Florentine tradition, opening onto the square. An elegant decoration is provided by four shields representing the cardinal virtues, a band decorated with seven coats of arms which have been damaged, a graceful frieze of small trefoiled arches and a slender roof balustrade (*terrace accessible from the Uffizi during the high season only*). Restored statues dating from the days of the ancient Romans and the Renaissance have been placed in the loggia. The admirable statue of **Perseus★★★** brandishing the head of the Medusa (*front left*) was made between 1545 and 1553 by Benvenuto Cellini. The low-relief depicting Perseus Delivering Andromeda is a copy (*original in the Bargello*). Rape of the Sabine Women (*right*) dates from 1583. *Hercules Slaying the Centaur, Nessus* (*behind*) (1599) is by Giambologna.

Palazzo Vecchio★★★ (Palazzo della Signoria)

Allow 2hrs. ◔*Open daily Apr–Sep 9am–11pm (Thu 2pm), Oct–Mar 9am–7pm (Thu 2pm). Last entry 1hr before closing.* ◔ *Guided tours available.* ◔*Closed 25 Dec. Restaurant. Bookshop.* ◔€12,50. Tower and tour of battlements: €12,50. Combined ticket Palazzo Vecchio, Torre and tour of battlements: €19,50. ◔ ℘055 27 68 325. cultura.comune.fi.it/musei.

At the end of the 13C, Florence decided to build a city hall worthy of its importance, and it was probably Arnolfo di Cambio, the cathedral architect, who drew the design for the new city hall.

The impressive mass of the *palazzo*, surmounted by an elegant belfry (94m-/

For the Whole Family…

The 👥 **Museo dei Ragazzi** is aimed at children and families with interactive displays, as well as hosting tours (*about 1hr 15min, secret passageways, etc*). Explore themes such as light and shadow, Galileo's telescope and Torricelli's experiments on vacuums, while maintaining a link with the history of the palace and the city. ◔*Open daily 9am–6pm (2pm holidays). Information available about the different activities and prices.* ℘055 27 68 224. www.museoragazzi.it

309ft-high), dominates the square. It is in an austere Gothic style with an almost total absence of doors or windows on the lower level. On the upper storeys there are twin windows with trefoiled arches, machicolations, parapet walkways and crenellations. The merlons on the *palazzo* are Guelf and those on the tower are Ghibelline.

The building was designed to house the city government (**la Signoria**) composed of six representatives of the guilds (**priori delle arti**), which held great power in Florence at that time, and a magistrate (*Gonfaloniere di Giustizia*) whose post combined judicial and military authority. These officials were elected for only two months and, during their period of office, lived almost like recluses within the *palazzo*, where they worked, ate and slept. They were permitted to leave only for exceptional reasons. Dante lived there in 1300 as a member of the magistrature. In the 16C Cosimo I made the building his residence and also adapted it to suit the lavish lifestyle of the grand-ducal court by enlarging it and making radical alterations to the interior. The work was supervised by Giorgio Vasari who, for almost 20 years, from 1555 until his death, was employed there as architect, painter and decorator. When Cosimo I left the building to his son and moved to the Pitti Palace, it became known as Palazzo Vecchio (Old Palace) instead of Palazzo della Signoria.

The luxurious, elegant Renaissance interior forms a striking contrast to the exterior. The **courtyard**★ with its tall portico was almost totally redesigned in the 15C by Michelozzo and was elegantly decorated a century later by Vasari, who added stuccowork on a gold background to the columns and painted grotesque figures on the vaulting. In the centre is a graceful fountain with a porphyry basin, surmounted by a small winged genius, a copy of a bronze by Verrocchio, which can be seen on the Juno Terrace inside the building.

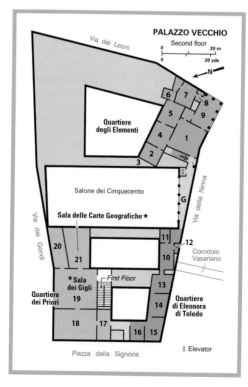

Palazzo Vecchio Tour: Second Floor Apartments

Refer to the floor plan, p137.

Apartments of the Elements

These rooms, which are situated above Leo X's Apartments, were built at the same time and to an identical layout. The decoration, based on ancient mythology, was designed by Vasari using complex symbolism with the aim of exalting the virtues of Cosimo I.

The **Elements Chamber (1)** is named after the allegorical scenes in its decoration. On the walls are illustrations of Water (the Birth of Venus), Fire (Vulcan's forge) and Earth (Saturn receiving fruit). On the ceiling, in the rectangular coffer above the allegorical representation of Earth is Air (Apollo's chariot).

The **Ceres Chamber (2)** is dedicated to Ceres, daughter of Saturn and Opis and goddess of agriculture. On the central coffer in the ceiling Ceres seeks her daughter Proserpina after her abduction by Pluto, god of the Underworld.

The **Study of Calliope (2)** originally housed miniatures, small bronzes, medals and rare and precious artworks from Cosimo I's collection, either on shelves or in cabinets and cases.

The **Room of Opis (3)** is named after Opis, wife of Saturn and goddess of prosperity. It lies immediately above the Room of Lorenzo the Magnificent, whose diplomatic talents were acknowledged and appreciated by numerous monarchs just as Opis was worshipped by numerous peoples. The goddess appears in the centre of the ceiling surrounded by allegories of the seasons and of the months of the year, each shown with its matching star sign.

On the central coffer in the ceiling of the **Jupiter Chamber (5)** Vasari and his pupils described the mythical childhood of Jupiter.

The antechamber of the **Juno Terrace (6)** contains the small statue by Verrocchio of a winged Cupid holding a dolphin. It was designed to be placed in the entrance courtyard.

On the ceiling of the **Hercules Chamber (7)** are paintings of the Twelve Labours of Hercules. The central coffer shows Hercules as a child with his parents, Jupiter and Alcmene; he is strangling the serpents sent to kill him by Juno, Alcmene's rival.

The **Study of Minerva (8)** was designed to host the small marble statues in Cosimo I's collection. (*Closed win.*)

The adjacent **Saturn Terrace (9)** looks out onto one of the most attractive stretches of countryside in the Florence district. In the centre of the ceiling is a painting of Saturn devouring his sons. The four triangular coffers contain representations of the Four Ages of Man. The 12 rectangular coffers round the edge are decorated with illustrations of the 12 hours of the day. (*Closed win.*)

A **gallery (G)** overlooks the Hall of the Five Hundred and gives a good idea of the exceptional height of the hall. Through the windows opposite there is a view of the cathedral dome and the Tuscan hills in the distance.

Eleonora of Toledo's Study

When Cosimo I came to live in the Palazzo della Signoria with his 18-year-old wife, he commissioned court architect Battista del Tasso to refurbish some of the austere apartments once occupied by the guild representatives (*priori*). A few years later, Vasari and Flemish artist Jan Van der Straet, better known as Lo Stradano, decorated the ceilings with scenes constituting a sort of hymn to femininity.

The **Green Chamber (10)**, the only one on which Vasari did not work, was Eleonora's bedchamber. On the vaulting is a shield bearing the coats of arms of the Medici and the House of Toledo. This room opens into a tiny study (**12**) with a small window, used by the Duchess as her office (*scrittoio*). It also opens into her private chapel (**11**), which was decorated from 1541 to 1545 with scenes from the story of Moses by Bronzino. The artist is said to have taken Cosimo and Eleonora's eldest daughter as his model for the Virgin Mary in the *Annunciation*, which hangs on the back wall next (*right*) to the *Deposition from the Cross*.

The **Sabine Chamber** (**13**) was used by Eleonora's ladies-in-waiting. On the ceiling is a painting of the Sabine women standing between their fathers and their Roman husbands to prevent the men fighting.

The **Esther Chamber** (**14**) contains an attractive 15C marble wash basin. Almost the entire ceiling is covered with a large coffer decorated with an illustration of Courage and Determination in the person of Esther, the Hebrew woman who succeeded in saving her people.

In the **Penelope Chamber** (**15**) the great central medallion is an exaltation of faithfulness symbolised by the wife of Ulysses dressed in 16C Florentine costume. In several places the Medici shield with its five roundels appears together with the chequerboard shield of the House of Toledo as well as the emblem of Cosimo I, the tortoise, a symbol of prudence, and a sail, which evokes a sense of opportunity.

The **Gualdrada Chamber** (**16**) is dedicated to Virtue, embodied in the young Florentine girl who gained fame in the 13C by refusing a kiss from Emperor Otto. The frieze below the ceiling contains a number of buildings in Florence which are easily recognisable.

Priors' Chapel

These apartments were laid out a century earlier than the remainder of the palazzo, which was altered by Cosimo I.

The **Priors' Chapel** (**17**) was decorated in the late 15C by Rodolfo Ghirlandaio. It was here that the officials (*priori*) gathered to pray before making decisions of a legal nature, as is evident from the quotations from the Old and New Testaments contained in the series of panels round the walls.

The **Audience Chamber** (**18**), which was decorated in the second half of the 15C, has a sumptuous coffered ceiling by Giuliano da Maiano.

The **Lily Chamber★** (**19**) is one of the most beautiful chambers in the *palazzo*. It owes its name to the golden fleurs de lys on a blue background decorating its walls. This is not the Florentine lily, but the emblem of the King of France, with whom the Republic of Florence was on friendly terms. The superb gold and blue coffered **ceiling★** was made, like the ceiling in the previous chamber, by Giuliano da Maiano (1478). The marquetry doors are decorated with portraits of Dante and Petrarch. The admirable sculpture entitled **Judith and Holofernes★** by Donatello is displayed in this chamber.

Machiavelli worked in the **Sala della Cancelleria** (**20**) for his last 15 years in office as Secretary to the Chancery, playing a leading role in Florentine politics, until he was forced into exile following the return of the Medici in 1512. The room contains two portraits of Machiavelli – a terracotta bust and a posthumous painting by Santi di Tito.

The **Map Chamber★** (**21**), designed by Vasari for Cosimo I, was where the Medici kept their state dress and their valuables. The decoration on the cupboards, completed in the second half of the 16C, consists of a collection of maps of outstanding interest since all the areas of the world known at that time are shown. The enormous globe in the centre of the room dates from the same period.

On the left of the Palazzo Vecchio, in Via dei Gondi, on the corner with Piazza S Firenze, stands the **Palazzo Gondi★** (1490), by Giuliano da Sangallo.

To reach the first floor, climb up the superb double staircase built by Vasari.

Salone dei Cinquecento (Hall of the Five Hundred)

The hall is a huge chamber (1,200sq m/ 12,912sq ft in area, 18m/59ft high), built in 1495 during the days of the Republic instituted by Savonarola. It was designed to accommodate the Grand Council which had so many members (1500) that only one third of their number could participate in the government of the city at any one time. Here Savonarola spoke in 1496, during his brief reign as master of Florence, and here he was condemned to death two years later.

When the Medici returned to power, they used the hall as their audience chamber and also for receptions, including the one given to celebrate the marriage of Francesco and Joan of Austria. The walls and **sumptuous coffered ceiling★★** were decorated by Vasari and his assistants with allegories and scenes in honour of Florence and Cosimo I. He is depicted like a god in the central coffer, amidst a circle of cherubs and coats of arms representing the city's various guilds. Battle scenes cover the walls along the entire length of the chamber, in honour of the victories won by Florence, mainly over its two great rivals, Pisa and Siena.

Most of the sculptures placed along the walls were already in the chamber in the 16C. Among them (*left of the door opposite the entrance*) is *La Vittoria*, an admirable group representing Genius slaying Might. Michelangelo created this work for the tomb of Julius II but, as it was never finished, it was given to Cosimo I by Michelangelo's nephew.

Studiolo★★

Access to the right of the entrance. Visible from the door. ⚷ *No admission to the room itself. (The Secret Passages Tour offers better access).*

The exquisite but visually challenging room was the study (*studiolo*) of Francesco I. Originally it could only be reached from his bedchamber via a small concealed door (*behind the bare panel to the right at the end of the room*). It has no external source of light, reflecting the solitary character of the prince and his taste for secrets.

It was Vasari who designed this tiny but elegant room. The walls themselves are covered in panels painted by several of the Florentine Mannerist painters.

Using a symbolism that is often difficult to comprehend, they illustrated the myth of Prometheus (decoration on the ceiling), the four elements – Water, Air, Earth and Fire – or human enterprise, scientific discoveries and the mysteries of alchemy. The two portraits placed opposite each other at the ends of the room depict Francesco's parents, Cosimo I and Eleonora of Toledo. Both were painted by Bronzino's studio.

Leo X's Apartments

Access from the Hall of the Five Hundred by the door opposite the Studiolo.

This wing of the *palazzo* was added in the 16C by Cosimo I. The rooms in Leo X's apartments were designed as reception rooms for the guests of the grand-ducal court. Their decoration glorified the merits of the Medici, each feature being dedicated to one illustrious member of the family. The decoration comprises not only a series of historical documents but also a veritable portrait gallery.

Leo X's Chamber, the largest chamber in Leo X's apartments, bears his name and is dedicated to the son of Lorenzo the Magnificent who re-established the family's authority in Florence in 1512 and was elected Pope in 1513. He is depicted arriving in Piazza della Signoria during his visit to his birthplace two years later (*on the wall opposite the fireplace*).

Access to the second floor from this room.

The second floor contains three suites of **apartments** (*quartieri*) – the Elements Apartments, Eleonora of Toledo's Apartments, and the Priors' Apartments (*See Apartments panel, previous page*).

Museo Galileo★

Piazza dei Giudici 1. ⏱*Open 9.30am–6pm (Tue 1pm).* ⏱*Closed 1 Jan, 25 Dec.* ✎€10. ✆*055 26 53 11. www.museogalileo.it.*

The medieval **Palazzo Castellani** is the science museum, renovated and renamed Museo Galileo in 2010. It has a good collection of scientific instruments acquired in part from the Medici and Grand Dukes Hapsburg-Lorraine, passionate Humanist Renaissance promoters of science. The Museo Galileo is home to the only surviving instruments designed and built by Galileo himself. The most important are two original telescopes and the objective lens of the telescope with which Galileo discovered Jupiter's moons.

Interactive rooms help to explain the functioning of certain instruments.

First Floor – The Medici Collections – Mathematical instruments 16C–17C: celestial globes, armillary spheres, astrolabes, quadrants, compasses, etc. Personal effects of Pisan physician and astronomer Galileo **Galilei** (1564–1642): the lens that enabled his 1609 discovery of the moons of Jupiter, his two telescopes, the compass he made, and in a reliquary, one of his fingers.

The optic rooms include 17C innovations: origin and evolution of the telescope, prisms (for light studies) and optical tricks. Cosmography, study of the heavenly skies, includes a splendid collection of Earth and celestial globes and armillary spheres. Instruments for observation and research include a 17C microscope, glass and meteorological instruments (17C–18C) and Florentine astronomy (18C–19C).

Second Floor – The Lorraine Collections – Clocks (appeared in the West in the 13C). Mathematical instruments and calculators 18C–19C, (which led to innovations in England, Germany, and France) and precision instruments.

The 18C instruments were used to demonstrate electrical and magnetic phenomena. The pneumatic and hydrostatic instruments date from 17C–18C.

Mechanical instruments document 17C progress from Descartes to Newton, and 18C instruments were used to demonstrate various theories such as centrifugal force and gravity.

A section on medicine includes surgical instruments and teaching models for obstetrics, the history of pharmacies and modern chemistry, concluding with a room of weights and measures.

Santa Maria Novella District

Near the Duomo and the Arno, the Santa Maria Novella neighbourhood is a transport hub for buses to other cities but is also home to cafés, shops, hotels, medieval *palazzi* and frescoes by Ghirlandaio.

⌚ **Michelin Map:**
pp104–105 CD12.

▷ **Don't Miss:** Frescoes in Santa Maria Novella, Sassetti Chapel in Santa Trinità.

👥 **Kids:** Knights' armour in Museo Stibbert; Alinari museum; family exhibit kit at Palazzo Strozzi.

👣WALKING TOUR

SANTA MARIA NOVELLA
Piazza Santa Maria Novella★★

The church and cloisters of Santa Maria Novella stand at the north end of the irregularly shaped **Piazza Santa Maria Novella**, which was laid out in the 14C.

It had a major renovation in the early 21C. The south side is lined by the Renaissance arches of the long, slightly elevated **Loggia de San Paolo**.

In the Middle Ages the square hosted numerous tournaments and other pageants. From the mid-16C–20C it hosted the Palio dei Cocchi, the chariot race

Farmacia Di Santa Maria Novella

The **Pharmacy of Santa Maria Novella** was founded in 1221 when the Dominicans first came to Florence. It has also sold spices since the 16C and their scents waft out into the street. The large shop is set out in an old chapel with ogival vaulting which was dedicated to St Nicholas. It was built in 1332 and redecorated in the neo-Gothic style in 1848. The room which opens onto the cloisters, now a herbalist shop selling a range of fragrant herbs, has stuccowork vaulting and 17C furnishings including display cabinets containing numerous stills. The frescoes in **St Nicholas' Sacristy** depict Christ's Passion.
⏱*Open daily 9am–8pm.* ⏱*Closed 1 Jan, 25–26 Dec.* ♿ ☏*055 21 62 76; www.smnovella.it.*

held on St John's Day (24 June), which was introduced by Cosimo I and based on the two-horse chariot (*biga*) races of ancient Rome. The Grand Dukes presided over the event from a canopied box set up on the steps of the loggia. The 17C marble obelisks were designed by Giambologna.

Santa Maria Novella★★

1hr. ⏱*Open Mon–Thu, 9am–5.30pm (Apr–Sept 7pm), Fri open 11 am; Sat 9am–5.30 pm (Jul–Aug 6.30pm). Sun and holidays: 1pm–5.30pm, (Jul–Aug noon–6.30pm, Sept 5.30pm).* ☜€7,50 *(includes Cathedral and Cloisters). www.chiesasantamarianovella.it.*
Although the Dominicans commenced work on Santa Maria Novella in 1279 in an attempt to heal the rift between the Guelfs and Ghibellines, the main building was not completed until 1360.

Exterior

The lower part of the extremely elegant **façade** with its light geometrical design picked out in green and white marble, dates from the mid-14C. In 1458 Leon Battista Alberti blended the existing Gothic features with the Renaissance style by employing simple harmonious forms such as squares and circles. The central doorway, pillars and the whole of the upper section of the façade were built to his plans. The remarkable voluted consoles in coloured marble marquetry were designed to fill the space between the aisles and the higher nave. This treatment influenced many Renais-

sance churches and Baroque façades. The Rucellai, a rich merchant family, are cited in the dedicatory inscription – IOHANES.ORICELLARIVS.PAV.F.AN. SAL.MCCCLXX – on the pediment. The Rucellai coat of arms, a billowing sail, appears in the middle frieze. A sundial (*right*) and an armillary sphere (*left*) also appear.

The small **cemetery** (*right* – ⚷ *closed to the public*), where Domenico Ghirlandaio was buried, is enclosed by a screen composed of a series of Gothic recesses that, like those on the façade, contain the remains of Florentine families. At the base of the recesses are marble sarcophagi carved with the People's Cross and the coats of arms of the families of the deceased.

From Piazza dell'Unità Italiana and Piazza della Stazione (*north*), is a remarkable **view★** of the powerful chevet, surmounted by a slender, austere Romanesque Gothic bell tower.

Interior

The interior of Santa Maria Novella was bright and vast (almost 100m/328ft long) for the preaching of sermons. Its Latin cross layout has a very short transept and flat chevet. The outstanding feature of the interior is its austerity. The elegant, spacious nave is lined with arches that become narrower towards the chancel, thus accentuating the feeling of depth. Alternating black and white archstones and the ogival vaulting in the nave and aisles are highlighted by geometrical designs, also in black and white.

Inside the Church

The **east aisle** contains the austere elegant tomb (**1**) (*second bay far right*) of the Blessed Villana delle Botti, a Dominican nun who died in 1361. Carved by Bernardo Rossellino almost one century later, it shows her recumbent figure lying beneath a canopy of flowing draperies. At the end of the **east transept** above the altar in the raised **Ruccellai Chapel** (**2**) is Nino Pisano's sweetly smiling marble **Madonna and Child★**.

The **Filippo Strozzi Chapel** (**3**) is decorated throughout with **frescoes★** painted by Filippino Lippi, who portrayed scenes from the life of St Philip and St John the Evangelist against a backdrop of exuberant architecture. The rich merchant to

Holy Trinity *by Masaccio*

© DEA/G NIMATALLAH/De Agostini Editore/age fotostock

whom the chapel is dedicated and who commissioned the Palazzo Strozzi, one of the finest mansions in Florence, is buried in an ornate basalt sarcophagus.

The dazzling **frescoes★★★** with which Domenico Ghirlandaio covered the walls of the **sanctuary** in 1485 at the request of Giovanni Tornabuoni are considered his finest work. In his illustration of the lives of the Virgin Mary (*left*) and St John the Baptist (*right*), he modelled his figures on members of the Tornabuoni family and their friends, and painted a brilliant and detailed picture of Florentine high society.

The **west transept** contains the **Gondi Chapel** (**4**) and its famous **Crucifix★★** by Brunelleschi. The walls of the slightly raised **Cappella Strozzi di Mantova** (**5**) are decorated with unusually large **frescoes★** painted by Florentine artist Nardo di Cione, c. 1357. Facing the entrance is a fresco of the Last Judgement; Hell (*right-hand wall*), depicted in dark, earthy colours, and Paradise (*left-hand wall*), with its light, golden tones, are based on the work by Dante. Above the altar is a Flamboyant Gothic **polyptych★** in which Andrea Orcagna, Nardo di Cione's brother, showed Christ surrounded by seraphim handing St Peter the keys to the Kingdom of Heaven and giving St Thomas Aquinas the Book of Wisdom.

The **Sacristy** (**6**) contains a **Crucifixion★** painted by Giotto. There is also a lavabo consisting of a marble basin surmounted by a glazed terracotta **niche★** which is one of the most delightful of all Giovanni della Robbia's works.

Located in the **north aisle** is the famous fresco of the **Trinity★★** (**7**), for which Masaccio needed only 27 days to complete. In this fresco, which is of vital importance in the history of art, the artist broke away from the attractive elegance of Gothic painting by painting God the Father in a Renaissance setting, holding the upright of the Cross and presenting the sacrifice of his crucified son. The outline of the Holy Ghost in the form of a dove stands out on his chest. Christ is flanked by the Virgin Mary (her face and outstretched hand also show that she has accepted the sacrifice), St John and the donors, on their knees. In this work Masaccio made use of new mathematical theories on perspective, drawn up by Brunelleschi, and so achieved one of the finest Renaissance examples of architectural perspective. The marble pulpit (**8**) (*against the following pillar*) has decorations in gold leaf designed by Brunelleschi. The panels recount the story of the Virgin Mary.

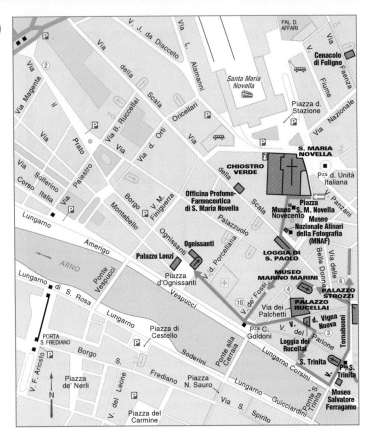

Cloisters★

🕐*Opening hours: see Santa Maria Novella (p142).* 🎧*Guided tour available. The visit is included in the Santa Maria Novella tour.* ☎*055 28 21 87.* ♿. *www.cultura.comune.fi.it.*

Chiostro Verde★

The **Green Cloisters** were built in the mid-14C in Romanesque style, with wide semicircular arches. The name refers to the green of the decorative **frescoes**, which were painted c. 1430 by Paolo Uccello and his students, depicting scenes from Genesis. The frescoes on the wall between the cloisters and

the church are the work of the master alone. They are painted in sombre tones and depict (*left to right*) scenes ranging from the Creation to the story of Noah. Only two bays are still in good condition: (**9**) the creation of animal life, Adam and Eve and Original Sin are all clearly visible; and in the fourth bay (**10**), depicting the Flood (the storm is particularly interesting) and Noah's drunkenness.

Cappellone degli Spagnoli★★

North Gallery. Behind the elegant Gothic twin windows with multifoiled arches and delightful twisted columns, is the

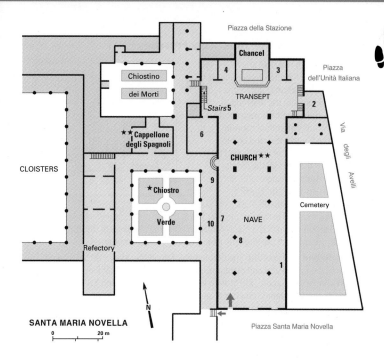

SANTA MARIA NOVELLA

0   20 m

chapterhouse built in the 14C. Also known as the **Spanish Chapel**, in the 16C it was frequented by the courtiers of Eleonora of Toledo. The walls and vaulted roof are covered with highly complex symbolic **frescoes★★** painted 1365–70 in vivid colours by Andrea di Bonaiuti, known as **Andrea da Firenze**, in honour of the Dominicans.

Left-hand wall – The Triumph of Divine Wisdom and the Glorification of St Thomas Aquinas. On the vaulting is a representation of Pentecost (the dove of the Holy Ghost coming down to the Apostles who are grouped round the Virgin Mary). Below them a Dominican theologian personifies Catholic doctrine. He sits on a throne surrounded by the Wise Men of the Old and New Testaments, above whom are the Virtues. Through Roman Catholic doctrine, the Holy Spirit brings to life the Liberal and Sacred Arts, symbolised by 14 female figures sitting in Gothic niches with figures representing these disciplines at their feet.

Right-hand wall – The Triumph of the Church. Activities of the Dominicans.

Domenico Ghirlandaio (1449–94)

Ghirlandaio painted a large number of frescoes including the cycles in Santa Maria Novella and Santa Trinità, and the Last Supper scenes in the refectories of San Marco and Ognissanti. He ran a leading studio in which Michelangelo was a pupil. The main characteristics of his style are his sense of decoration, his taste for detail and his love of line and colour. His works depict the finery of the wealthy bourgeois society from whom most of his clients came. The portraits, costumes, headdresses, buildings and furniture are all excellent descriptions of contemporary life in Florence.

On the vaulting is St Peter's boat, representing the Church. At the bottom of the wall, in front of a building that is one of the projects drawn by the artist for Florence Cathedral, are the

Deciphering the Sanctuary Frescoes

On the **left-hand wall** are
(**I**) Joachim chased from the Temple
because he has no children (the
young man with the fine mop of
hair to the left of the foreground
is Giovanni Tornabuoni's son-in-
law; the figure with hand on hip,
in the group to the right, is said to
be the artist himself; the Loggia
di San Paolo is recognisable in
the background); (**II**) The Birth
of the Virgin Mary; (**III**) Mary

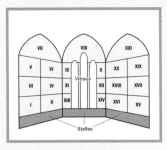

being presented in the Temple; (**IV**) The marriage of the Virgin Mary;
(**V**) The Adoration of the Magi (damaged); (**VI**) The Massacre of the Innocents;
(**VII**) The Death of the Virgin Mary and (*above*) the Assumption.

On the **end wall** are (**VIII**) The Coronation of the Virgin Mary; (**IX**) St Dominic
committing heretical and orthodox books to the flames; (**X**) St Peter the Martyr;
(**XI**) The Annunciation; (**XII**) St John in the wilderness; (**XIII** and **XIV**) the patrons
of the work, Giovanni Tornabuoni and his wife, Francesca Pitti, at prayer.

On the **right-hand wall** are (**XV**) The angel appearing to Zachariah;
(**XVI**) The Visitation; (**XVII**) The birth of St John the Baptist; (**XVIII**) Zachariah,
having lost the power of speech, is writing down the name to be given to
his son; (**XIX**) St John the Baptist preaching; (**XX**) The Baptism of Christ;
(**XXI**) Herod's feast.

Pope and the Holy Roman Emperor. In front of them (*left*) are various religious orders and orders of chivalry. Among the group of Christian believers (*right*) is a standing figure, dressed in a great brown cloak, shown full face and said to be Cimabue. Beside him, depicted in profile and wearing a green hood, is Giotto. Boccaccio is further to the right, dressed in purple and holding a closed book. Above him, wearing a cloak and hood of white ermine, is Petrarch. The figure beside him, shown in profile wearing a white cap, is Dante.

On the same register the Domini-cans are shown (*right*) protect-ing the Faithful from attack by Sin. The name "Dominicans" comes from the Latin *Domini Canes* meaning the Hounds of God; symbol-ised as dogs, they tear to pieces heretics depicted as wolves.

Above them, being welcomed into Heaven, are the souls of believers who succumbed to mortal sin but who were saved through their Confession received by a Dominican. Only three sins are depicted: Avarice, Lust and Pride are sitting next to a woman playing a viol. The Faithful are shown contemplating the Almighty, who is surrounded by angels with the Virgin Mary in their midst (she is in the group on the left). At the foot of the throne is the Lamb of God and the symbols of the Evangelists. **End wall** – The paintings (*left to right*) depict the climb up to Calvary, the Cru-cifixion and the descent into Hell. On the vaulting is the Resurrection. To the left of the tomb are the Holy Women who have come to embalm the Body of Christ. To the right, Christ appears to Mary Magdalen.

Entrance wall – This was not inte-grated into the overall decoration and was used to depict the first Dominican martyr – St Peter the Martyr. On the vaulting is the Ascension.

**Chiostrino dei Morti
(Little Cloisters of the Dead)**
Right of the Spanish Chapel.

The pavement and walls of these irregularly shaped cloisters and the small entrance gallery are almost entirely covered in gravestones.

Refectory

From the entrance lobby there is a view into the **Great Cloisters** (part of the Police College). The refectory and the room preceding it house the treasure of Santa Maria Novella – gold- and silverware, reliquaries, frontals, vestments – and a number of frescoes that have been removed from the church walls, including Orcagna's 35 busts of figures from the Old Testament which once decorated the chancel before it was painted by Ghirlandaio. They were found during restoration work.

Museo Novecento

Piazza Santa Maria Novella 10.
Open *Apr–Sep 11am–8pm (Thu 2pm, Fri 11pm); Oct–Mar 11am–7pm (Thu 2pm). Last entry 1 hr before closing.* €9.50. 055 28 61 32. *www.museonovecento.it*
On a par with the world's best, this museum is dedicated to 20C Italian art and exhibits some 300 works in 15 rooms.

Museo Nazionale Alinari della Fotografia (MNAF)★

Piazza Santa Maria Novella 14a. *Closed at the time of publication.* 055 23 95 235. *www. alinarifondazione.it; www.alinari.it.*
Since 2006 this former convent has been devoted to the story of the Alinar brothers, who in 1852 founded their photographic studio (*which still operates as an agency at Largo Alinari 15. Visits for groups. For information:* 055 23 95 232).
The collection (*bought in 2020 by the Tuscan Region*) owns some 3.5 million photographic records (vintage photos, glass plates, negatives, equipment).

In the SW corner of Piazza di Santa Maria Novella turn left into Via della Scala. Turn right into Via de' Fossi and a further right onto Borgo Ognissanti.

Ognissanti

Borgo Ognissanti 42. Open *9.30am–12.30pm and 4–7.30pm.* Closed *Wed am and Sun.* 375 56 52 013.
All Saints' Church, which dates from the 13C, was completely rebuilt during the 17C, with the exception of the bell tower (13C–14C) standing on the south side. The Baroque façade was designed by Matteo Nigetti and is decorated with a glazed terracotta Coronation of the Virgin Mary produced in della Robbia's workshops (*lunette above the doorway*) and Florence's coat of arms characterised by its lily (*centre of the pediment*).
The interior contains two frescoes by Domenico Ghirlandaio (*behind the second altar on the right*) depicting a Descent from the Cross and a Virgin Mary of Mercy protecting the members of the family of Amerigo Vespucci, the Florentine navigator, whose tombstone can be seen at the foot of the altar (*left*). It is interesting to compare Botticelli's fresco of St Augustine (*between the third and fourth altars*), with Ghirlandaio's fresco on the north wall of the nave opposite, portraying St Jerome, as both works were painted in 1480. Botticelli is buried in the south transept (*chapel on the right towards the entrance*) beneath a circular marble slab bearing his real surname, Filipepi.
The habit worn by St Francis of Assisi when he received the stigmata in September 1224 has been kept in the second chapel of the north transept since 1503.

Cenacolo (Old Refectory)

Open *Mon, Sat 9am–1pm.* Closed *1 Jan, 25 Dec.* 055 28 67 00 or 055 23 88 754. *Off the cloisters on the south side of the church, access from the transept.*
The former refectory was decorated by Domenico Ghirlandaio in 1480 with a huge fresco of the **Last Supper★**, painted after his version in the Monastery of San Marco. Compared to the fresco in San Marco the Last Supper in Ognissanti conveys a greater sense of serenity and is more natural owing to the slightly more austere decor and the varied poses of the Apostles.

Retrace your steps to the Carraia Bridge. At the junction turn left and walk into Via della Vigna Nuova towards the Palazzo Rucellai.

Palazzo Rucellai★★

Via della Vigna Nuova 18. (⚊closed to the public).

The mansion, built between 1446 and 1451 by Bernardo Rossellino to plans by Leon Battista Alberti, was constructed for Giovanni Rucellai, a member of a leading Florentine family. The Rucellai were related to the Strozzi and Medici and owed their name and fortune to imports from the Orient of a lichen, rocella (*oricella*), used to produce red dye. Their family emblem, a sail billowing in the wind, is depicted on a frieze on the first floor, on the loggia opposite and in Santa Maria Novella.

The mansion is the first example since Antiquity of a **façade** articulated by three orders superimposed. A rigorous sense of uniformity is created vertically by the alignment of pilasters and horizontally by the cornices that run along the top of each storey. The windows are set within these grid-like divisions against a background of slightly rusticated stonework, which contrasts greatly with the heavy rustication on the ground floor of the Palazzo Medici and throughout the façade of the Palazzo Strozzi, which dates from a later period.

Opposite stands the **loggia** that accompanied every notable family's residence. It is also attributed to Leon Battista Alberti. Although the bays are walled up, they have retained a certain elegance.

Take via del Purgatorio and turn right onto Via Panoncino. Turn right onto Lungarno Corsini. Take a left onto Via Maggio.

Museo Salvatore Ferragamo

Palazzo Spini Feroni, Piazza Santa Trinita 5r. ⚊ ⏰Open 10am–7.30pm. ⏰Closed 1 Jan, 1 May, 15 Aug, 25 Dec. ⚊€8. ☎055 35 62 846. www.ferragamo.com/museo.

After a stint in Hollywood shoeing the stars, in 1927 Salvatore Ferragamo set up his shoe business in Florence. Shoes from 1937–early 1960s are shown, made in exotic materials and shapes, including shoes for Brigitte Bardot, Marilyn Monroe and Sophia Loren.

Santa Trinità

Piazza Santa Trinità. ⏰Open daily 8am–noon (Sun and holidays 10.45am) and 4–6pm.

Holy Trinity Church was built in the second half of the 14C. The Baroque façade by Buontalenti was added in the late 16C. The extremely austere, slender interior is a fine example of the beginnings of Gothic architecture in Florence. The façade of the Romanesque church built in the 11C can be seen incorporated into the current façade. The church's crypt also dates from this period.

The chapels contain some interesting works of art. The *Madonna in Majesty with Saints* (*third chapel in the south aisle*) is a 15C altarpiece by Neri di Bicci. The **Chapel of the Annunciation★** (*fourth chapel*), enclosed by a fine 15C screen and decorated with Lorenzo Monaco's frescoes recounting the Life of the Virgin Mary, contains a fine Gothic altarpiece by the same artist depicting the Annunciation; the predella includes the Visitation, the Nativity, the Adoration of the Magi and the Flight into Egypt. The fifth chapel has an early 16C marble altar set in a splendid carved tempietto surround. The main feature of interest in this church is, however, the decoration in the **Sassetti Chapel★★** (*second chapel on the right in the south transept*) undertaken by Domenico Ghirlandaio in 1483. Using a technique he was later to employ in the chancel of Santa Maria Novella, the artist created a colourful portrait gallery of his contemporaries to depict episodes from the life of St Francis of Assisi. The vaulting is decorated with four splendid female figures representing Sibyls. The donors, Francesco Sassetti and his wife, are depicted kneeling. Their magnificent tombs have basalt sarcophagi, probably the work of Giuliano da Sangallo, on each side of the altar. Above is an Adoration of the Shepherds, another famous work by Domenico Ghirlandaio (1485) in which certain critics have observed the influence of the Portinari Triptych by Van der Goes (*now in the Uffizi*).

The chapel, on the other side of the altar, parallels the Sasetti chapel and has a monument with a garland of glazed polychrome terracotta by Luca Della Robbia. Further along, the wooden Mary Magdalene was begun by Desiderio da Settignano and completed by Benedetto da Maiano. Neri di Bicci painted St John Gualberto surrounded by saints and monks, as well as the *Annunciation*; the *Coronation of the Virgin* is by Bicci di Lorenzo (1430); in the fourth chapel is the 1503 *St Jerome in Penitence* and *Annunciation* by Ridolfo del Ghirlandaio. The crypt was part of the primitive Romanesque church.

On the corner with Via Delle Terme stands the **Palazzo Bartolini-Salimbeni** (1517–20), designed by Baccio d'Agnolo, with fine mullioned windows.

▷ Take Via Tornabuoni to the corner of Via degli Strozzi.

Here are several typical Florentine mansions: **Palazzo Spini-Ferroni★** (*no 2*), 13C with crenellations and **Palazzo Tornabuoni-Beacci** (*no 3*), a fine 14C mansion. After passing Piazza Strozzi, look at the **Palazzo dello Strozzino** (*no 7*), apparently a smaller replica (hence its name) of its prestigious neighbour, although it is an earlier building begun in 1458 by Michelozzo. The first floor by Giuliano da Maiano dates from the early 1460s. Also look at the **Palazzo Larderel** (*no 19 – blue*), built by Dosio in 1580. In **Piazza degli Antinori** (*north end of Via Tornabuoni*), see the **Palazzo Antinori** (*no 3*), built 1461 to 1466, which is attributed to Giuliano da Sangallo.

Palazzo Strozzi★★

Piazza Strozzi. 🕐*Open during exhibitions only: 10am–8pm (Thu 11pm).* 📞*055 26 45 155.* *www.palazzostrozzi.org.*

The last of the great private mansions to be built during the Florentine Renaissance, this is one of the period's finest achievements in vernacular architecture. Rich merchant Filippo Strozzi (d. 1491) commissioned Benedetto da Maiano, architect and sculptor, to design the building. The patron symbolically laid the first stone of his residence in 1489.The mansions of the Medici inspired this work. Giuliano da Sangallo produced a scale model of his future residence, however, a third architect, Simone di Pollaiolo, called Il Cronaca, took charge of the work. He designed the splendid stone cornice at the top of the building. The stately, elegant **courtyard**, surrounded by a high portico and overlooked by an open loggia on the upper floor in the Florentine tradition, is also the work of Cronaca. The building was completed in 1504, remaining in the Strozzi family until 1937. Now restored, Palazzo Strozzi houses various cultural institutes, the Biennial International Antiques Fair, and prestigious art exhibitions.

👪 A fun and imaginative visiting kit is on offer to families for the temporary exhibitions.

▷ Walk south along Via Tornabuoni to Piazza S Trinità.

Museo Marino Marini★

Piazza San Pancrazio. 🕐*Open Sat– Mon 10am–7pm (Rucellai chapel 11am–16.30pm), Tue–Fri by reservation. Permanent collection: free admission.* 💶*€6. €9.50 combined ticket exhibition and Rucellai chapel.* ⚑ 📞*055 21 94 32.* *www.museomarinomarini.it.*

The Church of San Pancrazio houses works by **Marino Marini** (1901–80)-sculptures, paintings, drawings and engravings. His favourite themes are Woman, the Horseman and the Warrior. The huge equestrian group *Aja* in the chancel is brilliantly lit.

OTHER SIGHTS
Cenacolo di Fuligno

Via Faenza 42. 🕐*Open Tue, 1st Sun of the month 8.30am–1.30pm.* 🕐*Closed Easter, 15 Aug, 25 Dec.* 💶*Free, donation suggested.* ⚑ 📞*055 53 81 123.*

The refectory of the former convent of Franciscan Tertiaries in Foligno has the **Last Supper★** fresco attributed to

Perugino c. 1491, the year in which Neri di Bicci, the artist originally commissioned for this work, died.

Museo Stibbert★

Via Federigo Stibbert 26; take bus no 4 (Piazza della Stazione behind the chancel of Santa Maria Novella). ◐*Open Mon–Wed 10am–2pm (Fri–Sun 6pm). Guided tours every hour.* ◐*Closed Thu, 1 Jan, Easter, 1 May, 15 Aug, 25 Dec. Bar. Bookshop.* ◔€8. ♿ ✆*055 47 55 20. museostibbert.it.*

The Stibbert Villa (19C) houses armour, sculptures, paintings, furniture, faïence, tapestries, embroidery, objects and costumes of varying origins and periods of history. Note the malachite and gilded bronze table made by Thomire for King Jerome, Napoleonic memorabilia, including his coronation robes, and 18C Venetian costumes. Ancient **armour★★** worn by Tuscans, Turks, Moors, Spaniards, Indians and Japanese are dramatically displayed on men and horses, guaranteed to stir the imagination of older kids.

San Lorenzo District★★

Florence under Lorenzo de'Medici

Lorenzo de' Medici was a true patron of the arts and many creative projects were undertaken during his reign. Starting at San Lorenzo, wind your way through the local market stalls.

SIGHTS
Church★★★

Piazza di San Lorenzo. ◐*Open 10am–5.30pm, Sun and holidays 1.30–5.30pm.* ◐*Closed Sun Nov–Feb.* ◔€7. €9.50 combined ticket Church and Library. ✆*055 21 40 42. www.operamedicealaurenziana.org.*
St Lawrence's Church is situated close to the Medici Palace (now the Palazzo Medici-Riccardi), and was formerly the Medici parish church, serving as their burial place for over three centuries. Construction of the church was begun c. 1420 by Brunelleschi, who was commissioned to undertake the work by Giovanni di Bicci, Cosimo the Elder's father. Subsequent generations of the Medici family added their own embellishments. As in the case of a number of other Florentine churches, the harsh façade never received the marble cladding included in the designs. The huge dome that caps the rear of the building is part of the Princes' Chapel (◔*See p153*), which was added in the 17C.

◔ **Michelin Map:** pp104–105 DE12.
▶ **Don't Miss:** San Lorenzo complex including the Medici Laurentian Library, Michelozzo frescoes in Palazzo Medici-Riccardi.
👥 **Kids:** Explore San Lorenzo central food market (morning).

For the interior Brunelleschi broke with Gothic conventions and introduced a style that became typical of the Florentine Renaissance. He adopted the traditional basilica layout – nave and two aisles – of the former building with 11C restorations, and combined its Romanesque semicircular arches with ancient Greek and Roman architectural features, such as Corinthian columns, fluted pilasters and cornices. San Lorenzo thus came to represent a new style of church with an austere, pure architectural design. The building has a coffered ceiling decorated, in the nave, with four reproductions of the Medici coat of arms. The barrel-vaulted aisles are flanked by shallow chapels surmounted by oculi.
In 1516 Pope Leo X, Lorenzo the Magnificent's son, commissioned Michelangelo to complete the east front that had been left unfinished on Brunelleschi's death in 1446. Michelangelo drew up a number of grandiose plans but only the inside

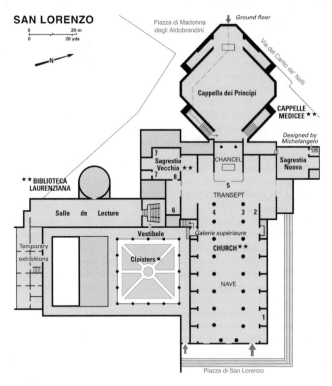

SAN LORENZO

0   20 m
0   20 yds

—N—→

Piazza di Madonna
degli Aldobrandini

Ground floor

Via del Canto de' Nelli

Cappella dei Principi

CAPPELLE MEDICEE ★ ★

Designed by
Michelangelo

7
Sagrestia
Vecchia ★ ★

CHANCEL

Sagrestia
Nuova

★ ★ **BIBLIOTECA
LAURENZIANA**

7

8

5

TRANSEPT

Salle   de   Lecture

6

4   3   2

Vestibule

Galerie supérieure

CHURCH ★ ★

Temporary
exhibitions

Cloisters ★

NAVE

1

Piazza di San Lorenzo

was completed with a small gallery designed to display relics to the faithful. In the *Marriage of the Virgin Mary* (**1**) (*second chapel on the right*) by the Mannerist painter, Rosso Fiorentino, the forms in the painting are gracefully elongated and the colours dazzlingly vivid. The delightful marble **relief**★ in the shape of a small temple (**2**) (*end of the south aisle*) was carved by Desiderio da Settignano. The work was inspired by Donatello and it formed the basis for the many such elegantly structured compositions with exquisite decorative effect called **tabernacles** (*tabernacoli*), which were produced in great numbers in Florence during the 15C. The work also shows a remarkable sense of perspective, one of the main features of Renaissance art. The two **pulpits**★★ (**3** and **4**) are faced with splendid panels produced by Donatello during the last years of his life and completed after his death by his pupils. In front of the chancel is a large circular slab (**5**) with an inlay of multicoloured marble. In the corners of the surround-

ing square is the Medici coat of arms. This marks the spot above the crypt where Cosimo the Elder is buried.

The **Martelli chapel** (**6**) contains the **Annunciation**★ painted c. 1440 by Filippo Lippi, a work which is remarkable for the perspective in the arches, buildings and pergolas.

Sagrestia Vecchia★★

Work on the new church of San Lorenzo began with the **Old Sacristy**, which is considered to be one of the most successful achievements of the Early Renaissance. It was a joint project involving Brunelleschi, who was responsible for the architecture, and Donatello, who undertook the decoration. This square chapel, with its hemispherical dome on pendentives and various architectural features highlighted by grey *pietra serena* admirably conveys the well-proportioned unity of geometrical lines that is characteristic of Brunelleschi's style. Donatello produced the cherubs comprising the frieze round the entablature, the polychrome medallions depicting the four Evangelists and scenes from the life of Saint John, and the remarkable **bronze doors★** (**7**) containing 40 figures of Holy Martyrs and Apostles. He also designed the splendid traceried marble screen and the altar in the tiny domed apse. To the rear of the altar is a remarkable triptych (*Madonna and Child*) by Taddeo Gaddi. In the centre of the room within the marble sarcophagus, which is capped by an altar table, lie Giovanni di Bicci and his wife Piccarda Bueri. The elegant **tomb★** (*left of the entrance*) (**8**) was produced in 1472 by Verrocchio, who was commissioned to undertake the work by Lorenzo the Magnificent and his brother Giuliano in honour of their father, Piero, and uncle, Giovanni. The lavish porphyry and bronze tomb is set in a bay connecting the sacristy to the adjoining chapel and is surmounted by an unusual trellis in which the mesh represents ropes. On a cabinet to the right of the door stands the terracotta bust of Lorenzo as an adolescent, a work attributed to Donatello.

Chiostro★ (Cloisters)

Entrance via the north aisle or by the doorway on the left of the façade.

The cloisters were built in the 15C in the elegant style of Brunelleschi.

From just before the entrance to the cloisters a staircase leads up to the Laurentian Library (Biblioteca Medicea Laurenziana).

Biblioteca Medicea Laurenziana★★

Entrance via a staircase from the upper gallery of the cloisters. ◷*Open Mon–Fri 9.30–13.30am.* ◷*Closed Sat, Sun, holidays.* ✆*055 29 37 911. www.bmlonline.it.*

The area of the Monumental Vestibule, Staircase and Michelangelo's Library is open to the public during library and book exhibitions.

The **Laurentian Library** was founded in the 15C by Cosimo the Elder and considerably extended by Lorenzo the Magnificent. It was not until the following century, in 1523, that Michelangelo was commissioned by Pope Clement VII (a member of the Medici family) to construct a dedicated building in the cloisters of San Lorenzo to house the library's priceless collection.

To decorate this exceptionally small yet disproportionately tall **vestibule**, the artist divided the walls into sections in an unusual way using architectural features that are normally found only on façades, while at the same time playing on the contrast between the white surfaces and grey *pietra serena* relief. The unusual use of huge twin columns, heavy cornices on brackets and window frames set flat against the wall already heralds the Baroque era. This style is further emphasised by the volutes on the consoles and the splendid monumental three-flight **staircase★★**. Michelangelo left for Rome in 1534, where he settled permanently, and the staircase was left at the planning stage. It was completed in 1559 by the Mannerist architect, Ammannati, who used the original drawings and acted in accordance with the numerous instructions sent to him by Michelangelo from Rome.

Although the architectural style is more austere, the **Reading Room** has its own charm because of the strict geometrical lines that are systematically repeated along the whole length of the room, creating a remarkable sense of perspective. The desks and lavish coffered ceiling, carved in warm-coloured wood and shown off by skilful lighting, were both designed by Michelangelo. The fine terracotta flooring from the same period is by Tribolo (the designer of the Boboli Gardens), who added decorative features reflecting the design of the ceiling.

A selection of the library's 10,000 manuscripts are exhibited in rotation. They include a 5C Virgil, a Horace annotated by Petrarch, Lorenzo the Magnificent's Book of Hours, Leonardo da Vinci's notebooks, a letter from Caterina de' Medici to Michelangelo and manuscripts by Petrarch, Ariosto, Machiavelli and Michelangelo.

Cappelle Medicee★★★

Entrance in Piazza della Madonna degli Aldobrandini 6. ◐Open daily 8.15am–2pm (last entry 40 min. before closing). ◐Closed 1st, 3rd, 5th Mon in the month, 2nd and 4th Sun in the month, 1 Jan, 1 May, 25 Dec. ⊚€9. ℘055 29 48 83. www.bargellomusei.beniculturali.it.
The term **Medici Chapels** is used to refer to the **Cappella dei Principi** (Princes' Chapel) and the **Sagrestia Nuova** (New Sacristy). Entrance to the **Princes' Chapel** is by way of a huge crypt in which the Medici Grand Dukes were buried. The stone just in front of the staircase to the right marks the tomb of Anna Maria Ludovica, the last member of the dynasty.

The Princes' Chapel was built to immortalise the Grand Dukes for whom it was intended as a funeral chapel. The most immediately striking features of the building are its overwhelming proportions and severe appearance. It is octagonal in design with walls and floor faced with *pietra dura* and precious marble, an impressive piece of workmanship produced in the Medici Pietre Dure workshop. At the base of the walls are 16 coats of arms with lapis lazuli, coral and mother-of-pearl inlay representing the towns within the Grand Duchy of Tuscany. In this breathtaking mineral decor are the huge tombs, made of Oriental granite and green Corsican jasper, of Cosimo I (*left of the altar*) and his descendants, all of whom are buried below. The altar is also lavishly inlaid with *pietra dura*.

The **Sagrestia Nuova** is in fact a funeral chapel, designed to house **Le Tombe Medicee★★★**, the tombs of the Medici family. In 1521, Cardinal Giuliano, the future Pope Clement VII, commissioned Michelangelo to construct the New Sacristy. It was Michelangelo's first commission as an architect. It is called the New Sacristy because it is symmetrically opposite the Old Sacristy and is reminiscent of the latter's architectural design. It uses the same grey *pietra serena* decoration, which forms a stark contrast with the pale-coloured marble and white walls. In the layout of windows, arches, cornices, niches and pediments – features that are mainly borrowed from classical architecture – Michelangelo gives the spatial layout a new rhythm that conveys a moving solemnity. In 1534, when Michelangelo left Florence for Rome, the work was unfinished and was not completed until 20 years later by Vasari and Ammannati. The sculptures on the **Medici Tombs** were also produced by Michelangelo. Closely combining his work as both sculptor and architect, the brilliant artist executed the famous tombs of the two members of the senior branch of the Medici family between 1526 and 1533.

The monumental group was to be composed of four mausoleums but only two were in fact completed. On the right is the tomb of Giuliano, Duke of Nemours (son of Lorenzo the Magnificent), who died in 1516 at the age of 35. Giuliano is portrayed as a Roman Emperor holding the baton of an army commander on his knees. At his feet are the famous semi-reclining allegorical figures of **Day** (unfinished), conveying a powerful energy, and **Night**, sleeping in a pose of graceful abandon. Opposite is the tomb of Lorenzo, Duke of Urbino (the grandson of Lorenzo the Magnificent and father of Caterina de' Medici), who died in 1519 at the age of 27.

He is shown in meditation and at his feet lie the other two famous statues depicting **Dusk**, in the guise of a melancholy old man, and **Dawn**, portrayed as a woman rising uneasily from her slumber. Each of these marble figures conveys a tragic grandeur and remarkable vigour. It is possible that the two idealised figures were intended to represent Action and Thought triumphing over Time which, through the different stages of life, leads man to his death. The only work to be produced for the tomb of Lorenzo the Magnificent (*right of the entrance*) is the admirable *Madonna and Child*. Lorenzo, the most famous of the Medici, lies with his brother Giuliano in the plain sarcophagus below. A small room beneath the chapel displays some mural **drawings**, attributed to Michelangelo, which were discovered in 1975. They may have been drawn during the few months the artist spent in hiding in the monastery of San Lorenzo, while being sought by the Medici for his part in the 1527 revolt that had driven the powerful family from Florence.

▶ In nearby Via Cavour stands the Palazzo Medici-Riccardi.

Palazzo Medici-Riccardi★★

(Medici Palace). Allow 30min. ◷*Open daily 9am–7pm.* ◷*Closed Wed, 1 Jan, 25 Dec.* ⊛€7. *Bookshop.* ♿ ☏*055 27 60 340. www.palazzo-medici.it*

The **Medici Palace**, the Medici family residence, was begun in 1444 on the orders of Cosimo the Elder to the design of his friend, Michelozzo. Cosimo did not, however, live in the building, which he deemed too large, until 1459; he died here five years later. His grandson, Lorenzo the Magnificent, held a princely court here, frequented by his poet, philosopher and artist friends. The building was also once the home of the young Caterina de' Medici, who became Queen of France.

In 1540 Cosimo I left the residence to settle in Piazza della Signoria. The mansion remained in the possession of the Medici family for another hundred or so years before being sold to the Riccardi. The noble building, which was considered the prototype for the aristocratic residences of the Florentine Renaissance, reflects a medieval austerity. Breaking with medieval tradition, however, Michelozzo structured the building around a fine courtyard with a tall portico. Between the arcades of the portico and the first floor, a stringcourse decorated with medallions carved in Donatello's workshop and depicting the Medici coat of arms or classical motifs, adds a graceful touch to the general architectural austerity.

Cappella★★★ (Chapel)

First floor. Entrance via the first staircase on the left on entering Michelozzo's courtyard. The tiny chapel with its rich gilt coffered ceiling and splendid marble flooring was designed by Michelozzo. The walls are decorated with **frescoes★★★**, painted in 1459 by **Benozzo Gozzoli**.

In a style that still echoes the influence of the international Gothic, the artist has produced a brilliant and picturesque illustration of Florentine life based on the theme of the **Procession of the Magi**. It was intended to honour the refined court of the Medici and to commemorate the Council, which met in Florence in 1439, and made a great contribution to the prestige of both the Medici and the city. The Three Kings, representing the ages of life, are portrayals of other major figures of contemporary society. At the head of the procession (*left-hand corner*) is the patriarch of Constantinople who died in Florence during the Council. Behind him, dressed in a splendid green and gold coat and Oriental headress, is the Byzantine Emperor John VIII Palaeologus (*wall opposite the altar – right of the entrance*). At the end (*right-hand wall*), clothed in a beige and gold jerkin and mounted on a palfrey (the harness bears the Medici coat of arms), is the young Lorenzo the Magnificent. Behind him on the white horse is his father, Piero I. In the middle of the group behind him is a self-portrait of Benozzo; his cap bears the inscription "Opus Benotii". Gozzoli's *Adoration of the Angels* is on the chancel walls.

Sala di Luca Giordano★★

Second floor. Entrance via the staircase (right), before Michelozzo's courtyard.
This bright and elegant gallery was built towards the end of the 17C, at the request of the Riccardi family. Its decoration of gilded stuccowork alternating with mirrored panels is dazzling. The room's crowning glory, however, is its barrel-vaulted ceiling decorated with a huge fresco painted in 1683 by the Neapolitan artist **Luca Giordano** (1632–1705). This fine exponent of Baroque decorative art earned the nickname "Luca Fa Presto" ("Luke works quickly") because of the extraordinary speed with which he executed his works. He learnt the art of grand decorative compositions and acquired his taste for light colours from his master, Piero da Cortona (who painted the ceilings in the Palatine Gallery in the Pitti Palace). Here the artist has depicted an **Apotheosis of the Second Medici Dynasty**. Above a frieze full of scenes borrowed from mythology, figures soar upwards into the clouds, while the use of foreshortening gives a sense of movement.

San Marco District

On this walk, history and art take precedence over less serious sightseeing, as there are many museums in this district. It is a good idea to choose according to one's preferences, as none of the museums can be seen in a hurry; it would take a whole day to visit all of them.

SIGHT

Convento e Museo di San Marco★★

Allow 1hr. Piazza San Marco 3. ○*Open daily 8.15am–1.50pm (4.50pm Sat, Sun and holidays).* ○*Closed 1st, 3rd and 5th Sun in the month, 2nd and 4th Mon in the month, 1 Jan, 25 Dec.* ⊙€8. *Bookshop.* ♿ ℘055 29 48 83. *www. polomusealetoscana.beniculturali.it.*
St Mark's Convent adjoins the church of the same name and houses the museum which contains **works★★★** by **Fra Angelico**.

- ♿ **Michelin Map:** pp104–105 E12.
- ▷ **Don't Miss:** Fra Angelico frescoes in Museo di San Marco; sculptures by Michelangelo in the Accademia; Etruscan works and the 19C Egyptian Gallery in Museo Archeologico.
- ♟ **Kids:** Mummies in Museo Archeologico; art workshop (reserve in advance) at Ospedale degli Innocenti; Michelangelo's slaves trying to free themselves from the marble, Galleria dell'Accademia; beautiful inlaid wood and marble at Opificio delle Pietre Dure.
- ○ **Timing:** A day to see all the museums. Reserve Accademia tickets in advance to avoid 2–3hr wait outdoors.

Fra Angelico

Fra Giovanni da Fiesole, better known as Fra Angelico, was born in the latter years of the 14C in Vicchio, 30km/19mi northeast of Florence. He entered the Dominican Order in Fiesole and later came to St Mark's in Florence where he spent about ten years covering the walls of the cells and conventual rooms with edifying scenes designed to inspire meditation.

Through his art this modest monk achieved fame within his own lifetime. Pope Nicholas V called him to Rome and commissioned him to decorate the Papal chapel in the Vatican. Orvieto Cathedral has some admirable frescoes painted by him. He also produced numerous altarpieces. He died in 1455 during a visit to Rome, where he is buried. For several centuries he bore the title "Blessed" (*Beato*) until he was eventually canonised in 1983.

His paintings are characterised by their serenity, tenderness and humility. Although he was deeply attached to the Gothic tradition and therefore often worked on triptychs, creating golden backgrounds and using the precious style of the miniaturist, he was also attracted by the new Renaissance theories. Some of his works express humanity in the figures and space hints at perspective. His altar paintings and frescoes, true acts of faith, are impressive for the simple mysticism of his vision and the purity of line and colour. In many cases he worked with his pupil, Benozzo Gozzoli, and with Filippo Lippi, and it is sometimes difficult to distinguish what was actually painted by him.

The convent was built for the Dominicans on the orders of Cosimo the Elder in 1436. It was his loyal friend and favourite architect, Michelozzo, who completed this extremely simple building in about seven years. Fra Angelico and Fra Bartolomeo, another artistic monk who also lived in the monastery but over half a century later, worked on its decoration. St Antoninus (1389–1459) and Savonarola were both priors of St Mark's.

Ground Floor

The elegant Renaissance **cloisters** in the shade of a huge cedar tree contain tympani decorated with frescoes (late 16C to early 17C) recounting the life of St Antoninus.

Ospizio

On the right, at the entrance to the cloisters.

The **Former Hospitium** contains numerous altar paintings that rank among the Dominican's best-known works.

Although the large Descent from the Cross (*right of the entrance*) is a triptych of all Fra Angelico's works, it is the one that most reflects the spirit of the Renaissance – background of buildings and landscape, humanity in the attitudes and facial expressions.

In the famous **Last Judgement** (1425) (*next wall*) Fra Angelico combines elements inherited from the Gothic tradition – golden colouring, details treated with the delicacy of the miniaturists – with features characterising the spirit of the Renaissance – sense of perspective in the receding line of tombs and the semicircular composition, dramatic realism in the depiction of the open graves. The admirable series of small panels (*farther along*), illustrating the Life of Christ, once covered the door of a church cabinet (*Armadio degli Argenti*). Among the scenes depicted (*from left to right*) against the exquisite backdrop of buildings and landscapes, the most outstanding include the Flight into Egypt, the Prayer on the Mount of Olives, the Kiss of Judas and the Arrest of Jesus. The tiny Virgin with the Star (*next pillar*) forms a stark contrast to the moving Lamentation over the Body of Christ (*farther along*).

The famous **Linaioli Madonna** (*far wall*), painted in 1433, was Fra Angelico's first public work, commissioned by the Linen Merchants' Guild to adorn a marble tabernacle. There is evidence of Masaccio's influence in the substance of the bodies and the feeling of space. The predella contains the Preaching of St Peter before St Mark, the Adoration of the Magi and the Martyrdom of St Mark.

One of the two tiny square panels (*towards the door against a pillar*) is a remarkable miniature depicting a Coronation of the Virgin Mary. Then comes the magnificent **Annalena Madonna**, named after the monastery for which it was painted. The small Gothic panel (*next pillar*) with two registers depicting the Annunciation and the Adoration of the Magi is also a masterpiece of miniature painting.

The **Lavabo Room** (*end of the next gallery on the right*) contains Fra Angelico's *Crucifixion between St Nicholas of Bari and St Francis*, which was extensively damaged by a flood in 1557.

In the **main refectory** (*right*) the main wall is decorated with a huge fresco by Giovanni Antonio Sogliani depicting St Dominic and his brother monks fed by the angels (1536). Two rooms (*other side of the Lavabo Room*) contain works by Fra Bartolomeo and Alessio Baldovinetti.

Sala Capitolare

The **chapterhouse** leads off the gallery opposite the entrance containing a 15C bell. This bell has been an anti-Medici symbol ever since it was rung to call the people to defend Savonarola, then prior of St Mark's, when he was arrested in 1498. The main wall of the room is covered with a huge, austere Crucifixion in which Fra Angelico depicted the people present at the historical event and the founder saints of the Dominican Order or saints who had links with the monastery (St Mark) and the Medici family (Saints Cosmas and Damian).

Refettorio Piccolo

Entrance from the small corridor on the left of the chapterhouse.

The **Small Refectory** is decorated with Domenico Ghirlandaio's **Last Supper★**, which preceded a variation on the same subject painted by the artist in 1480 in the refectory in Ognissanti. Another room contains architectural fragments from central Florence.

First Floor

The monks' cells are all decorated with scenes portraying the Life of Christ and the Life of the Virgin Mary and the mysteries of the Christian religion. The artistic value of the works varies depending on whether they were executed by Fra Angelico or his assistants. These frescoes were intended to encourage the meditative contemplation of the monks rather than as altarpieces or tabernacles to impress the faithful.

Overlooking the staircase is a huge **Annunciation★★★**, one of the artist's masterpieces. The cells line three corridors under bare rafters.

Fra Angelico's finest frescoes (*left side of the corridor*) include a fresh, poetic Apparition of Jesus to Mary Magdalen (no 1), another admirable **Annunciation** (no 3), a Christ on the Cross (no 4), a Transfiguration (no 6), Christ being mocked (no 7), the Holy Women at the Tomb (no 8), a Coronation of the Virgin in which the colours seem to be absorbed by the light (no 9) and the Presentation of Jesus in the Temple, in which the reddish background is in fact an undercoat from which the actual colour has worn away (no 10).

The two cells (*end of the next corridor*) once occupied by Savonarola contain his missal, rosary, hair-shirt, Crucifix and (*small vestibule*) his ardent, obstinate and zealous portrait by Fra Bartolomeo whom he had converted.

▷ Return to the staircase.

St Antoninus' cell (*no 31, immediately to the left in the right-hand corridor*) contains his death mask and a number of his manuscripts.

The splendid **library★** (*before the cell on the right*) is a bright, spacious room, containing three aisles with elegant arches, and is one of Michelozzo's most accomplished works.

The plaque (*near the entrance*) marks the place where Savonarola was arrested on the night of 8 April 1498. He was executed two months later in Piazza della Signoria. His own cell (*no 33*) is decorated with the *Kiss of Judas* by Fra Angelico. The two adjoining cells (nos 38 and 39 far right),

which were used by Cosimo the Elder, the monastery's munificent benefactor, during religious retreats, are decorated with *Christ on the Cross* (*first*) by Fra Angelico and an Adoration of the Magi (*second*).

👣 WALKING TOUR

Galleria dell'Accademia★★

30min. Via Ricasoli 58–60. 🕐*Open Tue–Sun 8.15am–6.50pm (6.20pm last admission).* 🕐*Closed 1 Jan, 1 May, 25 Dec.* €12. & ✆055 29 48 83. www.galleriaaccademiafirenze. beniculturali.it.

The Accademia is of exceptional interest for its collection of sculptures by Michelangelo. The gallery also houses an art collection of mainly Florentine works dating from the 13C–19C.

The first room contains paintings from the late 15C and early 16C, including a fine Deposition by Filippino Lippi and Perugino (*opposite the entrance*). The plaster-cast group in the middle of the room is the model produced by Giambologna for his *Rape of the Sabine Women* in the Loggia della Signoria.

Michelangelo Gallery★★★

On either side of the gallery are four of the famous **Slaves** (the other two are in the Louvre Museum in Paris), allegories for the soul imprisoned in the body, made for the tomb of Pope Julius II in Rome. A number of designs were produced for this mausoleum which was originally intended to include 40 huge statues and to be erected in the centre of St Peter's in Rome; the final version is in the Church of St Peter in Chains in Rome. In their contorted movements, the unfinished figures (1513–20) seem to be attempting to break free from the marble from which they emerge.

Flanked by the two Slaves (*right*) is St Matthew, part of a series of 12 statues of the Apostles that Michelangelo was commissioned to produce for the cathedral. This statue too is only roughly carved and the others were never produced.

The so-called **Palestrina Pietà**, together with the Pietà in the Museo dell'Opera del Duomo and the *Rondanini Pietà* in Milan, represents the final apotheosis of Michelangelo's art. The overdeveloped arms and torso and roughly carved legs, portrayed with unusual foreshortening, suggest the heaviness of Christ's dead body and illustrate the artist's remarkable knowledge of human anatomy.

At the end of the room stands the huge statue of **David**, in an apse that was specially built for the work in 1873. Michelangelo was 25 years old and already immensely famous when he carved this masterpiece (1501–04), one of his most famous sculptures, from an enormous block of marble that was considered to be unusable. The biblical hero who defeated the giant Goliath symbolised the determination of the Florentine Republic to defend its freedom in the face of its enemies. In contrast to older works, David is nervously poised for action with sling in hand, not yet experiencing the serenity and pride of victory. He stands with his body weight on his right leg to suggest, using the **contrapposto** technique, the tension arising immediately before movement. The artist also broke with tradition by portraying the character not as a frail adolescent, but rather as a muscular young man whose consummate beauty makes him reminiscent of an Apollo from Antiquity. The statue was placed in front of the Palazzo Vecchio, where it remained until 1873.

Pinacoteca★ (Art Gallery)

The first of the three small adjoining rooms (*right of the main gallery*) displays the front panel of the famous **Adimari Chest** (*second bay on the right*) depicting the wedding celebrations held in Florence for a member of this aristocratic family; in the background are the Baptistery and surrounding houses.

The room also contains works providing a remarkable insight into the transition from Gothic to Renaissance art. In the first bay is the Gothic-style Virgin Mary with a girdle (*Madonna della Cintola*) flanked by St Francis and St Catherine of Alexandria, by Andrea di Giusto Manzini (first half of the 15C). The *Mystical Marriage of St Catherine* (*first bay opposite the entrance*), painted in the mid-15C by Mariotto di Cristoforo, retains a Gothic feeling, but the overall layout (rectangular form) and the sketched-in landscape in the far distance are characteristic of the Renaissance style. This evolution towards Renaissance art is illustrated in the two following rooms. The third room contains two exquisite paintings by Botticelli: the famous **Madonna of the Sea** (actually of uncertain origin) and a delightful **Madonna and Child with the young St John and Angels**, a work displaying a wonderful freshness and tenderness.

In the continuation of the art gallery (*after the Michelangelo gallery*) is a statue of David flanked by 16C Italian paintings. The large *Deposition from the Cross* (*far right*) by Bronzino depicts in the background a descent from the cross. Alessandro Allori's *Annunciation* (*left*) unusually depicts the Virgin with her back almost turned towards the Archangel Gabriel and her hands raised as if she were already aware of her son's destiny, while at her feet, her book and embroidery form a fine still-life.

The **Gipsoteca** (Plasterwork Gallery) (*opposite end of the gallery*) contains works by two 19C sculptors, Bartolini and Pampaloni, professors at the Academy of Fine Arts. The plaster casts are the original models for marble sculptures.

The three rooms (*back towards the David Gallery*) contain 13C–14C Tuscan paintings, including three eye-catching Crucifixion scenes. The first floor displays a collection of 14C–15C Tuscan paintings and a collection of icons.

▶ Turn into nearby Via degli Alfani to the Opificio delle Pietre Dure.

Opificio delle Pietre Dure★

Via degli Alfani 78. ◷*Open Mon–Sat 8.15am–2pm.* ◷*Closed holidays, 24 Jun.* ◉*€4. Free admission with the Uffizi ticket.* ♿ *☏055 26 51 348. www.opificiodellepietredure.it.*

The **Pietra Dura Workshop** upholds one of the grand traditions of Florentine craftwork. The art of working hard stone (*pietra dura*) which had been fairly popular during the days of ancient Rome and Greece, was brought back into fashion in the 15C by the Medici family. Lorenzo the Magnificent's liking for ancient objects made of semi-precious stones stimulated skills in restoration and reproduction which his successors maintained and diversified with similar enthusiasm. In the 16C Cosimo I and his son, Francesco I, brought artists to their court from all over Italy and other European countries. They included cameo carvers, rock-crystal engravers, stone cutting specialists and goldsmiths. In Florence this period marked the beginning of the assembly (*commesso*) of hard stones, a form of mosaic in which the main feature is the juxtaposition of stones carved with such precision that the joins are invisible to the naked eye. The most commonly used stones were granite, porphyry, quartz, onyx and jasper, sometimes in conjunction with softer stones such as marble and alabaster.

In the early 17C the workshops were involved in the decoration of the Princes' Chapel in the Church of San Lorenzo. Their innovations included the production of superb pieces of furniture (known as *stipi*) made of precious woods and decorated with rare stones. There are several examples in the Pitti Palace.

After three centuries of activity, the workshops began to decline in 1859 with the fall of the Grand Duchy of Tuscany. The formation of the museum in the late 19C was inspired by the work produced by the old workshops, one of which has been fitted up on the first floor.

The first exhibits in the **Museum** show marvellous inlay in decorated panels for cabinets (*stipi*), mosaics and reliefs in hard or soft stone (17C). Motifs include **flowers**, **fruits and birds**, indicative of the naturalism cultivated by the Medici. The subjects chosen were particularly well adapted to this technique, where the bright colours of the stone stand out magnificently against the black marble background.

Ten panels have survived from the project of decorating the **Princes' Chapel** with *pietra dura* work. They depict landscapes (two of which evoke the Tuscan countryside) and scenes from the Bible (early 17C).

▷ Retun to Piazza San Marco and walk westwards.

Cenacolo di Sant'Apollonia

Via XXVII Aprile 1. ◷*Open 8.15am –1.50pm.* ◷*Closed 1st, 3rd and 5th Sun in the month, 2nd and 4th Mon in the* month, 1 Jan, 25 Dec. ☜*Free, donation suggested.* ☎*055 29 06 56. www. polomusealetoscana.beniculturali.it.*

St Apollonia's Refectory, a large hall once used as a refectory by the nuns of this Camaldolese convent, is preceded by a small room containing a number of 15C Florentine paintings, including *Madonna and Child surrounded by Saints* by Neri di Bicci, in which the Child is rather unusually depicted placing his hand inside his mother's bodice.

The huge **Last Supper★** covering one of the refectory walls is a masterpiece by Andrea del Castagno. The artist painted it towards the end of his very short life (c. 1450), at the same time as the other frescoes. It conveys great dramatic force because of the well structured framework, the abundance of mineral decoration, the relief achieved in the representation of the characters and the degree of realism.

The depiction of the Passion of Christ (*above*), which shows the Crucifixion (*centre*), the Deposition (*right*) and the Resurrection (*left*), is painted in a freer style against a single landscape background.

Chiostro dello Scalzo

Via Cavour 69. ◷*Open Mon, Thu, 1st, 3rd, 5th Sat in the month, 2nd and 4th Sun in the month 8.15am–1.50pm.* ◷*Closed 1 Jan, 25 Dec.* ☜*Free, donation suggested.* ☎*055 53 65 640. www.polomusealetoscana.beni culturali.it.*

The **Scalzo Cloisters**, small and intimate, contain a cycle of frescoes by Andrea del Sarto. Two of the 12 scenes depicting the life of St John the Baptist, the patron saint of the cloisters, were completed by Franciabigio. Andrea del Sarto worked sporadically in the cloisters between 1512–24 (interruptions in the work included a visit to the court of François I of France). The cycle is a fine example of his drawing skills and his gentle expressiveness.

▷ Return to Piazza San Marco and take a left along Via Battisti.

Piazza Santissima Annunziata★

This is the name of one of the prettiest squares in Florence and of one of the Florentine people's most beloved churches. Renaissance arcades run along three sides of this elegant square. At the far end (*approaching from the south*) stands the tall church porch and (*right*) the famous elevated portico of the Foundling Hospital. The portico of the Order of the Servants of Mary (*left*) was built to the same design by Antonio da Sangallo the Elder and Baccio d'Agnolo in the early 16C. In the middle of the square stands a bronze equestrian statue of Ferdinand I, the last work to be produced by Giambologna.

The square is also adorned with two delightful Baroque fountains made in 1629 by Pietro Tacca, who also worked on the completion of the equestrian statue that his master had left unfinished (d. 1608).

Santissima Annunziata (Annunciation)

🕐*Open daily 7.30am–12.30pm and 4–6.30pm, Sun and holidays also 8.45pm–9.45pm. annunziata.xoom.it*

The church was built in 1250 for the Order of the Servants of Mary, founded in the 13C by St Filippo Benizzi. It was rebuilt in the 15C in the Renaissance style by Michelozzo. It is preceded by cloisters (*Chiostrino dei Voti*), surrounded by a portico now covered with a glass roof, which was built between 1447 and 1452. Its decoration was begun in 1460 and continued sporadically over some 50 years. The restored **frescoes★** portray a cycle (*right of the entrance*) painted by several artists, including Rosso Fiorentino, Pontormo and Andrea del Sarto, that relates to the Virgin Mary. The *Life of St Filippo Benizzi* (*last two walls*) is a cycle painted mainly by Andrea del Sarto. The church interior, including the sumptuous coffered ceiling, was lavishly renovated in 17C Baroque style.

The marble chapel (*left after entering the church*) in the form of a small temple (*tempietto*) was built to plans by Michelozzo and designed to house the miraculous picture of the Virgin of the Annunciation which was said to have been completed by an angel after its artist fell asleep.

At the entrance to the choir on the wall (*right*) is a funerary monument to Monsignor Angelo Marzi Medici (1546) by Francisco da Sangallo; it is the first example in Italy of the renaissance of the Etruscan-style tomb where the dead man is shown reclining on one elbow on the coffin lid.

The choir in the form of a rotunda with nine radiating chapels is capped by a dome of impressive proportions (*to reach the dome follow the signs in the north transept to Sagrestia and Confessioni*). The Lady Chapel, which was altered by Giambologna to receive his own tomb, contains a bronze Crucifix of his own design. The large Resurrection (*next chapel on the left*) was painted c. 1550 by Bronzino. Andrea del Castagno painted the two frescoes (*last two chapels in the north aisle*) – the *Trinity* and *St Julian and the Saviour*. The **Cloisters of the Deceased** (*entrance in the north transept or by the doorway in the front of the church on the left-hand side beneath the porch*) are in the Renaissance style. The door (*at the end of the gallery opposite the street*) is surmounted by a famous fresco by Andrea del Sarto (*under glass*), the *Rest during the Flight into Egypt* (1525), known more familiarly as the **Virgin of the Sack★** because of the magnificent sack on which St Joseph is leaning.

The Chapel of the Brotherhood of St Luke (*further along in the next gallery*), which belonged to an association founded in the 14C by Florentine artists, is the burial place of Benvenuto Cellini and Pontormo, among others.

Ospedale degli Innocenti★

Piazza SS Annunziata 12. 🕐*Open Apr–Oct 10am–7pm; Nov–Mar 11am–6pm.* 🕐*Closed Tue, 1 Jan, 25 Dec.* ⬤€9. 📞*055 20 37 308. www.museodeglinnocenti.it.*

The **Foundling Hospital**, one of the city's most popular institutions, was built in the early 15C to designs by Brunelleschi.

The buildings are slightly elevated above the square and in front of them stands an elegant **portico**★★ consisting of nine semicircular arches set on very slender columns. This work was the first attempt to demonstrate the new theories formulated by Brunelleschi, and it marked the beginning of the era of great architectural achievements created during the Italian Renaissance. In 1463 Andrea della Robbia decorated the arches with a frieze of touchingly fresh **medallions**★★ depicting infants in swaddling clothes. The tiny window (*left beneath the portico*), which is now walled up and surrounded by a large door frame, recalls the wheel where, for four centuries until 1875, infants were abandoned anonymously.

The small inner courtyard was also the work of Brunelleschi. The door at the end of the gallery on the left of the entrance is surmounted by Andrea della Robbia's graceful, flowing **Annunciation**★, a statue made of glazed terracotta.

The **art gallery** (*second floor*) specialises mainly in 14C–17C religious paintings. In the great hall (*right of the entrance*) are the **Coronation of the Virgin Mary**, a fine composition in warm tones (15C) by Neri di Bicci, and the *Madonna and Child* by Filippo Lippi. In the small adjoining room (*end wall*) hangs a huge **Adoration of the Magi** (1488) by Domenico Ghirlandaio. The fine *Virgin Mary with Saints* (*right wall*) painted in brilliant colours is by Piero di Cosimo. Beside it is an enamelled terracotta Madonna and Child by Luca della Robbia.

They run art workshops for children, in English upon request.

▷ Walk E along Via della Colonna.

Museo Archeologico★★

Piazza della SS. Annunziata 9b.
🕐*Open Mon, Sat, 1st and 3rd Sun in the month, holidays 8.30am–2pm (7pm Tue–Fri).* 🕐*Closed 1 Jan, 25 Dec.* 🎫€8. *Free admission with Uffizi ticket.* ✆*055 23 575. www. polomusealetoscana.beniculturali.it.*

This under-visited museum contains numerous objects and works of art from many Etruscan settlements and ancient Egypt, Greece and Rome. A huge painting depicts the Franco-Tuscan expedition to Egypt showing Ippolito Rosellini, the father of Italian Egyptology. The Egyptian rooms retain their delightful 19C exhibit cases; collections, which include mummies, come mostly from Thebes (18th and 19th dynasties) and Saqqarah (26th to 30th dynasties).

Among the Etruscan funereal sculptures are cinerary urns, used only in the north of Etruria around Volterra, Chiusi and Perugia. They contained the ashes of the deceased who were depicted on the lids in a seated or standing position (6C BC) or lying down at a banquet (from the 5C BC onwards). Men were depicted holding a chalice or horn, and women holding a mirror, fan or pomegranate. The Sarcophagus of the Amazons is outstanding for its painted decoration.

The large collection of bronzes includes the **Chimera**★★, which dates from the first half of the 4C BC. It was discovered in 1553 in Arezzo, perhaps from an Etruscan workshop near Chiusi or Arezzo. The mythical monster lion has two extra heads – of a goat and a snake – and bears a votive inscription on its front right paw.

The Etruscan *Arringatore* statue of an orator demanding silence, probably dates from 100–80 BC because of its aristocratic Roman garb. The *Minerva* found in Arezzo in 1541 may be a Roman copy (1C BC) of a Greek variation on an original statue carved by Praxiteles (340–330BC).

The collection of ceramics includes the famous **François Vase**★★ named after the Florentine archaeologist who found its pieces in 1844–45 scattered in an Etruscan grave near Chiusi. The vase, a superb example dating from 570 BC, indicates the popularity of Attic ceramics among the Etruscans. Its decoration includes hunting scenes, festivities and battles taken from Greek mythology, all remarkably crafted.

Santa Croce District★★

Faith and Intrigue

This neighbourhood is built around the main church, and is rich in frescoes, chapels and cloisters. Santa Croce has a provincial air. Home to artisans, shopkeepers and merchants, the area is popular with Florentines, with plenty of good food, especially centred around the Sant'Ambrogio Market.

- ♿ **Michelin Map:** pp104–105 EF23.
- ▶ **Don't Miss:** Frescoes in Santa Croce and its cloisters.
- 👫 **Kids:** Look for artisans working leather and other trades; visit markets.
- 🕐 **Timing:** Half a day; Sant'Ambrogio market is in the morning.

SIGHTS

Piazza Santa Croce

The white marble façade of the **Church of the Holy Cross** fills the east side of a vast square, **Piazza Santa Croce**, one of the oldest and most grandiose squares in the city. It still has several of its old houses – (*no 1 opposite the church*) Palazzo Serristori, built in the 15C; (*nos 21 and 22*) the early 17C Palazzo Antella decorated with frescoes and flanked (*left*) by an old, similarly corbelled house. In the Middle Ages the people of Florence used to gather in this square to hear the great Franciscan preachers including St Bernardino of Siena in the 15C. From the 16C onwards, one of major events in Florence, Calcio Storico Fiorentino, was staged in the square (♿*See PLANNING YOUR TRIP*). This was one of the worst affected districts during the 1966 floods, and Santa Croce was one of the historic buildings of Florence which suffered most from the mud that reached a height of 3m/10ft inside the church and up to 5m/16ft in the cloisters.

Basilica di Santa Croce★

Allow 1hr 30min. Piazza Santa Croce at Largo Bargellini. 🕐*Open 9.30am–5pm (2–5pm Sun and holidays).* 🕐*Closed 1 Jan, Easter, 13 Jun, 4 Oct, 25–26 Dec.* ☞*€8 (includes Museo dell'Opera di Santa Croce).* 📞*055 24 66 105. www.santacroceopera.it*

Building began in 1295 to designs by Arnolfio di Cambio and was completed in the second half of the 14C, except for the present bell tower (the original bell tower collapsed in the 16C) and the neo-Gothic west front which only dates from the 19C. This is the Franciscan Order's church in Florence. It is a huge building (140m/459ft long and 40m/131ft wide) because it was designed for preaching. The Florentine Gothic interior is remarkably elegant. Because of the 276 gravestones set in the pavement and the lavish tombs contained in the church (most of them the tombs of famous men), Santa Croce has been nicknamed the "Italian Pantheon".

👣WALKING TOUR

Route on local map, ♿*p166. From Piazza di Santa Croce, take Via de'Benci.*

Museo della Fondazione Horne★

Via de' Benci 6. 🕐*Open 10am–2pm.* 🕐*Closed Wed, holidays.* ☞*€7.* 📞*0552 44 661. www.museohorne.it.*

Herbert Percy Horne (1864–1916), English scholar and collector, restored Palazzo Corsi to the atmosphere of a Florentine house during the Renaissance. Period furniture and art includes the Virgin and Child bas-relief by Sansovino, a St Stephen by Giotto, and the paintings of Dosso Dossi, Luca Signorelli, Masaccio, Pietro Lorenzetti, Benozzo Gozzoli, Domenico Beccafumi, Filippino Lippi and Simone Martini.

The first floor is distinguished especially by its leaded windows with lead rods and its *lettuccio* (bed). The tour concludes in the kitchen.

 **Santa Croce Tour**

South Aisle

The highly decorative *Madonna and Child* (**1**) (*against the first pillar*), carved by Antonio Rossellino in 1478, surmounts the tomb of Francesco Nori, who was killed during the Pazzi Conspiracy. The tomb of Michelangelo (**2**) (*opposite*) who died in 1564 was designed in 1570 (Rome also laid claim to his body) by Vasari, who also designed the great *Climb to Calvary* (**3**) above the next altar. The memorial to Dante (**4**), who died in 1321 and is buried in Ravenna, dates from the 19C.

A monument by Canova (**5**) marks the tomb of Alfieri, an Italian playwright who died in Florence in 1803. Opposite is a superb marble **pulpit★**, carved with scenes from the life of St Francis in 1476 by Benedetto da Maiano.

Beyond the pulpit is a monument (**6**) to Machiavelli (d. 1572) dating from the late 18C. The allegorical figure representing Diplomacy is a reminder of his diplomatic missions.

Donatello's **Annunciation★★** (**7**) (c. 1430) is one of the most harmonious examples of *tabernacoli,* a type of low-relief set in a frame in the shape of a small classical temple.

For the **tomb of Leonardo Bruni★★** (**8**), a Humanist and chancellor of the Florentine Republic (d. 1444), Bernardo Rossellino employed funerary architecture in which the sarcophagus bears a sculpture of the recumbent figure of the deceased. Many such tombs were created during the Italian Renaissance.

Beside it is Rossini's tomb (**9**) (d. 1868) and the tomb of Ugo Foscolo (1778–1827), one of the great poets of modern Italy (**10**).

South Transept

Taddeo Gaddi painted the **frescoes★** decorating the **Baroncelli Chapel** (**11**) from 1332 to 1338. They depict the Life of the Virgin Mary. On the altar is a fine **polyptych★** representing the Coronation of the Virgin Mary.

Sacristy★

A Renaissance doorway created by Michelozzo leads into the **sacristy**, a fine 14C chamber which still has its painted rafters and one wall covered with frescoes. Inside one of the inlaid cupboards (15C–16C) is a reliquary containing the habit and belt of St Francis of Assisi.

The **Rinuccini Chapel** (**12**) (*opposite the door*) is decorated with **frescoes★** recounting the life of the Virgin Mary (*left*) and the life of Mary Magdalen (*right*). The scenes were drawn by Giovanni da Milano, one of Lombardy's main artists in the 14C, who became a citizen of Florence.

▶ Beyond the Sacristy is a passageway towards the Leatherwork School.

Medici Chapel (13)

🔒 *Open only for religious rites. Visible through a window in the door.*

The delightful **Medici Chapel** built by Michelozzo in 1434 contains a graceful terracotta **reredos★** glazed by Andrea della Robbia.

Cappella Maggiore e Cappelle Adiacenti

The sanctuary is flanked by ten small chapels. The Giugni Chapel (**14**) contains the tomb of Giulia Clary, Joseph Bonaparte's wife (*right*) and the tomb of their daughter Charlotte Napoleon Bonaparte (*left*).

The **Bardi Chapel** (**15**) is decorated with the admirable **Frescoes of the Life of St Francis★★** (restored) which were painted c. 1320 by Giotto, recalling his famous frescoes in the basilica in Assisi.

The **sanctuary** (**16**) **frescoes★** recount the legend of the True Cross. They were painted in 1380 in a late-Gothic style by Agnolo Gaddi.

The frescoes in the Pulci Chapel (**17**) were painted c. 1330 by Bernardo Daddi and his pupils.

North Transept
The **Bardi Chapel** (**18**) contains a shockingly realistic wooden **Crucifix★★** by Donatello, a work that Brunelleschi wanted to surpass when he created his statue in Santa Maria Novella.

North Aisle
The **Tomb of Carlo Marsuppinia** (**19**), Humanist and secretary to the Florentine Republic (d. 1453), brought fame to its sculptor, Desiderio da Settignano.

Lorenzo Ghiberti (d. 1455) and his son, Vittorio, are buried opposite the fourth pillar (**20**). Galileo's tomb (**21**) (d. 1642) was built in the 18C.

Cloisters
These delightful 14C **cloisters** lead to the Pazzi Chapel (*at the end*) and the Santa Croce Museum (*to the right*). The closed gallery (*left*) contains a large and varied number of gravestones and tombs.

Cappella dei Pazzi★★
The **Pazzi Chapel**, one of the most exquisite of the designs generally attributed to Brunelleschi, was built for the Pazzi family, who were the main rivals of the Medici.

The interior is a masterpiece of Florentine Renaissance architecture owing to its unusual design, majestic proportions, purity of line and harmonious decoration.

Chiostro Grande
A superb Renaissance doorway opens into the **Great Cloisters**. The vast and elegantly proportioned construction was designed by Brunelleschi shortly before his death and completed in 1453.

Museo dell'Opera di Santa Croce (Santa Croce Museum)
Open 9.30am–5pm (2–5pm Sun and holidays). Closed 1 Jan, Easter, 3 Jun, 4 Oct, 25–26 Dec. €8 (includes Basilica di Santa Croce). 055 24 66 105.
The old Franciscan chapterhouse displays Cimabue's famous **Crucifixion★** (**22**), which has been restored with exemplary care after the considerable damage it suffered during the floods in 1966.

The end wall is covered by a huge fresco representing the Last Supper; above is the Tree of the Cross (**23**), painted in the 14C by Taddeo Gaddi, to represent the genealogy of the Franciscans. Among the other remarkable exhibits are a gilded bronze statue of St Louis of Toulouse (**24**) by Donatello (*left*) and small fragments of frescoes by Orcagna found on the wall of the church but which had been concealed by restoration work carried out in the 16C by Vasari: (*left*) are fragments of *Hell*; (*right panel 3*) is a group of beggars that was once part of the *Triumph of Death*.

The rooms between the cloisters contain underdrawings for frescoes (*sinopie*), 14C and 15C frescoes from the church and Tino da Camaino's tomb.

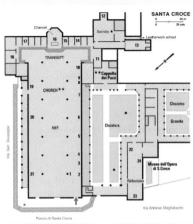

165

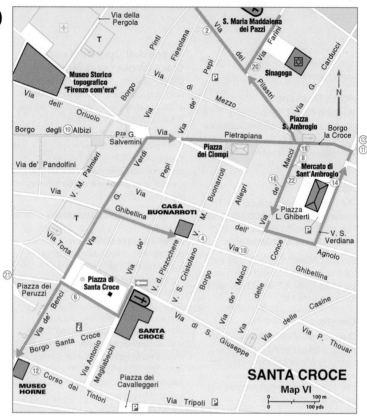

SANTA CROCE

Map VI

0 ——— 100 m
0 ——— 100 yds

WHERE TO EAT

Acquacotta.............②	Gilda.....................⑭	Osteria Da Que' Ganzi ......⑩
Baccarossa ....④	Il Pizzaiuolo ....⑯	Ristorante Cibrèo...........⑧
Boccadama................⑥	l' Trippaio	Ruth's ....⑳
Del Fagioli................⑫	di Sant'Ambrogio..........⑱	Trattoria Cibrèo............㉒
Dolci e Dolcezze...........⑪	La Corte de' Pazzi..........⑲	
Enoteca Bonatti ....⑬	Note di vino...............㉑	

▶ Take Via de' Benci to Via G. Verdi, right on Via della Ghibellina.

Casa Buonarroti★

Via Ghibellina 70. ⏱*10am–5pm (4.30pm Nov–Feb).* ⊘*Closed Tue, 1 Jan, Easter, 15 Aug, 25 Dec.* ⊛€8. ✆*055 24 17 52. www.casabuonarroti.it.*

The **Buonarroti House** consists of a group of houses purchased in March 1508 by Michelangelo at the corner of Via Ghibellina. Probably he lived in one of them. When he moved to Rome in 1534,

he sold the houses to his nephew, Leonardo, and left him the plans for alterations designed to convert the units into the present residence, in which Michelangelo never lived. The building was sold to Florence City Council in 1858 by the last surviving member of the Buonarroti family.

The ground floor houses the collections of ancient Roman and Etruscan sculptures acquired by the Buonarroti family. In the first room (*right of the hall*) are portraits of Michelangelo and a bronze

sculpture of the artist, cast in two parts by Daniele da Volterra and Giambologna. On the first floor are works by Michelangelo, including the unfinished marble relief (*right of the door*) depicting the **Battle of the Centaurs** (before 1492) and the famous **Virgin Mary and Staircase** (1490–92). A large model of a statue of the river god was intended to decorate one of the two Medici tombs in San Lorenzo and a wooden scale model shows the west front of the church.
The room behind the staircase contains rotating exhibitions of Michelangelo's works.

▶ Take Via Verdi to Piazza Salvemini; from Piazza Salvemini take Via Pietrapiana.

Piazza dei Ciompi

Piazza dei Ciompi has a small flea market (Mercato delle Pulci) Mon–bargelloSat, with antiques, used furniture, paintings, photographs, old postcards, used clothes, miscellaneous objects and bric-a-brac from yesteryear and today.

Mercato di Sant'Ambrogio

On **Via de' Macci** are a number of merchants: fish, meat, and one of the last of Florence's tripe vendors set up mornings against the façade of famed Cibreo. The street has more eateries and artisans (carpenters, framers). Take Via dell'Agnolo, then left on Via San Verdiana to Piazza Lorenzo Ghiberti, with **Sant'Ambrogio market halls**.

▶ Take Via della Mattonaia.

About 50m/55yds ahead at the intersection, Borgo la Croce has lingerie, ceramics and homeware shops.

▶ Return to Piazza Sant'Ambrogio to Via dei Pilastri, then right on Via Farini.

Sinagoga

Via Farini 4. ◷*Open Apr 14–Oct 12 Sun–Thu 9.30am–6.30pm (Fri 5pm); Oct 13–Apr 13 Sun–Thu 10am–5.30pm (Fri 3pm).* ◷*Closed Sat, Jewish*

The Florence Synagogue

© slovegrove/iStock

holidays. €6.50. ♿ ☎ *055 24 52 52 www.moked.it/firenzebraica.*
The Florence **Synagogue** was built between 1874 and 1882 and was based on the Byzantine Hagia Sophia in Constantinople. The interior has a rich Moorish decoration including frescoes and mosaics, in addition to a superfluous pulpit in the Christian tradition. Part of the furniture originates from the two synagogues of the **old ghetto**, which was located near Piazza della Repubblica. The Jews of Florence lived in a ghetto between 1571 (with authorisation from Cosimo I) and 1848, the year in which the restrictions were abolished. It was gradually demolished in the late 19C.

Santa Maria Maddalena dei Pazzi★

Borgo Pinti 58. ◷*Open 7.30am –12.30pm, 3.30–6pm.* ☎ *055 247 84 20.*
Access by the vestry of the church (*far right*) and an underground passage through the crypt.
Perugino painted this fresco 1493–96 depicting the Crucifixion in the Chapterhouse of the Benedictine Monastery of Santa Maria Maddalena dei Pazzi. Divided into three panels within the arcades of the room, the composition shows, from left to right, St Bernard

and the Virgin, Mary Magdalene at the base of the Cross, St John and St Benedict. The beautiful landscape of Lake Trasimeno in Umbria unifies the scenes bathed in a deep, soft morning light. In 1966, during the great flood of the Arno (&See p62), the waters went down to the feet of the fresco.

EXCURSION
Cenacolo di San Salvi★
1.5km/2mi E from Piazza Beccaria or from Piazza Santa Maria Novella Bus 6 or 20/stop DeAmicis, Via San Salvi 16. ⏱*Open 8.15am–1.50pm.* ⏱*Closed Mon.* ⌨*Free.* ☎*055 23 88 603.*

In the old refectory of the Vallombrosan Abbey on the outskirts of Florence, Andrea del Sarto sculptures and his dynamic 1520 frescoes of the Last Supper, inspired by Leonardo da Vinci's cycle in Milan. The harmony of colours and use of light were probably inspired by Raphael's works. The refectory has additional works by him, as well as by Pontormo.

Pitti Palace★★ and Giardino di Boboli★

Stroll across the Arno on Ponte Vecchio amongst the jewellers' stalls, to this green artisans' neighbourhood. Palazzo Pitti is a luxurious extension of the Uffizi with brilliant stars like Titian, Raphael and del Sarto, graced by the romantic Boboli Gardens. A delight for the senses.

- ⌖ **Michelin Map:** pp104–105 DE3.
- ⚏ **Kids:** Travel back in time with the costumes in Galleria del Costume. The Artichoke Fountain and grottoes.
- ⏱ **Timing:** Allow at least a half-day.
- ▷ **Don't Miss:** Paintings in the Palatine Gallery by Raphael, Caravaggio, Titian and others and Imperial and Royal Apartments.

👣WALKING TOUR

Ponte Vecchio★★
The **Old Bridge** is, in fact, the oldest bridge in Florence, and was built near where a Roman bridge once spanned the river carrying the road linking Rome to northern Italy.

Over the centuries the bridge was destroyed on a number of occasions; the current structure dates only from 1345. In 1944 it was the only bridge in Florence to be spared by the Germans who, in order to block the advance of American troops approaching from the south, razed the surrounding old districts almost entirely to the ground. The Ponte Vecchio did, however, suffer extensive damage during the 1966 floods.

The arcades that initially lined the bridge housed the tanners' workshops and, later, the stalls of butchers for whom the river provided a handy "sewer". In the 16C, on the orders of Grand Duke Ferdinand II, the butchers were forced to make way for craftsmen whose activities were of a less insanitary and more decorative nature – jewellers and gold- and silversmiths who built most of the tiny corbelled shops above the Arno, still occupied by craftsmen today. The shops attract a continuous flow of visitors, who come to browse or buy, and who throng the bridge during the summer season until late in the evening.

The esplanade in the middle of the bridge contains a bronze bust of the most famous goldsmith of all, Benvenuto Cellini, placed there in the 19C. From here, there is a fine **view** of the banks of the Arno and the succession of bridges that span it.

© MartinM303/iStock

Walk towards the Palazzo Pitti, passing in front of the Church of Santa Felicità.

Above the entrance porch is a sumptuous chamber, resembling a box at the theatre, where the Grand Dukes could attend Mass without ceremony, having entered from the Vasari Corridor.

The chapel (*immediately to the right of the entrance*), built in the early 15C by Brunelleschi, contains the famous **Deposition★★** by Pontormo, painted in clear sharp tones with undulating, elongated forms in a style characteristic of Tuscan Mannerism.

Museo di Storia Naturale La Specola★

Temporarily closed at the time of publication. Via Romana 17; at the top of the flight of steps on the left at the end of the street. ℘055 27 56 444 or 055 27 55 100. www.msn.unifi.it.

This natural history museum, which was founded in 1775 by Grand Duke Leopold, is named after the astronomical and meteorological observatory

PITTI-BOBOLI
Map VII

0 ——— 300 m
0 ——— 300 yds

WHERE TO EAT

Caffè Pitti	①	Osteria Antica Mescita	⑦
Caffé Bianchi	②	Pitti Gola e Cantina	⑧
Enoteca Bevo Vino	③	Trattoria Bordino	⑨
Enoteca Fuori Porta	④	Vip's Bar	⑩
Il Rifrullo	⑤	Zeb	⑪
La Mangiatoia	⑥		

(*specola* in Italian) which was installed at the request of the Grand Duke. It houses an extensive zoological collection of vertebrates and invertebrates and over 600 amazingly lifelike **anatomical waxworks**. Several rooms hosting the Cere Collection have been closed indefinitely.

Giardino Bardini★

Via dei Bardi 1r and Costa San Giorgio (Palazzo Pitti). ◷*Open Jun–Aug 8.15am–7.30pm; Apr–May, Sep–Oct 8.15am–6.30pm; Mar 8.15am–5.30pm; Nov–Feb 8.15am–4.30pm.* ◷*Closed 1st and last Mon of month, 1 Jan, 1 May, 25 Dec.* ✆€6. *Free admission with the Giardino di Boboli ticket.* ✆*055 20 06 62 33. www.bardinipeyron.it.*

👥 Restored from 2000–5, the Bardini Garden offers a green terrace amidst medieval Florence and the Arno Valley. Instead of being enclosed by a fort like Boboli, the 4ha/10acre ring the hillside, with successive changes brought by various families that owned it: Mozzi, during the Renaissance, Cambiagi, Jacques Louis Leblanc, Princess Wanda Carolath Benthen, up to Stefano Bardini, in the early 20C, antiquarian and collector.

Garden paths lead to various settings: rose garden, ancient sculptures (mythology inspired, notably Venus), botanical collections among iris, camellias and wisteria, "agrumeria" citrus greenhouse, Baroque and English gardens… The best route is along Via dei Bardi to go directly to the Boboli Gardens and exit through Palazzo Pitti.

Museo Bardini★

Via dei Renai 37. ◷*Open Mon, Fri, Sat–Sun 11am–5pm.* ◷*Closed 1 Jan, Easter, 15 Aug, 25 Dec.* ✆€7. ♿ ✆*055 23 42 427. museicivicifiorentini.comune.fi.it/en/bardini.*

The collections of this museum, displayed in a 19C mansion, include sculptures, stuccowork, paintings, small bronzes and medals, Persian rugs (16C–17C), 18C Florentine tapestries, ceramics and old musical instruments. All were bequeathed to the city in 1922 by Stefano Bardini (1854–1922), a famous antique dealer, and all indicative of his eclectic taste. The palazzo

where the museum is housed was bought and renovated by Bardini himself in 1881 so he could carry out his antique business. With some changes to the structure and the addition of some authentic architectural elements such as tympanums, portals and stairs, Bardini transformed the old building, once the church and convent of San Gregorio della Pace, into a charming neo-Renaissance palazzo.

The notable works here include a group representing Charity by Tino di Camaino; a graceful relief of the Madonna and Child by a 15C Sienese artist and another Madonna and Child set within a mandorla with angels and cherubs; an exquisite polychrome terracotta relief of the Madonna and Child by Donatello, a fine 15C inlaid ceiling and (*above the fireplace*) *St Michael the Archangel* painted on canvas by Antonio Pollaiolo.

Palazzo Pitti★★

🕐*See the detailed infos on the following panel pages. Allow half a day.*

The **Pitti Palace** is a huge Renaissance palace built round three sides of a sloping square overlooked by the building's long, severe façade. Only the shading of the heavy rustication work softens the imposing architectural style and breaks up a unity verging on the monotonous. Work began on the palace in 1458. It was designed for the Pitti, a family of influential merchants and bankers who were initially friends but later great rivals of the Medici. The building then consisted of no more than the section comprising the seven central bays. Several years later the Pitti family was financially ruined and the residence designed to outshine their rivals was left unfinished.

The palace was bought in 1549 by Eleonora of Toledo, wife of Cosimo I, and she turned it into a princely residence to which Cosimo I transferred his court c. 1560. The work of conversion was entrusted to the architect and sculptor Ammannati. The hillside was laid out as a magnificent garden but it was not until the 17C that the front of the building attained its current length (over 200m/650ft). The two projecting wings were added in the 18C.

© Sergio Hernán Gonzalez/iStock

Palazzo Pitti

The Pitti Palace provided the inspiration for the Palais du Luxembourg in Paris that was built by Marie de Médicis who as Maria de' Medici had lived in the Pitti Palace in her youth. It is also a remarkably rich repository of works of art, furniture and priceless objects.

Galleria Palatina★★★

See the detailed tour on the following panel pages. The entrance is up the staircase designed by Ammannati (in the corner of the courtyard to the right of the entrance). Persons with special needs can access the lift near the courtyard. Open Tue–Sun 8.15am–6.50pm (last entry 5.45pm). Closed 1 Jan, 25 Dec. Bookshop. Mar–Oct €16, Nov–Feb €10 combined ticket for: Galleria d'Arte Moderna, Tesoro dei Granduchi, Museo della Moda e del Costume, Appartamenti Imperiali e Reali. ☎055 23 88 614. www.uffizi.it (see Palazzo Pitti).

The **Palatine Gallery** takes its name from the title of the last of the Medici, Anna Maria Ludovica (1667–1743), who was married to the Elector Palatine. The luxurious interior houses an outstanding collection of 16C, 17C and 18C works, including a series of **paintings★★★** by **Raphael** and **Titian**, which make the Pitti Palace one of the richest art galleries in the world. The works were collected from the 17C onwards by the Grand Dukes of the Medici family and later by the Grand Dukes of Lorraine. They are exhibited regardless of didactic or chron-

ological order, as was the fashion of the great stately collections of the time.

Appartamenti Imperiali e Reali★

See the detailed tour on the following panel pages. Access via the foyer of the Palatine Gallery. First floor. Open Tue–Sun 8.15am–6.50pm (last entry 5.45pm). Closed 1 Jan, 25 Dec. Mar–Oct €16, Nov–Feb €10 (combined ticket: see Galleria Palatina). ☎055 23 88 614. www.uffizi.it.

The **Imperial and Royal Apartments** extending from the centre of the façade to the end of the right wing had always been used as state rooms or private apartments by Tuscany's three ruling families – the Medici, the Grand Dukes of Lorraine and the House of Savoy, sovereigns of Italy when Florence became the capital city (1865–70).

Galleria d'Arte Moderna★

Above the Palatine Gallery. Open Tue–Sun 8.15am–6.50pm (last entry 5.45pm). Closed 1 Jan, 25 Dec. Mar–Oct €16, Nov–Feb €10 (combined ticket: see p171, Galleria Palatina). ☎055 29 48 83. www.uffizi.it (see palazzo Pitti).

The **Gallery of Modern Art** is housed in a neo-Classical setting created for the Grand Dukes of Lorraine by the architect Poccianti. The gallery's rich collection of mainly Tuscan works from the late 18C to the early decades of the 20C is arranged according to the following themes: Historical Romantic painting, including

🐾 Galleria Palatina "Planet Rooms" Tour

Ferdinand II de' Medici commissioned Pierro da Cortona (1597–1669) to paint frescoes in the new reception rooms on the first floor. Each of these rooms was given the name of a planet from the solar system, as a tribute to Galileo Galilei, who had discovered Jupiter's satellites and decided to name them "Medicean Stars" in honour of Grand Duke Cosimo II, Ferdinand's father.

Painted in various stages between 1640 and 1665, the "Planet Rooms" focused on two main actors: Hercules, mythological figure who was dear to the Medici family, and Prince Ferdinand II. This latter, room by room, was set out to create a path of education and human and spiritual growth under Hercules' watchful eye, to conquer eternal glory and fame, like gods and heroes, receiving his crown from the hands of Jupiter.

At the time of their creation, the "Planet Rooms" were visited in reverse order to the way they are today, starting with the Room of Venus, immediately after the Room of the Niches. Each room, together with its group of pictorial decorations, corresponds to one of the ages in the life of the sovereign prince, from his youth until adulthood: the renunciation of pleasures offered by Venus to take the path of virtue (**Room of Venus**); the artistic and literary education (**Room of Apollo**), the acquisition of the heroic virtues of war (**Room of Mars**); the triumph of the virtues linked to good governance (**Room of Jupiter**),and lastly, the valour of old age, crowned by the ruler's fame and glory (**Room of Saturn**).

Pitti Palace Building History

Pitti Palace is the result of no less than three centuries of transformations and expansions, brought together to form the spectacularly stunning facade that welcomes visitors. In the late 15C the palace belonged to a rich Florentine banker, Luca Pitti. Wishing to have a new building that would stand out within the Florence's urban setting, he ordered the building of a monumental façade in rustic ashlar stone, set out on three perfectly equal floors: the bottom floor had three large doors – two of which would then be closed and reduced to the windows we see today –, while the first and second floors were perfectly symmetrical, each with seven large windows. The style of the palace was thus not unlike those of the typical Florentine models of the same century, such as the Medici, Strozzi or Rucellai Palaces.

Luca Pitti's brief fortune also led to the suspension of the works, although the façade and some rooms were left to complete. It was not until 1549, when Eleanor of Toledo, wife of Grand Duke Cosimo I, bought the palace to build a noble residence, surrounding by greenery, and Larger and more light and airy than the residence of Palazzo Vecchio, which was now too small to meet the needs of the court. The renovations were carried out between 1551 and 1559 by Giorgio Vasari and Bernardo Buontalenti; however, the most consistent transformation of the palace was the work of Bartolomeo Ammannati, begun in 1561. This architect and sculptor extended the old palace towards the Boboli Hill adding two Large wings at the back to create a building in the shape of a horseshoe and then realizing a monumental courtyard on three Levels with open Loggias on the central side.

From 1618, the needs of the court led Cosimo II to commission architect Giulio Parigi, Ammannati's nephew and his son Alfonso, to enlarge the palace again. The ground and first floors were extended to the right and left, adding eight windows per side, corresponding to the large reception rooms opening onto the square. On the ground floor were the apartments destined for summer use, which today house the Treasury of the Grand Dukes. On the first floor was the group of winter apartments, used by the Grand Duke and his family. The palace was gradually taking on its definitive shape.

Room of Venus

This room starts the famous series of elegant rooms in the winter apartment on the first floor of Pitti Palace.

It was the first to be painted by Pietro da Cortona on his return to Florence in 1641 and is the room where the change of spatial organization is felt less with respect to the renaissance construction below: the pattern of the lunettes, of the rib vaults and pendentives, although softened by the presence of the gilt stucco telamons and the white stucco medallions, follows a pattern that still reflects the order of the renaissance interior. The room was the antechamber for people waiting to be admitted to the presence of the Grand Duke, and for this reason, above, behind the *Story of Antiochus and Stratonice* lunette, a small window was inserted between the stuccoes so that the sovereign was able to spy on and listen to what happened or was said in the room below.

In the centre of the ceiling of the Room, a young prince is torn from the arms of a goddess, a symbol of pleasure, and driven by Minerva toward Hercules, a symbol of virtue. In the eight lunettes, bearing explanatory inscriptions in Latin, illustrious characters of the ancient world are portrayed, and in the white stucco ovals there are portraits of the most important members of the grand duchy, as well as the two popes of the Medici family, Leo X and Clement VII.

Room of Apollo

During the period of the Medici court, this room was used as antechamber for the "ordinary nobility", meaning it was used by gentlemen who were waiting to be received by the Grand Duke inside the Throne Room. Pietro da Cortona painted the main fresco in the centre of the vault, depicting the *Medici Prince brought before Apollo by Fame*. The fresco was painted not long before the artist left Florence to return to Rome in 1647 and Ciro Ferri, a loyal pupil of Cortona, completed the decorations in the room, fifteen years later (1659–61). His are the frescos in the lunettes and the superb stucco cornice – a model that was then copied

throughout Europe, based on the designs and cartoons left by his teacher.

The scene continues the ideal path of the prince's political and moral education, illuminated by Apollo and then guided along the path of knowledge by the laws governing the cosmos, as evoked by the celestial globe supported by Hercules, an obvious reference to Galileo's recent discoveries. To warn the future sovereign of the weight of responsibility from government and the need to be educated for the task by the Arts and by study, some of the best-known feats of the Greek god are shown in the stucco medallions below. The square frames show the emperors and *condottieri* from antiquity who favoured the development of culture – including Augustus, intent upon listening to the reading of the *Aeneid*, or Alexander the Great receiving the poems of Homer – and in the corbels, Apollo's companions, the Muses. A significant new element is introduced not only by the pictorial cycle but also by the articulated group of white stucco and gilt figures that disrupt the renaissance style of the architectural setting, and animate the ceiling with an illusion of male sculptures holding up the heavy festoons and satyrs wrapped in vine tendrils.

Room of Mars

This room was once used as a waiting room for ambassadors and visitors waiting to be admitted into the presence of the Grand Duke. The fresco covers the entire vault with an allegorical representation of the education of the young prince, instructed in the art of warfare and command by Mars, god of War. The prince is depicted in the naval battle which rages along the perimeter, watched over by Mars who bestows strength to the young man by lighting him with his star. At the end of the battle, Hercules, the prince's alter-ego and patron god of the Medici family, makes a trophy with the enemy spoils given to him by the Dark Gods, while a parade of prisoners, their weapons discarded in the hope of a lasting peace, advances towards the female figures of Victory, Plenty and Peace.

In the centre of the vault, the Medici coat of arms is held aloft by a cluster of cherubs, topped with a crown inscribed with the name of Ferdinand II de' Medici. Due to the theatrical composition and the lively arrangement of characters on the ceiling, this room, perhaps more than any other room in the Pitti Palace, reaches the level of Baroque illusionism found in the famous vault in Palazzo Barberini in Rome, where Pietro da Cortona had just completed his *Triumph of Divine Providence* fresco.

Room of Jupiter

In the Medici period, this room was used as an Audience Chamber or Throne Room, and, under the frescoed vault, it is still possible to see the hooks used to hang the canopy over the podium, where the Grand Duke held his public audiences. The richly decorated area is full of frescoes, white and gilt stucco works and plumes decorated with shells. It enhances the public role of this area and represents the crowing artistic achievement of Cortona, who has dotted it with extraordinarily detailed inventions. The finished work is the result of his direction, starting with the preparatory designs – many of which are in the Collection of Prints and Drawings at the Uffizi – through to the direct coordination of the workers on scaffolding: painters, gilders, masons and stucco artists.

The theme chosen here, Jupiter crowning the prince, to whom Hercules has consigned his club, highlights the commanding role of the Medici dynasty and legitimises the young heir's ascent to Grand Duke, completing the educational journey shown in the previous rooms, and evoked in the frescoed lunettes that show the many gods of Olympus – Minerva, Apollo, Mercury, and Mars – who accompanied and supported him in this ideal education, from adolescence to old age. The victorious prince thus disembarks from the ship of the Argonauts, followed by Victory, who is engraving the letter M (Medici) on her shield; he is met by Jupiter, surrounded by four female characters, probably allegorical depictions, and a tribute by the iconographer to the *Medicea Sidera*, the four satellites of the planet Jupiter, discovered by Galileo and announced in his *Sidereus Nuncius*, dedicated to Cosimo II de' Medici in 1610.

Room of Saturn

Known as the Audience Chamber, this room is the work of Ciro Ferri, a pupil of Cortona. The central fresco concludes with the parable of the prince's earthly life, now close to an end, having completed the journey of identification with the Medici's hero, Hercules, and as an immortal being, he is conducted into the Empyrean, by Prudence and Mars. Here he is awaited by Kronos/ Saturn, the divinity who symbolises Time, to be crowned by Fame, while Perfection points him towards the heavens and therefore to eternity. In the room the are around twenty works by Raphael – among them the small panel *Vision of Ezekiel*, the *Portrait of Julius II* (which can be compared with the illustrious copy by Titian on display in the Room of Venus), the *Portrait of Cardinal Bibbiena*, the *Young Man with an Apple*, the *Madonna del Granduca* and the *Madonna della Seggiola* – and other artists, including Perugino and Carlo Dolci.

Madonna della Seggiola *(1513–14)* by Raphael

👣 Imperial and Royal Apartments Tour

The rooms that lie along the right side of the palace façade are known as the Imperial and Royal Apartments. In the second half of the 17C, these were the private rooms of the Ferdinand (son of the Grand Duke Cosimo III). Here he assembled his impressive collection of Renaissance and Baroque masterpieces. After the Restoration (1815), the Apartments were enlarged and completely redecorated and refurnished according to the taste of the Hapsburg-Lorraine Grand-Dukes, who ruled Tuscany after the Medici family died out (1737) When Florence became the capital of the newly founded kingdom of Italy (1865-1870), the Pitti Palace was chosen by King Vittorio Emanuele II of the Sa- voy to be the new royal palace. Later still, Umberto I and his wife Margherita introduced some furniture and precious works of art from the "Palazzo Ducale" in Parma.

The tour of the Apartments starts from the **Green Room**. It was known as the Guards Room in the time of Ferdinand, and then it became kind of antechamber with access into the actual apartment. The name comes from the green colour of the wall coverings, curtains and the upholstery on some of the furniture, which are all in silk – textured or plain, fitted by Florentine manufacturers between 1854 and 1855.

The tour proceeds to the **Audience Room** and the **Chamberlains' Room** in the Lorraine period. With the arrival of the Savoy this room was used as the Throne Room and for this reason the canopy with the House of Savoy's coat of arms was hung.

Continuing the tour we find the **Chapel**, the only part of the apartments that preserves its original Late Baroque decoration dating back to the Medici period. The Grand Prince Ferdinand de' Medici had intended this space to be an alcove, or rather, an official bedroom, designed to receive a small group of people. During Savoy rule the furnishings were updated, cushioning the echoes of Medici-style and the accents that were probably considered too severe.

The **Parrot Room**, then as today, was the passageway between the Apartments of Queen Margherita and King Umberto. It gets its name from the design on the silk-hung walls.

The **Queen's Bedroom** adds a taste of the elegant disorder that – according to the eclectic tastes that were dominant around the end of the 19C – made it possible to create casual mixes of different furniture, objects, materials, periods and styles. A propensity to overload, to add the superfluous that only escapes forming a chaotic sense of bric-a-brac only because of the doubtless high quality of the pieces and their certain origin.

The **White Hall** (or Stucco Hall) is the former palace ballroom. It is illuminated by 11 magnificent crystal chandeliers and adorned with 11 mirrors, a larger one in the centre and 10 on the sides of the room (4 on the long sides and 2 on each of the shorter ones).

Like the Green Room, the **Blue Room** was renewed between 1854 and 1855 when it was known as the new "Quartiere delle Stoffe". After the addition of new wallpaper, in this case in a shade of blue, the room was also given a carpet made by French weavers in Tournai, which stands out for the neo-baroque decorative style, updated to the fashions of Paris and London in the mid-19C.

The Parade or, as it is better known, **Oval Room** ends the series of rooms that were set out along the facade. Its oval layout, which is unusual compared to the rest of the Palace, was devised by Ignazio Pellegrini, Veronese architect still sensitive to the late Baroque echoes of Francesco Borromini.

Samson and *The Two Foscari* by Hayez; Realism in Florence and Naples, including *Cloisters* by Abbati; portraits from the period when Florence was capital of Italy; the Banti and Martelli collections; genre scenes from between the end of the Grand Duchy and the Unification of Italy, including *The Moneylender* by Induno; democracy and patriotism, among which is Fattori's *The Italian Camp after the Battle of Magenta* by Fattori; Stefano Ussi and the theme of the World Exhibition (note the carved, painted ceiling dating from the 17C in this and the next room; the Macchiaioli and other schools; landscape painting; naturalism in Tuscany; and Divisionism, Symbolism and social themes (Medardo Rosso).

Tesoro dei Granduchi★★
Ground floor and mezzanine.
The entrance is situated at the left of the Ammannati courtyard. ◷*Open Tue–Sun 8.15am– 6.50pm (last entry 5.45pm).* ◷*Closed 1 Jan, 25 Dec.* ◒*Mar–Oct €16, Nov–Feb €10 (combined ticket: see p171,*

Galleria Palatina). ℘*055 29 48 83. www.uffizi.it.*

Formerly known as Museo degli Argenti (Silver Museum), the **Treasury of the Grand Dukes** is located on the ground and mezzanine floors of Pitti Palace, and occupies the rooms of the Medici's summer apartment, entirely frescoed on the occasion of the marriage between Ferdinando II de' Medici and Vittoria della Rovere. The Museum houses the grand ducal treasures consisting of jewellery, vases, plates and other furnishings in gold, silver, precious and semi-precious stones, ivory and amber. Among the many objects that reflect the splendour of the court there are vases which belonged to Lorenzo the Magnificent and the bizarrely shaped Mannerist vases of the end of the 16C, the 16C jewels which belonged to Anna Maria Luisa (the last descendant of the Medici, ancient and Renaissance cameos and the **Treasure of Salzburg** brought to Florence by Grand Duke of Tuscany Ferdinand III in 1815. An important col-

The Macchiaioli

The most lively artistic expression during this period came from the "Macchiaioli", and the Galleria d'Arte Moderna owns an outstanding collection of their **works★★**. The movement, a contemporary of Impressionism, grew up in Florence in the mid-19C and breathed new life into painting, which had become entrenched in rigid academic conventions. The Macchiaioli were enamoured of the truth and rejected subjects borrowed from mythology or the great historical paintings. Instead, they took their models directly from nature but they sought to give an impression of their subject rather than render an exact description. They generally painted small-sized works, translating reality by means of splashes (*macchie*) of colour with light playing upon them.

The Livorno artist, **Giovanni Fattori** (1825–1908), a complex character with a nevertheless sober and vigorous style, and the more poetic **Silvestro Lega** (1826–95) were the movement's most illustrious members. **Telemaco Signorini** (1835–1901), who was also a controversial writer, moved away from the group to seek an even sharper sense of realism. **Adriano Cecioni** (1836–86), who was more of a sculptor than a painter, was the theorist and critic of the movement. **Giuseppe Abbati** (1836–68) gave a touch of seriousness to his works and his contemplation of nature is tinged with melancholy. The Ferrara artist, **Giovanni Boldini** (1842–1931), spent only a brief time with the Macchiaioli before going on to become a fashionable portrait painter, especially in Paris. The work of **Giuseppe de Nittis** (1846–84), who came from the Puglia region, is characterised by the use of typical Mediterranean colours. He also emigrated to Paris, where he enjoyed a career as a society painter.

lection of jewellery, made between the 17 and 20C by prestigious European and Italian craftsmen is on display. There is also a large section dedicated to contemporary jewellery, reflecting the vitality of this historic museum and including important donations by prestigious noble families, collectors and goldsmiths. The collection of antique oriental and European porcelain and majolica, inspired by Asian models, enriches the already important collection of Chinese and Japanese porcelains, begun by the Medici dynasty in the 15C.

Museo della Moda e del Costume★

Meridian Pavilion. Access by lift situated in the ticket office and staircase leading to the Palatine Gallery. Open Tue–Sun *8.15am–6.50pm (last entry 5.45pm).* Closed 1 Jan, 25 Dec. Mar–Oct €16, *Nov–Feb €10 (combined ticket: see p171, Galleria Palatina).* 055 29 48 83. *www.uffizi.it.*

The **Museum of Costume and Fashion** (formerly known as the Costume Gallery) is located in the Palazzina della Meridiana next to the southern wing of Pitti Palace. Started under Grand Duke of Tuscany Peter Leopold by architect Gaspero Maria Paoletti in 1776 and completed in 1830 by Pasquale Poccianti under Grand Duke Leopold II, the building takes its name from the astronomical instrument made by Vincenzo Viviani in 1699. The instrument is in the vestibule – with the gnomon pinhole – of Ferdinand de' Medici's apartment. Anton Domenico Gabbiani depicted the Allegory of Time and the Arts (1693) in the vault of the vestibule. All the successive dynasties, from the Habsburg-Lorraine family to the House of Savoy, including the regency of Maria Luisa of Parma and the brief reign of Elisa Baciocchi, left their mark on furnishings and decorative wall paintings. Founded in 1983, it was the first State museum in Italy dedicated to the history of fashion and its social significance. Its collections include clothes and accessories as well as underwear, jewellery and costume jewellery, dating from the 18C to today.

The 16C funeral clothing of Cosimo I de' Medici, Eleonora of Toledo and their son Garzia de' Medici has been completely restored and is part of the permanent collection on display.

Giardino di Boboli★

1hr 30min. Open daily *8.15am–6.30pm (5.30pm Mar; 4.30pm Nov–Feb; 7.30pm Jun–Aug) (last entry 1hr before closing).* Closed 1st and last *Mon in the month, 1 Jan, 25 Dec. Bar, restaurant.* Mar–Oct €10, Nov–Feb *€6 combined ticket with the Museo delle Porcellane and Giardino Bardini.* 055 29 48 83. www.uffizi.it.

The **Boboli Gardens** were begun in 1549 when Cosimo I commissioned Niccolò Pericoli, known as Tribolo, to convert the hill behind the Pitti Palace into a vast garden. Together with Ammannati's courtyard and the terrace, it was to be the setting for the lavish pageants held by the Grand Dukes. When Tribolo died the following year, he had only drawn up the plans. He was succeeded in 1550 by Ammannati then in 1583 by Buontalenti, both of whom added a number of refinements to the original design.

The park is a fine example of an Italian terraced garden with many different perspectives, interspersed with ramps, flights of steps and terraces and dotted with statues and fountains. The entrance is situated on the far side of the inner courtyard. The terrace is separated from the rear of the palace by the elegant Artichoke Fountain (*Carciofo*), built in 1641.

The 17C **amphitheatre** dominates the centre of the park. In 1841 the Royal House of Lorraine had a Roman granite basin and a 2C BC Egyptian obelisk from Thebes placed in the centre.

▶ Walk towards the top of the hill; before reaching the first terrace, turn right onto an uphill path which leads to a circle.

This part of the gardens, covering the hillside, was not laid out until the early 17C. The long and steep **Viottolone★** (*opposite*) descends majestically between a double row of age-old pines and cypress trees to the charming circular **Piazzale dell'Isolotto★**. At the centre is a round lake adorned with statues. In the middle of the lake is an island with orange and lemon trees and the Ocean Fountain, carved by Giovanni da Bologna in 1576.

On turning back towards the palace, visitors see **Neptune's Pool**, adorned with a bronze statue (16C) of the sea-god and, on the following terrace, a statue of Plenty which was begun by Giovanni da Bologna and finished in 1636 by the Florentine, Pietro Tacca.

▷ A short path (right) leads to the Porcelain Museum (below).

The path (*left*) leads to the foot of the **Belvedere Fort** (*access now restricted by a gate*). Further down stands the **Kaffeehaus**, an extravagant and predominantly red edifice built by Zanobi del Rosse in 1776. From the bar patio, there is a **fine view★** of Florence.

▷ Walk back down towards the palace and turn right into the wide ramp.

At the end is a path leading to the **Grotta Grande**, a fanciful creation designed mainly by Buontalenti (1587–97) and consisting of several chambers deco-

rated with basins, statues, paintings, stalactites and a form of Rococo decoration depicting sheep, goats, shepherds, etc. The small **Bacchus Fountain** (*right near the exit*) includes a monstrous figure, one of Cosimo I's midgets, astride a tortoise.

Museo delle Porcellane★

ⓘOpen daily 8.15am–6.30pm (5.30pm Mar; 4.30pm Nov–Feb; 7.30pm Jun–Aug). ⓘClosed 1st and last Mon in the month, 1 Jan, 25 Dec. ⸙Mar–Oct €10, Nov–Feb €6 combined ticket with the Giardino Boboli and Giardino Bardini. ℘055 29 48 83.

The **Porcelain Museum** is comprised of three rooms. The first room contains numerous porcelains from Sèvres, including a portrait of Napoleon (early 19C). The second room is dedicated to Viennese porcelain from the 18C and early 19C, with pieces brought to Florence by the Royal House of Lorraine. The third room contains German ware from Frankenthal and Meissen.

▷ Walk along Via Mazzetta towards Piazza S Spirito.

On the southeast corner stands the **Palazzo Guadagni★**, surmounted by a splendid loggia (1503) and attributed to Baccio d'Agnolo or Simone del Pollaiolo, known as *Il Cronaca*.

Grotta Grande, Boboli gardens

© irisphoto2/iStock

Santo Spirito District

Santo Spirito and its cloister dominate this neighbourhood. Masterpieces by Lippi and Masacio are in the Brancacci Chapel, but the Oltrarno (across the Arno), also has artisans and shops to explore. The narrow streets lead to art galleries, cafés and restaurants for *dolce farniente* (pleasantly doing nothing).

- ⌚ **Michelin Map:** pp104–105 CD23.
- 🗎 **Don't Miss:** Brancacci Chapel in Sant Maria del Carmine.
- 👥 **Kids:** See city life at a slower pace.
- 🕐 **Timing:** A walk from Santo Spirito to San Frediano could be a pleasant day away from the crowds.

🐾 WALKING TOUR

South of Ponte Vecchio, west along the Arno, this historic neighbourhood is populated by artisans.

Borgo San Jacopo

From Ponte Vecchio turn right to Borgo San Jacopo with its shops selling antiques, leather and regional produce, and cafés with their small terraces. To the left the 12C Torre di Belfredelli rises followed by Torre dei Marsili, also 12C, with its door surmounted by an Annunication in two niches. A marble fountain marks the corner of Borgo San Jacopo with Via dello Sperone and Via Maggio. Take Via di Santo Spirito (the extension of Borgo San Jacopo) with its artisans' workshops. The street continues as Borgo San Frediano, also with artisans workshops, and ends at Porta San Frediano, built by Andrea Pisano as a monument to Florentine conquests, for the road that links to Pisa.

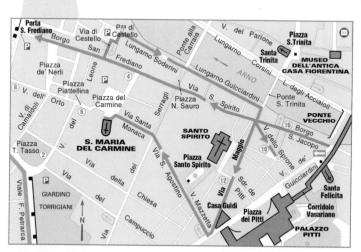

SANTO SPIRITO Map VIII	WHERE TO EAT	
0 — 200 m 0 — 200 yds	Al Tranvai .... ②	l'Brindellone .... ⑥
	Del Carmine .... ④	La Casalinga .... ⑫
	Il Guscio .... ⑧	L'Osteria del
	Il Magazzino .... ⑩	Cinghiale Bianco .... ⑯

The Brancacci Frescoes★★★

Masolino da Panicale

Masolino was the first artist to be commissioned, in 1424, to undertake the decoration of the chapel built for the Brancacci, a family of silk merchants. Although the spirit of his work is still noticeably Gothic, as is obvious from his kindly, serene treatment of the subject matter, there is already an attempt to render perspective and volume. He was probably influenced in this respect by his pupil, Masaccio. On the upper section, he depicted the Temptation of Adam and Eve (**VII**), St Peter raising Tabitha from the Dead (**VI**) and St Peter Preaching (**III**).

Masaccio

This chapel is a fine example of the innovatory genius of this artist, who pointed the way forward to the Renaissance through his feeling for relief and expression. In 1427, shortly before his untimely death, he created this set of frescoes that are now considered one of the most consummate examples of Italian painting in existence.

Masaccio (1401–28)
and the Introduction of Volume in Painting

Masaccio died prematurely at the age of 27 after travelling to Rome with Donatello and Brunelleschi. He was to painting what his two friends were to sculpture and architecture. From the former, he acquired a taste for powerful figures, realistic expressions and heavy, draped clothing; from the latter, he learned about perspective which he then applied not only to illustrations of buildings but also to human figures, as in his frescoes in Santa Maria Novella. He discovered that light contained sculptural resources and concentrated on giving volume to his figures and improving his spatial layout, leaving aside the grace, ornamentation and excessive detail of the Gothic style. He paved the way for the Renaissance style in painting, and his works had a huge impact on successive generations because of their lifelike realism.

In his famous painting of **Adam and Eve being expelled from Paradise** (**I**), symmetrically opposite the Temptation painted by Masolino, he totally excluded idealism in order to express, with poignant intensity, the shame and despair of the figures. The light projected onto the scene and the splashes of shadow that conceal certain parts of the bodies and faces add to the dramatic effect and accentuate the impression of relief, giving the figures a striking reality.

The Tribute Money (**II**) depicts the Apostles as vigorous figures radiating supreme gravity. The fresco includes three episodes, reduced to their main elements. They show the tax-collector (*rear view*) at the Capernaum Gate, demanding payment of the toll from Jesus, who is showing Peter the water in which he will find the fish with the silver coin in its mouth (*central scene*). The Apostle takes the fish (*left*), then hands the coin to the tax-collector (*right*).

Another fresco depicts St Peter baptising (**IV**) and St Peter curing the lame man (**V**). Painted by Masolino, his regular, more anecdotal style is evident in the two elegant figures crossing the square.

The subjects treated by Masaccio (*on the lower register*) are St Peter and St John giving alms (**XII**), St Peter curing the sick by the sole power of his shadow (**XI**); and St Peter on the episcopal throne (**X**).

Filippino Lippi

Still incomplete by the time Masaccio left for Rome, the chapel was completed in 1481 by Filippino Lippi who masterfully united the earlier scenes with his elegant style (*on the lower section of the wall*): St Paul visiting St Peter in prison in Antioch (**VIII**); St Peter raising the Son of Theophilus, Prefect of Antioch, from the dead (**IX**), a fresco that had been started by Masaccio; St Peter set free by an Angel during his second term of imprisonment in Jerusalem (**XIV**) and St Peter and St Paul arguing with Simon Magus before the Emperor and the Crucifixion of St Peter (**XIII**).

The two faces beside the altarpiece are portraits of Masaccio and Masolino.

Michelangelo's Crucifix

In 1492, Michelangelo sculpted a wooden Crucifix and gave it to the church of Santo Spirito in recognition of the services of the Church's prior, who had helped him with his dissections in his study of anatomy. According to the art historian Vasari, with this wooden Crucifix, Michelangelo gave a hint of his future genius. At the time, the Crucifix was located above the master altar. After its restoration, it was placed in the sacristy.

▷ Take Via di Cestello to Piazza di Cestello. Take the Lungarno Soderini, which offers a lovely view of Ponte Vecchio continuing on Lungarno Guicciardini. Turn right onto Via Maggio.

Palazzo Ricasoli-Ridolfi (*no.7*) and Palazzo di Bianca Cappello (*no. 26*) are the "souvenirs" of the Venetian courtesan who became second wife of Francesco I, built in the second half 16C by Buontalenti (graffiti is by Poccetti). Further along is **Casa Guidi**, where the poets Robert Browning and Elizabeth Barret Browning resided (*Piazza San Felice 8; ⏱Open Apr–Nov Mon, Wed, Fri 3–6pm; ✎Donation; ☏055 35 44 57*).

▷ Continue to Piazza Santo Spirito.

Chiesa di Santo Spirito★

Piazza Santo Spirito. ⏱*Open 10.00am–1pm (Sun and holidays 11.30am–1.30pm), 3–6pm.* ⏱*Closed Wed.* ☏*055 21 00 30.*
This Renaissance **church** designed by Brunelleschi is situated at the end of a peaceful, shady square off the main tourist track. Building began in 1444, but the great architect died two years later. Construction work on the modest façade continued until 1487 using the original plans, although a number of changes were made.
The building includes 38 small semi-circular chapels which, according to

Brunelleschi's plans, were intended to be visible from the outside. The chapels open into the aisles through arches of the same height as those in the nave and it is this that gives the church its remarkably spacious character.
Santo Spirito contains numerous **works of art★**, including *Madonna of Succour* barring the path of a glowing red, cloven-hoofed devil, by an unknown 15C Florentine painter; Filippino Lippi's **Madonna and Child**; and the **Corbinelli Chapel** containing an ornate carved marble reredos dating from the early 16C by Andrea Sansovino.
The splendid **sacristy★** (*entrance in north aisle by the door next to the second chapel*) is a monumental construction designed in 1489 by Giuliano da Sangallo in the spirit of Brunelleschi's designs.

Cenacolo di Santo Spirito

Left of the church – no 29. The fine Gothic hall with bare rafters is the **former refectory** of the Augustinian friary adjoining the church. One of its walls is covered by a large Crucifixion, a fresco painted c. 1360, and the remains of the Last Supper (*above*), which are attributed to Andrea Orcagna and Nardo di Cione. The refectory also displays sculptures dating from the Romanesque to the Baroque periods, including a low-relief (*end wall*) of St Maximus by Donatello.

▷ Walk along Via S Agostino and then along Via S Monaca as far as S Maria del Carmine.

Santa Maria del Carmine: The Brancacci Chapel★★★

Allow 15min. ⏱*Open Wed–Mon 10am–5pm, Sun and holidays 1–5pm.* ⏱*Closed Tue, 1 Jan, 7 Jan, Easter, 16 Jul, 15 Aug, 25 Dec. Reservations required.* ✎*€8.* ☏*055 27 68 224.* *cultura.comune.fi.it*
An extraordinary series of **frescoes★★★** decorates the walls of the Brancacci Chapel at the end of the south transept. Three different artists describe original sin and the life of St Peter; the latter subject was probably chosen because Florence had political links with the Papacy.

Passeggiata to Piazzale Michelangelo★★

The splendid hillside route (Viale dei Colli), which is subdivided into Viale Michelangelo (at the east end), Viale Galileo (in the middle) and Viale Machiavelli (at the west end), overlooks Florence from the south bank. It was built between 1865 and 1870 and its superb route was selected by the architect Giuseppe Poggi, who was in charge of urban improvement during the brief spell when Florence was the capital of the Kingdom of Italy. The road, which is lined with luxurious mansions, wends its way in wide curves across the hillside between two majestic rows of pines and cypresses.

☞WALKING TOUR

At the end of the Ponte Vecchio, go left on Via de'Bardi.

After about 500m/550yd, it passes Renaissance palaces. At no 36, the Palazzo Capponi delle Rovinate (15C) presents its beautiful façade. At no 28, Palazzo Canigiani, Sir John Pope-Hennessy (1913–94), English art historian and honorary citizen of the city of Florence, resided and died. At no 22 is the small 11C church of Santa Lucia dei Magnoli.

Via de'Bardi extends to Via di San Niccolò. Some craftsmen and cabinetmakers still have workshops. After 200m/220yds, at the crossroads, is a lively area for shopping, with pleasant outdoor cafés and restaurants. Via San Miniato leads to the Porta San Miniato. Through the gate take Via del Monte alle Croci then to the stairs of Via San Salvatore al Monte. The ascent is steep. Between 1 May and mid-June, look for roses blooming in Giardino delle Rose (*Rose Garden, 8am–10pm*), spread over an acre, lending lovely colours to Florence.

▷ **Don't Miss:** View from Piazzale Michelangelo.

👫 **Kids:** A *gelato* or fruit shake at Piazzale Michelangelo.

🕐 **Timing:** On foot allow 2.5hr (or Bus 12 from S Maria Novella).

▷ Take the stairs up the hillside. The Viale Galileo leads to Piazzale Michelangiolo.

Piazzale Michelangelo

From this vast esplanade overlooking the city, there is a magnificent **panoramic view★★★** of Florence and the Appenines.

The memorial to Michelangelo, erected in 1875 in the centre of the square, is decorated with copies of some of the artist's most famous statues.

▷ From Piazzale Michelangelo continue uphill away from the city along Via Galileo (part of Viale dei Colli).

San Miniato al Monte★★

A steep flight of steps leads up to the church (left).

The church of San Miniato was built in an outstandingly beautiful **setting★★** overlooking Florence, at the top of a wide flight of steps commissioned by Poggi. It is flanked by a graveyard from which there is a view of the countryside, including the Boboli Gardens laid out on the hill below the Belvedere Fort, which is distinguished by its 14C fortifications. A Benedictine monastery was founded here in the 11C and its church is one of the finest examples of Florentine Romanesque architecture. It was built in memory of **St Minias**, who fell victim to the persecutions ordered in AD 250 by the Roman Emperor Decius. Minias, probably a Tuscan of humble origins who, according to popular belief, was a king from Armenia, had already miraculously escaped a number of executions.

San Miniato al Monte

© KavalenkavaVolha/iStock

When he had finally been beheaded, he crossed the River Arno holding his head in his hands, returning to die on the hillside where he had lived as a hermit (then known as Mons Florentinus).

The 12C **west front** is exceptionally elegant and is reminiscent of the Baptistery. On the left is the unfinished 16C bell tower. Michelangelo, who was commissioned to add fortifications to the hillside, decided to use the tower as a base for artillery when Florence was besieged in 1530 by the troops of Charles V in an attempt to re-establish the Medici.

Like the west front, the **Interior** is remarkable for the pleasing geometric combination of green and white marble. The superb pavement (1207), inset with white and black marble, is like a piece of lace.

The tiny **Crucifix Chapel** was built in 1447 on the orders of Pietro I to designs by Michelozzo. Its purpose was to house a miraculous Crucifix. The glazed terracotta coffering decorating the roof is by Luca della Robbia. Agnolo Gaddi painted the panels above the altar in the late 14C. In the centre, dressed in red, is St Minias.

The **Chapel of the Cardinal of Portugal★** which was built in the 15C opens off the north aisle and is a fine example of Renaissance architecture, designed by one of Brunelleschi's pupils. It houses

the tomb of James of Lusitania, Archbishop of Lisbon and nephew of the King of Portugal, who died in Florence in 1459.

The **pulpit**, and the **choir screen** against which it stands, form a superb **set of furnishings★★** including some magnificent craftwork with inlays of white, green and pink marble dating from the early 13C.

Above the **apse** is a huge late-13C mosaic representing Christ giving His Benediction. He is flanked by the Virgin Mary and St Minias.

In the **sacristy**, Spinello Aretino painted **frescoes★** in 1387 (restored) in a style reminiscent of that of Giotto; they illustrate the Legend of St Benedict.

The **crypt** includes seven aisles separated by a multitude of wonderful, slender columns crowned by classical capitals. The altar contains the remains of St Minias.

The tour continues through a series of sweeping curves to the Porta Romana. Some way along this long avenue (*about 2km/1mi from Piazzale Michelangolo*) a narrow road (*one-way*) branches off to the right, leading down to **Forte del Belvedere** (*the road ends at Lungarno Torrigiani quay. Start from this quay if you wish to climb up to the Fort on foot*). The splendid **panoramic view★★** has provided inspiration to many painters.

The centre of Florence has such a rich concentration of famous architecture and art treasures that visitors often overlook its surrounding area, which ranges from pastoral countryside dotted with castles and villas, to one of central Italy's major manufacturing areas. The southern half of Florence is cupped by the Chianti Colli Fiorentini hills, lined with vineyards and olive groves, which form a gateway south to other famous Chianti wine zones.

Don't Miss

The area around Florence offers a rich variety of sights and activities. Medici villas and gardens adorn the countryside, especially to the north in the Mugello area. The town of Sesto Fiorentino is noted for its ceramics, while Borgo San Lorenzo has a lovely medieval centre to explore. The city of Prato is a manufacturing centre for industrial and fashion textiles, but has retained its medieval centre with its Duomo and frescoes by Filippo Lippi. Pistoia, also industrial, has a delightful medieval centre, too, and lively events from a Bear Joust to a Blues Festival. Relax at Montecatini Terme with its stylish Art Nouveau spa facilities that surround you while you drink the waters and enjoy pampering treatments.

Highlights

1 Visit **Medici villas and gardens** for an atmosphere of Renaissance country life (p188)

2 Explore the Etruscan heritage of **Fiesole** and savour the **views** of Florence (p190)

3 Relax in **Art Nouveau** elegance at the Montecatini Terme and ride the **historic cable car** to Montecatini Alto (p201)

4 Visit the **birthplaces of artists** from Leonardo da Vinci to Filippo Lippi (p208, p214)

5 Discover the world of textiles in **Prato** and stroll through its historic centre (p211)

Art and Culture in the Suburbs

Art lovers can enjoy a break from the crowds of the Uffizi and still see favourite masters. Visit Leonardo's birthplace in Vinci, examine models of his inventions and wander landscapes like those in his paintings. Admire masterpieces by Filippo Lippi and Pontormo in lovely towns and city centres. Discover ancient treasures from the Etruscan civilisation in towns like Fiesole.

Enquiring minds can see how textiles, glass, terracotta and ceramics are made; also a treasure trove for shoppers. Wander through parks that vary from elegant formal Medici gardens to a Pinocchio fantasy. Explore archaeological areas and castles. Visit farms to experience the rhythm of country life, and dine or stay at an *agriturismo* – some are humble, others have castles or manor houses.

Cuisine and Wine

Gourmets have plenty to enjoy here. Chianti Colli Fiorentini, the northern tip of the Chianti region, has over 30 wineries. Look also for excellent olive oil, for the prized chestnut Marrone del Mugello, and for *zafferano* (saffron). The *carciofo empolese* is a spring artichoke from around Empoli, which also produces white Bianco dell'Empolese wine. Chianina cattle are raised for the famous steaks. Pecorino cheese and salamis are excellent. Look for other wines, too, especially red. Winemakers like to tinker with grapes to make wines other than Chianti or Chianti Classico. Often these wines are economical and delicious; a passion of the winemaker rather than to satisfy market demands. The valleys are bountiful with fruit orchards and vegetables so check the local markets to see what's in season.

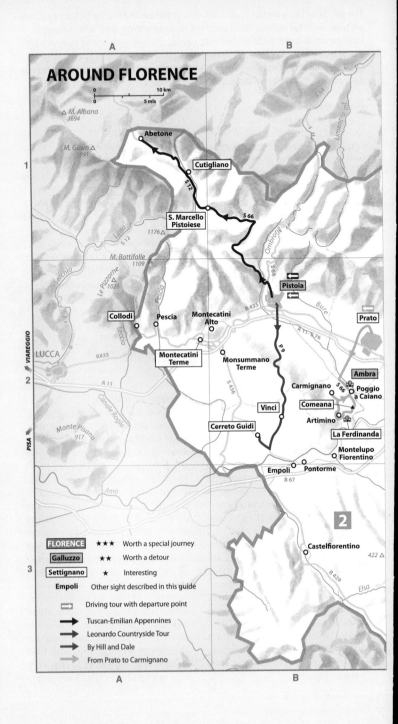

AROUND FLORENCE

| 0 | | 10 km |
| 0 | 5 mls | |

△ M. Albano
1694

M. Giovo △
1991

Abetone

Cutigliano

S 12

S. Marcello
Pistoiese

S 66

1176 △

M. Battifolle
1109

Le Pizzorne
△ 1026

Ombrone

Pistoia

Bure

Prato

Collodi

Pescia

Montecatini
Alto

R 435

A 11-E 76

Montecatini
Terme

Monsummano
Terme

LUCCA

VIAREGGIO

R 435

Serchio

Teccio

A 11

Canale Roggio

Monte Pisano
917

Arno

S 436

P 9

Carmignano

S 66

Ambra

Poggio
a Caiano

Vinci

Comeana

Artimino

Cerreto Guidi

La Ferdinanda

Montelupo
Fiorentino

Empoli

Pontorme

R 67

2

Castelfiorentino

422 △

R 429

Elsa

FLORENCE	★★★	Worth a special journey
Galluzzo	★★	Worth a detour
Settignano	★	Interesting
Empoli		Other sight described in this guide

⇦ Driving tour with departure point

➤ Tuscan-Emilian Appennines

➤ Leonardo Countryside Tour

➤ By Hill and Dale

➤ From Prato to Carmignano

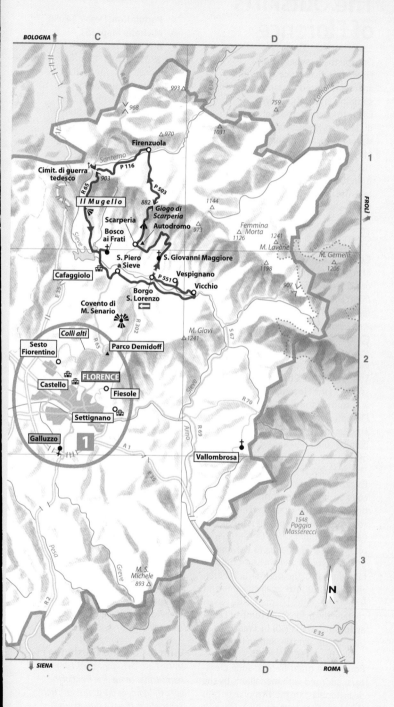

The Outskirts of Florence

Outside the busy centre of Florence, Renaissance artists and architects graced the landscape with stunning art and buildings. La Certosa (charterhouse) di Galluzzo, Medici villas, the Vallombrosa Abbey and the town of Fiesole are situated in the typical Tuscan countryside. This is a break from the mad sightseeing dash, to take the measure of the land and see things slowly.

SOUTH OF FLORENCE

Certosa del Galluzzo★★

6km/4mi S of Florence. On the W side of Via Senese/Via Cassia (the road from Galluzzo to Siena). ✒Guided *tours only (1hr) at 10am, 11am, 3pm, 4pm, 5pm (last tour at 4pm in winter).* ⊙*Closed Sun morning and Mon.* ⊜*Donation.* ℘*055 20 49 226. www.certosadifirenze.it.*

The **Galluzzo Charterhouse**, also known as the **Florence Charterhouse**, was founded in the 14C by the great Florentine banker, Niccolò Acciaiuoli. The Carthusian monks occupied the premises until 1957 and were succeeded by a Cistercian community.

The monastery buildings include Palazzo Acciaiuoli, which displays frescoes by Jacopo Pontormo (1523–25), originally in the cloisters. The church separated the lay brothers from the Carthusian monks. The Gothic Chapel of S Maria (*right*) leads to the underground chapels with the Acciaiuoli family tombs. The parlour (*left of the church*), leads into small cloisters and from there to the chapterhouse which contains the magnificent **tomb of Leonardo Buonafé** (1550) by Francesco di Giuliano da Sangallo and an intricately carved door (16C).

Round the great Renaissance **cloisters**, adorned with medallions by the della Robbias, are the 18 monastic cells (⊙*one is open to the public*). The visit

● **Population:** Fiesole 14,088.
⏦ **Michelin Map:** 563.
🅘 **Info:** Via Portigiani 3, ℘055 59 61 311. www.fiesoleforyou.it. www.comune.fiesole.fi.it.
▶ **Location:** 7km/5mi from Florence. Bus 7 Stazione S.M. Novella.
⊛ **Don't Miss:** Fiesole's view of Florence and San Francesco convent, the Certosa di Galluzzo charterhouse, Medici villas and gardens, and the Vallombrosa Abbey.
👥 **Kids:** Explore Fiesole's archaeological area, then find tombs in the museum, and take a walk through Medici gardens.
⏱ **Timing:** Allow half a day.

continues via the refectory, lay cloisters and guesthouse. Stop in their bar to have a coffee or sample the liqueurs made here or at other monasteries.

Scandicci

8km/5mi SW through Porta al Prato, or Tram 1/Resistenza stop.

Castello dell'Acciaiolo (*Via Pantin 7*) hosts occasional events and exhibitions. Nearby is the **Badia di San Salvatore a Settimo** medieval abbey, partly restored (*6km/4mi NW, via Via San Lorenzo 15;* ⊙*Open on Sun only, 3.30–6pm;* ⊜*€5;* ℘*055 73 10 537*).

NORTH OF FLORENCE

In the 16C, it became fashionable to have a second home. All the great Florentine families had their villas, designed by prestigious architects, from Michelozzo to Giuliano da Sangallo and Buontalenti.

Villa di Castello Gardens★

NW in Castello (signposted). Large semicircular car park in front of the villa; the gardens are at the rear; from Santa Maria Novella station Bus 2

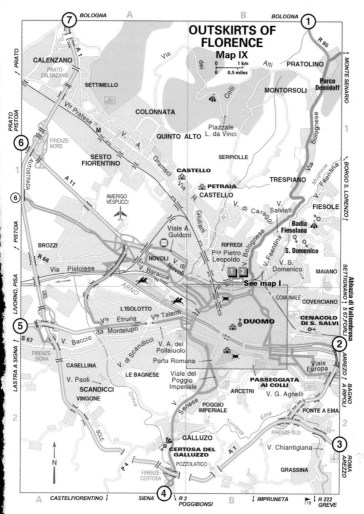

OUTSKIRTS OF FLORENCE
Map IX

0 — 1 km
0 — 0.5 miles

or 28 (stop "Sestese 03"). ⏰Open daily 8.30am–6.30pm (Mar and Oct 5.30pm; Nov–Feb 4.30pm); hours may vary. ⏰Closed 25 Dec, 1 Jan. ☞Free admission. ♿ www.polomuseale toscana.beniculturali.it.

The villa (☞ closed to the public) was purchased by the Medici in 1477 and in 1527, Duke Cosimo I commissioned Tribolo to refurbish it and lay out the gardens, which include a large Italian-style flowerbed set superbly in proportion to Tribolo's beautiful central fountain. A grotto contains reproductions of Giambologna's animal statues (the original bronze sculptures are in the Bargello

Museum loggia in Florence). A Secret Garden is open Apr–Oct.

Villa della Petraia★

NE in Castello, at the end of Via della Petraia (signposted). ⏰Open daily 8.30am–6.30pm (Mar and Oct 5.30pm, Nov–Feb 4.30pm); ☞Guided tours only, every hour from 8.30am. ⏰Closed 2nd and 3rd Mon of the month; 1 May, 25 Dec, 1 Jan. ☞ Free admission. ✆055 45 26 91. www.polomusealetoscana. beniculturali.it.

In 1576 Cardinal Ferdinand Medici commissioned the architect Buontalenti to transform this former fortress into a villa with gardens. Later, in the 19C, King Victor Emanuel II made the villa his summer residence. He had the State apartments, the courtyard and the Renaissance portico all glassed in to create a ballroom. The **gardens** (16C) consist of flowerbeds in front of the villa and a wooded park at the rear. On the right-hand side of the villa stands a superb Tribolo fountain. Giambologna's admirable statue of Venus adorns the first floor of the villa.

NORTHEAST OF FLORENCE

Fiesole★

8km/5mi NE of Florence. From Piazza San Marco take Bus 7 to Fiesole (20min). The Etruscans founded this city in the 7C or 6C BC, strategically built high in the hills with a healthy climate. The most important city in northern Etruria, Fiesole dominated its rival Florence until the 12C. The hills covered with olive groves, gardens and roads lined with cypress trees afford magnificent views.

WALKING TOUR

The centre of Fiesole is the vast, sloping **square**, which occupies the site of the old Roman Forum. The Santa Maria Primerana oratory has a late-16C portico; the small 14C–15C **Palazzo Pretorio** bears the coats of arms of the magistrates (*podesté*) who resided here. Opposite the cathedral entrance (*southwest corner*), a narrow and steep street, Via S Francesco, leads up to where the Acropolis of Faesulae stood in the Roman era.

Halfway up, turn left into the small public park for a fine **view★★** of Florence; the park projects like a balcony, overlooking the Arno Basin spread out below.

▶ This walking tour begins on Via S Francesco and heads E to Piazza Mino, the main square. 10min.

Basilica di Sant'Alessandro

Via S Francesco.

The **basilica** (c. 9C) was built on the site of a Roman temple that had been converted into a church by Theodoric (6C). The neo-Classical façade, added in 1815, is not inviting, but the austere interior has a certain nobility; its nave and aisles are separated by superb ancient Roman columns.

Convento di San Francesco★

Via S Francesco 13. ◷*Church: open daily 7/7.30am–7/8pm. Museum: open Tue–Sat 9.30am–noon, 3–7pm (Sat 10.30am), Sun and public hols 9–11am, 3–7pm; closing time at 5pm in Aut–Win.* ☏*055 59 175.*

This very modest **friary**, which is admirably located on the highest part of the hill, has been occupied by Franciscans since the early 15C. The tiny 14C cloisters (*entrance to the right of the church*) are visible through a wrought-iron grille. On the first floor are several of the tiny humble cells, where the friars lived. One of them was occupied by **St Bernardino of Siena**, who was Prior here for a few years.

The adjacent 14C **church** has an early-15C Gothic façade with a simple small multifoiled canopy that is utterly charming. The church's interesting **paintings★** include an Immaculate Conception by Piero di Cosimo and, opposite it, an Annunciation by Raffaellino del Garbo. The eclectic **Museo Etnografico della Missione Francescana** (Franciscan Missions Ethnographic Museum) has objects from the Orient (sculptures, paintings, clothing, porcelain) and a small archaeology section (artefacts excavated near the friary, Egyptian objects and a mummy found by missionaries in Egypt).

Cattedrale di San Romolo★ (Duomo)

Piazza della Cattedrale. ◷*Usually open 7.30am–noon (Aut–Wint 8am), 3–5.30pm.* ☏*055 59 400.*

This Romanesque **church** was begun in the 11C and extended in the 13C and 14C, and now has a 19C façade. The 18C addition of merlons and machicolations made the 1213 bell tower look like a belfry. The stark **interior★** is laid out like

The Roman theatre, Fiesole

a basilica. Most of the crypt's columns have ancient capitals. The polychrome glazed terracotta niche by Giovanni della Robbia features a statue of St Romulus, Bishop of Fiesole, to whom the cathedral was dedicated. The Salutati chapel decorated with frescoes by Cosimo Rosselli (15C), contains two delightful **works**★ by Mino da Fiesole: the tomb and bust of Leonardo Salutati and a carved reredos of the Virgin Mary in Adoration with the young St John and other saints.

Area Archeologica
Via Portigiani 1. ◔*Open daily Apr–Sep 9am–7pm, Mar and Oct 10am–6pm; Nov–Feb 10am–3pm, closed Tue.* ◔*Closed 25 Dec.* ✆€7; €10 combined with Museo Archeologico; €12 combined with Museo Archeologico and Museo Bandini.* ♿ ✆*055 59 61 293. www.museidifiesole.it*
In an enchanting **setting**★ on a hillside clothed in cypress trees lie the **remains** of several Etruscan and Roman buildings. The archaeological finds from the site have been placed in a small museum (*to the right of the entrance*).
The **Roman theatre**★ (*teatro romano*) set into the hillside dates from 80BC and has 23 tiers of well-preserved seats, the first four rows for VIPs. The semicircular orchestra was paved with multicoloured marble. The slightly higher stage had openings in the backdrop by which the actors made their entrances and exits. A small 4C BC **Etruscan temple** (*tempietto etrusco*) is marked by the rectangular foundation and steps, near fragments of the **Etruscan walls**. The 1C AD **baths** (*terme*) were built by the Romans. Two large rectangular swimming pools were open-air; under cover, the hot baths (*caldarium*) were on the floor supported by small brick pillars around which hot air circulated (*hypocaust*).

Museo Archeologico★
◔*See Area Archeologica.* ✆€10 *combined with Area Archeologica.*
The Archaeological Museum is organised geographically, thus objects from very different periods are clustered together. Artefacts came from an Etruscan necropolis and from the Archaeology Zone: antefixes (a sort of gargoyle) in the shape of female figures; tiny bronze votive offerings, some of which are shaped like feet or legs; 8C–7C iron belt ornaments; pearls from a necklace; and silver hairpins found beneath the skull of a female burial. A tombstone (5C BC) is decorated with a funeral meal, a dance and an animal combat. Also see the Greek vases and Etruscan buccheroware in the Costantini collection.

Museo Bandini

◷Open Fri–Sun Apr–Sep 9am–7pm, Mar and Oct 10am–6pm, Nov–Feb 10am–3pm. ◷Closed Mon–Thu, 25 Dec. ⬡€5; joint ticket with Area Archeologica and Museo Archeologico €12. ☎055 59 61 293.

Paintings from the 14C and 15C Tuscan School include the Florentine School's Petrarch's Triumphs: *The Triumph of Love and Chastity* and *The Triumph of Time and Religion*.

Piazzale Leonardo

🚶45min.

This walk leads to one of of the most amazing and avant-garde experiments of Leonardo da Vinci. From the Piazza Mino da Fiesole, take Via Verdi then go left on Via Montececeri to Piazzale Leonardo. Within the park, Montececeri Terrace offers a remarkable **panorama** of Florence. Historical records and legends suggest that here Leonardo affixed wings to the shoulders of an assistant. The flight probably lasted only a few metres, and ended on the lower slope of the Maiano park, with difficulty and some breakage. Nevertheless it is called the **first flight of man**. ⬡Free admission, all year.

Badia Fiesolana

3km/2mi SW of Fiesole. Almost halfway between Fiesole and Florence, turn right into the Via dei Roccettini.

◷Open Mon–Fri 8am–7pm (opening times of the European University Institute). ☎055 46 85 399.

The Badia Fiesolana (Fiesole Abbey), now home to the **European University Institute**, was originally a Benedictine convent. The ornate Romanesque **façade★**, in green and white marble, has been rather strangely integrated into the newer 15C façade, which remained unfinished on the death of Cosimo the Elder.

San Domenico di Fiesole

2.5km/2mi to the SW, beside the Florence road (left), just after the junction with Via Badia dei Roccettini on SP85. ◷Open Mon–Sat 8am–noon, 4–6pm, Sun and hols 4–6pm. ☎055 59 230.

Fra Angelico took his vows here, c. 1420, and spent several years in the adjacent monastery (⬤private). The church contains his delicate but vividly coloured **painting★** representing the Virgin Mary in Majesty surrounded by angels and saints (c. 1430).

EAST OF FLORENCE

Settignano★

On the hills NE of Florence, near Fiesole. From Santa Maria Novella in Florence take Bus 10.

Settignano, a small residential town, was the birthplace in the 15C of many

The Rise and Fall of Fiesole

The Etruscan town of Fiesole was the largest town in northern Etruria. The site had been chosen for its position on a rise commanding the routes which passed over the barrier of the Apennines (*north*) into the Arno Plain and continued south to Rome. This was, moreover, a healthier spot than the plain, which in those days consisted largely of swamps.

Within its mighty walls, Fiesole was a town of greater power and importance than Florence for several centuries. Sulla set up a colony of Veterans here c. 80BC. In 63BC the town rallied in support of Catiline, who sought refuge here before the Battle of Pistoia, where he was fatally wounded. From then on the destiny of Fiesole was linked to that of Rome. New buildings were erected on the ruins of the Etruscan structures and the Roman town, known as Faesulae, with its temples, theatre and baths, became the main centre of the region. From the 1CAD onwards it began to fall into decline and was overtaken by Florence, its rival and neighbour. In 1125 Faesulae was finally conquered by Florence and almost razed to the ground.

sculptors. Here Michelangelo spent his childhood among the stonecutters who worked *pietra serena*, the bluish-grey stone used for so many of the architectural features in Florence. The local beauty early on drew the great families of Florence who had superb villas built throughout this area. Boccaccio set the beginning of his *Decameron* in the grounds of a country house at the foot of the hills here. In the 19C the area was fashionable with English high society. In the 20C D'Annunzio had a villa here while he carried on his love affair with the great actress Eleonora Duse.

Viale Gabriele D'Annunzio★

This long **avenue** winds out of Florence through **Coverciano** and up the hillside; the view reveals the beauty of the landscape and the magnificent country houses. Halfway up (*left of the road in a right-hand bend*) stands the neomedieval 19C **Villa Contri di Mezzaratta**, set high above the valley. The road leads to the heart of the village, Piazza Tommaseo, and the small **Church of L'Assunta** which was built in the 15C and altered in the following century.

◐ From the square take the very narrow Via di San Romano; turn right into Via Rossellino; when the street bears right, go straight on and park (right) in front of the villa.

Villa Gamberaia: Gardens★

No 72; entrance on the right in front of a short vaulted passageway.
◐*Open Mon–Sat 9am–7pm, Sun 9am–6pm (last admission 1hr before closing); closing dates vary, visitors are recommended to check in advance.* ◐€20. The interior can be visited on appointment Tue–Sat 9am–noon (additional ◐€20). ℘055 69 72 05. www.villagamberaia.com.
Erected in the 14C by Benedictines who worked the surrounding land, in the 17C it was transformed into a plain quadrangular villa, soon embellished with magnificent gardens laid out with immense artistry. Below the loggia is a formal layout

of topiary work in cypress, yew and box, redesigned at the beginning of the century; it ends in a terrace from which there is a fine panoramic view of the Arno Valley. On the east side the grassy walks are flanked by azaleas, camellias, hydrangeas and rhododendrons; there are groups of lemon trees in pots, grapefruit trees and mandarin trees, and also two grottoes decorated with shells, niches and statues.

Abbazia di Vallombrosa★

36km/22mi E of Florence. Drive E to Pelago, then take SP85 for 12km/7.5mi. Via San Benedetto 115, Vallombrosa.
◐*Open daily 9am–6pm; hours may vary.* ℘055 86 22 51.
Celebrated by Milton in *Paradise Lost,* Vallombrosa is known for its abbey, its natural beauty, its views, its magnificent pine forest and excursions in the Pratomagno range.
The **monastery** was founded c. 1028 by Giovanni Gualberto, a young Florentine nobleman, with a companion and the two hermits they met when they retired to this place. As beneficiary of important gifts, it rapidly became influential. Its noble white façade was designed by Gherardo Silvani (1635–40).
A walled courtyard, dominated by a tall 13C bell tower and (*right*) a 15C tower, are the only surviving features of the earlier buildings.

🚗 DRIVING TOURS

① COLLI ALTI SCENIC ROUTE★
26km/16mi from Florence by S65 (Via Bolognese).

◐ Beyond Montorsoli turn left into the Monte Morello road.

The road climbs sharply at first and then winds across the southern slopes of Mount Morello, providing views (*south*) over Fiesole and Florence and the Arno Basin. The most extensive **view★** extends over a considerable distance (3km/2mi) from Piazzale Leonardo da Vinci (6km/3.5mi beyond Montorsoli – alt 595m/1 952ft – *restaurant*). The view embraces Florence and the Arno Valley; in the background are the Chianti Hills (*south*) and the Prato Plain (*west*). Beyond the Gualdo Refuge (alt 428m/ 1,404ft) the road narrows and runs down a steep hillside in a series of bends with views through the pines of Prato and Sesto Fiorentino.

 In Colonnata take the road to Sesto Fiorentino. In Quinto Alto turn left into Via Fratelli Rosselli, a long road.

The Etruscan Montagnola **tomb**★ dates from the 7BC or 6BC and is interesting for its remarkable domed roofing system concealed beneath an earth tumulus.

Sesto Fiorentino★

The small town of Sesto Fiorentino is situated at the sixth (*sesto*) mile northwest of Florence. Its medieval character was lost with development of manufacturing, notably porcelain and ceramics.

② TOUR OF MONTE SENARIO★

38km/24mi N of Florence by SS/SR 65 (Via Bolognese) following the same route as the previous tour as far as Montorsoli.

From the Trespiano hill there are views (*right*) over Florence in the valley below, to Fiesole, followed by a few rare glimpses of the Mugnone Valley.

 800m/875yd beyond the junction with the winding road (left) to Monte Morello turn right at the traffic lights into the villa entrance, a huge gate surmounted by two lions.

Parco Demidoff★

Near to Pratolino. ⏲ *Open Apr–Oct Fri–Sun and public hols 10am–8pm (Oct 6pm).* ⬿ *Free admission.* ✆ *055 40 80 721. www.firenzeturismo.it/pratolino.* Within this park, a masterpiece of Tuscan Mannerism, used to stand the most luxurious of all the Medici villas, known as the **Villa di Pratolino**. Its present name is that of the prince who purchased the property in 1872. Traces of its past splendour include the huge statue of the **Appennino**★ (1579–80) by Giambologna containing grottoes decorated with frescoes and fountains. To the right of the avenue is the chapel by Buontalenti.

 Continue to Pratolino; turn right off S65 into the road to Bivigliano. At the following junction, where the road divides on a bend (before the junction with the road to Olmo), turn into the road up to Monte Senario.

© Claudiovidri/Shutterstock

Statue of the Appennino *(1579–80) by Giambologna, Parco Demidoff*

From the hilltop approach road there are some delightful views of the surrounding hills and the monastery glimpsed among the fir trees.

▶ After 2.5km/1.5mi turn right; drive to the top of the hill (car park). A short private drive leads to the monastery.

Convento di Monte Senario

Alt 817m/2 655ft. Via di Montesenario 1, Vaglia. ⏱*Usually open 7am–12.45pm, 3–7.30pm.*

The **monastery** lies in a superb **setting**★★ on a wooded promontory above the Sieve Valley. Founded in the 13C, the present monastery dates from the 17C and 18C. Its tiny **church** has an elegant Baroque interior and a few works of art including a 15C terracotta *Pietà* in the Chapel of the Apparition (*on the altar*).

▶ On returning down the hill, turn right at the road junction towards Bivigliano (signposted).

Bivigliano is a pleasant shady residential village near a fine pine wood. The road continues along delightful terraces above the Carza Valley.

▶ From Pratolino take SS65 to return to Florence.

ADDRESSES

🏨STAY

⊜⊜🛏 **Dino** – *Via Faentina 329, Olmo, 9km/6mi NW of Fiesole.* ℰ*055 54 89 32. www.hotel-dino.it.* 🅿. *18 rooms.* 🍽. *Restaurant*⊜🛏. In the tranquil hills near Fiesole, this simple family hotel has comfortable rooms with rustic decor.

⊜⊜🛏 **Pensione Bencistà** – *Via Benedetto da Maiano 4.* ℰ*055 59 163. www.bencista.com.* 🅿. *41 rooms. Restaurant* ⊜🛏. This old mansion is set among olive groves and furnished with antiques. Its pleasant terrace overlooks a garden graced with view of Medici villas and the Arno Valley.

⊜⊜🛏🛏 **Marignolle Relais & Charme** – *Via di San Quirichino 16, Galluzzo.* ℰ*055 22 86 910. www.marignolle.com. 10 rooms.*

This hilltop villa 3km/1.8mi south of Porta Romana is beautifully decorated and the service is attentive. Swim in the pool, take a cooking course, play on neighbourhood tennis courts or let them book a game of golf.

⊜⊜🛏🛏 **Castello di Bibbione** – *Via Collina 66, Località Montepiridolfi, San Casciano in Val di Pesa.* ℰ*055 82 49 231. www. castellodibibbione.com.* The hunting castle of Machiavelli is still owned by his descendants. Tastefully furnished apartments: one in the castle itself, others in estate buildings.

🍽/EAT

⊜⊜ **Osteria Vinandro** – *Piazza Mino da Fiesole 33, Fiesole.* ℰ*055 59 121. vinandro.it.* Typical Tuscan cuisine, simple and flavourful, from market produce. Homely eclectic furnishings.

⊜⊜🛏 **Trattoria Bibe** – *Via delle Bagnese 1, Ponte dell'Asse, Galluzzo.* ℰ*055 20 49 085. www.trattoriabibe. com. Closed Wed and Mon–Fri lunchtime.* Immortalised by the Italian writer Montale in his poetry, this trattoria has been run by the same family for almost two centuries. The menu features traditional Tuscan dishes, such as pici pasta with wild boar sauce. Alfresco dining in summer.

HAVE A DRINK

Bistrot Caffè al n. 5 – *Piazza Mino da Fiesole 5, Fiesole.* ℰ*055 59 250.* Enjoy the view and life in the main square in the town's oldest caffè, here since 1908.

CHIANTI COLLI FIORENTINI
Among the Chianti winemakers from Colli Fiorentini, good wines to sample are made by I Mori, Tenuta Il Corno, Malenchini, Castello di Poppiano and Fattoria Zucconi delle Massete.

EVENT

Estate Fiesolana – ℰ*055 66 75 66. www.estatefiesolana.it. June–Jul.* Multicultural festival: classical music, pop songs, performances, acrobats, jazz, film, opera and dance held in the Roman theatre in Fiesole or other venues.

Open City Scandicci Estate – *www.comune. scandicci.fi.it. June–Sept.* Theatre, dance or circus performances, concerts and film take place in over ten venues in Scandicci (including Castello dell'Acciaiolo) and the surrounding hills.

Il Mugello★

As early as the 14C this delightful valley was popular with the Florentine aristocracy and wealthy middle classes as a summer resort, due to its mild climate, beautiful rolling hills, well-stocked forests and year-round lushness.

The region was the birthplace of the Medici family and was particularly popular with Cosimo the Elder, who commissioned the construction of the Villa di Cafaggiolo.

The Mugello's idyllic landscape is ideal scenery for nature walks. It is best known, however, as the site of the Autodromo, used by Formula 2 and the Motorcycle Grand Prix racing circuits.

- **Michelin Map:** Atlas p 38 and Map 563 – J/K 15/16 or Map 735 Folds 14 and 15.
- **Info:** Via P. Togliatti 45, Borgo San Lorenzo. ℘055 84 52 71 85/6. www.mugellotoscana.it.
- **Location:** The region of the River Sieve to the N of Florence.
- **Don't Miss:** Palazzo Pretorio in Scarperia, Castello di Cafaggiolo, the baptismal fonts in San Piero a Sieve, scenic views over the Mugello Valley.
- **Timing:** Allow a day.

🚗 DRIVING TOUR

BY HILL AND DALE

100km/62mi. Allow about 5hrs.
See regional map pp186–187.

Borgo San Lorenzo

Although badly damaged during the 1919 earthquake, Borgo San Lorenzo is nonetheless still the main town in the Mugello area. The Palazzo Pretorio in Piazza Garibaldi was reconstructed exactly as it had been, so too was the west front of the church of San Lorenzo, visible from the square.

The **church** dates from the 12C, but its unusual hexagonal bell tower dates from the 13C. The extremely bare interior contains a number of fine works by the Florentine School including a Madonna and Child attributed to Taddeo Gaddi (15C) and a fragment of a reredos depicting the face of the Virgin Mary, attributed to Giotto.

From Piazza Garibaldi the route to Piazza Cavour passes beneath the clock tower in Corso Matteotti. Just before **Porta Fiorentina** (14C) (*second street on the right*) there is a lane (*right*) which runs beside the old rounded town walls to Piazza Cavour.

Take SR302 towards Faenza. After 3km/2mi turn left into the lane leading to the church (400m/433yd).

San Giovanni Maggiore

This pretty little country **church**, set behind an elegant arched portico and flanked by a graceful octagonal bell tower, contains a marble pulpit with symbolic inset motifs (vases) in black stone on all four sides.

Return to SS302; continue towards Faenza; then turn left towards Grezzano and Scarperia.

Autodromo Internazionale del Mugello (Mugello Motor Racing Track)

1km/0.5mi E of Scarperia.
mugellocircuit.com.
The race track hosts Formula 2 races and motorcycle world championships.

Scarperia

This is a small, well-maintained town with a thriving and traditional cutlery trade. It still has its splendid crenellated **Palazzo Pretorio★★** (or Palazzo dei Vicari), built in the small central square in the early 14C to serve as a residence for the deputies of the Mugello region. Opposite the Palazzo Pretorio stands the **church** which contains (*high altar*) two extremely delicate marble sculptures, the first a tabernacle by Mino da Fiesole and the second a tondo of the Madonna and Child by Benedetto da Maiano.

Just outside the church on the left side of the square is a small **oratory** known as the **Madonna di Piazza**. Inside is a Gothic shrine with wreathed columns containing a Madonna and Child by Jacopo del Casentino, which is held in great veneration by local people.

▷ Take SP503.

The road climbs sharply up the range of hills on the north side of the Sieve Valley. The steep and winding road provides fine views south over the Mugello region before entering a wooded area. Further on, the road crosses the pass, **Giogo di Scarperia**, before heading down to Firenzuola, which is visible in the distance.

Firenzuola

Although Firenzuola was badly damaged during World War II, it has nevertheless retained its grid layout bisected by a picturesque thoroughfare lined with porticoes. At the southern end of the street is the Porta Fiorentina, surmounted by a pinnacle turret, and at the north end is the Porta Bolognese.

▷ From Porta Bolognese turn left into SP503. After approx. 1.5km/1mi bear left into SP116 towards Passo della Futa. At SR65 junction turn right and continue approx. 100m/108yd.

Cimitero di Guerra Tedesco

Beside the road (*left*) in the **German Military Cemetery** stands a huge, towering building erected in memory of the 30,653 German soldiers who were killed in this area during World War II.

▷ Take SS65 S towards Florence.

The road soon crosses the pass (**Passo della Futa**) and then descends into the Sieve Valley through pine and beech trees. South of Montecarelli the view

widens out to embrace the scenic Mugello Valley, bounded by gently rolling hills.

▷ 8km/5mi S of Montecarelli, at the crossroads after the right-hand turn to Barberino di Mugello, turn left towards Galliano. After 150m/162yd turn right to Bosco ai Frati.

Bosco ai Frati

This Franciscan **friary** lies off the beaten track and retains the ideal of solitude, one of the basic tenets of the Franciscan Order. Cosimo the Elder commissioned Michelozzo to rebuild it between 1420 and 1428. In front of the church is a small porch with two columns crowned by capitals bearing the Medici coat of arms, which also appears on the tall façade.

▷ Return to R65 and drive S.

Castello di Cafaggiolo★

Temporarily closed for restoration at the time of publication. ☏ 055 84 79 396. www.castellodicafaggiolo.com.
On the right-hand side of the road just before a bend stands the old Florentine **fortress** that Cosimo the Elder commissioned Michelozzo to convert into a country manor in 1451. The villa has retained the proud appearance conveyed by its central tower, fairly massive size and crown of battlements, which are now slightly obscured by the roofs erected over the old parapet walks. Lorenzo the Magnificent and his brother Giuliano spent part of their childhood here. The small town of Cafaggiolo was also famous in the 15C–16C for its majolica ware.

▷ In S Cafaggiolo turn left at the second junction from the hamlet.

San Piero a Sieve

San Piero is a small, relatively modern village overlooked to the west by **San Martino Fortress**, which was built on a high wooded hilltop by Buontalenti in the late 16C. It can be glimpsed on entering the village. From the high brick walls of the pentagonal fortress, there is a panoramic view of the Mugello

The Medici's Resort

Mugello was a strategic shift towards the Romagna in the Middle Ages, and from the 14C became a resort for nobles and wealthy citizens of Florence. Its mild climate, the harmony of gentle mountains that surround its evergreen landscape with an abundance of water and forests full of game, ensured its favour for many centuries. Origin of the Medici, Fra Angelico and Giotto, it benefited especially from Cosimo the Elder, who built nearby fortresses Cafaggiolo and Trebbio and modified the Franciscan convent of Bosco ai Frati *(See p197)*. Mugello unfortunately suffered heavy damage during the earthquake of 1919.

Valley. The parish church in the village (*main street*) contains a magnificent glazed ceramic baptismal **font**★.

▶ Take the road along the south bank of the Sieve. The road passes through superb scenery in the lush Mugello Valley, bounded by wooded hills.

Vicchio

A public park is laid out in the centre of the main square facing the loggia of the town hall (*municipio*).

▶ Take Via Garibaldi; right on Piazza Giotto into Corso del Popolo.

Benvenuto Cellini's house is where the famous sculptor spent his last 12 years.
A raised terrace nearby offers a fine view over the rolling hillsides of the Mugello region.
The **Museo di Arte Sacra Beato Angelico** (*Piazzetta Don Milani;* ◐*Open Apr–Oct Thu–Sun 10am–1pm, 3.30–7.30pm (Apr 2–6pm; Oct only Fri–Sun); rest of the year only Sun 10am–1pm, 3–6pm;* ◉*€4 combined with Casa di Giotto in Vespignano);* &. ℘*055 84 48 251)* is named after

the Vicchio-born **Fra Angelico**; however, it contains no works by the Dominican artist. Instead, it is comprised of a collection of works of art from churches and religious buildings throughout the Mugello region, including a bust of St John the Baptist by Andrea della Robbia.

▶ From the main square opposite the town hall take the Gattaia road.

On the outskirts of the village the road skirts a splendid purpose-built fishing **lake**.

▶ Take SP551 W. After 3.5km/2mi turn right to Casa di Giotto (1km/0.5mi).

Vespignano (District of Vicchio)

Tradition has it that Giotto was born here c. 1266. **Casa di Giotto** (◐*same opening hours as Museo Beato Angelico in Vicchio;* ◉*€4 combined ticket;* ℘*055 84 47 82; www.comune.vicchio.fi.it*) displays a number of documents relating to his life and works. There is a wonderful view of the Mugello Valley from the church overlooking the house.

ADDRESSES

◈STAY

◔ **Agriturismo Poggio di Sotto** *– Via di Galliano 17/19, Galliano, 10km/6mi NW of Borgo S. Lorenzo.* ℘*055 84 28 447. 9 rooms, 1 casale (14 beds). Restaurant*◔◔. This comfortable farm offers spacious rooms decorated with taste in country style. Breakfast is served in the adjoining restaurant. Organised horse riding and mountain bike excursions are available.

◔◔ **Casa Palmira** *– 15km/9mi SW of Borgo San Lorenzo by S302.* ℘*055 84 09 749. www.casapalmira.it. 7 rooms.* ▭. This fascinating medieval farm, surrounded by a beautiful garden, provides its guests with a warm welcome. The bedrooms contain fine old furniture. Afternoon coffee and *aperitivi* are offered. Numerous activities upon request: mountain biking, horse riding, cooking courses and artists' studio.

ℛ/ EAT

⊜⊜⊜ **Badia di Moscheta** – *Via di Moscheta 898, Firenzuola, 8km/5mi S of Firenzuola by SS503 towards Giogo di Scarperia.* ℱ *055 81 44 015. www.badiadimoscheta.it. 6 rooms, 2 apts., 1 haven (3 rooms with 6 beds, 2 with 2 beds). Closed Mon–Tue. Reservations suggested.* This farmhouse inn and restaurant is located at the heart of the little village. It prepares Emilian and Tuscan specialities such as potato pasta (*tordelli*) with mushroom sauce. In summer you could sit by the stream or in the shade of the gazebo, to rest after walking or horse riding.

⊜⊜⊜ **Fattoria Il Palagio** – *Viale Dante 99/101, Scarperia.* ℱ *055 84 63 76. www.fattoriailpalagio.it.* This 18C farmhouse is surrounded by a park. The country-style furniture and the menu, featuring steak and suckling pig, emphasise local tradition.

Empoli

and Around

The town of Empoli has experienced massive development since World War II, especially in the glass-making and clothing industries. Once mainly agricultural, the region has now been largely taken over by the industrial suburbs.

A BIT OF HISTORY

After the defeat of Florence at Montaperti in 1260, a Ghibelline parliament was set up in Empoli to decide on the future of the Guelf capital. The Ghibellines were in favour of razing Florence to the ground in order to emphasise their enemy's defeat, but a passionate plea that the city should be spared was made by **Farinata degli Uberti**, the Ghibelline leader of Florence, who had been banished from Florence by the Guelfs in 1258 and was so delighted to return home that he could not bear his city's destruction. He died four years later, and when the Guelfs defeated the Ghibellines in 1266 and returned to power in Florence, they took their revenge by demolishing the Uberti houses and banishing the Uberti descendants.

SIGHTS

Piazza Farinata degli Uberti★
In the city centre, S of Via del Giglio.
This **square** is one of the few surviving parts of the old town and its name commemorates **Farinata degli Uberti**, who persuaded the Ghibelline parliament assembled in Empoli in 1260 to spare Florence from destruction. The

▶ **Population:** 48,795.

⚲ **Michelin Map:** Michelin Atlas p 37 and Map 563 – K 14 and Map 735 Fold 14.

▯ **Info:** Via Ridolfi 70, at MuVe – Museo del Vetro, ℱ0571 76 714. www.toscananelcuore.it.

▷ **Location:** Empoli lies in the fertile plain of the lower Arno Valley approximately 30km/19mi W of Florence on the Florence–Pisa motorway (*superstrada* Firenze–Pisa).

⚘ **Don't Miss:** A walk around Piazza Farinata degli Uberti, then the Museo della Collegiata.

⚎ **Kids:** A visit to the glass museum, Museo del Vetro.

square is surrounded by a portico and decorated with a large central fountain erected in the 19C. Opposite the collegiate church is the **Palazzo Ghibellini**, where the famous parliament met. The **Collegiata Sant'Andrea** has a delightful Romanesque **façade★**, built of white and green marble, which marks the westernmost limit of the use of the Florentine style. Only the lower arches are original. At the end of the tiny square to the right of the church is the **Museo della Collegiata★** (⊙*Open Tue–Sun 9am–noon, 4–7pm;* ⊙*Closed public hols;* ⊜*€3.10 combined with MuVe – Museo del Vetro; free admission Sun afternoons;* ℱ*0571 76 284*), which contains a superb collection of 14C–17C paintings and sculptures. There is a **fresco★** representing a Pietà by Masolino da Panicale, works by Filippo Lippi and Lorenzo Monaco, sculptures by Bernardo and Antonio Rossellino and painted terracotta pieces by Andrea della Robbia (*upper floor in the cloisters*).

The visit continues with a guided tour of the **Church of Santo Stefano**, built by the Augustinians in the 14C in the Gothic style and reconstructed after World War II. It contains a reredos (*first chapel in the north aisle*) by Bicci di Lorenzo of St Nicholas of Tolentino protecting Empoli from the Black Death; an emotive fresco (*tympanum of the door into the sacristy*) by Masolino of the Madonna and Child; an Annunciation (*Mercy Chapel near the sacristy*) by Bernardo Rossellino; and traces of other frescoes by Masolino (*1st chapel in the south aisle*).

♁♁ MuVe – Museo del Vetro

Via Ridolfi 70. ◷*Open Tue–Sun 10am –7pm.* ◷*Closed Mon.* ◉€3.10 combined with Museo della Collegiata. *✆0571 76 714. www.museodelvetrodiempoli.it.*
The ancient Magazzino del Sale (warehouse for salt, mainly from Volterra) in 2010 became a glass museum, one of the town's most important industries, especially in the 19C and 20C. Multimedia displays show ancient and modern phases of production.

EXCURSIONS

Pontorme
1km/0.5mi E. Take the narrow street to the left of the Florence road.
This village was the birthplace of the painter Jacopo Carrucci, better known as **Il Pontormo**. The tiny brick Church of San Michele contains two Saints painted by the artist. There is also the **Pontormo House Museum** (*Via Pontorme 97;* ◷*Open Thu–Fri 10am–1pm, Sat–Sun and public hols 4–7pm;* ◉*free admission; ✆0571 99 43 46; casapontormo.it*).

Montelupo Fiorentino
7.5km/4.5mi E of Empoli.

The modern-looking village is the site of the **Museo Archeologico** (*Via S. Lucia;* ◷*Open Apr–Oct Fri 2–6pm, Sat 9am–1pm, Nov–Mar Fri–Sat 9am–1pm; other days by appointment; ✆0571 54 15 47*) and the **Museo della Ceramica★** (*Piazza Vittorio Veneto 10/11;* ◷*Open Mon 2–7pm, Tue–Sun and public hols 10am–7pm (Thu also 9–11pm);* ◷*Closed 1 Jan, Easter Sun, 1 May, 25–26 Dec;* ◉€5; free first Sun of the month; ♿; *✆0571 51 352; www.museomontelupo.it*) housing archaeological exhibits from Prehistory to the Middle Ages and a fine set of ceramics produced in Montelupo between the 14C and the end of the 18C.

Castelfiorentino
18km/11.8mi S of Empoli on SS429.
This town, whose name means Florentine Castle, became the property of the Bishop of Florence in the 12C. It was here that Siena and Florence signed the peace treaty after the Battle of Montaperti in 1260.

From **Piazza Gramsci**, a large square, the Siena road leads to the brick-fronted **Church of San Francesco** and then to the **Church of Santa Verdiana** (*18C Florentine frescoes; museum has works by Tuscan masters of the Middle Ages and Renaissance*), one of the most significant examples of early 18C architecture in Tuscany, standing at the end of a superb esplanade of trees.

In the centre of the village, the **BE-GO Museo Benozzo Gozzoli** (*Via Testaferrata;* ◷*Open Mon and Fri 9am–1pm, Tue and Thu 4–7pm, Sat–Sun and public hols 10am–noon, 4–7pm;* ◷*Closed Wed, 1 Jan, Easter Sun, 25 Dec;* ◉€3; ♿ *✆0571 64 448; www.museobenozzogozzoli.it*) is a small art collection worth visiting because it contains **frescoes★** and underdrawings for frescoes (*sinopie,* ◐*See PISA, p255*) by **Benozzo Gozzoli** (1420–97). The painter's style is remarkably well represented both in the frescoes of the Madonna della Tosse Tabernacle, which depict the Virgin Mary, St John and Two Saints, the Funeral of the Virgin Mary and the Assumption, and in the frescoes from the Visitation Tabernacle.

Montecatini Terme★

and Around

The therapeutic quality of the spring water here has been famous for centuries. Recommended for metabolic disorders, liver, stomach and intestinal complaints and rheumatism; numerous therapies are used but the most common form of treatment is drinking the water straight from the spring. The spa pools generally are for physical therapy rather than swimming. The mud packs are used to sooth aches and pains. The town makes for an enjoyable break – with parks, entertainment and a race track. Though the Romans were aware of the town's thermal waters, it was an unpleasant, mosquito-infested place until the late 18C, when the Grand Duke of Tuscany commissioned drainage improvement projects. Montecatini's heyday was in the 1920s, when many of the current facilities were built or enlarged, all in the Art Nouveau style, keeping alive its past architectural glamour.

▶ **Population:** 20,673.
Michelin Map: Michelin Atlas p 37 and Map 563 – K 14 and Map 735 Fold 14.
Info: Viale Verdi 66/68, ℘0572 77 22 44. www.montecatini. turismo.toscana.it.
Location: Between Florence and Lucca on the motorway (*autostrada* Firenze–*mare*).
Don't miss: Art Nouveau spa facilities and Montecatini Alto.
Time: 3hrs for a leisurely stroll, more for spa treatments.
Kids: Castello Garzoni Garden, Butterfly House and Parco di Pinocchio in Collodi.

SIGHTS

Accademia d'Arte

1.5km/1mi N of city centre. Viale Diaz 6. ↝Temporarily closed for restoration at the time of publication. &.
This **art** gallery contains sculptures by Dupré, a dramatic fresco by Pietro Annigoni (*Life*), personal souvenirs of Verdi and Puccini and other works.

Terme

From the town centre, follow Viale Giuseppe Verdi.
Terme Tettuccio was the most lavish of Montecatini's baths. In 1300 known as Bagno Nuovo, a canopy was added in 1370, and in 1417 Ugolino of Montecatini wrote about its healing properties. The building went up in 1779–81 at the request of Grand Duke Pietro Leopoldo, with significant revisions that were inaugurated in 1928. Designed as

GETTING THERE

Montecatini's popularity with Florentines makes it easy to reach by **train** on the Florence–Lucca–Viareggio line, arriving at Piazza Italia, or by **bus**, which serves Florence, Montecatini, Empoli and Pontedera. The historic 1898 *funicolare* (cable car) at Viale Diaz 22 makes for an easy, fun connection uphill to Montecatini Alto. ◦€4 one–way, €7 round trip. www.funicolare-montecatini.it.

a mini-city with piazzas, walks, a park and a ground plan based on Roman spas in neo-16C style, Tettuccio was built with Monsummano travertine. Galleria delle Bibite, the drinking hall, has 1,927 lovely ceramic panels by Basilio Cascella. A grand piano on the stage platform is under the dome of Tribuna della Musica. The pavilion **Tamerici★**, a 19C Art Nouveau treasure, hosts temporary exhibitions.

EXCURSIONS

Montecatini Alto

5km/3mi NE on SS633.

Pinocchio, the Little Wooden Puppet

Since the 19C the story of Pinocchio has achieved international recognition, due in particular to numerous film adaptations, including Walt Disney's version in 1940. This outstanding classic of Italian children's literature is much more than a children's tale, however; it depicts life among the Italian provincial poor, imbued with resignation and pessimism. Indeed, the original story is far darker than the movies suggest.

This is a small but elegant hillside village overlooking the Nievole Valley. A 1315 meeting between Ghibellines Uguccione della Faggiuola from Lucca and Castruccio Castracani from Pisa led to an alliance that defeated the Guelfs of Florence. **Piazza Giusti** is pretty with its medieval tower known as Casa di Ugolino, coats of arms, homes and cafés.

Monsummano Terme

4km/2.5mi SE on SS435 to SP14.
Poet Giuseppe Giusti (1809–50) is remembered in his birthplace at **Casa Giusti museum** (*Viale Martini 18;* ○*Open Wed–Mon 8am–2pm, 3–6pm;* ○*Closed Tue;* ∞*free admission;* ℘*0572 95 09 60; www.polomusealetoscana.beniculturali.it*).
Grotta Giusti Spa (℘*0572 90 771; www.grottagiustispa.com*) offers therapeutic treatments in a large thermal cave.

Pescia

10km/6mi W on SS435.
Historically the main town in the Nievole Valley, Pescia was the object of dispute among Lucca, Pisa and Florence for many years. The 12C town, founded to link the routes across the Apennines, is now famous for horticulture and its huge biennial flower show.
Porta Fiorentina is a gate that was built in 1732 in honour of Gian Gastone de' Medici. The **Duomo** is an old parish **church**, built in 857, and seat of

the bishop since 1726. The bell tower is massive.
Opposite is the church of Santa Maria Maddalena. The church Sant'Antonio Abate has a 13C wooden carving of the *Deposition from the Cross* and frescoes attributed to Bicci di Lorenzo (1373–1452).
The San Francesco **church** altarpiece depicts St Francis of Assisi, who visited Pescia in 1211, and illustrations of his life by Bonaventura Berlinghieri, c. 1235. Also worthy of note is the *St Anne Triptych*, the *Martyrdom of St Dorothy* and Brunelleschi's Cardini Chapel dating from the 15C. The monastery buildings are now law courts. Opposite is the 18C **Affiliati Theatre**.
Palazzo del Vicario, on the opposite side of the river, is a 12C building on the corner of Piazza Mazzini that has an attractive façade decorated with coats of arms. Its council chambers are open to the public and display the banner of Pescia surmounted by a dolphin, the municipal symbol.
On the other side of the square stands the 1447 **Oratory of Santi Pietro e Paolo**, also called the **Cappella della Madonna di Piè di Piazza**. The gilded wooden ceiling painted with a fresco of the Virgin dates from the 15C.

▷ Continue towards Piazza Obizzi.

San Stefano e San Niccolao

The church has been here since 1068. Palazzo del Podestà, also called Palagio, now houses the **Gipsoteca Libero Andreotti** (○*Open Fri 3–6pm, Sat–Sun 10am–12.30pm, 4–7.30pm; other days by appointment.* ♿ ℘*0572 49 00 57 or 0572 49 22 57; www.comune.pescia.pt.it*), with 230 works by Andreotti, the local sculptor.

Collodi★

3.5km/2mi W of Pescia on SS435.
Everything in this town set among rural hills relates to the famous puppet **Pinocchio**, a storybook character created by Carlo Lorenzini (1826–90). The author chose the village where his mother was born for his pen name.

♣ Castello Garzoni Garden★★ and Butterfly House

🕐 *Open daily Mar 9am–5.30pm, Apr–Oct 9am–7pm; low season (7 Jan–Feb, Nov–Dec) Sat–Sun and public hols 10am–sunset (daily 21 Dec–6 Jan).* 🎟 *€13; €22 combined with Parco di Pinocchio (€10; €18 in low season).* 🖉 *0572 42 73 14. www.pinocchio.it.*
Exuberant Italian Baroque landscaping of these highly formal 17C **gardens★★** includes terraced flowerbeds. The 18C **castello**, built by the Marquesses of Garzoni, lords of Collodi, has the kitchen where Lorenzini, the chef's nephew, began writing *Pinocchio*.
Hundreds of colourful tropical or equatorial butterflies and moths live freely in the **Butterfly House**.

♣ Parco di Pinocchio★

Signposted. 🕐 *Same opening hours as Castello Garzoni Garden.* 🎟 *€13; €22 combined with Castello Garzoni Garden and Butterfly House (€12; €18 in low season).* ♿ 🖉 *0572 42 93 42. www.pinocchio.it.*
Inspired by the story of Pinocchio, this park is situated in a pine wood on the banks of the tumbling Pescia near the Villa Garzoni. Laid out in a winding trail its panels recount episodes from the puppet's adventures, illustrated at intervals by bronze sculptures. On one, the path enters the jaws of the enormous shark that swallowed Geppetto. The trail ends in the Laboratory of Speech and Figures, hosting temporary exhibitions evoking the adventures of Pinocchio.

ADDRESSES

🏠 STAY

🛏 **Good to know:** Keep in mind that for all spa hotels, if you wish spa treatments, it may be more economical to book a package of treatments and/or meals. Almost all will accommodate special diets. Some hotels have their own spa facilities, some share with other hotels, and others book directly with the Terme. Many visitors use these spa hotels as an economical base to see Florence and Siena, but few offer spa treatments in the evenings, so you may wish to plan on a half day here.

⊜⊜ **Villa Le Magnolie** – *Viale Fedeli 13,* 🖉 *0572 91 17 00. 6 rooms.* This charming villa has all comforts and a lovely garden.

⊜⊜⊜⊜ **Grand Hotel & La Pace** – *Via della Torretta 1.* 🖉 *0572 92 40. www.grandhotellapace.it. 130 rooms. Restaurant*⊜⊜⊜⊜. The hotel offers spa treatments on the premises, set in a park with outdoor pool and clay tennis courts.

⊜⊜⊜⊜ **Grand Hotel Plaza and Locanda Maggiore** – *Piazza del Popolo 7.* 🖉 *0572 75 831. www.hotelplaza.it. 100 rooms.* Modern hotel with a historic section. Spa treatments are at Excelsior Hotel and at Grotta Giusti.

🍴 EAT

⊜⊜ **La Cantina di Pinocchio** – *Piazza della Pace 2, Collodi.* 🖉 *0572 42 86 34 or 339 83 11 766. www.lacantinadipinocchio.it.* Friendly family pizzeria-trattoria; traditional Tuscan fare.

⊜⊜⊜ **Ristorante Caffè Giusti** – *Piazza Giuseppe Giusti 24, Montecatini Alto, 5km/3mi NE of Montecatini Terme.* 🖉 *0572 70 186. www.cafferistorantegiusti.it.*
Gaze at medieval towers or people outdoors. Innovative, traditional cooking.

⊜⊜⊜ **La Torre** – *Piazza Giuseppe Giusti 8/9, Montecatini Alto, 5km/3mi NE of Montecatini Terme.* 🖉 *0572 70 650. Closed Tue.* Authentic family cooking, served for over 40 years on this square. Good wines.

⊜⊜⊜⊜ **La Pecora Nera** – *Via San Martino 18.* 🖉 *0572 70 331. www. ercoliniesavi.it.* Murano glass chandeliers and elegant period flooring provide a contrast to the fresh, contemporary-style decor of this restaurant. Imaginative cuisine with a focus on fish dishes.

TAKING A BREAK

Gelateria L'Altromare – *Viale Adua 3a/b.* 🖉 *320 24 32 416.* Few but authentic ice cream flavours. The custard is delicious.

Terme Tettuccio Bar – *Viale Verdi 41, inside the thermal complex, accessible by entry to baths only.* 🖉 *0572 77 81. www. termemontecatini.it.* A lovely bar for a drink, delicate apple strudel or light lunch.

SHOPPING

Bargilli – *Viale Grocco 2.* 🖉 *0572 79 459. www.cialdedimontecatini.it.* Almond cakes (*cialde*) have been the speciality since 1936.

Pistoia★★

The very industrial town of Pistoia has a surprisingly old town centre with one of the most delightful medieval squares in Italy. The town is particularly proud of its 12C religious buildings, dating from the days when it was a free borough and enjoyed its greatest period of prosperity, generated by its merchants and bankers. Set in the foothills of the Apennines, the town hosts a Bear Joust and a Blues Festival.

▶ **Population:** 90,358.

Michelin Map: Michelin Atlas p 33 and Map 563 – K 14 or Map 735 Fold 14.

Info: Piazza del Duomo (Palazzo dei Vescovi), ℘0573 21 622. territorio.pistoia.it.

Location: Pistoia lies 36km/22mi from Florence.

Don't Miss: The birthplace of Leonardo da Vinci.

Timing: Half a day for Pistoia, plus a day excursion to Vinci.

Kids: A castle and Leonardo's fantastic inventions in Vinci, Zoo (Giardino Zoologico di Pistoia).

SIGHTS

Piazza del Duomo★★

This vast **square** is attractive for its size and the layout of its main buildings. The cathedral (*south side*) is preceded by its Baptistery and flanked by the bell tower and the old **Bishop's Palace** (*Palazzo dei Vescovi*).

Facing each other across the square are the town hall (*east*) linked to the cathedral by an archway and the Palazzo Pretorio (*west*). Set slightly back from the main line of buildings is the medieval **Cataline Tower**, named for the famous Roman conspirator who was killed in 62 BC beneath the walls of Pistoia, then a Roman fortress. Each year in July the square is the setting for the **Bear Joust** (*Giostra dell'Orso*). Competitors dress in 14C costume and the best horsemen from the four urban districts (*rioni*) of medieval Pistoia ride at full speed at the target, held by a dummy shaped like

a bear, and tilt at it with lances. In the adjacent square (*Piazza della Sala*) is the graceful **Pozzo del Leoncino**, a 15C well crowned by a lion cub (*leoncino*) resting its front left paw on the shield of Pistoia.

Cattedrale di San Zeno★★ (Duomo)

Open daily Apr–Oct 8.30am–7pm, Nov–Mar 8.30am–12.30pm, 3–5.30pm; Free admission to the cathedral; St James Altar €5 (audioguide included). ℘0573 25 095 or 334 16 89 419.

The **cathedral** of San Zeno was destroyed by fire in 1108 and rebuilt in

Cattedrale di San Zeno

© Alberto Masnovo/iStock

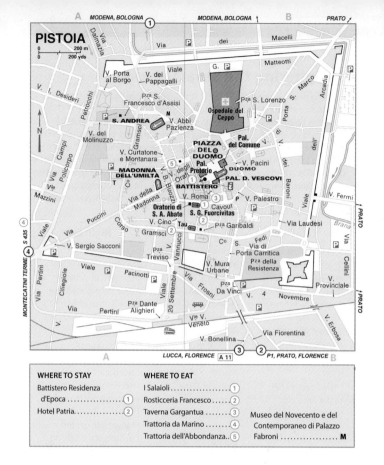

PISTOIA

Map legend and labels (as shown on map):

MODENA, BOLOGNA · MODENA, BOLOGNA · PRATO
Via Macelli · dei · Via Matteotti
G. P · Pza S. Lorenzo · Via S. Marco · Porta · Arcadia
V. Porta al Borgo · V. dei Pappagalli · Viale
Pza S. Francesco d'Assisi · M · Ospedale del Ceppo
S. ANDREA · V. Abbi Pazienza
V. del Molinuzzo · PIAZZA DEL DUOMO · Pal. del Comune
V. Curtatone e Montanara · Pal. Pretorio · DUOMO · V. Pacini
MADONNA DELL'UMILTÀ · Orat. degli · BATTISTERO · PAL. D. VESCOVI
Via della Madonna · V. Roma · V. Palestro · V. Fermi
Oratorio di S. A. Abate · Cavour · S. G. Fuorcivitas
V. Cino · Tau · Pza Garibaldi · Via Laudesi · Brana
Gramsci · Co · Fedi · Via di · Porta Carritica
Pza Treviso · V. Mura Urbane · Pza della Resistenza
Pacinotti · Via Frosni · Pza Da Vinci · V. 4 Novembre · V. Provinciale
Pza Dante Alighieri · 20 Settembre · Vle V. Veneto
V. Bonellina · Via Fiorentina
LUCCA, FLORENCE · A 11 · P1, PRATO, FLORENCE
MONTECATINI TERME S 435 · PRATO

the 12C–13C but major alterations continued until the 17C.

The marble-clad **west front★** is a delightful combination of the very austere Pisan Romanesque style and the Florentine Renaissance style. The three upper tiers were added in 1300. The strange **bell tower** (almost 70m/227ft high) also combines architectural styles, 13C–16C. The **interior** with its Romanesque nave and 17C Baroque chancel is most notable for the famous **St James Altar★★★** (*Dossale di San Jacopo*), an outstanding example of the silversmith's craft. Made of *repoussé* and embossed silver, the enormous altar includes 628 figures. The motifs are set around two large figures: St James (*sitting on a throne*) and Christ in Glory (*surrounded by cherubim and a choir of angels*). The front of the altar is covered with 12 episodes from the Life of Jesus and three scenes relating to St James.

The nine small panels (*right*) show episodes from the Old Testament but the depiction of the life of St James (*left*) is the most outstanding part of the work. The chapel (*left of the chancel*) contains a very fine **Virgin Mary in Majesty★**, a tranquil work in a subtle range of colours by Lorenzo di Credi – like Leonardo da Vinci, a pupil of Andrea del Verrocchio.

Battistero di San Giovanni in Corte

ⓘ *Open Jun–Sep daily 10am–6pm; Oct–May Wed–Mon 10am–1pm, 3–6pm; hours may vary.* ✆*Free admission.* ☎*334 16 89 419.*

This octagonal Gothic Baptistery (14C), clad in alternating strips of white and green marble, was designed by Andrea Pisano. The main entrance has a tympanum decorated with a Madonna and Child between St John the Baptist and St Peter; the statues are attributed

Deciphering the St James Altar

Weighing nearly a tonne, the St James Altar, dedicated to Pistoia's patron saint, is made almost entirely of silver. City elders commissioned the altar in 1287 in order to house a relic of St James that had been recovered from Santiago de Compostela in Spain, where the saint's remains are held. Work on the altar lasted almost 200 years and was carried out by numerous gold- and silversmiths, including Filippo Brunelleschi, to whom the figures of St Gregory and prophets Isaiah and Jeremiah are attributed. Because it took so long to complete, the altar contains Renaissance and Gothic stylistic elements. The altar consists of 628 figures, which were created using a *cire perdue* (lost wax) method, and scenes from the lives of Christ and his disciple, St James.

Left Side	Altar Front	Right Side
St James and his brother, St John the Evangelist, answer the call	Annunciation and Visitation of the Virgin Mary	Creation of Adam and Eve
Their mother, Mary Salome, recommends them to Jesus	Birth of Jesus	Original sin: Adam and Eve expelled from the Garden of Eden
St James' apostolic mission	Christ in Glory, between the Virgin Mary and St James	Cain's crime and punishment
St James preaching	Procession of the Three Kings	Construction of Noah's Ark
His arrest	Adoration of the Magi	Noah and his family receiving the divine blessing; Sacrifice of Isaac
Trial and conviction of the saint	Massacre of the Innocents	
St James baptises his accuser, who has been converted to Christianity	Judas' kiss	Moses receives the Tablets of the Law on Mount Sinai and gives the Law to the Hebrews
	Crucifixion	
Martyrdom of St James	The Women at the tomb	David receives the divine blessing and is crowned king
His followers take his body to Spain	Christ appears to St Thomas	
	Ascension	Birth and presentation of the Virgin Mary in the Temple
	Presentation of Jesus in the Temple	
	St James preaching	Marriage of the Virgin Mary
	Conviction of St James	
	Martyrdom of St James	
	On the sides – the Prophets	

to Andrea Pisano's two sons, Nino and Tommaso.

Below are small low-reliefs depicting the martyrdom of St John the Baptist, including the scene of Salomé presenting the saint's head that she requested on a platter.

Palazzo Pretorio

Formerly the Palazzo del Podestà, the palace was altered many times from the 14C–19C. The only traces that remain of the original building are the entrance, the Gothic double windows on the first floor and the staircase leading to the upper floor (*in the courtyard*).

Palazzo del Comune

This Gothic **town hall**, constructed 1294–1385, has a massive **façade★** over arcades facing the square. In the centre of the façade is the Medici coat of arms with its six balls.

The building was linked to the cathedral by an archway in 1637. Now the town hall, it also houses the **municipal museum**.

In the centre of the courtyard is a huge bronze sculpture (1953) from the *Miracoli* series, one of Marino Marini's most famous works.

The **Museo Civico** (🕐*Tue–Fri 10am–2pm, Sat–Sun and public hols 10am–6pm;* 🕐*Closed Mon;* ⊜*€3.50, €6 combined ticket with Museo dello Spedale del Ceppo and Palazzo Fabroni;* 👤*;* 📞*0573 37 12 14/96*) collection has 13C–19C paintings and sculptures. On the first floor are a St Francis surrounded by scenes illustrating his life and posthumous miracles and four large Renaissance altarpieces illustrating the theme of the Holy Conversation. Two of them are by Florentine artists Lorenzo di Credi and Ridolfo del Ghirlandaio.

Upstairs are mainly 17C–18C canvases including a Vision of St Jerome painted by Piero Paolini, who was strongly influenced by Caravaggio.

Palazzo dei Vescovi★
Museo di S. Zeno

Piazza del Duomo. 🕐*Open Thu–Tue 10am–6pm.* 🕐*Closed Wed and 25 Dec.* 🚶*Guided tours at 10.15am, 11.45am, 1.15pm, 3pm, 4.30pm.* ⊜*€5.* 📞*0573 28 782. www.fondazionepistoiamusei.it.*

The history of the **Bishop's Palace** (11C) and of the land, told through interesting remains of Roman town walls, remains from the Via Cassia, Etruscan funerary urns and Lombard vases, excavated during the palace restoration.

The tour includes a visit to the **cathedral museum** and a collection of church plate and vestments. See the **sacristy** from which the treasure was stolen in the 13C by Vanni Fucci, as told by Dante in Canto XXIV of his *Inferno*.

The **room★** contains frescoes by Giovanni Boldini (Ferrara 1842–Paris 1931) the Macchiaiolo painter, and the **Cappella San Niccolo** (13C) is also decorated with frescoes and bears inscriptions scratched on the walls by 15C prisoners when the chapel served as a jail.

Ospedale del Ceppo★

Piazza Giovanni XXIII 14. 🕐*Museum: open Tue–Fri 10am–2pm, Sat–Sun and public hols 10am–6pm.* 🕐*Closed Mon.* ⊜*€3.50.* 👤*.* 📞*0573 37 10 23.*

The name of this **hospital**, founded in 1277, means "hollow tree trunk" (*ceppo*), which was the vessel once used to receive offerings. Its portico is decorated with an admirable glazed terracotta **frieze★★**, which is one of the main sights of Pistoia. Created shortly before 1530 in the workshop of Giovanni della Robbia, the seven panels illustrate the *Seven Works of Mercy*. Between the panels are graceful female figures representing the Virtues of (*left to right*) Prudence, Faith, Charity, Hope and Justice. Medallions surrounded by garlands of leaves, fruit and flowers decorate the squinches between the arches. The Medici coat of arms has the chequered emblem of Pistoia beside it.

Sant'Andrea★

🕐*Open Tue–Sat 9am–1pm, 2–5pm, Sun 9–10am, 11.30am–4pm; hours may vary.* 🕐*Closed Mon.* ⊜*€2.50.* 📞*338 61 70 784.*

This attractive Pisan Romanesque **church** was built in the 8C but extensively altered in the 12C. The plain **interior★★** has a tall and narrow nave separated from the aisles by low arches with a narrow span. The columns are crowned by capitals with varied decorations.

A 15C marble niche carved with slender foliage (*beyond the first altar on the right*) contains a gilded wooden **Crucifix★** by Giovanni Pisano.

The most outstanding feature in the church is Pisano's **pulpit★★** 1298–1301. Designed to resemble the pulpits in the Baptistery in Pisa and the cathedral in Siena, the hexagonal pulpit is covered with five marble panels depicting (*from left to right*): the Annunciation and the Nativity; the Adoration of the Magi; the Massacre of the Innocents; the Crucifixion; and the Last Judgement.

Palazzo Fabroni – Museo del Novecento e del Contemporaneo

Via Sant'Andrea 18. 🕐*Open Tue–Fri 10am–2pm, Sat–Sun and public hols 10am–6pm.* 🕐*Closed Mon.* ⊜*€3.50; €6 combined ticket with Museo Civico and Museo dello Spedale del Ceppo.* 👤*.* 📞*0573 37 18 17. musei.comune.pistoia.it*

Madonna dell'Umiltà★

The huge dome of this octagonal basilica is reminiscent of Brunelleschi's dome in Florence. The Renaissance basilica was built to house the miraculous picture of the Virgin Mary of Humility, the patron saint of Pistoia.

San Giovanni Fuorcivitas

Via Cavour. Open 8.30am–noon (Sun 10–11am), 5.30–6.30pm; hours may vary. Free admission. 0573 24 784.

The 12C–14C Church of St John outside the walls has a north **wall★** with a long and spectacular striped façade overlooking Via Cavour.

The sombre basilica interior is without aisles or apse. Near the basin, carved partly by Giovanni Pisano, is an all-white glazed terracotta sculpture of the **Visitation★★** by Luca della Robbia. The severe yet beautiful 1270 **pulpit★** (*right-hand wall*) by Fra Guglielmo of Pisa has white marble panels depicting the Life of Jesus and the Virgin Mary. A polyptych shows Mary surrounded by saints by Taddeo Gaddi (14C).

Oratorio di Sant'Antonio Abate (near the church) was once connected to San Giovanni Fuorcivitas by an archway. Nearby is the **Church and Palace of Tau**.

Chiesa del Tau – Museo Marino Marini

Corso Silvano Fedi. Museum: open Tue–Sat 11am–6pm, Sun 2.30–7.30pm; hours may vary in Jul–Aug. Free admission to the church; museum €7; 0573 30 285. www.fondazionemarinomarini.it.

The word "Tau" refers to the letter "T" which appeared on the tunics and cloaks of monks of the Order of Hospitallers of St Anthony, who lived here in the 14C. The small 14C church (deconsecrated since the 18C) is known for its Gothic **frescoes★** painted by local artists.

The former monastery now houses the documentation centre dedicated to **Marino Marini** (1901-80). It was set up with a donation from the sculptor himself and contains sculptures, drawings, lithographs and etchings by the artist who is well known for his sense of movement and the dramatic tension in his work.

🚗 DRIVING TOURS

LEONARDO COUNTRYSIDE TOUR

25km/15.5mi. See map pp186–187.

▶ From Piazza Leonardo da Vinci, take Via C. Battisti, then left to SS9 towards Empoli, follow signs to Vinci, then San Baronto and Mont Albano.

Vinci★

It was near this village, not far from Monte Albano, that the genius Leonardo da Vinci was born in 1452. The gentle and harmonious **landscape★★** of silver-leafed olive groves, vineyards, terraced plots and hills on the horizon is enhanced by transparent light.

Perched on the hillside of this medieval village is the 11C **castle** of the Counts Guidi, now one of the exhibition sites of **Museo Leonardiano★** (*ticket office in Piazza Leonardo da Vinci 26;* Open daily 9.30am–7pm (Nov–Feb 6pm); €11 (includes Casa Natale in Anchiano); 0571 93 32 51; www.museoleonardiano.it). It contains a collection of about 100 **models of machinery** recently built to the artist's plans and designs and exhibited on three floors.

Among the models built according to the artist's innovative vision are a mechanical wing, a helicopter, a clock mechanism, a tank, a bronze smelting kiln, a speed gauge for wind or water, a spotlight and a ventilator, a bicycle, rack-and-pinion steering, a diver's breathing apparatus and a parachute. The second floor features temporary exhibits inspired by Leonardo's drawings and a small auditorium.

The house thought to have been his **birthplace** is in **Anchiano** (**Casa Natale**; *2.5km/1mi to the N of Vinci on the road to S Lucia and Faltognano; car park 50m/54yd;* Open daily 10am–7pm (Nov–Feb 5pm); €11 (includes Museo Leonardiano in Vinci); 0571 93 32 48; www.museoleonardiano.it) and has a few 15C features: the fireplace, the stone sink, the family coat of arms in the main room and the paving in the lower room.

Halfway from Vinci and Anchiano, the historic estate Villa del Ferrale displays

Leonardo da Vinci (1452–1519)

Leonardo was an illegitimate child, who took his name from the village of Vinci, where he was born. He was a creative genius whose "gaze was four centuries ahead of its time". Very early on in life, he showed a gift for drawing, painting and science. In 1469 he travelled to Florence where he studied painting with Verrocchio. Florence did not, however, enable him to exploit his many talents and in 1482, he moved to Milan. There he entered the service of Ludovico il Moro and worked in every conceivable sector as painter, sculptor, civil and military engineer, hydraulics engineer, town planner, musician and organiser of festivities and special events. At the same time, he continued his research into human anatomy, water, air, bird flight, physics and mechanical engineering. In 1499, owing to the fall of Ludovico il Moro, he was forced to leave Milan. Eventually, in 1516, after extensive travels, he found a patron worthy of his enormous intelligence, François I of France. He died in Amboise, France, in 1519.

the museum section "**Leonardo and Painting**" (*included in the ticket price*): full scale, HD reproductions of all Leonardo's paintings and of some of his drawings.

Cerreto Guidi★

This village grew up around the castle that once belonged to the Counts Guidi, which passed into the hands of the Medici family, and was totally rebuilt by Cosimo I, c. 1560. It was used as a hunting lodge for the Medici and their courtiers, but fell into decline after the tragic death of Cosimo I's daughter, Isabella Orsini, Duchess of Bracciano. The villa has since been restored to its 16C glory.

Villa Medicea★

Via dei Ponti Medicei, 7. ⏱*Open Mon–Sat 10am–6pm (Apr–Sept 9am), Sun 10am–7pm.* ⏱*Closed 2nd and 3rd Mon of the month, 1 Jan, 25 Dec.* ✒*Free admission.* ☎*0571 55 707. www.polomusealetoscana.beniculturali.it.*
Buontalenti designed this austere hilltop **villa**. The approach is embellished by two majestic, monumental flights of brick steps, known as the *ponti*. The terrace affords a wonderful view of the Arno Valley hills and (*left*) of San Miniato and its high tower.
The entrance hall is hung with portraits (*right*) of Isabella Orsini and her husband and (*left*) of Bianca Cappello, wife of Francesco I Medici. On the first floor is the Medici portrait gallery. From the balcony (*loggia*), there is a delightful view of the garden and its pergola.

TUSCAN-EMILIAN APENNINES
55km/34.1mi. 👜*See map pp186–187.*

▶ From Pistoia take the road towards Bologna, then SS66.

San Marcello Pistoiese★

Alt 650m/2 112ft. 20km/12mi SE.
The largest town in the Pistoia mountains is set amidst beautiful scenery. The district is home to the interesting hamlet of **Gavinana**, where, on 3 August 1530, the militiamen of the Republic of Florence, under the command of Francesco Ferrucci, valiantly resisted the troops of the Emperor Charles V. The battle is recalled in the nearby **Museo Ferrucciano** (⚰ *closed for restoration at the time of publication;* ☎*0573 63 80 37*).
Nearby in Pian de' Termini is an **observatory** (*Osservatorio Astronomico;* ⏱*Open by reservation: Tue and Sun mornings in summer; Tue and Thu mornings in winter; Fri and Sat evenings (also Mon in summer);* ☎*0573 62 12 89; www.gamp-pt.net*).
In **Mammiano** is a recently restored 1922 **suspended bridge**, which crosses the Lima River and was forged in metal foundries in villages on the opposite bank.

▶ 14km/9mi SE.

Cutigliano★

Alt 670m/2 178ft.
Cutigliano, a delightful village built in terraces up the northern slopes of the Lima Valley, has become one of Tuscany's main

winter sports resorts, owing to the **Doga-naccia cable car**.

Historic buildings here include the **Palazzo Pretorio**. Its façade is decorated with the coats of arms of the 14C–18C Captains of the Mountain who held legal and administrative authority over Cutigliano and the neighbouring hamlets. The church, known as the **Madonna di Piazza** (Our Lady on the Square) contains a superb altar front by Andrea della Robbia.

▷ Leave Cutigliano North via SP37, then SS12.

Abetone

Occupying an attractive setting in the Tuscan Apennines, Abetone is one of the most famous winter resorts in central Italy. The mountain pass is indicated by two pyramid-shaped stones that serve as a reminder of the old border between the Grand Duchies of Tuscany and Modena. "Abetone" refers to a giant pine that was chopped down in the 18C to create the Ximenes–Giardini road.

ADDRESSES

⌂STAY

⊜⊜⊜ **Battistero Residenza d'Epoca** – *Vicolo dei Fuggiti 4.* ✆ *0573 07 92 20.* *www.residenzabattistero.it. 13 rooms.* ⌂. *Restaurant*⊜⊜⊜ A small modern design hotel in Pistoia centre. Good restaurant.

⊜⊜⊜ **Hotel Patria** – *Via Crispi 8/12.* ✆ *0573 35 88 00. www.patriahotel.com. 27 rooms.* 17C *palazzo* in Pistoia centre, comfortable.

⑂/EAT

⊜⊜⊜ **Trattoria da Marino** – *Via Provinciale Lucchese 102, Ponte Di Serravalle, 10km/6mi SW of Pistoia* ✆ *0573 510 42. www.trattoriadamarino.com. Closed Tue.* The cuisine of this welcoming trattoria focuses on regional specialities with the occasional updated twist, such as *tortelli* with a shellfish ragù. The steak (one of the more expensive options) is excellent, while the generous desserts, especially the "Trionfo", are well worth a photo.

⊜⊜⊜ **I Salaioli** – *Piazza della Sala 2.* ✆ *0573 20 225. www.isalaioli.it.* High-quality contemporary cuisine, with cheeses and charcuterie from the best producers in the area, and excellent wines!

⊜⊜⊜ **Trattoria dell'Abbondanza** – *Via dell'Abbondanza 10/14.* ✆ *0573 36 80 37. www.trattoriadellabbondanza.it. Closed Wed. Reservations suggested.* The cuisine here showcases regional traditions, with particular attention paid to the carefully chosen ingredients. Welcoming atmosphere, young and enthusiastic staff.

TAKING A BREAK

Rosticceria Francesco – *Corso Gramsci 10.* ✆ *0573 22 216. www.rosticceriafrancesco.it. Closed Sun afternoon, Mon.* Popular little *trattoria*, delicious Tuscan specialities.

Taverna Gargantua – *Piazzetta dell'Ortaggio 12.* ✆ *0573 23 330. www.tavernagargantua.com.* Popular taverna for an aperitif with slices of cold meats, fish or cheese; or for a quick dinner.

SHOPPING

Visit **markets** at Piazza della Sala for fruits and vegetables (except Sun); Piazza del Duomo holds its general market Wed and Sat mornings.

Bruno Corsini – *Piazza San Francesco 42.* ✆ *0573 20 138. www.brunocorsini.com. Closed Sun.* Famous sweets shaped like hedgehogs (*riccio*), a speciality that dates from 1372.

Galleria Vittorio Emanuele – *Via degli Orafi 54/56.* This Liberty-style building now houses a shopping centre.

SPORT AND LEISURE

▲⁑ **Giardino Zoologico di Pistoia** – *Via di Pieve a Celle Nuova 160a, 4km/2.5mi W of Pistoia. Bus 59 from Pistoia railway station.* ✆ *0573 91 12 19. www.zoodipistoia.it.* An oasis in a green valley committed to conservation and educational activities. Among the animals you can see bears, red pandas, capybaras, lemurs, gibbons…

EVENTS

Giostra dell'Orso – *Piazza del Duomo. 25 Jul.* The best horsemen of the four medieval districts of Pistoia compete in a traditional jousting contest in which they try to spear a bear-shaped target (*orso*).

Pistoia Blues – *www.pistoiablues.com.* A week-long musical festival featuring major international blues acts.

Prato★

Despite the peaceful atmosphere and provincial air of the central districts, Prato is the fourth-largest city in central Italy after Rome, Florence and Livorno. It is also one of the busiest and most highly industrialised. Its traditional wool industry was already producing cloth famous throughout Europe in the 13C. Today, it specialises in man-made fibres and fabrics, as well as "recycled" wools. Prato has the second-largest Chinese population after Milan, many employed in the garment industry. Less attractive upon approach, its centre merits a visit for a charming cluster of Medieval and Renaissance treasures.

▶ **Population:** 194,590.
Michelin Map: 563 – K 15 or Map 735 Fold 14.
Info: Piazza del Comune (Palazzo Pretorio), ℘0574 24 112. www.pratoturismo.it.
Location: Prato is situated only 17km/10.6mi from Florence and is easily reached either by A1 Bologna–Firenze or by the Firenze–*mare* motorway.
Don't Miss: Frescoes by Filippo Lippi in the Duomo, harmonious lines of Santa Maria delle Carceri, and the air of intrigue in the Medici villas. The Virgin Mary's Holy Girdle (Sacro Cingolo), which is unveiled several times a year in Prato's Duomo.

SIGHTS

The main sights all lie within the fortified town walls built in the 14C, beyond which the town did not extend until the beginning of the 20C.

The Pratomusei card (€16) is valid for 3 days and gives unlimited access to Prato's main museums for information visit: www.prato-musei.it/en/card.

Cattedrale di Santo Stefano★★ (Duomo)

Frescoes in the Duomo: open Mon and Wed–Sat 10am–1pm, 2–5pm, Sun and public hols 2–5pm.
Closed Tue. Free admission to the church; €8 frescoes and Museo dell'Opera del Duomo. ℘0574 29 339. diocesiprato.it.

The **cathedral**, which was built mainly in the 12C and 13C, then considerably extended in the 14C and the 15C, is a harmonious combination of Romanesque and Gothic styles.

The elegant Gothic façade, which has an unusually tall central section, is partly clad in green marble and white stone. The famous corner **pulpit** has a fanshaped canopy which was probably designed by in the early 15C so that the Holy Girdle could be shown to the con-

---

During the Time of the Communes

Prato, which means "meadow", was originally the name of one of the districts which grew up outside the walls around a vast expanse of land used for markets. In the 11C this district dominated the others. The town belonged to the Alberti, who were named Counts of Prato by the Holy Roman Emperor and who later possessed land throughout northern Tuscany. In the middle of the 12C the town became a free, democratically governed borough. In 1351, after many years of internal dissension and opposition to Florence in the rivalry between the Guelfs and Ghibellines, Prato came under Florentine rule until the end of the 18C. Prato was also a major centre of artistic activity, attracting famous architects, sculptors and painters, who left a heritage of fine buildings and art. It was the birthplace of **Filippino Lippi** (1457/8–1504), the son of Filippo, and more recently, of the writer, Curzio Malaparte, who built the famous red villa on Capri.

gregation. Donatello, in whose studio Michelozzo was then employed, carved some remarkable decorative panels for the pulpit. The present panels are copies of the originals.

A glazed terracotta Madonna and Child by Andrea della Robbia (1489) surmounts the entrance.

The **interior** is laid out with massive green marble columns supporting Romanesque arches emphasised by alternating strips of light and dark stone. **Holy Girdle Chapel** was built in the late 14C to house the precious relic. The two very elegant bronze **screens★** are decorated with roses, cherubim and animals. Between 1392 and 1395 Agnolo Gaddi and his pupils covered the walls of the chapel with frescoes. On the altar is the exquisite, tiny marble statue of the **Madonna and Child★** known as the *Madonna della Cintola*

carved by Giovanni Pisano towards the end of his life in 1317.

The marble **pulpit★** (*left-hand side*), shaped like a chalice, is by Mino da Fiesole and Antonio Rossellino (1473).

The touching **Virgin Mary with the Olive★** (*Madonna dell'Ulivo*) (*end on the right-hand side*), set in a niche, is a terracotta statue made by Benedetto da Maiano (1480).

The **frescoes★★** are one of Filippo Lippi's most accomplished works (1452–65). His mature talent portrays the lives of St Stephen and St John the Baptist.

His famous **Herod's Feast★★★** shows **Salome's Dance** with the same undulating lines, melancholic gentleness and ethereal grace that can be seen in the finest female figures painted by Botticelli, Lippi's famous pupil.

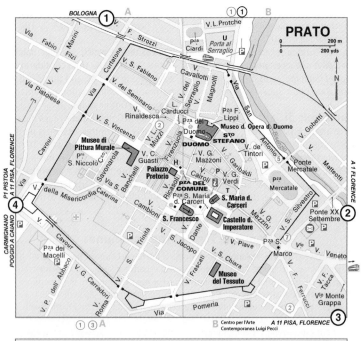

WHERE TO STAY	
Bed & Breakfast Villa Rucellai	(1)
Borgo al Cornio	(2)
Hotel Paggeria Medicea – Tenuta di Artimino	(3)
Hotel San Marco	(7)

WHERE TO EAT	
Biagio Pignatta	(1)
Il Piraña	(2)
Osteria Cibbè	(5)

The Bocchineri Chapel is decorated with 15C **frescoes★** begun c. 1436 by Paolo Uccello, and completed by Andrea di Giusto, a Florentine contemporary.

Museo dell'Opera del Duomo

Piazza Duomo 49. ⏲*Same opening hours as the frescoes in the Duomo.* 🎟€8 (includes the frescoes). ☎0574 29 339. www.diocesiprato.it/museo-dellopera-del-duomo.

The **Cathedral Museum** rooms are set out around a courtyard flanked on one side by the **arches★** of delightful little Romanesque cloisters where the white marble of Carrara and the green marble of Prato form charming geometric motifs above graceful white columns crowned by attractively carved capitals. A room off the courtyard contains the seven original **panels★** from the outdoor pulpit. Carved 1428–1438 by Donatello and his pupils, they depict an exquisite circle of children dancing. Also, a coffer in the shape of a temple decorated with cherubim is a superb piece of Renaissance goldsmiths' work designed to hold the Holy Girdle, and a charming painting of St Lucy was painted by Filippino Lippi in his youth.

Palazzo Pretorio★

This tall, fortress-like building stands in **Piazza del Comune**, which has a graceful bronze fountain with Bacchus as a Child (*original in the Palazzo Pretorio*) by Ferdinando Tacca (1659). During the Middle Ages this was the residence of the Captain of the People (*Capitano del Popolo*) who held executive power.

It now hosts the **Museo di Palazzo Pretorio** (⏲*Open Wed–Mon 10.30am–6.30pm;* ⏲*Closed Tue (except public hols) and 25 Dec;* 🎟€8; ☎0574 24 112 or 0574 18 37 860; www.palazzopretorio.prato.it). The collection has 14C–15C Tuscan **polyptychs★**, two outstanding works by Bernardo Daddi including the Predella (1337) with seven scenes telling the story of the Holy Girdle, a polyptych by Giovanni de Milano, a triptych in brilliant "international Gothic" style attributed to Lorenzo Monaco, and the *Madonna del Ceppo* (1453) by Filippo

Lippi. A reconstruction was made of the small 1498 tabernacle destroyed in a bombing raid in 1944.

Palazzo Comunale

Piazza del Comune. ⏲*Open by reservation only.* 🎟*Free admission.* ♿ ☎0574 18 36 220.

This medieval building with its late-18C façade by Giuseppe Valentini houses the sumptuous municipal council salon, beautifully embellished with wood, and displays portraits of benefactors and governors (15C–19C).

Castello dell'Imperatore

🎟*Free admission.* ♿ ☎0574 38 207.

Frederick II constructed this mighty **imperial fortress** c. 1248 to strengthen the position of the Ghibelline faction. Its rigorous geometrical architecture and a square fortress layout around a central courtyard resembles other castles in Frederick's territory in the Holy Roman Empire and the Kingdom of Sicily, but is an anomaly in central and northern Italy.

Santa Maria delle Carceri

The **church** derives its name from a miraculous painting in the prison (*carcere*) that previously stood on this

© Claudio Giovanni Colombo/iStock

Bacchus as a Child (1659) fountain outside Palazzo Pretorio

site. The exterior early was never completed on this 15C church by Giuliano da Sangallo. The austere **interior** dispays geometric rigour and majestic proportions. *Pietra serena* contrasts with the light-coloured walls. Andrea della Robbia crafted a graceful frieze of glazed white and blue terracotta and four medallions of the Evangelists.

Museo di Pittura Murale

Piazza San Domenico 8.
⚬┅Temporarily closed for restoration at the time of publication. www. diocesiprato.it/museo-di-pittura-murale.

The cloister and Gothic Church of San Domenico leads to the museum, which displays detached frescoes from various churches around Prato. A Crucifix made by Filippino Lippi for the city of Prato was auctioned in 2010 at Christie's in New York.

Museo del Tessuto di Prato

Via Puccetti 3. ⓘ*Open Tue–Thu 10am–3pm, Fri–Sat 10am–7pm, Sun 3–7pm.* ⓘ*Closed Mon.* ◉*€8.* ℘*0574 61 15 03. www.museodeltessuto.it.*

The 19C Campolmi building is now a museum that traces the past and present textile industry in Prato, which today employs 40,000 workers in some 8,000 buildings. The museum can also direct you to factories that allow visitors.

San Francesco

Begun in the late 13C, the church's tall façade striated with green marble dates to the 14C and its triangular pediment to the Renaissance. The chapterhouse, **Migliorati Chapel**, is lit by a Gothic window opening into the small 15C cloisters. **Frescoes★** by Nicolò di Pietro Gerini, a Florentine influenced by Giotto, depict the lives of the Apostles.

EXCURSION

Centro per l'Arte Contemporanea Luigi Pecci

Viale della Repubblica 277. Bus LAM Blu departing also from the station. ⓘ*Open Tue–Thu and Sun 10am–8pm, Fri–Sat 10am–11pm.* ⓘ*Closed Mon.* ◉*€10.* ℘*0574 53 17. www.centropecci.it.*

Back in the late 1980s the Associazione Centro per l'Arte Contemporanea Luigi Pecci has been the first Italian museum to have a building built from scratch for the presentation, collection, documentation and promotion of the most recent developments in art. The

---

An Artistic and Libertine Monk

While Fra Filippo Lippi (1406–69), then aged 50, was engaged in painting the Prato cathedral's frescoes, he made the acquaintance of and was captivated by the delightful Lucrezia Buti, a nun in the convent to which he was chaplain. He had entered Holy Orders at the age of 15 but later left his monastery. He was captured by Barbary pirates and sold in Africa where his talents as an artist so amazed the Moors that they granted him his freedom. He returned to the monastic life until he fell in love with Lucrezia. Their son Filippino was born the following year. Despite the scandal, Cosimo the Elder obtained the Pope's permission for Lippi to be released from his vows. Filippo married Lucrezia, whose smooth, angular face and delicate blonde hair he used time and again in his paintings of the Madonna and Salome. His amorous ways may have been his undoing: reportedly poisoned by a jealous husband, Filippo died in Umbria, where his son Filippino designed his father's tomb in Spoleto's Duomo. A pupil of Lorenzo Monaco, Lippi was also strongly influenced by Masaccio. His paintings express grace and freshness. The main characteristics of this artist, who painted exclusively religious subjects, were his sincere inspiration, his natural, simplistic view, his pure lines and his subtle use of colours. In his early works Filippino used his father's style but his painting shows greater melancholy.

collection includes over 1000 works by more than 300 artists, among which: Andy Warhol, Aleksandra Mir, Vito Acconci, Sol LeWitt, Anish Kapoor, Mario Merz, Jannis Kounellis, VALIE EXPORT, Bruno Munari, Massimo Bartolini, Thomas Hirschhorn, Jan Fabre.

A lawn dotted with contemporary sculptures surrounds the building.

🚗DRIVING TOUR

1 FROM PRATO TO CARMIGNANO

From Prato, S on Via Roma continuing 9.5km/16mi on SP22 on a road that goes past olive groves and vineyards.
See regional map pp186–187.

Villa "Ambra" di Poggio a Caiano★★

Piazza de' Medici 14. ◷Park and garden: open daily Jun–Aug 8.15am–7.30pm, rest of the year 8.15am–1hr before dusk; last admission 1hr before closing; Monumental apartments: entry every hour from 8.30am; Museum of Still Life by reservation only: visits every hour from 9am, except 1pm. ◷Closed 2nd and 3rd Mon of the month, 1 Jan, 25 Dec. ⬡Free admission. ℰ055 87 70 12. www.polomusealetoscana. beniculturali.it.

Surrounded by pleasant gardens, the Villa of Poggio a Caiano was built in 1485 by Giuliano da Sangallo for Lorenzo the Magnificent.

Built to a plan by Giuliano da Sangallo, this was the first example of a real Tuscan villa rather than a refurbished fortress. The classical style emphasised symmetry, which became the hallmark of Renaissance villas.

Francesco I and his second wife **Bianca Cappello** died here in 1587, probably of poison. Pope Leo X (son of Lorenzo the Magnificent) commissioned the magnificent drawing room on the first floor, where there is a strange coffered ceiling and frescoes by Andrea del Sarto, Franciabigio, Alessandro Allori and Pontormo. The latter created the

delightful lunette fresco, based on a story from Ovid's *Metamorphoses*. Elisa Bonaparte is rumoured to have had an affair with the famed violinist Paganini when she lived here in the early 19C. King Victor-Emmanuel II also lived here during the short time when Florence was the capital of Italy.

Reserve in advance to see its **Museum of Still Life**, created in 2007 with some 100 works from the 16C to 18C, with special attention given to the lively compositions by painter Bartolomeo Bimbi (1648–1730).

▷ 5km/3.5mi S on SP45.

Etruscan Graves in Comeana★

◷*Open Mon–Sat 9am–2pm.*
◷*Closed Sun. ℰ055 87 19 741. www. parcoarcheologicocarmignano.it.*

Among these 7C BC graves is the **Tomba di Montefortini★** (*43 Via di Montefortini*) with a passage (*dromos*) (13m/43ft long) closed off by a stone slab (still visible) and a rectangular burial chamber. Unusual is the continuous bracket running along the top of the walls, which was used as a shelf for funeral articles. The **Boschetti Grave** (*near the cemetery, SW from Comeana on SP45, the Poggio–Caiano road towards Artimino*) is smaller.

Artimino

The area around the Artimino hill was inhabited in the Paleolithic era. In the 7C BC an Etruscan town was built on the site and probably gained prosperity because of its control of the natural trade routes along the Arno and Ombrone rivers.

Pieve di San Leonardo

Via della Chiesa, 19/A.
This Romanesque parish **church**, said to have been commissioned by Countess Matilda of Canossa in 1107, was partly built with materials from the Etruscan graveyard, including urns (some of them carved). The interior has a nave and two aisles with ogival vaulting.

▷ 26km/16mi west of Artimino.

Villa La Ferdinanda★

Via Papa Giovanni XXIII 1. *Private property, but open days and events are organized with guided tours to the villa and its garden.* *055 87 18 124. www.artimino.com/en/visit-villa-dei-cento-camini.*

Grand Duke Ferdinando I commissioned Buontalenti to design this vast **mansion** towards the end of the 16C. Its dominant position affords views south over the Arno Valley to Florence and north over Prato and Pistoia); the lawn is dotted with amusing metal statues.

Museo Archeologico

Piazza San Carlo 3. *Open Mar–Oct Mon–Tue and Thu–Fri 9.30am–1.30pm, Sat–Sun and public hols 9.30am–1.30pm, 3–6pm; closed Wed; Nov–Feb only Sat–Sun and public hols 9.30am–1.30pm, 2–4pm.* *€4.* *055 87 18 124. www.parcoarcheologicocarmignano.it.* Archaeological finds from the ancient **Etruscan** town include imported Greek vases, Etruscan buccheroware, coins, sculptures and tomb artefacts.

▶ 6km/4mi NW on SP45.

Carmignano

This small town, surrounded by vines and olive trees, is home to the 16C **Church of San Michele** (*free admission;* *055 87 12 046*). Inside is a splendid **Visitation★★** by **Pontormo**.

▶ SP44 then SS66 to return to Prato.

ADDRESSES

☞STAY

Borgo al Cornio – *Via Convenevole da Prato 30.* *347 78 04 653. www.borgoalcornio.com. 3 apartments.* Three small, economical two-roomed flats with kitchen in the centre of Prato, near the Duomo.

Hotel San Marco – *Piazza S Marco 48.* *0574 21 321. www.hotelsanmarco prato.com. 39 rooms.* Near the motorway, the railway station and the historic centre. The rooms are simply decorated and the buffet breakfast well-supplied.

Bed & Breakfast Villa Rucellai – *Via di Canneto 16, 4km/2.5mi NE of Prato towards Vaiano Verno.* *0574 46 03 92. www.villarucellai.com. 11 rooms.* Slightly old-fashioned 16C mansion has a garden with swimming pool, offering a bit of elegance at a reasonable price. Breakfast is served on the terrace or in the pretty dining room.

Hotel Paggeria Medicea – Tenuta di Artimino – *Viale Papa Giovanni XXXIII, Artimino. 21km/13mi SW of Prato.* *055 87 51 41. www.artimino. com.* P. *37 rooms.* In the grounds of Villa Ferdinanda enjoy stylish rooms or apartments, set in a luxuriant park with swimming pool and tennis courts.

☞/EAT

Osteria Cibbé – *Piazza Mercatale 49.* *0574 60 75 09. www.cibbe.it. Closed Sun. Reservations advised.* Wooden or marble tables covered with paper and unpretentious service. Main dishes based on the traditional regional cooking.

Biagio Pignatta – *Viale Papa Giovanni XXXIII, Artimino. 21km/13mi SW of Prato.* *055 87 51 406. www.artimino. com.* Facing hotel *Paggeria Medicea,* set on two floors, this restaurant is graced with a panoramic winter garden and serves traditional Tuscan cuisine, including the "Duck breast Caterina de' Medici style".

Il Piraña – *V. G. Valentini 110.* *0574 25 746. www.ristorantepirana.it. Closed Sat lunchtime, Sun dinnertime. Reservations advised.* For fish lovers, this excellent restaurant offers cuisine anchored in tradition.

SHOPPING

Good to know: Prato Textile Museum indicates Prato factories open to visitors or with outlets. They work textiles from cashmere, mohair and merino as well as synthetics. *www.pratoturismo.it.*

OpificioJM – *Piazza San Marco 39.* *0574 16 63 233. www.opificiojm.it.* Actor John Malkovich in 2010 launched his TechnoBohemian fashion line for men, a riot of textures and colours, based on his drawings, made with Prato textiles and workmanship.

Antonio Mattei – *Via Ricasoli 20/22.* *0574 25 756. www.antoniomattei.it. Closed Sun afternoon and Mon.* Famous for *cantucci,* crunchy biscuits, made here since 1858.

The medieval walled city of Lucca is the capital of its own province and offers an especially lively city life, by day or night. There's plenty to explore right in town, from medieval architecture to Puccini's birthplace or a museum dedicated to comics. But don't miss the famous villas and gardens of the surrounding area, lovely for an hour, a day or an overnight stay.

The Versilia in northwest Tuscany offers the enchanting setting of the sea, framed by the Apuan Alps, which at first glance appear to be snowcapped but are actually gleaming with white Carrara marble.

Marvel at the Marble

A closer look at the mountain itself will show the enormous scale not only of the marble as it is quarried, but of the size of the machines needed to cut and move marble; the dangerous, complex work that's required before marble is sent to the sculptor's studio or to an architectural site. Explore sculptors' studios in Pietrasanta.

Something for Everyone

The beaches are lovely in this area, some shaded by forests of umbrella and maritime pines, others open and still surprisingly pristine, perfect for observing waterfowl and the splendours of nature. Forte dei Marmi attracts the jet-set, while in the back country trails beckon for those more eager to rub shoulders with nature. Opera lovers come for the Puccini festival and to see his birthplace. Children will delight in the beach, watching the marble being cut or loaded onto ships, to seeing museum dedicated to comics, or the underground wonders of caves with dramatic formations and underground lakes. Summer is the season for many of the festivals, but the natural beauty of the area as well as its artistic treasures makes for an enjoyable visit year-round.

Highlights

1 A walk through **medieval Lucca** and on top of its walls and visits to Luccan villas and gardens (p220)

2 Sun and swim with the jet-set in **Forte dei Marmi** or in quiet nature reserves, or a beach picnic under the shady cover of umbrella pines (p230)

3 Marble quarries and stonecutting in **Carrara** (p236) and sculptors' workshops in **Pietrasanta** (p231)

4 Boat excursions on **Lago di Massaciuccoli** to observe wildlife and marsh habitats (p233)

5 Viareggio's **Carnevale** with its elaborate witty floats, many of which praise or mock national and world leaders (p235)

Viareggio

© Jon11/iStock

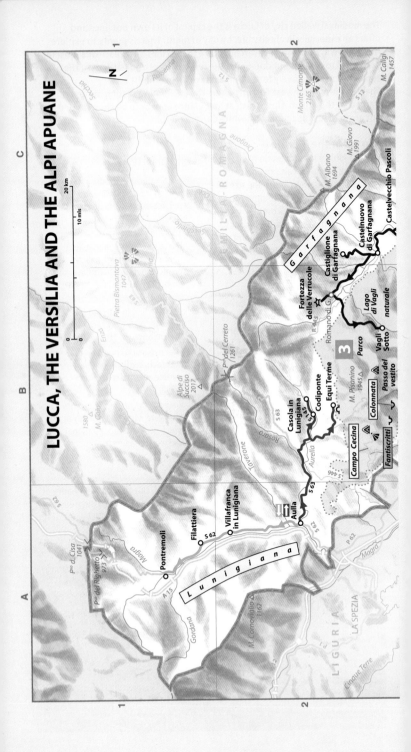

LUCCA, THE VERSILIA AND THE ALPI APUANE

N

20 km
10 mls

C

B

A

1

2

Secchia

Rossenna

S 12

Monte Cimone
2165

M. Albano
1694

M. Giovo
1991

M. Caligi
1457

S 12

E M I L I A - R O M A G N A

Dragone

Dolo

Scoltenna

Pietra Bismantova
1047

S 63

M. Cusna

1580
M. Cusna

Alpe di
Succiso
2017

P.so del Cereto
1261

Garfagnana

Castelnuovo
di Garfagnana

Castiglione
di Garfagnana

Castelvecchio Pascoli

Fortezza
delle Verrucole

Lago
di Vagli
naturale

Romano di G.

Serchio

R. 445

3

Parco

Vagli di
Sotto

Enza

Taverone

Rosaro

Aurella

S 63

Casola in
Lunigiana

Codiponte

Equi Terme

M. Pisanino
1945

Colonnata

Passo del
vestito

M. Cornoviglio
1162

Campo Cecina

Fantiscritti

S 446

S 63

Aulla

Aurella

Magra

Villafranca
in Lunigiana

Filattiera

S 62

Pontremoli

P.so d. Cisa
1041

P.so del Righetto
973

Magra

Gordana

Lunigiana

P. 62

S 62

L I G U R I A

LA SPEZIA

Cinque Terre

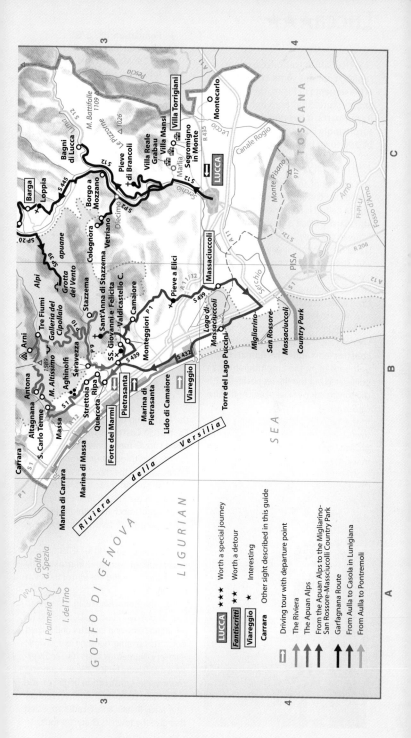

Barga

Loppia

S 445

Bagni
di Lucca

Alpi apuane

SP 39

Grotta
del Vento

Borgo a
Mozzano

Pieve
di Brancoli

M. Battifolle
1109

Le Pizzorne

△ 1026

Pescia

3

Galleria del
Cipollaio

Arni

Antona

Altagnana

Carrara

S.Carlo Terme

Massa

Marina di Carrara

Tre Fiumi

M. Altissimo
1589

Aghinolfi

Seravezza

Strettoia

Querceta Ripa

Forte dei Marmi

Stazzema

Sant'Anna di Stazzema

SS. Giovanni e Felicita

Valdicastello C.

Colognòra

Vetriano

Pietrasanta

Camaiore

Marina di
Pietrasanta

Lido di Camaiore

Marina di Massa

Monteggiori

Pieve a Elici

Massaciuccoli

Villa Reale
Grabau

Villa Mansi

Villa Torrigiani

Montecarlo

Segromigno
in Monte

Marlia

LUCCA

Diecimo

S 12

SP 2

Sèrchio

S 12

Canale Rogio

Lago di
Massaciuccoli

Viareggio

Torre del Lago Puccini

Migliarino

San Rossore

Massaciuccoli

Country Park

A 11/12

S 439

S 432

Sèrchio

PISA

Monte Pisano
917

Arno

Fosso d'Arno

TOSCANA

C

A 12

S 1

P 1

FI-PI-LI

R 206

LIGURIAN

SEA

GOLFO DI GENOVA

Golfo
d. Spezia

I. Palmeria

I. del Tino

Riviera della Versilia

P 9

Lècchio

4

A   B   C   4

LUCCA ★★★ Worth a special journey

Fantiscritti ★★ Worth a detour

Viareggio ★ Interesting

Carrara Other sight described in this guide

☐ Driving tour with departure point

The Riviera

The Apuan Alps

From the Apuan Alps to the Migliarino-
San Rossore-Massciucolli Country Park

Garfagnana Route

From Aulla to Casola in Lunigiana

From Aulla to Pontremoli

Lucca★★★
and nearby villas

This city, which was once a minor capital, contains some of the finest achievements of Pisan Romanesque architecture. Sheltered behind its ramparts, it has remained surprisingly lively and untouched by 20C town planning.

A BIT OF HISTORY

The origins of the town of Lucca are remembered in its name, which comes from a Celto-Ligurian word, *luk*, meaning "marshy place". It was colonised by Rome in the early 2CBC and still has the layout of a Roman military encampment, with streets intersecting at right-angles along each side of two main perpendicular thoroughfares. It was already a large town when Caesar, Pompey and Crassus met there to form the First Triumvirate.

In the Middle Ages a network of narrow winding alleys and uneven squares was constructed within the Roman chequerboard plan; the amphitheatre was obliterated but the site reappeared with the construction of Piazza dell'Anfiteatro (⌾ *See p224*).

In the 12C–13C, after becoming a free town, Lucca continued to enjoy economic growth from manufacturing and trading in silk. Its greatest prosperity came under

▶ **Population:** 387,876.
⚙ **Michelin Map:** Map 563 – K 13 or Map 735 Fold 14.
🗊 **Info:** Piazza Curtatone, ℘0583 44 20 90; Piazzale Verdi, ℘0583 58 31 50; Palatucci car park, Viale Carlo del Prete, ℘0583 46 22 81. www.turismo.lucca.it.
◗ **Location:** Lucca is situated on the major road from Florence to the sea, 74km/46mi from Florence and 20km/12mi from Viareggio.
🕑 **Timing:** A half-day to see the highlights or a day to explore more fully; best would be a stay overnight to enjoy the evening and morning before the tourists arrive; an extra half-day to see some villas in the outlying areas.
👥 **Kids:** Climb to the top of Guinigi Tower, walk along the top of the city walls, see the Botanical Gardens.

the leadership of the great *condottiere*, **Castruccio Castracani** in the early 14C, when Lucca's merchants exported their famous silks throughout Europe and the Orient. Most of the churches were rebuilt and the splendid façades were constructed in the Pisan Romanesque style. A number of imposing Gothic residences, some of which still have their towers, have survived.

Another major figure in local history was **Paolo Guinigi**, who came from a wealthy merchant family and was lord of the town in 1400.

During the **Renaissance**, in the second half of the 16C, Lucca abandoned its declining trade and industry and turned instead to **farming**, boosting its economic recovery. Numerous villas (⌾ *See Excursions p227*) were built in the surrounding countryside. Construction began on the town walls, completed almost a century later. Many Renaissance façades appeared that give the town its character today.

San Martino bell tower

© sansa55/iStock

In the early 19C, Lucca was briefly a principality. Life in the city was dominated by one woman, **Elisa Bonaparte**, crowned Princess of Lucca and Piombino by her brother, Napoleon, after his conquest of Italy. From 1805 to 1813, aided by her husband Félix Baciocchi, she ruled decisively and wisely over her principality with a remarkable talent for managing affairs.

THE CITY TODAY

An independent republic as late as 1799, Lucca had to protect itself from various rivals. Today, one of the rare cities still completely enclosed within 16C and 17C walls, it preserves many medieval and Renaissance structures. These iconic fortifications also close Lucca's historic centre to cars, making it a paradise for pedestrians and cyclists. A favourite pastime of the Lucchesi is a stroll or ride atop the ramparts, with tree-lined walkways and gardens.

ᕦᕤ WALKING TOUR

OLD LUCCA★

The atmospheric streets and squares of old **Lucca** (*la città vecchia*) lead to Gothic and Renaissance palaces, the towers of the nobility, old shops, sculptured doorways and coats of arms, wrought-iron railings and balconies.

▷ Walk to Piazza San Martino.

Cattedrale di San Martino★★ (Duomo)

Piazza San Martino. ◔*Open Mon–Fri 9.30am–7pm (winter 5pm), Sat 9.30am–6.45pm, Sun and public hols noon–7pm (winter 6pm).* ◔*Closed 25 Dec.* ◔€3; €9 combined ticket with bell tower, Museo della Cattedrale, Santi Giovanni e Reparata (archaeological area). ₲ ☏ 0583 49 05 30. www.museocattedralelucca.it.

Lucca **cathedral**, which is dedicated to St Martin, was rebuilt in the 11C. Its outside and interior were redesigned in the 13C and 14C–15C respectively. The splendid alternating white and green marble **façade★★** by architect

Guidetto da Como was the first example of Pisan Romanesque architecture in Lucca.

The distinctive 13C **bell tower★** (*campanile*) displays impressive elegance. From the top (*217 steps*), a wonderful **view★★** extends over Lucca and the surrounding mountains and green hills (◔*Open daily 10am–6pm (winter Mon–Fri 3pm, Sat–Sun and public hols 5pm);* ◔€3; €9 combined ticket).

The **decorative features★** in the portico include pillars with colonnettes and sculptures, blind arcades picked out in red marble, a marble marquetry frieze and narrative carvings. Scenes recount the life of St Martin.

The **Gothic interior**'s inside wall of the façade contains a freely-carved Romanesque sculpture (**1**) depicting the famous scene of St Martin sharing his cloak with a beggar. In the north aisle is a Presentation of the Virgin Mary at the Temple by Bronzino (**2**). A small private chapel takes the form of an elegant Renaissance temple (*tempietto*) built in 1484 by **Matteo Civitali** (1436–1501),

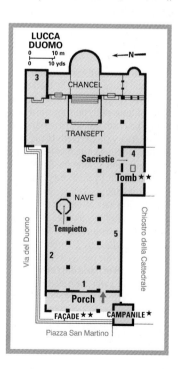

the local sculptor and architect, to house the **Volto Santo**. The blackened wood 11C **large Crucifix★**, bears the figure of Jesus stiffly portrayed in a long tunic. The north transept's entrance to the Sanctuary chapel leads to the altar with a Madonna and Child flanked by St Stephen and St John the Baptist (**3**), painted in 1509 by the Florentine artist Fra Bartolomeo.

The sacristy (*south aisle*) contains a delightful brightly coloured Madonna and Child surrounded by Saints (**4**) (*above the altar*) by Domenico Ghirlandaio. The masterpiece is the white marble **Tomb of Ilaria del Carretto★★**, Paolo Guinigi's wife, who died in 1405. It is one of the purest examples of Italian funerary sculpture, created in 1406 by the Sienese artist Jacopo della Quercia. The spectacular **Last Supper★** (**5**) is by Tintoretto.

Museo della Cattedrale

Piazza Antelminelli 5. ⏰*Open mid Mar–Oct daily 10am–7pm; rest of the year Mon–Fri 10am–2pm, Sat–Sun and public hols 10am–6pm.* ⏰*Closed 25 Dec.* ✆€4; €9 combined ticket with Duomo, bell tower, Santi Giovanni e Reparata. ♿ 𝄞 0583 49 05 30. www.museocattedralelucca.it.

Objects, paintings and carvings from the cathedral include the statue of an apostle by Jacopo della Quercia and the ceremonial vestments for the Volto Santo festival.

Santi Giovanni e Reparata (archaeological area)★

Piazza San Giovanni. ⏰*Same opening hours as Museo della Cattedrale.* ✆€4; €9 combined ticket with Duomo, bell tower, Museo della Cattedrale. 𝄞 0583 49 05 30. www.museocattedralelucca.it.

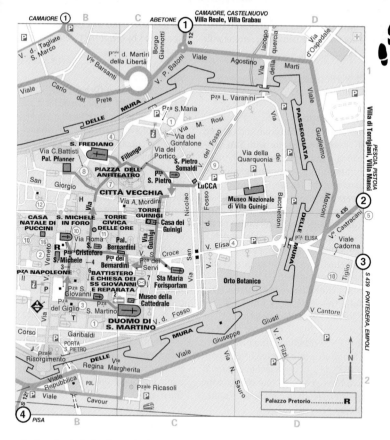

Archaeological digs brought forth the remains of a Roman house and baths, in addition to the initial site and successive extensions of the **original cathedral** and **Baptistery**.

Across Piazza del Giglio is the neo-Classical building **Teatro del Giglio**.

Piazza Napoleone★

Plane trees shade this square built for Elisa Bonaparte. **Palazzo Ducale** was begun in the 16C by Florentine architect **Bartolomeo Ammannati**.

▷ Via Beccheria leads to Piazza San Michele.

Piazza San Michele

This square rests on the site of the ancient Roman forum, surrounded by 13C and 14C buildings. The **Palazzo Pretorio** – the Podesta's ancient palace – opens its

Renaissance arcades and a loggia toward Via Vittorio.

San Michele in Foro★★

Piazza San Michele. ◷*Open daily 8.30am–6pm (winter 9am–5.30pm); hours may vary.* ℘*0583 53 576.*

This 12C–14C **church** in **Piazza San Michele** is flanked by a massive bell tower built above the transept. The exceptionally tall 13C **façade★★** displays the most exuberant and delicate features produced by the Pisan Romanesque style, despite major restorations. The pediment is surmounted by a huge statue of St Michael slaying the dragon, flanked by two angel musicians.

The **interior** is Romanesque, except for the 16C ceiling vaulting. Above the first altar is a white glazed terracotta **Madonna★** by Andrea della Robbia. The south transept contains a splendidly vivid

223

painting★ by Filippino Lippi portraying St Roch, St Sebastian and St Jerome with St Helena.

▷ Via Beccheria, then Via Roma to the right leads to Via Fillungo.

Via Fillungo★

Lucca's most picturesque and elegant business street begins with **San Cristoforo**, a deconsecrated church transformed into a temporary exhibition space; on the façade (St Christopher) covered in alternating light and dark marble, its lovely portal has a lintel sculpted with floral motifs and a pretty rose window. Inside, its noble sobriety is bathed in rose light; names engraved in stone on the walls honour citizens who died defending Lucca.

Along the street is 13C **Torre Civica delle Ore** (*Civic Clock Tower:* ⊙*Open 9.30am–7.30pm (Mar and Oct 5.30pm, Apr–May 6.30pm).* ⊙*Closed Nov–Feb.* ⊚*€5; €9 combined ticket with Torre Guinigi and the Botanical Gardens;* ℘*0583 48 090; www.lemuradilucca.it/ torri/torre-delle-ore*). Your climb up the 207 steps leads to a marvelous **panorama**★★.

Left on Via degli Asili, is 17C **Palazzo Pfanner**: its monumental staircase has arcades and balustrades; its garden landscaped in the 18C and its ramparts testify to its former splendour.

The final stretch on Via Cesare Battisti is dominated by the robust *campanile* of San Frediano.

San Frediano★

Piazza San Frediano. ⊙*Open daily 9.30am–5pm (Sat 5.30pm).* ⊚*€3.*
This 12C Romanesque **church** occupies the site of a 6C basilica by St Frediano, Bishop of Lucca, to whom the miracle of the damming of the River Serchio is attributed. The 13C **façade** was built with stone that was originally in the Roman amphitheatre. Like the façade, the Romanesque basilica-shaped **interior** has a noble simplicity. The Classical columns are crowned with splendid capitals, probably from the amphitheatre. The 14C–15C chapels interrupt the overall harmony.

The admirable 12C Romanesque **baptismal font**★ is decorated with carved panels. A fine door surround adorns an extremely graceful glazed terracotta **Annunciation** by Andrea della Robbia. The **Trenta Chapel** (*north aisle*) contains a Gothic marble **polyptych**★ portraying the Madonna and Child surrounded by saints, intricately carved by Jacopo della Quercia.

Piazza dell'Anfiteatro

Access through a vaulted alleyway from Via Fillungo.
Passages beneath the houses lead into this astonishing enclosed oval

Piazza dell'Anfiteatro

© PeteSherrard/iStock

space, which occupies the site of a 2C Roman **amphitheatre** that fell into ruin during the Barbarian invasions. It was exploited for building materials during the Middle Ages to reconstruct the town's churches, particularly the marble façades. It was not until 1830 that this space was laid out within the medieval quarter.

Piazza San Pietro is a small, irregularly-shaped square surrounded by stately 16C façades. It is overlooked by the dual-coloured bell tower of the 12C Romanesque church of **San Pietro Somaldi**; its 14C façade has two registers of arcades in the Pisan tradition. In the lintel above the central doorway Jesus hands St Peter the Keys of Heaven.

Lu.C.C.A (Lucca Center of Contemporary Art)

Via della Fratta 36. ⊙*Open Tue–Sun 10am–7pm.* ⊙*Closed Mon.* ⊗€10. ℘ *0583 49 21 80. luccamuseum.com.*
At the intersection of Via della Fratta with the typical **Via dei Fossi** stands Palazzo Bocella, an elegant Renaissance building, which hosts a lovely space dedicated to contemporary art; its multifunctional design extends even to the bathrooms.

▷ Follow Via Guinigi.

♟♟ Torre Guinigi★

Via Sant'Andrea 45. ⊙*Open 9.30am–7.30pm (Mar and Oct 5.30pm, Apr–May 6.30pm; Nov–Feb 4.30pm).* ⊙*Closed 25 Dec.* ⊗€5; €9 combined ticket with Torre delle Ore and the Botanical Gardens. ℘*0583 48 090. www.lemuradilucca.it/torri/torre-guinigi.*
This typical 13C–15C tower house once belonged to the powerful Guinigi family, and is a landmark in Lucca. This 14C red-brick tower, 41m (135ft) high, was one of the last to continue the Italian tradition of planting oak trees at the top. A climb up 230 steps concludes with a panoramic view over the city.
Across from it, at nos 10 and 22 are two important brick houses, which also belonged to the Guinigi.

▷ Walk along Via Guinigi.

Santa Maria Forisportam

The name of the 13C **church** indicates that it stood outside the Roman gates. The Pisan-style marble façade has three doors with architraves beautifully carved with floral and animal motifs. The bas-relief above the central doorway depicts the Coronation of the Virgin Mary.
The Romanesque interior was modified in the 16C with vaulting and the small dome. Two paintings are by Guercino: *St Lucy (last altar, south aisle)* and *The Virgin Mary, St Francis and St Alexander (north transept)*.

Via Santa Croce, Piazza dei Servi and Piazza dei Bernardini, overlooked by the austere **Palazzo dei Bernardini** (16C), lead to Piazza San Michele.

PASSEGGIATA DELLE MURA

The **ramparts★** that give Lucca its characteristic appearance encircle the town (4km/2.5mi). They took the entire 16C and the first half of the 17C to complete and include 11 forward-projecting bastions (*baluardi*) connected by curtain walls (30m/100ft wide at the base). The walls' original four gateways were joined by a fifth in 1804 added by Elisa Bonaparte on the east side, known as Elisa's Gate. The ramparts were planted with two rows of trees in the 19C; they now offer an unusual public park for pedestrians and cyclists.

♟♟ Orto Botanico

Via del Giardino Botanico 14. ⊙*Open daily Jul–Sept 10am–7pm; May–Jun 10am–6pm; end of March–Apr and Oct 10am–5pm; rest of the year Mon–Fri 9.30am-12.30pm by reservation (except public hols).* ⊗€5; €9 combined ticket with Torre delle Ore and Torre Guinigi. ℘*0583 95 05 96. www.lemuradilucca.it/orto-botanico.*
Created in 1820 by Maria Luisa di Borbone, this botanical garden is a lovely, green, flowering place within the San Micheletto complex.

ADDITIONAL SIGHTS

Museo Nazionale di Palazzo Mansi

Via Galli Tassi 43. ◷*Open Tue–Sat at 9.30am (only this fixed entry time in the morning) and noon–7.30pm.* ◷*Closed Mon, Sun and public hols.* ⊷€*4;* €*6.50 combined ticket with Museo Nazionale di Villa Guinigi.* & ℘ *0583 55 570. www.luccamuseinazionali.it.*

The **picture gallery** housed in the Palazzo Mansi (17C) displays large compositions by Italian painters including Veronese, Giordano, Pontormo (*Portrait of a Young Man*) and Tintoretto. Portraits and small paintings are from abroad, particularly the Flemish School.

The **Apartments** display remarkable 17C–18C **decorative features★**. Morning rooms have ceilings painted with frescoes of mythical subjects and the walls are hung with sumptuous 17C Flemish tapestries; the 18C-style Conjugal Chamber has a canopied bed beneath a fresco of Eros and Psyche.

Museo Nazionale di Villa Guinigi

Via della Quarquonia. ◷*Open Tue–Sat at 9.30am (only this fixed entry time in the morning) and noon–7.30pm.* ◷*Closed Mon, Sun and public hols.* ⊷€*4;* €*6.50 combined ticket with Museo Nazionale di Palazzo Mansi.* & ℘ *0583 49 60 33. www.luccamuseinazionali.it.*

This impressive Romanesque and Gothic brick building (built 1418) was the country seat of Paolo Guinigi.

The **museum** displays archaeological finds from the region and exhibits local sculpture and paintings. Splendid inlaid wood intarsio panels show scenes illustrating Lucca's importance, and gold-embroidered **vestments** gleam with silk or silver thread made in Lucca in the 15C–18C.

Puccini Museum – Casa Natale di Puccini

Corte San Lorenzo 9. ◷*Open daily Apr–Oct 10am–7pm (Oct 6pm); rest of the year Wed–Mon (closed Tue except public hols) Mar 10am–6pm, Nov–Feb 10am–5pm.* ◷*Closed 25 Dec.* ⊷€*7; guided tour in English (included in the ticket price) every Fri at noon in Jun–Sept.* ℘ *0583 58 40 28. www.puccinimuseum.org.*

The great composer **Giacomo Puccini** (1858-1924) was born in Lucca. The house where he was born was recently renovated and is now home to a museum where fans of *La Bohème, Turandot* and *Tosca* can see letters, documents relating to his work, as well as his piano. You can continue the pilgrimage to Torre del Lago Puccini and the villa he lived in from

---

Legend of the Holy Face

The Holy Face (**Volto Santo**) is the miraculous Crucifix worshipped in the Cathedral of San Martino. According to various traditions it was carved from memory by Nicodemus after the Entombment or his hand was guided by angels as he worked; that is why Christ's face is such a good likeness. The Volto Santo is said to have been washed up on the shores of Luni, north of Viareggio, in the 8C. The story as to how it arrived there differs; some say it was cast into the sea by Nicodemus himself, in obedience to an order from on high, while others believe that it was found by an Italian bishop on a pilgrimage to the Holy Land and that he left it to float with the tide. When the devout Christians of Luni and Lucca began to argue about ownership of the holy image, the Bishop of Lucca settled the matter by placing it on an ox cart and leaving the animals to decide on its destination; they headed towards Lucca.

In the Middle Ages the Volto Santo was famous far beyond Lucca. Its story was told by merchants from Lucca and soon spread to northern Europe.

The **Luminara di Santa Croce** (*evening of 13 Sep*) commemorates the mysterious arrival of the Volto Santo. The whole town joins with various religious orders from the region and representatives from other Tuscan towns, to take part in a huge candlelit procession that makes its way through the streets.

Villa Torrigiani

© Maui01 /iStock

1891 onwards (⎣ *See p234*), where he is now buried.

Chiesa di San Paolino

Via San Paolino. ⏱ *Open 8.30am–6pm.* Dedicated to the city's patron saint, this 1522–36 church has the 19C organ, which Puccini, a parishoner of San Paolino, often came to play.

EXCURSIONS
Villa Reale di Marlia★

8km/5mi N of Lucca by SS12, or by SS435; after 6km/4mi turn right towards Marlia (signposted) and cross the railway line. Bus 59 from Lucca. ⏱ *Open daily Mar–Oct 10am–6pm; last admission 1hr before closing.* ⏱ *Closed Nov–Feb.* ⊜ €9 (park); €14 (park + villa). ℘ 0583 30 108. *www.parcovillareale.it.*

The villa is surrounded by magnificent 17C **gardens★★** that include the flower garden, lemon grove, grotto and park with its statues, niches, terraces and topiaried yew trees. Also a Green Theatre, a Water Theatre and a Clock Mansion.

The interior of the villa is under renovation but some rooms are open to visitors. Furnishings and decorations still evoke the original splendour of the times of Elisa Bonaparte, Napoleon's sister and owner of the house in the early 19C century.

Villa Grabau

8km/5mi N of Lucca by SS12; Via di Matraia 269, San Pancrazio. ⏱ *Open Jul–mid Sept 10am–1pm, 2.30–6pm;* *Easter–Jun 11am–1pm, 2–5.30pm; rest of the year 11am–1pm, 2.30–5.30pm (Nov–Easter only Sun and public hols).* ⏱ *Closed Mon mornings and Wed except public hols.* ⊜ €7. ⎣ ℘ 0583 40 60 98. *www.villagrabau.it.*

The 16C neo-Classical villa has belonged to the Grabau family since 1868. Fountains with bronze mascarons and white marble statues add to the elegant appearance of the **park★★**, an area of 9ha/22 acres. The layout includes an outdoor theatre, an informal English garden, an Italian garden, a winter greenhouse and an unusual 17C–18C **Lemon House**.

Villa Torrigiani★

12km/7.5mi NE of Lucca by the Pescia road (Pesciatina); in Zone turn left to Segromigno in Monte. ⏱ *Open daily Jun–Sept 10am–1pm, 2.30–6.30pm; first Sun of Mar–May and Oct 10am–1pm, 2.30–5pm; rest of the year by reservation only; hours may vary.* ⊜ €7 (park); €12 (park + villa). ℘ 0583 92 80 41. *villatorrigiani@villeepalazzilucchesi.it.*

The 16C Villa Torrigiani was, in the 17C, a luxurious summer residence of Marquess Nicolao Santini, Ambassador of the Republic of Lucca to the papal court. The gardens have fountains, caves and grottoes.

Villa Mansi

11km/7mi NE of Lucca by the same route as above for Villa Torrigiani; from Segromigno follow the signs. Via Selvette

242 Segromigno in Monte. ◑Open end of Mar–end of Oct Mon–Thu 1–4pm, Fri 8am–4pm; hours may vary; rest of the year by reservation only. ◐Closed Sat–Sun. ◉€7 (park only). ℘0583 92 02 34. This superb 16C villa has numerous statues on its façade. It stands in the middle of a huge **park★** with a large lake and lanes lined with statues.

Montecarlo

15km/9mi E of Lucca.

A lovely town in a panoramic setting, at the top of a hill covered with vineyards and olive groves. Beyond its walls are the vestiges of a 14C castle and an elegant neo-Classical theatre.

Also getting top billing is the **Strada del Vino e Olio** (℘338 22 11 779. www.stradavinoeoliolucca.it), wine roads that lead to Montecarlo DOC red and white wines, as well as Colline Lucchesi wines.

ADDRESSES

🏠STAY

🏡 **Good to know:** The villa area has numerous options for lodging, generally on the expensive side and sometimes with a minimum stay. Some may be in the villa itself, others in an outbuilding. Some offer tours and meals, while others expect guests to be self-sufficient; so state your preference. If these are priced beyond your budget, consider an *agriturismo* or country *palazzo*, which offer the pleasures of country life at economical prices. If only a grand *villa Lucchese* will do, check those that offer accommodation on www.villeepalazzilucchesi.it.

⊖⊖ **Piccolo Hotel Puccini** – *Via di Poggio 9.* ℘0583 55 421. www.hotelpuccini.com. *14 rooms.* A taste of modern life in a small family-run atmosphere.

⊖⊖⊟ **Albergo San Martino** – *Via Della Dogana 9.* ℘0583 46 91 81. www.albergosanmartino.it. &. *9 rooms.* High comfort, modern decor near the cathedral. Enthusiastic owners offer tours.

⊖⊖⊟⊟ **Alla Corte degli Angeli** – *Via degli Angeli 23.* ℘0583 46 92 04. www.allacortedegliangeli.com. 🅿. *21 rooms.* Rooms painted in lively colours; fresh flowers in the breakfast room.

🍴EAT

⊖⊖ **Osteria Baralla** – *Via dell'Anfiteatro 5.* ℘0583 44 02 40. www.osteriabaralla.it. *Closed Sun. Reservations required.* Medieval mansion, local dishes, vaulted ceiling.

⊖⊖ **Buca di Sant'Antonio** – *Via della Cervia 3.* ℘0583 31 21 99. *Closed Sun dinnertime, Mon.* Over 50 years of local cuisine and products, including prosciutto, which doubles as decor.

⊖⊖ **Trattoria da Leo** – *Via Tegrimi 1.* ℘0583 49 22 36. Lively trattoria, simple local fare. Outdoor tables.

⊖⊖ **Osteria dal Manzo** – *Via Cesare Battisti 28.* ℘0583 49 06 49. *Closed lunchtime.* A diverse clientele comes for typical Tuscan tradition and delicious desserts.

⊖⊖ **Gli Orti di Via Elisa** – *Via Elisa 17.* ℘0583 49 12 41. www.ristorantegliorti.it. *Closed Thu lunchtime and Wed.* Traditional and original cuisine. Grilled dishes, bistro decor.

⊖⊖⊟ **Giglio** – *Piazza del Giglio 2.* ℘0583 49 40 58. www.ristorantegiglio.com. *Closed Wed lunchtime, Tue.* In a 18C palazzo, three young chefs share the same vision of modern cuisine with its roots firmly anchored in the region yet also with a hint of Japanese influence.

⊖⊖⊟ **Ristorante All'Olivo** – *Piazza S. Quirico 1.* ℘0583 49 62 64. www.ristorante olivo.it. Refined fish and meat dishes. Really pleasant service on the veranda.

⊖⊖⊟ **La Griglia di Varrone** – *Viale Europa 797/f.* ℘0583 58 36 11. grigliavarrone.com. *Closed Sat lunchtime.* Trendy steakhouse, including exotic (kangaroo, antelope, zebra).

⊖⊖⊟ **Osteria Verciani "il Mecenate a Lucca"** – *Via del Fosso 94.* ℘0583 51 18 61. www.ristorantemecenate.it. Occupying the premises of a historic local laundry and dyeworks, this authentic trattoria serves excellent regional cuisine.

⊖⊖⊟ **I Diavoletti** – *Via Stradone di Camigliano 302, 11km/7mi NE of Lucca, nearby Villa Torrigiani.* ℘0583 92 03 23. www. ristorantepizzeriaidiavoletti.it. In this charming restaurant, with brightly coloured dining rooms, three sisters delight guests with their delicious regional cuisine. Specialities include locally produced meats and vegetable tarts.

TAKING A BREAK

Betty Blue Cafè – *Via del Gonfalone 16–18.* ℘0583 49 21 66. www.bettybluelucca.it. Disco-pub and Internet café with live music.

Pasticceria Taddeucci – *Piazza San Michele 34.* ℘0583 49 49 33. www.buccellatotaddeucci. com. Open 8am-8pm. Since 1881 the family has proffered pastries typical of Lucca.

The Versilia★

The Versilia is scenically situated between the sea coast and the mountains, which bestow it with a mild climate. Superb sea resorts boast fine sandy beaches (up to 100m/108yd wide) that slope gently into the sea and are ideal for families. The gently rolling hills give way to a lush coastal plain. In the distance is the white-capped Apuan Alps National Park, including Camaiore, Pietrasanta, Stazzema and Seravezza.

🚗 DRIVING TOURS

THE RIVIERA

28km/17.5mi. 🖐 See map pp230–231.

Viareggio★

This is the main seaside resort in Versilia and one of Italy's most popular. The small fishing and shipbuilding village was transformed in the early 19C into a seaside resort by Marie-Louise de Bourbon, who made sea-bathing fashionable. Lined with wooden pavilions with cafés, bathing houses or shops, the 1917 fire left only **Chalet Martini** standing. Fine late-1920s architecture replaced it, such as the splendid **Gran Caffè Margherita**, with coloured Baroque-style cupolas.

The long, broad beach has fine sand; certain sections are reserved for hotel guests. There is also a fairly busy fishing harbour. The **Carnival** in Viareggio is internationally famous for the procession of allegorical papier-mâché floats, traditionally caricatures of Italian and international political figures.

Galleria d'Arte Moderna e Contemporanea (GAMC)

Palazzo delle Muse, Piazza Mazzini.
🕐Open Wed–Sat 3.30–7.30pm, Sun 9.30am–1.30pm, 3.30– 7.30pm (mid Jun–Aug also Tue 9.30am–1.30pm).
🕐Closed Mon–Tue. ⊛€8; free admission third Sun of the month.
🖉0584 58 11 18. www.gamc.it.

- 🖐 **Michelin Map:** 563–J 12-K 12/13 or Map 735 Fold 14.
- ℹ️ **Info:** Piazza Curtatone, Lucca, 🖉0584 44 20 90/91. www.turismo.lucca.it; www.inversilia.com.
- ▷ **Location:** Versilia is easily accessible from the Genoa–Livorno motorway or from the motorway from Florence to the sea.
- ⊘ **Don't Miss:** Carnevale at Viareggio, a walk along the sea at Viareggio, the jet-set at Forte dei Marmi, Pietrasanta, Cave dei Fantiscritti and the Migliarino–San Rossore–Massaciuccoli Country Park.
- 🕐 **Timing:** A half-day at the beach, a half- to full day in the backcountry to see nature or explore quarries.
- 👪 **Kids:** Sandy beaches at Marina di Pietrasanta. A boat trip through the Migliarino–San Rossore–Massaciuccoli Park.

Some 3,000 works of 19C and 20C European artists are displayed, including local Expressionist painter **Lorenzo Viani** (1882–1936).

Gran Caffè Margherita

© NickNick_ko/iStock

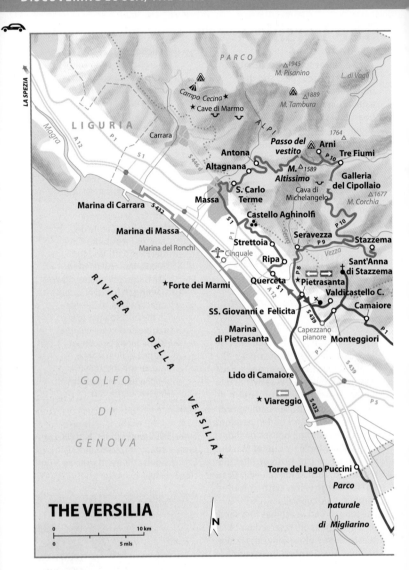

THE VERSILIA

0 —— 10 km
0 —— 5 mls

N

▶ N of Viareggio the coastline consists of an almost unbroken line of seaside resorts facing the Gulf of Genoa.

Lido di Camaiore

Lido di Camaiore is more modern and more of a family resort than Viareggio, its prestigious neighbour, but they are so close that one runs into the next. They share the same pine woods and a delightful esplanade.

Marina di Pietrasanta

This seaside resort has a long beach (over 5km/3mi), delightful paths through the pine woods ideal for walking or cycling, sports and excellent nightlife. Nearby is the **Versiliana Park** (about 80ha/198acres), a woodland that hosts various cultural events in summer.

Forte dei Marmi★

This elegant resort, long popular with artists and the Italian jet-set, has attracted an influx of wealthy Russians

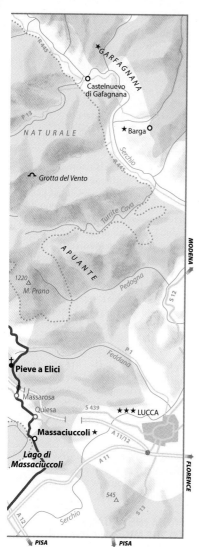

Between them is the harbour from which marble is exported. Often huge blocks of marble sit at the water's edge, awaiting ships.

THE APUAN ALPS
85km/52mi. Allow 3hrs.

This route through Upper Versilia skirts **Monte Altissimo** in the heart of the Apuan Alps. Famous for its excellent marble since the days of the Etruscans and Romans, quarrying was abandoned in the Middle Ages but began again in the Renaissance, encouraged by Pope Leo X. He entrusted the enterprise to Michelangelo, who worked here from 1515–18 and one of the quarries still bears his name. He selected the routes leading to the quarries from Seravezza and for transporting quarried marble down into the valley.

Pietrasanta★

The crossroads of Via Francigena with Via Aurelia, which leads to France, gave this area strategic importance. Its Rocca was constructed in the 14C. Since 1960 Pietrasanta has been a favourite of modern sculptors, from Botero to Moor and Miró, who came to work both in marble and bronze. Some artists' studios with original works are being restored.

The Porta a Pisa leads to the **Duomo di San Martino**, with 1389 Baptistery fonts. **Palazzo Moroni** hosts an archaeological museum, with artefacts from prehistoric to medieval times. Church of **Sant'Antonio Abate** (or Chiesa della Misericordia) on Via Mazzini has Botero's **Gate of Paradise** and **Gate of Hell frescoes★** which include Mother Theresa, Hitler, the Italian flag and a Conquistador. Piazza Matteoti has a bronze Warrior sculpted by Botero.

The route moves through **Querceta** and rejoins the road at **Ripa** and the quieter villages on the Alp slopes. After **Strettoia**, the route climbs up to the **canale di Murli** and descends alongside pine trees and vineyards.

▶ Beyond Capanne the road rejoins Via Aurelia (S1) to Massa.

in recent years. The beach has rows of delightful, colourful cabins.

▶ To the N the mountains of Liguria turn W towards the coast and plunge into the sea, marking the end of the gentle Versilian coastline.

Marina di Massa and Marina di Carrara

A somewhat deserted stretch of coast precedes these two resorts, with some fine late 19C–early 20C buildings.

The Versilian Pievi

The Versilia district used to belong to Lombardy until it was annexed in the Middle Ages by Lucca, which was seeking an outlet to the sea to facilitate its exports as well as for its strategic military position. The Romanesque churches (*pievi*) built in the 12C–13C therefore reflect Luccan influence as regards their structure and carved ornamentation. Their main features are their harmonious austerity, their smooth façades defined within a square and their interiors with rafters.

Massa
See CARRARA.

From Massa take SP4 E inland towards S Carlo.

The road passes through **San Carlo Terme** and **Altagnana**, affording a superb view of the Apuan Alps, and **Antona**. Beyond the mountain pass (**Passo del Vestito**) the road runs close by **Arni**.

At the junction (left to Castelnuovo di Garfagnana) bear right into SP10 to Seravezza and Pietrasanta.

Tre Fiumi has a succession of marble quarries. South of the **Galleria dei Cipollaio** (*tunnel – about 1km/0.5mi long*) the road is flanked (*right*) by **Monte Altissimo** (*alt 1589m/5,213ft*), the mountain that contains Michelangelo's famous quarry.

At the junction by the River Vezza turn left; after 2km/1mi, in the main square in Ponte Stazzemese, turn right onto a narrow and winding road to Stazzema (5km/3mi).

Stazzema
The summit of Monte Procinto casts its shadow over the winding streets and flower-decked balconies of this village (*alt 440m/1,444ft*), a popular holiday resort. Near the entrance to Stazzema stands the Romanesque church (*left*) of **Santa Maria Assunta**, which has a wonderful 14C ceiling.

Return downhill. In Ponte Stazzemese bear left and continue W down the Vezza Valley to Seravezza.

Seravezza
This village takes its name from the confluence of the Serra and Vezza rivers. Since the early 16C it has been closely linked to marble quarrying, an activity revived by the Medici.

Grand Duke Cosimo I commissioned a mansion, **Palazzo Mediceo★** (1561–65) (*www.palazzomediceo.it*). In the centre of the splendid inner courtyard is a delightful well carved out of a single block of marble to represent a trout; it is said to be a copy of the fish caught by Marie-Christine of Lorraine in the River Vezza in 1603.

In the centre of Seravezza stands the **Cathedral of Santi Lorenzo and Barnaba**, built 1422–1569. It was badly damaged by bombs during World War II but has retained the early 16C marble font carved by Stagio Stagi, a local artist.

South of Seravezza the road runs along the N bank of the River Vezza; turn left over the river into SS439 to return to Pietrasanta.

FROM THE APUAN ALPS TO THE MIGLIARINO–SAN ROSSORE–MASSACIUCCOLI PARK
40km/24mi. *See map pp230–231.*

Pietrasanta★
See p231.

Take S439 S towards Lucca; on the outskirts of Pietrasanta turn left.

Pieve dei Santi Giovanni e Felicità
Among the olive trees stands the oldest church (9C) in the Versilia region.

Continue up the valley to Valdicastello Carducci.

Valdicastello Carducci

Poet Giosuè Carducci's **birthplace** (*casa natale*) houses a small museum relating to his life. ◐*Open Jul–Aug Tue–Sun 5–8pm; rest of the year Tue 9am–noon, Sat–Sun 3–6pm.* ℘*0584 79 55 00.*

Return to SS439. After 3.5km/2mi turn left (shortly before Capezzano Pianore) towards S Lucia and Monteggiori.

The road climbs through olive groves and cypress trees to **Monteggiori**, a medieval village clinging to the mountainside.

Follow the same road to Sant'Anna.

Ossario di Sant'Anna di Stazzema

On 12 August 1944 three SS battalions marched towards Sant'Anna. The village men took refuge in the forest, leaving women, elderly and children, believing that no one would harm them. Three hours later, 560 innocent victims were massacred. The goal of the SS was to destroy the villages it believed were aiding Resistance fighters in the area. The victims are remembered on this monument, in the **Parco Nazionale della Pace** (℘*0584 77 20 25; www.sant annadistazzema.org).*

Camaiore

This Roman village (Campus Major) is now a major farming and commercial centre at the foot of Monte Prana (alt 1,220m/3,965ft). Of its medieval past, one of few remaining monuments is the **Romanesque Church of Santa Maria Assunta** (1278) flanked by a solid 14C *campanile* in Piazza S Bernardino da Siena.

Beyond the 14C gate (*follow signs to Badia and Cimitero; 1km/0.5mi from the centre*) stands the church of an 8C Benedictine abbey (*badia*).

From Camaiore take the road E towards Lucca. At the T-junction by a river, turn right to Massarosa. Continue for 5km/3mi.

In a bend (*right*) stands the 11C Church of San Pantaleone di **Pieve a Elici**. Immediately beyond Pieve a Elici there is a view of the former Massaciuccoli Marshes.

In Massarosa take SS439 S to Quiesa. Turn right to Massaciuccoli.

Massaciuccoli★

This village, with neighbouring lake, has retained some links with the Roman era. Its **Padiglione Espositivo Guglielmo**

Low hills around Lake Massaciuccoli

© t-lorien/iStock

Lera (○*Open Fri 10.30am–1.30pm, Sat 3.30–7pm, Sun 10.30am–1.30pm, 3.30–7pm; hours may vary, reservation advised; ℰ0584 97 45 50*) displays the various ceramics found on the site. The impressive ruins of the **Roman baths★** (*guided tour by reservation only, ℰ0584 97 45 50*) are set on a hilltop amid the olive trees (*left of the road; access on foot only along a path signposted Zona Archeologica*). From in front of the church of San Lorenzo (*first on the left after the villa*) there is a fine **view★** downhill over the baths and the lake to the sea.

▷ Continue S and W; turn right into Via Aurelia (SS1) N towards Viareggio; left to Torre del Lago.

This road crosses part of the **Migliarino–San Rossore–Massaciuccoli Country Park** including the lake, the Massaciuccoli Marshes and the remains of the ancient Pisan Forest.

Torre del Lago Puccini

Here **Puccini** (1858–1924) composed most of his works: *La Bohème*, *Tosca* and *Madame Butterfly*. On the shores of **Massaciuccoli Lake** stands his house, **Villa Puccini** (○*Open 10am–12.40pm, 2–5.20pm (Feb–Mar 2.30–5.50pm); last admission 40 min before closing, mornings and afternoons);* ○*Closed Mon mornings (except public hols), 25 Dec; ◎€7; ℰ0584 34 14 45; www.giacomopuccini.it*), with memorabilia and his grave.

▷ Return to Pietrasanta via Viareggio and Lido di Camaiore (tour B).

ADDRESSES

🕍STAY

⊜⊜ **Locanda Le Monache** – *Piazza XXIX Maggio 36, Camaiore. ℰ0584 98 92 58. www.lemonache.com.12 rooms. Restaurant ⊜⊜.* Conceived in 1923 as a way station for travellers and pilgrims, it has recently been tastefully renovated.

⊜⊜⊜ **Hotel Arcangelo** – *Via Carrara 23, Viareggio. ℰ0584 47 123. www.hotel arcangelo.com. 19 rooms.* Former house, with private garden. Bedrooms are furnished in the 1950s style.

⊜⊜⊜ **Hotel Miramare** – *Via Donati 32, Forte dei Marmi. ℰ0584 78 72 77. www.miramarehotel.org. ℙ. 18 rooms.* In a residential district, near Forte dei Marmi. Restful, welcoming and reasonable. Some rooms have a small terrace.

⊜⊜⊜ **Hotel Pardini** – *Viale Carducci 14, Viareggio. ₺ ℰ0584 96 13 79. www.hotelpardini.com. 14 rooms.* On Viareggio's promenade. Spacious, modern, simply furnished rooms; attentive service.

⊜⊜⊜ **Hotel I Pini** – *Via Roma 43, Lido di Camaiore. ℰ0584 66 103. www.clubipini.com. ℙ. 22 rooms.* Painter Galileo Chini's Art Déco former villa. Romantic garden, artistic atmosphere and warm hosts. Excellent restaurant with good wines.

⊜⊜⊜ **Hotel Piccolo Mondo** – *Via Manfredi 20, Lido di Camaiore. ℰ0584 61 86 66. www.hotelpiccolomondo.net. ℙ. 26 rooms.* Good value. Tranquil, near the beach. Garden.

⊜⊜⊜ **Hotel Sylvia** – *Via Manfredi 15, Lido di Camaiore. ℰ0584 61 79 94. www.hotelsylvia.it. ℙ 34 rooms.* 🛏 Quiet, near the sea, with garden. Large, light rooms and home cooking. Library on the ground floor.

⊜⊜⊜⊜ **Hotel Byron** – *Viale della Repubblica 59, Forte dei Marmi. ℰ0584 78 70 52. www.hotelbyron.net. 29 rooms. Restaurant ⊜⊜⊜⊜. Reservation required.* This charming Art Nouveau villa only a few blocks from the beach has its own pool hidden in the garden. Its elegant and superb restaurant, La Magnolia, is one of the town's best and in summer also offers an informal poolside barbecue. The chef demonstrates his ability to collect and develop traditional Mediterranean recipes, while adding his own authentic, distinctive and original touches.

⊜⊜⊜⊜ **Grand Hotel Principe di Piemonte** – *Piazza Puccini 1, Viareggio. ℰ0584 45 151. www.principedipiemonte.com. ℙ 106 rooms.* 🛏 *Open Mar–Oct. Restaurant ⊜⊜⊜/⊜⊜⊜⊜. Reservation required.* Founded in the early 1920s, the rooms of this hotel are laid out across five floors, each decorated in a different style, either with a sea view or looking out at the Apuan Alps. On the fifth floor of the hotel, a panoramic roof garden acts as a delightful setting for the creative and sophisticated cuisine of the Il Piccolo Principe restaurant (*ℰ0584*

40 18 06. www.ristoranteilpiccoloprincipe.it),
here dishes are refined, inspired (sometimes
original) and beautifully presented. The
Regina restaurant focuses on the traditional
cuisine of Versilia and Tuscany.

⏷/ EAT

🍽 **Rino** – *Via della Chiesa 7, Bargecchia di
Massarosa, 4km/2.5mi S of Camaiore. 📞0584
95 40 00. Closed Wed.* Traditional food –
fresh pasta and grilled meat. Summer
meals in the garden.

🍽 **Da Cecco** – *Belvedere Puccini, Torre
Del Lago Puccini. 📞0584 34 10 22.* Near the
lake and Puccini's house; serves seafood
and local produce, with game in winter.
Also eel and frogs' legs.

🍽 **La Martinatica** – *Via Della
Martinatica 20, Pietrasanta. 📞0584 17 88 946.
www.martinatica.it. Closed Tue. Reservation
suggested.* This renowned restaurant
occupying an old mill with rustic yet elegant
decor has recently been taken over by new
chefs who have come here from elsewhere
in Versilia. The menu offers a selection of fish
and meat dishes, all of which are prepared in
the same modern and unfussy style. Simply
a good meal.

🍽 **Ristorante Da Miro** – *Via Coppino
289, Viareggio. 📞0584 38 40 65. www.
ristorantedamiro.com. Closed Mon–Thu
lunchtime. Reservation suggested.*
Overlooking the dock, this restaurant has
been serving fish and seafood dishes from
Viareggio since 1954. Its most famous
speciality is the *spaghetti alla trabaccolara*
(with a seafood sauce).

🍽 **Ristorante La Barca** – *Viale
Italico 3, Forte de Marmi. 📞0584 89 323. www.
ristorantelabarca.org. Closed Mon lunchtime
and Tue.* Forte dei Marmi's oldest restaurant,
facing the sea, was founded in 1906 by
Captain Leo Tacchella on the *barca* with
his cargo of wine from the island of Elba.
Regular, tourist and tasting menus are
largely inspired by the bounty of the sea.

🍽 **Ristorante Il Porto** – *Via Coppino
118, località Darsena, Viareggio. 📞0584
38 47 33. www.ristoranteilporto.eu. Closed
Tue. Reservations suggested.* The waiter will
announce the classic seafood specialities,
which are made with very fresh ingredients.

🍽 **Romano** – *Via Coppino 118,
località Darsena, Viareggio. 📞0584 38 47 33.
www.ristoranteilporto.eu. Closed Tue.
Reservations suggested.* The waiter will
announce the classic seafood specialities,
which are made with very fresh ingredients.

TAKING A BREAK

Pasticceria Patalani – *Via Zanardelli 183,
Viareggio. 📞0584 47 279.* Excellent pastries
for a tiptop breakfast.

ENTERTAINMENT

Clubbing in Versilia – *Seaside promenade
between Lido di Camaiore and Forte dei
Marmi.* Every evening the seafront is
transformed into a dancefloor. From
Viareggio to Forte dei Marmi there is a
chain of clubs, each one different. The
oldest, founded in 1970, is La Bussola
(now **Bussola Versilia**, *Viale Roma 44,
Marina di Pietrasanta. 📞349 19 93 837. www.
bussolaversilia.it*) which has given Versilia
its reputation for a lively nightlife. The
25- to 30-year-olds prefer **Seven Apples**
(*Viale Roma 108, Focette, Marina di Pietrasanta.
📞0584 20 458. www.sevenapples.it*), with its
pool, **La Capannina** (*Viale della Repubblica
16, Forte dei Marmi. 📞0584 80 169 or 371 37
99 456. lacapanninadifranceschi.it*), which has
orchestral evenings, or **Twiga Beach Club**
(*Viale Roma 2, Marina di Pietrasanta. 📞0584 21
518 or 393 93 56 127. twigabeachclub.com*).

SHOPPING

Markets
Lido di Camaiore – *Viale J. F. Kennedy
and Via del Secco Mon mornings (and Sun
mornings in summer).*

Camaiore – *Historic centre, Fri mornings, 2nd
weekend of the month, crafts.*

Forte dei Marmi – *Piazza Marconi Wed
mornings (and Sun in summer) antiquarian;
crafts first weekend of the month.*

Pietrasanta – *Piazza Statuto, Thu mornings;
crafts, 2nd Sunday of the month; antiquarian,
1st Sun of the month; flowers,
3rd Sun of the month.*

Seravezza – *In the centre, Mon mornings.*

Viareggio – *Piazza Cavour area, Thu
mornings; antiquarian, last weekend of the
month; crafts, 3rd weekend of the month.*

EVENTS

Carnevale di Viareggio – *ilcarnevale.com.*
World-famous carnival, with elaborate
colourful floats, many feature timely
political caricatures.

Festival Puccini – *Torre del Lago. www.
puccinifestival.it. July–Aug.* Opera festival.

La Versiliana Festival – *Marina di
Pietrasanta. versilianafestival.it.July–Aug;
additional events throughout the year.*
Theatre, dance, music events and art shows.

Carrara
Massa and the Quarries

This town, whose name comes from the Ligurian root "kar", meaning "stone", is world-famous for its exceptionally pure, fine-grained white marble. Carrara marble (*marmo*) has been quarried since Roman times. Michelangelo used to come to the local quarries to choose blocks of stone for his masterpieces. In 1769 Maria Teresa Cybo Malaspina (the last of the aristocratic family which controlled events in Massa and Carrara for many centuries) set up an Academy of Fine Arts, which teaches artistic technique and skills.

▶ **Population:** 62,285.

Michelin Map: Atlas p 32 and Map 563 – J 12 and Map 735 Fold 14.

Info: Lungomare Vespucci 24, Marina di Massa. ℰ0585 24 00 63. www.aptmassacarrara.it.

▶ **Location:** Carrara lies in a delightful valley on the edge of a ruggedly spectacular limestone mountain range, the Apuan Alps, which have tops so white that they seem to be covered in snow. It is easily reached by the Genoa–Livorno (Leghorn) motorway.

Don't Miss: Fantiscritti, the rugged marble quarries.

Kids: In the marble quarries watch enormous machines and marble blocks in movement (be sure to visit during work hours).

TOWN
Duomo
The **cathedral** was built (11C–14C) in the Romanesque-Gothic style with a façade in the Pisan style, pierced by a rose window, decorated with superb marble tracery and flanked by an elegant 13C bell tower. The interior has interesting statues including a wooden Crucifix and a marble Annunciation, both 14C.

Beside the cathedral is a huge 16C fountain decorated with a statue by Baccio Bandinelli (1493–1560).

Museo del Marmo★
Viale XX Settembre 85, loc. Stadio.
🕐*Open Jun–mid Sept Tue–Sun 10am–6pm; mid Sept–May Tue–Wed 9.30am–12.30pm, Thu–Sun 9.30am–12.30pm, 3–5pm.* 🕐*Closed Mon and public hols.* ✆€5. 📞*Call for guided tour.* ♿ ℰ0585 84 57 46. www.musei.carrara.ms.gov.it/museo-del-marmo.*

From Antiquity to the present day, marble is presented beginning with how marble was quarried during the days of the ancient Romans, with information obtained from archaeological excavations. The **Marmoteca★** is a "library" of more than 300 samples of marble and granite from the largest seams in the world. Quarrying techniques from the 17C to the early 20C are shown. Various aspects of the use of marble precede a collection of modern sculptures.

EXCURSIONS
Marble quarries★
The untamed scenery, the white scree slopes and the gigantic scale of the work undertaken by man are an amazing sight. Beside the road stand small viewing platforms (*during working hours*) showing the machinery in operation. To extract the marble, the quarrymen use a "diamond wire", a steel wire containing small cylinders covered with diamond dust, which acts as a high-power abrasive. The blocks of stone are then taken down to the plain where they are divided in stonecutting plants; after being processed in marble works, the stone is exported from the harbour in **Marina di Carrara**.

Fantiscritti Quarries★★
4km/2.5mi NE beyond Miseglia.
This is the most impressive of all the quarry sites because of its ruggedness and terracing. The site is reached by a particularly steep road, which crosses three viaducts known as the *Ponti di Vara*, built

Carrara Marble

The marble seams in the Apuan Alps extend over several square miles but the largest of all is in Carrara. It is famous for its translucent whiteness and fine grain, qualities which are highly prized in statues, hence its title – *statuario*. Once polished, it acquires the pearly sparkle that is its characteristic quality. Carrara also produces veined or coloured marbles (dark red, green, grey-blue, orange). The colours result from the presence of mineral salts (or other elements) in the original limestone which, after crystallising for several million years, has turned into marble.

Neptune Carrara marble statue by Bartolomeo Ammannati, Neptune Fountain (1565), Piazza della Signoria, Florence

On this side of the Apuan Alps, quarrying has been in progress for some 2,000 years. Quarrying is now concentrated in three valleys – Colonnata, Fantiscritti and Ravaccione. Over the centuries, quarrying has undergone constant expansion and the industry now produces 800,000 tonnes of marble a year. This has been made possible, since the 19C, by new techniques and the opening, in 1876, of a railway linking the quarries to the sea, thereby facilitating the transport of the stone.

From the reign of Caesar Augustus until the 5C, Imperial Rome obtained three-quarters of its building stone from Carrara. Thereafter, Carrara marble was used for such prestigious works as the main staircase in the Hermitage in St Petersburg, London's Marble Arch and the Kennedy Center for the Performing Arts in Washington, DC. Since the Renaissance many sculptors – Michelangelo, Giambologna, Bernini, Canova and Henry Moore – have come to the quarries in the vicinity to choose stone for their work.

Carrara marble continues to be a sought-after building material. Today, the Carrara Marmotec exhibition takes place every two (even-numbered) years and attracts builders and architects from around the world. The stonecutters here are so expert that other types of marble are shipped from around the world to be cut here and then shipped back or on to their final destination.

Carrara marble quarry

in the 19C for the railway, which are now road bridges.

Colonnata Quarries★

8km/5mi E via Bedizzano or Carrara along the valley floor.

These quarries are more easily accessible than the others; the road mounts from one level to the next, passing several stonecutting plants. The setting is less grandiose but more attractive owing to the greenery. Its marble caves are used to cure *lardo* (pork fatback).

Campo Cecina Road★

20km/12mi N of Carrara by the Fosdinovo road (S446d) to the viewing point.

The road climbs above a wooded valley and passes through Gragnana and Castelpoggio. The first view (*left*) is over the final outcrops of the Apuan Alps and down to the sea, including the beach at Marina di Carrara and the promontory at Montemarcello.

▶ Turn right into the winding Campo Cecina road which is used by the large trucks transporting the marble from the quarries.

The road runs along the south-facing, pine-clad slopes of Monte Pizza. There are more views (*right*) over the Carrara area. A picturesque trip along a road cut into the bare marble hillsides of Monte Uccelliera, interspersed with forest sections, leads to **Piazzale dell'Uccelliera**, from which there is a magnificent **view★★** of the Torano quarries, the beaches at Marina di Massa and Montignoso, the islands in the Tuscan archipelago and the peaks in the Southern Alps.

Massa

In the plains at the foot of the Apuan Alps, 4km/2.5mi inland from the Riviera.

This modern town has squares adorned with large fountains and marble sculptures. The many white marble façades are from nearby quarries. Two **historic buildings** from the 15C–18C remain, during the powerful Malaspina family rule. Their 15C–16C Castello Malaspina is incorporated into the half-ruined medieval fortress (*Rocca*) on the stony hillside overlooking the town; their 16C–17C residence, **Palazzo Cybo Malaspina**, now houses the Prefettura (*Piazza Aranci in the town centre*).

The **cathedral** (*Duomo*) has a modern marble façade and interesting art including a Madonna by Pinturicchio, and the Malaspina family tombs.

Massa's **botanical garden** features plants indigenous to the Apuan Alps.

Garfagnana★

Region

Inhabited since prehistoric times, this region is particularly interesting for its landscape and its geology. The rough configuration of the Apuan Alps is visibly different from the Apennines and the softer outline of the foothills.

🚗DRIVING TOUR

150km/31mi. See map pp218–219. Depart from Lucca, heading N, to Vagli Sotto.

- ♿ **Michelin Map:** 563 – J 13 and 735 Fold 14.
- 🛈 **Info:** Piazza delle Erbe, Castelnuovo Garfagnana. 📞0583 64 10 07. www. castelnuovogarfagnana.org.
- ▶ **Location:** Easily reached from Lucca by the SS12.
- 👪 **Kids:** Grotta del Vento.
- 🕐 **Timing:** Allow one day, more if you go hiking.

Two roads, parallel along the banks of the Serchio, lead from Lucca to Borgo a Mozzano. The west branch of SS12 and Ludovica SR2, built by Charles Ludovic de Bourbon arrives in Borgo a

Mozzano; the east branch at **Bagni di Lucca** (*8km/5mi NE of Borgo a Mozzano*), lovely thermal baths nestled at the foot of where the Garfagnana mountains begin. Very popular in the 19C with royalty and artists, the town built Europe's first casinos (1840).

▷ SS12 to Vinchiana, turn right toward Pieve di S. Giorgio di Brancoli.

Pieve di Brancoli

Cited in written text c. 1062, this interesting Romanesque church is built on a basilica plan with three naves and retains its 12C pulpit and baptismal fonts. From the piazza enjoy a beautiful view of Lucca and Serchio Valley.

▷ SS12. After crossing the Serchio take SP2. At Diecimo turn left to Vetriano.

Teatrino di Vetriano

The gem of this hamlet is a tiny theatre, 71sq m/764sq ft, built in 1890 and restored, with money from productions by Accademia del Teatro alla Scala in Milan. ◷ *Open by reservation only.* ◷ *Closed 23 Dec–2 Jan.* ✆€5. ✆*0583 35 81 31. www.fondoambiente.it/luoghi/ teatrino-di-vetriano.*

▷ Follow the road to Colognora.

Pretty town **Colognora** has a chestnut museum: **Museo del Castagno**. Chestnut flour is used in local cuisine. *Località Colognora, Val di Roggio.* ◷*Open Sun and public hols 3–6pm, other days by reservation.* ◷*Closed winter.* ✆*0583 35 80 04 or 328 57 22 956. www.museodelcastagno.it.*

▷ Take SP2.

Borgo a Mozzano

This village on the road to Abetone is known for its unusual Magdalen Bridge, **Ponte della Maddalena** (12C), spanning the River Serchio. Its name derives from the statue of Mary Magdalen, now conserved in the parish church. Also called the **Devil's Bridge** (Ponte del Diavolo) for the legend of the builder who asked the Devil to help him complete it. The Devil accepted in exchange for the first soul to cross the bridge. To prevent a human soul from going to hell, the builder ensured that the first living thing to cross the bridge was a dog.

Barga★

At Fornaci di Barga an excursion to the right leads to the Romanesque **Pieve di Santa Maria di Loppia**, rebuilt in the 16C.

The town stands amid trees and vineyards in a delightful setting on a plateau on the northern slopes of the Serchio Valley over which it had control during the Middle Ages. Its "castle" (*castello*) is the upper town, a medieval district of winding, steep and narrow streets behind the remains of the town walls. Above the upper town is an elegant **Duomo**, a superb Romanesque **cathedral** built of white limestone. Its portal is flanked by two engaged columns, each crowned by a lion in the Lombard-Romanesque style. From the terrace in front of the church there is a pleasant view over the rooftops of the upper town to the mountains.

Inside the cathedral is a superb 12C marble **ambo★** (pulpit) decorated with bas-relief carvings (scenes from the Life of Mary and the Life of Christ); also an eagle-lectern, the stoup decorated with carved heads and St Christopher carrying the Child Jesus (18C).

▷ 5km/3mi W of Barga.

Castelvecchio Pascoli

The village is linked in the Italian mind with the *Songs of Castelvecchio* composed by **Giovanni Pascoli** (1855–1912), a pupil of Carducci. **Casa di Giovanni Pascoli** is here (◷*Open Tue 3.30–6.45pm (winter 2–5.15pm), Wed–Sun 10.30am–1pm, 3.30–6.45pm (winter 9.30am–1pm, 2.30–5.15pm).* ◷*Closed Mon;* ✆*0583 76 61 47; www. fondazionepascoli.it).*

▷ Drive S for 5km/2.5mi to Gallicano, then 9km/6mi to Fornovolasco.

⁂ Grotta del Vento

14km/9mi SW of Fornovolasco.
Guided tours (1hr) 10am–6pm;
2hr and 3hr tours available Apr–Oct
and public hols only. Closed 25
Dec. €9 (1hr); €14 (2hr); €20 (3hr).
0583 72 20 24.
www.grottadelvento.com.

The **Windy Cave** lies on a winding road bristling with sheer rocky cliffs and providing a breathtaking view down over the Calomini hermitage set in a wall of rock at an altitude of more than 100m/325ft. Inside the cave, the temperature is a steady 10.7°C/51°F. The "wind" is sucked into the cave during the winter when the temperature outside is lower and, in summer, the phenomenon is reversed.

Its stalactites and stalagmites are bright from a film of water. Also see polychrome flowstone, alabaster draperies, crystal-brimmed lakes, underground water-courses and bizarre forms of erosion.

▷ Return to Gallicano and continue 8km/5mi to Castelnuovo di Garfagnana.

Castelnuovo di Garfagnana

This small industrial town is the starting point for long-distance walks in the Apuan Alps Park (*www.parcapuane.it*). Its 12C **Rocca Ariostesca** houses a small archaeological museum. The 16C **Duomo** has paintings attributed to Verrocchio and Ghirlandaio. A large market moves in every Thursday. Ludovico Ariosto, author of the epic Renaissance poem *Orlando Furioso*, lived for three years (1522–25) in this brigand-infested province.

▷ Take SP72, which climbs up to Castiglione di Garfagnana.

Castiglione di Garfagnana

The village, which occupies a panoramic position above the valley, is crowned by the remains of the Rocca. It has the church of S Michele (15C), with red and white façade, and the older church of S Pietro (13C).

▷ Return towards Castelnuovo di Garfagnana, then head for San Romano.

3km/1.2mi north of **San Romano di Garfagnana**, the **Fortezza delle Verrucole**, built 11C–12C, stands 600m/660yds high on a hill. *Park the car in the hamlet of Verrucole and walk to the fortress, which offers a beautiful view of the Garfagnana and the Apuan Alps.*

▷ Take SR445 S towards Camporgiano, then turn right to Vagli.

Lago di Vagli

A beautiful 10km/6mi road leads to the artificial lake of Vagli, created in 1947 to supply the power plant. It houses a ghost town, the Fabbriche di Careggine (13C), which becomes reachable every time the basin is emptied for the dam maintenance and repairs.

ADDRESSES

⌂ STAY

Albergo-Ristorante da Carlino – *Via Garibaldi 15, Castelnuovo di Garfagnana. 0583 64 42 70. www.dacarlino.it. 23 rooms. Restaurant.* This friendly hostel, situated in the heart of the Apuan Alps park, offers rooms decorated with rustic furnishings and spacious marble bathrooms.

⊖ EAT

Antica Locanda di Sesto – *Via Ludovica 1660, Sesto di Moriano, 2.5km/1mi NW of Ponte a Moriano. 0583 57 81 81. www.anticalocandadisesto.it. Closed Sat.* Family run, friendly and warm, this old inn with medieval origins has preserved a naturalness and authenticity. The beef with black pepper and rosemary is highly recommended for meat lovers.

EVENTS

My Flower – Biennale dell'Azalea – *In Borgo a Mozzano. Apr. giardinoazalea.it.*

Festival Opera Barga – *In Barga. Jul–Aug. 0583 71 10 68. www.operabarga.it.* An international opera festival which has been running every July since 1967.

Barga Jazz – *Barga. Aug. www.barganews. com.* Jazz festival.

Lunigiana★

Region

This historical and geographical region with a backdrop of castles and Romanesque parish churches runs along the River Magra on the borders of Tuscany, Liguria and Emilia. Although it combines a number of different cultures, it still retains a strongly discernible character of its own.

🚗DRIVING TOURS

FROM AULLA TO CASOLA IN LUNIGIANA
35km/22mi. About half a day.
🕰*See regional map pp218–219.*

Aulla
The town is overlooked by the **Fortezza della Brunella**. This quadrangular fortress dates from the early 16C and is believed to have been built by Giovanni dalle Bande Nere. It now houses the **Natural History Museum** (*Via della Brunella;* 🕙*Opening time varies;* 👝 *€3.50;* 📞*0187 40 90 77*), which contains a reconstruction of the natural environments of La Lunigiana region, ranging from the caves to the Mediterranean scrub (*macchia*).

▶ Take S63 E. Beyond Rometta turn right into S445. On the outskirts of Gragnola follow the signs to Equi (S).

Equi Terme
This **spa resort** with its sulphur-rich springs provides treatment for respiratory and skin disorders and bone and joint ailments. In addition to its therapeutic virtues, the locality is also of special archaeological and speleological interest.
The karst **caves** (🕙*for opening hours, guided tours and prices contact the Grotte di Equi Geo-Archeo-Adventure Park:* 📞*338 58 14 482; www.grotte-diequi.it*) are open to the public and contain a wealth of stalactites and stalagmites. In some of their deep,

rugged cavities, remains have been found showing evidence of human settlements in the Paleolithic and Neolithic ages. There are also traces of cave bears.

▶ Return to SS445. Continue E towards Codiponte and Casola in La Lunigiana (Aulella Valley).

Codiponte
Its main attraction is the Romanesque parish church (*pieve*) with Lombard-Carolingian decorative motifs. It has retained its old font.

Casola in Lunigiana
A stroll through the old village with its typical 15C–16C buildings is highly recommended. The lone brick tower, the symbol of the city, once served as the bell tower for the church of Santa Felicita, which has a rich Baroque interior.

"La Pieve"

The Italian word *pieve* is derived from the Latin *plebs*, meaning the common people, and is used to indicate the local place of worship – the parish church. These churches are often rich in symbolic carvings depicting both sin and redemption.

⏱ **Michelin Map:** 563 – I–J, 11–12 or 735 Folds 13–14.

ℹ **Info:** Lungomare Vespucci 24, Marina di Massa, 📞0585 24 00 63; Piazza Gramsci 1, Aulla, 📞0187 40 94 74. www.aptmassacarrara.it; www.visittuscany.com/en/areas/lunigiana.

▶ **Location:** A thin strip of land along the course of the River Magra, between Tuscany, Liguria and Emilia.

👫 **Kids:** Museo Etnografico della Lunigiana.

🕐 **Timing:** One day.

Historical Note

La Lunigiana was first inhabited in Paleolithic times. Later there were Etruscan settlements in the area and the Romans founded a 2,000-strong colony in the town of Luni (now in Liguria) from which the name La Lunigiana is derived. During the Middle Ages the region was still a single entity, under the authority of the Bishop.

FROM AULLA TO PONTREMOLI

22km/13.5mi. Allow about half a day.
See regional map pp218–219.

Aulla

See p241.

▷ Take SS62 N
towards Pontremoli.

Villafranca in Lunigiana

This small town is best known for its ▲▲ **Museo Etnografico★** (*Ethnography Museum, Via dei Mulini 71;* Open Mar–Nov Thu–Sat 9.30am–12.30pm, 3–6pm; Dec–Feb Fri–Sat 9.30am–12.30pm; €3; 0187 49 34 17; www.museoetnografi-codellalunigiana.it), which provides a clear illustration of the cultural identity of La Lunigiana's rural civilisation through numerous displays and audio-visual presentations. Exhibits include weights from the Roman era, wooden ex-voto statuettes, utensils for peeling chestnuts, looms, cheese moulds, butter churns, etc.

▷ Continue N on S62.

Filattiera

Beside the road stands the parish church, **Pieve di Sorano**, built in the Tuscan and Lombard style. The finest example of this architectural style can be seen in the splendid apse.

▷ Continue N on SS62
to Pontremoli.

Pontremoli

Pontremoli lies at the confluence of the rivers Magra and Verde. **Piagnaro Castle**, begun in the 10C, bears witness to the town's cultural history. It gets its name from the slate slabs (*piagne*) used to roof buildings in the Lunigiana region. The castle houses the interesting **Museo delle Statue Stele della Lunigiana** (Open daily Jun–Sept 10am–6.30pm (Aug 7.30pm); Oct–May 9.30am–5.30pm; Closed 25 Dec; €7 (castle and museum); 0187 83 14 39; www. statuestele.org), a collection of female anthropomorphic sculptures representing the Mediterranean mother goddess and symbol of fertility, and male sculptures whose weapons may be intended to indicate deified heroes or tribal chiefs. The statues span a long period dating from the second millennium BC to the 5C BC.

The large **bell tower** (*campanone*), situated between Piazza della Repubblica and Piazza del Duomo, is the symbol of the town. It was once part of the wall known as the war-guard (*cacciaguerra*), built in the 14C on the orders of Castruccio Castracani to separate the Guelf and Ghibelline districts of the town.

ADDRESSES

🛏 STAY

🍴🍴🍴🍴 **Agriturismo Costa d'Orsola** – *Località Orsola, 2km/1mi SW of Pontremoli.* 0187 83 33 32. www.costadorsola.it. *14 rooms.* The ancient 16C hamlet was restored and transformed into a delightful country hotel. Situated on the top of a hill overlooking a valley. Pleasant rooms and good food.

🍴 EAT

🍴🍴 **Da Renato** – *Località Guinadi, Pontremoli. 10km/6mi NW of Pontremoli.* 0187 83 47 15. The woodland setting of the picturesque town of Guinadi explains the presence on the menu of this restaurant of specialities based on the local mushrooms; other typical dishes are wild boar stew accompanied by polenta, as well as diamond-shaped pasta (*testaroli*).

This lesser explored area of western Tuscany is full of famous art treasures, like the Leaning Tower, but is also full of the unexpected, from "Venetian" canals in Livorno, to a coastal wildlife refuge near a winery, eerie *fumaroles* and spooky pipes that spout steam, and a museum full of Vespas near a gourmet chocolate factory. The Island of Elba is full of outdoor activities. Mainland beaches tend to be laidback and reasonable, rather than glitzy.

Pisa

Pisa's glorious past dates back to the Etruscans, and then the Romans. As a major sea power in the Middle Ages, it is quite different from its rival and conqueror, Florence. Its Leaning Tower provides not only a curiosity – and a degree of suspense – but is only one part of a stunningly beautiful complex of buildings in Piazza dei Miracoli. As a university town, Pisa's youthful buzz is matched by enthusiasm for modern trends, including public art. Take a leisurely ride on the Arno canals, which as in Livorno, the Medici family modelled after Venice. Celebrate festivals centred around the water.

Back on land, celebrate the Vespa at the Piaggio Museum in Pontedera. Or rent a Vespa, buzz off to the Amedei gourmet chocolate factory, and then follow the open road.

The Coast

The Etruscan Coast stretches from Livorno to Piombino, and offers an amazing array of landscapes and activities. Explore archaeological ruins – especially Etruscan – and see literary associations that are very familiar to Italians. Beaches range from simple to elegant, especially lovely where framed with beautiful maritime pine groves. Or muse like the poet Carducci over the elegant and melancholy cypresses between Castagneto and Bolgheri. For those who can't resist a mystery or a puzzle, head to Pieve di San Giovanni and try to figure out what is written in the magic square in the parish church.

Wine and Cuisine

The Etruscan Wine Road offers wines from the humble to the very pricey. The cuisine offers bounty from the sea, the hills and the mountains. Piombino offers access to the Island of Elba, famous for Napoleon's exile here. Rugged, mountainous Elba has activities, from swimming and other water sports, to rock climbing, hiking and paragliding, and can be quite economical.

Geological Wonders

Further south, the Metalliferous Hills offer a world of metals like iron and copper (and crafts) and an underworld of mining. The wide variety of minerals create a spooky landscape as they shoot up steam and bubble to the surface.

The Via Aurelia, the SS1, offers easy access to beaches and hill towns.

Highlights

1 Marvel at Pisa's **Leaning Tower** and **Piazza dei Miracoli**, for their "miraculous" beauty (p249)

2 Taste precious white truffles and wander through medieval **San Miniato** (p265)

3 Admire the **poetic landscape**, swim in the sea and taste wine along the Etruscan Riviera (p270)

4 Enjoy water sports and visit Napoleon's villa on the **Isola d'Elba** and swim off the Island of Giglio (p275)

5 Explore **Volterra** and its "metal" hills, mines and alabaster and spooky landscape (p282)

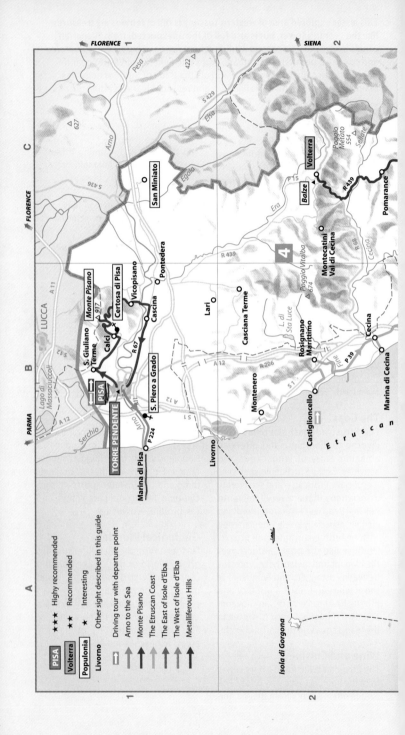

Legend:

PISA	★★★	Highly recommended
Volterra	★★	Recommended
Populonia	★	Interesting
Livorno		Other sight described in this guide

Driving tour with departure point

- Arno to the Sea
- Monte Pisano
- The Etruscan Coast
- The East of Isole d'Elba
- The West of Isole d'Elba
- Metalliferous Hills

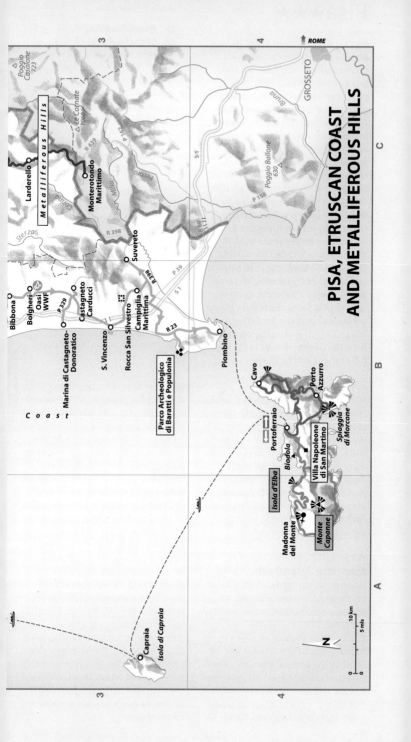

PISA, ETRUSCAN COAST AND METALLIFEROUS HILLS

245

Pisa★★★

Pisa's iconic buildings tell of its long and illustrious history. The city is more spacious than Florence and less austere – thanks to its yellow, pink or yellow-ochre house fronts – but it shares the same river, the Arno, which bisects the city here in a majestic meander. Pisa has the atmosphere of a minor capital that has lost some of its bustle, but the city's charm lies in its aristocratic air and genteel Mediterranean lifestyle. Pisa is almost totally encircled by walls and is traversed from north to south by a main street lined with shops. On the south bank the thoroughfare is called Corso Italia. On the north bank, the road narrows and is flanked by arcades, known as Borgo Stretto. The noble, cheerful, winding Via Santa Maria links Piazza del Duomo with the Arno. The interesting streets on the north bank flank the busiest district in the city, full of shops and restaurants.

▶ **Population:** 88,880.
⚙ **Michelin Map:** 563: K13.
🄸 **Info:** Piazza Duomo 7. ℰ050 55 01 00. www.turismo.pisa.it.
◗ **Location:** Pisa is near the mouth of the Arno. Migliarino–San Rossore–Massaciuccoli Park is between Pisa and the sea.
👥 **Kids:** Take the mini train from Piazza Arcivescovado, a horse-drawn carriage from Piazza dei Miracoli, or a cruise on the Arno. In Pontedera admire vintage Vespas and other motos in Museo Piaggio, and taste Amedei gourmet chocolate.
🕐 **Timing:** For Piazza dei Miracoli allow half a day, and two days to explore the riches of the city.
🎭 **Don't Miss:** Piazza dei Miracoli, the riverbanks of the Arno, Piazza dei Cavalieri.

THE CITY TODAY

Modern Pisa has a decidedly youthful atmosphere, thanks to the University of Pisa, one of Italy's largest and best universities. Popular among students and contemporary art lovers is a giant mural (at Sant'Antonio Convent) by the American pop artist Keith Haring. Pisa's population is supplemented by millions of tourists, who flock to see the Leaning Tower, one of the world's most distinctive architectural structures.

A BIT OF HISTORY

Maritime Splendour

When it was founded c. 7C BC, Pisa was on the coast. The shoreline receded as alluvium accumulated at the mouth of the Arno.

The Etruscan city was an ally of Rome for many years. From 180BC it was colonised by the Romans who saw its geographical advantage on the Arno near the sea, and turned it into a naval base free from the risk of attack by pirates, a role that continued until the AD 476 fall of the Roman Empire in the West. In AD 888 the city became an independent republic, but only later in the Middle Ages did it use its geographical location for economic development. Like Genoa and Venice, this powerful maritime republic resisted Muslim domination; its "merchant-warriors" fought stubbornly throughout the Mediterranean Basin. Pisa took possession of Sardinia in 1015 and later of Corsica, which it controlled through the 11C. In 1114 it captured the Balearic Islands, then Tunisia, and set up Mediterranean trading posts east as far as Syria. Pisa developed into a very active port in the 11C and reached the peak of its prosperity in the 12C and first half of the 13C. Its ships plied the Mediterranean carrying arms, wool, furs, leather and timber from the Apennines to the Orient, together with iron mined on the Isle of Elba: they returned with spices, silk and cotton. They constructed the finest buildings and founded the university, which still has a reputation for excellence.

GETTING THERE

BY AIR: Galileo Galilei International Airport (*Information Desk in the Arrivals Area, ✆050 84 93 00; www.pisa-airport.com*) is served internationally by Alitalia, British Airways, Lufthansa and by a number of low-cost carriers including easyJet and Ryanair. The airport is linked to Pisa Central Railway Station in the city centre (*2km/1.2mi*) by the PisaMover, a high-speed automated people mover service (*5min; daily 6am–midnight, every 5–8min; €5; pisa-mover.com*).

BY TRAIN: Pisa **Central Railway Station** (**Piazza della Stazione**) is linked to Genoa (Genoa–La Spezia–Pisa line), Rome (Pisa–Livorno–Grosseto–Rome line), Lucca and Florence; change at Empoli for Siena (*www.trenitalia.com*).

BY BUS: Buses run from Pisa Airport to Florence (*Sky Bus: 1hr; www.caronnatour.com*), Lucca and Viareggio (*lucca.cttnord.it*).

BY CAR: Pisa is approached by road from Florence by the express route Florence–Pisa–Livorno and from north or south by the coastal motorway A12, which runs north–south between Pisa and the sea.

GETTING AROUND

TRAFFIC AND PARKING: Driving in Pisa is difficult owing to the pedestrian precincts and the one-way system designed to take traffic away from the city centre. The larger car parks are outside the town walls (near Piazza dei Miracoli). There are numerous small car parks or parking spaces in the streets or along the banks of the Arno in the centre near the main sights.

When the Investiture Controversy broke out between the Papacy and the Empire in the late 11C, Pisa, a resolutely Ghibelline city, rallied to the Emperor's camp. At sea it resisted the threat of Genoa, its main maritime rival in the Mediterranean. On land it withstood its two Guelf rivals, Lucca and Florence. When Pisa was deprived of the support of Emperor Frederick II (d. 1250) and of King Manfred (his son, d. 1266), the city began its decline.

In August 1284 at the great **Battle of Meloria** (a small island off Livorno), the Pisan fleet was wiped out by Genoese ships. The city was forced to transfer its rights in Corsica to Genoa and to give up Sardinia. Unable to access its commercial empire in the East by sea, it was also undermined by internal strife. Pisa was taken over by Florence in 1406.

The Medici dynasty was particularly interested in Pisa. Lorenzo the Magnificent reorganised its university and began to build a new one. In the 16C Pisa was incorporated into the Grand Duchy of Tuscany and Cosimo I founded the Order of the **Knights of St Stephen** in the city. During this period the city enjoyed a renewal of its influence, mainly in the sciences.

PISAN ROMANESQUE

An innovative artistic style emerged in the 11C–13C, while Pisa was increasing in economic prosperity and political power, expressed in both the city's architecture and its sculpture.

Architecture

Pisan religious architectural style differed from Romanesque elsewhere in Italy. Its heyday was in the 13C and spread throughout Tuscany, including Lucca, Pistoia and Arezzo – and to churches in Sardinia and Corsica.

The style, Pisan Romanesque, brought together a pleasing combination of several influences, most markedly of Lombardy. To it was added a wealth of decoration inspired by the shapes and motifs of articles brought back from the Orient or the Islamic world by the Pisan fleet. This trend led to outstanding elegance and unity, of which the cathedral in Pisa is the most rigorous and solemn example. The west front, side walls and apse are all skilfully faced with green and white marble, a costly building material popular in Pisa and other Tuscan towns, in particular Florence. Whereas the architects of Florence emphasised the geometric divisions on the façades of churches by framing them in marble, the craftsmen of Pisa made extensive use of relief – tall but shallow blind arcading running all round the building and galleries with exuberant colonnettes, dappling the upper section of the gable with light and shade. Rose windows, diamond shapes and other small motifs picked out in marble marquetry show Oriental inspiration in their use of colour.

In the second half of the 11C and early 12C the architects whose names are inextricably linked with the great buildings of Pisa were **Buscheto**, **Rainaldo** – his direct successor who was a contemporary of **Diotisalvi**, and **Bonanno Pisano**, architect and sculptor. **Giovanni di Simone** was the main architect working in the second half of the 13C.

Sculpture

Medieval Pisan sculpture has pride of place in the history of Italian art.

Local artists such as Bonanno Pisano and **Fra' Guglielmo**, or Lombards such as **Guido da Como**, worked on the decoration of the Romanesque churches of Pisa in the 12C and early 13C. However, Nicola Pisano, a sculptor perhaps from Apulia, is credited with paving the way for a succession of artists in the second half of the 13C. In their eyes Pisa was the birthplace of Italian Romanesque and especially of Gothic sculpture.

These sculptors, who were also architects and interior decorators, were responsible for the creation of huge and unusual pulpits, masterpieces of harmonious structure, intricate decoration and the aesthetic beauty of their carvings.

Nicola Pisano (born c. 1220, d. shortly after 1280) studied classical sculpture. He assimilated its majesty and power but added the humanity and the realism seen in the paintings of his contemporary, Giotto. His main works are the pulpit in the Baptistery in Pisa and in the cathedral in Siena. With the assistance of his son, Giovanni, who worked with him in Siena, he also built the Fontana Maggiore in Perugia. One of his pupils was Arnolfo di Cambio, the architect of the cathedral in Florence.

Giovanni Pisano (born c. 1250, d. c. 1315–20) was undoubtedly the greatest of all the sculptors. He had a more flexible technique and captured dramatic intensity. He worked with his father until the latter's death. His compositions became increasingly complex with figures that were more and more tormented, yet were filled with an outstanding intensity that gave them a wonderful lifelike quality. His genius created the splendid pulpit in Siena cathedral and in Sant'Andrea in Pistoia. He was also the first person to direct work on Siena cathedral, which he wanted to cover with huge statues like the Gothic cathedrals in France that he had visited c. 1270. Giovanni was the last member of the first Pisano dynasty and his death marked the end of the great period of powerful and monumental Gothic sculptures in Tuscany. His most able pupil was Tino di Camaino, from Siena.

Andrea da Pontedera, named after a town near Pisa and also known as **Andrea Pisano**, was born at the end of the 13C and worked mainly in Florence where one of his major works was the first bronze door for the Baptistery. His elegant and refined style (developed while training as a goldsmith) and his attractively drawn scenes were not inspired by his Pisan predecessors. His powerful high reliefs decorate the bell tower by Giotto in Florence.

Andrea's son, **Nino Pisano**, who died c. 1365–70, preferred to work in the round. He was a master in the art of relief and he created graceful Madonnas including the famous *Madonna del Latte* (*See Museo Nazionale di San Matteo, p258*). This second Pisano dynasty, which also included **Tommaso**, Nino's brother, enjoyed a reputation in the late 14C that made their workshop an obligatory training ground for a number of great Sienese and Florentine sculptors in the early 15C, including Lorenzo Ghiberti and Jacopo della Quercia.

Renaissance Revolutionary Genius

Pisa's most famous son was the astronomer, mathematician, philosopher and physicist **Galileo Galilei** (1564–1642), whom 21C scientist Stephen Hawking credits as the single person most responsible for the birth of modern science. Galileo first taught design in Florence's Accademia, then returned to Pisa as chair of mathematics in 1589 at the university where he had studied medicine. His patron was Cosimo II, Grand Duke of Tuscany. Nevertheless Galileo had to defend his theory of heliocentrism before the Inquisition in 1633 on trial of heresy and was forced to recant his theory that the Earth revolved around the sun.

SIGHTS

PIAZZA DEI MIRACOLI★★★

(Miracles Square) *Allow 3hr.*

This prestigious **square**, which is also known as **Piazza del Duomo** (Cathedral Square), contains four buildings which constitute an exceptionally beautiful sight, one of the most famous in the world and in 1987 designated a World Heritage Site by UNESCO. It resembles a vast enclosure, lined on two sides by a slim wall of red brick to which crenellations were added in the mid-12C. Within are the dazzling white marble mass of the Baptistery and the cathedral with its famous bell tower, known as the Lean-

ing Tower of Pisa. In the background is the cemetery (*camposanto*). This succession of buildings is best seen from **Porta Santa Maria** and it is also from this point that the angle of the Leaning Tower is most spectacular.

All the monuments are open daily; last admission 30min before closing.

Torre Pendente (Leaning Tower)★★★

Check the calendar on the website: tickets for the Tower are at set times and limited in number, so you must choose a time when you buy your ticket. €18 (includes Cathedral). For safety reasons, under-8s are not permitted to enter. 050 83 50 11/12. www.opapisa. it (online tickets).

The **Torre Pendente**, the bell tower (58m/189ft high) of the cathedral, is the pre-eminent symbol of the city. Its famous angle (approximately 5m/16ft off the vertical) has made it one of the most popular tourist attractions in the world. Its angle is caused by the alluvial soil, which is not compact enough to bear the weight of the building.

The building work was begun by Bonanno Pisano in 1173 and had reached the first floor when the first subsidence occurred. The architect, however, ignored it and another two storeys were built. When the second subsidence occurred in 1185, work

Baptistery, Duomo and the Leaning Tower

© The_Chickenwing/iStock

I abjure, curse, and detest!

Galileo Galilei was born in 1564, two months before William Shakespeare, into a well-educated family whose father was a renowned musician and composer in Pisa. Galileo abandoned his medical studies, taught design in Florence's Accademia, then returned to Pisa to pursue physics and astronomy. In 1589 he became chair of mathematics at the university.

Portrait of Galileo Galilei

He was only 19 when, watching a swinging lamp in the cathedral in his native town, he realised that the oscillations always took the same amount of time whatever their range. From this observation he developed the principle of the pendulum and decided to apply the measurement of its movement to the measurement of time. He used the Leaning Tower of Pisa to study the laws of falling bodies and uniformly accelerated motion. He also built one of the earliest known microscopes.

In 1609 Galileo invented the telescope that now bears his name and began to study the stars, measuring the height of relief on the moon's surface, discovering Saturn's rings and Jupiter's satellites and observing sunspots. Although favourably received when he first visited Rome in 1611, Galileo's discoveries would increasingly put him at odds with Jesuit and Dominican theologians. Galileo upheld the autonomy of science over theological interpretation of scripture, and so he was reported to the Inquisition. In 1616 in Rome Galileo was warned not to support Copernicus, whose book, *De Revolutionibus*, had been temporarily banned pending "correction". Galileo engaged in a dispute (1617–19) over the nature of comets. Galileo was a strong supporter of Copernicus' theory of the movement of the planets around their own axes and around the sun, in particular the theory of the double rotation of the Earth. In 1623 Galileo published *The Assayer* and attacked the Jesuits' scientific methods. Prohibited from openly arguing in favour of Copernicus' system, Galileo's *Dialogue Concerning the Two Chief World Systems* (1632) refuted both the Aristotelian and Ptolemaic positions. The Holy Office ordered a trial. Galileo was called to Rome, taken into custody and tried in 1633. Guilty of "vehement suspicion of heresy", his *Dialogue* was banned. Galileo was forced to pronounce in the famous words, "I abjure, curse, and detest" his beliefs as a scientist. He also had to declare that he would never concern himself again with the Earth's motion. According to legend, as he rose to his feet, he added in exasperation a remark that has remained famous to this day – *Eppur si muove!* (Yet it does turn!). Condemned to house arrest in a villa near Florence, although almost 70 and becoming blind, he continued his earlier research and published major work on the motion of falling objects. He died, blind, in 1642 and was buried in Florence in Santa Croce; in later centuries his tomb was moved to a more prominent position in that church.

stopped and did not start again until a century later when another architect, Giovanni di Simone, tried to correct the angle of slope by ensuring that the side which was sinking into the ground carried less weight. He died at the Battle of Meloria before his work was completed.

The top of the bell tower was added by Tommaso Pisano in 1350.

The peculiarity of the tower cannot conceal the beauty of its architecture. It was built as a cylinder, like the towers in Byzantium, and has six floors of galleries which seem, because of the angle of incline, to be unwinding in an ethereal spiral. On the lower level, in the purest of Pisan Romanesque styles, is the circle of blind arcading decorated with diamond-shaped motifs.

Cattedrale di Santa Maria Assunta★★ (Duomo)

🕐 *Opening time varies, see the website.*
🎫 *No charge, but free ticket is needed.*
♿ 🖉 *050 83 50 11/12. www.opapisa.it.*
The two architects of the **cathedral** were Buscheto, who began the building work in 1063, and Rainaldo, who completed it towards the middle of the 12C.

It was the fabulous booty brought back to the city after major victories over the Saracens in Sicily that provided the funds required for the construction of this lavish building.

Pisa Cathedral is a vast building in the shape of a Latin Cross and it gives an impression of being wonderfully well-balanced with its long nave, huge transept and boldly projecting apse. To counterbalance this solemnity, a light touch is created by the rows of galleries on the west front, the blind arcading, the three rows of windows flanked by pilasters round the building and the bonding with alternating light and dark marble string-courses. All these features formed the major characteristics of the Pisan Romanesque style.

Set in the **west front★★★** decorated with elegant geometric motifs picked out in marquetry and mosaics of marble and multicoloured glazed terracotta is the tomb of Buscheto (*first arch on the left*). Bronze **doors★** cast in 1602 to designs by Giambologna replaced the original doors which were destroyed by fire in the late 16C. They depict the Life of the Virgin Mary (*centre*) and the Life of Christ (*sides*). The most famous of the doors is the one named **San Ranieri** (*here replaced by a copy: the original door is on display at the Museo dell'Opera del Duomo*), which opens into the south transept opposite the Leaning Tower. Cast in the late 12C, its admirable Romanesque bronze **panels★★** were designed by Bonanno Pisano.

Using a rigorous economy of figures but showing prodigious inventiveness, he depicted the Life of Christ in 20 small tableaux in a manner that was highly stylised and gracefully naive.

The **interior** of the building (best seen from the end of the nave) is less uniform than the exterior. It is a very impressive sight with its nave (100m/325ft long), four aisles, deep apse, triple-bay transept and slightly oval dome. The 68 columns, each carved out of a single block of stone, provide an amazing variety of perspectives.

The splendid **pulpit★★★** on which **Giovanni Pisano** worked for almost ten years (1302–11) is a masterpiece of strength and delicacy. The pulpit itself is supported by porphyry columns, two of which stand on lions, a motif taken from the Lombard tradition, and by five pillars decorated with statues. The female figures on the central pillar symbolise the theological virtues – Faith, Hope and Charity. The pillar stands on a base decorated with small figures representing the Liberal Arts. On the pillars round the edge of the pulpit the carvings represent St Michael, the Evangelists carrying Christ, the cardinal virtues – Fortitude, Justice, Prudence and Temperance – supporting a woman with a baby at her breast, an allegorical representation of the Church being nourished by the Old and New Testaments, and Hercules. The pulpit is almost circular owing to the eight slightly convex carved panels.

In a set of tumultuous carvings filled with human figures Giovanni Pisano gave full vent to his talent for expressiveness and his sense of the dramatic. The first panel depicts the Annunciation and the Visitation of the Virgin Mary, followed by the Nativity, the Adoration of the Magi, the Presentation in the Temple and the Flight into Egypt, the Massacre of the Innocents, Christ's Passion, the Crucifixion and the Last Judgement (*two panels*). The Pisan New Year, 25 March, is determined when at noon a ray of sun hits the marble egg above the pulpit. Near the pulpit is the bronze lamp, known as

"Long live the Tower of Pisa, which leans and leans but does not fall…"

Since 1178, when the Tower was first observed to lean, over 8,000 projects have been drawn up to remedy the problem, with varying degrees of success. The tower was closed to the public in 1990 because of the inherent danger of collapse and a committee was formed to debate how best to find a long-term solution to the problem. In 1992 two stainless steels rings were placed around the first floor.

In 1991 the tower was attached to the ground by 18 steel cables and in 1993 the foundations were strengthened with a reinforced concrete sheath containing 670 tonnes of lead (1m/3.28ft in length) to counterbalance the lean. The progression of the lean was effectively stopped for several years.

Early in 1994 it was noted that the tower had moved back towards the vertical by 9mm/0.036inch, but the work was then stopped owing to a lack of funds.

Another restoration attempt in September 1995 ended in disaster when the tower shifted 2.5mm/1 inch in one night, double the annual rate. Engineers dumped lead on the base of the north side, and the tower was prevented from falling. No further restoration work took place until 1998, when steel-cable "braces" were attached to the tower. They were removed in 2001 when the tower had moved a further 40cm/1.3ft towards the vertical, returning the tower to the angle it was at in 1838. The tower was reopened to the public later that year. Some 300 steps wind their way to the top, from which there is a superb **view**★ of the square and the city spread out below. In fine weather the view extends across the countryside to the coast. In this prestigious university town, however, it is worth recalling the age-old curse that is well known to Italians – "Any student hoping to graduate should never risk the climb to the top."

Galileo's Lamp. According to tradition it was while watching the lamp swing as it was lit by the sexton that Galileo was inspired to develop his famous theory about the movement of a pendulum. In fact Galileo had already made his discovery a few years before the lamp was placed in the cathedral.

The Crucifix above the high altar was made by Giambologna, who also created the two bronze angel candlesticks at the corners of the choir screen. Two 16C paintings face each other on pillars on each side of the chancel – (*right*) *St Agnes* by Andrea del Sarto and (*left*) *Madonna and Child* by Antonio Sogliani.

Battistero★★★ (Baptistery)

🕐 *Opening time varies, see the website.* €5; €7 *joint ticket for two monuments;* €8 *joint ticket for three monuments;* €9 *joint ticket for all the four monuments (Camposanto Monumentale; Museo delle Sinopie; Museo dell'Opera del Duomo).* ✆ *050 80 50 11/12. www.opapisa.it (online tickets).*

This is a majestic, circular building (almost 110m/358ft in circumference and just under 55m/179ft high) almost equal to the height of the Leaning Tower. It took 250 years to build. Work began in 1153, with a break of 50 years in the 13C, until 1400. The project and the early work were directed by Diotisalvi. Nicola and Giovanni Pisano also worked on the Baptistery, producing many of the carvings and sculptures. Although the first two levels were designed in the Pisan Romanesque style, there is a decidedly Gothic flavour about the second floor and the gables and pinnacles above the arches on the first floor. At the very top of the building is a strange dome rising to a small, truncated pyramid and a statue of St John the Baptist.

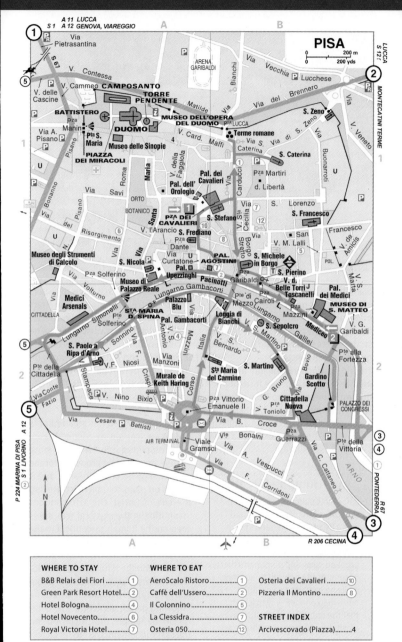

The doors are among the most decorative features in the building. The one opposite the cathedral, the most ornate of the four, is flanked by columns carved with foliage in the 13C. On the lintel, carved in a Byzantine style, are episodes from the Life of St John the Baptist; above is a representation of Jesus between the Virgin Mary and St John with the four Evangelists on either side, alternating with angels. On the jambs are labours of the 12 months of the year (*left*) and carvings of the apostles (*right*). The **interior** (35m/114ft in

253

Battistero

© zm_photo/iStock

diameter) is impressive for its tall rows of arcading, its deep dome, its striking majesty and the amount of light that floods into it. A custodian will demonstrate the remarkable echo that can be heard in the Baptistery.

The alternating strips of light and dark marble create an austere form of decoration. Elegant monolithic columns with attractively carved capitals alternate with huge pillars to form a uniform peristyle on the lower level with a wide

The Triumph of Death

Part of this painting is taken from the story of the Three Living and Three Dead Men, a legend known throughout Europe. St Macaire is depicted (*left*) holding an unrolled scroll and pointing to the decomposed bodies of three kings, while he explains to a group of noblemen on their way to a hunt that the only reality is death, the inevitable. Above are Anchorite monks calmly preparing for death as they go about their daily business. Death (*right*) is ignoring a group of beggars pleading for his attention (*in the centre*) and preparing instead to swoop down triumphantly on a party of carefree young people in an orchard.

gallery above which is open to visitors (*staircase left of the entrance*). The effect of the near-perfect spatial layout can be seen at its best from the gallery. The circular building, articulated by the ring of columns and pillars, converges on the superb octagonal **font★**. It was designed in 1246 by Guido Bigarelli, an artist from Como, and was used for christenings.

The Baptistery also has an admirable **pulpit★★**, carved by Nicola Pisano, who completed it in 1260. It is more austere than the one produced for the cathedral by his son, Giovanni, and it stands on plain columns. In retracing the Life of Christ, the artist sought inspiration in the classical sculptures seen on the Roman sarcophagi in the Camposanto. This influence is particularly strong in the first two pulpit panels representing the Nativity and the Adoration of the Magi in which the Virgin Mary resembles a Roman matron. The following panels depict the Presentation in the Temple, the Crucifixion and the Last Judgement; the face of Lucifer (*bottom right-hand corner*) is much like masks used in classical theatre.

Camposanto Monumentale★★

○*Opening time varies. See the website.* €5; €7 joint ticket for two monuments; €8 joint ticket for

254

three monuments; €9 joint ticket for all the four monuments (Baptistery; Museo delle Sinopie; Museo dell'Opera del Duomo). &. ☎050 83 50 11/12. www.opapisa.it (online tickets).

The cemetery is almost as famous as the other buildings in Piazza del Duomo. Building began in 1277 under the direction of Giovanni di Simone, the second architect to work on the bell tower, but was interrupted by the war against Genoa which ended in the Battle of Meloria (1284). The cemetery was not finished until 1464.

Originally designed like an unroofed cathedral nave, this huge graveyard now resembles vast cloisters, as the tall Romanesque arches were converted in the 15C into wonderfully light four-bay Gothic windows. In the middle is the **Sacred Field** (*Camposanto*), reputedly laid out using earth brought back from Golgotha in the early 13C by Crusaders. The earth was said to have the power to reduce dead bodies to skeletons in a few days. The galleries are paved with 600 tombstones and contain several superb Greco-Roman sarcophagi, most reused in the Middle Ages for the burials of Pisan noblemen. The walls used to be covered with admirable **frescoes** painted in the second half of the 14C and in the following century by artists such as Benozzo Gozzoli, Taddeo Gaddi, Andrea di Buonaiuto and Antonio Veneziano. In July 1944 artillery caused a fire which melted the lead roof, destroying or badly damaging most of the frescoes. Some of them, however, were saved and restored, including the famous fresco depicting the cycle of the *Triumph of Death* (1336–1341), attributed to **Buonamico Buffalmacco**, which consists of three different scenes: the *Stories of the Holy Fathers*, the *Last Judgement* and the *Hell* and the *Triumph of Death*.

▷ Walk round the Camposanto anticlockwise.

The **North Gallery**, now totally bare like the South Gallery, has rooms with the most remarkable frescoes.

Beyond a small chapel, containing the St Rainier Altar carved by Tino di Camaino, is a room showing a photographic reconstruction of the frescoes as they were originally. A very fine Attic marble urn (2C BC) is carved with Dionysian scenes in light relief.

The great chamber beyond contains the **Fresco Room**. Among the frescoes (*left wall*) is the **Triumph of Death★★**, attributed to Buonamico Buffalmacco, one of the most interesting examples of 14C Italian painting. Probably painted shortly after the plague epidemic of 1348, it illustrates very popular themes in western Europe at that time – the vanity of earthly pleasures and the brevity of life.

The two magnificent frescoes covering the end wall of the room and part of the next wall represent the **Last Judgement★★** and **Hell★** and were originally part of the same cycle. The *Story of the Anchorites in the Thebaid* (*beyond*) depicts various details of the hard, lonely and ascetic life led by the early Christians who sought refuge from persecution in Egypt. On the last wall (*right of the entrance*) are *Satan's Pact with God* and *The Sufferings of Job* by Taddeo Gaddi.

The **West Gallery** was the first one to be filled with the lavish tombs of Pisan noblemen from the 16C onwards. Each tomb was placed symmetrically in relation to the others. The **East Gallery** was organised in the same way. In the 18C the custom became so popular that the tombs began to spread into the longer North and South galleries.

In 1807 Carlo Lasinio was appointed curator and he introduced the ancient sarcophagi which had lain along the sides of the cathedral and in the many monasteries and churches in Pisa.

Museo delle Sinopie★

🕓*Opening time varies. See the website.* ⊜*€5; €7 joint ticket for two monuments; €8 joint ticket for three monuments; €9 joint ticket for all the four monuments (Baptistery; Camposanto Monumentale; Museo dell'Opera del Duomo).* &. ☎*050 83 50 11/12. www.opapisa.it (online tickets).*

Sinopia

Although frescoes (⚭ See INTRODUCTION) can withstand the passage of time and the effects of the elements, they must be painted on a fresh (fresco) base. They therefore have two main disadvantages – they have to be completed quickly and, once dry, the colours are sealed in place and cannot be touched up with the same technique. In order to overcome these disadvantages, artists used to draw a sketch called an underdrawing (sinopia) on the wall, after the initial base had been prepared. This type of sketch got its name from a town, Sinope, on the shores of the Black Sea, which provided the reddish-brown pigment usually used to draw them. Once the scene had been roughly sketched in, the artist could take his time to produce the final work, preparing the base only for the area he wanted to paint on a particular day. Many of these underdrawings have come to light over the past few decades as frescoes have been removed from walls for restoration.

This **museum**, formerly the Santa Chiara hospice built in the 13C and 14C, features the underdrawings of the Camposanto frescoes.

These preparatory drawings for frescoes displayed on the **ground floor** were sketched in the 15C and are very rough since it was customary for artists to work at their studies on paper and only the main lines of the work were sketched on the wall. During the restoration work on the frescoes, which had been damaged in 1944, the underdrawings were also removed and restored. They are now skilfully displayed in a high-ceilinged chamber covering two floors.

On the **upper floor** a series of platforms (staircase at the end of the room) gives a panoramic view of the gigantic underdrawings created for the most famous frescoes in the Camposanto. At the end of the room is the underdrawing for the Crucifixion, the first fresco to be painted c. 1320–30 by Francesco di Traino, Pisa's most important 14C artist. The grandiose compositions used for the Triumph of Death, the Last Judgement and Hell and the Story of the Anchorites in the Thebaid show the remarkable drawing talents of Francesco di Traino, especially in the facial expressions. Other artists include Buonamico Buffalmacco, Spinello Aretino, Taddeo Gaddi and Benozzo Gozzoli. Two higher galleries provide different views of the works.

Museo dell'Opera del Duomo★★

🕓 Opening time varies. See the website. 🎫 €5; €7 joint ticket for two monuments; €8 joint ticket for three monuments; €9 joint ticket for all the four monuments (Baptistery; Camposanto Monumentale; Museo delle Sinopie). ♿ ☎ 050 83 50 11/12. www.opapisa.it (online tickets).

The works in the **museum** come from the buildings in Piazza dei Miracoli. At the end of the recent and extensive restoration (2014–2019), the exhibition itinerary was completely renewed and enriched with some works.

On the ground floor, there are the **Porta di San Ranieri** – the transept door of the cathedral designed by Bonanno Pisano, the only bronze door miraculously surviving the 1595 fire –, and a room dedicated to the Romanesque Duomo. The following foreign works are part of the cathedral's furnishings and the shapes imported from distant lands enrich the early, mainly classical, Romanesque architecture. Most of the additions were from the Islamic world, familiar to Pisans because of their maritime trade. New geometric and iconographic motifs were introduced, with a taste for polychrome marble inlay, a craft form that was already known through Byzantine art and architecture. Sculptures from Provence and Burgundy verify links with French Romanesque artists.

The other buildings in the square – the Baptistery and the tower – are celebrated together with their glorious Pisan sculptures. After **Nicola Pisano**'s Gothic heads and half busts, there are the full-size statues by his son, **Giovanni Pisano**, who also realized some other marble masterpieces, such as the splendid Madonnas with the child and statues of saints. The itinerary continues with the followers of Giovanni, including the Sienese sculptor **Tino di Camaino**, active in Pisa for many years: the statues of the Emperor, four of his advisers, an Annunciation and two angels (1315) come from his mausoleum for Henry VII of Luxembourg, who died in 1313. **Nino Pisano** also created a number of the tombs in the cathedral in the second half of the 14C. The tomb of Archbishop Giovanni Scherlatti so delighted Archbishop Francesco Moricotti that he asked Nino to create an identical one for him. The main figure in the 15C art world was the Florentine **Andrea di Francesco Guardi**, a pupil in Donatello's workshop whose main work was Archbishop Pietro Ricci's tomb.

On the upper floor, the atmosphere of the celebrations of the Christian cult is recreated, with furnishings, clothes, fabrics, goldsmith's art, and liturgical books. Among the illuminated manuscripts and antiphonies are two 12C–13C "Exultet". On one side of these rolls was a transcript of the liturgical chant sung on Easter Saturday while the reverse showed the congregation scenes from the mystery of the Resurrection.

Some colossal busts, which adorned the top of the Baptistery loggia, by Giovanni Pisano are in the cloister gallery to give visitors one last greeting.

From the loggia and the cloisters you have a lovely view of the Leaning Tower.

WALKING TOURS

After enjoying the treasures of Piazza dei Miracoli, be sure to enjoy the lovely city of Pisa. This walk begins at a gem of a piazza.

1 CAVALIERI TO THE ARNO

Piazza dei Cavalieri★

This spacious, tranquil **square** lies in the heart of the medieval town and is now frequented by students. One of the most majestic and best-preserved areas in Pisa, here in 1406 the end of the Pisan Republic was proclaimed.

The square was totally transformed when Cosimo I de' Medici commissioned his architect, Vasari, to erect the buildings designed for the **Knights of St Stephen** (Cavalieri di Santo Stefano). This holy, military order, which was subject to the Rule of St Benedict, was founded in 1562 to lead the fight against the Infidel, its main task being to capture the Muslim pirates who infested the Mediterranean. The brotherhood died out in 1860.

The square is lined by 16C and 17C buildings and dominated by the **Palazzo dei Cavalieri** on which the long, unusual, slightly curved **façade★** is decorated with grotesque figures and foliage. The upper storeys are separated by a frieze of niches containing the busts of the six members of the Medici dynasty who were Grand Dukes of Tuscany. Their coat of arms – six balls – is visible in several places, as is the Cross of the Knights who were instructed here. The building is now the seat of the university founded during Napoleon Bonaparte's rule. In front is a 1596 statue of Cosimo I 1596 by Francavilla.

The Church of **Santo Stefano** dates from 1569 but its white, green and pink marble west front, including the Medici coat of arms and the Cross of St Stephen, was built some 40 years later. The **Palazzo dell'Orologio** (Clock House), also known as the **Gherardesca**, was reconstructed by Vasari in 1607 on the site of two older buildings. He incorporated the remains of a tower (Torre della Fame) in which, following the defeat of Pisa in 1284 at the Battle of Meloria, Count **Ugolino della Gherardesca**, the commander-in-chief of the Pisan fleet, was accused of treason and sentenced to death by starvation with his children. Dante described this

Statue of Cosimo I de' Medici, Piazza dei Cavalieri

© ClaudioStocco/iStock

episode in his *Inferno* (*Divine Comedy, Canto XXXIII*). It now houses the university library.

Santa Caterina

Leaving Piazza dei Cavalieri to the east is Via Carducci. Go left to see the elegant **façade★** of Santa Caterina, built of white marble discreetly marked with lines of darker marble. It harmoniously combines austere, wide Romanesque blind arches on the lower level with two successive rows of graceful Gothic columns and multifoiled arches on the upper sections. The interior contains two white marble tombs. Nino Pisano sculpted the left tomb, as well as the two sculptures of the Annunciation flanking the chancel.

San Michele in Borgo

Head south towards the river from Piazza dei Cavalieri. The church **façade★** shows a remarkable transition between the Romanesque and Gothic periods. It has three rows of galleries with trefoiled pointed arches and colonnades decorated with masks, a sharp contrast with the robust lower section where, unlike most of the churches in Pisa, there is no blind arcading.

From Piazza Garibaldi turn left through the narrow Rigattieri, which runs

through the medieval quarter to the church of **San Pierino**. Built in the 11C–12C, its impressive crypt has columns that may have been taken from ancient Roman port structures.

Via Rigattieri becomes Via delle Belle Torri, named for tower houses that once lined the street.

From Borgo Stretto turn onto a left lane to the picturesque **Piazza delle Vettovaglie**, which hosts a busy market. On nearby Via del Campano the medieval **Torre del Campano** rises from the street.

The last stop on Via Curtatone e Montanara is **La Sapienza University** founded in the 12C. On **Piazza San Frediano**, its University Church (11C–12C) houses a large crucifix from the 13C.

② LUNGARNO AND THE LEFT BANK

Museo Nazionale di San Matteo★★

Piazza San Matteo in Soarta (Lungarno Mediceo). ⏰*Open Tue–Sat at set times: 8.30am, 10.30am, 12.30pm, 2pm, 4pm, 6pm; Sun 8.30am–1.30pm (last admission 1pm).* ⏰*Closed Mon, 1 Jan, 25 Dec.* 🎫*€5; €8 combined with Museo Nazionale di Palazzo Reale.* ♿ 𝒫*050 54 18 65. polomusealetoscana. beniculturali.it.*

Turn left along the river from San Michele in Borgo to reach this **museum** set around the cloisters in the former St Matthew's Monastery (15C). The rooms contain an extraordinary collection of sculptures and paintings from Pisan churches and monasteries, by local artists, all showing what a major centre of artistic creativity Pisa was in the 13C–15C.

The **ground floor** gallery gives access to the collections of **ceramics**. Pisa acquired a large quantity of Islamic ceramics and was also famous in the 13C–17C for its original work. From the 14C onwards production was exported throughout the Mediterranean basin from Spain to Turkey, including Provence, Corsica and Greece. Locally it is an unusual feature in the architectural decoration of churches (*See Driving Tour, p263*). From the mid-13C, Pisan workshops were among the largest in Tuscany, and succeeded in making their ceramics waterproof by coating them in pewter-based vitreous enamels. This "early majolica" has brown and green painted decoration. From the 15C onwards the designs were etched into the ceramics and usually highlighted by a brown ochre tint. The item itself could be left white or uniformly painted in pale yellow, yellow-ochre or green. These incisions (*a stecca*) evolved into the decorative style known as "peacock's feather eye". The following rooms contain ceramics imported from Liguria, southern Italy, Islamic countries or the Middle East. The collection of 10C–13C Islamic items is extensive.

The upper gallery in the **first floor** cloisters displays architectural sculpture, dating from the 12C.

The tour of **Pisan painting** begins in the room (*left at the top of the staircase*) with 12C–13C works. The huge Crucifixes are characteristic of this period, which was still strongly influenced by Greek and Byzantine works. 14C works (*right of the staircase*) show Pisa's openess to new artistic trends. The great freestanding polyptych, which is painted on one side with the *Glory of Saint Ursula* and on the other with the *Glory of Saint Dominic*, is by Francesco di Traino (1344). A magnificent polyptych of the Virgin and Child was painted c. 1320 by Simone Martini for the Church of Santa Caterina.

The room on the right is filled with **Pisan sculptures** from the 14C, a period that was dominated by the workshop of Andrea Pisano and his sons, Nino and Tommaso (*See p248*). Note the delightful marble Madonna and Child by Nino Pisano and, more particularly, the **Madonna del Latte** on which the nursing Virgin Mary gracefully leans with a serene smile on her face. The tour of painting continues in the room opposite (*and in the cloister gallery at right angles to it*). Although the outbreak of plague in 1348 interrupted the flow of commissions and shifted the choice of subject matter, Pisa remained a major centre of creativity. The other rooms reveal the artistic activity in Pisa in the 15C. After coming under Florentine control in 1406, Pisa attracted prestigious artists from the Tuscan capital. The cloister gallery has the *Virgin Mary of Humility* by Gentile da Fabriano and a **St Paul** which is stupefyingly lifelike. This was once part of a polyptych painted in 1426 by Masaccio. There is also a Madonna and Child (*stucco low relief*) by Michelozzo, a delightful Madonna and Child by Fra Angelico and a gilded bronze bust of St Rossore by Donatello. The following room contains works by Benozzo Gozzoli and the *Holy Conversation* by Ghirlandaio.

In the same gallery are life-sized sculptures in painted and gilded wood; most are by **Francesco di Valdambrino**, who learned his craft from the Pisano family of artists. These mainly feminine figures were used to decorate Pisa's convents.

Lungarno Mediceo

The superb **Palazzo Toscanelli** (no 17) has a majestic Renaissance façade. Byron wrote part of his *Don Juan* there between the autumn of 1821 and the summer of 1822. The **Palazzo dei Medici** (now the Prefettura) dates from the 13C–14C but later was much altered. Its most famous guest was Lorenzo the Magnificent of Florence.

Walk by the Ponte di Mezzo, site of the **Gioco del Ponte** in June (*p265*).

Lungarno Pacinotti

From Piazza Solferino and the bridge of the same name, there is a view east along the **quays** of a bend in the Arno, with Monte Pisano in the background. To the west is the tall brick tower of the old citadel. The slender, white church of Santa Maria della Spina stands out on the south bank. The 17C **Loggia di Banchi** formerly housed the linen market. The **Palazzo Upezzinghi** (no 43) was built in the early 17C and is now part of the university. Its façade flanks a large gateway, surmounted by a balcony, and a huge coat of arms with a

lion. The 15C **Palazzo Agostini★** (nos 28–25) has a decorative brick façade with two rows of Gothic windows.
The famous ground floor **Caffé dell'Ussero** (Hussars' Café) was established in 1794 and frequented by the writers of the Risorgimento.

Museo di Palazzo Reale

Lungarno Pacinotti 46. ⏰*Open Mon and Wed–Sat 9am–2pm (last admission 30min before closing).* ⏰*Closed Tue, Sun and public hols.* 🎟€5; €8 combined with Museo Nazionale di San Matteo. ♿ ☎050 92 65 73. polomusealetoscana. beniculturali.it.

The Royal Palace in the 16C building designed by Bernardo Buontalenti for Francesco I de' Medici was the former seat of the Medici, the dukes of Lorraine and Savoia. Museum artefacts evoke Pisan court life and customs in paintings, portraits, furniture, tapestries, armour and other objects. Among the most important objects are the Medici tapestries, the 15C and 16C armour of the Giochi del Ponte, and the predella of San Nicola da Tolentino by young Raphaël (1500).

Santa Maria della Spina

© Ryszard Stelmachowicz/iStock

Behind Palazzo Reale stands the 11C–14C church of **San Nicola**, dominated by a *campanile* crowned with a small loggia.
Piazza Solferino and its eponymous bridge mark the bend of the Arno and its docks in the background, dominated above by Monte Pisano, while to the west on the other bank stands the tall brick tower of the Church of Santa Maria della Spina, with its fine white façade.

Lungarno Simonelli

Here stand the **Medici arsenals**, built on the orders of Cosimo I who, along with his sons Francesco I and Ferdinand I, wanted to make Pisa an major maritime base. The construction, begun in the mid-16C, was completed in 1588.

▷ Walk across Ponte della Cittadella.

San Paolo a Ripa d'Arno

As its name suggests, this 11C–12C church stands on the bank of the Arno. Its attractive **façade★** with three rows of columns, its alternating rows of black and white marble and the blind arcading decorating the sides are all typical of the Pisan Romanesque style.
The 12C **Cappella Sant'Agata** behind the apse is a strange little octagonal brick chapel with a pyramid-shaped roof that is usually attributed to Diotisalvi.

▷ Continue on the Lungarno Sonnino.

Santa Maria della Spina★★

⏰*Opening time varies.*
Standing alone, white and ethereal on the banks of the Arno, this tiny marble Romanesque-Gothic **church** looks like a reliquary with its spires, gables, pinnacles, niches and rose windows. For many years, it contained one of the thorns (*spina*) from Christ's Crown, hence its name. Built in the early 14C at the river level, it was demolished in 1871 because of water damage and rebuilt on its present spot.

Several of the statues that decorated the exterior, created by the Pisano School, have been replaced by copies. The plain rectangular room forming the nave and chancel is lit, on the side facing the Arno, by an almost unbroken row of Gothic double windows beneath a Romanesque arch. The church contains a graceful Madonna and Child by Nino Pisano.

◉ Continue along the Arno.

Palazzo Blu

Lungarno Gambacorti 9. ◔*Open Mon–Fri 10am–7pm, Sat–Sun and public hols 10am–8pm; last admission 1hr before closing.* ◉€3. ☎*050 22 04 650. palazzoblu.it.*

With its beautiful blue façade, the Palace Dell'Agnello Giuli, built in the late 14C and enlarged in the 16C, traces the line of the Lungarno. Restored and managed by the bank Cassa di Risparmio di Pisa, it now houses the CariPisa Foundation **art collection★** (mid-14C–20C Pisan works) and an auditorium, and hosts **major exhibitions**.

Nearby are the 17C Loggia di Banchi, formerly the textile market, and the severe Gambacorti Palace, town hall, built in the late 14C in grey-green stone streaked with pink: a major restoration is evident in its three levels of bifurcated windows inscribed with round arches.

◉ Follow Via San Martino, an ancient route that led to medieval Florence, along which merchants once ran Turkish and Arab shops.

San Sepolcro

Named for the Holy Sepulchre in Jerusalem, this **church** is built to a similar layout. Its octagonal design with pyramid-shaped roof was created in the 12C by Diotisalvi. The **interior★** has an ambulatory and majestic central chancel around which very tall, mighty pillars support high arches surmounted by a high dome surrounded by brick bonding.

Take Via San Martino to **San Martino** (14C), which has fragments of frescoes and a Pisan crucifix (1250).

Walk along Via Piazza Toniolo to the pleasant **Giardino Scotto**, a new garden set inside the Cittadella Nuova built by Giuliano da Sangallo.

Take Viale Benedetto Croce to Piazza Vittorio Emanuele (near the railway station), to admire the bold colours of the *Tuttomondo mural* (1989) by Keith Haring.

Return to the Arno by Corso Italia, a pedestrian shopping street along which stands the church of **Santa Maria del Carmine** (17C organ).

ADDITIONAL SIGHTS
San Francesco

The slim bell tower marks the 13C–17C **church** (*Piazza San Francesco;* ⊶*Closed for restoration at the time of publication*) with a beautiful 15C marble altar carved by Tommaso Pisano and the tomb of Count Ugolino della Gherardesca. The cloister leads to the chapter room, covered with late-14C frescoes.

Ancient Church of San Zeno

Piazza San Zeno.

Built in the 10C–11C above older (probably Roman) buildings, its beautiful façade is preceded by a portico of pillars and decorated with ceramic. The interior, divided into three naves by columns with Romanesque capitals, hosts temporary exhibitions.

♠♣ Museo degli Strumenti di Calcolo

Vecchi Macelli, Via Bonanno Pisano 2/B. ◔*Open Mon–Fri 9am–5pm.* ◔*Closed Sat–Sun and public hols.* ◉€2.50. ☎*050 22 15 212. www.msc.sma.unipi.it.*

In a city where science has always played a leading role, this small museum run by the university traces the history of **calculating instruments**, from the time of Galileo to modern computers, to the huge CEP (Calcol Elettronica Pisana) used by Enrico Fermi.

EXCURSION
Cascina
21km/13mi SE by R67.

The town specialises in the small-scale and mass production of furniture, hence its size. Before 1364 it was controlled by Pisa, but after the **Battle of Cascina** it fell to Florence. Michelangelo chose it as the subject of a major fresco that was never painted; however, the battle remained famous because of the artist's magnificent cartoon. It was designed for the Hall of Five Hundred in the Palazzo Vecchio in Florence where it would have appeared opposite Leonardo da Vinci's fresco of the Battle of Anghiari.

Michelangelo, who was fascinated by the anatomy of the human body, chose to illustrate this episode, which allowed him to depict Florentine soldiers bathing naked in the Arno when they were subjected to a surprise attack by Pisan troops.

The **old town**, laid out in a grid pattern, is traversed by Corso Matteotti, a street lined with arcades. At one end, there is a clock tower containing a small bell; this is all that remains of the walls that encircled the town in the Middle Ages. At the other end is the Oratory of San Giovanni (late 14C) which has a *Crucifixion* by Martino di Bartolomeo (1398) above the altar, including (*top right*) the beginning of a cycle of frescoes on Genesis. Set back from the Corso Matteotti and flanked by two other churches is **Santa Maria**, a 12C church with a typically Pisan **façade★**.

Pontedera
25km/15.5mi E of Pisa on Superstrada FI PI LI towards Florence or by train.

♣♦ Museo Piaggio
The museum is near the train station. Viale Rinaldo Piaggio 7. ○*Open Tue–Sat, 2nd and 4th Sun of the month 10am–6pm (Jul–Aug every Sun).* ○*Closed Mon, 1st and 3rd Sun of the month.* ✆*Free admission.* ✆*0587 27 171. www.museopiaggio.it.*

A museum perfect for kids and motorcycle fans, this is where Vespas were once assembled. Now full of marvellous motorcycles and other machines, this Piaggio design studio and Tuscan manufacturing centre in Pontedera brought great design, mobility and fun into the world with its Vespas and Gileras. See also the Vespa prototype, a three-wheeler cycle that became a tiny workhorse aptly named the Ape ("Bee"), a fetching bright-red Gilera with its spare tyre, and a tiny sky-blue button of a car.

Amedei Chocolate Factory
Via San Gervasio 29. ⬡*Guided tours only, reservation required.* ⬡*Prices vary.* ✆*0587 48 48 49. www.amedei.it.*

From the Vespa factory the ideal next move is on to this factory in the La Rotta section of Pontedera. Their boutique chocolate is made from cacao beans that Amedei manages from harvest to storage and production. Especially good chocolates are Chuao, Toscano Black, Madagascar and 9 Amedei. Book a tasting and decide for yourself!

If you don't have the time, stop by **La Bottega del Caffè** (*Corso Matteotti 79*), **Caffè Giannini** (*Piazza Martiri della Libertà 56*) or **Enoteca La Cantina** (*Via Roma 284*) where you can buy Amedei chocolates.

Vespa Drives
Try **Noleggio Moto Toscana** (*Via Pisana 78;* ✆*0587 21 26 25; www.noleggiomototoscana.it*), which rents the Vespa Piaggio 125cc (⬡€60/day) or Piaggio MP3 250 (⬡€75/day) for a full day or weekend – a fun way to tour Pisa or head for the sea. **The Vespa Trip** (*thevespatrip.com*) organizes tours (*Mon–Sat* ⬡€540) from the stretched farmlands around Pisa, through the hills of the Chianti region and the mountainous area around Lucca to medieval cities like Siena and Florence. The Giro Classico starts and ends in Pisa, the daily trips are always between 70 and 120 km. Every day you can choose to drive the routes on your own (using a road book & GPS), or you can follow the guide to drive completely carefree. Newbies can take a "Start-to-Vespa" class (⬡€50).

🚗 DRIVING TOURS

ARNO TO THE SEA
30km/19mi. Allow 3hr.
See map pp244–245.

▷ From Pisa take the road along the south bank of the Arno and follow signs for Mare and Marina di Pisa and then for San Piero.

San Piero a Grado★
The 11C Romanesque **basilica★** of San Piero a Grado (St Peter's on the Quay) is said to stand on the old quayside in the Roman port of Pisa where St Peter is believed to have landed. The 14C frescoes in the interior, depicting the life of St Peter, are said to be copies of the ones that decorated the original basilica of St Peter's in Rome.

Tirrenia and Marina di Pisa
Tirrenia (*second turn to the right after the basilica*) is an elegant resort famous for its extensive pine woods, its white sandy beach and its film studios, 22km/14mi from Piazza dei Miracoli. **Marina di Pisa** is a popular beach at the mouth of the Arno. There is a view of Livorno (*south*). Nearby is the vast pine wood on the **San Rossore** estate which belonged to the Medici family and then to the House of Savoy. It is now part of the Migliarino–San Rossore–Massaciuccoli Country Park.

MONTE PISANO★
60km/38mi round trip. About 2hr30min. See map pp244-245.
From Pisa take S12 (*blue signs to Lucca*) and A11 (*green signs to Firenze*).
This small outcrop of the Apuan Alps, lying between Pisa and Lucca, rises to a peak in Monte Serra (917m/2,980ft).

San Giuliano Terme
This small **spa** town was once frequented by such famous 19C figures as Byron and Shelley. In the distance is a large yellow-ochre portico with five arches, which marks the entrance to the pump rooms. The two hot springs, famous since Roman times, produce water at temperatures of 38˚C/100˚F and 41˚C/106˚F. **Bagni di Pisa** luxury spa resort offers various thermal water treatments (✆*050 88 501; www.bagnidipisa.com*).

▷ Take the road to Calci (8km/5mi from San Giuliano)

At the junction where the left turn leads to Agnano, Monte Pisano comes into view. The small "Verruca" hill, site of a now-ruined 13C Pisan fortress, is the final promontory before the descent.

Calci
The 11C parish **church** (**pieve**) has a fine Pisan Romanesque west front. The interior contains a 12C christening font.

▷ Continue straight at the lights (700m/758yd) to the charterhouse.

Certosa di Calci★
Guided tours only, Tue–Sat and first Sun of the month at set times: 9am, 10.30am, noon, 1.30pm, 3pm, 4.30pm, 6pm (last tour); other Sundays and public hols at 9am, 10.30am, noon, 12.30pm. Closed Mon, 1 Jan, 25 Dec. €5. ✆050 93 84 30. www.polomusealetoscana.beniculturali.it.
The **Calci Charterhouse** (*also known as Certosa di Pisa*) was begun in 1366. The daily routine of the Carthusian monks alternated between their solitary cells and the **church**; these buildings form part of a harmonious group, which includes the **Great Cloisters★** and the prior's lodgings.
In the 18C the buildings resounded less to the murmur of monks at prayer and more to the voices of the guests in the Grand Duke's apartment. The monks' numbers dwindled, and they left in 1969.
Organised by the **Calci Charterhouse National Museum,** the guided tour also passes from the pharmacy to the monks' chapels, to the cemetery and past the monks' gardens to the refectory. The monks were mainly vegetarian, although their rules permitted them to eat fish.

One wing of the monastery houses a **natural history museum** (⏱ *Open Jun–Sept 10am–8pm; Oct–May Mon–Sat 9am–7pm, Sun 9am–8pm; last admission 45min before closing;* ⏱ *Closed 25 Dec;* ⊕ *€8;* ☎ *050 22 12 970/980, www.msn.unipi.it*) run by the University of Pisa. The highlight of the collection is a magnificent gallery of cetacean skeletons. The grounds afford a view of the surrounding mountains and the ruins of the Verruca fortress.

▶ Return to the crossroads in Calci and turn right at the lights to Monte Serra.

The Arno Plain is visible (*right*) with the river winding majestically through the countryside at the foot of the mountain range. There is a superb **view★** from a layby (*5.3km/3mi from the crossroads in Calci*). At the fork the road (*left*) continues to climb Monte Serra; the other road, (*right*) to Buti, soon crosses to the opposite side of the range where the scenery becomes less rugged.

▶ In Buti take the road to Pontedera. At the T-junction, opposite the river, turn right; first left, cross the bridge; bear left. At the fork, turn left uphill. At the end, Vicopisano and its keep come into view.

Vicopisano

The Pisan Romanesque church (12C–13C) contains a rare woodcarving of the **Deposition from the Cross★** (11C). The old village has picturesque traces of its medieval walls, including three towers. On the hilltop stand the crenellated keep and the Palazzo Pretorio.

▶ Take the road along the north bank of the Arno to return to Pisa.

Near **Uliveto Terme** the road skirts the rugged slopes of Monte Pisano. As it approaches Caprona, the outpost of the fortress on Verruca comes into view high above a quarry which produces the *verrucano*, a yellow-ochre veined stone.

▶ Follow signs taking SS67 to Pisa.

ADDRESSES

🛏 STAY

🛏🛏 **Hotel Novecento** – *Via Roma 37.* ☎ *050 50 03 23. www.hotelnovecento.pisa.it. 14 rooms.* In the Santa Maria university quarter, near Piazza dei Miracoli, this pretty former residence dates to 1900. Elegant decor and contemporary furniture. Pleasant interior garden.

🛏🛏 **B&B Relais dei Fiori** – *Via Carducci 35/37.* ☎ *050 80 53 552. www.relaisdeifiori.com. 12 rooms.* Elegant, refined B&B in an Art Nouveau house with pastel rooms, each decorated with different flowers.

🛏🛏 **Royal Victoria Hotel** – *Lungarno Pacinotti 12.* ☎ *050 94 01 11. www.royalvictoria.it. 48 rooms.* Along the Arno, this restored 14C palace has been managed by the Piegaja family since 1837.

🛏🛏🛏 **Hotel Bologna** – *Via Mazzini 57.* ☎ *050 50 21 20. www.hotelbologna.pisa.it. 64 rooms.* Located in the Sant'Antonio quarter, within walking distance of the city centre, this beautifully restored palace offers every comfort.

🛏🛏🛏 **Green Park Resort Hotel** – *Via dei Tulipani, Calambrone.* ☎ *050 31 35 711. 148 rooms. www.greenparkresort.com.* Set among five villas surrounded by bougainvillea and hibiscus. Relax in the spa with heated pool, sauna, Turkish bath and massages. The restaurant serves traditional Tuscan fare.

🍴 EAT

🍴 **Pizzeria Il Montino** – *Via Monte 1.* ☎ *050 59 86 95. Closed Sun.* In the centre, this is economical and popular with students. *Cecína* (chickpea pie), pizza.

🍴🍴 **Il Colonnino** – *Via Sant'Andrea 37/41.* ☎ *050 54 49 54. www.ristorante ilcolonnino.it.* This *enoteca-osteria* is in a 15C Baptistery, where an Etruscan column (*colonnino*) was found. Regional specialities.

🍴🍴 **Osteria 050** – *Via San Francesco 36.* ☎ *050 54 31 06. www.biosteria050.it. Closed Mon, Sun lunch.* This *"biOsteria"* chooses local and seasonal ingredients.

🍴🍴 **AeroScalo Ristoro** – *Via Roma 8, Pontedera.* ☎ *0587 52 024.* With fragrant bread, excellent Tuscan ham, *lardo*, *crostini* topped with tomatoes or chicken-liver pâté, good fresh pastas and grilled Tuscan meat, best accompanied by local red wine.

⊖🍽🍷 **Osteria dei Cavalieri** – *Via San Frediano 16.* ☏*050 58 08 58. www.osteria cavalieri.pisa.it. Closed Sat lunchtime, Sun, 3 weeks in Aug. Reservations advised.* A stone's throw from the university, an establishment renowned for its home-made and aromatic cuisine, at really reasonable prices. Informal, warm hospitality.

⊖🍽🍷 **La Clessidra** – *Via del Castelletto 26/30.* ☏*050 54 01 60. www.ristorante laclessidra.net. Closed lunchtime and Sun. Reservations suggested.* Simple but pleasant in an elegant district of Pisa. Typical Tuscan food plus interesting variations.

TAKING A BREAK

Caffè dell'Ussero – *Lungarno Pacinotti 27.* ☏*050 58 11 00. www.ussero.com.* On the ground floor of Palazzo Rosso, this 18C café and was the meeting place for Pisa's intellectuals.

EVENTS

Capodanno Pisano (Pisan New Year) – *25 Mar.* From medieval times Pisans celebrated the New Year on 25 March, until a 1749 decree abolished it. In the 1980s Pisans reinstated the tradition.

Historical Regatta of the Maritime Republics – *May–Jun.* Since 1956 the Regatta of the Four Maritime Republics (Amalfi, Genoa, Venice and Pisa) has been held in each city in turn. The regatta boat race matches the old rival republics. A historic costumed procession arrives at the Duomo before noon.

The Luminara di San Ranieri – *16 Jun.* On the evening before the Feast Day of St Rainier, the Lungarno Mediceo and Lungarno Galilei quays are lit with hundreds of tiny lanterns. The lanterns are reflected in the Arno where other tiny lights float on the water. At sunset the sky turns red, followed by spectacular fireworks.

Historic Regatta in Honor of San Ranieri – *17 Jun.* The afternoon regatta is held on the Arno with historic boats. Racers are dressed in traditional costume.

Il Gioco del Ponte – *Last Sat in June.* Based on the game of *mazzascudo* played at least as far back as the 12C. Two groups seek to gain control over the bridge. Before the game the two "armies", each bearing their local colours and 16C armour, parade along the quaysides in two processions.

San Miniato★

The charming town of San Miniato, through which the medieval Via Francigena passes (*See PLANNING YOUR TRIP, p15*), has retained its old appearance, set along a hilltop that forms an amphitheatre. Formerly called San Miniato *al Tedesco* (of the German), from the 10C onwards it was the official residence in Tuscany of the Holy Roman Emperors and the seat of imperial vicars. Its proud outline is broken up at the top by the fortress tower and its northeast side is buttressed by the San Francesco Monastery, which was built on the site of the 8C San Miniato Church. A few tower-houses and aristocratic mansions dating from the 15C, 16C and 17C suggest its prosperous past.

▶ **Population:** 27,959.
👣 **Michelin Map:** Michelin Atlas p 37 and Map 563 – K 14 and Map 735 Fold 14.
ℹ **Info:** Piazza del Popolo 1. ☏0571 42 745. www. sanminiatopromozione.it.
▶ **Location:** San Miniato is situated halfway between Florence and Pisa just south of the motorway.

👣WALKING TOUR

Prato del Duomo★

This tour of historic buildings begins with the 12C **cathedral**, which has a bell tower that originally served as defensive tower of the old castle (**Torre di Matilde**: ◷*Open Apr–Sept*

Mon–Fri 11am–2pm, Sat–Sun 11am–2pm, 3–6pm; Oct–Mar Sat 10am–1pm, 2–5pm, Sun 2–5pm; ⏰Closed public hols; ℘342 68 60 873). The cathedral has a Romanesque façade studded with a number of 13C ceramic bowls in the Pisan tradition, a style also seen at San Piero a Grado. The three doors date from the 15C.

The **Museo Diocesano di Arte Sacra** (*left of the cathedral;* ⏰*Open daily Apr–Sept 9am–1pm, 2–4pm; Oct–Mar Thu 2–4pm, Fri 9am–1pm, 2–4pm, Sat–Sun 9am–1pm;* ⏰*Closed public hols;* ☞€2.50; €5 combined ticket with Torre di Matilde and Rocca di Federico II; ℘342 68 60 873) contains paintings and sculptures from the 15C–19C by Filippo Lippi, Neri di Bicci, Cigoli and Verrocchio, as well as sacred art objects.

Opposite the cathedral the 12C **Bishop's Palace** initially served as the residence of the captain of the citadel's militia. Later it was the residence of the *Signori Dodici* (the 12 magistrates of the town) and then of the Captain of the People. Since 1622 it has been the bishop's residence.

The **Palazzo dei Vicari dell'Imperatore** (formerly the residence of the imperial vicars but now a hotel) is surmounted by a tower. It dates from the 12C, although tradition has it that Countess Matilda of Tuscany was born there in 1046. A narrow street between these two buildings leads to a tiny terrace from which there is a view of the rooftops of San Miniato and the Tuscan countryside.

Below in **Piazza della Repubblica** is the **Palazzo del Seminario★**, a building with a concave façade decorated early in the 18C with frescoes and Latin aphorisms by the Fathers of the Church; the lower part preserves part of the medieval shop fronts.

▷ From the terrace to the left of the cathedral walk up the steep street and steps (15min return on foot).

Rocca di Federico II (Frederick II Fortress)★

⏰*Open Apr–Sept Tue–Sun and public hols 10am–6pm (Apr–May and Sept from 11am); Oct–Mar Sat–Sun and public hols 10am–3pm (Oct–Nov 5pm).* ☞€3.50; €5 combined ticket with Museo Diocesano di Arte Sacra and Torre di Matilde. ℘348 71 87 908.

This tall brick tower, reconstructed as it appeared when it was the fortress (**rocca**) of Frederick Barbarossa (Redbeard), dominates the hilltop. Dante recounts that here Pietro Vigna, Frederick II's chancellor, accused of treason, committed suicide (*Inferno*, Cantico XIII). From the terrace the lovely **view★★** extends over San Miniato, the Val d'Arno, the Pisan hills, Pistoia and Florence, up to the Apennines.

Santuario del Crocifisso

Behind the cathedral, the 17C **Crucifix Chapel** is capped by a circular drum and contains a 10C Ottonian wooden Crucifix. A dramatic flight of steps leads to Via delle Vittime del Duomo.

▷ Walk along Via delle Vittime del Duomo.

Palazzo Comunale

⏰*Opening time varies.* ☞€2.50. ℘348 71 87 908.

The building contains frescoes by Giotto's School and a small church, **Chiesa del Loretino**, which has a precious altar made of marquetry with gilding and painting, a tabernacle painted by Lanfranco and 16C frescoes of the Life of Jesus.

▷ Walk along Via Ser Ridolfo to Piazza del Popolo.

San Domenico

Construction of this 1194 church was interrupted several times and its façade never completed. Inside, in a chapel on the right, note the funerary monument of physician and Humanist Giovanni Chellini, attributed to Bernardo Rossellino (15C).

City Museums

Ask Fondazione San Miniato tourist office in Piazza del Popolo for opening hours and prices: Mon 9am–1pm, Tue–

Fri 9am–5pm. ☏*0571 42 745. www.
sanminiatopromozione.it.*

The museum tour includes the Archaeology Museum (Etruscan objects) and
Museo dell'Oratorio del Loretino (altar),
as well as the Confraternità della Misericordia (Brotherhood of Mercy), Con-
servatorio di Santa Clara (paintings by
Cigoli and embroideries) and Via Angel-
ica (three chapels to visit). The tour ends
by Accademia degli Euteleti, the palace
and its tower.

ADDRESSES

🛏 STAY

🍽🍽🍽 **Villa Sonnino** – *Via Castelvecchio
9/11, località La Catena, 4km/2.5mi E
of San Miniato.* ☏*0571 48 40 33. www.
villasonnino.com. 13 rooms.* This elegant
15C–17C villa offers all conveniences
and good food.

🍴 EAT

🍽🍽🍽 **Il Convio** – *Via San Maiano 2.
1.5km/1mi SE of San Miniato.* ☏*0571 40
81 13. www.ristoranteilconvio.com. Closed
Wed.* Situated in the green valley, here
is a warm welcome, a lovely view, and
in warm weather, outside dining. Local
specialities.

SHOPPING

The white truffle is undisputed king,
especially during autumn and winter.
In food markets (and restaurants) look
for *pomodoro grinzoso sanminiato*, a
pumpkin-shaped tomato excellent for
sauces, and for *carciofo sanminiatese*,
the tender, meaty local artichoke.
The main industry is high-quality leather
tanning, coloured with vegetable dyes;
the hides are mostly shipped elsewhere,
but keep an eye open for local leather
artisans. Tobacco grows locally, used to
produce the *sigaro Toscano*, Tuscan cigar.

Il Cantuccio di Federigo – *Via P Maioli 67.*
☏*0571 41 83 44.* Paolo Gazzari offers a
good selection of sweets and wines.
Market – *Tue morning.*
Brocante – *First Sun of each month.*

EVENTS

Festa del Tartufo Bianco – *Last three
weekends in Nov.* The surrounding hills
are a treasure-trove of white truffles,
sold at this major fair.
Theatre Festival – Since 1947, every July
a new play is performed.

Livorno

The commercial harbour of
Livorno (Leghorn) is one of the
main ports on the Mediterranean,
shipping mainly wood, Florentine
craftwork, marble, rough-cut or
crafted alabaster, and cars.
From here ferries also depart for
Sardinia and Corsica, as well as
ocean liners like *Queen Mary II*.
The local fishing trade has given
rise to culinary specialities like
fish soup (*cacciucco*) and red
mullet (*triglia*).

▶ **Population:** 157,783.
🕐 **Michelin Map:** Michelin
Atlas p 36 and Map 563 –
L 12 or Map 735 Fold 14.
Town plan in the
Michelin Guide Italia.
🛈 **Info:** Via Pieroni 18/20.
☏0586 89 42 36.
www.comune.livorno.it/
portaleturismo.
▶ **Location:** The city can be
reached by the A12 Genova–
Livorno major road, the A11
Florence–sea coast major
road or the motorway
(*superstrada* Firenze–Livorno).

👣 WALKING TOURS

HISTORIC CENTRE

*From Piazza Micheli, walk to the old
port (Darsena Vecchia).*

Monument "I Quattro Mori"★

In Piazza Micheli, the Four Moors Monument celebrates the victory of Ferdinand I de' Medici and the Knights of
St Stephen over the Moors. Bronze by
Pietro Tacca, 1623–26.

Duomo

On Piazza Grande, the rebuilt cathedral contains Fra Angelico's *Christ's Head Crowned with Thorns*, 1438.

Piazza del Municipio

Livorno's governing centre has its Chamber of Commerce and Provincial Palace.

Quartiere Venezia★

In 1629 the Medici created this area, which like Venice has building foundations that rise from the water, with principal entrances on the canal. The 16C **Fortezza Vecchia** is by Antonio Sangallo the Elder (1455–1534), while the late 16C **Fortezza Nuova** was built aided by Buontalenti (1536–1606). Via Borra, the most elegant street, was the 19C seat of consulates and wealthy merchants. In the church of S Caterina (1720), note the painting by Giorgio Vasari (Coronation of the Virgin). Via della Madonna has three churches: SS Annunziata or Church of the Greeks, Church of the Madonna and S Gregorio degli Armeni (of the Armenians), now a cultural centre.

▶ From Piazza Grande take Via Grande to Piazza Guerrazzi.

Cisternino

On Via Grande near Piazza Guerrazzi the Cisternino (1837) connects to the aqueduct, **Acquedotto Leopoldino**, now a cultural centre. The Cisternone is the imposing neo-Classical (1842) cistern. Via Grande leads to Piazza della Repubblica, then to Fortezza Nuova.

The **Mercato Centrale** (1894) is still the central market (vegetables, fish, meat and baked goods). See the outline of the neo-Gothic Dutch church on Fosso Reale.

▶ Fosso Reale leads to Piazza Cavour. Walk up Via Cairoli, then left to Piazza Benamozegh.

Synagogue

Piazza Benamozegh. ⸙*Guided visits by reservation.* ℘0586 89 62 90.
The sumptuous Baroque synagogue, destroyed in World War II, was rebuilt in

1962. Architect Angelo di Castro's form was inspired by Moses' tent during the Exodus. The luminous interior has two red windows that represent the Shoah and a precious "Ark" armoire (1708).

OUTSIDE THE CENTRE

Walk to the seafront, then to piazzas Mazzini, Orlando and Vittime della Moby Prince to Viale Italia.

Viale Italia

This elegant 1835 street connects south to **Ardenza**, with lovely views of the sea, hotels, and villas.

▲▲ Aquarium

Piazzale Mascagni 1. ⏱*Open 10am–6pm (Jul–Aug 7pm); hours and prices may vary, check on the website; last admission 1h before closing.* ⏱*Closed 24–25 Dec.* ⸙€10/17. ℘0586 26 91 11. www.acquariodilivorno.it.
On the beautiful Terrazza Mascagni over the sea, this offers science and history, with temporary exhibits.
On Viale Italia is the prestigious Italian "Naval Academy".

Museo Civico Giovanni Fattori★

Villa Mimbelli, Via San Jacopo in Acquaviva 65. ⏱*Open Tue–Sun 10am–1pm, 4–7pm.* ⏱*Closed Mon, 1 Jan, 1 May, 15 Aug, 25 Dec.* ⸙€6. ♿ ℘0586 80 80 01. www.museofattori.livorno.it.
Paintings by **Giovanni Fattori** (1825–1908), leading exponent of the Macchiaioli movement, and by his contemporaries, among them Telemaco Signorini, Giovanni Boldini, Silvestro Lega and Vittorio Corcos.

Museo Ebraico "Yeshiva Marini"

Via Micali 21, between Piazza XX Settembre and Viale Marconi, SW of Piazza della Repubblica. ⸙*Guided tours by reservation only,* ℘0586 83 97 72.
The synagogue in the 19C palace of merchant Marini houses a small museum with religious objects from the ancient

Livorno's History

In 1571, Cosimo I de' Medici constructed the first canal to link Livorno with Pisa. His son Francesco I called in architects and artists, including Buontalenti, to plan and construct an "ideal city". His brother, Ferdinand I, in 1587 gave Livorno port authority, creating a major player in commerce. In 1591, *Leggi Livornine* (Livornese Laws) granted all nationalities access to trade and freedom of religion, attracting Armenians, Greeks, Dutch, English and especially Jews. This renowned open, tolerant *porto franco*, a duty-free port, saw major 18C expansion. After 1868, as part of the Kingdom of Italy, it lost that status and business declined. Mussolini's racial laws of 1938 forced most Jews to close their businesses. Livorno's strategic military importance, especially for oil refineries, made it a target for bombardments on 28 May 1943, when much of the historic centre was decimated.

synagogue and works by artisans (textiles, coral). This building served several years as the *scuolina* (school) for Jewish students who were expelled from public schools under Mussolini's racial laws (1938).

Casa Natale Amedeo Modigliani

Via Roma 38, S of Piazza Cavour near Via Ricasoli. 🔊 *Guided tours by reservation only.* 🎫€10. 📞320 88 87 044. www.casanataleamedeomodigliani.com. The painter's former house is dedicated to his life and works.

EXCURSIONS
Montenero

10km/6mi S. Exit Livorno by SS1. After Ardenza, follow the signs. This road offers a panoramic view of the coast and Livorno.
This Baroque sanctuary (1721), a pilgrim destination, is dedicated to Our Lady of Graces, the patron saint of Tuscany. Adjacent rooms are covered with curious ex votos mostly with themes inspired by the sea.

Lari

35km/22mi E. Exit Livorno by Superstrada FI PI LI going towards Florence.
Perched on a hilltop that overlooks the Valdarno, this pretty village is dominated by the massive 13C–16C **Castello dei Vicari** (🔒*Temporarily closed for restoration at the time of publication;* 📞*334 39 63 782; www.castellodilari.it),* seat of the governors of Florence, who controlled the village.

Casciana Terme

15km/9mi S of Pontedera, on the axis of the Florence–Leghorn motorway.
Casciana Terme is surrounded by hills planted with grapevines and peach and olive trees. This ideally quiet yet varied holiday town is perfect for taking the waters, before exploring nearby towns on day trips.
Known under Caesar Augustus, its fame increased with 11C legend of **Matilda of Canossa** (1046–1115), who observed a blackbird heal its swollen foot in these waters. The springs are strongly recommended for treating circulatory disorders, hypertension, arthritis, rheumatism, asthma and bronchitis. Terme di Casciana (www.termedicasciana.com) offers a thermal pool (€15–17), mud baths, inhalations and drinking water.

ADDRESSES

🏨STAY

🛏 **Al Teatro** – *Via Mayer 42.* 📞*0586 89 87 05. www.hotelalteatro.it. 8 rooms.* 19C, small, elegant, musical themed decor. Lovely private garden.

🍴EAT

🍽 **Da Galileo** – *Via della Campana 20.* 📞*0586 88 90 09. www.dagalileo. com. Closed Sun dinnertime and Wed.* Old-fashioned with authentic Livorno *cacciucco* and other specialities.

🍽🍷 **Osteria del Mare** – *Via Borgo dei Cappuccini 5.* 📞*0586 88 10 27. Closed Thu. Reservations recommended.* Port-area bistro, seafood at reasonable prices.

🍽🍷 **Il Merlo Pizzorante** – *Piazza Minati 5, Casciana Terme.* 📞*0587 64 40 40. www.ristoranteilmerlo.it. Closed Thu.* Delicious pizzas and traditional Tuscan cuisine, in the centre of Casciana Terme.

🍽🍷🍷 **Ristorante Oscar** – *Via Franchini 78, Ardenza.* 📞*0587 50 12 58. www. ristoranteoscar.it. Open Wed–Sun, closed Tue dinner in summer.* Situated off the tourist trail in a charming residential district, this restaurant is popular with locals who come here to enjoy the fresh fish on offer – the vast selection on the buffet makes dining here a real treat. In summer, choose a table on the delightful outdoor veranda.

🍽🍷🍷🍷 **Locanda Martinelli** – *Piazza Mazzini 11, Nibbiaia, 22km/13.5mi SW of Livorno.* 📞*0587 74 01 61. locandamartinelli. it. Closed Tue. Reservation recommended.* It's well worth leaving the coast and climbing into the foothills to get to this small restaurant serving excellent cuisine. Housed in a rustic-style house with individual furnishings, in what could be the sitting room of a private house, the restaurant serves meat and fish specialities prepared with imagination from local produce and ingredients from further afield. As well as being a wine expert, the female owner gathers herbs, flowers and berries to flavour her recipes.

TAKING A BREAK

Bar Civili – *Via del Vigna 55.* 📞*0586 40 13 32. Closed Sun.* For over 100 years locals have gathered for the "Livorno punches".

ACTIVITIES

👥 **Giro in Battello dei Fossi Medicei** – *Departures from Scali della Darsena, in front of the monument "I Quattro Mori". For other departures call 📞333 15 73 372. €12. livornoinbattello.it.* Glide along the Medici canals in picturesque New Venice.

Terme di Casciana – *Piazza Garibaldi 9, Casciana Terme.* 📞*0587 64 461. www. termedicasciana.it.* A few hours or a full day of relaxation and pampering at the thermal baths.

EVENT

Settimana Velica Internazionale "Accademia Navale e Città di Livorno" – *www.settimanavelicainternazionale.it.* International regattas.

Etruscan Coast

The Etruscan Riviera, the strip of land along the coast between Livorno and Piombino, is rich in natural features, archaeological remains and literary associations. On its southern border lie the parks of the Val di Cornia – Parchi costieri della Sterpaia e di Rimigliano, Parco Archeologico di Baratti e Populonia, Parco Archeominerario di San Silvestro, Parco Naturale di Montioni and Parco Forestale di Poggio Neri.

🚗 DRIVING TOUR

Circuit of 120km/75mi.
🕐See regional map pp244–245.
Begin in Castiglioncello, 21km/13mi S of Livorno. The motorway to Piombino; inland to Castagneto Carducci, Bolgheri and Campiglia Marittima.

ⓘ **Michelin Map:**
Michelin Atlas p 36 and p 42 and Map 563 – I/M 13 or Map 735 Fold 14.

ⓘ **Info:** Livorno tourist office, Via Pieroni 18/20. 📞0586 89 42 36. www.visittuscany. com/en/areas/etruscan-coast-area.

▶ **Location:** The towns of the Riviera degli Etruschi are accessible via the SS1 motorway (Via Aurelia).

Castiglioncello

This is an elegant seaside resort on the Etruscan Riviera, well known for its delightful beaches sheltering in creeks in the shade of pine woods. The resort has an excellent climate owing to its ideal situation, protected by a headland and by hills descending to the water's edge.

Rosignano Marittimo

The remains of the medieval centre are in the upper part of the village. The **archaeological museum** (*Via del Castello 24;* ◷*Open Jul–Aug Tue–Sun 10am–1pm, 5–8pm; Sept–Jun Tue–Sat 9am–1pm, Sun and public hols 10am–1pm;* ◷*Closed Mon;* ✆€5; ✆*0586 72 42 88*) in the castle (**Palazzo Bombardieri**) provides local history from the Etruscans to the Middle Ages.

Cecina

Cecina is a farming and industrial town which was founded in the mid-19C following local land improvement. Set at the heart of the Etruscan Riviera, it extends to the coast as **Marina di Cecina**, a seaside resort sheltered by a wonderful pine wood. Its numerous Etruscan remains are studied by archaeologists. The **archaeological museum** (*Via Guerrazzi, località La Cinquantina;* ◷*Open Jul–Aug Tue–Sun 10am–1pm, 5–10pm; May–Jun and Sept Tue–Fri 4–8pm, Sat–Sun 10am–1pm, 4–8pm; Oct–Apr Sat–Sun 3–7pm (mid Dec–mid Jan only Sun);* ◷*Closed 1 Jan, 6 Jan, 25 Dec;* ✆€4.50; ✆*0586 61 12 66; www.museoarcheologicocecina.it*) contains Etruscan buccheroware, Greek vases decorated with painted figures dating from the classical and Hellenistic periods, urns dating from the 6C BC and funeral items from the days of imperial Rome.

Bibbona

Bibbona is a pretty medieval village set in the lovely Tuscan countryside. The Pieve di Sant'Ilario was founded in the 11C and enlarged in the 14C. Santa Maria della Pietà, a Renaissance church (1482), is attributed to Ranieri Tripalle and Vittorio Ghiberti.

Bolgheri

In this village the poet Giosuè Carducci lived 1838–48. The long avenue lined with large cypress trees from San Guido (*west*) was described in his elegiac poem, *In Front of San Guido*, well known to Italians. Today it is famous for Sassicaia, dubbed "father of Supertuscans", and for its local red wine, Bolgheri DOC.

The protected marsh ♟♟ **Oasi WWF Palude di Bolgheri** (*Km 269.4 SP 39 "Vecchia Aurelia";* ↞ *Guided visits by reservation,* ✆*328 193 70 95 or 389 95 78 763; bolgheri@wwf.it; www.wwf.it/oasi/toscana/padule_di_bolgheri*) is a refuge for aquatic fowl.

Castagneto Carducci (formerly Castagneto Marittimo)

Evocatively situated on a hilltop landscape of olive trees, the town belonged to the counts della Gherardesca, whose castle is reduced to the ruins of one tower (*Torre di Donoratico, 3.5km/2mi S*). Here the infamous Ugolino della Gherardesca, having been accused of treason by Pisa after the Battle of Meloria (1284), was locked in the tower to starve with his children in 1289; Ugolino was dubbed the "cannibal count" from Dante's depiction of their ambiguous fate.

Castagneto had belonged to Pisa since the 12C, then came under Florentine jurisdiction in 1406. The village was renamed after the Italian poet **Giosuè Carducci** (1835 Valdicastello–1907 Bologna), who stayed in the village during his youth and wrote poetry in honour of the beautiful Tuscan countryside. His life and work is recalled in the **Museo Archivio Giosuè Carducci** in the Palazzo Municipale (*town hall, Via Carducci 1;* ◷*Open daily mid Jun–mid Sept 10am–1pm, 4.30–7.30pm; rest of the year Tue–Fri 10am–1pm, Sat–Sun 10am–1pm, 3–6pm;* ✆*free;* ✆*0565 76 50 32; carducciecastagneto.wordpress. com*), and in his house along the same street, **Casa Carducci** (*no 59;* ◷*Open daily mid Jun–mid Sept 10am–1pm, 4.30–7.30pm; rest of the year Sat–Sun 10am–1pm, 3–6pm;* ✆€2).

Wine lovers come to taste the Bolgheri DOC, the heady red wine produced at **Tenuta Ornellaia** (◷*Open by appointment only for tours and tastings;* ✆*0565 71 811; www.ornellaia.com*) and other wineries.

♟♟ **Marina di Castagneto-Donoratico** is a lovely sandy beach bordered by a forest of maritime pines.

San Vincenzo

This well-equipped sandy beach is 5km/3mi long, with some rocky sections.

Campiglia Marittima

Campiglia developed on a hilltop (210m/ 682ft above sea level) in what was once the Pisan section of the Maremma district. The village, a strange collection of stone houses surrounded by walls that were once impregnable, dates from at least 1004 when a document states that Count Gherardo II della Gherardesca granted ownership of the town to a monastery near Chiusdino. From 1259 the community was governed by a captain from Pisa, then in 1406 by Florence after it conquered Pisa. In the 16C its military power waned and influential families ruled.

From Piazza della Repubblica, the street climbs to Palazzo Pretorio.

Palazzo Pretorio

The building is decorated with the coats of arms of the captains who lived here until 1406. The column to the left served as the base of the cage in which wrongdoers were publicly ridiculed.

Rocca

Overlooking the Florentine Gate, with coats of arms from the four rulers of Campiglia, are the remains of the 12C–13C **fortress**, probably built on the site of an earlier 8C fortress.

Pieve di San Giovanni

In the cemetery. This 12C parish **church** built in the shape of the Greek letter *tau* (T) has two particularly interesting features. Beneath the side portal is a low-relief depicting the Boar Hunt in Meleagre.

Beneath the roof of the side chapel is an inscription of the mysterious **magic square** which dates from the beginning of the Christian era, if not earlier. The five words are set out in a square of five lines which read the same both backwards and forwards and up and down –

```
S A T O R
A R E P O
T E N E T
O P E R A
R O T A S
```

Although its meaning remains obscure, it seems to have been used as a magic spell to ward off evil spirits.

Parco Archeominerario di San Silvestro

Via di San Vincenzo 34/b. For opening hours see the website; last admission 2h before closing. €20 (€10–17 partial tours). 0565 22 64 45. www.parchivaldicornia.it.

In the hills north of Campiglia Marittima is an **archaeological mining site** (450ha/1,112 acres) with waymarked routes illustrating mining techniques in the Etruscan period.

Rocca San Silvestro, 10C, is a village devoted to the extraction of minerals

---

Carducci and the Maremma

"I cipressi che a Bólgheri alti e schietti
Van da San Guido in duplice filar,
Quasi in corsa giganti giovinetti…"

The tall and blunt Bólgheri cypresses
Go to San Guido in double row,
Almost running as young giants…

So opens the 1874 poem "Davanti San Guido" by 1906 Nobel prize Giosue Carducci (1835–1907), who blends the beauty of the gentle Maremma countryside with the melancholy of change and loss after the death of his grandmother, and celebrated his boyhood spent in Tuscany. Part of that landscape today is Tenuta San Guido, the famous winery that makes Sassicaia (*See Wine Road box, opposite*) and is near the wildlife preserve. Today's visitors will find the landscape much as it was in Carducci's time. The town name, though, changed from Castagneto Marittimo to Castagneto Carducci.

Wine Road

The Etruscan Riviera has been an agricultural district since the 15C. Bolgheri has become famous especially for two wines: Sassicaia, called "the father of Supertuscans" and Ornellaia. However, these can cost easily €100 per bottle, so it's best to know that the two wineries that produce them prefer serious wine collectors or merchants. However, don't hesitate to seek out the lesser-known wines – this route has some 60 smaller wineries making Bolgheri DOC, Val di Cornia and Bibbona wines. Try them in *enotecas* or restaurants if you can't arrange a tasting at the winery (*make an appointment*).

The Wine Road (SP16) begins in Rosignano Marittimo and finishes in Piombino. It is a good route (*160km/99mi*) for cycling and we would recommend the stages between Bibbona, Bolgheri and Castagneto Carducci.

🛈 **Consorzio La Strada del Vino e dell'Olio Costa degli Etruschi** – *Località San Guido 45, Bolgheri. ℘0565 74 97 05. www.lastradadelvino.com.*

(copper, lead, silver) and to the making of alloys (♿ *museum*).

Suvereto

This charming medieval hamlet nestled in the hills overlooking the sea and surround by remains of ramparts, is lined with cobblestone streets, stone houses, churches and buildings that include the 13C municipal palace. The cloister of San Francesco (13C–16C) is now a hotel (♿ *See Addresses*). The *Rocca* above town is 9C, modified in the 12C by the Aldobrandeschi.

Among local wineries is **Petra** in San Lorenzo Alto, designed by architect Mario Botta (2003). It offers tasting and visits (🕐 *by appointment. ℘0565 84 53 08; www.petrawine.it. €35–60*) to fully explore viticulture, architecture, the pure essence of wine and the charm of Tuscan hospitality.

Parco Archeologico di Baratti e Populonia★

Località Baratti. 🕐*For opening hours see the website; last admission 2h before closing.* ☜*€20 (€10–17 partial tours). ℘0565 22 64 45. www.parchivaldicornia.it.*

The **necropolis** of the Etruscan town of Pupluna stands below the acropolis overlooking the sea. It dates from the Iron Age (9C–8C BC), when Baratti Bay was the site of all the great burial grounds. Economic activity was probably based on the mineral mines on the Isle of Elba and in the hills around Campiglia (*northeast*). From

Medieval village of Suvereto

© Lady-Photo/iStock

the 4C BC, when people began to mine iron on the island, the burial grounds were gradually covered with scoria and waste from the kilns, concealed until the early 20C.

Different types of graves were excavated – pits, ditches and chambers (being the oldest) and oriental-style barrows. Among the tumuli with cylindrical bases are the **Tomb with Funeral Beds** (*letti funebri*) and the **Tomb with the Pear-Shaped Urn** (*a small Grecian urn*). The **Funnel Tomb** (*dei colatoi*) has a tall barrow; the **Fan Tomb** (*dei flabelli*) and **Goldware Tomb** (*delle oreficerie*) are the only tumuli to have remained intact; the **Small Bronze Offering Tomb** is a tomb with an aedicule and was named after the bronze fans found among other funeral items.

Populonia Alta

2km/1.2mi past Baratti Park.
This little village has three narrow streets lined with artisan shops and a small **Etruscan museum** (*Palazzo Gasparri, Via di Sotto;* ⏰*Open daily 10am–7pm (mid Jun–mid Sept 8pm and Jul–Aug Sat–Sun 10pm; Nov–6 Jan 6pm; 7 Jan–21 Mar only Fri–Sun 10am–6pm or by reservation);* ⏰*Closed 25 Dec;* ✎€3; ✆0565 17 66 345; www.pastexperience.it).*

▶ From SS1, Via Aurelia, take the exit for Venturina.

Piombino

Midway down the coast of ancient Etruria, Piombino was built on a promontory and was the site of three successive harbours since Antiquity – the Etruscan port of Baratti, the port of Marina (12C–early 20C) and the Falesia harbour, now known as Portovecchio. The town is the **passenger ferry port** for the Tuscan Archipelago (⏰*See opposite*).

Piazza Verdi is the starting point for walks through the town centre. The buildings in the square include the Rivellino (1447), Piombino's old main gate, and the Torrione, a massive tower built in 1212. South of the square on Corso Vittorio Emanuele is the 1444 **Palazzo Comunale**, restored in 1935. The 13C **Casa delle Bifore** (nearby in Via Ferruc-

cio) houses the municipal archives. At the far southern end of Corso Vittorio Emanuele is Piazza Bovio, a square shaped like a ship's prow, with a fine **view**★ of the Tuscan Archipelago. From Piazza Bovio turn right towards the tiny port of Marina to see the **Fonti dei Canali**. These 13C public marble **fountains** are attributed to Nicola Pisano and have provided the local water supply for almost seven centuries. Head west from Piazza Verdi on Via Leonardo da Vinci to see the bastions of the town walls. At the end of the road is the citadel, built 1465–70 on the order of Jacopo III Appiani which has a remarkable marble **cistern**.

Head southeast from Piazza Verdi (*Piazza del Castello*) to the 13C–16C castle (*cassero*) and fortress (*fortezza*), off Via Giordano Bruno, built in 1552 on the order of Cosimo I.

Museo Archeologico del Territorio di Populonia

Piazza Cittadella 8. ⏰*For opening hours see the website; last admission 1h before closing.* ✎€7. ✆0565 22 64 45. www.parchivaldicornia.it.*
Palazzo Nuovo brings together a rich collection of archaeological finds from Baratti and Populonia.

ADDRESSES

🛏STAY

🍴 **Hotel Massimo** – *Via Zaccaria 3, Marina di Cecina.* ✆0586 62 02 16. www.hotelmassimo.it. 28 rooms.* Near the beach and the pine grove. A family hotel with simple modern style; some rooms with balcony. It also offers a beauty centre.

🍴 **Hotel Miramare** – *Via Marconi 8, Castiglioncello.* ✆0586 75 24 35. www.albergo-miramare.it.* 🅿. 45 rooms.* Restaurant 🍴. Churchill, Pirandello and Macchiaioli visited this mansion overlooking the bay to the beach. Pleasant rooms, some with sea view. Choose half or full board.

🍴 **Agriturismo "Tra Gli Ulivi"** – *Località Felciaino 189/B, Bolgheri.* ✆0565 76 52 01. www.chiappinitragliulivi.com. 6 apts, 6 rooms.* Apartments and rooms among vineyards, olive groves and cypresses;

this farm produces olive oil and wines including Bolgheri.

Podere La Cerreta – *Via della Cerreta 7, Sassetta, 8km/5mi S of Castagneto Carducci on S325. ℘0565 79 43 52. www. lacerreta.it.* ⓺ *9 rooms.* A few miles from the sea this farm offers traditional rooms, thermal baths and country food.

Il Chiostro Apartments and Suites – *Via del Crocifisso 14, Suvereto. ℘0565 82 70 67. www.vacanzeilchiostro.it. 15 suites.* Spacious rooms or small apartments in the rustic style, in town.

Il Chiassetto – *Via Lauretta 2, Bolgheri. ℘339 66 30 171. www.ilchiassetto bolgheri.it. 3 rooms.* Pretty rooms in the centre at the foot of a castle.

ⵏ/EAT

Bagno Nettuno – *Via Costa 2, San Vincenzo. ℘0565 70 10 95. www.bagno ristorantenettuno.it. Closed Nov–Mar.* On the beach, enjoy an economical fish meal.

Il Garibaldi Innamorato – *Via Garibaldi 5, Piombino. ℘0565 49 410.*

www.ristoranteilgaribaldinnamorato.com. Simple, local specialities from the sea.

Locanda Il Canovaccio – *Via Vecchio Asilo 1, Campiglia Marittima. ℘0565 83 84 49. www.locandailcanovaccio.it. Closed lunchtime, Mon except in Jul–Aug. Reservations suggested.* Light seafood or vegetable dishes. Veranda overlooks the square.

Tarabaralla – *Via Curtatone 19, Cecina. ℘0586 68 42 38. Closed lunchtime.* Innovative, traditional cooking; dine by candlelight in the garden.

Osteria del Contadino – *Via Don Sturzo 69, Guasticce. ℘0586 98 46 97. www.osteriadelcontadino.com. Closed Sun. Reservations suggested.* First-class ingredients in dishes served with flair. Relax in the "cantina" room.

Osteria Magona – *Via Bolgherese, località Vallone dei Messi 199, Bolgheri. ℘0565 76 21 73. www.osteriamagona. com. Closed Mon.* On a picturesque village square, enjoy a Fiorentina steak or traditional Mediterranean cuisine.

Isola d'Elba and the Tuscan Archipelago★★

The Tuscan Archipelago is a string of seven islands, of which Elba is the largest. Giglio, Capraia, Montecristo, Pianosa, Giannutri and Gorgona are mountainous, with a rich unspoiled natural environment that is seen at its best during the seasons when the climate is mild and the coastline free from crowds of tourists.

ISOLA D'ELBA★★

Elba, island of seahorses, is the largest island in the Tuscan Archipelago. It is popular for its solitary beauty, its silence, its mild climate, its untamed nature and its varied landscapes.
The Isle of Elba was part of the Tyrrhenian continent that was partially submerged beneath the sea in the Quaternary era, leaving behind the islands of Corsica, Sardinia, the Balearics, Elba and

- **Michelin Map:** 563 – L, M 11 and N, O, P 12, 13, 14; Map 735 Folds 14, 24, 25.
- **Location:** North to south, the islands of the Tuscan Archipelago: Gorgona, Capraia, Pianosa, Montecristo, Giglio and Giannutri.
- **Take Note:** Gorgona, Montecristo and Pianosa cannot be visited.
- **Elba Population:** 31,904.
- **Elba Info:** Calata Italia 44, Portoferraio, www.visitelba. info. www.visittuscany.com.
- **Elba Timing:** Allow two days to tour the island by car (rentals in Portoferraio).
- **Giglio Info:** Via Umberto I, Giglio Porto. ℘0564 80 94 00. www.isoladelgiglio.it.

two mountain ranges on the French Riviera (Les Maures and L'Estérel). Elba is a mountainous island; its highest peak is **Monte Capanne** (1,018m/

275

GETTING THERE

BY SEA: Elba is easily reached from Piombino, port of departure for ferries going to Portoferraio and Rio Marina. Contact: **Moby Portoferraio**, Via Giuseppe Ninci 1, Portoferraio, &0565 91 67 58, www.moby.it; **Toremar**, Calata Italia 36, Portoferraio, &0565 91 80 80, www.toremar.it; **Blu Navy**, Calata Italia 8, Portoferraio, &0565 26 97 10, blunavytraghetti.com.

BY BUS/TRAIN: Buses and trains go only as far as Piombino (◖See above). **Piombino Marittima train station** is reachable from all major cities (transfer at Campiglia Marittima; Ferrovie dello Stato, www.trenitalia.com). **ATM–Tiemme buses** (Via L. da Vinci 13, Piombino, &0565 26 01 11, www.atm.li.it) have routes to

Piombino Porta and a direct bus from Florence (mid Jun–8 Sept).

BY AIR: Direct flights operate from Pisa and some international destinations to **Elba airport** (www.elbaisland-airport.it).

GETTING AROUND

BY CAR: You can take your car from the mainland to Elba via a car ferry. Otherwise, you can hire a car (multiple options available at the port).

BY BUS/TAXI: CTT operates intra-island bus routes as well as city routes in **Portoferraio** (Viale Elba, Portoferraio, &0565 88 26 02, livorno.cttnord.it). For taxi service from the port or elsewhere in Portoferraio, call &0565 18 22.

3,308ft). It has a jagged coastline consisting of natural, well-sheltered coves with small beaches. Professional fishermen regularly catch tuna and anchovies along the island's rocky shores.

Elba is perhaps best known as the place of exile for Napoleon from 1814 to 1815. From his homebase in Portoferraio he commanded a small court and initiated several public works projects.

🚗 DRIVING TOUR

THE WEST★★
70km/44mi. About 5hr anticlockwise from Portoferraio, following the route indicated in orange on the map, below.

Portoferraio★
The capital of Isola d'Elba lies on the shores of a beautiful bay, protected by the remains of outer walls and two fortresses.

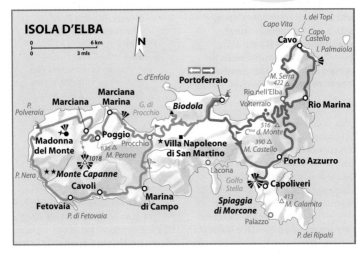

Portoferraio

© LaraBelova/iStock

In the upper part of the town overlooking the sea (*north*) is the **Museo Nazionale delle Residenze Napoleoniche – Palazzina dei Mulini★** (*Mill House, access from the town centre; follow signs for a fatiguing climb on foot up a long flight of steps or by car up a rough narrow road;* ◷*Open Mon and Wed–Sat 8.30am–7.30pm (mid Sept–Oct 6.30pm), Sun and public hols 8.30am–1.30pm; Nov–Mar Wed–Mon 8.30am–1.30pm;* ◷*Closed Tue, 1 Jan, 25 Dec;* ⬤*€5; €8 joint ticket with Villa di San Martino, valid for 3 days;* ☏*0565 91 58 46; polomusealetoscana. beniculturali.it*), a simple house with a patio and garden, where Napoleon lived during his brief period of sovereignty. The house contains a museum consisting of the officers' mess, Napoleon's library, his bedroom and the antechamber; from the first floor there is a fine view of the garden and the sea; downstairs are the WC, the servants' room, Napoleon's salon, his study and the door to the garden, where one can take a stroll. The **road★** west from Portoferraio to Marciana Marina is particularly recommended for the views it provides of Procchio and Procchio Bay. A small detour leads to **Biodola**, a vast, beautiful sandy beach.

Marciana Marina

This is a harbour protected by two jetties, one of which holds the ruins of the Medici Tower (*Torre Medicea*).

Napoleon, Sovereign of the Isle of Elba

After signing the Act of Abdication in Fontainebleau, the deposed French Emperor lived on Elba from 4 May 1814 to 26 February 1815.

Napoleon had with him a small court governed by Bertrand, the Grand Marshal of the Palace. He also commanded about 1,000 soldiers, of whom 300 had accompanied him at the outset, together with 100 grenadiers and infantrymen from his imperial guard, and 600 more came to join him, including Polish lancers under the orders of Drouot and Cambronne. He also had his own navy consisting of one brig, *L'Inconstant*.

During his short stay he directed Cambronne's men to build roads, and the Polish lancers developed iron mines, wrote texts and made improvements in farming methods, and modernised the road network in Portoferraio. In less than a year, Napoleon escaped from exile, returned to power, then four months later was defeated at Waterloo on 18 June 1815.

Gemstones

Where the Isle of Elba is not green with vegetation, it is red with iron ore in the east and white with granite in the west. It's a good hunting ground for minerals; golden or silvery pyrites in various shapes cubes – dodecahedrons and octahedrons – can be found near Rio Marina. You can look for light-blue beryls, the famous aquamarines in the granite of Monte Capanne, the Oggi Cave, Fonte del Prete, Speranza and Gorgolinato. The island mines are no longer in operation, but there are many minerals in the old workings. The local pyrites is likely to be found near deposits of haematite, which is reddish or brown, and the velvety black ilvaite, which is also known as lievrite – the name Elba is derived from the Latin *ilva*. A search for aquamarines may turn up other beryls like pink morganite or black heliodor – or you might find tourmalines, garnets or topaz.

Monte Capanne★★

15min by cable-car. Operates daily Easter–Oct 10am–1pm, 2.15–5pm *(Jul–Sept 5.30pm).* €18 return trip. 0565 90 10 20.

From the rocky summit (*15min on foot from the top station*), there is a superb **panoramic view★★** over the entire island of Elba, (*east*) to the coast of Tuscany and (*west*) to the east coast of Corsica.

Marciana★

The village lies at the foot of its ruined castle on the eastern slopes of Monte Giove, providing a wonderful **view★** of Poggio, Marciana Marina and Procchio Bay.

The small **archaeological museum** (*Open mid Apr–Sept 10.30am–12.30pm (Jul–Aug 11am–1pm), 4–7pm (Sept 3.30–6.30pm);* Closed Tue and Thu; €2; 0565 90 12 15; www.visitmarciana.it) has exhibits dating from the Iron and Bronze ages and a collection of Greek pottery.

Madonna del Monte★★

Alt 627m/2,037ft. 45min there and back on foot from the road to the castle above Marciana.

A rocky path runs through the trees at the beginning of the walk but later provides panoramic views as it climbs to the 16C chapel built on the north slope of Monte Giove. Near the chapel is a strange semi-circular fountain dating from 1698 and the "hermitage" where Napoleon lived with Maria Walewska for a few days in the summer of 1814.

From the adjacent rocks the **view★** embraces the creeks on the north coast, Marciana Marina and Procchio Bay, and the villages of Marciana and **Poggio★**. The road continues along the west coast, passing the beaches of Sant'Andrea and **Fetovaia**. East of Fetovaia the road reaches **Cavoli**, a seaside resort with a sandy beach.

Marina di Campo

Marina di Campo lies on the edge of a plain dotted with olive trees and vineyards and is popular for its superb beach. Fishermen make the delightful little harbour a bustling place.

▶ Take the road that runs up the Galea Valley, bordered to the right by the uninhabited Lacona region, to return to Procchio. From Procchio take the road towards Portoferraio; in San Martino, turn right to Villa di San Martino.

Museo Nazionale delle Residenze Napoleoniche – Villa di San Martino★

Open Apr–mid Oct Tue, Thu, Sat–Sun 8.30am–1.30pm, Wed and Fri 2–7.30pm; rest of the year Tue–Sun 8.30am–1.30pm. Closed Mon, 1 Jan, 25 Dec. €5; €8 joint ticket with Palazzina dei Mulini, valid for 3 days. 0565 91 46 88. polomuseale-toscana.beniculturali.it.

The silent hillsides planted with oak trees and vineyards have not changed since Napoleon's day; nor has the view, except for the neo-Classical palace built by Prince Demidoff. Above it stands the modest house used by Napoleon as his summer residence; the interior decoration has been restored to what it was during Napoleon's occupation. From the terrace, there is a pleasant view of Portoferraio Bay.

THE EAST★

68km/42mi. About 3hr – clockwise from Portoferraio following the route indicated in purple on map p276.

◗ From Portoferraio (&*See p276*) take the road S; after 3km/2mi turn left towards Porto Azzurro. The road skirts Portoferraio harbour before bearing S across the the narrowest part of the island. It then crosses the Monte Calamita peninsula. Turn right to Capoliveri.

Capoliveri

On the western outskirts of this small town, the point known as **Three Seas Panorama★★** offers views of three bays: Portoferraio Bay (*north*), Stella Bay (*west*) and Porto Azzurro Bay (*east*); below (*south*) is the beach at Morcone. Out to sea (*southwest*) are the islands of Pianosa and Montecristo.

◗ Return to the road to Porto Azzurro.

Porto Azzurro

This town faces a delightful harbour commanded by a fortress that is now a prison. The vegetation consists mainly of cacti and agaves.
The road then winds north across the eastern slopes of Monte Castello and Cima del Monte.

◗ Before reaching Rio nell'Elba turn right to Rio Marina.

Rio Marina

This fine village and mining harbour is protected by a small tower with merlons. The **coast road★** to Cavo provides a number of attractive views of the tiny rocky islands of Cerboli and Palmaiola in the Piombino Strait and of Follonica Bay and the mainland.

Cavo

This is a pretty little harbour, the nearest to the mainland, protected by Cape Castello.

◗ Take the road via Rio nell'Elba towards Porto Azzurro. At the crossroads, turn left and then first right.

The **Volterraio road★** runs high above the sea, providing a number of breathtaking views of the ruins at Volterraio and Portoferraio Bay.

ADDITIONAL SIGHTS

OTHER ISLANDS IN THE ARCHIPELAGO
Isola del Giglio★

The mountainous island of Giglio (Lily Island) lies just off Monte Argentario. There are only three villages – **Giglio Porto**, where the boats from the mainland dock, **Giglio Castello**, the medieval village encircled by the walls of its fortress, and **Campese**, a village with accommodations, which overlooks a delightful bay fringed with a sandy beach. The sheer, rugged coast carpeted with scrub blends harmoniously with the natural beauty of the wild and emotive environment, which is the product of the very dry climate. A range of sports is available including sub-aqua, windsurfing and horse riding.

Isola di Giannutri★

Giannutri, which lies southeast of Giglio, is privately owned but open to visitors for a few hours every day (⊘ *no camping or picnics*). There are traces of a 1C Roman villa which may have belonged to Domitian Enobarbus.

Isola di Capraia★

Capraia lies nearer the northern tip of Corsica than Italy. The western side is mountainous; the eastern side is gentler and more hospitable. The natural environment is rugged, and only the centre and harbour are inhabited. It is this untamed nature that makes the island a paradise for walkers who come to admire the tiny lake (*laghetto*) in an old volcanic crater.

Sailors like to view the island from the sea and admire the nesting birds and the deep colours of the Cala Rossa (Red Creek). The coastline is perfect for sub-aqua and windsurfing activities.

Gorgona, Pianosa★ and Montecristo

⚓ *Little or no access to visitors.*

There are prisoners on **Gorgona**, an agricultural penal colony, which lies offshore from Livorno (Leghorn).

Pianosa, which is south of Elba, held a maximum security prison until 1998 (famous for holding a future president of Italy, Pertini, a political prisoner, as well as Mafia criminals). Tourists can make day trips to Pianosa Apr–Oct in groups that depart from Marina di Campo, to see Roman ruins and other sights. Emperor Augustus exiled Agrippa Postumus (son of Marcus Agrippa, whose name is inscribed on Rome's Pantheon) here under maximum security in 9 AD. Novelist Joseph Heller set *Catch 22* on Pianosa.

Montecristo, south of Pianosa, is a granite island dominated by Monte Fortezza (645m/2,096ft), classified as an uninhabited nature conservation zone.

The island is famous as the setting chosen by Alexandre Dumas (1844) for his novel *The Count of Monte Cristo*. Visitor permission is granted to a few who must go through the Italian Forestry Corps, with a wait that may take three years or more.

ADDRESSES

🛏 STAY

Hotel Brigantino – *Campo all'Aia, Procchio, 15km/9mi E of Marciana.* ℘*0565 90 74 53. www.hotelbrigantino.com. Closed 21 Oct–22 Mar. 46 rooms.* The best feature of this hotel is the vast and shady garden a few yards from the sea, which also has a pool, tennis and ping pong. Rooms are spacious and adequately furnished.

Da Giacomino – *Capo Sant'Andrea, Marciana, 6km/4mi NW of Marciana.* ℘*0565 90 80 10. www.hoteldagiacomino.it. Closed Nov–Easter. 33 rooms. Half-board.* The ideal place for a holiday – set in a magnificent garden that runs to the edge of the steep cliff, with a fine view of the sea, a saltwater pool and tennis courts. The rooms are light and pleasant, and the owners are charming.

Hotel Residence Villa Giulia – *Località Lido di Capoliveri, Porto Azzurro, 7.5km/5mi NW of Capoliveri.* ℘*0565 94 01 67. www.villagiuliahotel.it. Closed Oct–Mar. 35 rooms.* 🅿. The comfortable rooms, in four separate buildings, have cane furniture and a balcony or small garden. In summer, meals for residents are served on the terrace overlooking the sea. Swimming pool.

Hotel Campese – *Località Campese, Isola del Giglio.* ℘*0564 80 40 03 or 366 26 49 722. www.hotelcampese.com. 47 rooms.* Restaurant. 🅿. The hotel, which overlooks its private beach, is a quiet family-run hotel and has recently been refurbished.

Montecristo Island

© M. Piacentino/Sime/Photononstop

Hotel Dino – *Pareti, 4km/ 2.5mi S of Capoliveri. ℘0565 93 91 03. www.elbahoteldino.com. Closed Oct–Apr. 30 rooms. ⌑. Half board, restaurant ☺☺.* All the rooms at this hotel are spacious with a view of the sea and far enough (although not too far) from the noise of the beach. The hospitality of the staff will add to your enjoyment.

♀/EAT

La Guardiola –*Campo all'Aia, Procchio. ℘339 68 68 338. Closed dinnertime.* This tiny, 5-table restaurant sits just 5m from the waterfront, and is one of the nicest places on Elba island for a plate of spaghetti or even just a simple espresso.

La Vecchia Pergola – *Via Thaon de Revel 31, Giglio Porto, Isola del Giglio. ℘0564 80 90 80. Closed Wed and Nov–Feb.* In the port, hovering on stilts above the water, this restaurant's peaceful island-village atmosphere is ideal for dining.

Affrichella – *Via S Chiara 7, Marciana Marina. ℘0565 99 68 44. Reservations required.* Small, near the cathedral. Fish specialities and extensive wine list. Ideal in summer for romantic candlelit dinners in the adjoining square.

Da Pilade – *Località Marina di Mola, Capoliveri, on the road to Capoliveri. ℘0565 96 86 35. www.hoteldapilade. it. Closed mid-Oct–Easter. Reservations required.* Not far from the sea, this hotel-restaurant specialises in grilled Angus steak and a huge choice of hors d'œuvres.

Publius – *Piazza del Castagneto 11, Poggio, 3km/2mi E of Marciana. ℘0565 99 208. www.ristorantepublius.it. Closed Dec–Mar.* Choose a table on the veranda to enjoy splendid views of Marciana, the hills and the sea. The cooking is authentic with an emphasis on fish.

Trattoria Moderna – *Piazza Garibaldi 9, Capoliveri. ℘391 41 49 585. facebook.com/Trattoria-Moderna-di-Matteo. Closed Sun in winter and Nov–Feb.* A beautiful family bistro with an attractive outdoor area. Simple, informal dishes at lunchtime, followed by a larger selection in the evening. The courteous welcome and enthusiasm of the owner-chef will make you want to return here.

Da Maria – *Via della Casa Matta, località Castello, Isola del Giglio. ℘0564 80 60 62. Closed Wed and Jan–Feb.* This restaurant, possibly the most typical of the island, is located in the picturesque centre of medieval Castello,

with a panoramic view from the terrace of Campese Bay. Local specialities, such as fish and seafood, are served in a simple setting.

Sapereta – *Via Provinciale ovest 73, località Mola, Porto Azzurro. ℘0565 95 033. www.sapereta.it.* Housed in a historic winery, this simple, rustic-style restaurant is surrounded by a garden where farmyard animals roam freely. Don't be fooled by appearances, however – the cuisine here is modern, with meat dishes taking pride of place on the menu.

ACTIVITIES

The Island of Elba is a paradise for sports enthusiasts, where activities are set amidst natural beauty.

Free climbing – In Chiessi, Pomonte, Marciana and the north slope of San Bartolomeo.

Paragliding – At Monte Capanne, Monte Perone, Monte Volterraio and Monts Orello and Norsi.

Trekking – Numerous hiking trails throughout the island. Easy route *(1hr30min)*, from Santa Lucia to San Martino; medium difficulty *(2hr)*, through the mining area on the island of San Felo to Ortano; for experienced hikers *(2hr)*, along the east ridge between Parata and Volterraio.

Cycling – Many trails for mountain bikers.

Riding – Excursions on horseback from 1–3hrs, or a day with picnic or restaurant stop included.

Diving – Especially beautiful sea floor at: Corbelli Islands off the coast of Mount Calamita; the Formiche della Zanca, near Cape Sant'Andrea, the rock of the Ogli near the beach Pomonte and the Scoglietto north of Portoferraio.

Centro Velico Naregno – *Naregno beach, Capoliveri. ℘338 92 40 201. www.centroveliconaregno.it. Closed mid Oct–Mar.* This sailing school offers Naregno sailing and rents windsurfing boards, catamarans, and sea scooters.

Nautilus – *Departs from Marciana Marina and Portoferraio. ℘0565 97 60 22 or 328 70 95 470. Closed Nov–25 Apr. Reservation recommended. www.aquavision.it/nautilus. html.* An alternative to diving, a submarine boat to discover marine life.

Canoing-kayaking – Around the granite rocks of Marina di Campo.

Good to know: It is also the perfect spot for fishing, tennis, golf and sailing.

Volterra★★

Volterra stands on a hill between the Cecina and Era valleys, enclosed within Etruscan and medieval walls. It is set in an unusual and fascinating landscape★★. To the west the outline of the hill is broken by the grandiose crags★ (*balze*) caused by erosion and rock falls. West of the town are vast salt pans where table salt and soda are produced.

THE LANDSCAPE★★

Volterra is a piece of the Middle Ages, set upon rolling hills defined by their geological features formed of clay and sand (erosion ditches), or even salt (to the west, the salt flats are used for the manufacture of refined salt and soda).

●●WALKING TOUR

Piazza dei Priori★★

The **square** is flanked by austere and sober mansions. The **Palazzo Pretorio** (13C) has twin-bay windows. Beside it rises a massive crenellated tower which, owing to the wild boar on its upper section, is called *Porcellino* (Piglet). Opposite stands the 13C **Palazzo dei Priori** (◐*Open daily mid Mar–1 Nov 9am–7pm; rest of the year 10am–4.30pm (26–31 Dec 6pm);* ◐*Closed 25 Dec;* ⊚€6; €16 with

- ▶ **Population:** 10,159.
- ♿ **Michelin Map:** Michelin Atlas p 37 and Map 563 – I 14 or Map 735 Fold 14.
- ▯ **Info:** Piazza dei Priori 20. ℘0588 87 257. volterratur.it. www.comune. volterra.pi.it.
- ◗ **Location:** Volterra is found on S68, which links Poggibonsi and Cecina.

"Volterra card"; ℘0588 86 099), decorated with the emblems of Florentine magistrates. It is now used as the town hall and contains frescoes, paintings and sculptures (14C–19C).

◉ **Volterra card** (€16; volterratur.it), valid for 3 days, gives unlimited access to Volterra's main sights: Palazzo dei Priori, Pinacoteca, Ecomuseo dell'Alabastro, Museo Etrusco Guarnacci, Acropoli and Teatro romano.

◗ Take Via Turazza (along left side of the Palazzo dei Priori).

Duomo and Battistero★

◐*Open daily 8am–6pm; hours may vary in winter.*

The **cathedral** in picturesque Piazza San Giovanni was built in the Pisan Romanesque style. The nave is divided from the aisles by 16C monolithic col-

Medieval town of Volterra

© Photogillio/iStock

WHERE TO STAY

Albergo Nazionale .... ①
Chiostro Delle Monache
 Hostel Volterra .... ⑦
Hotel Villa Porta all'Arco .... ④
Villa Rioddi .... ⑩

WHERE TO EAT

Don Beta .... ⑥
Il Poggio .... ②
Il Sacco Fiorentino .... ③
Osteria dei Poeti .... ⑬
Trattoria Albana .... ⑨

STREET INDEX

Museo di Arte Sacra .... **M**

umns with capitals. The coffered ceiling represents Paradise with the saints of Volterra and (*above the sanctuary*) the Assumption of the Virgin Mary.

The Addolorata Chapel (*left*) contains the *Procession of the Magi*, a fresco by Benozzo Gozzoli (1420–97) serving as the background to a multicoloured terracotta crib by Zaccaria Zacchi da Volterra (1473–1544). Opposite is another polychrome terracotta work by Zacchi. In the south transept is a touching 13C **Deposition from the Cross★★** made of polychrome, silvered and gilded poplar wood. It represents Christ, Nicodemus, Joseph of Arimathaea, Mary and John, and is one of the best-preserved groups of its day. The octagonal **Baptistery** dates from 1283. It has a marble doorway and one side decorated with white and green marble.

⬤ Walk along Via Porta all'Arco.

Porta all'Arco★ (Arch Gate)

This Etruscan archway, dating from the 4C BC, is built with huge quadrangular blocks of stone.

⬤ Return to Piazza dei Priori. Take the street which slopes N and turn right into Via Buomparenti.

The street contains the remarkable Buomparenti 13C tower-houses, linked by a slender arch.

Via dei Sarti

The elegant Via dei Sarti is lined with palaces, the most interesting are: no 1 in the Palazzo Minucci Solaini, attributed to Antonio da Sangallo and now home to the art museum; and at no 41, the

Palazzo Viti with its beautiful Renaissance façade designed by Ammannati.

Pinacoteca

Via dei Sarti 1, in the Palazzo Minucci Solaini. ◐Open daily mid Mar–1 Nov 9am–7pm; rest of the year 10am–4.30pm (26–31 Dec 6pm). ◐Closed 25 Dec. ◈€8 (includes Ecomuseo dell'Alabastro); €16 with "Volterra card". ℘0588 87 580 / 86 347. volteratur.it.

The **art gallery** has some interesting works of religious art by Tuscan masters of the 14C–17C – a Madonna and Child by Taddeo di Bartolo (c. 1362–1422); a superb Annunciation by Luca Signorelli (c. 1445–1523); a dramatic **Deposition from the Cross★★** with stylised outlines by Rosso Fiorentino (1495–1540); and a Christ the Redeemer by Domenico Ghirlandaio (1449–94). This is a major work of Italian Mannerism.

Ecomuseo dell'Alabastro

Via dei Sarti 1, in the Palazzo Minucci Solaini. ◐Open daily mid Mar–1 Nov 9am–7pm; rest of the year 10am–4.30pm (26–31 Dec 6pm). ◐Closed 25 Dec. ◈Included in Pinacoteca's ticket.

The older part of Palazzo Minucci Solaini has one of the three parts of this "museo diffuso" dedicated to alabaster and works made from it, its use, decorative styles, and economic impact on this area. The other two sections of the museum are located in other towns.

Palazzo Viti

Via dei Sarti 41. ◐Open daily Apr–1 Nov 10am–5.30pm; rest of the year by reservation. ◈€5; €4 for "Volterra card" holders. ℘0588 84 047. www.palazzoviti.it.

This mansion houses collections belonging to the Viti family, who once owned the most famous stone, marble and alabaster factory in Volterra; the factory closed down in 1874. Giuseppe Viti was also a Vizier and Emir of Nepal. His beautiful Indian garments are exhibited in the museum, as are fine collections of Chinese drawings and porcelain.

▷ Continue to Piazzetta San Michele.

The Romanesque west front of the church of **San Michele**, which houses a Madonna and Child terracotta by Giovanni della Robbia, is flanked (*right*) by an unusual tower-house.

▷ Walk down Via Guarnacci.

Porta Fiorentina at the bottom of the street leads to the **Roman theatre and ruins** (*Teatro romano, rovine romane; ◐Open daily mid Mar–1 Nov 10.30am–5.30pm; Dec–8 Jan 10am–4.30pm; rest of the year Sat–Sun 10am–4.30pm; ◐Closed 25 Dec; ◈€5; €16 with "Volterra card"*) which date from the 1C BC. The theatre seated about 2,000 spectators.

▷ Return to Piazzetta San Michele and descend the long flight of steps in Via di Docciola.

The fortified gateway, **Porta di Docciola**, dates from the 13C. The Docciola Fountain was built in 1245.

▷ Return up the steps to Piazzetta San Michele. Turn left into picturesque Via Matteotti and left again into Via Gramsci.

The small **church of Sant'Agostino** has a 16C terracotta Assumption of the Virgin Mary in the style of the della Robbias and hosts the Museum of Sacred Art.

Museo Diocesano di Arte Sacra

Piazza XX Settembre. ◐Open mid Apr–Oct Tue–Sun 11am–6pm; rest of the year 10am–3pm. ◐Closed Mon. ◈€5. ℘0588 87 733. volteratur.it.

This museum displays some beautiful statues, bells, furnishings and paintings from the cathedral and other nearby churches. Note the altarpiece of the Villamagna Rosso, made the same year as the Deposition in the Pinacoteca. There also is a beautiful reliquary by Andrea Pollaiolo.

Museo Etrusco Guarnacci★

Via Don Minzoni 15. ◐Open daily mid Mar–1 Nov 9am–7pm; rest of the year 10am–4.30pm (26–31 Dec

6pm). ⓐClosed 25 Dec. ⊜€8; €16 with "Volterra card". ℰ0588 86 347. volterratur.it.

The **Etruscan Museum** houses the **archaeological collection** and private library of Monsignor Mario Guarnacci, who bequeathed them to the town in 1761. His extensive collection includes Etruscan pieces from the Villanovan period (8C BC) to the Hellenistic period (4C–1C BC), a time of extraordinary artistic creativity seen mainly in the tufa, alabaster and terracotta **cinerary urns**. Among the small bronze votive offerings is the famous **Ombra della Sera** (Evening Shadow); it was named because of the elongated pose of the body.

Parco archeologico (Acropoli etrusca)

Via di Castello. ⓐOpen daily mid Mar–1 Nov 10.30am–5.30pm; rest of the year Sat–Sun 10am–4.30pm (26–31 Dec daily). ⓐClosed 25 Dec. ⊜€5; €16 with "Volterra card". ℰ0588 86 347. volterratur.it.

Below the walls, this vast park with its pleasant garden is dotted with evidence of the **Etruscan acropolis**, which contains the remains of two 3C and 2C BC temples. From the garden enjoy a beautiful view over the surrounding countryside and the fortress that dominates the park (ⓒSee below).

Viale dei Ponti

This promenade provides superb **views**★★ over the Metalliferous Hills. Above it is the Fortezza, an impressive piece of military architecture now used as a prison and consisting of the Rocca Vecchia (14C) and the Rocca Nuova, built in 1472, which comprises a keep and four corner towers.

Balze★

1.5km/1mi from Porta San Francesco, towards Pontedera.

Before leaving Volterra, it's worth the time to take a ride to this deep chasm dominated by the former Badia monastery. Carved by erosion, it engulfed the Etruscan and Roman necropolis and the oldest churches.

EXCURSION
Montecatini Val di Cecina

20km/12.5mi west of Volterra.

Museo delle Miniere

Località La Miniera. ⌒Guided tours only (1hr), opening hours vary. ⊜€7. ℰ0588 31 026, ℰ0586 89 45 63. www. museodelleminieremontecatini.it.

Set in this lovely town's Palazzo Pretorio, the mining museum traces the history of the copper mines and mining activity of the Val di Cecina. The tour ends at the old mine Caporciano, 1km/0.6mi from the village.

🚗DRIVING TOUR

METALLIFEROUS HILLS★

Driving tour 50km/30mi. Allow a day. From Volterra to Monterotondo Marittimo, ⓒSee regional map pp244–245.

The Metalliferous Hills, named for the metals, pyrites and other minerals found here, form a peculiar, eerie landscape. The gentle hills contrast sharply with towers of steam and shiny steel tubes that snake their way over the hills and along the roads, which create a sinister effect. The landscape is dotted with fumaroles that bubble with the persistent odour of sulphur, which explains its name, Valley of the Devil.

▷ From Volterra southwest on SR 68. At Saline di Volterra, about 9km/5.5mi, take the left panoramic road SS439 that weaves through the Metalliferous Hills and connects with Massa Marittima (ⓒMASSA MARITTIMA).

The road passes through **Pomarance**, the hometown of two painters, Cristoforo Roncalli (1552–1626) and Niccolò Circignani (c. 1530–92), both known to Pomarancio.

Shortly after the Canneto fork, the landscape bursts with fumaroles and geysers of steam emitted at high pressure and temperature (up to 230°C/450°F) from the depths of the earth, which contains boric acid, hydrogen sulphide, carbon dioxide, methane, ammonia and other gases, which now generate power. A surreal effect can be seen in **Larderello**, a name that derives from Frances of Larderel, who in 1818 began the extraction of boric acid from the Monteacerboli "lagoons", full of muddy boiling water. Palazzo Larderello (*Piazza Leopolda*) hosts the **Museo Geotermico** (🕐*Open daily mid Mar–Oct 9.30am–6.30pm; Nov–mid Mar Tue–Sun 10am–5pm; 🕐Closed 25, 26, 31 Dec, 1, 6 and last two weeks of Jan; ☜free admission; 𝄐0588 67 724; www.museivaldicecina.it*), which traces the history of geothermal research and explains the techniques used in drilling. Near the medieval town of **Monterotondo Marittimo** extends the impressive Parco delle Biancane (*explore on foot or by car*), home to an active natural lagoon with geothermal phenomena such as fumaroles.

ADDRESSES

🏠STAY

😑😑 **Chiostro Delle Monache Hostel Volterra** – *Via del Teatro 4, località San Girolamo.* 𝄐0588 86 613. www. ostellovolterra.it. 23 rooms. Located just outside the Etruscan walls of Volterra, the hotel is sited in a 15C Franciscan monastery. Simple but comfortable rooms.

😑😑 **Hotel Villa Porta all'Arco** – *Via Mazzini 2.* 𝄐0588 32 49 88. 🅿. 10 rooms. Just steps from the Porta all'Arco close to the historical centre and surrounded by a garden, this renovated villa is furnished in antique style, and has a panoramic view of the surrounding hills.

😑😑😑 **Albergo Nazionale** – *Via dei Marchesi 11.* 𝄐0588 86 284. www.hotel nazionale-volterra.it. 40 rooms. Restaurant. Next to Piazza dei Priori and close to major attractions, this hotel and restaurant dates from 1890, has renovated rooms and is quiet and comfortable.

😑😑😑 **Villa Rioddi** – *Località Rioddi, 2km/1.2mi W of Volterra on S68.* 𝄐0588 88 053. www.hotelvillarioddi.it. 🖺🅿🏃 13 rooms, 1 apt. This refurbished 15C

establishment has its own large garden and a panoramic view of the town and the Cecina Valley.

🍴EAT

😑😑 **Don Beta** – *Via Matteotti 39.* 𝄐0588 86 730. www.donbeta.it. The cuisine of this restaurant is typical of the region, with home-made pasta and cakes. Truffles and mushrooms are on the menu year-round.

😑😑 **Il Poggio** – *Via Porta all'Arco 7.* 𝄐0588 85 257. www.ilpoggiovolterra. it. Reservations recommended. In an old tower, near the old town, this family trattoria serves Tuscan food on its small terrace in the summer.

😑😑 **Il Sacco Fiorentino** – *Via Giusto Turazza 13.* 𝄐0588 88 537. This restaurant offers simple unpretentious fare; a good place to enjoy the culinary delights of Tuscany.

😑😑 **Trattoria Albana** – *Mazzolla, 2km/1.2mi S of Volterra.* 𝄐0588 39 001. www.trattoriaalbanamazzolla.com. Reservations recommended. A road lined with majestic cypress trees leads to this tiny village and the main square, where this welcoming trattoria offers unusual game specialities.

😑😑😑 **Osteria dei Poeti** – *Via Matteotti 55.* 𝄐0588 85 100. Closed Thu. Located in the historic centre, this famous gourmet restaurant with its beautiful stone walls is loved by the locals.

SHOPPING

Rossi – *Piazza della Pascheria, 100m/110yd from Piazza dei Priori, towards Teatro Romano.* 𝄐0588 86 133. www. rossialabastri.com. An alabaster workshop founded in early 20C with a well-established reputation for original creations and Etruscan reproductions, Rossi is now one of the best-known craftsmen and his work is displayed in a small private museum.

EVENTS

Feast day of the patron saint – *5 June.*
Medieval festival – *3rd and 4th Sun in Aug.*
Roman Theatre Festival – *www. teatroromanovolterra.it. Jul–Aug.*
Volterra Jazz – *www.volterrajazz.it.* Concerts in Piazza dei Priori.
VolterraTeatro – *www.guasconeteatro. it. Jul.* Biennial International Theatre Festival.

The Maremma often is divided into three areas that belong respectively to the Provinces of Pisa, Grosseto and Latium.

Mineral Deposits and Waters

The Metalliferous Hills, rich in mineral deposits, abut Maremma's northern edge, and lead to interesting mining museums. Saturnia bubbles with thermal waters and chic spas.

Provincial Capital and Antiquities

Grosseto, the pleasant provincial capital, is a short distance from the sea. Throughout the province small museums and sites are rich with artefacts from Etruscan and Roman civilisations, as well as medieval and Renaissance art treasures and urban scenes.

Sea and Nature

The Monte Argentario is a popular summer retreat for Italians, with its scenic views, trails, clear water and easy access to the island of Giglio.

Cowboys and Herd Dogs

The enduring Maremma image in the romantic Italian imagination is the *buttero*, the cowboy herding long-horned Maremma cattle from the seashore to the hills, assisted by the famous white Maremma herd dogs. Now rare, this lifestyle still exists here, especially around Parco Regionale della Maremma. The park offers tours on foot, bike or horseback, with expert riders able to ride with the *buttero*.

Cuisine and Wine

Maremma has its own wine and food specialities. The mountain forests have Castagna del Monte Amiata, a local chestnut, and a peculiar honey, *miele di melata*, while nearby vineyards produce Montecucco. The wine roads in northern Maremma lead to wineries that produce Monteregio di Massa Marittima wine. The area's best-known wine is luscious red Morellino di Scansano. Further east is Bianco di Pitigliano white wine. Meat includes *vitellone bianco* veal and beef, *prosciutto toscano* and wild boar, also

Highlights

1. See Etruscan and Roman treasures in **Grosseto's archaeological museum** (p290)

2. Explore the **Parco Naturale della Maremma** and watch the *butteri* herding cattle (p292)

3. Try Morellino di Scansano wine-tasting and a walk in the **Tarot Garden** (p294, 296 *Events*)

4. Enjoy a **swim and sunset** from Castiglione della Pescaia (p292) or Monte Argentario (p299)

5. Be pampered in the **thermal waters** of Saturnia (p302)

© Romaoslo/iStock

Monte Argentario, the Maremma

made into sausage and salami. Unique to the coast are *anguilla sfumata* (eel) and *bottarga di cefalo* (fish eggs).

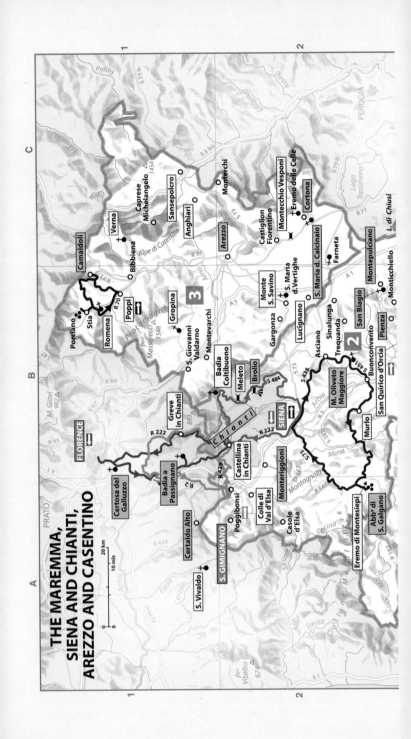

THE MAREMMA,
SIENA AND CHIANTI,
AREZZO AND CASENTINO

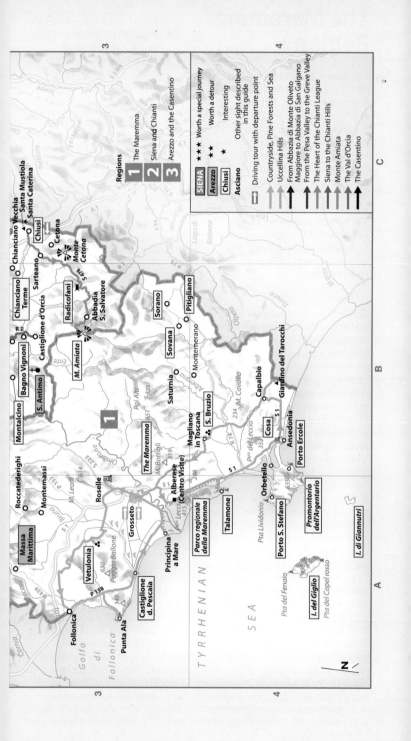

Regions

1 The Maremma
2 Siena and Chianti
3 Arezzo and the Casentino

SIENA
★★★ Worth a special journey
★★ Worth a detour
★ Interesting

Arezzo

Chiusi
Other sight described in this guide

Asciano
Driving tour with departure point

Countryside, Pine Forests and Sea
Uccellina Hills
From Abbazia di Monte Oliveto
Maggiore to Abbazia di San Galgano
From the Pesa Valley to the Greve Valley
The Heart of the Chianti League
Siena to the Chianti Hills
Monte Amiata
The Val d'Orcia
The Casentino

289

The Maremma Region ★

This huge sub-region of Tuscany includes a range of hills, mineral deposits, marshes, lakes and coastal dunes (*tomboli*), which act as natural dams. The vast Parco Regionale della Maremma was one of Italy's first nature preserves. The popular white Maremma sheepdog, or Maremmano, takes its name from this area, as does the long-horned cattle and even a horse. The *buttero*, sometimes called *mandriano*, is the legendary cowboy of the area, who on a handful of farms stills herds cattle and other livestock.

A BIT OF HISTORY

The Etruscans, who founded Populonia, Roselle and Vetulonia, were the first to attempt to drain this marshy area, but the first major hydraulic work was undertaken during the Pax Romana. After the decline of the Roman Empire, the region returned to its wild marshy state and malaria became rife. In 1826 the Dukes of Lorraine resumed land reclamation, work which continued throughout the Fascist regime. Now drained, agriculture is the land's main economy.

GROSSETO

The capital of its own province lies on the Aurelian Way in the fertile Ombrone plain 13km/8mi from the sea. The old centre is enclosed within huge hexagonal brick ramparts fortified with late-16C bastions built by the Medici. The heart is around Piazza Dante Alighieri, flanked by the cathedral and the provincial palace, a Gothic-Renaissance pastiche.

The 12C **Duomo** is dedicated to St. Lawrence. The gallery and the rose window are Romanesque. In the right corner, the Roman column is where notices were posted in the Middle Ages. The interior has a baptismal font (1506) adorned with aquatic subjects, while the 1470 font and the Our Lady of Grace altar

▶ **Population:** Grosseto 82,353; Capalbio 4,068.

⚲ **Michelin Map:** Michelin Atlas p 43, p 48 and Map 563 – N/O 15 and Map 735, folds 24–25.

▣ **Info:** Corso Carducci 5, Grosseto, ☎0564 48 85 73 / 48 88 25. Via Collacchioni 2, Capalbio, ☎0564 89 66 11. quimaremmatoscana.it. www.visittuscany.com.

▶ **Location:** The Maremma extends north from Massa Marittima south to the Argentario and east towards Siena province.

⊘ **Don't Miss:** Parco Naturale della Maremma, watch a buttero, swim in the Argentario.

▲▲ **Kids:** A bike or horseback ride in the park; Giardino dei Tarocchi; mining museums.

◷ **Timing:** Allow one day for Grosseto, a day per driving tour.

near the Annunciation reveal the influence of Andrea della Robbia.

From the cathedral, walk along Strada Ricasoli to Piazza del Sale and the 14C Cassero del Sale (Salt Castle), where salt was brought and distributed after being gathered along the coast, a commodity so valuable that the Sienese began to tax it in the early 14C.

▶ From the piazza take Corso Carducci to Piazza Baccarini.

Museo Archeologico e d'Arte della Maremma ★

◷*Open Jun–mid Sept Tue–Fri 10am–7pm, Sat–Sun and public hols 10am–1pm, 5–8pm; rest of the year Tue–Fri 10.30am–5pm (Nov–Mar 9.30am–1.30pm), Sat–Sun and public hols 10am–1pm, 4–7pm.* ◷*Closed 1 Jan, 1 May, 25 Dec.* ⊜€5. ☎*0564 48 87 50 / 52 / 60. www.museidimaremma.it.*

This museum has five sections tracing the history of Roselle, the Maremma and the Grosseto. The Diocesan Museum section is rich in works by Sienese artists.

Continue to Piazza dell'Indipendenza to the 13C Gothic church of **San Francesco**, which has small frescoes by the Sienese School (14C–15C) and a painted Crucifix attributed to Duccio di Buoninsegna (c. 1255–c. 1318). Its cloisters have a portico-covered well (1590), called the buffalo well, where animals came to drink.

AROUND GROSSETO

Ruins of Roselle

North of Grosseto and Roselle, on a hilltop, are the **Rovine di Roselle** *(10km/ 6mi NE of Grosseto on SP223;* ◷*Open daily 10.15am–6.45pm; last admission 6pm;* ◷€4; ℘*0564 40 24 03).* One of the most illustrious towns in northern Etruria, this was separated from Vetulonia *(northwest)* by a lake, Lacus Prilius. According to Livy, the Etruscan town of Russel *(Russelae* in Latin) was colonised by the Romans in 294 BC. After the fall of the Roman Empire it declined and was almost abandoned after 1138. **Excavations** begun in 1942 are still in progress, and have revealed a wall (over 3km/2mi long and up to 2m/6ft high) built of polygonal stone blocks. An outer line of brick fortifications probably dates from the 7C BC. The wall itself was built in the 6C *(north)* and in the 2C BC *(west).* Three huge gateways have been discovered. Remains of a Roman

amphitheatre, an imperial forum, cobbled streets, a villa with a mosaic floor and a residential district with late 6C craft workshops have been found.

⬡ DRIVING TOURS

COUNTRYSIDE, PINE FORESTS AND SEA

135km/84mi. Allow 1 day.
◷*See regional map pp288–289.*

The Grosseto province, typical of the Maremma region, consists of a plain which rises from below sea-level along the coast to rolling countryside further inland. The hills are planted with olive trees and vines and interspersed with farmland. Near the sea the intense colours vary with the seasons. The coast's fine sandy beaches are fringed with pine forests.

▷ From Grosseto/Roselle take SS1 (Via Aurelia) towards Buriano. The road crosses the plain S of Vetulonia on the hillside and climbs N along a series of terraces to the burial ground and an archaeological excavation before reaching the village.

Necropoli di Vetulonia★

Vetulonia dominates the Grosseto plain. The Tombe Etrusche, Etruscan tombs, are along the unsurfaced track (800m/866yd long), rough but

Ruins of Roselle

© M. Marca/Michelin

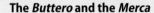

The *Buttero* and the *Merca*

Although the work of the cowboy (*buttero*) has undergone fundamental changes, it remains governed by the rhythms of nature. Maremma cowboys (*butteri* or *mandriani*), similar to those of the Camargue in France, carry out their ancient and taxing tasks on horseback. A buttero's day began at dawn when he selected his horse, and began his tasks, supervising and sorting the cattle and pens and helping cows with birthing. The highlight of the year is the branding of the cattle (*merca*), on 1 May in Alberese. Exhausting and hazardous, this work was also entertainment. The saying goes: "Anyone whose heart has not been seared by the *merca* could not really have been there." The glorious finale was entrusted to the women, who spent several days preparing a grand feast including pasta, meat and cakes. Only a handful of farms today have working *butteri*, but interest is strong in keeping the tradition alive. Working with herds, which might include the Maremma ox, a huge beast with lyre-shaped horns, are the Maremma horse, probably descended from the Berber horse, and the popular Maremma sheepdog, or Maremmano. The dog's thick white or yellowish- white coat easily distinguishes it from wolves.

passable. ⏱Archaeological area: open 10am–7pm in summer, 8am–5pm in winter. ⏱Closed Tue and Fri. ℘0564 94 80 58. www.museidimaremma.it.
The huge walls of Vetulonia, which was one of the largest towns in northern Etruria, are the only relics of the original citadel (6C–5C BC). The interesting necropolis remains include the **Tumulus della Pietrera** (7C BC), a grave with two chambers: the upper chamber is roofed with a pseudo-dome and has a quadrangular layout; the lower chamber, which has a pillar in the middle, was probably circular. The **Tombe del Diavolino** (Little Devil's Tomb) is quadrangular beneath a pseudo-dome.
The excavations in progress on the Greek and Etruscan-Roman town (*northeast*) are open to the public. An ancient paved road was once lined by shops and houses.

▷ To reach Follonica take the road through Gavorrano or take SS1.

Follonica

This seaside resort facing Follonica Bay is popular for its mild climate, pine forests and local artistic sights.

Punta Ala

This modern and luxurious resort is set in a picturesque pine forest on southern Follonica Bay. The superb sheltered beach is complemented by a large yachting marina, sports facilities and an 18-hole golf course.

Castiglione della Pescaia★

The fishing harbour and seaside resort of Castiglione was built as a canal port at the foot of a hill.
On the slope is a walled medieval town with steep paved streets, covered passageways and fortified gates. From the castle-capped summit there is an interesting view of the canal port and the fine sandy headland beaches.
South of Castiglione the road skirts the umbrella pines of Pineta del Tombolo.

Principina a Mare

This peaceful seaside town lies in the heart of the pine forest that stretches south along the coast from Follonica. The pine trees and fine sandy beaches make for splendid walks.

UCCELLINA HILLS

160km/100mi. Allow 1 day.
See regional map pp288–289.
From Grosseto take the SS1
(Via Aurelia) to the Alberese exit.
In Alberese, park by the visitor centre (centro visite) to enter or for a coach tour of the park.

Butteri in the Parco Naturale della Maremma

Parco Naturale della Maremma★

🕐 *Visitor centre: Via del Bersagliere 7/9, Alberese. Open daily 8.30am–8pm in summer, 8.30am–2pm in winter.*

🔊 *In summer, only guided visits are possible. Self-guided tours along the paths in winter.* 🎫 *€10 (itineraries on foot), €18–€30 depending on tour (bike, canoe, chariot, horseback). It is advisable to call ☎ 0564 39 32 38. www.parco-maremma.it.*

The **park** consists almost entirely of the **Monti dell'Uccellina** (almost 4,000ha/ 9,884 acres), an area of forest (Mediterranean scrub), running parallel to the coastline between Principina a Mare and Talamone.

There is much evidence of the first human settlements from the Paleolithic era through the Bronze Age up to the days of the Romans. Man has been able to hunt here since ancient times, owing to the great mammals which have always dwelt in the Maremma. In the past, however, the coastal areas were infested with mosquitoes carrying malaria, making permanent settlements impossible.

Flora and Fauna: Wildlife of the Maremma

The many local species of flora and fauna are influenced by the varied climate, which includes features typical of continental, Mediterranean and, in certain cases, desert conditions. The **wild boar** is the symbol of the Maremma and its most popular denizen, the quarry during the hunt (*cacciarella*), a traditional event bringing together hunters, hounds and beaters. The **fallow deer** is another common inhabitant of the region; its hide is reddish-brown, dotted with white in the summer and grey-brown in the winter.

The woods are also home to **roedeer**. Local **porcupine** and **badgers** often share the same set. As for the **fox**, it is the undisputed lord of Maremma, at home in all types of natural environment, whether fields of crops, pastureland, woods, rocky areas, pine forests, marshes or dunes. The area also boasts **wildcats**, **stone martens**, **weasels** and other mammals, as well as a multitude of beautifully coloured birds including **falcons**, **buzzards**, **owls**, **shoveller ducks**, **seagulls**, **hoopoes**, **herons**, **cormorants** and **kingfishers**, which are of great interest to bird-watchers.

Like the fauna, the plantlife varies depending on the environment. **Juniper** and **lentiscus** can be found growing between the **marine lilies** of the coastal dunes and the pine forest. The rocks are covered with **thyme** and **red valerian**, while the hills are overrun by scrub and **heather**. Among the many other species native to the region are the **dwarf fan-palm**, **rosemary**, **asphodel**, **broom**, **yellow poppies** and **orchids**.

The park offers tours on bike, canoe, chariot, horseback or on foot; self-guided tours follow theme-based itineraries with various aspects of the park (forest, wildlife and panoramic views).

Other "Parkland" itineraries include San Rabano (*5hr – one departure per day*) and delle Torri (*tour of the Towers – 3hr*) or a tour of the outlying area around Alberese featuring the flora and fauna.

▶ Continue S to rejoin S1.

Fonteblanda

This town (Talamone road junction) is famous for its spa, **Terme dell'Osa** (○━*Closed at the time of publication*).

Talamone★

This typical little fishing harbour is overlooked by a 15C fortress. The town has both Etruscan and legendary origins. The hill rising above the town is said to be the burial mound of Telamon, who took part in the Argonauts' expedition to Colchis in search of the Golden Fleece. In 225 BC two Roman consuls defeated the Gauls in the plain of Campo Regio.

Argentario and Orbetello★

&See PROMONTORIO DELL'ARGENTARIO.

Rovine di Cosa★

11km/7mi SE of Orbetello, at the base of the Tombolo Meridionale.

On the top of a promontory north of **Ansedonia** overlooking the Laguna di Orbetello and the Argentario peninsula stand the **ruins** of Cosa. A Roman colony from the 3C BC–4C AD, Cosa was built beside the **Via Aurelia**. In the town is the **Museo Archeologico** (*Via delle Ginestre, Ansedonia;* ○*Open daily Apr–Oct 10.15am–6.30pm; Nov–Mar 8.15am–4.30pm;* ○*Closed 1 Jan, 25 Dec;* ✆€2; ⅙; ✆*0564 88 14 21; www. polomusealetoscana.beniculturali.it*). The **excavations** reveal two distinct centres of interest, only a few hundred yards apart. On the top of the promontory is the acropolis, its outer walls consisting of huge blocks of stone enclosing the surviving walls and columns of the capitol, a temple and other smaller buildings. Further north is the town itself – paved streets intersecting at right angles, foundations of the buildings within the forum (basilica, temples, *curia*, shops), cisterns and houses. The massive south gate (Porta Romana) is still standing.

Capalbio

Capalbio occupies a favourable position on a hilltop (209m/679ft above sea level), overlooking undulating hills to the south of the Tuscan Maremma, near the sea. Dominated by a crenellated tower, medieval Capalbio is visible from all directions. In summer the jet-set arrives and plays host to Capalbio Cinema, a festival of short films.

Two gates, Porta Senese (Siena Gate) and Porticine (Little Gate), lead into the walled medieval village. The Romanesque Church of San Nicola contains 14C frescoes (*north side*) and 15C frescoes (*south side*) and has a 12C bell tower. Nearby is the Aldobrandeschi fortress (*Rocca*).

Outside the walls, in Piazza Provvidenza, the Oratorio della Provvidenza is

---

Historical Perspective

The first document to mention Capalbio dates from 1161. In the 14C the Aldobrandeschi family gave the village to the Republic of Siena and thereafter the destinies of the two places were linked. In 1555 Capalbio, like Orbetello, was invaded by the Spaniards (allies of the Medici). In the 18C and 19C the town suffered from the neglect of the surrounding farmland which had been allowed to return to marsh, causing malaria and the general impoverishment of the whole area. Not until the 20C did Capalbio see an increase in its population, due to a revival of farming. It is between the rugged Ansedonia coast and the "little Jerusalem" town of Pitigliano.

decorated with a 15C fresco influenced by Perugino and Pinturicchio.

⏵ 6km/4mi E on SP75 to Garavicchio.

Contemporary art lovers come to see **Giardino dei Tarocchi** (⏱*Open daily 1 Apr–15 Oct 2.30–7.30pm; Nov–Mar first Sat of the month 9am–1pm; ✆€12; free first Sat of the month Nov–Mar; ✆0564 89 51 22; ilgiardinodeitarocchi. it*), the Tarot Garden, by French sculptor Niki de Saint-Phalle (1930–2002), who, inspired by Gaudi's Park Güel in Barcelona, began her tarot figures in 1979.

Ruins of San Bruzio★

Just beyond the village beside the road to Magliano from Marsiliana are the remains of a 12C church standing solitary in the middle of a vast field.

Magliano in Toscana

30km/19mi N of Orbetello.

At the top of a hill covered with olive trees, Magliano is half concealed by its 14C and Renaissance walls. Via di Mezzo has two churches: San Giovanni Battista, which has a Renaissance façade, and Romanesque San Martino. A nearby Etruscan **necropolis** is visible. The town later became a Roman colony. ▤ *Info Point Magliano, Via Garibaldi 12, ✆0564 59 30 56 / 59 21 02.*

ADDRESSES

🛏 STAY

◎◎ **Argentario Camping Village** – *Albinia, 10km/6.2mi N of Orbetello. ✆0564 87 00 68. www.argentariocampingvillage. com.* On the sea, between the Argentario and Talamone, camp in a pine forest near a WWF oasis. Also bungalows or villas.

◎◎ **Talamone International Camping Village** – *Strada Provinciale Talamone Ovest 2, Talamone. ✆0564 18 38 489. www. talamonecampingvillage.com. 300 sites. Restaurant◎. ⚓.* This huge campsite has a view of the bay and of Talamone, a swimming pool and a private beach.

◎◎◎ **Agraria Grazia** – *Via Aurelia 4/b, Orbetello Scalo. ✆0564 88 11 82. www. agriturismograzia.com. 1 room, 5 suites.*

Restaurant◎◎. Farm in a wildlife reserve with deer, sheep and wild boar. Riding. Comfortable, well-lit rooms.

◎◎◎ **Agriturismo La Rombaia** – *Località La Rombaia, Castiglione della Pescaia. ✆0564 94 40 12. www. agriturismolarombaia.it. 5 rooms and 11 suites.* Farmhouse rooms decorated with agricultural themes. Comfortable and tranquil.

◎◎◎ **B&B La Casa della Tartaruga** – *Via della Tartaruga 1, Castiglione della Pescaia. ✆333 20 92 992. www. lacasadellatartaruga.it. 2 rooms.* A cosy, relaxing retreat for all art lovers. The house is soaked in original paintings and crafts made by the host for a unique boho-chic atmosphere. Healthy homemade breakfast.

◎◎◎◎ **Antica Fattoria La Parrina** – *Località Parrina, Albinia, 5km/3mi N of Orbetello Scalo. ✆0564 86 26 26. www. parrina.it. ⊠. Restaurant◎◎. ⚓* A working farm, with a 19C house furnished in grand period style. Wine, olive oil and cheese.

◎◎◎◎ **Azienda Agrituristica Ghiaccio Bosco** – *Strada della Sgrilla 4, Capalbio. ✆0564 89 65 39. www.ghiacciobosco.com. 13 rooms.* This large Maremma farm near the sea has classic decor. Home-made cakes and jams.

🍴 EAT

◎◎ **Vineria da Romolo** – *Via Vinzaglio 3, Grosseto. ✆0564 27 551. Closed Tue.* In the heart of Grosseto, this traditional trattoria is a longstanding local favourite, where you can enjoy wood-fire pizzas and delicious grilled meats in a warm, informal atmosphere.

◎◎ **Il Canto del Gallo** – *Via Mazzini 29 (or Piazza Tognetti 2), Grosseto. ✆339 18 44 146. Reservations suggested.* Situated near the ramparts, chicken and organic produce are its specialities, with many vegetarian dishes.

◎◎ **Osteria del mare** – *Via IV Novembre 15, Castiglione della Pescaia. ✆0564 93 47 63. www.osteriadelmarecdp.it. Closed Mon and Nov.* The chef at this restaurant adds his own individual touch to top – quality ingredients to create intriguing, personalised dishes such as *pici* pasta with a tuna *amatriciana* sauce, fish soup, and chocolate fondant with orange cream. In the evening, enjoy fish and seafood (which varies according to the catch of the day) in the Crudosteria annexe. Excellent wine list.

⊜⊜ **Taverna Osteria nel Buco** – *Via del Recinto 11, Castiglione della Pescaia. 339 28 78 439. Closed lunchtime Mon–Fri. Reservations required*. Traditional dishes, with music played by the owner.

⊜⊜⊜ **La Bussola** – *Piazzale Facchinetti 11, Porto Santo Stefano. 0564 81 42 25. ristorantelabussola.biz.* Small restaurant in front of the port that offers simply prepared sea specialities that delight the palate. Attractive outside seating.

⊜⊜⊜ **Il Cavaliere** – *Via Pantini 3, Orbetello Scalo. 0564 86 43 42. www. ristoranteilcavaliereorbetello.it. Closed Wed, dinnertime Mon–Tue, lunchtime Thu–Fri. Reservations suggested*. Family-run, simple, although passing trains cause some noise. Hors d'œuvres and fish specialities.

⊜⊜⊜ **Tullio** – *Via Nuova 27, Capalbio. 0564 89 61 96*. Traditional family restaurant features local Maremma dishes; served on the terrace in summer.

⊜⊜⊜ **L'uva e il malto** – *Via Mazzini 165, Grosseto. 0564 41 12 11. www. luvaeilmalto.it. Closed Sun*. Run by a dynamic young couple in the city centre, this intimate and modern restaurant has a wine-bar annex. Mostly fish-based menu.

⊜⊜⊜⊜ **La Trattoria Enrico Bartolini** – *at L'Andana Resort, Badiola, Castiglione della Pescaia. 0564 94 43 22.*

www.andana.it. Open Apr–Oct. Renowned chef Bartolini has brought a breath of fresh air to this charming restaurant with a rustic yet elegant feel. While remaining true to regional traditions and cooking methods, such as charcoal grills, the cuisine also demonstrates the occasional modern twist.

ACTIVITIES

Maremma Equestrian Show – *Equinus, 335 65 11 774. www.cavallomaremmano. com.* Dinner on a Maremma farm with horse show.

Horseback rides with *butteri, www.butteri-altamaremma.com.*

Cycle tourism and horseback riding in the Maremma region, visit *www.maremmainbici.it.*

EVENTS

International Short Film Festival – *Capalbio, June.*

Sant'Antonio Abate feast day and blessing of the animals; *butteri* take their horses to be blessed. *17 Jan.*

Festa dell'Uva – *Scansano, Sept.* Harvest festival; taste Morellino di Scansano red wine.

Massa Marittima★★

The name Massa Marittima perhaps indicates that the territory formerly extended as far as the sea. This old medieval town stands in the southern foothills of the Metalliferous Hills. Twice a year in May and August, Massa recalls the Middle Ages during the Balestro del Girifalco, a historic pageant featuring pennant-throwers in 14C costume. This is also a good approach to the eerie, otherworldly Metalliferous Hills (*See VOLTERRA; Driving Tour, p285*).

▶ **Population:** 8,303.
 Michelin Map: Michelin Atlas p 43 and Map 563 – M 14 and Map 735 Fold 14.
 Info: Via Todini 5. 0566 90 65 54. www.turismo massamarittima.it. www. coopcollinemetallifere.it.
 Location: Massa Marittima is on the road between Follonica and Siena.
 Don't Miss: Massa Marittima's Pisan Romanesque Duomo.

– the Palazzo del Podestà with double window bays, the town hall capped with merlons and the Duomo (cathedral).

WALKING TOUR

Piazza Garibaldi★★
In the city centre. The **square** is surrounded by three Romanesque buildings

Duomo★★
This majestic Pisan Romanesque **cathedral** was extended by Giovanni Pisano

in 1287. Dedicated to St Cerbone, Bishop of Populonia from 570–3, note the lintel above the central doorway depicting his life. The **interior** contains a marble low-relief originating from a 3C Roman sarcophagus. The chapel (*north side*) contains a Virgin of the Graces attributed to **Duccio di Buoninsegna** (c. 1255–c. 1318). The chancel houses St Cerbone's marble sarcophagus (*arca*), carved by Goro di Gregorio (1324). Its fine **bell tower★** has four bellcotes and its window bays increase in number from ground floor to the top.

Palazzo del Podestà

This 13C former residence of the most eminent magistrate (*podestà*) now houses the **Museo Archeologico** (*Piazza Garibaldi;* ⏰ *Open Apr–Oct Tue–Sun 11am–1pm, 3–6pm; Nov–Mar Sat–Sun 10am–1pm, 3–5pm;* ⊗ €3; €5 *combined ticket with Torre del Candeliere;* ✆ *0566 90 65 25*). An interesting stele from Vado all'Arancio is the only example found in Etruria of a style typical of northwest Tuscany and southern France. Also see Etruscan collections from the burial ground at Accesa Lake.

Fortezza Senese and Torre del Candeliere★

⏰ *Open Apr–Oct Tue–Sun 11am–1pm, 3–6pm; Nov–Mar Sat–Sun 10am–1pm, 3–5pm.* ⊗ €3; €5 *combined ticket with Museo Archeologico.* ✆ *0566 90 65 25.*

Massa is surrounded by 13C walls which were partly destroyed by the Sienese in 1337 and rebuilt by them during the 14C. The **Sienese fortress**, with its five towers, was built in 1335 and divides the town into two sections joined by the Porta alle Silici. It is connected by an arch to the **tower** (Torre del Candeliere) (22m/72ft wide), which is all that remains of an earlier fortress built in 1228.

Museo di Storia e Arte delle Miniere

⛏ *Closed at the time of publication.* ✆ *0566 90 65 25.*

The **History and Art of Mining Museum** contains collections of tools, some dating from the Middle Ages, minerals, scale models of mine shafts and documents illustrating the town's ancient mining industry.

Antico Frantoio

Via Populonia.

⛏ *Temporarily closed at the time of publication.* ✆ *0566 90 65 25.*

Antique wooden olive oil press (18C).

Chiesa e Chiostro di Sant'Agostino

N to Piazza XXIV Maggio.

This early-14C church has a large unadorned Romanesque façade, a beautiful Gothic apse and a crenellated bell tower added in the 17C.

Duomo

© Clodio/iStock

Two wings (left) remain of the original Romanesque cloister. Inside, the vaulted wood interior is illuminated by intense red and blue windows.

Museo degli Organi Meccanici

Corso Diaz 28. ⏱*Open summer Wed–Sun 10.30am–1pm, 3.30–7pm; winter Wed–Sun 10.30am–12.30pm, 3–6pm.* ⏱*Closed Mon–Tue; 15 Jan–Feb only by reservation.* ✆€5. ☎*0566 94 02 82. www.museodegliorgani.it.*
Collection of antique mechanical organs and keyboard instruments, showing the evolution from the harpsichord to the piano (1600–1904).

Chiesa di San Francesco

At the end of Via San Francesco, SW of Piazza Matteotti.
Subject to major restoration, the Gothic church was part of the convent (and seminary) in the tradition founded by St. Francis c. 1220. Although only the apse remains almost intact, the building displays the simple charm of Franciscan churches. Modern windows (lovely green colour) depict St Francis, St Bernardino and St Cerbone.

Museo della Miniera

Near Piazza Garibaldi. ⏱*Guided tours only at 11am, noon, 3pm, 4pm, 5pm, Apr–Oct Tue–Sun; Nov–Mar Sat–Sun.* ✆€5. ☎*0566 90 40 67.*
The **Mining Museum** explains the mining of iron ore in the region, with a long gallery (700m/2,300ft) housing reconstructions of various pit props (wood, iron, concrete). The recesses display trucks, machinery and tools.

Piazza Matteotti

Città Nuova. Around this square, the heart of the "new city", are the fortifications of the Torre del Candeliere and the Fortezza dei Senesi.

EXCURSIONS
Roccatederighi

25km/15.5mi SE of Massa Marittima.
This characteristic medieval village, surrounded by ramparts, reveals charming streets and squares. The top of the rock, where the church of S Martino stands, offers a beautiful view of the countryside.

Montemassi

8km/5mi S of Roccatederighi.
The silhouette of this town seem familiar to art lovers: it refers to the famous fresco by Simone Martini in Siena's Palazzo Pubblico of Guidoriccio da Fogliano at Montemassi. In addition, the town's atmosphere encourages a stroll.

ADDRESSES

🏨STAY

🛏 **Hotel Girifalco** – *Via Massetana Nord 25.* ☎*0566 90 21 77. www.ilgirifalco. com. 7 rooms. Restaurant* 🛏🍽. ⛷. Near the centre, this simple 1970s-style hotel is convenient for motorists and cyclists. Lovely views of valley to the sea.

🛏🛏 **Podere Riparbella** – *Località Sopra Pian dei Mucini, 6km/4mi N of Massa Marittima on S441 towards Prato.* ☎*0566 91 55 57. www.riparbella.com. 11 double rooms, half board.* This small family organic farm prepares creative home-cooked meals. Light, airy rooms have wooden furniture.

🛏🛏 **Agriturismo Tenuta del Fontino** – *Località Accesa. 12km/7.5mi S of Massa Marittima.* ☎*0566 91 92 32. www.tenutafontino.it.* ⛷. *26 rooms, 6 apts.* Fontino is in the hills surrounded by vineyards and olive trees, southeast of Massa Marittima. Various sports, hiking trails and mountain biking.

🛏🛏 **Agriturismo Valentini** – *Podere Fiordaliso 69, Valpiana, 12.5km/8mi SW of Valpiana by S439.* ☎*0566 91 80 58. www.agriturismo-valentini.it. 5 suites.* ⛷. Near the sea, this modern property has comfortable country-style rooms, family cooking and a swimming pool situated by a small mountain lake.

🛏🛏🛏 **Agriturismo Azienda Pereti** – *Località Pereti-Roccatederighi.* ☎*334 34 85 100. www.agriturismo-pereti.com. 3 rooms.* ⛷. Romantic farm setting with panoramic sea view, tasteful rooms and garden. Home-made bread and jams.

⍭/EAT

⊜⊜ Osteria da Tronca – *Vicolo Porte 5, Massa Marittima.* *☏0566 90 19 91.* The motto "I love wine so much that damned be those who eat the grapes" sets the tone of this establishment. Local cooking, informal service and plenty to drink!

Ristoro il Gatto e la Volpe – *Vicolo Ciambellano 12, Massa Marittima.* *☏0566 90 35 75. Closed Mon.* Hidden in a picturesque alley in the medieval centre, this friendly spot has family cooking and a wine cellar for buffs. Also doubles as an attractive craft shop (basketry, ceramics).

TAKING A BREAK

I Tre Archi – *Piazza Garibaldi 7.* *☏0566 90 22 74. www.itrearchidiastorino.it.* This café, sheltered under old arches, has a terrace over-looking the main square.

EVENTS AND FESTIVALS

In May and August, during Massa's **Balestro del Girifalco**, people dressed in 14C costume give spectacular demonstrations of flag tossing accompanied by trumpet blasts and drum rolls.

In July, at the **Mineral Market** collectors exchange and buy prized minerals.

In August by Duomo San Cerbone, **opera** is performed.

Promontorio dell'Argentario

The small limestone massif of Mount Argentario, a former island, is connected to the mainland by sand spits, the Tomboli of Feniglia to the south and Giannella to the north. This promontory surrounded by a lagoon, now a nature reserve, has become a favourite resort of Italians. Take a scenic drive to discover the most attractive sights.

SIGHTS

Orbetello

The town lies on the middle causeway which crosses the lagoon and carries the main access road to the peninsula (*S 440*). In AD 805 Charlemagne gave the town to the Abbey of the Three Fountains in Rome.

The fortifications date from the days of Sienese then Spanish occupation, when Orbetello was the capital of the Garrison State. The **cathedral** stands on the site of an ancient Etruscan-Roman temple. An inscription on the architrave on the central portal notes that the late-Gothic façade was altered in 1376 under the direction of Nicolo Orsini. The two aisles date from the days of the Spanish occupation.

▶ **Population:** Orbetello 14,731; Monte Argentario 12,397.

◔ **Michelin Map:** 563 O15.

▯ **Info:** Piazza della Repubblica, Orbetello. *☏0564 86 04 47. quimaremmatoscana.it.*

◗ **Location:** On the Maremma coast, W of Ansedonia and Capalbio.

♠♠ **Kids:** Swim in the sea, take a boat or fishing excursion. Observe fish in the Porto Santo Stefano aquarium.

◔ **Timing:** Allow a day to tour the promontory and a day for an island boat tour.

The Lombard-style chancel rail is decorated with entwined vine shoots.

Between the edge of the lagoon and Porto Santo Stefano, the road (*SP440*) runs uphill along the north coast of the peninsula between hedgerows, villas and hotels, finally providing a view of the Talamone headland on the mainland and Porto Santo Stefano on the island.

Porto Santo Stefano★

The main town on the peninsula is the embarkation point for boat trips to Giglio (*⌕See ISOLA D'ELBA AND THE*

A Troubled History

The promontory had an eventful history both in the Middle Ages, when it belonged to the Aldobrandeschi and Orsini families, and in the 16C when it passed out of the hands of the Republic of Siena and became a Spanish fortress. In the 18C it passed to the Austrians, then to the Bourbons and later to the Grand Duchy of Tuscany before being annexed to the Kingdom of Italy in 1860.

TUSCAN ARCHIPELAGO). The houses are built on the hillside, flanking the 17C Aragonese fortress (*Rocca*) from which there is a superb **view★** north over the harbour and Talamone Bay.

From Porto Santo Stefano take the scenic route (Strada Panoramica) N.

Beyond the headland at Lividonia, a succession of views look over the west coast and the island of Giglio. The corniche road descends between cypress trees, passing above Cala Grande Bay, distinguished by the tiny island of Argentarola, and the small seaside resort of Cala Piccola and its bay. Further south the island of Giannutri is visible.

Beyond the junction with a road running across to Porto Santo Stefano, the road twists and turns downhill; there is no retaining wall.

At high altitude, there are several **views★** of the rocky creeks along the southwest coast, the island of Rossa (reddish rocks) and of the terraced fields and peaks of Monte Argentario. One part of the road looks down on the rugged headland of Torre Ciana (*crowned by a tower*), the south coast and then on the island of Isolotto and Fort Stella. The road then passes Rocca Spagnola, a 16C bastioned citadel, before reaching Porto Ercole.

Porto Ercole★

The seaside resort stands at the foot of the Rocca Spagnola, to which it is linked by two parallel walls capped with battlements. A medieval gate leads into the old town. Piazza Santa Barbara is flanked by the arcades of the former Governor's Palace (16C); from the square there is a view of the yachting marina, the bay and the two old Spanish fortresses, opposite on Monte Filippo. After his flight from Rome, Caravaggio died here in 1610.

The road completes the round tour by skirting the eastern slopes of the Argentario promontory, where it soon runs at sea level between the headland and the Levante lagoon before joining (right) the road (SP440) to Orbetello.

Porto Santo Stefano

© StevanZZ/iStock

ADDRESSES

🏨 STAY

🛏️🍽️💰 **Bi Hotel** – *Lungomare Andrea Doria 30, Porto Ercole.* 📞*0564 83 30 55. www.bi-hotel.it. 12 rooms.* By the Porto Ercole seafront, this charming renovated hotel offers comfortable contemporary rooms, most with harbour views. Also a wellness centre.

🛏️🍽️💰 **Hotel Vittoria** – *Via del Sole 103, Porto Santo Stefano.* 📞*0564 33 20 33. www.hvittoria.com. 28 rooms. Restaurant*🍽️💰. 🏊. Lovely quiet location, 150m/164yd above the bustling harbour, with panoramic views and a fine restaurant with terrace. Excellent value upscale resort.

🛏️🍽️💰💰 **Il Pellicano** – *Località Sbarcatello, Porto Ercole.* 📞*0564 85 81 11. www.pellicanohotel.com. Restaurant*🍽️💰💰💰. This legendary spot has a heated saltwater pool carved out of rock. Rooms and cottages over the sea offer comfort and privacy that suited guests Charlie Chaplin and Jackie Onassis. A memorable splurge.

🍽️ EAT

🍽️💰 **L'Oste Dispensa** – *Strada Provinciale Giannella 113, Orbetello, 6km/4mi E of Porto Santo Stefano.* 📞*0564 82 00 85. www.ostedispensa.it.* This restaurant focuses on local cuisine from the lagoon and also has a shop where you can buy homemade products such as jams and biscuits.

🍽️💰💰 **Alicina Hosteria** – *Via San Sebastiano 54, Porto Ercole.* 📞*0564 83 26 30. www.alicina.it. Reservation suggested.* Seafood cuisine with an individual touch on a menu featuring daily specials which change according to market availability.

Pitigliano★

Sorano, Sovana, Saturnia

The town was an Etruscan settlement before being colonised by the Romans. From the 13C–17C, it belonged to the Aldobrandeschi family and later to the Orsini family, before being annexed to the Grand Duchy of Tuscany. From the late 15C–early 20C, Pitigliano had a large Jewish population and became known as "Little Jerusalem". Its synagogue in Via Zuccarelli was built in 1598.

- ▶ **Population:** 3,744.
- 🕰️ **Michelin Map:** Michelin Atlas p 49 and Map 563 – O 16–17 or Map 735 Fold 25.
- 🛈 **Info:** Piazza Garibaldi 10. 📞0564 61 71 11. quimaremmatoscana.it.
- ▷ **Location:** Pitigliano is set picturesquely high above the Lente and Meleta rivers.
- ✦ **Don't Miss:** The **view★** of the town by Madonna delle Grazie. The spa in Saturnia.

GETTING THERE

BY BUS: The company **Tiemme** leaves from Grosseto and Albinia (10km/6.2mi N of Orbetello) for Pitigliano, from Albinia for Sorano, from Manciano for Saturnia. *www.tiemmespa.it.*

👣WALKING TOUR

Arrival in Pitigliano by SS74 is particularly striking. The remains of the wall (Etruscan base) and aqueduct (16C arches) can be seen from the south. Piazza della Repubblica offers a fine view of the valley below. A pleasurable stroll on its narrow streets finds everything "within reach".

The Medieval Town

The town is traversed by cobbled streets lit by old lanterns. Streets are linked to each other by covered alleyways or flights of steps.

At the lower end of the town stands the small **Church of San Rocco** (12C), which has a Renaissance west front and a bell tower decorated with arcading and tracery. An 11C low-relief depicts a man with his hands in the mouths of two dragons.

Palazzo Orsini

This vast square building retains its 14C appearance with crenellations, machicolations and an austere loggia with two arches of unequal size. The 16C alterations include a courtyard with a well bearing a coat of arms and with a wing of arcades supported by Ionic columns. The other wing has a delicately carved Renaissance entrance.

Duomo

The 18C Baroque façade of the **cathedral** contrasts sharply with the fortified medieval bell tower. Nearby is a travertine column (1490) carved with coats of arms and surmounted by a bear, the Orsini family emblem.

EXCURSIONS

Sorano★
9km/5.6mi NE of Pitigliano.

Medieval Sorano is picturesquely set above the superb wooded limestone **Lente Gorge★** dotted with natural or man-made caves (Etruscan tombs). In the Middle Ages it passed from the Aldobrandeschi to the Orsini family in 1293 and entered the Grand Duchy of Tuscany in 1608. The town is dominated by the half-ruined Orsini Fortress, built in the 15C. The 18C district, *Masso Leopoldino*, built on a flattened rock platform, provides a breathtaking view down into the gorge.

Sovana★
8km/5mi N of Pitigliano.

Sovana was the birthplace of **Pope Gregory VII** (Ildebrando di Sovana, c. 1020, elected Pope in 1073). Now a sleepy village, Sovana still boasts some reminders of its glorious past. The church of **Santa Maria** (12C) has a typically Romanesque interior and some 16C frescoes. The intricately carved **ciborium★** dates from the 9C. At the west end stands the Romanesque and Gothic **cathedral★**.

The **Etruscan Graveyard** (*1.5km/1mi W of Sovana towards San Martino*) contains numerous Etruscan graves (7C–2C BC); the main graves are reachable by footpaths or narrow **gorges★** (*tagliate*) cutting into the cliffs. The **Tomba Ildebranda** has a majestic set of terraces and caves surmounted by a temple, within view of Sovana Cathedral.

Saturnia
30km/19mi NW of Pitigliano.

Saturnia, famous for its thermal waters and for Etruscan and Roman remains, has a number of excavated burial grounds, including the 7C BC **Necropoli del Puntone** (*signposted*).

The 15C **castle** (*cassero*), built in the days of Sienese control, has been reduced to a few remains. Ruins of the **Roman baths** are visible on Piazzale Bagno Secco.

The town is now popular with people taking the waters in chic **Terme di Saturnia★★**, where the sulphur-rich water rises from the spring at a temperature of 37°C/98.6°F. It is particularly recommended for the treatment of skin diseases and respiratory disorders.

ADDRESSES

⚑/EAT

◿◼◼ **La Taverna Etrusca** – *Piazza del Pretorio 16, Sovana.* ☏0564 61 41 13. *Reservation suggested.* This converted, rustic 13C *palazzo* serves local specialities.

◿◼◼ **Il Tufo Allegro** – *Vicolo della Costituzione 5, Pitigliano.* ☏0564 61 61 92. *Reservation advised. Closed Tue.* Close to the synagogue, a small restaurant with a well stocked wine cellar and two dining rooms hewn out of the rock. Tuscan dishes.

ACTIVITIES

Free spirits might take a drive to see where thermal waters gush forth in the hillside fields, a free "spa". Saturnia is known for its chic spas with a good range of treatments and its pretty settings.

Terme di Saturnia – ☏0564 60 01 11. *www.termedisaturnia.it.*

Mystical Siena, its province and Chianti have beckoned visitors for centuries. The city of Siena is a surprising contrast to Renaissance Florence, steadfast in its Gothic tradition in architecture and art that expressed its own delicate beauty. Symbolism and spirituality were foremost over realism and logic, a message carried through to small towns and country churches that are full of art treasures. Siena was a powerful military and commercial rival to Florence, with bankers whose influence spread to Rome and beyond. As today, much of that wealth was based on agriculture.

Working Farms

One of the best ways to experience Tuscany is to visit local working farms. Perhaps stay on one for a few days or a week, to experience not only the rhythm of nature, but a major force in the Tuscan economy. Tuscany's key agricultural products are wine and olive oil. Harvest time in late summer through to autumn is a joyous time, but you can taste and enjoy these products year-round right in the territory where they are made.

Wine

Some wines are made in grand castles and estates, others on small modest farms. Seek both out to compare differences in style and quality. Begin in an *enoteca* and sample several glasses of Chianti, Vino Nobile di Montepulciano or Brunello di Montalcino.
Excellent olive oil often is produced by wineries, too. Tuscan oil is prized worldwide. Visit wineries to try – and purchase – both.

Slow the Pace

Explore the countryside on horseback, by bicycle or through hikes. They slow down the pace yet are a wonderful way to have a more active holiday.

Take the Waters

Try water tasting, or even cures. In Chianciano Terme, for centuries travellers have come to benefit from the properties of various mineral waters that gush forth. Have a soak in thermal waters and get spa treatments in the little spa towns or in a luxurious accommodation.

Highlights

1 A break soaking in the atmosphere at **Piazza del Campo** (p310)

2 Chianti **country castles**, farms, vineyards and tasting wine (p331)

3 Climb a **medieval tower** in San Gimignano (p340)

4 Taste Brunello di Montalcino in a town **enoteca** (p347)

5 Montepulciano wineries under the city streets and an excursion to **San Biagio** (p354)

Taking it to the Piazza

When Italians have issues to discuss, traditionally they "take it to the piazza". Generally, the piazza is a place to catch up, tell tales, play games and otherwise enjoy the passing show. Pause in grand Piazza del Campo in Siena or in small squares in the planned Renaissance town of Pienza. Cool off in Piazza della Cisterna under the medieval towers of San Gimignano with a cool *gelato* or glass of white Vernaccia di San Gimignano.

Mysterious Etruscans

Etruscan traces of civilisation are throughout the region.
Visit tombs in Sarteano, a labyrinth in Chiusi, or see a home interior recreated in Chianciano Terme. Small museums with one or two special objects can spark hours of imagination and wonder. Enquire about a guided tour to further enjoy the sights.

Siena★★★

Siena is a mystical, refined city of art and architecture with a passionate and generous soul, welcoming visitors with its motto inscribed above the Camollia Gate: *"Cor magis tibi Seni pandit"* or, **"Siena opens its heart even wider to you"**. This Gothic city of yellow-brown buildings – the "burnt Sienna" of paintboxes – has always held a unique fascination for visitors. Set on three steep hills of reddish clay and enclosed by extensive walls, the city is overlooked by the elegant tower of the Palazzo Pubblico and the black-and-white striped cathedral, which rise above the rooftops and are visible for miles. Siena is perhaps best known for the Il Palio horse races, held annually in the summer. These races carry on a medieval tradition of competitive rivalry between the city's neighbourhoods.

THE CITY TODAY

Though Siena has a youthful populace, thanks to its university, it has retained much of the culture and values espoused during medieval times. True Sienese are loyal first to *contrada* (*See p306*), then city, then country. This civic pride is on

- ▶ **Population:** 53,937.
- **Michelin Map:** Michelin Atlas p 44 and Map 563 – M 15/16 or Map 735 Fold 15.
- **Info:** Palazzo Squarcialupi, Piazza Duomo 1. ℘0577 28 05 51. www.terresiena.it.
- ▶ **Location:** Siena is located 68km/42mi S of Florence by the motorway ("Tangenziale") or 72km/45mi by Via Chiantigiana (S222) through Chianti.
- **P Parking:** Paid car parks are available in Via Esterna Fontebrande and Via Baldassarre Peruzzi, and several are located near Fortezza Medicea. Rates start at €1 per hour.
- **Don't Miss:** The Piazza del Campo is one of the most famous squares in the world, site of the Palio horse race. Torre del Mangia for views of Siena and the Chianti Senese. Siena's magnificent Duomo. Sienese paintings in the Pinacoteca.

Historic centre of Siena

© Storisov/iStock

GETTING THERE

BY RAIL: The railway station is on the north side of the city (*Piazza Fratelli Rosselli*). Siena is linked by rail to **Florence**, **Rome** (*Via Chiusi*) and **seaside resorts** as far south as Orbetello (*Via Grosseto*).

BY COACH: There is a frequent coach service between **Florence** and **Siena** provided by **TIEMME** (*www.tiemmespa.it*) by the direct route (*1hr 15min*) or by the longer route via Poggibonsi (*2hr 10min*); departures (*morning and evening*) from the coach station near Santa Maria Novella Railway Station in Florence and Piazza Gramsci in Siena. TIEMME buses also link Siena to the **surrounding towns** (Montalcino, Murlo, San Gimignano and others) and **Grosseto**.

The bus station in Siena is nearer the city centre than the railway station, the journey is swift and the cost moderate, a better option than by train between Siena and Florence or Rome.

TO REACH THE CITY CENTRE
TIEMME runs a bus service (*5min*) from the railway station in Piazza Fratelli Rosselli on the north side of the city to the centre (*Piazza del Sale*) – no 8 (*station to centre*) and no 4 (*centre to station*); also no 9 and no 10.

BY BICYCLE: For information contact Amici della Bicicletta di Siena (*Via Di Vittorio 12, ✆0577 33 33 33; www.adbsiena.it*).

---

display year-round, but is most fervent during the twice-yearly Palio, a horse race that guarantees Siena a prominent place on the tourist itinerary along with its famed art.

A BIT OF HISTORY
A City of Uncertain Origins

Legend has made up for the lack of knowledge as to who founded Siena, and maintains that the city was founded in the early Roman era (8C BC) by Senius, son of Remus. The Sienese emblem shows Romulus and Remus being suckled by the she-wolf. One fact is certain: the site now occupied by the city was a small town in the days of the Republic of Rome and Caesar Augustus repopulated it (1C BC) by setting up the Roman town of Sena Julia.

In the 12C Siena became an independent republic. Having prospered through its merchants and bankers, it became a threat to neighbouring Florence. Political rivalry was rife between the two cities, Siena being a supporter of the Ghibellines while Florence supported the Guelfs. Until the 15C the history of the two cities, which had little in common, was marked by alternating success and failure. In 1230 the Florentines besieged Siena and cat-

apulted manure and donkeys over the town walls. In 1258 Siena breached a treaty it had signed with Florence and opened its gates to Ghibelline exiles. The most memorable episode in this long struggle took place on 4 September 1260, a dozen or more miles to the east in **Montaperti**, where the Ghibellines of Siena defeated the Guelfs of Florence.

This period of unrest – from the mid-13C to the mid-14C – was nevertheless the heyday of Siena. Its most prestigious public buildings were erected, as were most of its palaces and patrician mansions.

The great plague which ravaged the Western world between 1348 and 1350 reduced the city's population by one-third. In the early 15C internal struggles finally took the city into decline.

Although at first Siena accepted the peace-keeping role of Emperor Charles V and celebrated his arrival in the city in April 1536, the city then rebelled against his authority and placed itself under the protection of the King of France, Henry II. The town was besieged by imperial troops from early in 1554 to April 1555. Four years later Siena was annexed to the Grand Duchy of Tuscany governed by Cosimo I of Florence.

Administrative Structure

The medieval administrative structure has partly survived to this day. The three hills correspond to three urban districts: Città, Camollia and San Martino. Each district (*terzo*) was divided into 59 sub-districts (**contrade**) or parishes, of which 17 still exist. A *capitano* heads each sub-district, with administrative, judicial and territorial powers.

The emblem of each district was borne on a standard or pennant which was the responsibility of the standard-bearer. Every citizen was required to take an oath of allegiance before the Cart of Freedom (*carroccio*), the symbol of the community, which was taken into battle.

These days the 17 *contrade* spend the entire year in preparation for the *palio* (See below). Each *contrada* has a centre containing a museum which displays its trophies, a church, a public fountain in the shape of its emblem, a band, stables and warehouses in which weapons were stored. Each also has its own local social life based on gastronomic evenings, dances and preparations for the *palio*. The emblems of the 17 *contrade* represent one of the 17 virtues of Siena: the Porcupine symbolises sharpness, the She-wolf faithfulness, the Goose perspicacity, the Forest power, the Dragon ardour, the Giraffe elegance, the Wave joy, the Panther daring, the Eagle the willingness to fight, the Snail prudence, the Tower resistance, the Tortoise obstinacy, the Caterpillar skill, the Ram perseverance, the Owl finesse, the Shell discretion and the Unicorn science.

The "Palio delle Contrade"

The *palio*, the horse race which dates from the 13C, is the most famous of its kind in Italy. Held twice a year on 2 July and 16 August, only 10 *contrade* compete so the 17 must take turns (See box above). During the days of preparation intrigue is rife and betting is heavy. The streets are draped in the colours of each *contrada*, young people practise throwing the flag, the edge of the Piazza del Campo is covered with sand to form the race track and dangerous corners are protected with mattresses. The outer edge is lined with tiers of seats but the centre, from which anybody can watch the race free of charge, is left open. Emotions surge in the last two days before the race, when a solemn drawing of lots in the Campo to assigns horses to the participating *contrade*. The animals are then carefully prepared; doping is allowed. If a horse dies, the *contrada* that it represented has to retire from the race but its standard, set at half-mast, is entitled to take part in the opening procession and the horse's hooves are solemnly carried on a silver tray. The jockeys (*fantini*) are accommodated within the *contrade* and watched day and night to ensure that they are not bribed by a competitor to lose the race.

On the morning of the race a Mass is said in the church of each *contrada* and horse and rider are blessed. In the afternoon a lavish procession around the Campo involves all the representatives of the 17 *contrade* dressed in 15C costume and carrying their emblems while the flag-bearers (*alfieri*) skilfully brandish their pennants. Behind them come six black horses mounted by riders in mourning in memory of six *contrade* that no longer exist – the Viper, Rooster, Oak Tree, Sword, Bear and Lion – and that were probably taken over by more powerful *contrade*. At the very end of the procession is the triumphal chariot, built to the design of the ancient *carroccio*. The town archers follow. The high spot of the festival occurs at the end of the afternoon when the famous *corsa al palio* is run. This is a dangerous horse race in which no holds are barred and it is all over within a matter of minutes, the time it takes the jockeys to ride bareback three times round the Campo. The winner receives the banner (*palio*), hence the name of the race. The banner bears a representation of the Virgin Mary which is painted by a leading artist

Although the city has a coat of arms, its true face is reflected in the colours of the *contrade*.

Wave

Shell

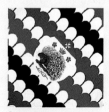
Porcupine

Eagle

Unicorn

Forest

Owl

Tortoise

Ram

She-wolf

Snail

Goose

Giraffe

Caterpillar

Dragon

Panther

Tower

© MICHELIN

especially for the occasion. After the race all the *contrade* continue the festivities in their streets and community centres where the dinner may be an occasion for feasting or bitterness, depending on the result.

SIENESE ART

Whereas Florence was a great Renaissance city, Siena enjoyed its main period of artistic development during the flowering of Gothic art and has remained very conservative in this respect. The Gothic style expressed here was particularly elegant, affected and expansive.

Architecture

Although most of the architects who worked in Siena were born elsewhere, the Gothic style which developed, particularly in vernacular buildings, has certain specific characteristics – the combined use of brick and stone; double-arched openings on the lower levels of buildings consisting of a pointed arch with surbased arch below and known as **Sienese arches**; an abundance of windows – usually triple bays with slender colonnettes and tympani; merlons supported by a frieze of small arches to cap the top of buildings.

Religious architecture in Siena also had its own characteristics. Like the west front of Orvieto Cathedral (*See Green Guide Italy*), which was designed by Sienese artist **Lorenzo Maitani**, the façade of Siena Cathedral indicates the transition from the Tuscan Romanesque to the Flamboyant Gothic style.

Siena made its contribution to the Renaissance through a talented architect named **Francesco di Giorgio Martini** (1439–1502) who left very few traces of his artistry in the city of his birth but who worked in other towns in Tuscany, Umbria and the Marches, in particular in Urbino.

Sculpture

This art was originally a Pisan speciality and its greatest exponents were Nicola and Giovanni Pisano, who came to work in Siena, where they had pupils.

Tino di Camaino, who was born in Siena c. 1280 and died in Naples in 1337, may have had a weaker personality than Giovanni, his master, but his talent was robust as well as delicate. He too worked on the cathedral where his skills are most apparent in the complex tombs carved like reliquaries.

The leading figure, however, in Sienese sculpture in the 15C was **Jacopo della Quercia** (born c. 1371, d. 1438) who rivalled the greatest artists of the day and who competed with Brunelleschi and Ghiberti for the commission to design the doors for the Baptistery in Florence. He was trained in the Gothic tradition but was equally open to the Florentine Renaissance culture, and he combined both styles to produce a very personal synthesis. His austere and pure style was very different from the exquisite gracefulness which had been the main feature of Sienese work until that time.

Sienese School of Painting

It was mainly the Primitives in the 13C–14C who earned Siena its reputation as a major city of art. Filled with fervent but calm piety, they painted hieratic figures against golden and engraved backgrounds, initially in a style strictly inspired by Byzantine art. Their expressiveness compares to Mannerism. The favourite subject of these artists was the Madonna and Child; for several centuries the people of Siena regarded the Virgin Mary as their supreme saviour. So many similar representations of her appeared in Siena that her image seems to have been mass-produced.

The first of the Sienese Primitives to make a name for himself was **Guido da Siena** who, in the second half of the 13C, produced a Maestà for the Palazzo Comunale.

It was through **Duccio di Buoninsegna** that Siena made its brilliant entry into history. The artist, born in Siena c. 1255 and d. c. 1318, slipped from the Byzantine tradition to a new Gothic sensitivity. To the Byzantine atmosphere he introduced exquisite line and colour. Their naive grace and Mannerist charm, and the golden backgrounds from Byzantine art, characterised the Sienese School.

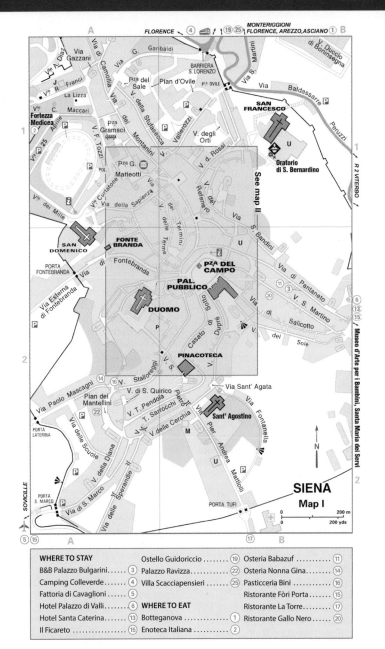

His pupil, **Simone Martini**, born c. 1285, was one of the great exponents of Gothic painting and his influence spread as far as Provence, Catalonia, Aragon, England, Flanders and Bohemia. He shed the constraints of Byzantine hieratic painting, approaching a more natural art form.

Foremost among Simone Martini's pupils were the Sienese painters **Lippo Memmi**, his brother-in-law and assistant, and **Barna da Siena** (d. c. 1380) whose cycle of frescoes in the collegiate church in San Gimignano shows pathos and great vivacity.

The **Lorenzetti** brothers, who were contemporaries of Simone Martini, both trained with Duccio and were influenced by the expressive, tormented works of Giovanni Pisano and the naturalistic and dramatic style of Giotto. The work of **Pietro** (born c. 1280), the elder of the brothers, was still close to the severity of Byzantine art but from Pisan sculpture he borrowed the way of depicting a tender dialogue.

Ambrogio, the younger brother, was very well known in Siena for his wisdom. He painted several pictures of the Madonna and the Virgin Mary in Majesty but he was most famous for his "civilian" fresco cycle in the Palazzo Pubblico. Both the brothers died of the plague in 1348. The techniques of these Gothic masters was continued in the second half of the 14C and later by lesser artists such as **Lippo Vanni**, **Luca di Tommé**, who was strongly influenced by Pietro Lorenzetti, **Bartolo di Fredi**, who also worked on the frescoes in the collegiate church of San Gimignano, and **Taddeo di Bartolo** (1362–1422).

The 15C brought attractive and in some cases innovatory artists. While Florence was moving towards the Renaissance, Sienese art maintained a fundamental link with Gothic values. **Lorenzo Monaco** (1370–c. 1425), a native of Siena, was still considered a major artist of his day in Florence, where he taught Fra Angelico, with compositions that have all the intricacy of a miniaturist and all the colours of an illuminated manuscript, making him one of the most brilliant exponents of the international Gothic style. **Giovanni di Paolo** (c. 1403–c. 1483) retained close ties with the Sienese tradition. Other artists were more open to the Florentine influence. Stefano di Giovanni, also known as **Sassetta** (born c. 1400, d. 1450) attempted perspective while showing ingenuity in his flowing figures and delightful harmonies of colour. His pupil, **Sano di Pietro** (1406–81), paid minute attention to detail, and introduced a refreshingly new narrative aspect in his wonderful predellas.

Lorenzo di Pietro, better known as **Vecchietta** (born c. 1410, d. 1480), was responsible for a real change in style. In close contact with the Florentines, he introduced perspective into Sienese painting and gave it new vigour. His most famous pupil was **Matteo di Giovanni** (c. 1430–1495) who created elegantly refined paintings of the Madonna as well as dramatic works full of movement. He also influenced **Francesco di Giorgio Martini**, whose attention to perspective was handed on from the Florentines, but emphasised Sienese lyricism and gentleness.

In the 16C **Pinturicchio** from Umbria settled in Siena (1502) and created the brilliant decoration for the Libreria Piccolomini (*See p317*), marking an artistic renaissance in the city. Siena was also the adopted home of **Il Sodoma** (1477–1549), Leonardo da Vinci's pupil who originally came from Lombardy. His works influenced the Sienese artist **Domenico Beccafumi** (c. 1486–c. 1551) who adopted the Mannerist style, of which he became one of the greatest exponents in Tuscany.

PIAZZA DEL CAMPO★★★

The Campo is one of the most famous squares in the world. The harmony of its buildings has rarely, if ever, been surpassed. It is a pink and white "shell" or "fan" set on a slight slope and is a consummate example of the "drawing room squares", which are main sights in any Italian city, representing a place for exchange, where life and history are lived to the full. Established in the 13C as a marketplace, in the Campo over the centuries the great proclamations were heard by the citizens, where feuding factions confronted one another, and where St Bernardino addressed the people from a pulpit erected in front of the Palazzo Pubblico.

In the mid-14C the square was paved with bricks within an outer circle of cobblestones. On the southeast side, also in brick and stone, is the long façade of the Palazzo Pubblico. From its centre radiate eight white lines dividing the Campo into nine sections, which symbolise the government "of the Nine", the nine magistrates from among the craftsmen, traders

Piazza del Campo and Palazzo Pubblico

© Fotonio/iStock

and bankers who brought the greatest period of prosperity (1287–1355).

At the top of the square is the **Fonte Gaia** (Fountain of Joy), named for the general joy that accompanied its inauguration in 1348. In 1419 it was decorated with marble panels by Jacopo della Quercia, which were replaced by copies in 1868. The originals are currently undergoing restoration and those finished are displayed in Santa Maria della Scala.

Behind the fountain beneath a small tower (*right*) is the 13C **Palazzo Sansedoni**, extensively altered in the late 19C.

Palazzo Pubblico★★★

🕘*Museo Civico open daily 15 Mar–Oct 10am–7pm; rest of the year 10am–6pm; last admission 45min before closing.* 🕘*Closed 25 Dec.* ⊛€10 (€9 with reservation); €15 joint ticket with Torre del Mangia; €20 combined ticket with Torre del Mangia and Santa Maria della Scala Complex. ℘0577 29 22 32 or 0577 29 26 15. www.comune.siena.it.

This is one of the finest vernacular buildings in Italy. Exceptionally elegant and austere, it synthesises all the characteristics of the Sienese Gothic style. It served as a model for most of the other palaces in the city.

Construction began at the end of the 13C and by the middle of the following century, it was almost complete, except for the second floor of the two wings,

which was added in 1680. The pale travertine used for the lower section contrasts sharply with the yellow ochre of the remainder of the building. The large number of doors and windows along the ground floor and the slightly concave façade give an impression of lightness despite its size. Two crenellated bell turrets flank the top of the main building, in the centre of which is a huge copper circle with Christ's monogram (IHS – *Iesus Hominum Salvator* – Jesus Saviour of Mankind) which always accompanied St Bernardino. The Sienese shield decorates the tympani of the trefoiled windows, each with three bays beneath a relieving arch.

Soaring heavenwards from the east end of the façade, crowned with a white stone belfry elegantly designed by Lippo Memmi, is the slender **Torre del Mangia** (*88m/286ft high*). It took ten years to build and was only just finished when the Black Death broke out. Its name derives from the nickname of the first of the bellringers. Visitors can climb to the top of the tower (👞*See below*).

At the foot of the tower is the **Cappella di Piazza**, a chapel in the form of a loggia built in 1352 to express gratitude at the cessation of the plague. A century later it was altered and decorated in the Renaissance style.

The doorway (*right of the chapel*) leads into the narrow and austere courtyard, called the **Cortile del Podestà** (Magistrate's Court), of the Palazzo Pubblico.

The palace has been the seat of successive governments of Siena and still houses the local authority offices.

The interior of the palace was decorated by most of the great names in the Sienese School. Combined, these rooms make up the **Museo Civico★★★** (Municipal Museum). **The first floor** is home to the ancient apartments *podestats* and Council members. The first rooms (**2–5**) display a collection of 16C–18C paintings (*Quadreria*).

The **Sala de l Risorgimento** (**6**) was painted between 1886 and 1891 and depicts the life of the first King of Italy, Victor Emmanuel II.

The **Sala di Balìa** (**7**) is also known as the **Priors' Chamber** because, from 1445, it was the meeting place of the influential magistrates who were members of the Balìa, a very old Sienese institution. Its walls, vaulted ceiling and dividing archway are covered with frescoes.

Between 1405 and 1407 Spinello Aretino painted the highly descriptive frescoes depicting the struggle in the 12C between Pope Alexander III, who was born in Siena, and the Holy Roman Emperor, Frederick Barbarossa, in which the Pope was victorious. The most outstanding events were the naval battle in which the Venetians defeated the imperial navy (party wall with Room **8**) and (opposite) the Pope's return to Rome.

The allegorical frescoes decorating the vault of the **Sala del Concistoro** (Council Chamber) (**9**) were painted c. 1530 by Domenico Beccafumi. The classical subjects allude to the civic and patriotic virtues of the Sienese government. Among the priceless pieces of gold and silver plate (12C–17C) in the **Vestibolo della Cappella** (ante-chapel) (**10**) is a small and intricately worked gold rose tree by Simone da Firenze, which was given to the city by Pope Pius II Piccolomini.

The **Cappella★** (chapel) has a superb wrought-iron **screen★** which is said to have been designed by Jacopo della Quercia. The frescoes are by Taddeo di Bartolo narrating the Life of the Virgin Mary (1407–14). The backs of the choir **stalls★★** consist of wonderful marquetry panels illustrating the Creed, which are the work of Domenico di Niccolò, assisted by Matteo Vanni, over five years (1425–29). Above the altar is a *Holy Family* by Il Sodoma.

Two Great Saints

St Catherine was born in Siena in 1347, the daughter of a dyer-fuller who had 25 children. Tradition holds that at age seven she decided to devote her life not to a human but to a heavenly husband. She entered the Dominican Order at age 16. Her mystical marriage with Christ was a favourite subject with artists. (St Catherine of Alexandria was instead given a wedding ring by the Child Jesus.) The golden legend of St Catherine of Siena is one of the most eventful in the hagiography. She had numerous visions and ecstasies and received the stigmata in Pisa in 1375. She also wrote a religious treaty. In 1377 she persuaded Pope Gregory XI to return the papal court, resident in Avignon since 1309, to Rome. She died in Rome in 1380. She is a Doctor of the Church, patron saint of Europe, the ill, nurses, and Italy (with St Francis).

In the same year **St Bernardino** was born in Massa Marittima. He gave up his university studies in order to help plague victims in the hospital of Santa Maria della Scala in Siena, of which he took charge. At the age of 22 he entered the Franciscan Order. He founded the Congregation of Observants who complied strictly with the Rule laid down by St Francis. He made the monastery of Osservanza north of Siena into a major centre for his teaching. An eloquent reformer, St Bernardino travelled throughout Italy preaching sermons filled with a degree of caustic sarcasm. Two have remained famous to this day. He died in 1440 in L'Aquila.

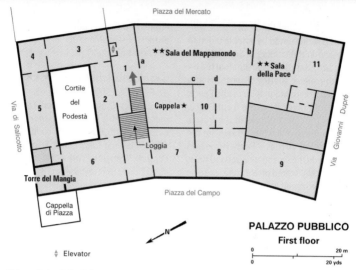

Piazza del Mercato

Via di Salicotto

4 · 3

Cortile del Podestà

5

★★ Sala del Mappamondo · b

a

1

2

c · d

★★ Sala della Pace

11

Cappela ★ · 10

Loggia

6 · 7 · 8

9

Torre del Mangia

Cappella di Piazza

Piazza del Campo

Via Giovanni Dupré

N

Elevator

PALAZZO PUBBLICO
First floor

0 ————— 20 m
0 ————— 20 yds

Although the **Sala del Mappamondo★★** (Mappamundi Room) was named after Ambrogio Lorenzetti's rotating map of the world, which was formerly attached to the wall beneath the equestrian portrait of Guido Riccio, it is famous for the two frescoes by Simone Martini. The admirable **Virgin Mary in Majesty★★** seated beneath a canopy and flanked by the Apostles, angels and saints (**a**). It was the artist's first known work, created in 1315 but badly damaged by the damp which has risen from a salt store below. It is unusual in that it was restored by the artist himself in 1321. The flowing composition, expressive faces, wonderfully fluid clothes, delicate colours and intricate decoration make this one of the most graceful and poetic examples of work from the Sienese Gothic period.

Opposite it is the famous **equestrian portrait of Guido Riccio da Fogliano★★** (**b**). The Sienese general is portrayed between the two fortresses where he put down rebellions in 1328. Although the Republic of Siena paid for the artist to travel to the scene of the rebellions so that the background could be depicted accurately, the rugged chalky landscapes of the Maremma area seem unreal because of the contrast with the inky blue sky. Conversely, the *condottiere*, proudly sitting astride a horse that, like its rider, is covered with a rich piece of cloth on which the motifs are picked out in detail, is painted with a certain realism. The fresco immediately below the portrait, representing two men and a castle, was rediscovered early in the 1980s. It is thought to date from the early 14C and to be the last work by Duccio di Buoninsegna. The concentric circles left by the rotation of the old world map are clearly visible.

On the same wall are two frescoes representing two saints painted by Il Sodoma. On one of the pillars St Catherine (**c**) was painted in 1461 by Vecchietta; on the next pillar (**d**) is St Bernardino painted by Sano di Pietro in 1460.

The **Sala della Pace★★** (Peace Room) contains a number of priceless paintings, unfortunately in very poor condition. This chamber was used by the government of the Nine for their meetings and it is to them that Ambrogio Lorenzetti dedicated the two vast compositions painted 1335–1340, illustrating the **Effects of Good and Bad Government**. As lively as it is natural, the artist combined the noble and doctrinal tones inherent to allegorical painting with the detailed narrative style which he supported with great fervour and thus created scenes that are variously amusing or poetic. Not only was it unique in medieval times in its profane inspiration, but it is also of inestimable artistic value and its documentary interest is priceless.

Good Government (*wall facing the window*) is represented by a noble old man dressed in the colours of Siena. Beside him are seated the cardinal virtues – Temperance, Justice, Fortitude and Prudence with Magnanimity and Peace; the room takes its name from Peace, one of the finest figures in the fresco, shown dressed in white. Above are the Theological Virtues – Faith, Hope and Charity. Justice is shown a second time, majestically seated on a throne (*extreme left of the scene*). At her feet is Concord, with a plane in her lap, an allusion to the equality that must reign between the citizens depicted on the fresco in rows. They are all holding ropes, the symbol of agreement, running down from the scales of Justice.

The effects of Good Government (*above the door*) can be seen in town and country. Against the backdrop of Siena as it was in the Middle Ages with many towers, are a number of elegantly dressed men and women on horseback. A tavern scene shows young men playing and young girls dancing. A clog-maker is at work in his workshop. Masons are building a house. The fields are depicted in the two best seasons of the year (spring and summer). The peasants tend the fields while noblemen set off to hunt wild boar. Bad Government (*on the wall opposite the door*), the most severely damaged fresco, shows figures representing the Vices surrounding Lucifer, who is sowing discord in the town where citizens are being arrested or killed. The countryside appears as it is in the dead seasons of the year (autumn and winter).

The **Sala dei Pilastri (11)** contains works by Sienese artists from the 13C, 14C and 15C including a Maestà by Guido da Siena (*right-hand wall*) and a surprising Massacre of the Innocents by Matteo di Giovanni (*opposite the door*).

From the corridor between the Balìa Room (**7**) and the Risorgimento Room (**6**), a flight of 51 steps leads up to a superb **loggia** containing the original fragments of the Fonte Gaia. From the loggia, which looks down on the marketplace below, there is an extensive view southeast of the countryside, which penetrates into the city between the urban districts of Santa Maria dei Servi (*left*) and San Agostino (*right*).

CATHEDRAL PRECINCT★★★

€8-15 OPA SI PASS combines 5 monuments (Duomo, crypt, Baptistry, museum and the Facciatone panoramic terrace). €20 ACROPOLI PASS combines OPA SI PASS and Santa Maria della Scala Complex. Both passes are valid for 3 days. Tickets next to museum. ℘0577 28 63 00. www.operaduomo.siena.it.

Piazza del Duomo★

Cathedral Square, dominated by the famous cathedral, is situated at the top of the hill.

The southwest side is lined by the long façade of the hospital of Santa Maria della Scala dating partly from the 13C. Its name, St Mary of the Steps, is derived from the steps (*opposite*) leading up to the main entrance to the cathedral. On the two short sides are (*northwest*) the neo-Gothic Archbishop's Palace and (*southeast*) the 16C prefecture.

Cattedrale di Santa Maria Assunta (Duomo)★★★

See floor plan p315. Open Mon–Sat 10.30am–7pm (2 Nov–Feb 5.30pm; 26 Dec–8 Jan 6pm), Sun and public hols 1.30–6pm (2 Nov–Feb 5.30pm). €5-8; free Nov–24 Dec and 7 Jan–Feb; see above for OPA SI PASS. ℘0577 28 63 00. www.operaduomo.siena.it.

The history of the **cathedral** is complex. The present building was built mid-12C–early 14C. The final work was mainly due to the Cistercian monks of San Galgano, who sought inspiration in the design of their own abbey. In the 14C, when Siena was at the height of its prosperity, the citizens decided to create a cathedral to be larger than the one in the rival city of Florence. The existing building would have become simply the transept of the new edifice. The work began in 1339 and was proceeding with great speed when it was suddenly interrupted in 1348 by the outbreak of the Plague.

Siena lost much of its manpower and abandoned the vast project. Some of

Pavement of the Duomo

1. Hermes Trismegistus (1481–98)
2. Coat of arms of Siena and 12 other towns (mosaic)
3. Imperial altar
4. Allegory of Fortune (Pinturicchio)
5. Wheel of Fortune (Marchese d'Adamo, 1406)
6.–15. Sibyls (1481–98)
16. The Seven Ages of Man (c. 1450)
17. The theological virtues – Faith, Hope and Charity – and Religion
18. Story of Jephthah (1481–98)
19. Story of Eli and Ahab (Beccafumi 1518–47) (certain scenes were repainted in 1878 by Alessandro Franchi)
20. Moses smiting the rock to bring forth water (Beccafumi 1518–47)
21. Moses on Mount Sinai (Beccafumi 1518–1547)
22. Emperor Sigismond (1434)
23. Death of Absalom (1443)
24. Battle of Samson against the Philistines (c. 1425)
25. Moses and the tablets of the Law (c. 1425)
26. Goliath the giant (c. 1425)
27. David singing psalms (c. 1425)
28. Young David armed with his sling (c. 1425)
29. Joshua (c. 1425)
30. Hanging of the five Amorite kings (c. 1425)
31. Abraham's sacrifice (Beccafumi 1518–47)
32. Prudence (Marchese di Adamo, early 15C)
33. Temperance (Marchese di Adamo, early 15C)
34. Mercy (Marchese di Adamo, early 15C)
35. Justice (Marchese di Adamo, early 15C)
36. Fortitude (Marchese di Adamo, early 15C)
37. Judith liberating Bethulia (1473)
38. Massacre of the Holy Innocents (Matteo di Giovanni, 1481–95)
39. Herod losing his throne (1481–98)

the new building was deemed dangerous since the ground had been insufficiently prepared to take its weight and it was demolished. In the last quarter of the 14C, therefore, work began on the completion of the original cathedral – the upper section of the west front, raising the roof level of the nave, construction of the apse. The only relics of the grandiose 14C project are the arches of the nave and what was to be the façade of the new building (*south side of the present cathedral*).

Although somewhat lacking in unity, the **west front** is attractive for its rich ornamentation and the gentle colouring in its marble. The lower section is Romanesque but shows signs of the impending Gothic style. It was designed by Giovanni Pisano, who worked on it from 1285 to 1296 and

Façade, Duomo

Splendid interior of the Duomo

© YinYang/iStock

decorated it with statues that have now been replaced by copies (*originals in the Cathedral Museum*).

The upper section, built a century later, was strongly influenced by the west front of the cathedral in Orvieto, showing the full exuberance of the Gothic style. The mosaics on the gables date from the end of the 19C. The **campanile** (bell tower), completed in 1313, is Romanesque.

The most characteristic and breathtaking features of the **interior** are the densely alternating horizontal bands of light and dark marble, the short but very broad transept, the rectangular apse and the large number of pillars which provide infinite perspectives in the transept and chancel.

The **pavement★★★** is unique. It is composed of 56 marble panels depicting figures from mythology (Sibyls, Virtues and allegories) and Old Testament scenes, outstanding for their intricacy and liveliness.

They were produced between 1369 and 1547 by some 40 artists, including Matteo di Giovanni, Pinturicchio and Beccafumi. The designs for 35 of the panels are due to Beccafumi's remarkable talent for drawing and decoration. Some have been restored, others replaced by copies.

Good to know: *60 percent of the pavement is protected from excessive wear by a temporary floor which is moved from time to time so that all the panels can be admired in succession.*

The oldest panels were made using the *graffito* technique. They consist of white outlines on a black background and the details and reliefs are engraved in the marble then blackened using asphalt. From 1518 onwards, Beccafumi used inlay techniques with different coloured marbles.

The Baroque **Cappella della Madonna del Voto** (**A**) contains (*flanking the door*) marble statues of St Jerome and St Mary Magdalen carved by Bernini in the 17C. He also produced the altar and the two angels.

The right-hand wall in front of the entrance is covered with votive offerings, including a few caps hung there by jockeys (*fantini*) after the *palio* (*See p306*). The superb 16C marble altar in the **sanctuary** has a fine bronze tabernacle, made c. 1470 by Vecchietta, and four candlesticks at the corners, made a few years later by Francesco di Giorgio Martini (*the two lower candlesticks*) and Giovanni di Stefano. The back panels of the choir **stalls★★** are a fine example of woodcarving with marquetry. The ones at the end of the chancel date from the 16C; the ones on the sides, which are the finest, date from the 14C and were further embellished by wonderful marquetry panelling by Fra Giovanni da Verona (1503). The circular stained-glass window in the sanctuary (recently restored) depicts the Annunciation, the Coronation and the Burial of the Virgin

Mary. It was made in 1288 to designs by Duccio di Buoninsegna.

The **Cappella di Sant'Ansano** (**B**) was dedicated to the first patron saint of Siena. Set in its pavement is the gravestone of Bishop Pecci carved by Donatello (1426); against the wall is a marble Gothic tomb (1318) by Tino di Camaino and his father, Camaino di Crescentino.

The splendid carved marble **pulpit★★★** is a masterpiece by Nicola Pisano made from 1266 to 1268, six years after the one in the Baptistery in Pisa, with the assistance of Giovanni, his son and a few other pupils such as Arnolfo di Cambio. The pulpit resembles the earlier one but shows greater Gothic influence in its light design and flowing sculptures.

On seven panels the artist depicted episodes from the Life of Christ with the same grandeur and power as on the pulpit in Pisa but with heightened drama – (*left to right*) the Nativity, the Adoration of the Magi, the Flight into Egypt and the Presentation of Jesus in the Temple, the Massacre of the Innocents, the Crucifixion and the Last Judgement (*two panels*). The various panels are separated by statues of prophets and angels. On the sill is a lectern shaped like an eagle, the emblem of St John. Between the trefoiled arches are seated female figures representing the Virtues. The pulpit is supported by nine marble, granite and porphyry columns.

Shaped like a rotunda, the Renaissance **Cappella di San Giovanni Battista** (**C**) contains a statue of St John the Baptist by Donatello (1457) in a niche (*below the window*). The frescoes (restored) are by Pinturicchio.

A highly decorative marble doorway flanks the entrance to the **Libreria Piccolomini**, a very famous room, which was built c. 1495 on the orders of Cardinal Francesco Piccolomini to contain the library of Enea Silvia Piccolomini, his uncle, who had become Pope Pius II.

On the floor and in the friezes round the ceiling is the Piccolomini emblem, the crescent moon set on a blue background. All of the walls were painted by Pinturicchio. In the **frescoes★★** that he produced between 1502 and 1509 he used his light, attractive narrative talents to illustrate the main episodes in the life of the Pope.

The series of ten panels shows (*starting right of the window and going clockwise*) his departure from Genoa to attend the Council of Basel, his return from the Council, his meeting with James I of Scotland, his consecration as a poet by Frederick III, his submission to Pope Eugene II, Enea at the betrothal of Emperor Frederick III and Eleonora of Aragon near the Camollia Gate, Pope Calixtus III presenting him with the Cardinal's hat, his election as Pope, his decision to go to war against the Turks taken at the Congress in Mantua, the canonisation of Catherine of Siena and the welcome extended to the Christian fleet on its return from Turkey. The ceiling is richly decorated with allegories, mythological scenes and grotesques. A fine marble group representing the *Three Graces*, a 3C Roman sculpture showing the influence of the Greek tradition, stands in the centre of the room. The display cases beneath the frescoes contain 15C psalters. Outside the Libreria (*on the right*) is the impressive **Piccolomini Altar**, a late 15C work with statues attributed to Michelangelo.

Cathedral Crypt★

Beneath the choir of the cathedral, recent restoration work revealed frescoes by artists from Siena in the second half of the 13C, shedding light on the fundamental development of the Sienese School of painting. The crypt was sandy and full of stones used to build the cathedral. The panels are remarkably preserved and surprising for their vivacious colour.

Battistero di San Giovanni★

Open 10.30am–7pm (2 Nov–Feb 5.30pm; 26 Dec–6 Jan 6pm). See p314 for OPA SI PASS. ℘0577 28 63 00. www.operaduomo.siena.it.

The unfinished 14C Baptistery of St John, beneath the apse of the cathedral, has a white marble façade (1382) and was built in a more austere Gothic style than the cathedral.

The interior is vaulted and has three aisles. It was decorated with frescoes in the 15C. In the centre stands the 15C **font★★**, a hexagonal basin decorated with gilded bronze panels capped by a delightful marble tabernacle. Attributed to Jacopo della Quercia, it is one of the most successful Tuscan sculptures from the transitional period between Gothic and Renaissance.

Several masters depicted episodes from the life of St John the Baptist: *Zachariah being expelled from the Temple* (*beside the altar*) was also by della Quercia; *The Birth of St John the Baptist* (*next on the right*) was by Turino di Sano; *The Preaching of St John the Baptist* was by Giovanni di Turino, one of Jacopo della Quercia's pupils; *The Baptism of Jesus* and the *Arrest of St John the Baptist* were carved by Lorenzo Ghiberti, who designed the Paradise Door in the Baptistery in Florence; and *Herod's Feast* was by Donatello. Donatello also carved two of the statues of the Virtues of Faith and Hope placed at each of the corners of the basin.

Santa Maria della Scala Complex (SMS)★

Piazza Duomo 1. ⏰*Open 15 Mar–15 Oct 10am–7pm (Thu 10pm); 16 Oct–14 Mar Wed–Mon 10–5pm (Thu 8pm, Sat–Sun 7pm; closed Tue); 23 Dec–6 Jan daily 10am–7pm (Thu 8pm; closed 25 Dec).* ⏰€*9;* €*20 combined ticket with Museo Civico in Palazzo Pubblico and Torre del Mangia;* €*20 ACROPOLI PASS.* ☎*0577 53 45 04 or 0577 28 63 00. www.santamariadellascala.com.*

Built in the 10C in front of the cathedral (hence the name St Mary of the Stairs), this building was intended for the pilgrims on the Via Francigena (which crossed the city from the Porta Romana to the Porta Camollia), the poor and abandoned children. Over the centuries the hospital remained in operation until the 1990s when it was converted into a museum and cultural centre. Today it houses exhibitions; **SMS Contemporanea**, a contemporary art centre; the **Museo d'Arte per Bambini** (👥), a museum dedicated to children; the restoration project of Fonte Gaia in Piazza del Campo; and an archaeological section.

You enter the Pellegrinaio delle Donne, the hospital section reserved for women. Today it houses the ticket office and the bookshop with 15C frescoes. After crossing the Sagrestia Vecchia (frescoes and *Madonna del Manto Vecchietta* by Domenico di Bartolo, 1444) and the Cappella della Madonna (*Strage degli Innocenti* by Matteo di Giovanni, 1482), you reach the church of **SS Annunziata**, founded in the 15C and rebuilt 17C–18C. Above the altar, the bronze *Risorto Cristo*, by Vecchietta (1476), stands on the back of the apse adorned with a work of Sebastiano Conca, the *Probatica Piscina* (18C).

The Cappella del Manto (14C frescoes representing saints and doctors of the church and *Meeting at the Golden Gate* of Beccafumi, 1512, icon of the museum) and Passeggio (14C–16C statues) lead to a room even more complex, the **Pellegrinaio★★**, (14C–15C). The frescoes covering the walls, made mostly by Vecchietta (c. 1412–80) and Domenico di Bartolo (1428–47) illustrate the functions of the institution. The subjects often deal with human misery, surprising for their realism and attention to detail. Note the compositional qualities of *Charity Widow*, or treating the sick, the most famous fresco, in which, amid the frenetic activity of the hospital, the eye is captivated by objects: the urine bottle, slippers, a red stocking, the ponds.

The Passeggio Gallery leads to the children's art museum.

The attic is now home to the panels of *Fonte Gaia* by Jacopo della Quercia, the oratories of different fraternities, and the rich treasures of Santa Maria della Scala. The archaeological museum displays objects discovered in Tuscany, which help illustrate regional history, from prehistoric to Roman times.

Pinacoteca Nazionale★★★

Allow 2hrs. Palazzo Buonsignori, Via San Pietro 29. ⏰*Open Tue–Sat 8.15am–7.15pm, Sun–Mon and public hols 9am–1pm.* ⏰*Closed 1 Jan, 25 Dec.* ⏰€*8; free 1st Sun of the month.* ♿ ☎*0577 28 11 61. pinacotecanazionale. siena.it.*

The **picture gallery** is housed in the **Buonsignori Palace★** (mid-15C).

Few works are by Sienese masters Duccio and Simone Martini, but its outstanding collections show the development of Sienese painting from the 13C to the 16C. The **second floor** is devoted to the Primitives. The painted Crucifixes in Rooms **1** and **2** decorated the Romanesque churches in the region, and were the only pictures in existence in the late 12C–early 13C. The first room has two works of Byzantine inspiration, obvious in their hieratic character and brilliant colouring. Christ is shown in triumph and not in suffering, as depicted in later years. The first known artist from Siena was Guido da Siena. The three scenes from the Life of Christ (*wall opposite the door*) are among the earliest works on canvas attributed to his school.

The second room is almost entirely concerned with this great master, Guido da Siena. His works were all markedly Greek in style. The figures are shown from front view, although the heads are sometimes bent or seen from three-quarter view; the volume is suggested in the lines – the systematic emphasis of the ridge of the nose, the concentric lines used to suggest volume in the cheeks – and the folds or creases in the clothes are very marked and emphasised in dark colours or gold. The painting of St Francis (*right of the door*) by Margaritone d'Arezzo, another Tuscan artist, shows how the Byzantine influence continued until the second half of the 13C.

In some cases the end of the 13C was marked by a development in artistic techniques: facial shapes were more gentle, the attitudes more natural and fabrics given greater volume. Niccolò di Segna, in Room **3**, sought to accentuate the natural features of his figures; the eyes are no longer heavily outlined and the hair and beards are softer. His large painting of the Crucifixion (*opposite the window*) shows a suffering Christ. Duccio is the supreme representative of the great period of Sienese painting. The delicate little **Madonna dei Francescani** in Room **4** was one of his early works and it shows the solemnity and rigidity of expression typical of Byzantine art. There is a foretaste of the flowing, graceful lines that characterise the Sienese School in later years in the slight bend in the Virgin Mary's body and the curl along the hem of her cloak.

Room **5** contains paintings by Luca di Tommè and Bartolo di Fredi, who worked during the second half of the 14C, in the same style as the great masters (Simone Martini and the Lorenzetti brothers) but with additional refinement. An Adoration of the Magi by di Fredi (*right-hand wall*) shows brilliant narrative skill and exquisite command of colouring.

Simone Martini (d. 1344) is represented in Room **6** by his **Madonna col Bambino** painted with a softness and purity rarely equalled. There is also his attractive polyptych of the *Blessed Agostino Novello*. The Madonnas painted by Lippo Memmi, his closest pupil, show something of his elegance and grace but they lack the vibrant lyricism of his master.

Room **7** room has outstanding works by the Lorenzetti brothers, who died of the Plague in 1348. The great **Pala del Carmine** (*right of the door to Room 8*) was a reredos commissioned from Pietro, the elder brother, in 1329 by the Carmelites of Siena.

Although the severe and impressive *Virgin Mary in Majesty*, shown full face and sitting very straight, is still rather stiff, the scenes on the predella depicting the history of the Carmelite Order have a very lively narrative, supplemented by the landscapes and architectural perspectives.

The exquisite little *Virgin Mary in Majesty* (*opposite*) by Ambrogio, Pietro's brother, is a more precious and more refined work which is also more tender, like his other representations of the Madonna, several of which are in the same room. Ambrogio also painted two charming little views of a *Town Overlooking the Sea* and a *Castle on the Shores of a Lake* in which his Gothic grace is expressed in the extreme detail of the towers above the town and the graceful curve of the boat on the lake.

The golden *Assumption*, a work of unrivalled affectedness, was painted by

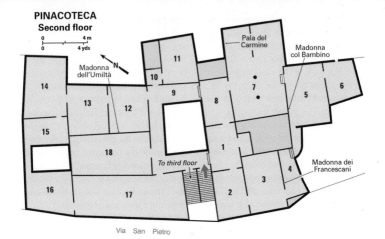

PINACOTECA
Second floor

the Master of Monte Oliveto who was strongly influenced by the monumental character of Pietro Lorenzetti's works. Most of the works on the left-hand side of the room are by this artist and by Paolo di Giovanni Fei.

Rooms **11** to **13** display works from the last Sienese Primitives to work in the late-Gothic style in the 15C. Taddeo di Bartolo (*Room 11*), who died c. 1425 is represented here by an Annunciation (*right-hand wall*). In Room 12 is the *Assumption of the Virgin Mary surrounded by four Saints* by Giovanni di Paolo (c. 1403–82), whose Mannerist tendencies are present – the flowing garments, the slight bend in the knees of John the Baptist and the very obvious veins and the almost excessive suffering of the *Ecce Homo* and saints on the predella. The artist's delightful **Madonna dell'Umiltà** (*Room 13 – left of the door*) is exquisitely unreal, with a long and sinuous outline, separated by a poetic curtain of rose trees from a minutely detailed background.

Rooms **14** and **15** contain Sienese works that have been influenced by the Renaissance masters. In the 15C Sienese art was open to the innovations of the Renaissance while at the same time retaining its own grace. In his religious paintings, Francesco di Giorgio Martini (1439–1502) shows the beginnings of the Florentine influence and in his descriptive landscapes show a fondness for Mantegna.

Matteo di Giovanni (c. 1430–95) had a vigorous drawing technique and he willingly accentuated and varied the attitudes and expressions of his figures; he produced a number of paintings of the Madonna and Child (*Room 14*) and an Adoration of the Shepherds (*Room 15*). Sano di Pietro (1406–81), featured in Rooms **16** and **17**, was very prolific but not very innovative. He remained most faithful to the Gothic style during this period. His great polyptych (*Room 16 – right-hand wall*) shows a Madonna and Child with Saints in brilliant, refined colours; the drawing is of good quality. He also painted exuberant polyptychs (*Room 17*) in the Gothic style.

The aesthetic innovations of the Florentine Renaissance are also evident in Room **18** in works by Vecchietta (c. 1400–80) whose great coffered panel (*centre of the room*), originally part of a reliquary chest (*arliquiera*), shows a keen sense of perspective. In works by Girolamo di Benvenuto and Benvenuto di Giovanni, this new style is accompanied by a certain harshness.

The **Spannocchi Collection** on the **Third Floor** contains paintings from the 16C–17C of Flemish, Dutch and German origin (*St Jerome* by Dürer); from Venice (works by Paris Bordon, *Nativity* by Lorenzo Lotto) and from Lombardy, Emilia and Rome.

Room **23** (*2nd room to the right beyond the courtyard*) contains a roundel (*tondo*) of *The Holy Family with the young St John* by Pinturicchio set against a background of gentle countryside suffused in the characteristic light of Umbrian skies.

The other two artists whose personality marked Sienese painting in the 16C, Beccafumi and Il Sodoma, are well represented. Among the outstanding works by Beccafumi is **Birth of the Virgin Mary** (*below Room 13 on the 2nd floor*) in which the colours are daringly graduated; the main subject is set against a fairly dark background that seems to absorb the colours because of the unreal lighting. Il Sodoma painted the pathos-filled **Christ on the Column** (*below Room 15*) which is an amazingly beautiful work. The following room contains his large *Deposition from the Cross* on which the clothes look like sails swirling in the wind, with rich and shimmering colours.

WALKING TOUR

Stroll through the streets of Siena, starting from the Piazza Banchi di Sotto, from the **Loggia del Papa** (*right*), a building with huge Renaissance arches supported by Corinthian columns. Its name recalls that it was built at the request of Pope Pius II Piccolomini.

Via Banchi di Sotto★
East from the junction of Via di Città and Via Banchi di Sopra.
This **street**, which skirts the north side of the mansions facing Piazza del Campo, includes the historic University of Siena (*left*). Opposite is the white travertine façade of the **Palazzo Piccolomini★**. Probably Bernardo Rossellino, the architect of the Palazzo Ruccellai in Florence, drew the plans for this fine Renaissance building and gave it its Florentine features – façade with light rustication becoming even less marked towards the top, small cornices emphasising the various levels, projecting roof with the coat of arms of the Piccolomini (crescent moon) set between the consoles. It houses the city archives.

▷ Take Via Banchi di Sopra.

Via Banchi di Sopra★

▷ N from the junction of Via di Città and Via Banchi di Sotto.

On the west side of Piazza Tolomei stands **Palazzo Tolomei**, dating from the early 13C, which now houses the Cassa di Risparmio di Firenze. This is the oldest privately owned mansion in Siena. Its façade is built entirely of stone and has two rows of Gothic double-bay windows over an unusually high ground floor, both austere and elegant. Robert of Anjou, King of Naples, stayed here in 1310.

Piazza Salimbeni★
One of the most noble squares in Siena is lined on three sides by buildings in which three different styles of architecture are represented. On the east side is 14C **Palazzo Salimbeni** (extensively restored 1879). The light-coloured stone façade has a row of Gothic triple-bay windows, each capped by a pointed arch. Its name is after an influential medieval Sienese family of merchants and bankers. Building began on the **Palazzo Spannocchi** (*south side*) in 1470 to designs by the Florentine architect Giuliano da Maiano, for the treasurer to Pope Pius II Piccolomini. Its Renaissance façade with double bays and three rows of smooth rustication flanked by cornices is similar to the mansion built during the same period in Florence.

The **Palazzo Tantucci** (*north side*) was designed almost a century later by the Sienese architect, Riccio. All three house the departments of the **Monte dei Paschi**, a Sienese credit institution founded in 1472; its very existence was closely linked to the prosperity of Siena. Its name comes from the pastures (*pascoli* or *paschi*) in the Maremma region, then owned by Siena. The income from the pastures guaranteed the financial viability of the institution.

▷ Take Via della Sapienza and turn left into Via della Galluzza.

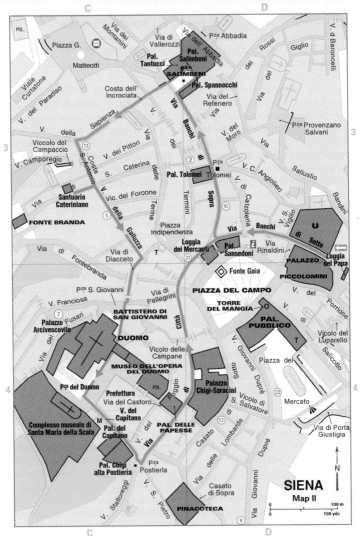

WHERE TO STAY	WHERE TO EAT	
		Osteria Il Carroccio ....(12)
Antica Residenza Cicogna.....(2)	Grotta di Santa Caterina ......(5)	Osteria la Chiacchera..........(13)
Boutique Hôtel	La Taverna di San Giuseppe ...(9)	Torrefazione Fiorella...........(21)
Alla Scala 1746..............(7)	Nannini ....(10)	Trattoria Papei.................(22)

Via della Galluzza

▷ N from Piazza del Campo.

This narrow, steeply-sloping **street** is one of the most picturesque medieval thoroughfares in Siena. It is lined with old brick houses and has eight arches, one of which includes an attractive triple bay.

Santuario Cateriniano (St Catherine's Birthplace)

Costa di Sant'Antonio, entrance Via Santa Caterina. ⏱*Open daily 9am–12.30pm, 3–6pm.* ⊛*Free admission.* ✆*0577 28 81 75.*
The birthplace of St Catherine of Siena became a sanctuary in 1465, and is now a group of superimposed chap-

els, surrounded by other buildings. On the lower floor (*staircase on the left at the end*), on the site of the dyeshop belonging to Catherine's father, there is a church dedicated to the Saint. On the upper floor (*left*), on the site of the former kitchen, is richly decorated with wooden panelling decorated in blue and gold and a superb majolica pavement dating from the 17C. The other (*right*) contains the 13C painted Crucifix to which the Saint is said to have been praying in Pisa when she received the stigmata.

⊳ Walk towards the Duomo.
At the Piazza, take Via del Capitano.

Via del Capitano★

⊳ From Piazza del Duomo SE to Piazza di Postierla (also known as Quattro Cantoni).

This **street** is one of the finest in Siena. **Palazzo Chigi alla Postierla** (*left, no 1*) is a 16C building attributed to the Sienese architect Riccio.
The late-13C **Palazzo del Capitano del Popolo** (*left, nos 15–19*), extensively restored in the 19C, is a fine Gothic building of stone and brick in the Sienese style. The powerful and austere lower level has only three tall doorways and contrasts sharply with the top of the building, which is relieved by a long row of Gothic double-bay windows and a cornice above tiny arches containing coats of arms and a row of merlons.

⊳ Turn into Via di Città.

Via di Città★

⊳ From Piazza di Postierla (S of Piazza del Duomo) to Via Banchi di Sotto (N of Piazza del Campo).

This **street**, like most in the historic centre, is a pedestrian precinct. Together with Via Banchi di Sopra, it is the main shopping area in Siena.
Both streets are narrow and winding, cobbled and without pavements but they are lined with patrician houses and superb **palaces★**.
In **Via di Città** (*about halfway from the southern end*) beyond several brick mansions is (*left*) Palazzo Piccolomini, also known as **Palazzo delle Papesse**, which now houses the offices of the Banco d'Italia. It was probably designed by Bernardo Rossellino and built of light-coloured stone in the second half of the 15C on the orders of Catherine Piccolomini, the sister of Pope Pius II. The lower section of its stone façade has marked rustication in the style of the Florentine Renaissance.

Palazzo Chigi-Saracini★

Almost opposite is the long and slightly curved Gothic façade of the **Palazzo Chigi-Saracini**, partially rebuilt in the 18C. The combination of stone and brick, the two rows of elegant triple-bay windows and the merlons along the top of the wall are all reminiscent of the Palazzo Pubblico. The building houses the Accademia Chigiana, a famous academy of music. From the top of its tower, since truncated, the victory of Montaperti is said to have been proclaimed to the citizens. At the north end of the street (*Croce del Travaglio*) is the **Loggia dei Mercanti** (*right*), the early 15C Merchants' Loggia, which was the seat of the Commercial Court. Its architecture is Renaissance but its decoration – niches with statues – shows traces of the Gothic style. Marble benches carved with low-reliefs representing philosophers and generals from the days of ancient Rome run along two sides. The upper storey is 17C.

⊳ Continue on Via di Città to Palazzo Sansedoni.

OTHER SIGHTS
Basilica di San Domenico★
Piazza San Domenico.
In this convent **church** near her home (⊙ *See Walking Tour, p321*) St Catherine of Siena experienced her ecstasies. The 13C–15C church is in a powerful and austere Gothic style.

The T-shaped interior is spacious and well-lit, with a wide nave and very small chancel.

Cappella delle Volte (*east*), is a chapel with (*above the altar*) the only authentic portrait of the Saint, painted by her contemporary, the Sienese artist, Andrea Vanni.

In **St Catherine's Chapel** (*mid-nave – right*) is the Renaissance marble **tabernacle★** carved in 1466 by Giovanni di Stefano, another Sienese artist, which contains the Saint's head (her body is in Rome). Il Sodoma painted the famous **frescoes★** (*end wall and left-hand wall*) which depict scenes from her life: St Catherine in Ecstasy, St Catherine receiving the Stigmata, St Catherine helping a Condemned Man. The modern stained-glass windows in the chancel (1982) are by B Cassinari.

The tabernacle and two angels (*high altar*) were carved in the 15C by Benedetto da Maiano. The delightful triptych of the *Madonna and Child surrounded by Saints* (*first chapel to the right*) is by Matteo di Giovanni, who also painted the exquisite *St Barbara between two Angels and two other Saints* (*second chapel to the left*). In the lunette (*right-hand wall*) is an Adoration of the Magi.

Fonte Branda★
Via di Fontebranda.
Downhill from the basilican church of San Domenico is the unusual brick-built **Branda Fountain**, the oldest in the city. It was already in existence in 1080, and in 1246 it acquired its present form, similar to the façade of Siena's Gothic mansions with its crenellated top and three wide arches as wide as doorways.

Basilica di San Francesco
Piazza San Francesco.
On the very top of one of the three hills on which Siena is built stands the Gothic basilican **church** dedicated to St Francis, extensively restored (west front 19C). In front of this church in 1425 **St Bernardino**, a Franciscan monk, preached one of his sermons, hence the small **chapel** (*right of the church*) bearing

the three initials IHS on its façade. The basilica always flies the colours of the *contrade*. The building has a single, magnificently wide **nave★**, in which the painted decor imitates the alternating black and white marble of the cathedral, and a chancel, flanked by small chapels. The church is lit by particularly fine stained-glass windows.

Pietro Lorenzetti painted the fresco (*first chapel to the left of the altar*) representing the Crucifixion, and other frescoes (*third chapel*) are by his brother, Ambrogio, depicting (*right-hand wall*) *St Louis of Toulouse*, great-nephew of St Louis and brother of Robert of Anjou, King of Naples, in front of *Boniface VIII* and (*opposite*) the *Martyrdom of the Franciscans in Ceuta*. Verdi chose this church for the first performance of his *Requiem*, with a choir of 400 singers, as is recorded on the plaque (*east end of the nave – left-hand side*).

Oratorio di San Bernardino – Museum of Sacred Art★
🕐*Open mid Mar–Oct 10.30am–1.30pm, 3–5.30pm.* 🕐*Closed Nov–mid Mar.* ⊚€3. ✆0577 28 30 48.

Here St Bernardino preached passionate eloquent sermons that made him famous. The lower chapel, with its starry vault, has a beautiful Madonna and Child by Sano di Pietro. The upper oratory has a beautiful fresco cycle dedicated to the Virgin, painted by Sodoma, Domenico Beccafumi and Girolamo Pacchia.

The Museum of Sacred Art assembles remarkable 13C–19C works, including a beautiful terracotta Madonna and Child by Jacopo della Quercia, a fresco of the Resurrection by Ambrogio Lorenzetti and *Madonna del Latte* by Pietro Lorenzetti.

Sant'Agostino
Prato di Sant'Agostino. 🕐*Open mid Mar–Oct Mon–Sat 2.30–5.30pm.* 🕐*Closed Sun.* ⊚€2.50.

This 13C **church** dedicated to St Augustine has a Baroque interior (18C) redesigned by Vanvitelli. The admirable **Adoration of the Crucifix★** (*second altar to the right*), set against a superb landscaped background, was painted in 1506 by Perugino. The Piccolomini Chapel (*door immediately beyond the altar*) contains some interesting **paintings★**: a remarkably fresh fresco of the Madonna with the Saints by Ambrogio Lorenzetti and an Adoration of the Magi by Il Sodoma (*above the altar*).

Santa Maria dei Servi
Piazza Manzoni.
The **church** presents an unfinished and rustic façade of brick at the top of a short avenue of cypress trees. Above it is an attractive Romanesque-Gothic bell tower. From the church steps, there is a magnificent **view★★★** of the steeply sloping hill on which the cathedral is built and of the rear of the Palazzo Pubblico.

The interior of the church, an unusual combination of Gothic and Renaissance styles, contains some outstanding **works of art★**: *Virgin Mary in Majesty* (1261) by the Florentine artist Coppo di Marcovaldo, who was taken prisoner at Montaperti and is said to have painted this work (*second altar on the right*) in exchange for his freedom; a highly expressive *Massacre of the Innocents* by Matteo di Giovanni (*fifth altar*); frescoes by Pietro Lorenzetti (*second chapel on the left of the chancel*) depicting *Salome's Dance* and the *Death of St John the Baptist* (*right*); *Adoration of the Shepherds*

(1404) (*above the altar*) by Taddeo di Bartolo.
A very gentle *Virgin Mary of Misericord* by Lippo Memmi (*end of the north transept*) is incorporated into another painting.

EXCURSIONS
Convento dell'Osservanza
3km/2mi NE of Siena by SP408 (to Montevarchi). After the level crossing, follow the yellow signs to Basilica Osservanza.

The **Observants' Monastery** founded by St Bernardino (⚫ *See box, p312*), stands on a hilltop which affords an attractive view of Siena. The brick basilica, which was rebuilt in its 15C style after being destroyed in 1944, contains some interesting **works of art★** – a terracotta Coronation of the Virgin Mary by Andrea della Robbia (*second chapel on the left*); a triptych of the Madonna and Child by Sano di Pietro (*first chapel on the left*); a fine Pietà (*second chapel on the right*) carved by the Sienese sculptor, Giacomo Cozzarelli (1453–1515).

Inside the monastery is St Bernardino's cell containing his personal effects and a cast of his face made in 1443, one year before his death.

Monteriggioni★★
15km/9mi NW of Siena.
🅸 *Piazza Roma 23. ☎0577 30 48 34. www.monteriggioniturismo.it.* 🅿

Monteriggioni

Traffic is restricted within the walls to residents and hotel guests only. Car park beside the approach road (too steep for caravan) 5min from the entrance.

Monteriggioni lies only 15km/9mi from Siena. Its towers are visible from the Florence–Siena motorway. It stands peacefully on top of one of the graceful hills north of Siena. It owes its picturesque beauty to the clear-cut outline of its enclosing wall and 14 square towers. The fortress was formerly a Ghibelline outpost, built by the Sienese in the early 13C, and was described by Dante in his *Divine Comedy*.

The **village**, set inside its walls, has a long main street running from south to north between the two gates (Porta Franca and Porta Senese) and passing along one side of the main square, Piazza Roma. The square is flanked (*east*) by the small Romanesque-Gothic church, Santa Maria Assunta, which served as a waypoint for pilgrims travelling the Via Francigena.

You can walk along a small section of the defensive walls, next to which a small museum displays medieval armour. Entry is at Piazza Roma or Piazzetta Fontebranda (*€3 for museum and walkway*).

🚗 DRIVING TOUR

FROM ABBAZIA DI MONTE OLIVETO MAGGIORE TO ABBAZIA DI SAN GALGANO
Circuit of 115km/71.5mi.
See regional map pp288–289.

Asciano
21km/13mi SE by SP438.

Asciano is separated from Siena by a line of hills. It is an old medieval fortified town on a rise overlooking the Ombrone river. The Corso Matteotti runs through it from one end to the other. The 12C Romanesque **Basilica di Sant'Agata** (St Agatha's Basilica), built entirely of travertine marble, has a Gothic façade approached by a wide flight of steps. The nave, with its bare rafters, has a wonderful fresco of the Madonna and Child attributed to Girolamo del Pacchia. The **Museo Amos e Giuseppe Cassioli** (*open Apr–Oct Tue and Sun 10am–1pm, 3–6pm (Jul–Aug 5–8pm); Nov–Mar by reservation only; €5; ℘0577 71 95 24*) is devoted to the works of Amos Cassioli (1832–92), famous in his day for portraits and historical paintings, and of Giuseppe Cassioli (1865–1942), his son.

Left of the basilica is the **Museo Civico Archeologico e d'Arte Sacra** (*Palazzo Corboli, Corso Matteotti 122; open Apr–Oct daily 10am–1pm, 3–7pm (Jul–Aug 5–10pm); Nov–Mar Sat–Sun and public hols 10am–1pm, 3–6pm; €5; ℘0577 71 95 24*). The museum, in a 13C palazzo, exhibits sculptures, majolicas and panels painted by the Sienese school (12-18C), and bronze and ivory archaeological finds from the 7-1C BC.

Abbazia di Monte Oliveto Maggiore★★
Open daily 9.15am–noon, 3–6pm (3.15–5pm in winter). Free. ℘0577 70 76 11. www.monteolivetomaggiore.it.

Monte Oliveto is in the heart of the area known as Toscana della Fede not far from the abbeys of San Galgano, Sant'Antimo and Farneta. It is about 10km/6mi from the Via Cassia and about 30km/18mi SE of Siena. The huge pink brick buildings of this famous abbey nestle among the cypress trees in a landscape of eroded hills. Monte Oliveto is the mother-house of the Olivetians, a congregation of Benedictine monks founded in 1313 by Blessed Bernardo Tolomei of Siena. A fortified tower with terra-cotta decorations by the Luca della Robbia School leads into the monastery grounds.

Main Cloisters
The cloisters were decorated with a superb series of 36 **frescoes★★** recounting the life of St Benedict. They were painted by Luca Signorelli from 1498 onwards and by Sodoma between 1505 and 1508.

Frescoes, Abbazia di Monte Oliveto Maggiore

The cycle (*left to right*) begins near the church door with the main arch on which are paintings of *Christ at the Pillar* and *Christ carrying the Cross*, both of them masterpieces by Sodoma. Like the frescoes on the north side, the first 19 scenes, starting with *St Benedict leaving his Father's House*, are by the same painter. They are followed by a fresco by Riccio and then eight frescoes by Signorelli.

Sodoma, who is portrayed in the third fresco facing the viewer, was a man of refinement and a genius, who was influenced by Leonardo da Vinci and Perugino. He was not particularly pious and was mainly attracted by the aesthetic portrayal of human types, landscapes and picturesque detail, as shown in the fourth fresco in which St Benedict receives the hermit's habit, the 12th fresco (*first on the south side*), where the saint welcomes two young men in the midst of a crowd of characters in varying poses, and the 19th fresco (*last on the south side*), in which lascivious courtesans are sent to tempt the monks. The work of **Signorelli** is distinguishable by the sculpture-like power of his figures and the dramatic settings in which the landscapes are reduced to a mere suggestion of space. This is evident in the 24th fresco where St Benedict restores to life a monk who has fallen from the top of a wall.

The cloisters give access to the 15C refectory which is decorated with frescoes dating from the same period (*Last Supper*).

Abbey Church

The interior has been refurbished in 18C Baroque style but the stained-glass windows are of modern design.

The chapel (*left of the entrance from the exterior*) contains a wooden Crucifix brought to the abbey by its founder in 1313. The nave is lined by magnificent **choir stalls★★** (1505) by Fra Giovanni da Verona; they include marquetry inlays of birds, architectural vistas, tabernacles and musical instruments etc. A staircase to the right of the chancel leads to the crib.

Buonconvento

Buonconvento stands at the confluence of the Arbia and Ombrone rivers, on the Via Cassia, the Roman road between Siena and Rome. The centre of a small farming community, the town is built entirely of brick and enclosed within 14C town walls. Emperor Henry VII, in whom Dante placed his hopes of a unified, pacified Italy, died here in 1313. On the north side of the fortifications stands the great **Porta Senese** (Siena Gate), topped with small relieving arches and battlements, from which Via Soccini traverses the town. In a small square to the left is the **Church of SS Pietro e Paolo** (St Peter and St Paul) which has a façade in the Jesuit style. Further on is the **Palazzo Pretorio** surmounted by an elegant tower based on Siena's.

Museo d'Arte Sacra della Val d'Arbia★

Via Soccini 18. ◐*Open Apr–Oct Tue–Sun 10am–1pm, 2.30–6pm; Nov–Mar Tue–Fri 9am–1pm, Sat–Sun 10am–1pm, 3–6pm.* ◐*Closed Mon.* ๑€3.50. ௸ ℘0577 80 71 81. www.museisenesi.org. This **Museum of Sacred Art** presents 14C to 17C paintings by the Sienese School, as well as church plate, liturgical vestments and reliquaries from the Buonconvento and the Arbia Valley.

Murlo★

⊟ *Piazza della Cattedrale 4.* ℘0577 81 40 99. Murlo is 24km/15mi S of Siena, between SP223 and the Via Cassia. The tiny medieval gem is formed of several buildings in a single row of houses backing onto the town walls. From the 11C to the 18C it belonged to the Bishops of Siena. Today it is famous for the Etruscan archaeological discoveries made in Poggio Civitate, near Vescovado (north).

Antiquarium di Poggio Civitate★★

◐*Open mid Mar–mid Oct Tue–Sun 10am–1.30pm, 3–7pm; rest of the year Fri–Sun 10.30am–1.30pm, 2.30–5.30pm.* ๑€5. ℘0577 81 40 99.

The **museum** is housed in the former bishop's palace (*palazzone*) and contains the remains of a patrician early Etruscan quadrangular villa (7C–6C BC) discovered in Poggio Civitate. It formerly had a central porticoed courtyard. It gives a rare insight into domestic architecture, including the roofing structure which has remained almost intact.

The reconstructed roof and its rich terracotta decoration was an architectural feature, which reflected the family's social status. The ridge is adorned with a series of statues (over 1.5m/5ft high), some 20 animal and human fig-

ures, including a man wearing a wide-brimmed hat and boasting a Pharaonic beard. The roof was further emphasised by a border of antifixae representing Gorgon heads and a large frieze decorated in the Greek style with banqueting and horse racing scenes.

In addition to this exhibit, there are also some fine ceramic vases imported from Greece and locally-produced buccheroware, crockery used in the kitchen or by servants, and ivory and bronze decorative objects and jewellery, a glimpse into the life of an aristocratic Etruscan family (mid-7C–late 6C BC).

Abbazia di San Galgano★★

Località San Galgano, Chiusdino. ℘0577 75 67 38. www.prolocochiusdino.it. The majestic and impressive ruins of this complex, set atop Monte Siepi, leave an indelible picture in the memory. A Cistercian abbey and a hermitage were built on the site where Saint Galgano died a pauper. The wayward knight lived out his last days on this hill after thrusting his sword into a stone – proof that here the Lord wished him to live as a hermit. Visitors can still see his legendary sword stuck in the rock.

Abbey

2min on foot from car park; restoration in progress. ◐*Open daily Apr–Oct 9am–6pm (Jun and Sept 7pm, Jul–Aug 8pm); Nov–Mar 9am–5.30pm.* ๑€4. ℘0577 75 67 38.

The unroofed **church** is flanked by one range of the cloister buildings – the chapterhouse and the scriptorium. The Romanesque-Gothic abbey was built in honour of **St Galgano** (1148–81) between 1224 and 1288 by Cistercian monks from Casamari (*southeast of Rome*) and contained the earliest Gothic church in Tuscany which provided the inspiration for Siena Cathedral. A tour of the buildings reveals the traditional features of Cistercian architecture.

Eremo di Montesiepi★

Separate approach road and car park. The **hermitage**, which stands on the hill (*200m/217yd from the abbey*), is a strange 12C Romanesque rotunda with an amazing **dome** (1181–5) devoid of ribs. Its design was inspired by Etruscan and Roman tombs, an ideal link between Classicism and the Renaissance.

Its main feature is the 24 red-and-white brick-and-stone circles. The number is a multiple of 12, which has sacred connotations – the 12 Apostles and the 12 tribes of Israel. The church was built to house the body of Galgano Guidotti and the rock in which in 1180 he planted his sword, henceforth considered to be a Cross.

SIENA TO THE CHIANTI HILLS
100km/62mi route.
See CHIANTI.

ADDRESSES

🛏 STAY

🛏 **Camping Colleverde** – *Strada di Scacciapensieri 47, 2.5km/1.5mi N; follow the signs FS.* 📞*0577 33 25 45.* 🏊. *200 places. Restaurant. www.sienacamping. com.* In the Sienese hills with swimming pool. Fine view of the towers particularly at night.

🛏🛏🛏 **Antica Residenza Cicogna** – *Via delle Terme 76.* 📞*0577 28 56 13. www.anticaresidenzacicogna.it. 5 rooms, 2 suites.* This beautifully appointed, stylish B&B offers the charm of a noble medieval palace.

🛏🛏🛏 **B&B Palazzo Bulgarini** – *Via Pantaneto 93.* 📞*0577 15 24 466. www.bbpalazzobulgarini.com. 6 rooms.* In an ancient *palazzo* 300m/330yd from Piazza del Campo, this B&B offers comfortable, newly renovated rooms.

🛏🛏🛏 **Boutique Hôtel Alla Scala 1746** – *Via Fusari 28.* 📞*391 709 9693. boutiquehotelallascala1746.business. site. 4 rooms.* Ideally located in a 1746 building in the city centre, steps from the Duomo and Piazza del Campo, services and furnishings are good quality.

🛏🛏🛏 **Hotel Santa Caterina** – *Via E. S. Piccolomini 7.* 📞*0577 22 11 05. www.hotelsantacaterinasiena.com.* 🅿 *22 rooms.* Near Porta Romana, this villa is decorated in the Tuscan style. Breakfast

or relax in its small garden. Sophisticated, familial atmosphere.

🛏🛏🛏 **Hotel Palazzo di Valli** – *Via E. S. Piccolomini 135.* 📞*0577 22 61 02. www. palazzodivalli.it.* 🅿. *11 rooms.* This 16C villa, near Porta Romana, has frescoed, vaulted ceilings and terracotta flooring. Italian garden. A good family respite.

🛏🛏🛏🛏 **Palazzo Ravizza** – *Pian dei Mantellini 34.* 📞*0577 28 04 62. www. palazzoravizza.it.* 🅿. *30 rooms.* Near, Piazza del Campo, a Renaissance mansion with coffered ceilings and frescoes. Austere Tuscan elegance with early 19C atmosphere and contemporary furniture. Garden with panoramic view on Sienese hills.

NEARBY

🛏 **Ostello Guidoriccio** – *Via Fiorentina 89, Fontebecci, 2,5km/4mi N of the city centre; Florence–Siena motorway, Siena North junction, 500m/550yd towards the centre.* 📞*0577 16 98 177.* 🅿. *47 rooms.* Convenient by bus or car. Simple rooms are furnished with wash basins and bunk beds. Buffet breakfast.

🛏🛏 **Il Ficareto** – *53018 Ancaiano, 13km/8mi SW of Siena towards Sovicille-Ancaiano on the SS73.* 📞*371 35 40 080. www.ficareto.it.* ♿. Off the usual tourist track, this farmhouse offers a friendly relaxing stay close to nature.

🛏🛏 **Fattoria di Cavaglioni** – *Via del Poggetto 1, Località San Rocco a Pilli, Sovicille, 9km/6mi SW of Siena, on S223 towards Grosseto.* 📞*0577 16 06 571. www. anfamtos.com.* 🅿. *Villa with 8 rooms.* This 17C house and its hamlet is ideal for country walks or total relaxation.

🛏🛏🛏 **Villa Scacciapensieri** – *Via di Scacciapensieri 10, 2km/1.2mi N of the city centre.* 📞*0577 41 441. www. villascacciapensieri.it.* 🅿 *31 rooms.* Elegant 19C manor house in a commanding hill setting with park and Italian garden. Family atmosphere. Great chimney-piece in common space.

🍽 EAT

🍽🍽 **Osteria Il Carroccio** – *Via Casato di Sotto 32.* 📞*0577 41 165. facebook. com/osteriailcarroccio16. Closed Wed.* Near Piazza del Campo, this *osteria* attracts the locals with its simplicity and Sienese cooking, traditional dishes and delicious salads.

🍴🍽 **Osteria Nonna Gina** – *Piano dei Mantellini 2*. *℘0577 28 72 47*. *www.osterianonnagina.com*. Since 1992, this simple *osteria* offers delicious food and family service. Try the daily-made *gnocchi*, you will not be disappointed! Good for traditional fare.

🍴🍽 **Trattoria Papei** – *Piazza del Mercato 6*. *℘0577 28 08 94*. *www.anticatrattoriapapei.com*. Lively, simple and well-kept. In summer tables are set in the crowded square by Torre del Mangia. Good value for money.

🍴🍽 **Grotta di Santa Caterina – Da Bagoga** – *Via della Galluzza 26*. *℘0577 28 22 08*. *www.bagoga.it*. Since 1973, traditional cuisine run by Bagoga (Tuscan dialect for apricot), a retired Palio *fantino* (jockey), and his family in a pleasant spot. A landmark cuisine!

🍴🍽 **Ristorante Fòri Porta** – *Via Tolomei 1*. *℘0577 22 21 00*. *www.foriportasiena.it*. Next to Porta Romana, this is a simple place for true Sienese fare. Attached to a wine shop and grocery.

🍴🍽🍽 **Bottganova** – *Strada Chiantigiana 29, towards Montevarchi*. *℘0577 28 42 30*. *Reservations suggested*. *www.anticatrattoriabotteganova.it*. One of Siena's best for dining, but away from the centre. Local dishes, plus fish, in an elegant country dining room.

🍴🍽🍽 **La Taverna di San Giuseppe** – *Via Giovanni Dupré 132*. *℘0577 42 286*. *www.tavernasangiuseppe.it*. *Reservation suggested*. This building evokes the origins of Siena, from the wine cellar (*open to visitors*) occupying an Etruscan house from the 3C BC, to the dining room itself, with its Roman brick walls. Courteous staff and authentic Tuscan cuisine, including *galletto al mattone con aromi* (brick-baked chicken).

🍴🍽🍽 **Osteria Babazuf** – *Via di Pantaneto 85*. *℘0577 22 24 82*. *www.osteriababazuf.com*. This modern inn serves traditional cuisine, plus a few seafood options, mushrooms and truffles in season.

🍴🍽🍽 **Osteria la Chiacchera** – *Costa di Sant'Antonio 4*. *℘0577 28 06 31*. *www.osterialachiacchera.it*. Summer wood tables set up in the side street between Santa Caterina and Piazza del Campo. Traditional Tuscan and Sienese dishes. Usually very crowded.

🍴🍽🍽 **Ristorante Gallo Nero** – *Via del Porrione 65–67*. *℘0577 28 43 56*. *www.gallonero.it*. Medieval ambience, service and cuisine. Several set menus.

ASCIANO

🍴🍽 **Ristorante La Torre** – *Monte Oliveto Maggiore*. *℘0577 70 70 22*. Pleasant restaurant in the abbey tower, run for over 40 years by the Giustarini family. Try the classical *pici* pasta or the *zuppa di fagioli* (bean soup).

TAKING A BREAK

Piazza del Campo – Choose from among the many cafés in this vast square, find a table on the terrace and enjoy the sun while savouring a drink, a *gelato*, or pastry products like the traditional *panforte* (a Sienese, a spiced vanilla cake with almonds and candied fruit), the *panpepato* (a cake with pepper and spices, enriched by candied fruit, almonds and hazelnuts) or the *cantucci* (crunchy biscuits).

Torrefazione Fiorella – *Via di Città 13*. *℘377 18 67 228*. This café roasts its own coffee beans, an alluring aroma.

Enoteca Italiana – *Piazza della Libertà 1, Fortezza Medicea*. The 16C Medici fort stocks over 1,000 Italian, particularly Tuscan, good-quality wines. Tasting and talks by winemakers.

Bar Conca d'Oro – Nannini – *Via Banchi di Sopra 22/24*. *℘0577 23 60 09*. *www.pasticcerienannini.it*. This, the most famous café in the city, is popular for Sienese cakes or ice cream. Other Nannini's bars in Siena are in *Via Massetana Romana 42-44, Viale Toselli 94/A* and *Piazza Matteotti 29*.

Pasticceria Bini – *Via Stalloreggi 91*. *℘0577 28 02 07*. *facebook.com/pasticceria bini1944*. Since 1943, this pastry shop features specialities like *panforte*.

EVENTS

Palio delle Contrade – *2 July and 16 August*. Since 1633, the most famous horse race in Italy. *www.ilpalio.org*.

Treno Natura – The "nature train" is a vintage steam locomotive which runs a tourist service on the occasion of food and wine festivals in the Orcia Valley (*departs from Siena at 9am*). For information and reservations, contact Visione Del Mondo Agenzia Viaggi (*℘0577 48 003*) or *www.terresiena.it/trenonatura*.

Chianti★★

Pesa Valley and Greve Valley

The soil of Chianti has been tilled for many centuries, as evidenced by the farmed and furrowed landscape of the region. Among the dark forests of chestnut, oak, pine and larch (two-thirds of the territory), lie row upon row of vineyards and silver-green olive trees, forming a bright carpet on gently sloping hillsides. Small villages, villas, an abbey, castles, fine estates and farms harmonise with the land.

A BIT OF HISTORY

The Chianti region is famous for its excellent wine (♿*See INTRODUCTION*), the key attraction for tourism and commerce.

The **Chianti Classico** (Black Rooster) communities are nine: Castellina, Gaiole and Radda (the three of the 13C Chianti League); and parts of Barberino Val d'Elsa, Castelnuovo Berardenga, Poggibonsi, San Casciano Val di Pesa and Tavarnelle Val di Pesa. The wine must be at least 80 percent (up to 100 percent) Sangiovese grapes, with the remaining varieties as stipulated in regulations. (The traditional addition of white grapes has not been allowed since the 2006 harvest.) Some 90 of these wineries bottle their own olive oil. Good Chianti wine is produced outside these areas, but may not use "Classico". An *enoteca* is a great place to do tastings of different wineries. However, don't miss the chance to visit a winery, whether a small farm or a grand castle.

🚗DRIVING TOURS

The three excursions described below all follow **Via Chiantigiana** (SR222). Visitors doing a rapid tour of Tuscany, including Florence and Siena, are advised to travel from one city to the other along this road, which provides wonderful views of the local forests and vineyards.

- ♿ **Michelin Map:** Michelin Atlas p 37 and Map 563–L 15, 16 and Map 735 Fold 14–15.
- 🛈 **Info:** Via Ferruccio 40, Castellina in Chianti, ✆0577 74 13 92. Piazza Matteotti 10, Greve in Chianti, ✆055 85 46 299. Piazza del Castello, Radda in Chianti, ✆0577 73 84 94.
- ▷ **Location:** Chianti is the region between Florence and Siena. It is traversed from N to S by S222, known as the Via Chiantigiana.
- 🕐 **Timing:** Expect to spend one day per tour (*below*).

The highway between Florence and Siena, known as the Raccordo, is particularly attractive in the Pesa and Staggia valleys.

FROM THE PESA VALLEY TO THE GREVE VALLEY

About 100km/62mi. ♿*Route in red on regional (pp288–289) and local (p333) maps.*

Florence★★★ ♿*See FLORENCE.*

▷ From Florence take Via Senese going to Galluzzo.

Certosa del Galluzzo★★
♿*See THE OUTSKIRTS OF FLORENCE.*

▷ Take R2 to Siena rather than the superstrada or the Raccordo autostradale Firenze–Siena. South of Tavarnuzze, pass under the motorway. After about 1.5km/1mi turn right to Sant'Andrea in Percussina, crossing the River Greve.

The first few miles are through forest, but the road emerges to the first glimpses of the vineyards. In the hamlet of **Sant'Andrea in Percussina** *(left)* is the **Albergaccio di Niccolò**

Vineyards near Badia a Passignano

© Alexmi156/iStock

Machiavelli, now a restaurant, where **Machiavelli** lived after being banished from Florence by the Medici and where he wrote *The Prince* in 1513. He was not allowed to return to Florence until 1526, one year before his death.

San Casciano in Val di Pesa

Set on a hilltop, between the valleys of the Greve and the Pesa, some of the 14C–16C town walls remain. From **Piazza Orazio Pierozzi** *(Via Roma at Via 4 Novembre)*, Via Morrocchesi leads to the Romanesque-Gothic Chiesa della Misericordia, with interesting works by 14C–15C Tuscan artists. Santa Maria del Gesù (Via Roma) contains the **Museo di Arte Sacra** (Museum of Sacred Art). Piazza della Repubblica, a large park, is flanked by fortification ruins and a 14C tower. The terrace affords a view over the Pesa Valley. Some good Chianti Classico wineries from San Casciano are Solatione, Savadonica and Poggiopiano.

▶ The road (SR2) descends into the Pesa Valley and follows the the Tavarnuzze River. Before reaching Sambuca, turn left towards Badia a Passignano.

Badia a Passignano★★

🕐 *Only visitable on Sun afternoons or by appointment.* 💶 *Free, donation suggested.* 📞 *055 80 71 171 or Tavarnelle Val di Pesa tourist office* 📞 *055 80 77 832.*

This splendid **abbey** stands on the top of a gentle rise planted with vines and cypress trees. **St Giovanni Gualberto** founded Passignano in 1049, died there in 1073 and is buried in the abbey.

Chianti League

In 1384, Florence set up the Chianti League, a military alliance to counter the territorial expansionist policies of Siena. The League, which included the three territories (*terzieri*) of Castellina, Gaiole and Radda, were administered by a magistrate (*podestà*), originally based in Castellina. In 1415 his offices were moved to Radda. In the middle of the 16C, when the Republic of Siena was annexed to the Grand Duchy of Tuscany, the League ceased to have any purpose.

Upon its formation, the League took as its emblem a black rooster (*gallo nero*), which was depicted later in Giorgio Vasari's ceiling painting in the Salone dei Cinquecento in the Palazzo Vecchio in Florence. The famous black rooster is now used by the Chianti Classico wine consortium of Tuscany as a symbol of Chianti produced within the nine communities.

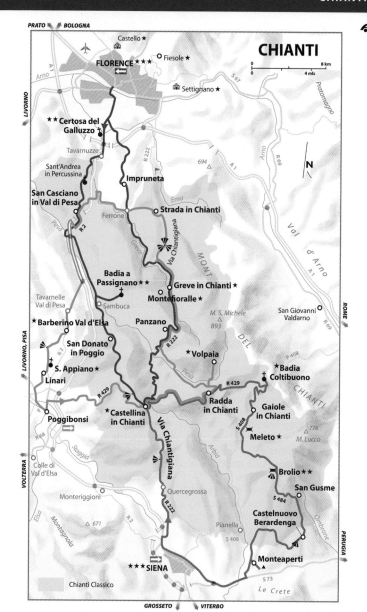

The façade is surmounted by a 13C marble statue of St Michael the Archangel. The interior is decorated with 16C paintings by Domenico Cresti, who is called Il Passignano.

▶ The road towards the Pesa Valley crosses a landscape of coppices, olive groves, vineyards and fields of grain.

In the valley the road skirts the old village of Sambuca before returning to the hilltops.

San Donato in Poggio

🅿 *Park at the rear of the abbey.*
This medieval hilltop village was once part of an old castle. In the central square is the Palazzo Malaspina and

333

a Renaissance cistern. The 12C **Parish Church of San Donato** contains the nave with pitched roof, and aisles ending in three apsidal chapels, with semicircular roofs. The crenellations of the bell tower betray its defensive purpose. The road to Castellina crosses vast stretches of countryside where the views are interrupted by copses and yellow broom. From a bare hilltop (*7km/4mi from San Donato*) there is an extensive view (*right*) over the Elsa Valley and beyond.

Castellina in Chianti★

See p335.

The road twists and turns as it descends into the Pesa Valley.

Panzano (*left*) is visible from some considerable distance because its church and bell tower stand on a rise. The next stretch of Via Chiantigiana passes through a delightful succession of olive groves, vineyards, copses and rows of cypress trees. Some good Chianti Classico wines from Castellina are Quattro Strade, Tenuta Canale, Casafrassi and Bartali. Several castles (Brolio, Meleto) have restaurants and wineries.

Greve in Chianti★

The village is situated in the valley of the River Greve. Its centre, attractive Piazza Matteotti, is bordered by irregularly shaped porticoes supporting flower-decked terraces and by the tiny Church of Santa Croce (rebuilt 19C), also preceded by a portico. The Renaissance interior (north side) has is a triptych (*left*) of the Madonna and Child with Saints and (*right*) a small Annunciation by Bicci di Lorenzo. Some good Chianti Classico wines from Greve are Casaloste, Solatio, Panzanello, Casasola and Villa Cafaggio.

The road continues north beside the Greve, through fairly wild countryside. In Le Bolle bear left to Ferrone (the major road S222 bears off right to Florence). North of Ferrone the road climbs up to Impruneta, lined with many trees – cypress, pine and oak.

Montefioralle★

Make a detour (*2km/1.2mi W*) to this delightful fortified hilltop village. Its unique circular street is lined with houses, medieval towers and the picturesque Gothic church of Santo Stefano. The navigator and explorer **Amerigo Vespucci**, who gave his name to America, was born in the Vespucci House recognisable by the V on the front.

It continues north along long the Greve River through a relatively wild stretch, then crosses the river, where a road (*left*) leads to Florence.

Impruneta

Impruneta is a pretty little town renowned for the manufacture of high-quality bricks, tiles and decorative terracotta ware. Many believe that Brunelleschi ordered Impruneta tiles for the roof of Florence Cathedral.

The centre of town is Piazza Buondelmonti, near which several of Impruneta's old brickworks are located.

Santa Maria dell'Impruneta★

Piazza Buondelmonti. The basilican church has a Renaissance portico with five arches opening into the huge main square. Little has survived from the Romanesque period except the 13C bell tower. Inside is a nave and on either side of the choir are two private **chapels★★** designed by Michelozzo to resemble the one in Santissima Annunziata in Florence (1456). The south chapel is decorated with glazed ceramics by the della Robbias; the north chapel contains the famous portrait of the Virgin, which is thought to date from the 13C. The building was bombed in 1944 (*photographs in the Baptistery*) and was reconstructed using sections that were not destroyed.

Museo del Tesoro

Next to Santa Maria dell'Impruneta.
Open Sat–Sun 9am–1pm, 4–7pm (Nov–Mar 3–6pm). Pro Loco Impruneta tourist office 055 23 13 729.

The Treasury contains the result of many centuries of devotion in the basilica to the Virgin Mary of Impruneta and the generosity of eminent Florentine families including the Medici: gold- and silverware, reliquaries, church plate, numerous ex-votos dating from the 14C–19C and a fine collection of illuminated liturgical works (14C–16C).

THE HEART OF THE CHIANTI LEAGUE

From Poggibonsi (or San Gimignano): about 100km/62mi. ⏱ *Route in green on regional (pp288–289) and local (p333) maps.*

Poggibonsi

This is a dynamic, modern town; its old town, however, is set slightly above the valley. In Piazza Cavour stands the small **Palazzo Pretorio**, decorated with coats of arms, dominated by a crenellated Gothic tower and surrounded by more recent buildings.

▷ Pass through the industrial estate to reach the hills on the other side of the valley. Here the road gradually climbs the Chianti uplands, giving way to frequent bends in the road until reaching the crest, where it runs through stretches of woodland. There are a few magnificent views of the hills below, particularly in the last stretch before Castellina.

Castellina in Chianti★

At the end of the 13C the town was on the border between the territories of Florence and Siena. It often changed hands because of its strategic position between the river valleys of the Elsa, Pesa and Arbia.

At the entrance to the town, opposite the neo-Romanesque Church of **San Salvatore**, is the start of an unusual street, **Via delle Volte★**, which is vaulted along almost its entire length. It skirts the interior of the town walls. From the 16C onwards, when Tuscany was unified and became the Grand Duchy of the Medici, openings were made to give views of the wooded hillsides in the Chianti area.

▷ At the end of the vaulted street, turn back along Via Ferruccio.

The impressive **Palazzo Ugolino** (*no 26*) has wine cellars dating from the Renaissance period. Opposite this *palazzo*, a narrow street climbs to the Rocca, the crenellated 15C castle; on the ground floor are two glass cabinets containing artefacts discovered in Poggino, the Etruscan graveyard in Fonteruoli (6C). From the second storey there is a panoramic view.

Radda in Chianti

An original member of the Chianti League, this medieval village became the main town in the League in 1415. It has retained one side of its town walls and its 15C town hall, which is decorated inside the double-arched porch with a fresco painted by the Florentine School.

Volpaia★

6km/3.7mi to the north, along a scenic winding road, is this beautiful medieval fortified village with remains of its wall. On the square stands a tower. This romantic spot is perfect to dally, in a village restaurant or bar.

▷ On SR222 NW of Radda along the upper valley of the Pesa, or take the alternative dirt road to reach Panzano.

From Panzano to Greve

⏱ *See first tour directions, opposite.*

▷ From Greve continue N on S222.

The area between Greve and Strada contains some of the most attractive scenery in the Chianti region. The magnificent road follows the crest of the hills in several places, providing an extensive **panoramic view★★** of the vineyards.

Strada in Chianti

In the past, travellers between Florence and the Chianti district would have had to pass through this village, hence its name (*strada* means road). All that the modern village has retained of its past is the Romanesque church of San Cristoforo.

▷ Take the road W Via Ferrone.

San Casciano in Val di Pesa
See p332.

Take the motorway (superstrada) S towards Siena. As the road runs downhill, there is a fine view over the Pesa Valley. Turn right off the motorway at the Tavarnelle exit. S of Tavarnelle there is a view (*right*) over the Colli Fiorentini and (*left*) of the Pesa Valley.

Barberino Val d'Elsa★
Barberino has now extended beyond the limits of the fortified hilltop village. The Porta Senese, the only gate in the 13C and 14C fortifications, leads into the main street, Via Francesco da Barberino. Further on is Piazza Barberini, flanked (*right*) by the Palazzo Pretorio. Beside it rises the simple east end of the church. From the church door there is an admirable view of the Pesa Valley.

On the outskirts of Barberino turn right off R2 to Sant'Appiano.

The road to this hamlet provides some outstanding **views★★** of the Colli Fiorentini, clothed in vineyards and olive groves.

Sant'Appiano★
Open Sat–Sun 3–6.30pm. €1.50. 055 80 52 290.
This pre-Romanesque church (10C–11C) has retained its original apse and part of the north aisle; its bell tower collapsed in 1171. The remainder of the church was rebuilt in the late 12C. In front of the façade are four sandstone pillars, the remains of a separate octagonal Baptistery that was demolished by an earthquake in the early 19C. Beside the church (*right*) is a set of buildings enclosing picturesque little cloisters which are reached via the Antiquarium at the rear of the building. After winding its way through woodland, the road provides a view of a promontory (*right*), crowned by the village of **Linari**.

Take the S429 to return to Poggibonsi.

SIENA TO THE CHIANTI HILLS
About 100km/62mi.
Route in purple on regional (pp288–p289) and local (p331) maps.

Siena *See SIENA.*

Between Siena and Castellina, the R222 passes through woods and very few vineyards. South of Quercegrossa, the road follows the contours of the land; then climbs, providing magnificent **views★★** (*left*) over the Staggia Valley.

Castellina in Chianti★
See p335.

Radda in Chianti
See p335.
East of Radda, a well-tended landscape of neat vineyards alternates with a succession of dark wooded hills.

At the junction of five roads follow Badia Coltibuono signs (900m/0.5mi).

Badia Coltibuono★
This prosperous abbey was built in the 11C. It was, however, vacated by its monks in 1810, under a Napoleonic edict, and turned into a farm.
The Romanesque church is devoid of aisles and surmounted by a crenellated bell tower; it and the neighbouring buildings together give some idea of past grandeur. From the east end of the church there is a view over the middle reaches of the Arno to the wooded uplands of Pratomagno. The winding road to Gaiole (*5km/3mi*) is flanked by dense woodland.

Gaiole in Chianti
This village is mainly a modern holiday resort in a small valley surrounded by vine-clad hillsides.

Take S408 south; after 2km/1mi turn left towards Meleto; after 400m/433yd turn right into a dirt track (700m/758yd).

Castello di Meleto★

This fine 12C quadrangular medieval castle has round towers at the corners. Badly damaged during numerous attacks over the centuries, it was restored and converted to a residence in the 18C. (*Winery, restaurant, rooms; www.castellomeleto.it.*)

▷ S and E by SP408 and SP484. The Brolio district abounds in vines and olive trees.

Castello di Brolio★★

1km/0.5mi from the entrance to the castle door. 🕐*Gardens: open daily 10am–6pm (27 Oct–mid Mar 4pm); ⌐€5 (includes a tasting of one wine). Guided tours with tastings (2hrs) of the castle, wine-making facilities and cellars at 10.30am by reservation; ⌐€30.* 📞*0577 73 02 80 / 0577 73 02 20. www.ricasoli.it.*

This huge crenellated **castle** has belonged to the Ricasoli family since the 11C. Its pentagonal fortifications include the first bastions built in Italy, probably designed by **Giuliano da Sangallo**. Inside the castle walls is access to the gardens and the parapet walk. The castle, which is still inhabited, underwent extensive 19C restoration. Beside it the Chapel of St Jacopo houses the Ricasoli family tomb in the crypt. From the top of the walls (*south*) a magnificent **view★★★** extends over the Arbia Valley. Beyond the towers of Siena is the high peak of Monte Amiata; to the west, downhill, is the castle winery.

▷ Return by car to the valley following a dirt track (4km/2.5mi) that loops through the Brolio vineyards with the castle on the right.

There are some fine views downhill over the castle.

▷ Beyond the estate farm buildings, turn right into S484, which returns past the entrance to the estate.

Between Brolio and San Gusme (*7km/4mi*) the country is still fairly wooded, except near San Gusme where it becomes more open.

▷ Turn left off S484 into a narrow road (700m/758yd to the village).

San Gusme

This stone-built farming village has retained its medieval character with outer walls, gateways and narrow streets. The village offers a lovely view over the southern part of the province of Siena with Monte Amiata in the background. The same view can be enjoyed from Castelnuovo Berardenga.

Castelnuovo Berardenga

This town in the most southerly of the nine Chianti Classico zones stands on a hilltop above the upper reaches of the River Ombrone. The road which skirts the village turns south towards the majestic 19C **Villa Chigi★**, built on medieval foundations and surrounded by a beautiful park full of very old trees which can first be seen from the San Gusme road. Next to a well-proportioned square with a central fountain is the **Church of Santi Giusto e Clemente** with a neo-Classical portico and a small bell tower and inside *Madonna and Child with Angels* by **Giovanni di Paolo** (1426). The Fèlsina winery (*www.felsina.it*), off Via della Regnaia del Chianti is an easy walk from the north edge of town, and makes one of the area's best Chianti Classicos and excellent olive oil. The small Miscianello winery (*www.miscianello.it*) on a narrow pebbled road through the woods makes a wonderful setting (**view** of Siena). It merits a visit for its Chianti Classico, and for its Rosso Toscana made according to the former Chianti formula of adding white grapes (10 percent Trebbiano and Malvasia). Other good Castelnuovo Berardenga Chianti Classicos to try are Il Castagno and Campacci.

On the outskirts of Castelnuovo, there is a breathtaking **view★★** over the gently rolling, bare hills of the Sienese countryside. West of town (*SS326*) Acqua Borra has an *enoteca* in a stone building that looks like one side is emerging from the earth (or sliding into it), where the springs ooze mud for therapeutic baths.

▶ After 1.5km/1mi turn right to Pianella (not left to Montaperti as this road is unsurfaced). At the next junction (beyond a stud farm) turn left into the road to Siena.

Monteaperti (also Montaperti)

Near this village on 4 September 1260 the famous battle took place in which the Ghibellines of Siena defeated the Guelfs of Florence. A memorial to the battle, a small pyramid flanked by cypress trees, stands on a prominence. On the outskirts of the village opposite the war memorial turn left into a narrow dirt track (*1.5km/1mi*).

▶ Take S73 west to return to Siena.

ADDRESSES

🛏️STAY

😴🛏️ **I Fagiolari** – *Via Case Sparse 25, 2.5 km/0.8mi SW of Panzano in Chianti along the SP 118.* ☎*055 85 23 51. www. fagiolari.it. 5 rooms.* Tucked away amid olive trees and lavender bushes, here the word "relaxation" takes on special significance. Terracotta floors, exposed wood beams and rustic furniture give the locale a special family atmosphere. Cooking and ceramic decoration courses available.

😴🛏️🛏️ **Albergo Bellavista** – *Via della Croce 2, Impruneta.* ☎*055 20 11 083. www.bellavistaimpruneta.it.* ♿. *12 rooms. Restaurant.* Family-run hotel on the piazza in Impruneta, service attracts tourists and business clientele. Breakfast on terrace.

😴🛏️🛏️ **Il Colombaio** – *Via Chiantigiana 29, 1km/0.6mi N of Castellina in Chianti on S222.* ☎*0577 74 04 44. www.albergo ilcolombaio.it. 15 rooms.* Stone farmhouse a short walk from Castellina. The rooms have iron bedsteads, solid wood furniture and spacious bathrooms.

😴🛏️🛏️ **Giovanni da Verrazzano** – *Piazza G. Matteotti 28, Greve in Chianti.* ☎*055 85 31 89. www.albergoverrazzano. it. 10 rooms.* Charming hotel on Greve's celebrated square, frequented by tourists

and business clientele. Rooms with a view of the piazza or with small terrace.

😴🛏️🛏️ **Podere Terreno** – *Località Volpaia 21, 5.5km/3mi N of Radda in Chianti; 3km/2mi towards Florence and then turn right.* ☎*0577 05 77 19. www. podereterreno.it. 5 rooms.* ☕. This 16C farmhouse has terracotta tiles, chestnut beams and country furniture. There is a convivial atmosphere round the large dinner table. Reading room.

😴🛏️🛏️🛏️ **Agriturismo Castel-vecchi** – *Località Castelvecchi, 6km/4mi N of Radda in Chianti, towards Volpaia.* ☎*0577 73 80 50. www.castelvecchi.com.* 🏊. *8 rooms.* ☕. This 18C winery offers well-appointed rooms. The swimming pool overlooks the wooded hills and vineyards.

😴🛏️🛏️🛏️ **Palazzo Squarcialupi** – *Via Ferrucio 22, Castellina in Chianti.* ☎*0577 74 11 86. www.squarcialupirelaxinchianti. com.* 🏊 🅿 ♿. *17 rooms.* A restored 14C *palazzo* in a medieval village with comfortable, spacious rooms.

😴🛏️🛏️🛏️ **Villa di Sotto** – *Via Santa Caterina 30, località Villa a Sesta, Castelnuovo Berardenga.* ☎*347 93 27 090. www.villadisotto.it.* 🏊. *8 rooms, 11 apt. Restaurant* 😴🛏️. Explore Chianti's southernmost area. Rooms overlook vineyards and olive groves. Run by efficient, enthusiastic owners.

😴🛏️🛏️🛏️ **Villa Il Poggiale** – *Via Empolese 69, San Casciano in Val di Pesa, 2km/0.6mi NW in the direction of Cerbaia-Empoli.* ☎*055 82 83 11. www. villailpoggiale.it. Restaurant* 😴🛏️🛏️🛏️. 🅿 🏊. *20 rooms.* Set in a harmonious corner of Tuscany, this magnificent historic villa surround by olive groves was restored with taste and refinement.

😴🛏️🛏️🛏️ **Villa Le Barone** – *Via San Leonino 19, Panzano in Chianti.* ☎*055 85 26 21. www.villalebarone.com.* 🏊. *28 rooms. Restaurant* 😴🛏️🛏️🛏️. One villa belonged to the della Robbia family on this ancient country estate, set amidst olive trees and vineyards. This distinctive classy place produces its own Chianti Classico.

🍴EAT

😴 **Il Carlino d'Oro** – *Località San Regolo 33, Gaiole in Chianti.* ☎*0577 74 71 36. Open lunchtime.* Although in a bland building in Gaiole, the ambience and cuisine are good.

⊖⊜ **Antica Trattoria La Torre** – *Piazza del Comune 15, Castellina in Chianti. ☎0577 74 02 36. www.anticatrattoria latorre.com. Closed Thu. Reservations suggested.* This classic-style inn is enlarged in summer by its veranda. Tuscan cuisine, attentive service.

⊖⊜ **Da Padellina** – *Corso del Popolo 54, 50027 Strada in Chianti, 8km/4.9mi SE of Impruneta. ☎055 85 83 88. Closed Thu. Reservations advised.* Serves local Chianti dishes, and doubles as the Club Dante Alighieri, offering poetry readings of Dante's works.

⊖⊜ **Antica Trattoria La Toppa** – *Via del Giglio 41, San Donato in Poggio. ☎055 80 72 900. anticatrattorialatoppa. business.site. Closed Mon.* In the heart of a romantic medieval hamlet, this typical Tuscan trattoria celebrates regional cuisine in all its glory. Highlights on the menu include soups and fresh pasta dishes. In summer, meals are served outdoors on the attractive street.

⊖⊜⊜ **Badia a Coltibuono** – *Località Coltibuono, Gaiole in Chianti. ☎0577 74 90 31. ristorante.coltibuono.com. Closed 8 Jan–15 Mar.* Set in the old Abbey of Coltibuono, Tuscan dishes are prepared in the style of Lorenzo the Magnificent. Meals are served on the terrace with a superb view of the hills.

⊖⊜⊜ **Osteria Le Panzanelle** – *Località Lucarelli 29, 7km/4.3mi NW of Radda in Chianti, towards Panzano. ☎0577 73 35 11. www.lepanzanelle.it. Closed Mon.* This rural trattoria has a simple, informal ambience. It serves generous portions of delicious regional cuisine, including homemade pasta and excellent meat.

⊖⊜⊜ **La Terrazza** – *Piazza Matteotti 22, Greve in Chianti. ☎055 85 33 08. www. osterialaterrazza.com. Closed Tue and Feb. Reservations suggested.* A pleasant inn with terrace facing the piazza. Tuscan specialities. *pappardelle, taglierini, ravioli*: all pasta is home-made and delicious.

⊖⊜⊜⊜ **L'Asinello** – *Via Nuova 6, località Villa a Sesta, 6km/4mi N of Castelnuovo Berardenga. ☎055 35 92 79. www.asinelloristorante.it. Open Wed–Sat dinnertime and Sun lunchtime. Reservations recommended.* This former stable has been converted into a quiet, elegant restaurant by a friendly young couple. The chef champions traditional cuisine which is minimalist in its choice of flavours and made from just a few well-balanced ingredients. A real culinary gem!

WINE TOURS AND ENOTECHE

Barone Ricasoli – *Via Cantine del Castello di Brolio, 10km/7mi S of Gaiole in Chianti towards Siena. ☎0577 73 02 20. www.ricasoli.it.* The Ricasoli family, which has belonged to the nobility since 1141, was the first to define "Chianti Classico". In 1997 Francesco Ricasoli created "Castello di Brolio", which is made with the best Sangiovese grapes.

Castello di Querceto – *Via François 2, località Dudda, 14km/9mi W of Greve in Chianti. ☎055 85 921. www.castellodiquerceto.it. Enoteca open Mon–Sat. Wine tours by reservation.* This crenellated castle, which has been owned by a French family for over 100 years, is superbly located in the centre of the Chianti district. This beautiful estate winery even has its attendant peacocks.

Castello di Verrazzano – *Via Citille 32A, località Greti, Greve in Chianti. ☎055 85 42 43. www.verrazzano.com. Wine tours by reservation.* This was the birthplace of the famous explorer Verrazzano. Since 1960 this estate has belonged to the Cappellini family who produce several Sangiovese wines in this gorgeous setting.

Enoteca Falorni – *Piazza delle Cantine 6, Greve in Chianti. ☎055 85 46 404. www. enotecafalorni.it. Closed Tue–Wed.* Wine lovers can't miss this marvellous locale, which offers 140 labels.

Fèlsina – *Via del Chianti 101, Castelnuovo Berardenga. ☎0577 15 23 789. www. felsina.it.* This *enoteca* on the lovely estate winery is a short walk from the town centre along a cypress-lined drive. Featured are Fèlsina; high-quality Chianti Classico; olive oil and other wines produced by the estate.

Miscianello – *Ponte a Bozzone, Castelnuovo Berardenga. ☎335 65 71 640. www.miscianello.it.* This small winery, on a narrow pebbled road through the woods, merits the drive for the setting (view of Siena), the good Chianti Classico, and for its tenacity in clinging to the old formula of adding white grapes (10 percent Trebbiano and Malvasia) to Rosso Toscana. The owners' collaborators (translated) are Mr Cuddles, Mr Cat and Mr Merlin.

San Donatino – *Località San Donatino 20, Castellina in Chianti. ☎0577 74 03 18. www.sandonatino.com.* Léo Ferré's last residence is rich in souvenirs and the personality of his wife Maria Cristina Diaz. This winery makes good olive oil.

San Gimignano★★★
and Around

Rising up from the Val d'Elsa like a city of skyscrapers, San Gimignano has all the charm of a small medieval town. Its 14 grey stone ancient towers and mainly brick structures have been amazingly well preserved. The town's historic centre was declared a UN World Heritage Site. Vernaccia di San Gimignano, the local white wine that dates from the 13C, was described by Michelangelo Buonarroti the Younger as the wine that "kisses, licks, bites, pinches and stings".

▶ **Population:** 7,760.

Michelin Map: Michelin Atlas p 37 and Map 563 – I 15 or Map 735 Fold 14.

Info: Piazza Duomo 1. ℰ0577 94 00 08. www.sangimignano.com.

Location: Take the north–south motorway S towards Siena from Florence; in Poggibonsi turn W and follow the signs to San Gimignano (13km/8mi from Poggibonsi).

Parking: Public car parks are available on the outskirts of the town, as parking within the walls is restricted to residents of the town and certain hotels.

Don't Miss: Views of the city from the medieval Torre Grossa and fresco cycles by Benozzo Gozzoli in Sant'Agostino and by Bartolo di Fredi in the Collegiata di Santa Maria Assunta.

A BIT OF HISTORY

Little is known about the origins of San Gimignano, a bishop who lived in Modena in the 4C, and the reasons that the town took his name. The town became a free commune in the mid-12C and continued to prosper for 200 years, although it did not escape the rivalry between the Guelf and Ghibelline factions, which were represented in the town by the Ardinghelli and Salvucci families, respectively.

The town supported the Pope and rallied to the side of Florence in her wars with Pisa, Siena, Pistoia, Arezzo, Volterra, etc. In 1353 the town took an oath of allegiance binding it to Florence. A number of great painters from Siena and, later, Florence, worked in San Gimignano, where they produced great masterpieces.

Piazza della Cisterna

© bluejayphoto/iStock

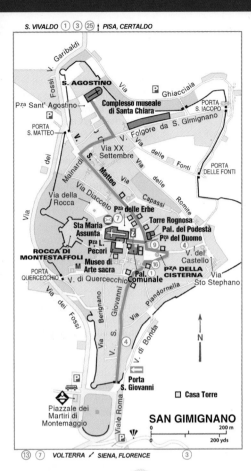

WHERE TO STAY

Agriturismo Il **Casale** del Cotone	①
Agriturismo Cesani . .	③
Bel Soggiorno	④
Casa de' Potenti	⑦
Hotel Leon Bianco . . .	⑨
Hotel Le Volpaie	⑬
La Cisterna	⑯
Poderi Arcangelo	㉕

WHERE TO EAT

Dulcis in Fundo	①
Da Pode	③
Osteria del Carcere . .	④
Osteria del Vicario . . .	⑦

👣 WALKING TOUR

This walking tour follows the shopping street Via San Giovanni and Via San Matteo, lined with tower-houses.

Porta San Giovanni

The massive 13C **San Giovanni Gate** (*south*) with its barbican and Sienese arch, opens into the picturesque street (Via San Giovanni) which leads up past medieval houses to the central square.

Piazza della Cisterna★★

Piazza della Cisterna is an irregularly shaped area paved, in medieval style, with bricks forming a herringbone pattern. The **well** (*cisterna*) has occupied the centre of the square since the 13C.

Around it are austere 13C–14C buildings, some with towers. The 13C **Salvestrini House** (*south side*) is now a hotel. At the entrance to Via del Castello (*east*) is the 14C **Palazzo Tortoli** which has two rows of Gothic twin windows.

Almost opposite is the **Devil's Tower** (*Torre del Diavolo*). The northwest corner of the square, which leads to Piazza del Duomo, is dominated by the two **Ardinghelli Towers** named after the most influential Guelf family.

Piazza del Duomo★★

The austere collegiate church, very old mansions (*palazzi*) and seven towers provide a majestic setting.

👁 **San Gimignano Pass** (€13), *valid for 2 days, gives unlimited access to Collegiata di Santa Maria Assunta, Museo di*

341

Arte Sacra and San Gimignano's municipal museums (Palazzo Comunale – Museo Civico, Complesso museale di Santa Chiara, Chiesa di San Lorenzo in Ponte).

Collegiata di Santa Maria Assunta

Open Apr–Oct Mon–Fri 10am–7pm, Sat 10am–5pm, Sun and hols 12.30–7pm; rest of the year Mon–Sat 10am–4.30pm, Sun and hols 12.30–4.30pm. Closed 1, 16–31 Jan, 12 Mar, 3rd Sun in Jun, 1st Sun in Aug, 16–30 Nov, 25 Dec. €4 (includes Cappella di Santa Fina); €6 combined ticket with the Museo di Arte Sacra. 0577 28 63 00. www.sangimignano.com.

The cathedral of St Mary of the Assumption is a 12C Romanesque building that was extended in the 15C by Giuliano da Maiano. The west front underwent major 19C restoration. The interior is covered in frescoes.

On the rear of the façade on the lower section of the wall (*coin box for lighting*) the Florentine artist Benozzo Gozzoli depicted the Martyrdom of St Sebastian (1465) flanked by two painted wooden statues representing the Virgin Mary and the Angel of the Annunciation carved c. 1420 by the Sienese sculptor Jacopo della Quercia. Above them Sienese artist Taddeo di Bartolo painted a Last Judgement (1393).

The north aisle was covered (second half-14C) with a cycle of **frescoes★** illustrating the major stories from the Old Testament by the Sienese artist, Bartolo di Fredi.

Influenced by Simone Martini and the Lorenzetti brothers, the artist illustrated the following scenes: top, the Creation of the World, the Creation of Man, Adam in the Garden of Eden, the Creation of Eve and the Forbidden Fruit. On the middle level, after two scenes which are no longer visible (Adam and Eve expelled from Paradise and Cain killing Abel), the Building of Noah's Ark, the Animals entering the Ark, the Departure of the Ark, Noah's Drunkenness, the Departure of Abraham and Lot, Lot taking Leave of Abraham, Joseph's Dream and Joseph being lowered into a well.

At the bottom, again beyond the first bay where the painting is now illegible (Joseph having his Brothers Arrested, and Joseph Recognised by his Brothers), there is Moses and the Brazen Serpent, Pharaoh's Army being swept away by the Red Sea, the Jews Crossing the Red Sea, Moses on Mount Sinai, Satan receiving God's permission to tempt Job, the Murder of Job's Servants and the Stealing of his Animals, the Collapse of the House of Job, Job giving Thanks to God, and Job, in his illness, being comforted by his Friends.

In the south aisle the Life of Christ is illustrated in a c. 1335–40 series of **frescoes★★** by Barna da Siena, who worked in Simone Martini's studio and painted these before those by Bartolo di Fredi. Vasari wrote that the artist died falling from scaffolding before this work was almost completed. This cycle remains an essential part of the history of Italian Gothic painting, because of its sheer size.

The paintings depict (*starting at the lunettes, top right*) the Annunciation, the Nativity, the Adoration of the Magi, the Circumcision, the Massacre of the Innocents and the Flight into Egypt; (*middle, from left to right*) starting at the great Crucifixion, they represent Jesus and the Doctors of the Law, Christ's Baptism, St Peter's Call, the Marriage in Cana, the Transfiguration, Lazarus being Raised from the Dead, and Christ's Entry into Jerusalem (two panels); (*lower level, from right to left*) the Last Supper, Judas receiving the Thirty Pieces of Silver, the Prayer on the Mount of Olives, Judas' Kiss, Jesus being brought before Caiaphas the High Priest, the Scourging, the Crown of Thorns and the Road up to Calvary, ending with the Crucifixion. On the left of this great panel are (*below*) the Deposition (*almost entirely missing*), Christ Descending into Hell (*badly damaged*), and (*above*) the Resurrection (*partly damaged*) and Pentecost.

The chapel, **Cappella di Santa Fina** (*at the end of the south aisle*) is dedicated to the local saint, Serafina di Ciardi, a paralysed girl who died in 1254 at the age of 15. On the day of her death, all the bells

Tower-houses
(Case Torri)

The main buildings in town were constructed in the 12C and 13C, when San Gimignano was a free borough. In the Middle Ages there were 70 towers but the number had dropped to 25 by the end of the 16C. Today 14 survive. Half of these, including the Torre Grossa (the tallest at 54m/177ft, built over the course of 11 years) and the Torre della Rognosa (one of the oldest, constructed around 1200) are located around the main square, Piazza del Duomo.

Torre Rognosa (left) and Torre Grossa, San Gimignano

These feudal towers, designed like castle keeps, were built in many Italian towns by the great families during the struggle for supremacy between the **Guelfs** and **Ghibellines** and, later, between local tyrants. Two of the main rival families in San Gimignano were the Ardinghelli (Guelf) and Salvucci (Ghibelline). The latter's twin towers (*torri gemelle*) are iconic.

For reasons of prestige the nobility built as tall as they could. The holes visible in their walls are said to have been used as supports for a network of footbridges linking the houses of allied families who could gather together quickly in times of danger.

A more prosaic explanation is that the towers are a legacy of the importance of San Gimignano as a major textile and saffron centre. The secret saffron yellow dye is produced from precious saffron, gathered from the three red stigma (threads) from the *crocus attivus* flower. To fix the colour, the cloth had to be kept away from dust and sunshine. A higher price could be commanded for longer pieces of cloth, which also needed space to dry. The rich cloth-producers built tall towers, then made holes in the walls to support drying rods and the staircases attached to the exterior to maximise the use of interior space.

San Gimignano tower-houses

began ringing and her bed was covered with flowers, as were the tops of the towers in the town.

In 1468 the townspeople commissioned Giuliano da Maiano to build this chapel in her honour. This elegant chapel with the harmonious marble and alabaster **altar★** with fine carvings and gold ornamentation was made by Giuliano's nephew, Benedetto. In 1475, Domenico Ghirlandaio painted some remarkable **frescoes★** depicting the life of the saint; these paintings exhibit a less refined elegance than his masterpiece in Santa Maria Novella in Florence, which he painted a few years later.

Palazzo Comunale (or del Popolo) – Museo Civico★

Open daily Apr–Sept 10am–7.30pm; Oct–Mar 11am–5.30pm. Closed 25 Dec. €9 (includes all municipal museums, valid for 2 days). 0577 28 63 00. www.sangimignanomusei.it.

This 13C–14C Palazzo Comunale, also called the People's Palace or the Magistrate's Palace, is surmounted by a tower (54m/176ft) (Torre Grossa). The small inner courtyard is on two levels, flanked by a portico, with an octagonal well.

The **Museo Civico★** occupies the upper floors. The Grand Council Chamber, where Dante made a speech in 1300, overlooks Piazza del Duomo and is decorated with frescoes by the 14C Sienese School representing hunting scenes and Charles of Anjou, King of Naples. In 1317 Lippo Memmi, the Sienese primitive, painted a masterpiece, **Maestà★**, restored c. 1467 by Benozzo Gozzoli.

The top of **Torre Grossa** (*staircase, 200 steps*) affords an unusual **view★★** of the towers, rooftops and countryside. On the second floor, a small room has frescoes depicting married life. The other rooms (Pinacoteca) display paintings, most by 12C–15C Florentine and Sienese schools. The finest exhibit is an **Annunciation** by Filippino Lippi in the form of two rondels (*tondi*). Also notable are two polyptychs by Taddeo di Bartolo (*Madonna and Child* and *Scenes from the Life of St Gimignano*).

Palazzo del Podestà

The 13C building Piazza del Duomo opens onto the square through a huge porch (*loggia*) with stone benches along each side, under a wide arch. It is surmounted by the mighty **Rognosa Tower** (51m/166ft high). To the left the 13C Chigi Palace has its own tower beside it.

Piazza Luigi Pecori

Access via a vaulted passageway to the left of the collegiate church.

One side of this charming little square is lined by a portico, called the **Baptistery loggia**; the remains of the 14C cloisters are where Domenico Ghirlandaio painted a harmonious Annunciation fresco in 1482. To the left of the vaulted passageway a 13C palace houses the Museum of Sacred Art.

Museo d'Arte Sacra

Open Apr–Oct Mon–Fri 10am–7pm, Sat 10am–5pm, Sun and hols 12.30–7pm; rest of the year Mon–Sat 10am–4.30pm, Sun and hols 12.30–4.30pm. Closed 1, 16–31 Jan, 12 Mar, 3rd Sun in Jun, 1st Sun in Aug, 16–30 Nov, 25 Dec. €3.50; €6 combined ticket with Collegiata di Santa Maria Assunta and Cappella di Santa Fina. 0577 28 63 00. www.sangimignano.com.

Highlights are an expressive marble bust by Benedetto da Maiano (c. 1493), a wooden Crucifix by Giuliano da Maiano and *The Madonna and the Rose* by Bartolomeo di Fredi.

Continue on V. S. Matteo. Turn right on Via XX Settembre.

Complesso museale di Santa Chiara

Via Folgore da San Gimignano.
Open daily Apr–Sept 10am–7.30pm; Oct–Mar 11am–5.30pm. Closed 25 Dec. €9 (includes all municipal museums, valid for 2 days). 0577 28 63 00. www.sangimignanomusei.it.

The ancient monastery houses three museums. **Museo Archeologico** has Etruscan, Roman and medieval objects. **Speziera di Santa Fina** has the apothecary collection of ceramics and glass from the ancient hospital. **Galleria d'Arte Moderna e Contemporanea** has an abstract collection, also exhibits.

Sant'Agostino

🕐*Open daily 10am–noon, 3–7pm (Nov–Mar 6pm); hours may vary.*
🕐*Closed Mon am Jan–Mar.*

At the northern end of the town, this 13C Romanesque-Gothic church has a chancel with 17 **frescoes★★**, painted 1464–1465 by Benozzo Gozzoli depicting intimate, personal details from the life of St Augustine. The most outstanding scenes are (*bottom left-hand wall*) Augustine being taken to school by St Monica, his mother; (*bottom right-hand wall*) Augustine teaching philosophy in Rome and his Departure for Milan; (*lunette*) his Funeral.

ADDITIONAL SIGHT

Rocca di Montestaffoli

This 1353 fortress has a panoramic view from its ramparts; very romantic at sunset. **Vernaccia di San Gimignano – Wine Experience** (🕐*open daily 11.30am–7.30pm; ℘0577 94 12 67; www.sangimignanomuseovernaccia.com*) is a museum dedicated to the local white wine.

EXCURSIONS

San Vivaldo★

17km/11mi NW to Montaione.

Vivaldo, a Franciscan lay brother from San Gimignano, withdrew here as a hermit c. 1300. He was found dead on 1 May 1320 beneath a chestnut tree. Franciscans established a community in the woods and constructed chapels, one with a gentle Nativity by Giovanni della Robbia, and Sacro Monte which reproduces in miniature holy places of Jerusalem and displays almost life-sized sculptures of New Testament events.

Certaldo Alto★★

11km/6.8mi N of San Gimignano.

This pleasant hill town offers a lovely stroll. Visit Giovanni Boccaccio's house (*museum*), the 13C Church of SS Jacopo e Filippo with the writer's tomb, and

Palazzo Pretorio (reconstructed 16C) with its emblems and prison with ancient graffiti of prisoners. The Church of St Thomas and Prospero has sinopias by Benozzo Gozzoli. Clever artisans' shops offer ceramics and prints.

Colle di Val d'Elsa★

3km/2mi from the Florence–Siena motorway (superstrada Firenze–Siena) on SS68 to Volterra. 🔲 *Via del Castello 33/b (Colle Alta). ℘0577 92 27 91.*

The lower town Colle Bassa is in the valley beside the River Elsa. Colle Alta, the upper town, clings to the hillside with its 16C bastioned walls and fortified gate, and has the main attractions. From Porta Vecchia (*north*) the road up to the castle (*castello*) runs south through the upper part of the town (*borgo*) beneath one of the arches of Palazzo Campana, a 16C mansion, and along the main street, Via del Castello, bordered by 16C mansions and medieval tower-houses with truncated towers.

The 17C **cathedral** has a neo-Classical façade, a robust quadrangular bell tower and Baroque interior. The Bishop's Palace (opposite) is flanked by (*right*) the Palazzo Renieri and the former town hall (13C).

Beside the bell tower stands the 14C Palazzo Pretorio, decorated with coats of arms; it now houses the **Museo Archeologico Bianchi Bandinelli** (👁*Temporarily closed for restoration at the time of publication; ℘0577 92 29 54; www.museocolle.it*), with interesting Etruscan collections. Next is Palazzo Giusti, the Old Seminary (17C). From the southwest corner of the square a strange 14C–15C street, Via delle Volte, leads down under the houses; it is arched-over for its entire length (*110m/120yd*).

Via del Castello

Access from Piazza del Duomo.

This **street** contains the **Palazzo dei Priori** (15C) and the tower-house reputed to be the birthplace of **Arnolfo di Cambio** (c. 1245–1302), the architect and sculptor who designed Florence Cathedral. The nearest bastion affords an extensive view over Colle Bassa, the Sienese Hills, the Chianti region and the countryside.

Museo del Cristallo

Via dei Fossi 8/A, Colle Bassa. 🕐*Open Tue–Sun 10am–noon, 4–7.30pm.* 💶*€3.* 📞*0577 92 41 35.* Glass and crystal museum recounts the town's major industry since the Middle Ages, once suppliers of 95 percent of Italian crystal.

Casole d'Elsa

22km/13.2mi S of San Gimignano. Guarded by ramparts with round towers this lovely town blends medieval architecture with public modern sculpture. There also is a museum of archaeology and sacred art.

ADDRESSES

🛏️STAY

🛏️🛏️ **Bel Soggiorno** – *Via San Giovanni 91.* 📞*0577 94 03 75. www.hotelbelsoggiorno.it. 21 rooms.* Near Porta San Giovanni, in the family since 1886. The restaurant features Etruscan and medieval dishes.

🛏️🛏️ **Casa de' Potenti** – *Piazza delle Erbe 10.* 📞*327 18 33 950. www.casadeipotenti.com. 9 rooms.* A 14C mansion in the centre; reasonably priced. Rooms look onto the square and have a fine view of the cathedral.

🛏️🛏️🛏️ **Agriturismo Cesani** – *Località Pancole 82/A, San Gimignano.* 📞*0577 95 50 84. www.agriturismocesani.it. 10 rooms, 1 apt.* 🏊. Two sisters make good Vernaccia and other wines and raise crocus for saffron. Pleasant guest rooms, pretty wine tasting room.

🛏️🛏️🛏️ **Agriturismo Il Casale del Cotone** – *Località Il Cotone 59, Cellole, 2.5km/1.5mi N towards Certaldo.* 📞*0577 94 32 36. www.casaledelcotone.com. 17 rooms and 2 apts.* 🏊. This isolated 18C farmhouse blends old furniture and rustic art.

🛏️🛏️🛏️ **La Cisterna** – *Piazza della Cisterna 23.* 📞*0577 94 03 28. www.hotel cisterna.it. 49 rooms.* Lovely *palazzo* on central piazza has spacious rooms, some with valley view.

🛏️🛏️🛏️ **Hotel Leon Bianco** – *Piazza della Cisterna 13.* 📞*0577 94 12 94. www.leon bianco.com. 26 rooms.* Charming 14C *palazzo*. Roof terrace, pretty patio.

🛏️🛏️🛏️ **Hotel Le Volpaie** – *Via Nuova 9, Castel San Gimignano.* 📞*0577 95 31 40. www.hotellevolpaie.it. 16 rooms.* 🏊. Excellent value, nicely decorated, with pool and garden. Situated between San Gimignano, Colle di Val d'Elsa and Volterra.

🛏️🛏️🛏️ **Poderi Arcangelo** – *Località Capezzano, San Gimignano.* 📞*0577 94 44 04. www.poderiarcangelo.it. Restaurant*🛏️🛏️. 🏊. Spacious, modern rooms furnished with flair. Sandra makes olive oil, honey and Vernaccia. Traditional cuisine. Very helpful touring advice.

🍴EAT

🛏️ **Dulcis in Fundo** – *Vicolo degli Innocenti 21.* 📞*0577 94 19 19. Closed Wed. Reservation suggested.* Some tables on the side street off Piazza della Cisterna. Traditional Tuscan cuisine.

🛏️🛏️ **Da Pode** – *Località Sovestro 63, 3km/2mi SE of San Gimignano.* 📞*0577 94 31 26. www.dapode.com. Closed Thu.* The building has retained some of the architectural features of its rural past. It serves delicious Tuscan cuisine prepared by Signora Lucia.

🛏️🛏️ **Osteria del Carcere** – *Via del Castello 13.* 📞*0577 94 19 05. Closed Wed, Thu lunch.* Near Piazza della Cisterna, the menu changes daily. Quality meat comes from the Panzano butcher in Chianti.

🛏️🛏️🛏️ **Osteria del Vicario** – *Via Rivellino 3, Certaldo Alto.* 📞*0571 66 78 09. www.osteriadelvicario.com.* Near Boccaccio's house, this restaurant has beautiful exposed brick walls, fine cuisine and a panoramic view. Decorated monks' cells for those who wish to stay over.

TAKING A BREAK

Caffè delle Erbe – *Piazza delle Erbe.* 📞*0577 94 04 78. Closed Tue.* The most elegant café in town. Tables in the square.

SHOPPING

Mezzetti Cristallerie – *Via Oberdan 13, Colle di Val d'Elsa.* 📞*0577 92 03 95. www.cristalleriemezzetti.com. Closed Sun–Mon morn.* Famous *calici degustazione*, magnificent crystal wine goblets, made by CALP, the greatest glassmakers in Italy.

Montalcino★
and Buonconvento

The hillside town of Montalcino still has part of its 13C walls and its fortress (*fortezza*) built in 1361. It was ruled by Siena for several centuries and served as a refuge for the members of the government of the Republic of Siena when their town was captured by Charles V in 1555.

Brunello is the local name for the Sangiovese grape grown here. Montalcino is known throughout the world for its excellent red wine, Brunello di Montalcino. In a 2011 competition of best wines in the world, four Brunellos (all 2006 vintage) were selected, with one ranked no 4. The wine-growing area is restricted to the communal territory of Montalcino.

 WALKING TOUR

Fortezza★★
Piazzale Fortezza. ○ *Open daily 9am–8pm (winter 6pm).* ∞€4. *℘0577 84 92 11.*
This fine 14C **fortress** has been remarkably well preserved despite its later vulnerability to artillery. The high walls, complete with a parapet walk and machicolations, form a huge pentagon in which the population could seek refuge. In the interior are the remains of a basilica and the keep (*mastio*) designed to house officials and noblemen in times of siege. There is **wine tasting** (*ground floor*) and the standard of the Republic of Siena painted by Il Sodoma (*second floor*). The **parapet walk** offers a vast panoramic **view** over the town and surrounding countryside.
As you walk through town, keep an eye out for shops with frescoes, including a pharmacy and butcher shop.

Palazzo Comunale★
The 13C building overlooking Piazza del Popolo is flanked by a 14C–15C arcaded loggia and surmounted by a tall belfry.

▶ **Population:** 5,843.
Ⓖ **Michelin Map:** Michelin Atlas p 44 and Map 563 – M 16 or Map 735 Fold 15.
🄸 **Info:** Via Costa del Municipio 1. ℘0577 84 93 31. www.prolocomontalcino.com.
▶ **Location:** Montalcino sits not far from the Via Cassia between Siena and San Quirico d'Orcia.
☺ **Don't Miss:** Brunello di Montalcino wine; 14C fortress (*Fortezza*).

Sant'Egidio
Piazza Garibaldi, behind the town hall. The church has a nave with wooden rafters and is divided by three arches. Near the entrance is a gilded 16C tabernacle.

Museo Civico e Diocesano
Via Ricasoli 31. ○ *Open Tue–Sun 10am–1pm, 2–5.40pm.* ○ *Closed Mon (except public hols), 1 Jan, 25 Dec.* ∞€4.50. ♿ *℘0577 84 60 14. www.prolocomontalcino.com.*
The **Civic and Diocesan Museum** contains prehistoric and Etruscan remains, 13C–18C ceramic ware from Montalcino, 14C–15C paintings and polychrome wooden statues by the Sienese School and a two-volume Bible and a Crucifix (both 12C) from the Abbey of Sant'Antimo.

Chiesa di Sant'Agostino
14C Romanesque-Gothic church has an elegant rose window and marble portal. The interior has 14C frescoes from the Sienese School.

Brunello di Montalcino
Wine is the town's main draw, in commerce as well as tourism. The best place for tastings is an *enoteca* (wine bar), in the Fortezza or cosy wine bars where the Brunello of various wineries and vintages can be sampled. There are over 200 producers that bottle Brunello. The historic pioneer is Biondi Santi Franco. Some especially recommended are Belpoggio, Brunelli, Campogiovanni, Cana-

Abbazia di Sant'Antimo

© Peter Zelei/iStock

licchio, Capanne Ricci, Tenuta Carlina, Casanova di Neri, Collelceto, Cupano, Fanti, Fornacella, L'Aietta, La Mannella, La Pescaia, La Poderina, La Serena, La Velona, Pecci Celestino, San Polino, Talenti, Tenuta La Torraccia, Tenuta Le Potazzine and Tenuta Vitanza.

EXCURSION

Abbazia di Sant'Antimo★★

⊙Open daily Apr–Oct 10am–7pm (Oct 6pm; Nov–Mar 10.30am–5pm. Services sung to the Gregorian chant. ☞€3/6. ℘0577 28 63 00. www.antimo.it.

The former abbey of Sant'Antimo founded in the 9C lies at the foot of the village of Castelnuovo dell'Abate and has preserved its solitude in the delightful Tuscan **landscape★** of hills planted with olive and cypress trees.

The abbey reached its peak prosperity and influence in the 12C. The **church** (12C) is particularly fine Romanesque Cistercian architecture. The Burgundian style is evident in the ambulatory with radiating chapels; on the other hand the porch and pilaster strips decorating the bell tower and various walls are typically Lombard in style.

The interior is spacious and austere. The raftered nave is separated from the rib-vaulted aisles by columns crowned with superb alabaster capitals. Note the graceful proportions of the ambulatory, the light apse with its double window, the frescoes dating from the 14C–17C, and the capitals (one is attributed to Maestro di Cabestany and depicts Daniel in the Lions' Den).

The abbey is now dedicated to spiritual retreats and prayer (**Gregorian chants**) and is run by an order of Augustinian monks founded in the 12C by St Norbert in Prémontré.

ADDRESSES

🛏STAY

⊜ **Foresteria dell'Abbazia di Sant'Antimo** – *Località Sant'Antimo 222, Castelnuovo dell'Abate. ℘0577 28 63 00. www.antimo.it. ⌁. Prices available at the house.* A step back in time to the Middle Ages. The view of the abbey and the sound of the Gregorian chants will remain in the memory. Only for a true, silent retreat.

⊜⊜⊜⊜ **Castiglion del Bosco Hotel** – *Località Castiglion del Bosco, Montalcino. ℘0577 19 13 001. www.castigliondelbosco. com.* Suites and villas, two restaurants, a cooking school and a Spa to celebrate of Italian heritage and natural beauty.

⌾/EAT

⊜⊜ **Podere Canapaccia** – *Via Cassia 2, località Canapaccia, 11km/7mi NE of Montalcino. ℘0577 83 45 47. www. poderecanapaccia.com. ⌕.* They make their own good Brunello, hard to find elsewhere. Casual place, good value, the menu rarely changes – soups, pastas, great Chianina steaks. In season hunters bring game to barter for wine.

⊜⊜ **Vigneria Le Potazzine** – *Piazza Garibaldi 9. ℘0577 84 60 54. lepotazzine. com. Closed Mon (except summer). Reservations suggested.* Informal rooms, regional seasonal fare. Brunello, Rosso and others also served by the glass.

🥘🍷🍽 **Boccon DiVino** – *Via Traversa Dei Monti 201, Località Colombaio Tozzi, 1,6km/1mi SE of Montalcino by SP14. ℘0577 84 82 33. www.boccondivino montalcino.it. Closed Tue. Reservations suggested.* In a farmhouse on the edges of town, this restaurant has a rustic dining area with modern tables and chairs and a beautiful summer terrace with a view. Authentic local dishes.

🍷🍽 **Taverna dei Barbi** – *Località Pordernovi, 5km/3mi S of Montalcino by SP55. ℘0577 84 11 11. www. fattoriadeibarbi.it. Closed Tue dinnertime and Wed. Reservations suggested.* Brunello winery has a rustic restaurant with elegant touches.

🥘🍷🍽 **Taverna del Grappolo Blu** – *Scale di Via Moglio 1. ℘0577 84 71 50. www.grappoloblu.it.* The name of this typical restaurant hints at Montalcino's main activity (*grappolo* is the Italian for a bunch of grapes), as the village is listed numerous times on the restaurant's wine list. Traditional Tuscan dishes made from carefully chosen ingredients served in a pleasantly convivial atmosphere.

🥘🍷🍽🍽 **Castello Banfi – La Taverna** – *Poggio alle Mura, 13km/8mi S of Montalcino, towards Sant'Angelo Scalo. ℘0577 87 75 24.*

www.castellobanfi.com. Closed dinnertime. Reservations recommended. The Banfi castle and winery in Brunello countryside is a memorable setting for lunch. Traditional cuisine.

TAKING A BREAK

Enoteca La Fortezza di Montalcino – *Piazzale Fortezza. ℘0577 84 92 11. www.enotecalafortezza.com.* The former guardroom with its terrace in the courtyard of the old fortress now houses this superb cellar and wine bar. On display beneath the great red-brick vaults are wines and produce from the Montalcino region.

Caffè Fiaschetteria Italiana – *Piazza del Popolo 6. ℘0577 84 90 43. Closed Thu only Nov-Mar.* The period furnishings – yellow marble tables, velvet seats and old mirrors – suit this historic wine bar, which was founded 1888 by Ferruccio Biondi Santi, the original vintner of Brunello.

EVENT

Thrush Festival *(Sagra del Tordo)* – The four districts of the medieval town stage a procession in period costume and an archery contest.

Pienza★★

Pienza, located in Val d'Orcia, is a perfect example of Renaissance town planning. It was commissioned by Pope Pius II, a scholarly man who wanted to build the ideal town, and who was born (1405) when the village was known as Corsignano. Florentine architect Bernardo Rossellino designed the Pope's perfectly proportioned city.

PIAZZA PIO II★★

In the city centre, off Corso Rossellino. This tiny **square**, named after Pope Pius II Piccolomini, is the earliest example of a real town planning policy. Flanked by the main monumental buildings constructed by Rossellino, it balances civil and religious authorities through architectural harmony.

▶ **Population:** 2,074.
⚲ **Michelin Map:** Michelin Atlas p 44 and Map 563 – M 17 or Map 735 Fold 15.
ℹ **Info:** Corso Rossellino 30. ℘0578 74 99 05. www. comune.pienza.si.it.
▶ **Location:** Pienza lies on SP146 between San Quirico d'Orcia and Montepulciano.

The cathedral (*south*) stands opposite Palazzo Comunale with an open loggia on the ground floor. The Bishop's Palace (*east*) has simple 15C restorations. An aristocratic mansion (*west*), surmounted by an architrave, bears the Piccolomini coat of arms.

A walk round the cathedral gives a lovely **view★** of the Orcia Valley.

Le Crete Senesi: A Voyage Without Moving

One of the most fantastic experiences of Tuscany requires doing almost nothing. Stand before the clay hills that form the Crete Senesi and they appear to be waves, ready to transport the viewer on any voyage – outside of time or even a destination. Suddenly the house perched on a hill seems as if it should be a ship. The sense of being transported is at once strong and comforting. The gentle, moving curves of these hills were in fact covered by sea 4.5–2.5 million years ago; the clay is composed of marine sediments and sand. The Crete Senesi undulate between Siena and Pienza. Pick a hill near Rapolano Terme, Asciano, Monterone d'Arbia, San Giovanni d'Asso or Buonconvento. Without moving, the voyage begins.

Cattedrale di Santa Maria Assunta★ (Duomo)

The 1462 **cathedral** has a simple yet grand Renaissance façade. The restored Gothic interior contains major 15C works by the Sienese School, including altarpieces (*south aisle*) by Giovanni di Paolo and (*south transept*) by Matteo di Giovanni.

Most remarkable are *Madonna and Saints* by Sano di Pietro (*north transept*) and **Vecchietta's** masterpiece (*north apse*) the **Assumption★★** of the Virgin Mary between Popes Pius and Calixtus, St Catherine of Siena and St Agatha. Note the golden backgrounds, the impression of relief, the delightful use of colour and the accuracy of the drawing.

Museo Diocesano★

Palazzo Vescovile. ◔*Open Mar–Oct Wed–Mon 10.30am–1.30pm, 2.30–6pm; rest of the year Sat–Sun and public hols 10am–4pm.* ◔*Closed Tue (except public hols).* ⊛*€4.50.* ♿ ℘*0578 74 99 05 or 349 28 68 318.*

The **museum** has 14C–15C paintings by the Sienese School, 15C–16C Flemish tapestries, a 14C panel with 48 painted compartments depicting the Life of Christ and an extraordinary 14C cope with narrative embroidery given to Pius II.

Palazzo Piccolomini★

◔*Open 15 Mar–15 Oct Wed–Mon 10am–6.30pm, rest of the year 10am–4.30pm.* ◔*Closed Tue, 7 Jan–14 Feb,*

Cattedrale di Santa Maria Assunta

© LianeM/iStock

*16–30 Nov. €7. ☎0577 28 63 00.
www.palazzopiccolominipienza.it.*
Rossellino's most accomplished work
was much inspired by the Palazzo
Rucellai in Florence. The three façades
overlooking the town are identical.
Well-ordered harmony is created by
the vertical pilasters and the horizontal
entablatures. The courtyard owes its
elegance to the slender Corinthian columns. The interior contains an armoury,
early printed books in the library and
a Baroque bed in the papal chamber.
This was the first mansion purposely
designed to look out over a wide expanse of countryside and it enjoys a
view over the Orcia Valley from its three-
storey loggia and hanging gardens on
the south side.

EXCURSIONS
Pieve di Corsignano
*1km/0.5mi W along the south side of
Pienza past the town walls.*
This was the old village church before
Pienza was built. It is an 11C–12C Romanesque building standing alone at the
foot of the town. The façade, built of
pale golden stone, is decorated with a
carved doorway and a window with a
column in the form of a statue. Beside it
is a short cylindrical bell tower.

Monticchiello
10km/6mi E.
This medieval hillside village, surrounded by walls dotted with crenellated towers, is riddled with lanes and
little squares steeped in charm. The village church has a pentagonal staircase
leading up to its austere Gothic doorway. From the car park at the entrance
to the town, there is a superb **view★** of
the Orcia Valley. On the right is Pienza
with a foreground of *crete* (arid hilltops),
a characteristic feature of the landscape
south of Siena, and (*left*) the summit of
Monte Amiata.

San Quirico d'Orcia★
40km/25mi S of Siena.
🛈 *Via Dante Alighieri 33. ☎0577 89
97 28. www.comunesanquirico.it/en/
tourism-area.*

Brunello di Montalcino

Brunello di Montalcino is available
for sale 1 January of the 5th year
following the harvest (6th year
for Brunello Riserva). Rosso di
Montalcino, also made from
Sangiovese, is released for sale 1
September of the year following
the harvest (and therefore is more
economical). The best way to
enjoy this wine is with food – with
nice juicy Chianina steak, game,
duck, Cinta Senese pig, wild
mushrooms, truffles and other
hearty Tuscan food.

This old town set on a small rise still has
its 12C walls and its huge gates. Very
early in the Middle Ages, San Quirico
gained importance because it straddled
Via Francigena, which passed through
the Orcia Valley linking Rome and the
north of Italy. In 1154 Frederick I of
Swabia (Frederick Barbarossa) received
ambassadors from Pope Adrian IV here.

Collegiata★★
This admirable 12–13C Romanesque-
Gothic **collegiate church** has an elegant but simple façade; beneath a row of
arcading are a fine carved rose window
and majestic **Romanesque portal★**. Its
columns and its lintel, which is carved
with monsters in confrontation, are set
in a great arch supported by entwined
columns resting on lions' backs. On the
right-hand side of the church are **two
Gothic portals**, the wider of the two
flanked by statue-columns supported
by lions and of a more complex design
than the Romanesque portal (*west front*).
Note the kneeling telamones supporting
the division in the double bay.
The most notable features of the interior are (*between the last two pillars to the
left of the nave*) the recumbent statue of
Count Henry of Nassau, who died in San
Quirico in February 1451 when returning from a jubilee in Rome, (*chancel*) the
early 16C carved wood panelling with
marquetry inlays (*north transept*) and,
most outstanding of all, a **reredos★**
painted by Sano di Pietro (15C), consist-

ing of a triptych depicting the Virgin Mary, the Child Jesus and four saints against a golden background; in the lunette is the Resurrection and Descent into Hell; the predella depicts the Life of the Virgin Mary.

Palazzo Chigi
One side of Piazza della Collegiata is filled by this 17C **mansion**. In poor repair, its past majesty is apparent. The coat of arms shows the six hummocks of the Chigi family and the crown of oak leaves of the della Rovere family.

Porta ai Cappuccini
Along the right side of the Palazzo Chigi is Via Poliziano, a narrow, medieval street leading to Porta ai Cappuccini, a 13C **gate** in the form of a polygonal tower.

🚗 DRIVING TOUR

THE VAL D'ORCIA
1hr 30min without visiting Rocca a Tentennano – about 10km/6mi from San Quirico to Castiglione and Rocca d'Orcia. 👆 *See regional map pp288–289.*

▷ From San Quirico take the Via Cassia (SS2) S towards Rome.

Val d'Orcia

© Heinz Wohner/Look/Photononstop

The road descends gently into the Orcia Valley between undulating hillsides. On the nearest hill is the mighty Rocca d'Orcia (fortress); in the distance is Monte Amiata and the fortress at Radicofani.

▷ Before crossing the River Orcia, turn right towards Bagno Vignoni.

The road climbs steeply along the sheer-sided river valley, giving a fine view of the nearby fortress.

Bagno Vignoni★
This hamlet is particularly popular for its thermal water used to treat arthritis and rheumatism as far back as Roman times.
A surprise is the bathing pool where one expects to see a piazza, flanked on one side, by St Catherine's Portico, a reminder of the Saint's visit.
Opposite the large car park is the Rocca d'Orcia, set high above the Orcia Gorge, which in the Middle Ages provided a means of communication with the Maremma region.

▷ Return to the bridge and cross the River Orcia. After 350m/380yd turn right into the Castiglione road.

Castiglione d'Orcia
Castiglione belonged to the Aldobrandeschi family but in the early 14C it passed to Siena. A few years later Siena sold the village and other property in the Orcia Valley, including the fortress at Tentennano, to the rich Sienese Salimbeni family. In 1419 the Republic recovered all the land when Cocco Salimbeni was forced to capitulate.
The triangular main square, **Piazza Vecchietta**, was named after Lorenzo di Petro, also known as the Vecchietta, who was said to have been born in Castiglione c. 1412. In the centre of the piazza is a 17C travertine well. Little remains of the fortress.
From the esplanade above the outer wall (*access by a flight of steps*) there is a view of the castle ruins and of Monte Amiata and the Orcia Valley.

Follow the signs to Rocca a Tentennano; car park below the fortress.

Rocca a Tentennano★

Open daily 10.30am–1.30pm, 2.30–6.30pm. €3. 392 00 33 028.
The promontory overlooks Via Francigena and the Orcia Valley, probably settled in the 9C. The fortress was designed by Tignoso di Tentennano and remained in the family until the mid-13C when the Republic of Siena took possession. Restored in the 1970s, the missing sections were replaced by brick. The **tour** of the fortress not only provides splendid views of the Orcia Valley and Monte Amiata but also reveals the medieval system of defence. The pentagonal fortifications enclose a military parade ground and a polygonal tower.

Rocca d'Orcia

Accessible on foot from the fortress.
This medieval town was built against the walls of the Rocca a Tentennano on which it was dependent.
Narrow streets, partly cobbled, meet around a huge polygonal cistern capped by a well.

ADDRESSES

⌂ STAY

Affittacamere Gozzante – *Corso Il Rossellino 23. 338 70 70 971. www.affittacameregozzante.it. 5 rooms.* Modest but comfortable rooms with iron and wood furniture in an old palazzo near Pienza Cathedral.

Agriturismo Aiole – *Strada Provinciale della Grossola 22, Poggio Rosa, 8.5km/5.3mi SW of Castiglione d'Orcia. 0577 88 74 54. www.agriturismo-aiole.com. 6 rooms.* Welcoming stone farmhouse with rustic Tuscan interior dark wood furniture, terra-cotta floors.

Agriturismo Castello La Grancia – *Località Spedaletto, 7.5km/4.5mi SE of Pienza. 0577 74 81 58. www.agriturismocastellolagrancia.com. 7 rooms.* This enchanting castle has pretty rooms, home-baking for breakfast and traditional Tuscan dinners.

Agriturismo il Rigo – *Località Casablanca, 4.5km/2.7mi SW of San Quirico d'Orcia. 0577 89 72 91. www.ilrigo.com. 10 rooms.* In the Orcia Valley, this 17C convivial family farm offers cooking classes and the opportunity to harvest saffron (*Oct*) or pick olives (*Nov/Dec*).

Agriturismo Santo Pietro – *Località Santo Pietro 29, 5km/3mi NE of Pienza by S146. 0578 75 41 51. www.tenutasantopietro.com. 12 rooms.* This farmhouse room is decorated in rustic style; authentic cooking using farm produce. Horse riding, tennis nearby.

ⵏ EAT

La Buca delle Fate – *Corso Rossellino 38/a. 0578 74 84 48. www.ristorantelabucadellefatepienza.it. Closed Mon. Reservation suggested.* The 15C Gonzaga *palazzo*, in the town centre, has large rooms and vaulted brick ceilings. Elegant country style. Traditional food at reasonable prices.

Trattoria Latte di Luna – *Via San Carlo 2. 0578 74 86 06. Closed Tue.* Near Porta al Ciglio and Piazza San Carlo, dine under umbrellas on terrace.

La Porta – *Via del Piano 1, Monticchiello, 7km/4mi SE of Pienza. 0578 75 51 63. www.osterialaporta.it. Reservations suggested.* Splendid terrace with "postcard" view of the surrounding hills dotted with cypress trees. Daily specials. Good wine list.

Trattoria al Vecchio Forno – *Hotel Palazzo del Capitano, Via Poliziano 18, San Quirico d'Orcia. 0577 89 73 80. www.palazzodelcapitano.com. Reservations suggested.* Local specialities served in a pleasant room with big fireplace in a medieval *borgo*. The garden has rustic tables and chaises made of tree trunks.

La Terrazza del Chiostro – *Via del Balzello via Corso il Rossellino, Pienza. 0577 74 81 83. www.laterrazzadelchiostro.it. Reservations suggested.* Gourmet cuisine takes pride of place here, with traditional Tuscan dishes featuring on the menu alongside more creative options, all of which delight guests with skilful preparation and intense flavours. There's also a simpler menu at lunchtime. Enjoy alfresco dining in summer on the terrace.

EVENT

San Quirico d'Orcia celebrates the "Festa del Barbarossa" (*June*) with historical re-enactments.

Montepulciano★★

Montepulciano is an attractive little town typical of the Renaissance period. It has a remarkably picturesque **setting★★** on the top of a tufa hill separating two valleys. The town, founded in the 6C by refugees from Chiusi fleeing the Barbarian invasion, was named Mons Politianus (even today inhabitants are known as Poliziani). Poets have long sung the praises of its ruby-red wine, Vino Nobile di Montepulciano. An exceptional feature of is that much of the tufa under the *palazzi* was carved out to form wineries, which still operate in the centre, as do others in the surrounding countryside. A stroll through town is a walk above hundreds of wine barrels! Antonio da Sangallo the Elder, of the famous family of Renaissance sculptors and architects, bequeathed some of his most famous works to Montepulciano.

WALKING TOUR

The walk lasts about 2hrs.

Within Porta al Prato, a fortified gate bearing the Tuscan coat of arms, and beyond the Florentine lion (*marzocco*), the main street lined with numerous interesting **mansions★** and churches climbs uphill. At the end of the first section (Via Roma) the street divides in two to enclose the historic landmarks.

The splendid Palazzo Avignonesi (*no 91 Via Roma*) dates from the late Renaissance period (16C) and is attributed to Vignola. The mansion (*no 73*), which belonged to the antique dealer Bucelli, is decorated with engraved Etruscan and Roman stones.

Further along (*right*) is the church of Sant'Agostino (restored) with its Renaissance **façade★** designed by Michelozzo of Florence in the 15C. The Jack-o'-the-clock on the tower (*opposite*) is none other than Mr Punch.

▶ **Population:** 13,824.
Michelin Map: Michelin Atlas p 44 and Map 563 – M 17 or Map 735 Fold 15.
Info: Piazza Don Minzoni 1. ☎0578 75 73 41. www.prolocomontepulciano.it. montepulcianoliving.it.
Location: Montepulciano is between San Quirico d'Orcia and Chiusi on S146.
Don't Miss: The view from Palazzo Comunale. The setting and Renaissance harmony of San Biagio. Tasting Vino Nobile di Montepulciano and Rosso di Montepulciano.

▷ Turn left at the Logge del Mercato (Corn Exchange) into Via di Voltaia nel Corso.

The Palazzo Cervini (*no 21*) was designed by **Antonio da Sangallo the Elder** and is a fine example of Florentine Renaissance style, with its rustication and rounded and triangular pediments.

▷ Continue along Via dell'Opio nel Corso and Via Poliziano.

Poliziano was born at no 1 Via Poliziano. At the end of the street stands the **Church of Santa Maria dei Servi**, which contains a Virgin and Child by Duccio di Buoninsegna.

Piazza Grande★★

The **main square** at the top of the town has an irregular layout. The different styles of façade avoid architectural monotony and combine to give an overall sense of harmony.

Palazzo Comunale★

West side. The Gothic **town hall** includes 15C alterations by Michelozzo. It is reminiscent of the Palazzo Vecchio.

The **tower** affords an extensive **panoramic view★★★** of the town and its outskirts including the Church of the

© miralex/iStock

Madonna di San Biagio (*west*) and the Tuscan countryside embracing Mount Amiata (*southwest*), Pienza (*west*), Siena (*northwest*), Cortona (*northeast*) and Lake Trasimeno (*east*).

On the other side of the square stands **Palazzo Contucci**, which was begun in 1519 by Sangallo the Elder, completed in the 18C.

Palazzo Nobili-Tarugi★

North side. This majestic Renaissance **mansion** opposite the cathedral is attributed to Sangallo the Elder. Six Ionic columns set on a very high base support the pilasters of the first floor. It features a portico and huge doorway with semicircular arches.

The bay windows with their rounded pediments are set on small consoles. The loggia (*left*) was open but has been walled up. (Tourism office and Vino Nobile *enoteca* are here.)

Next to Palazzo Tarugi is the Palazzo del Capitano (*north side*).

Well★

Two lions supporting the Medici coat of arms adorn this picturesque well.

Cattedrale di Santa Maria (Duomo)

South side. The 16C–17C **cathedral** never received its marble cladding the façade. The interior is austere and stylistically pure. A number of statues come from the dismantled Aragazzi's tomb, designed by Michelozzo (15C). The 14C Baptistery is surmounted by a fine terracotta by Andrea della Robbia. A 15C

portrait of the Madonna (*north aisle*) is by Sano di Pietro.

A monumental **reredos★** (1401) by Taddeo di Bartolo depicts the Assumption, the Annunciation and the Coronation of Mary.

▷ Continue N on the main street.

Piazza San Francesco

The **square** provides a fine view of the surrounding countryside and the church of San Biagio below.

EXCURSIONS

Chiesa della Madonna di San Biagio★★

Below the town (W); off S146 to Pienza.

This masterpiece of Antonio da Sangallo the Elder stands on an avenue of cypress trees that leads to the magnificent Our Lady of San Biagio. Built of pale golden stone set off by its silvery lead dome, beautifully situated on a grassy stretch high above the valley, it was inaugurated in 1529 by Pope Clement VII Medici. Sangallo was strongly influenced by Bramante's plan for the reconstruction of St Peter's in Rome. The harmonious lines convey majestic solemnity outside and in. Note a 14C Annunciation and the impressive marble high altar (1584). The elegant canon's residence (Canonica) with a portico stands opposite.

Sinalunga

21km/13mi N of Montepulciano.

The old town stands high above the Chiana Valley, which expanded into

Vino Nobile di Montepulciano

A tour of a winery's *cantina* in town and tasting of the elegant Vino Nobile is not to be missed. Then sample wines by other winemakers in an *enoteca*. The red wine must be made from at least 70 percent Sangiovese (locally called Prugnolo Gentile) grapes, with the remaining 30 percent being grapes authorised by the Tuscany region. There are 230 producers of Vino Nobile, but only 72 bottle their wines. Excellent wineries outside the centre include Poderi Sanguineto, Godiolo, Boscarelli, La Ciarlana, Avignonesi, Bindella, Fassati, Le Bèrne, Tenuta Valdipiatta and Il Macchione. The tourist office can give maps and make appointments at wineries in the centre or outside the city.

the plain after land improvement to the swamps and railway construction. In the vast main square, **Piazza Garibaldi** has three 17C–18C churches. The **Collegiata di San Martino**, above a large flight of steps, was begun in the late 16C on the site of the old fortress, using the stone from the castle. Inside the *Madonna and Child surrounded by two Saints and two Angels*, set on a golden background, is signed Benvenuto di Giovanni (1509). Piazza XX Settembre Via Mazzini leads to the historic town centre and the **Palazzo Pretorio**, decorated with coats of arms of the *Pretors* and of the Medici family who gained possession of the town in 1533.

Trequanda
7km/4mi SW of Sinalunga.

This small hilltop village has retained some of its crenellated walls and a few remains of Cacciaconti Castle, including one huge round corner tower. The 13C **Church of San Pietro** has a very unusual rustic façade with an alternating checkerboard design of white travertine and brown-ochre local stone. The interior presents an Ascension by Il Sodoma (*right-hand wall*) in a frame of carved and gilded *pietra serena*. Above the altar is a triptych by Giovanni di Paolo.

Chianciano Terme★
Chianciano is on SP146, which links Montepulciano and Chiusi.
🏢 *Piazza Italia 67.* ☏ *0578 67 11 22.*
Chianciano Terme (*pop. 7,079*) is a large spa town, delightfully situated adjacent to the old hilltop village of Chianciano Vecchia, overlooking the fertile Chiana

Valley to the west. The mineral water here was known to the Etruscans and Romans, and mentioned by Horace. In its mid-20C heyday, author Luigi Pirandello and film director Federico Fellini made annual visits to drink the water. (Fellini featured Claudia Cardinale as an attendant in an early scene of *8 1/2*.) Four separate thermal establishments dispense drinking water for cures: Acqua Santa and Acqua Fucoli for gastrointestinal and liver health; Acqua Sillene for the skin; and Acqua Sant'Elena for the kidneys. Some have pretty parks for walks and bandstands with music. Terme Sensoriale is ideal for a few hours of spa treatments.

The main street, Viale Roma, is the most elegant in the resort. Its many hotels make this an economical base for exploring Tuscany. The tourist office can arrange horseback excursions through wine country.

Museo d'Arte di Chianciano Terme
Viale della Libertà 280. ⏰*Opening hours may vary, check the website for information. www.museodarte.org.*
This is one of Central Italy's most interesting art museums to open in recent years (2009). The collection is in five sections: Etchings (Dürer, Rembrandt, Goya, Piranesi); Asian Art; Drawings (Veronese, Luca Giordano, Guercino, Tiepolo, Munch, Magritte); Historical (portraits); and Contemporary. The collection is well chosen and the contemporary art displays fine works (Salvador Dalì, Mario Schifano, Damien Hirst, Frances Turner, Albert Louden),

the most recent of which include British artists using strong imagery and vibrant colours.

Museo Civico Archeologico delle Acque★

Via Dante, in front of the Biblioteca Comunale. ⏰*Open Tue–Sun 10am–1pm, 4–7pm (Nov–Mar only Fri–Sun and public hols).* ⊕€5. ✆*0578 30 471. www.museoetrusco.it.*

The Archaeological Museum houses objects from Etruscan settlements, the necropolis at Tolle, fine jewellery, reconstructions of an Etruscan farmhouse and Selene temple excavations.

ADDRESSES

🛏STAY

⊜⊜⊜ **Il Marzocco** – *Piazza Savonarola 18, Montepulciano.* ✆*0578 75 72 62. www. albergoilmarzocco.it.* 🅿. *16 rooms.* A 16C palace with retro decor. Run by the same family since 1900. Some rooms have balcony.

⊜⊜⊜ **Palazzo Bandino** – *Via delle Stiglianesi 3, Chianciano Terme.* ✆*0578 61 199. www.palazzobandino.it. 4 rooms and 9 apts. Restaurant* ⊜⊜. This farm below town produces Vino Nobile and olive oil. New spa with indoor/outdoor pool. Horse excursions.

⊜⊜⊜⊜ **Agriturismo San Gallo** – *Via delle Colombelle 7, Montepulciano.* ✆*0578 75 83 30. www.agriturismo sangallo.com. 6 apts.* Set in a Vino Nobile winemaker's vineyard below town; self-catering rooms or apartments with lovely furnishings. Swimming pool. Barbecue.

⊜⊜⊜⊜ **Grand Hotel Admiral Palace** – *Via Umbria 2, Chianciano Terme.* ✆*0578 63 297. www.admiralpalace.it. 60 rooms. Restaurant* ⊜⊜⊜. 🅿 ⌇ In a residential area, rooms are light and modern. Spa. Generous *antipasto* buffet.

🍴EAT

⊜⊜ **Enoteca Canaebam** – *Viale della Libertà 448, Chianciano Terme.* ✆*0578 190 22 12. facebook.com/canaebam.* This friendly *enoteca* has a distinctly modern feel. Excellent wines and delicious Tuscan cuisine. Just order some *bruschette* and

a glass of wine or indulge in a complete meal all the way from appetizers to dessert. Try the *pici* pasta or the exquisite pork shank.

⊜⊜ **Hostaria Il Buco** – *Via della Pace 39, Chianciano Terme.* ✆*0578 30 230. Closed Wed.* Just below the old town centre in the upper part of the town stands this small establishment with a warm, family atmosphere. Two small rooms with round tables. The menu offers typical seasonal Tuscan recipes, home-made pasta, mushrooms and truffles. Home-made pasta, grilled beef, pizzas.

⊜⊜ **Hotel Tiziana** – *Via SS326, località Tre Berte, 12km/7.5mi E of Montepulciano.* ✆*0578 76 77 60. www.hotel-tiziana.com.* Simple decor, friendly service, popular with winemakers for reasonable prices and good traditional food – *pici* with duck or wild boar sauce, grilled meats – and good range of Vino Nobile and Rosso di Montepulciano, from small wineries.

⊜⊜⊜ **Le Logge Del Vignola** – *Via delle Erbe 6.* ✆*0578 71 72 90. www.leloggedel vignola.com.* This small establishment is a good spot in the old town centre. Its tables are a bit cramped but they have smart table settings and well-prepared, regional ingredients are served.

⊜⊜⊜⊜ **La Grotta** – *Località San Biagio, 1km/0.6mi SW of Montepulciano by S146.* ✆*0578 75 74 79. www.lagrotta montepulciano.it. Closed Wed. Reservations suggested.* Splendid vaulted ceiling in 16C *palazzo*; Tuscan cuisine with innovations. A picturesque place with its nice summer service in the garden across from evocative San Biagio.

TAKING A BREAK

Antico Caffè Poliziano – *Via Voltaia nel Corso 27/29.* ✆*0578 75 86 15. www. caffepoliziano.it.* Since 1868, artists such as Pirandello, Malaparte and Fellini frequented this beautiful café. Light lunch. Savour the red wines of Montepulciano. Patio.

Bar Pasticceria Centro Storico – *Via Casini 22, Chianciano Terme.* ✆*0578 31 444. www.barpasticceriacentrostorico.it.* Retro patisserie-tearoom (but also bar and restaurant) with small terrace overlooking the town and valley. In the historic centre. Have an aperitif with a *tagliere di affettati* and *formaggi* (platter of cold cuts and cheeses) and a glass of red wine.

Chiusi★

and around

Now a quiet, friendly little town, Chiusi was built on an easily defended hilltop, as it was once one of the 12 sovereign towns of the Etruscan confederation. Its prosperity derived not only from the farmland in the surrounding fertile plain but from its control of the Chiana, then a tributary of the Tiber, which linked the town to Rome and to the sea.

▶ **Population:** 8,429.
◔ **Michelin Map:** Michelin Atlas p 44 and Map 563 – M 17 or Map 735 Fold 15.
ℹ **Info:** Via Porsenna 79. ☏0578 22 76 67. visitchiusi. it. www.prolocochiusi.it.
▷ **Location:** Chiusi is on the boundary with Umbria on SS71 between Chianciano Terme and Città della Pieve.

A BIT OF HISTORY

In 507 BC **Porsenna**, the powerful King of Chiusi, attempted to reimpose on Rome the domination that had endured for over a century under three Etruscan kings, before the Romans set themselves free by instituting a republic. Once Rome regained its freedom, it gained in power and finally allied itself to Chiusi, which rallied to Rome in the 4C BC and began a period of Romanisation. In the early days of Christianity, these links led many inhabitants of Chiusi to convert to the new religion.

TOWN

The streets of Via Porsenna and Via Pietriccia meet in the town centre at Largo Cacioli, site of most attractions.

Museo Archeologico Nazionale★

Via Porsenna 93. ◔Open daily 9am–8pm. ◔Closed 25 Dec, 1 Jan. ☞€6; free 1st Sun of the month Oct–Mar. ♿ ☏0578 20 177. www. polomusealetoscana.beniculturali.it.
The **National Archaeological Museum** contains numerous Etruscan artefacts excavated in local graveyards. Displays illustrate art and civilisation in the Chiusi region.

The anthropomorphic, earthenware **funeral urns**, also known as canopic jars, date from the Villanovan period and were first used in the 7C BC. In the 6C BC they were replaced by busts carved of stinkstone, a local limestone that emits an unpleasant odour when being carved. From the 2C BC onwards Chiusi became famous for its high output of clay urns with moulded decoration. Realist art forms and Etruscan fantasy were expressed in architectural terracotta ornaments for temples and mansions, in bronze sculptures and utensils, gold jewellery, lamps, glassware, clay votives and decorated tableware.

Chiusi was a major producer of buccheroware, the glazed black pottery which in the 6C BC was decorated with low-relief motifs and from the 5C BC without decoration. Attic black-figure and later red-figure vases were initially imported but later made locally by Greek artists who settled in Etruria.

Painting, an art form that was rare in the north of Etruria, is shown in the reconstitution of a tomb (*tomba delle Tassinaie*), which dates from after the mid-2C BC, possibly decorated by artists from Tarquinia.

▷ A museum warden will accompany visitors who have a car to see a few of the tombs found along the Lake Chiusi road (*3km/2mi; at 11am or 2.30pm*).

Visitors are usually shown two tombs: the **Tomba del Leone** (Tomb of the Lion), which was originally painted and in which the burial chambers are set out in the shape of a cross around a central area, and the **Tomba della Pellegrina** (Tomb of the Pilgrim) at the end of a corridor (*dromos*) and containing 3C and 2C BC urns and sarcophagi decorated with reliefs drawn from Greek mythology or, on later artefacts, the war between the Galatians and the Romans.

Cattedrale di San Secondiano

The earliest **church** on this site, a 4C–5C paleo-Christian basilica, was destroyed by the Goths and rebuilt in the 6C by Bishop Fiorentino. After being destroyed again during the Barbarian invasions, it was rebuilt to an identical design in the 12C. The nave and aisles are separated by 18 ancient but dissimilar columns, revealing the reuse of Roman materials. In the 17C the body of St Mustiola was interred in the south transept.

Campanile

The 12C defence tower was converted in the 16C into a bell tower (*campanile*).

Museo della Cattedrale

Piazza del Duomo. ⏰*Open mid Apr–Sept Tue–Sun 10am–12.30pm, 2.30–4.45pm; rest of the year Tue–Fri 10am–12.30pm, Sat–Sun and public hols 10am–12.30pm, 2.30–4.30pm; hours may vary.* ✎€5 (includes *Porsenna Labyrinth, see box below).* ✆0578 22 69 75. www.prolocochiusi.it/ museo-della-cattedrale.

The ground floor of this **museum** displays Etruscan, Roman and paleo-Christian remains discovered beneath the cathedral. From the gardens, part of the 3C BC Etruscan wall is visible. On the first floor are furniture, religious ornaments and reliquaries, including two magnificent 15C chests from the Embraschi workshops. There is a valuable collection of illuminated antiphonaries, psalters and graduals (15C–16C) brought from the Abbey of Monte Oliveto Maggiore (🕭*See SIENA, Driving Tour).*

EXCURSIONS

Catacombe di Santa Mustiola e di Santa Caterina

On the lake road. ⏰*Only guided tours by reservation, enquire at the Museo della Cattedrale for hours and tickets.* ✎€5 (using your own vehicle). ✆0578 22 69 75.

These 3C **catacombs**, the only ones known to exist in Tuscany, were discovered in 1634 and 1848 respectively. They were still in use as burial places in the 5C. The earliest catacombs, where St Mustiola was buried in an extensive network of galleries bear a large number of inscriptions; the second catacombs are smaller, named for the tiny chapel dedicated to St Catherine of Alexandria.

Torri Beccati Questo e Beccati Quello

3km/2mi E.

Translating roughly as "Take This and Take That", these towers stand only a few yards apart. The first tower stands in Umbria and the second in Tuscany, recalling the former rivalry between the two regions. The octagonal Tuscan tower is dominated by the square taller Umbrian tower.

Lago di Chiusi

5km/3mi N.

This quiet **lake** offers boating, rowing and angling. Fish are cooked in the traditional dishes of Chiusi. Pike (*brustico*)

Porsenna Labyrinth

Excavations have revealed a complex system of underground galleries used originally by the Etruscans and later by the Romans to supply the town with water. Pliny the Elder records that the famous Porsenna "was buried beneath the town of Chiusi, in a monument with a square base (90m/300ft long) enclosing a maze". It is tempting to imagine that these galleries could be part of the tomb of the Etruscan king.

The tour of this ancient water system starts in the Museo della Cattedrale and finishes in the Etrusco-Roman cistern (2C–1C BC); the tank was probably used as an emergency water supply in the event of fire. Visitors exit at the bottom of the medieval tower, a bell tower since the end of the 16C.

is cooked directly on reeds from the lake. **Tegamaccio**, a fish stew, consists of lake fish cooked in tomato sauce served on slices of garlic toast.

Cetona
9km/6mi N.
During the Middle Ages Cetona lay on the border between the Republic of Siena and the Papal States and was fiercely possessed or angrily coveted by both parties. A fortress from that era crowns the hilltop. The restored village is fashionable with the Italian jet-set, many with holiday homes there.

The **Collegiata** church dates from the 13C and contains a fresco of the Assumption. The **Museo Civico per la Preistoria del Monte Cetona** (*in the Palazzo Comunale; ⊙ open Jul–Sept Tue–Sun 10am–1pm, 4–7pm; Oct–Jun Mon–Fri 10am–1pm (Tue and Thu also 4–6pm), Sat–Sun, public hols and the day before hols 10am–1pm, 3–5pm; ⊙ €4; €7 combined ticket with Parco Archeologico Naturalistico di Belverde; ⧫ ☏0578 26 94 16; www.preistoriacetona.it*) is housed in the town hall and illustrates the geology of Monte Cetona (⧫ *See below*). Objects give evidence of prehistoric settlements from the Paleolithic era to the end of the Bronze Age.

Monte Cetona – Parco Archeologico Naturalistico di Belverde
5.5km/3.5mi SW of Cetona by car; 500m/547yd on foot to the summit.
The summit of the bare rocky mountain (*1,148m/3,731ft*) provides a superb **panoramic view**. Humans have settled the natural caves in these slopes since the Paleolithic era. The period of major population growth occurred in the middle of the second millennium BC. Around **Belverde** some of these ancient **caves** are accessible and electricity has been installed (*signs to Parco Archeologico Naturalistico; ⊙ open Jul–Sept Tue–Sun 10am–1pm, 3–7pm; Oct–Jun Sun and public hols 10am–1pm, 3–5pm. ☏0578 23 92 19. ⊙ €6; €7 combined ticket with Museo Civico per la Preistoria del Monte Cetona*).

🚗 DRIVING TOUR

MONTE AMIATA
59km/36.5mi circuit from Sarteano.
⧫ *See regional map pp288–289.*

Sarteano
6.5km/4mi NW.
This spa resort consists of three swimming pools filled with warm, mineral-rich water. The 24°C water comes from a thermal spring known to the ancient Romans. The village is dominated by an 11C hilltop fortress, which was altered in the 15C by the Sienese; its walls and mighty square tower with machicolations are well preserved.

The **Church of San Martino** has a single nave and contains a number of interesting paintings: (*left*) a large **Annunciation★★** by Beccafumi; *Madonna and Child between St Roch and St Sebastian* by Andrea di Niccolò; a Visitation by Vanni; and two works by Giacomo di Mino del Pellicciaio: a Madonna and Child, signed and dated 1342, and a triptych.

Radicofani★
Fort Radicofani is perched on a natural promontory (over 800m/2,600ft high). It dominates the whole of the surrounding countryside and is easily recognisable for its mighty tower standing out

Radicofani
© Alkir/iStock

proudly against the skyline. The village of Radicofani, built in the same dark brown stone as the fortress above it, has medieval houses and steep streets nestling up against the fortress walls. To the left of the main street is a tiny square in which stand two churches, opposite one another.

From the adjacent public park, there is a fine **view★** of Monte Amiata and the surrounding countryside dotted with the sharp bare peaks of the **Orcia Hills**. The main street then leads to the 16C Palazzo Pretorio, decorated with coats of arms, and to the **fortress★** itself (*car park nearby*). The fortress was built in the 13C, altered in the 16C and destroyed by an explosion in the 18C. Its majestic ruins were shored up early in the 1990s.

Abbadia San Salvatore★

The small town of Abbadia San Salvatore is a summer and winter holiday resort at the foot of Monte Amiata. It has a large **medieval quarter**, a labyrinth of arched streets and alleyways and a fortress. It takes its name from an abbey which was once the wealthiest monastery in Tuscany.

Chiesa Abbaziale

The **abbey church** is all that remains of the monastery founded in 743 AD by Rachis, a Lombard king converted to Christianity. Building work on the church was completed in the 11C; slight alterations were made in the 16C. The austere façade contains a large bay with colonnettes; the tall bell tower is crenellated. The interior has a nave but no aisles. The chancel, raised above the level of the nave, has rounded arches painted with Renaissance friezes. The transept was decorated with frescoes in the late 17C and early 18C. A 12C painted wooden Crucifix adorns the south wall of the nave.

Beneath the chancel is the **crypt★** (8C) of the original church. It was built in the shape of a cross (one of the arms has been reconstructed) and is supported by a profusion of columns with decorated capitals. Beside the church are the traces of the cloisters.

Around the Mountain

A winding road (13km/8mi) runs round the mountain (recommended access from Abbadia San Salvatore, brown signs for "Vetta Amiata"), providing a number of impressive views.

From the south side, the most attractive, the road runs up to the summit marked by an iron cross (22m/72ft high) at the top of a paved path (*15min there and back on foot*) flanked by a 🎿 chair-lift and ski lifts.

ADDRESSES

🛏 STAY

🍽🍽🍽 **Azienda Agrituristica Il Poggio** – *Celle sul Rigo, 30km/19mi SW of Chiusi by S478.* ✆*0578 53 748. www.ilpoggio.net.* 🏊*. 7 apts, 5 suites. Closed 12 Jan-21 Feb.* This farm, which is also an approved equestrian centre, offers authentic traditional cooking and horse riding in the quiet Sienese country. Additional activities include swimming and archery.

🍴 EAT

🍽🍽🍽 **Osteria La Solita Zuppa** – *Via Porsenna 21, Chiusi.* ✆*0578 21 006. www.lasolitazuppa.it. Closed Tue (except Jul and Aug). Reservations advised.* Large, hospitable country-style *osteria* with Tuscan fare and soups on offer.

ACTIVITIES

Monte Amiata offers a wide range of sporting activities.

Hiking – The Anello della Montagna (*28km/17mi c. 12hr)* tour. Trails through nature reserves of Pigelleto and Monte Penna. Chestnut Trails (Sentieri della Castagna) among chestnut groves.

Trekking – Grosseto (Pitigliano, Saturnia, Scansano, Argentario promontory). Around Siena (Montalcino, Pienza, Montepulciano, Chiusi, Siena). The Florence–Siena–Rome trail through
Monte Amiata leads to Rome in 25 stages.

Cycling and mountain biking – Il Sentiero della Bonifica is an excellent easy new route, away from traffic, from Chiusi to Arezzo (*62km/38.5mi*).

Caving – Sassocolato (or Bacheca) Cave–Monte Penna nature reserve, inhabited by bats.

Monasteries at Camaldoli and Vallombrosa are set within enchanting forests, as is St Francis' sanctuary at La Verna, amid tranquil contemplative landscapes dotted with *pieve* (parish churches). Piero della Francesca, the Renaissance artist born in Sansepolcro, brings visitors to the city of Arezzo to admire his fresco cycle, Legend of the True Cross, one of the great Renaissance masterpieces.

Highlights

The Colour of the Area

Arezzo offers the pleasures of a great market city, with lively cafés and the bustling of trade. Cortona has the air of an ancient Tuscan hill town awakened to renewed vigour with the buzz of trendy international visitors looking for the Tuscan sun and festivals. Traversed by two major rivers, the Arno and the Tiber, the lush valleys are home to a variety of crops, while hills tend to be covered with vineyards and olive groves, and the mountains produce their own rich bounty. The Val di Chiana to the south is famous for its beef, while south towards Cortona and east towards Sansepolcro Arezzo shares a border with Umbria. Further north its mountain forests with their monasteries lead into the Marches and Romagna.

Arezzo

Etruscans made Arezzo and Cortona part of their League of Twelve Cities. Under the Romans, Arezzo grew to one of Italy's largest cities thanks to pottery production. Its flourishing economy in the Middle Ages and Renaissance made it a major art centre, attracting the best artists, some of whom were born in the city, like Giorgio Vasari, while others such as Michelangelo, Paolo Uccello and Piero della Francesca were born in provincial towns. Petrarch was born here and Dante set some of his memorable scenes here.

Arezzo gets its economic boost from industry, agriculture and gold, for which it is one of Italy's major trading centres. The latter happens behind closed doors, but not surprisingly some good gold-smiths are in town.

Artistic, Spiritual and Cultural Provincial Towns

Many of the towns, like Anghiari with its steep, narrow medieval streets, are like a step back in time, especially off season. Follow art trails that lead to the works of Piero della Francesca, Vasari and della Robbia. Tournaments, like jousting or crossbow, carry the experience further. Literary travellers will find landscapes from Dante. Besides the artistic and spiritual side, the enquiring mind will find the province has mills weaving quality Casentino wool in Stia near Poppi, or linen and cotton in Anghiari, while elsewhere smiths are forging wrought iron or carpenters are working wood. All make for good shopping, too. You could follow wine roads, some that begin on the outskirts of the capital. Active travellers will enjoy hikes in the lush mountains. All activities are ideal for the visitors seeking to escape the mass tourism of the big art cities. There are plenty of good restaurants and cafés for taking a break to savour it all.

Arezzo★★

As a supporter of the Ghibelline faction, Arezzo was involved in a long struggle against Guelf-leaning Florence before it merged with the latter larger town in 1384. During those days of conflict, Aretini built a large number of tower-houses, which now contribute to the picturesque aspect of the town.

- ▶ **Population:** 99,179.
- **Michelin Map:** Michelin Atlas p 38 and Map 563 L 17 or Map 735 Fold 15.
- **Info:** Piazza della Libertà 1. ☎0575 40 19 45.
- **Location:** Arezzo is 81km/50mi from Florence and 11km/7mi from the Florence–Rome motorway (*autostrada Firenze–Roma*). The old town is built in terraces on a hill crowned by a citadel. From the parapet walk of the citadel, there are a number of delightful views of the town and the surrounding countryside.
- **Don't Miss:** Piero della Francesca's frescoes in the Church of San Francesco.

A BIT OF HISTORY

A centre of Etruscan civilisation, Arretium became a prosperous Roman town famous for its production of "Aretine" vases. This pottery, invented by Aretine native Marcus Perennius, was made of very fine, reddish-brown, glazed clay, an "industry" that flourished for more than a century, between 30 BC and AD 40, spread to other towns and was exported throughout the Roman world from Gaul to Syria.

Long after the Roman period, the town was the birthplace of a number of major figures in the field of the arts: the Benedictine monk, **Guido of Arezzo** (c. 990–c. 1050), who was recognised as the inventor of a system of musical notation; the scholar and poet **Petrarch** (born 1304); the writer, **Pietro Aretino**, also known as **The Aretine** (born 1492); the painter and art historian, **Giorgio Vasari** (born 1511). The town owes it greatest claim to fame to **Piero della Francesca** (♿See p364), who was born in Sansepolcro and produced most of his work in Arezzo.

FRESCOES

Piero della Francesca (c. 1416–92), who divided his time mainly between his birthplace, Sansepolcro, the courts in Ferrara and Urbino, and Arezzo where he painted his masterpiece, was one of the most unusual and most outstanding representatives of the 15C, because of the austerity and powerful sincerity of his work. He was initially influenced by the painters of the Sienese School, for harmonious colours and accurate drawing.

As a young man, he worked in Florence for more than five years with Domenico Veneziano, who taught him how to produce a soft, unreal light and use pale, light colours. During this period Masaccio taught him about perspective and its links with a rigorous form of geometry; Uccello gave him a feeling for volume in his paintings. His admiration for Flemish painting may have added *chiaroscuro* (light and shadow), which lends his frescoes a resemblance to oil painting. His statuesque, impassive figures are robust and solid. His compositions are strongly structured and comply with geometric rules. Balance and solemnity characterise his work. Piero spent almost all his final 20 years writing two treatises, one on pictorial perspective and the other on the geometry of "pure forms".

San Francesco

Piazza San Francesco (at Via Cavour). ♿*Open by appointment only Mon–Fri 9am–7pm (Nov–Mar 6pm), Sat 9am–6pm, Sun 1–6pm (Nov–Mar Sat–Sun 5.30pm).* ✆€8. *Contact the ticket office for a booking number.* ☎0575 35 27 27. www.pierodellafrancesca.it.

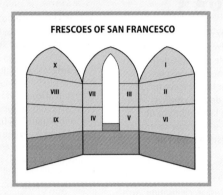

FRESCOES OF SAN FRANCESCO

Frescoes★★★ of San Francesco

The **frescoes★★★** were painted by Piero della Francesca on the walls of the apse between 1452 and 1466 and are considered one of the most outstanding examples of Renaissance painting in Tuscany. They illustrate the **Legend of the True Cross**, a common theme in Franciscan churches and friaries in the Middle Ages, and were inspired by the 13C *Golden Legend* by Jacopo da Varagine.

The artist did not intend to follow the chronological order of the tale in any strict fashion. Instead, the work "reads" as follows:

I–Death of Adam (*right*) and his burial (*left*). Three seeds, from which will grow the Tree of the Cross, are being placed in his mouth by his son, Seth. The tree divides the scene in two.

II–Adoration of the sacred wood. The Queen of Sheba, having received a divine revelation, refuses to cross the bridge (*left*) which has been built with the sacred wood. After travelling to Jerusalem, she explains her vision to Solomon (*right*).

III–The sacred wood is moved and buried.

IV–The angel tells the Virgin Mary of her son's Crucifixion. This scene forms a central point in the story of the wood of the True Cross (before and after the Crucifixion) without depicting the central episode in the story.

V–On the eve of his battle with Maxentius who is disputing his claim to the imperial crown, Constantine the Great (later to be the first Christian emperor) is advised by an angel in a dream to fight under the sign of the Cross. This is the first example of the use of *chiaroscuro* in Italian art.

VI–Constantine, brandishing the Cross, has defeated Maxentius at the Milvian Bridge (AD 312).

VII–The torture of the Jew. St Helena, Constantine's mother, while trying to trace the wood from the True Cross in Jerusalem, was told that only one Jew knew where the relic had been buried. As the man refused to speak, Helena had him dropped down a well where he remained for six days before agreeing to her request.

VIII–Empress Helena, aided by Judas, has the three Crosses excavated outside the walls of Jerusalem, which the artist depicts as an exotic version of Arezzo. The resurrection of a dead man (*right*) shows her which one was the Cross of Christ.

IX–Three hundred years later, Heraclius defeated the Persian King, Chosroes, who had stolen the Cross to decorate his throne.

X–Exaltation of the Cross, which is returned to Jerusalem by Heraclius.

This is a vast **church**, built in the Gothic style in the 14C for the Franciscan Order. The Franciscan monks, as keepers of the Holy Places, showed particular devotion to the True Cross. They commissioned Piero della Francesca to decorate the chancel of the church (ℰ *See box opposite*).

Other Works of Art★ – Ancient frescoes decorate the other walls – (*south wall*) an Annunciation by Spinello Aretino (early 15C); (*south apsidal chapel*) the **Assumption triptych** painted by Niccolò di Pietro Gerini in the early 15C; (*in front of the main chapel*) a huge 13C **Crucifix** painted on wood.

The oculus (*west wall*) is filled with a superb stained-glass window by artist Guillaume de Marcillat, which depicts St Francis giving roses to Pope Honorius III, in mid-January.

WALKING TOUR

Piazza Grande★

The **main sloped square** is surrounded by medieval houses, the Romanesque galleried apse of Santa Maria della Pieve (parish church), the late-18C Law Courts, the part-Gothic part-Renaissance (14C–15C) Palazzo della Fraternita dei Laici and the 16C galleries (*logge*), designed by Giorgio Vasari, now occupied by restaurant and cafe tables.

Casa-Torre Còfani faces the *palazzo*.

Santa Maria della Pieve★

This superb Romanesque parish **church** is crowned by a haughty *campanile*, which, owing to its numerous double bays (there are 40), is called the "One Hundred Holes". The church was constructed mid-12C–14C. The 16C alterations were directed, notably, by **Giorgio Vasari**. The **façade★★**, inspired by the Romanesque style used in Pisa, is very ornate with three tiers of arcades supported by colonnettes, decorated with a variety of motifs. The upper coving of the central doorway is wittily decorated with the 12 symbols of the zodiac.

The interior includes a half-rounded apse and a raised chancel in which the pillars are decorated with capitals carved with large human heads. Two marble low-reliefs depict Epiphany, of Byzantine origin (*rear of the façade*) and a 13C Nativity (*north aisle*). The High Altar displays a superb polyptych (1320–24) by Pietro Lorenzetti from Siena.

Casa Museo di Ivan Bruschi

Corso Italia 14. 🕐 *Open Tue–Sun 10am–1pm, 2–6pm.* 🕐 *Closed Mon, 25 Dec.* ⊕ *€5.* ℰ *0575 35 41 26. www.fondazioneivanbruschi.it.*

Ivan Bruschi founded the antiquarian fair in Arezzo. A great collector, he lived in this restored 14C palace, furnished with his acquisitions.

▷ Take Via Ricasoli.

The Legend of the True Cross

This legend tells the story of the Cross on which Christ was crucified. It begins with Adam who, as he was dying, asked his son Seth for holy oil. Seth is said to have placed three seeds from the Tree of Knowledge under Adam's tongue. After Adam's death these seeds grew into the tree cut down for the Cross on which Christ, the new Adam, was crucified. The tree was then used to build a bridge, the holy significance of which was recognised by the Queen of Sheba. Her prophecy to Solomon was that the wood from the bridge would bring disgrace to the people of Israel. Solomon ordered that the bridge be buried. The three Crosses from Calvary were later discovered by Helena, the mother of Emperor Constantine, who made an epic journey (c. 326–8) from Rome to search for them. The resurrection of a dead man indicated the Cross of Christ. Stolen by the Persian King, Chosroes, the Cross was later retrieved by Heraclius, who returned it to Jerusalem. Relics of the Cross appear in various churches.

WHERE TO STAY	WHERE TO EAT	
B&B Palazzo dei Bostoli .... ①	Antica Osteria l'Agania ..... ①	Trattoria il Saraceno .... ⑩
Badia di Pomaio .... ③	La Lancia d'Oro .... ②	Vita Bella .... ⑪
Casa Volpi .... ⑤	Le Chiavi d'Oro .... ⑧	
Hotel Continentale .... ⑦	Saffron .... ⑨	

Via dei Pileati

This **street**, which runs along the façade of Santa Maria della Pieve, is a strange sight with its palaces, Gothic towers and old houses. Palazzo Pretorio (14C–15C) has the coats of arms of the magistrates (*podestà*).

Cattedrale (Duomo)

The **cathedral** (built 1278–1511), has a neo-Gothic façade. On the south side is an attractive Romanesque-Gothic portal (first half 14C). Among its fine **works of art★** are (*south aisle*) stained-glass windows by Marcillat; (*near the vestry*) the fresco by Piero della Franc-

esca depicting Mary Magdalen; and (*behind the high altar*) the 13C tomb of St Donatus.

▶ Take Via Ricasoli and turn into Via Sasso Verde.

San Domenico

This 13C Gothic **church** has an asymmetrical façade. Frescoes are by the Duccio School, and by Spinello Aretino and his school. The admirable high altar **crucifix★★** is by Cimabue.

▶ From Via San Domenico, turn left on Via XX Settembre.

Casa del Vasari

Via XX Settembre 55. ○Open Mon and Wed–Sat 8.30am–7.30pm, Sun and public hols 8.30am–1.30pm. ○Closed Tue, 1 Jan, 25 Dec. ⊜€4. ♿ ℘0575 40 90 40. www.polomusealetoscana. beniculturali.it.

Still not forgiven for abandoning his native Arezzo for rival Florence, **Giorgio Vasari's house**, which he luxuriously decorated in 1540, gets little play. This Renaissance man was painter, sculptor, architect and writer (his *Lives of the Artists* was a 16C bestseller and is still in print). The house contains works by Tuscan Mannerist painters and a terracotta by Andrea Sansovino.

▷ Via XX Settembre to Via San Lorentino.

Museo Nazionale d'Arte Medievale e Moderna★

○Open Tue, Thu and Sat 9am–1.30pm, 3–7.30pm, Wed 9am–1.30pm, Fri and Sun 3–7.30pm; hours vary. ○Closed Mon, 1 Jan, 25 Dec. ⊜Free admission. ♿ ℘0575 40 90 50. www. polomusealetoscana.beniculturali.it.

The **museum of medieval and modern** art is in the fully furnished Palazzo Bruni-Ciocchi. It contains sculptures, gold and silverware and numerous paintings dating from the Middle Ages to the 19C. Early works include art by Luca Signorelli, Andrea della Robbia and Vasari. The 19C is represented by *Macchiaioli* artists such as Fattori and Signorini. Also, outstanding Renaissance **majolicaware★★** from Umbria, 17C–18C ceramics, coins, glassware, weaponry and ivories.

Badia delle Sante Flora e Lucilla

Piazza della Badia.

Simply called La Badia, this 13C church was remodelled in the 16C plan by Vasari; the *campanile* dates from 1650. Inside, the trompe-l'œil false dome (1702) was painted by Andrea Pozzo (also painted in S Ignazio in Rome). Note the Crucifix by Segna di Bonaventura (1319) and the majestic altar by Vasari, who painted an Assumption of the Virgin.

ADDITIONAL SIGHTS

Museo Archeologico

Via Margaritone 10. ○Open daily, hours vary; check on the website. ○Closed 1 Jan, 25 Dec. ⊜€6. ♿ ℘0575 20 882. www.polomusea letoscana.beniculturali.it.

The **Archaeological Museum** stands adjacent to the oval **Roman amphitheatre** (1C–2C). See interesting Etruscan and Roman bronze statuettes (from 6C BC to 3C AD), Greek vases (Euphronios' *krater*), Aretine vases and Hellenistic and Roman ceramics.

Santa Maria delle Grazie

1km/0.6mi S by Viale Mecenate.

This mid-15C **church** has a graceful, ethereal **portico★** designed by Benedetto da Maiano (15C) from Florence. Inside, a marble **reredos★** by Andrea della Robbia frames a painting by Parri di Spinello (*Virgin Mary of Pity*).

ADDRESSES

🏨STAY

⊖⊜🍽 **B&B Palazzo dei Bostoli** – *Via Mazzini 1, 2nd floor. ℘334 14 90 558. www.palazzobostoli.it. 5 rooms.* Charming rooms in renovated 13C *palazzo.* Breakfast served at the bar next door.

⊖⊜🍽 **Casa Volpi** – *Via Simone Martini 29, 1.5km/1mi SE of Arezzo. ℘0575 35 43 64. 15 rooms.* Set in a park near the city gates, this elegant 19C country home has beamed ceilings and frescoes. The superb terrace has a panoramic view of Arezzo.

⊖⊜🍽 **Hotel Continentale** – *Piazza Guido Monaco 7. ℘0575 20 251. www.hotelcontinentale.com. 73 rooms.* 🅿 *Paid parking.* Modern, with spacious rooms, in the city centre. Good value.

⊖⊜🍽🍽 **Badia di Pomaio** – *Località Badia di Pomaio, 7.5km/4.5mi NE of Arezzo. ℘0575 35 32 10. www.hotelbadia dipomaio.it. 17 rooms.* 🍴. *Restaurant.* The gardens and pool give a broad view over Arezzo and its surroundings; inside, each room has been renovated taking care to maintain the original style of the 18C abbey.

⍩ EAT

😊😊 **Antica Osteria l'Agania** – *Via Mazzini 10. ☎0575 29 53 81. www. agania.com. Closed Mon.* Modest, family place; local dishes and Tuscan wines.

😊😊 **Trattoria Il Saraceno** – *Via Mazzini 6. ☎0575 27 644. www.ilsaraceno.it.* Authentic local dishes, a wood-burning oven for pizzas and good wines. Friendly.

😊😊😊 **Le Chiavi d'Oro** – *Piazza San Francesco 7. ☎0575 40 33 13. www. ristorantelechiavidoro.it. Closed Mon.* Gourmet dining, refined atmosphere. Divine artichoke ravioli.

😊😊😊 **La Lancia d'Oro** – *Piazza Grande 18. ☎0575 21 033. www. ristorantelanciadoro.it. Closed Mon (except public hols and Jul–Aug). Reservation suggested.* Located under the frescoed *logge* built by Vasari, this has pleasant outdoor tables. Tuscan cuisine.

😊😊😊😊 **Saffron** – *Piazza Sant'Agostino 16. ☎0575 18 24 560. Closed Mon.* Restaurant featuring contemporary design mixed with rustic features.

The menu features traditional and imaginative fusion dishes, as well as raw fish options and sushi.

TAKING A BREAK

Vita Bella – *Piazza San Francesco. ☎0575 35 61 47.* Smallest of three lively cafés by San Francesco, with outdoor tables. Light, good food.

SHOPPING

Al Canto de' Bacci – *Corso Italia 65. ☎0575 35 58 04. Closed Sun–Mon.* Fine-quality Tuscan cured meats and wines.

Galleria Cesalpino – *Via Cesalpino 29. ☎0575 182 24 94. Closed Mon.* Quality artisans: clothing in Casentino wool, jewellery, art, wine and local products.

EVENTS AND FESTIVALS

Saracen Joust – *Giostra del Saracino, 3rd Sat of Jun, first Sun of Sept. www.giostra delsaracinoarezzo.it.* 14C–15C joust and costume parade, Piazza Grande.

Antiques Fair – *1st Sun and preceding Sat of each month. www.fieraantiquaria.org.*

Sansepolcro ★

Monterchi and Caprese

This small industrial town, once the centre of the Buitoni pasta empire, lies in the centre of the Upper Tiber Valley. Still enclosed within walls, its houses date from the Middle Ages–18C. Its name recalls two 10C pilgrims returning from the Holy Land who brought relics of the Holy Sepulchre, (*santo sepolcro***) and a chapel was built to hold them. A village, Borgo San Sepolcro, grew up around the chapel and was the birthplace of Piero della Francesca (born c. 1415–20), the son of a shoemaker. He died here in 1492.**

▶ **Population:** 15,801.
🜨 **Michelin Map:** Michelin Atlas p 39 and Map 563 – I 18 or Map 735 Fold 15.
🛈 **Info:** Via Matteotti 8. ☎0575 74 05 36. www. valtiberinaintoscana.it.
▶ **Location:** Sansepolcro is situated on the border of Tuscany and Umbria on the E45 motorway between Cesena and Perugia.
👁 **Don't Miss:** Piero della Francesca paintings in the Museo Civico.

👣 WALKING TOUR

Patrician Streets ★

In the heart of the old town is a vast square, **Piazza Torre di Berta**, a popular meeting place. Between the square

and the wide Via Matteotti, runs **Via XX Settembre**, flanked by Gothic, Renaissance and Mannerist mansions (*palazzi*); a few truncated medieval towers remain (*nos 127 and 131*). The narrow alleyway, **Via Del Buon Umore**, has buildings separated by five brick arches. Via XX Settembre has attractive shops and leads (*left into Via Luca Pacioli*) to the **Church of San Lorenzo**, with a superb **Deposition from the Cross★** by Rosso Fiorentino.

Cathedral (Duomo)
Via Matteotti.
The Cathedral of St John the Baptist (early 11C) has both Romanesque and Gothic elements. Its austere façade has an alabaster rose window. The square and pointed bell tower was rebuilt in the 14C in the Franciscan style. **Palazzo delle Laudi**, now the town hall, has, like **Palazzo Aggiunti** (*opposite*), a Mannerist design (late 16C–early 17C).

▶ From Via Matteotti pass through Porta della Pesa.

Museo Civico★★
Via Aggiunti 65.
🕙Open daily 10 Jun–25 Sept 10am–1.30pm, 2.30–7pm; rest of the year 10am–1pm, 2.30–6pm. 🕙Closed 1 Jan, 25 Dec. ✆€8. ✆0575 73 22 18. www.museocivicosansepolcro.it.
The **museum** highlights are **paintings★★★** by **Piero della Francesca** – the superb triptych of the *Virgin Mary of Mercy*, which shows echoes of Masaccio, especially in the Crucifixion, two fresco fragments (*St Julian* and *St Ludovic*) and a Resurrection.
Other artists born in Sansepolcro – Santi di Tito, Matteo di Giovanni, Raffaellino del Colle – are here, as are Bassano, Signorelli and the della Robbia School.

▶ Arrive at Piazza San Francesco.

Piazza San Francesco
The **Church of San Francesco** (12C–18C) with its pointed bell tower stands opposite the **Church of Santa Maria delle Grazie**, which is flanked by a small loggia with two arches; the door is decorated above with skeletons and two skulls.
The street right of San Francesco has the **Casa di Piero della Francesca** (*no 71*), the artist's 15C home.
The Medici fortress remains are on the outskirts, towards Perugia.

EXCURSIONS
Anghiari★
28km/17.3mi NE of Arezzo by SP43; or 31.5km/19.5mi by SS73.
🅘 *Corso Matteotti 103. ✆0575 74 92 79. www.valtiberinaintoscana.it.*
In 1440 a battle between the troops of Florence and Milan was fought on the wide Tiber Plain between Anghiari and Sansepolcro. Florence won. Leonardo da Vinci memorialised the Battle of Anghiari in the Hall of the Five Hundred in the Palazzo Vecchio (City Hall) in Florence. Perched on a hill overlooking the Tiber Valley, the walled town of Anghiari (*pop. 5,501*) occupies a picturesque **site★**. Narrow, winding, irregular streets run up and down the hillside, preserving its medieval charm. Its compact historic centre radiates from Corso Matteotti. Via Mazzini has the Busatti textile factory with a shop on the ground floor (*no 14*) for fine textiles.

Museo Statale di Palazzo Taglieschi★
Piazza Mameli. 🕙Open Tue–Thu 9.15am–6pm, Fri–Sun 10.15am–7pm; last admission 45min before closing. 🕙Closed Mon, 1 Jan, 25 Dec. ✆€4. ✆0575 78 80 01. www.polomusealetoscana.beniculturali.it.
The 15C *palazzo* exhibits relate to Upper Tiber Valley traditions – domestic, religious and farm. There is furniture, 15C–16C paintings and Renaissance sculptures including a superb painted Madonna by Jacopo della Quercia and a Nativity by the della Robbia school.

Museo della Battaglia d'Anghiari
Piazza Mameli 1–2. 🕙Open 9.30am–1pm, 2.30–6.30pm (2 Nov–Mar 5.30pm). 🕙Closed 25 Dec. ✆€4. ✆0575 78 70 23. www.battaglia.anghiari.it.
The battle is recounted in its political, military and local aspects. One room has 2,200 painted soldiers, others show rare manuscripts, reproductions of Leonardo's drawings; as well as armour, crafted here.

▶ A few yards farther along Via Garibaldi, turn right and then left. In the square stands the town hall with its many shields. Take the narrow street opposite leading to another small square.

Chiesa di Badi★

This much-altered Romanesque **church** has an unusual and asymmetrical layout. An altar (*second to the left*), with fine Renaissance *pietra serena* decoration, is attributed to Desiderio da Settignano.

Monterchi

17km/11mi S. SS73 to SP221.

Via della Reglia **exhibition centre** (*spazio espositivo;* ◷ *Open daily 15 Mar–3 Nov 9am–1pm, 2–7pm; 4 Nov–14 Mar 10am–1pm, 2–5pm;* ◷ *Closed 25 Dec;* ✆ €6.50; ⌛ ✆ 0575 70 713, www.madonnadelparto.it) houses an enigmatic work by Piero della Francesca, the **Virgin Mary giving Birth★** (*Madonna del Parto*). This fresco, restored, was painted at about the same time as the Legend of the True Cross cycle in Arezzo and its majesty is reminiscent of the other work.

Caprese Michelangelo

Take the E45 towards Cesena; in Pieve Santo Stefano follow the sign for Caprese Michelangelo (about 25km/15mi). Park at the top of the village. A cobbled street (pedestrians only) leads to the castle.

The controversy as to whether Chiusi della Verna or Caprese was the birthplace of Michelangelo on 6 March 1475 was settled in 1875 by the discovery of a copy of the artist's birth certificate – the original had been lost. Michelangelo was born in Caprese, where his father, a magistrate (*podestà*) employed by Florence, had been posted. After his birth, Michelangelo was placed with a wet-nurse in Settignano, near Florence.

Casa di Michelangelo

◷ *Open Apr–1 Nov and 26 Dec–6 Jan 9.30am–1pm, 3–6.30pm; rest of the year Sat–Sun and public hols 10am–1pm, 3–5.30pm.* ✆ €4. ✆ 0575 79 37 76. www.casanatalemichelangelo.it.

The 14C castle contains **Casa del Podestà**, the modest Magistrate's House adorned with coats of arms, where Michelangelo's family lived. Now the **Museo Casa Natale di Michelangelo** (Michelangelo's House and Museum), it displays plaster casts and photographs of the artist's sculptures and paintings; reproductions of paintings illustrate his life. Michelangelo was probably born in the small room at the end of the corridor. The modest 13C Church of St John the Baptist (San Giovanni Battista), below the castle, is where Michelangelo might have been christened.

ADDRESSES

🛏STAY

◷ **La Meridiana** – *Piazza IV Novembre 8, Anghiari.* ✆0575 78 81 02. www.hotella meridiana.it. **P**. A comfortable family-run hotel-restaurant in the centre.

◷◷◷ **Relais La Commenda** – *Località Commenda 6, Tavernelle di Anghiari, 3km/1.8mi W of Anghiari.* ✆0575 72 33 56. www.relaislacommenda.com. Charming, refined former monastery set in a park. Has a pool and patio.

◷◷◷◷ **Relais Palazzo di Luglio** – *Frazione Cignano 35, 2km/1.24mi NW of Sansepolcro.* ✆0575 75 00 26. www.relais palazzodiluglio.com. 4 suites. ⌛. Elegant 18C hilltop villa near olive groves with Tiber Valley view.

🍴EAT

◷ **Da Ventura** – *Via Aggiunti 30, Sansepolcro.* ✆0575 74 25 60. www. albergodaventura.it. Closed Sun dinnertime and Mon. A traditional restaurant offering mushroom and truffle specialities in season. Rustic furnishings and a beautiful collection of cartoons on the walls create a familial atmosphere.

◷◷◷ **Da Alighiero** – *Via Garibaldi 8, Anghiari.* 0575 78 80 40. Closed Tue. Hidden amid the maze of streets in Anghiari, this authentic and atmospheric trattoria is run by a Tuscan who is as organised as he is friendly and generous. Try the cantucci biscuits.

EVENT

Palio della Balestra – *Second Sun in Sept.* Sansepolcro holds a **crossbow competition** in Renaissance costume.

Cortona★★

Cortona occupies a remarkable **site★★** on the steep slope overlooking the Chiana Valley. The town once belonged to the League of Twelve Etruscan Towns before coming under the control of Rome. Its medieval town walls are commanded by a huge citadel (*fortezza*) that replaced the Etruscan precinct. Annexed to Florence in 1411, Cortona has barely changed since the Renaissance, with fine mansions (*palazzi*) and narrow, paved streets, mostly very steep, leading to irregularly shaped squares lined with arcades and public buildings.

WALKING TOUR

San Domenico

This early 15C Gothic church contains a Madonna with Angels and Saints by Luca Signorelli and a fresco by Fra Angelico of the Madonna and Child between two Dominican Friars. The promenade opposite the church offers delightful views of Lake Trasimeno.

Narrow street in Cortona

© Brigitta L. House/Michelin

▶ **Population:** 21,984.
🖋 **Michelin Map:** Michelin Atlas p 44 and Map 563 – M 17 and Map 735 Fold 15.
🛈 **Info:** Piazza Signorelli, Palazzo Casali 9; ℘0575 63 72 23. www.comunedicortona.it.
▷ **Location:** Cortona is just off SS71 between Arezzo and Lake Trasimeno.
⊚ **Don't Miss:** The views of the Chiana Valley.

Palazzo Comunale

The **town hall** building dates from the 13C but was completed in the 16C with a bell tower and a huge flight of steps leading up from Piazza della Repubblica. The **Sala del Consiglio★** (Council Chamber) overlooks Piazza Signorelli, the site of the original town hall. The medieval character is evident in the richly painted ceiling subdivided by wooden beams and the stone walls, one of which is decorated with a huge fresco.

Palazzo Casali★

Built in the 13C and named after its former owners, lords of the city, the Piazza Signorelli façade is early 17C, but the side decorated with coats of arms of *podestas* is Gothic.

Museo dell'Accademia Etrusca e della Città di Cortona (MAEC)★

🕓 *Open Apr–Oct daily 10am–7pm; Nov–Mar Tue–Sun 10am–5pm.*
🕓 *Closed 25 Dec.* ⊜ *€10.* ℘*0575 63 72 35. www.cortonamaec.org.*

Palazzo Casali houses the **museum**, with its most important exhibits around the main hall, including an Etruscan bronze **oil lamp★★** (second half of the 4C BC). There are bronze Etruscan and Roman statuettes, ceramics and 15C Italian ivories. Among the paintings are works by Signorelli and his followers, a superb Miracle of St Benedict by Andrea Commodi (17C), a Madonna by Pinturicchio and a huge Virgin and Child with Saints by Pietro da Cortona (17C). The smaller rooms display an Egyptian collection, 14C paintings, a lapidary collection dating from Antiquity and funeral urns. The Severini Room contains the works donated to the town by this artist, including *The Gypsy Woman* (1905) and **Motherhood★** (1906).

Piazza del Duomo

The **square** abutting the town walls provides an attractive view of the valley and the cemetery. The **cathedral** was originally built in the Romanesque period, but was altered in the Renaissance.

Museo Diocesano★★

Open Apr–Oct daily 10am–7pm; Nov–Mar Fri–Sun 10am–5pm (25 Dec–6 Jan daily). €5. 0575 62 830.

Opposite the cathedral in the Chiesa del Gesù (Church of Jesus), which has a superb carved ceiling dating from 1536, are the valuable collections of the **Diocesan Museum**.

Fra Angelico, who came to Cortona to paint, is represented by two of his best works – an **Annunciation** and a **Madonna** surrounded by the Saints. There are a number of superb paintings by the Sienese School – a Madonna by Duccio, a Madonna with the Angels and a huge Crucifixion by Pietro Lorenzetti (late 14C) and a triptych of the Madonna and Child (1434) (restored) by Sassetta. Select works by the local painter Luca Signorelli include *Communion of the Apostles* and the *Deposition* in which the horror is heightened by the gentle landscape.

Among the sculptures is a fine 2C Roman sarcophagus with low-reliefs (Lapiths and Centaurs). The former vestry displays church plate, including the Vagnucci reliquary made by Giusto da Firenze (1458). The small lower church is covered in 16C frescoes based on designs by Vasari; its expressive painted terracotta Pietà dates from the 16C.

▷ Return to Piazza della Repubblica and turn left on to Via Berrettini.

Art in Cortona

Cortona began to attract artists in the 14C and the Sienese School proceeded to predominate until the arrival of Fra Angelico. The town's main claim to fame, however, is as the birthplace of a number of famous Old Masters.

Luca Signorelli (1450–1523) was a painter who, through his dramatic temperament and sculpture-like forms, was a precursor of Michelangelo. He died when he fell from the scaffolding as he painted frescoes in the Villa Passerini (*east of Cortona*).

Among architects the most famous name is that of Domenico Bernabei (1508–49), known as **Boccador** (literally "Mouth of Gold"), who worked principally in France; at the age of 25 he was invited by King François I to Paris where he worked from 1533 to 1549 on the design of the City Hall.

Pietro da Cortona (1596–1669), painter and architect, was one of the great masters of the Roman Baroque style. He had a prodigious imagination and was a genius in interior decoration. His main works include the decoration of the Pitti Palace in Florence and the Barberini Palace in Rome and the façade of the Church of Santa Maria della Pace in Rome.

The painter **Gino Severini** (1883–1966) was born in Cortona and became one of the best representatives of Futurism, the great Italian avant-garde movement created in 1909.

The people of Cortona have a very special regard for St Francis, who set up a hermitage at Le Celle; for St Margaret, a 13C Magdalen; and for Brother Elias, St Francis' first friend and follower, who supervised the construction of the basilica in Assisi and is buried beneath the chancel in the Church of San Francesco.

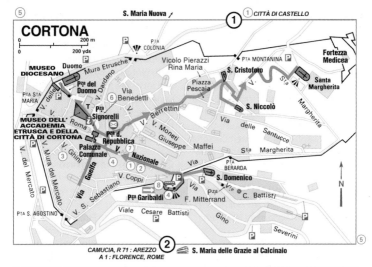

San Cristoforo

This small, elongated **church**, which is said to date from the late 12C, is surmounted by a bellcote. The sacristy serves as the entrance. Inside there is a 14C fresco of the Crucifixion, the Annunciation and the Ascension.

San Niccolò

An elegant porch extends across the façade and down one side of the 15C **church**. The Baroque interior includes two works by Luca Signorelli: (*left of the entrance*) a fresco of the Virgin Mary surrounded by the Saints and (*on the high altar*) the **Deposition of Christ★**.

Santuario di Santa Margherita

The **church**, which stands above the town, was built in the 19C, but the bell tower dates from the 17C. The interior contains (*left of the chancel*) the Gothic **tomb★** of the saint (1362); the saint's body lies on view at the high altar; (*right of the chancel*) a moving representation of the Crucifixion (13C).

From the esplanade there are some attractive **views★** of the town, the valley below and Lake Trasimeno. To the right of the terrace in front of the church is Via Santa Margherita decorated by Severini with mosaics representing the **Stations of the Cross**.

ADDITIONAL SIGHT
Santa Maria Nuova

Proudly standing below Porta Colonia, its square plan reflects the Renaissance ideal. The later dome is by Vasari. All are 16C. Among its paintings is *Birth of the Virgin* by Allori (*right of altar*).

EXCURSIONS
Santa Maria del Calcinaio★★
3km/2mi S of Cortona by exit ②.

This church was built between 1485 and 1513 in the style of Brunelleschi, to designs by Francesco di Giorgio Martini of Siena. It is constructed of a dark-coloured stone and is admirable for the elegance and coherence of its overall design and its well-balanced proportions. The oculus in the façade contains an outstanding stained-glass window (1516) by Guillaume de Marcillat depicting the Madonna of Mercy.

Tanella di Pitagora

3km/2mi S of Cortona by exit (2); at the left-hand hairpin bend, continue straight on towards Arezzo.

The circular Etruscan **tomb**, which dates from the 4C BC, stands in a delightful setting surrounded by cypress trees. It was misnamed the Tomb of Pythagoras because of an age-old confusion between Cortona and Crotona; Pythagoras the mathematician lived in Crotona (Calabria).

Eremo delle Celle

3.5km/2mi E of Cortona by exit (1); after 1.5km/1mi, at a right-hand bend, turn left into a narrow road.

On his return from Rome, after the Pope had officially recognised the Franciscan Order (1210), **St Francis** came to Cortona. He withdrew to Le Celle where he founded his first community here for its natural silence and austerity.

The **monastery** is occupied by Capuchins and retains the original chapel used by St Francis' first companions. Behind the altar is the tiny cell used by St Francis himself, to which he returned after receiving the stigmata in La Verna.

Abbazia di Farneta

15.5km/10mi SW of Cortona by exit S on SR71. ○*Open daily 9am–dusk.* ✎*Free.*

This austere T-shaped **church** was built by the Benedictines on the site of a Roman temple. The most interesting feature is the **crypt** (9C–10C), which has ribbed barrel vaulting and three multifoiled apsidal chapels supported by Roman columns from a variety of sources. Since 1937, the abbey has been closely linked with Don Sante Felici, a committed archaeologist with Tuscan roots who discovered the crypt, as well as numerous archaeological remains and fossils found at Farneta and the surrounding area, some of which can be seen here.

Castello di Montecchio Vesponi★

3.5km/2mi S by SS 71. ✆*333 76 76 408. www.castellodimontecchio.it.*

The **castle** stands on a rise on the east side of the road between Castiglion Fiorentino and Cortona. It is interesting for the size of its crenellated outer wall reinforced by eight small towers and for its keep (*30m/97ft*), which contained the main apartments. This was the largest fortress in the Chiana Valley, retaining its military importance until the 17C.

Castiglion Fiorentino

10km/6.2mi N on SP37, right on SS71.
🛈 *Piazza Risorgimento 19.* ✆*0575 65 82 78. www.prolococastiglionfiorentino.it.*
Once the site of an Etruscan settlement, the town's first stronghold (*castiglion*), was built on the hilltop during the 5C Barbarian invasions. It was replaced in the 11C–12C by a citadel (*cassero*) dominated by a slender tower.

The streets of Castiglion (pop. 11,644) radiate downhill from Piazzale del Cassero, location of the Pinacoteca. The Collegiata di San Giuliano lies at the eastern edge.

Pinacoteca★

Take the street to the right that climbs up behind the town hall. ○*Open May–Sept Thu–Sun 10am–1pm, 3.30–7pm; Oct–Apr Fri–Sun 10am–12.30pm, 3.30–6pm.* ✎*Free admission.* ✆*0575 65 94 57. www.museicastiglionfiorentino.it.*

The **art gallery**, in the Chapel of Sant'Angelo next to the citadel, contains a number of valuable paintings, including two Umbrian Crucifixion scenes painted on wood and dating from the 13C and 14C, a painting of St Francis of Assisi by Margaritone of Arezzo (13C), a Virgin Mary in Majesty (14C) by Taddeo Gaddi and two reredos panels by Giovanni di Paolo (15C).

There are also some superb pieces of church plate, including a bust-reliquary of St Ursula (14C Rhenish School), a Crucifix-reliquary from the Moselle (late 12C) and a French Crucifix dating from the second half of the 13C.

From the top room (*saletta della torre*), there is a wonderful view of the Church of San Giuliano, the countryside and the mountains.★

Collegiata di San Giuliano

This **church** has a 17C carved wooden presbytery and interesting works of art, including a painted earthenware St Anthony Abbot and an Annunciation from the della Robbia workshop, a Virgin Mary in Majesty by Bartolomeo della Gatta and *Mary and Joseph Adoring the Infant Jesus* by Lorenzo di Credi (15C). The 16C **Chiesa del Gesù** (Church of Jesus) close to the Collegiata has a fine Baroque interior.

Chiostro di San Francesco

These small **cloisters**, next to the uninspiring 13C Church of St Francis, were rebuilt in the 17C with an upper storey that forms a balcony with colonnettes.

ADDRESSES

STAY

 Albergo Ristorante Portole – *Località Portole, 7km/4.3mi above Cortona in the direction of Città di Castello.* 0575 69 10 08. www.portole.it. *20 rooms. Restaurant.* . Traditional stone building, comfortable rooms and splendid views over the Chiana Valley, Lake Trasimeno and Mount Amiata.

 Hotel San Luca – *Piazza Garibaldi 1.* 0575 63 04 60. www.sanluca cortona.com. *60 rooms.* In Cortona's historic centre, modern and elegant. Best views on the upper floors.

 Il Falconiere Relais – *Località San Martino a Bocena 370, 3.5km/2mi N of Cortona.* 0575 61 26 79. www.ilfalconiere. it. *22 rooms.* This 17C villa has beautifully furnished rooms and a spa. Elegant restaurant, cheerful and airy, has Tuscan specialities. Marvellous valley view.

EAT

 La Grotta – *Piazza Baldelli 3.* 0575 63 02 71. www.trattorialagrotta.it. *Closed Tue.* Small family-run trattoria serves local dishes. Just off the main square.

 La Bucaccia– *Via Ghibellina 17.* 0575 60 60 39. www.labucaccia.it. *Closed Mon in winter. Reservations required.* Housed in an old 13C palazzo built on a Roman road (part of which can still be seen in the main dining room), this restaurant serves exquisite regional cuisine including an excellent selection of cheeses and Chianina beef dishes.

 La Locanda del Molino – *Località Montanare 10. 8km/5mi SE of Cortona.* 0575 614016. www.locandadelmolino. com. *2 rooms. Reservations required.* This rustic yet charming restaurant occupies an old family mill. In the kitchen, the chef creates traditional specialities such as fried rabbit and nettle with ricotta cheese *gnudi* (ravioli filling without the pasta) in a fresh tomato sauce.

 Osteria del Teatro – *Via Maffei 2.* 0575 63 05 56. www.osteria-del-teatro.it. *Closed Wed. Reservations required.* A number of rooms with open fireplaces combine to create this friendly trattoria's warm and lively atmosphere that is unmistakably reminiscent of a love for the theatre and music. Chef (and owner) Emiliano prepares traditional and authentic tasty dishes.

 Tonino – *Piazza Garibaldi 1.* 0575 63 05 00. Restaurant with splendid terrace, overlooking the valley to Lake Trasimeno – a great photograph setting.

TAKING A BREAK

Caffè degli Artisti – *Via Nazionale 18.* 0575 60 12 37. Good humour, good house cocktails and family atmosphere.

Caffè La Saletta – *Via Nazionale 26/28.* 0575 60 33 66. Elegant wine bar adds jazz, blues or classical guitar concerts on Saturdays. A pleasant evening of music and wine.

Pasticceria Banchelli – *Via Nazionale 64.* 0575 60 10 52. This pastry shop makes gingerbread, Etruscan biscuits and home-made ices.

SHOPPING

Galleria "Il Pozzo" – *Via Nazionale 10.* 0575 60 37 30. www.cortonagiftshop. com. Converted from 11C wells, this gallery features local artists.

EVENTS

Giostra dell'Archidado – *Piazza Signorelli. Late May or beginning of Jun.* www.giostraarchidado.com. Crossbow competition.

Sagra della Bistecca – *14 and 15 Aug.* Huge barbecue in public gardens.

Mercato dell'Antiquariato – *Last week of Aug–1st week of Sept.* www. cortonantiquaria.it. Antiques fair.

Monte San Savino★

and Santa Maria delle Vertighe

This medieval town was the birthplace of the sculptor and architect, Andrea Contucci, otherwise known as Sansovino (1470–1529). A thoroughfare lined with some fine historic buildings runs right through the town, linking the two gates set within the walls of the old stronghold (*cassero*).

> ▶ **Population:** 8,702.
> ⚙ **Michelin Map:** Michelin Atlas p 44 and Map 563 – M 17 or Map 735 Fold 15.
> 🖥 **Info:** Piazza Gamurrini 25. ☎0575 84 94 18. www.monteservizi.it.
> ◐ **Location:** Monte San Savino is 21km/13mi SW of Arezzo.

TOWN

The main monuments of this village, enclosed within four medieval gates, lie on or near Piazza Gamurrini.

Piazza G F Gamurrini

The **square** lies near the Porta Fiorentina and is marked by a 17C obelisk. The humble 17C Church of **Santa Chiara** contains two examples of terracotta ware by Sansovino – a group depicting St Sebastian, St Lawrence and St Roch and a Madonna and Child between Four Saints, glazed by Giovanni della Robbia.

Museo del Cassero

🕐*Open Apr–Sept Wed 10am–1pm, Thu–Sun 10am–1pm, 3–6pm; Nov–Mar Wed and Sat 10.30am–12.30pm (Dec–6 Jan Wed 10.30am–12.30pm, Sat–Sun and public hols 10am–1pm, 3–6pm).* 🕐*Closed 1 Jan, 25 Dec.* ⊗*Free.* ☎*0575 84 94 18. www.monteservizi.it.* The fortress houses the **ceramics museum**: 18C and 19C local works from San Savino and Val di Chiana, medieval ceramics and majolica, and contemporary ceramics.

Loggia dei Mercanti★

The lines of this majestic loggia, attributed to Sansovino (1518–20), are emphasized by the use of *pietra serena*. Its Corinthian capitals display great finesse.

Palazzo Comunale★

The **mansion** stands opposite the loggia and was built for the del Monte family by Sangallo the Elder between 1515 and 1517. Its ground floor built in heavily rusticated stonework, supports a well-structured *piano nobile*, including windows surmounted by alternating rounded and triangular pediments. A fine del Monte family coat of arms decorates a corner. The Renaissance courtyard contains two wells; the upper storey has mullioned windows.

Chiesa della Misericordia

This Romanesque **church** has a nave with wooden rafters. It was redecorated in Baroque style during the 17C–18C. The tomb immediately to the left of the main entrance was an early work by Sansovino (1498).

Palazzo Pretorio

This 14C building, formerly the **residence** of the Florentine magistrate (*podestà*), is decorated with the coats of arms of those who held the office.

Sant'Agostino

This 14C **church** (extended in the 16C–17C) is decorated with a fine Gothic doorway and a rose window with stained glass designed by Guillaume de Marcillat. Inside are a number of early 15C frescoes. To the left of the church is the entrance to small cloisters with semicircular arcades built to plans by Sansovino. Beyond them is the **Baptistery of San Giovanni**, which has a splendid door designed by the artist.

EXCURSIONS

Gargonza

About 7km/4.34mi W on SS73.
The poet Dante came to a meeting here between Guelfs and Ghibellines to

decide who would be exiled. The hamlet has been converted to a hotel (⌖See Addresses).

Santuario di Santa Maria delle Vertighe

2km/1mi E.

A stand of chestnut trees flanks this 16C building, which was formerly a Marian church dating from the 11C. The nave and aisles, roofed with wooden rafters, incorporate the Romanesque chevet of the original chapel which was the subject of popular devotion. This ensured that the two successive portraits of the Virgin could be kept in their original setting. They consist of a fresco of the Assumption (partly preserved) which adorns the small oven-vaulted apse, and the **Virgin altarpiece★** by Margaritone of Arezzo (13C), which became the subject of worship after being placed on a lower level in the 15C.

Lucignano★

8km/4.9mi from E78 S to SP19.

🄸 *Piazza del Tribunale. ℰ0575 83 80 01. www.visitlucignano.it.*

Lucignano (*pop. 3,544*) is a peaceful village in the Val di Chiana. It has an unusual elongated shape as the main street rises in spirals before entering a picturesque maze of medieval streets.

Backing onto the town walls are the remains of the 14C **castle** (*cassero*). Opposite stands the **Collegiate Church of San Michele** built in the late 16C.

In front of the church is a beautifully designed staircase. It is concave then convex in shape and set around an oval stairhead. Inside the church, the barrel vaulting is highlighted by the *pietra serena* of the pillars and arches. The monumental Baroque altar was designed by Andrea Pozzo.

The street running along the left side of the church leads to Piazza del Tribunale; at one end stands the small **Palazzo Comunale** decorated with coats of arms. The **museum** (🕓*Open Apr–Oct Wed–Mon 10.30am–1pm, 2.30–6pm; Nov–Mar Fri–Mon 10.30am–1pm, 2.30–5pm;* 👓€5; ℰ0575 83 80 01) includes a number of Sienese paintings (13C–15C) and (*ground floor*) a remarkable gold gem-encrusted reliquary, which, owing to its shape, is known as the **Tree of St Francis★★**. It is a masterpiece produced in Sienese goldsmiths' shops during the 14C–15C.

The Church of **San Francesco** (*right of the Palazzo Comunale*) has a harmonious Romanesque façade of alternating black and white stone.

ADDRESSES

🛏 STAY

🍽🍽🍽 **Logge dei Mercanti** – *Corso San Gallo 40. ℰ0575 81 07 10. www.loggedei mercanti.it. 12 rooms.* In front of Loggia dei Mercanti, the village's oldest

Collegiate Church of San Michele, Lucignano

© Clodio/iStock

pharmacy was transformed into a hotel. Rooms have a view of the hills.

 Castello di Gargonza – *Località Gargonza, 8km/5mi W of Monte San Savino.* *0575 84 70 21. www. gargonza.it. 15 rooms.* A medieval hamlet transformed into a hotel removed from time. Modern comforts.

EAT

 Ristorante Belvedere – *Località Bano 226, 4km/2.5mi W of Monte San Savino.* *0575 84 42 62. www. ristorante-belvedere.net. Reservations required.* Good *Chianina* steak, mushrooms and truffles; all local produce. Massimo pairs wines well with food.

San Giovanni Valdarno

and Montevarchi

San Giovanni is one of the main industrial towns in the Arno Valley and is particularly famous for its steel works and the huge lignite mines in the vicinity. The first great painter of the Florentine Renaissance, Masaccio (d. 1428), was born here in 1401.

▶ **Population:** 16,823; Montevarchi 24,490.

 Michelin Map: Atlas p 38 and Map 563 – I 16 or Map 735 Fold 15.

 Info: Piazza Cavour 3. *055 91 26 268. www.prolocosangiovanni valdarno.it.*

 Location: San Giovanni Valdarno is about 40km/ 25mi from Florence on the motorway (A1) between Florence and Rome.

TOWN

San Giovanni is arranged around two central *piazze* – Piazza Cavour and Piazza Masaccio – between which stands the Palazzo Pretorio.

Palazzo Pretorio★

This building, which stands in the centre of the town, is emblazoned with the coats of arms of former magistrates (*podestà*). Said to have been designed by Arnolfo di Cambio, the building dates from the 13C and was altered during the Renaissance.

San Giovanni Battista

This early-14C **church** in Piazza Cavour stands opposite the main façade of the Palazzo Pretorio. It resembles its neighbour with its elegant portico decorated with glazed roundels (*tondi*) in the style of the della Robbias.

Santa Maria delle Grazie

Open 8am–noon, 2–7pm.
Behind the Palazzo Pretorio stands this 15C **basilican church** with a 19C neo-Renaissance façade facing Piazza Masaccio. Beneath the porch is an Assumption of the Virgin Mary, a superb, vividly coloured glazed ceramic by Giovanni della Robbia.

Inside the basilica, the high altar is decorated with the fresco of *Our Lady of Grace* (14C), from which the church takes its name. Behind the chancel is a small **museum** (*Open Wed–Sun 10am–1pm, 3–6.30pm; €3.50;* *055 91 23 735; www.museobasilica.it*) containing works by the Florentine School, mainly from the 15C–16C, including a superb **Annunciation★★** by Fra Angelico.

Oratorio di San Lorenzo

To the right on leaving the basilica.
The **chapel**, which is set behind a modest brick and stone façade, contains numerous 14C–15C frescoes and a reredos depicting the Coronation of the Virgin Mary by Giotto's School (*behind the high altar*).

EXCURSION

Pieve di Gropina★

Between Florence and Arezzo, 1.8km/ 1mi SE of Loro Ciuffenna (signposted to San Giustino Valdarno); after

1.2km/0.5mi turn right. ⏰*Open daily 8am–noon, 3–5pm. www.gropina.it.*

The church of San Pietro in Gropina dates from the first half of the 12C and is considered to be the first example of a Romanesque church in Tuscany. It stands on the lower slopes of the Pratomagno, slightly above the Arno Valley. The **interior** is laid out in three aisles. The semicircular central apse has an external gallery with colonnettes; the central colonnettes are interconnected. The richly **carved decoration★** inside the church is unequalled anywhere else in Casentino. The capitals and ambo in the south aisle (the first to be completed) date from the second half of the 12C and are carved in an early Romanesque style still using flattened sculpture. The capitals in the north aisle are more highly sophisticated and are thought to come from Emilian workshops. The most interesting designs are: (*south side, starting from the entrance pillar*) the sow, a symbol of the Church, suckling her litter; the knights-in-arms fighting the demon; the highly stylised vine stocks; the eagles crowning the ambo which is carved both in flattened relief and in the round; (*north side, third column*) the figures of Christ, St Peter and St Paul, Samson killing the lion, and St Ambrose presenting the new Law;

(*fourth column*) the punishment of lust: a man being dragged by his beard and three women whose breasts are being bitten by dragons.

Below the church are remains from two previous churches dating from the 5C and the 8C; both can be visited via the stairs on the right aisle.

Montevarchi
5km/3mi SE.
This village is famous throughout Tuscany for its market selling Arno Valley chickens and wine from the hillsides of Aretino. The streets in the historic old town form parallel arcs on each side of Via Roma. The 18C **Church of San Lorenzo** in Piazza Varchi (*in the middle of Via Roma*) supposedly contains an ampoule of breast milk from the Virgin Mary, kept in the tabernacle on the high altar.

ADDRESSES

🏠STAY
💶 🍽🍽🍽 **Agriturismo Villa Le Vigne** – *Via Caposelvi 84. ℘055 97 07 339. www.villalevigne.it. 8 apts.* 🛁. This 19C villa set among vineyards, offers apartments (*2–8 people*); tastefully decorated and well equipped.

Poppi★
and Bibbiena

The arcaded streets of Poppi are dominated by the proud castle, once the property of the Counts Guidi. It is visible at a distance, nestling in the mountains that were once dear to St Francesco and St Romualdo.

👣WALKING TOUR

UPPER TOWN
A long climb leads up to the entrance to the town, a gateway set among the houses. Overlooking the tiny Piazza Amerighi decorated with a central marble fountain is the **Church of Madonna**

▶ **Population:** 6,114.
🗺 **Michelin Map:** Michelin Atlas p 38 and Map 563 – K 17 or Map 735 Fold 15.
ℹ **Info:** Via Cavour 11. ℘0575 50 21. www. comune.poppi.ar.it.
▶ **Location:** Formerly the main town in the Casentino, Poppi dominates the Arno Valley. Easily reached from Arezzo, 33km/20mi by SS71.

del Morbo (17C) capped by a dome and flanked by porticoes on three sides. **Via Cavour** (*opposite*), also lined with shady porticoes, leads to the right-hand side of the **Church of San Fedele**, built in the 13C by the monks of Vallombrosa.

Castello dei Conti Guidi★

🕐*Open mid Mar–Oct daily 10am–6pm (end of Jun–Aug 7.30pm); rest of the year Thu–Sun 10am–5pm.* ☞€7. 🕿*0575 52 05 16. www.buonconte.com.*

At the top of the upper town beyond a tree-lined esplanade stands a 13C Gothic **castle** with trefoiled window bays, merlons, a barbican and keep. It was built for the *priori* and is now used as the town hall. In the strange **courtyard★**, which is decorated with coats of arms, stands a stone table (*at the rear*) from which justice used to be dispensed. Two rows of roofed wooden balconies and an outside staircase add to the impression of height. The rooms open to the public include the library (*first floor*), containing 20,000 books, some of which date from the 13C and 14C, and the great hall in which the ceiling beams still have their original painted decoration.

At the end of the chamber is a *tondo* representing a Madonna and Child by the Botticelli School and (*right of the door*) a glazed terracotta in the style of the della Robbias. The corner drawing room (*second floor*) has a wonderful fireplace (1512) bearing the coat of arms of the Marquess Gondi. The adjoining chapel is decorated with frescoes attributed to Taddeo Gaddi. From the windows of the drawing room there is a delightful view of the valley and the mountains north towards Camaldoli and east to La Verna.

Zoo

0.5km/0.3mi E of Poppi. 🕐*Open daily 10am–7pm.* ☞€8. 🕿 *0575 50 45 41. www.parcozoopoppi.it.*

This pleasant zoo, devoted to European wildlife, is traversed by a tree-lined circular path round a central lake.

EXCURSIONS
Bibbiena

5km/3.1mi SE of Poppi on S71.

Bibbiena used to extend no further than a hilltop; today it stretches down to the valley floor, making it the largest town in the Casentino area.

Cardinal **Bernardo Dovizi**, better known as **Cardinal Bibbiena** (1470–1520) was born here. He was secretary to Leo X and a friend of Raphael. He was also the author of *La Calandria* (1513), the first comedy in the history of Italian theatre. This type of theatre had not been seen since the days of Ancient Rome, but from the 16C onwards it enjoyed success throughout Europe. The old town, perched right on the top of the hill in a position that guarantees a panoramic view, has sloping narrow streets and is steeped in the discreet charm typical of rugged, mountainous areas like this where ostentation is out of place.

▶ The first entrance is at the top of a long climb, to the left of a major crossroads. The town centre is signposted. Turn into Via Dovizi.

Palazzo Dovizi★

Via Dovizi 26–28.

Palazzo Dovizi is the **residence** commissioned by Bibbiena early in the 16C. It is an austere building with brick facing yet it has a certain air of elegance. The central doorway is surmounted by a coat of arms, and the loggia above the building adds a touch of ethereal originality.

San Lorenzo

This church, standing opposite the palace, was built in the 15C. Its natural stone frontage conceals an interior with a nave and two aisles laid out in a uniform Renaissance style in alternating greys and whites. The aisles are decorated with two glazed **terracotta sculptures★★** by the della Robbias. On the third altar to the right is the *Adoration of the Shepherds*; on the third to the left the *Deposition*.

▶ Continue on Via Dovizi to Piazza Roma, where you will find the 16C Palazzo Comunale. Across the square turn into a narrow street and walk to the end.

Piazza Tarlati

Turn left off the square.

The **square** was named after the Tarlati family, one of whose members, Pier Saccone, had one of the four towers of the fortress (*cassero*) built on this very spot. Very little remains today except the crenellated **Clock Tower** and, to the rear of the square, a wall linking the clock tower to a lower tower.

Opposite it is the **Church of Santi Ippolito e Donato**, built in the early 12C as a private chapel for the Tarlati Castle. Romanesque style, it has an unusually wide transept crossing flanked by very short arms. The walls are covered with numerous 14C–16C frescoes. On the south side just inside the door is a Crucifixion painted by the Master of San Polo in Rosso (13C) followed by a sculpture of the Madonna and Child (14C Tuscan School). In the north transept is a Crucifixion by the School of Giotto (second half of the 14C). The apse contains a triptych of the Madonna and Child with Saints by Bicci di Lorenzo (1435). In the south arm of the transept is a rare painting by Arcangelo di Cola da Camerino, **The Madonna and Child with Angels★**.

To the left of Piazza Tarlati a terrace offers a superb **view★** of the valley with Poppi Castle (*right*) and the rolling wooded hills of Pratomagno in the background.

Santuario della Verna★

Chiusi della Verna, 26km/16mi E of Bibbiena. ◐*Open daily 6.30am–7.30pm (summer 10pm).* ℘*0575 53 41. www.laverna.it.*

The Sanctuary, which has its own hostel (*Foresteria, ℘0575 53 42 10*), sits at an altitude of 1,128m/3,666ft.

In 1213 Count Cattani from Chiusi gave Monte Verna to St Francis, who settled there with his brothers and received the stigmata there in 1224. The sanctuary remains a popular place of pilgrimage, owing to its atmosphere of serenity and meditation and its dramatic **site★★**, perched on the edge of sheer limestone cliffs among pine, fir and beech trees.

Life of St Francis

Halfway along the Corridor of the Stigmata is a door leading to the cave where St Francis used to sleep on a bare stone. The **Chapel of the Stigmata** was built to preserve the place where the miracle occurred. On the end wall is a **Crucifixion** by Andrea della Robbia. The 15C choir stalls are decorated with marquetry (restored in the late 19C) depicting the saints, popes and famous people who bore witness to St Francis' stigmata. The **church** contains two glazed terracotta pieces by Giovanni della Robbia (*on the screen dividing the church in two*) and a terracotta altarpiece (*high altar*) by Andrea della Robbia representing the Assumption of the Virgin Mary. From the square, a path (*88 steps*) leads down to a rock, **Sasso Spico**, where St Francis used to pray.

There also is a small **museum** containing works of art, sacred objects, pharmacy vases of the monks (◐*Open Sun and public hols 10am–noon, 2–5pm; ☞free*).

🚗DRIVING TOUR

THE CASENTINO: NATURE AND SPIRITUALITY

The tour makes a 50km/31mi loop around the Casentino, shown on the regional map (⌖pp288–289).

The Casentino covers about 700sq. km/ 270sq. mi and has 35,000 inhabitants. The Arno flows through the middle of the high valley through the plain of Arezzo before heading to Florence bounded by Mount Falterona, source of the Arno, the Pratomagno, which separates Casentino and Chianti, and Alpe Catenaia, the secondary chain of the Apennines between the Tiber and the Arno. **Parco Nazionale del Monte Falterona e delle Foreste Casentinesi** (▯*Palazzo Vigiani, Via Brocchi 7, Pratovecchio; ℘0575 50 301 or 0575 50 30 29; www.parcoforestecasentinesi.it*) spans more than 36,000ha/89,000acres on the ridge of the Apennines and the Romagna. Within 50km/31mi of the Tuscan capital, Florence, the area remains unspoiled and little visited, even by Italians. The dense forests of fir and chestnut trees, which in the fall sprout the famous porcini, are rich with streams and brooks, meadows with beautiful white cows, wild hills and varied fauna and flora. They are also home to two of the largest monasteries of Tuscany, as well as Romanesque Pieve, medieval castles and 50 works of glazed terracotta by della Robbia.

The main park centre is dedicated to man and the forest.

18km/11mi NE of Poppi, on the SP72 midway between Arezzo and Florence.

Camaldoli★★

The winding **road**★★ from Poppi (*18km/ 11mi*) provides views over the town, the castle and the Arno Valley before climbing the slopes of a small valley and passing through the forest.

St Romuald chose this area, among the mountains of the vast Casentino Forest, as the location for the headquarters of the Camaldolese religious order in the 11C. It is comprised of a monastery, where communal life took place, and the hermitage, where the select group of reclusive monks lived. The two different aspects of the monk's life are harmoniously reflected in the architecture.

Convento★

0575 55 60 12. www.camaldoli.it.
The **monastery** is impressively situated at the end of a dark valley on slopes covered with pine trees.
Within the section that has been converted into accommodation (*Foresteria*), one may see an 11C portico in the courtyard and small 15C cloisters leading to a number of rooms and chapels.
The left-hand entrance in the façade opens into the 16C church. The Baroque interior includes several paintings by Vasari including a Deposition above

St Francis of Assisi (1182–1226)

Francis, who had a brilliant mind, was the son of a wealthy Italian textile merchant of Assisi and a Frenchwoman. As a young man, being fond of society and fired with chivalrous ideals, he lived the life of a rich merchant's son. In 1202 he was taken prisoner during a border dispute with Perugia. On his return to Assisi he fell victim to a serious fever; during his illness he was touched by grace and decided to devote his life to prayer and the poor, hence his nickname, "the poor man" (*il poverello*).

Francis had several visions of the Virgin Mary and Christ; the most famous one, when he received the stigmata, occurred at La Verna. He died in 1226, 16 years after setting up the Order of Minor Friars, a mendicant order, known as the Franciscans. Throughout his life of prayer and penitence, he attracted a large number of followers and he encouraged Clara, a young noblewoman from Assisi, in her religious vocation; she founded the Order of Poor Clares. The real, or legendary, story of his life and the life of his followers was set down in an anonymous work in the 14C. It has now become famous and is called the *Fioretti*.

The simplicity of his lifestyle was evident in his language, which could be understood by even the poorest members of the community. This was the Umbrian vulgar, in which he wrote the *Canticle of the Creatures* (1224), one of the first great poems in the Italian language. As a lover of beauty and nature, preaching love of all living creatures, he celebrated the value of joy in the service of God and was nicknamed "God's juggler". The same simplicity can be seen in the joy with which he invented new and efficient ways of saving souls. He touched the hearts of the common people effectively with his promotion of the Christmas crib.

Camaldoli monastery

© Pegasophoto/iStock

the high altar. The monks' quarters are on the upper floor.

Round to the left of the building is the 15C **pharmacy★★**. Its origins can be traced to the 11C when the monks, having built a hospital, began to care for and treat the sick free of charge. Their hospital functioned until the beginning of the 19C.

Eremo★★
Alt. 1,027m/3,338ft. ℘0575 55 60 21. www.camaldoli.it.

The **Hermitage** is a monastic village of some 20 small houses built between the 13C and 17C, enclosed by a wall. In front of the Hermitage are a few buildings open to the public. On the inner courtyard is the superb 18C **church** with two bell towers and a façade decorated with statues. At the entrance is a fine low-relief by Mino da Fiesole. The interior is decorated in the Neapolitan Baroque style, with a mixture of stuccowork, gold leaf, marble, paintings, wood carvings and statues, together with a number of older works. In St Anthony's Chapel (*left of the entrance to the rear*) there is a glazed earthenware figure (15C) by Andrea della Robbia. The apse is flanked by two marble **tabernacles★★** (15C) by Desiderio da Settignano; the Crucifixion is attributed to Bronzino. Opposite the church is the tiny garden and St Romuald's cell, a small apartment with dark wainscoting laid out like the

other monks' lodgings with a living room where the monk lived, slept and worked, a private chapel, a woodshed, a washing area and a store-room off a single corridor.

▷ 5km/3mi N via the SP72.

Stia
This village lies at the confluence of the Stia and the Arno, which rises only a short distance away on Monte Falterona. It contains some relics of the time when it was known as Palagio.

In Piazza Bernardo Tanucci, an attractive but narrow and elongated square, stands the 12C church of **Santa Maria Assunta**, much altered over the years. The Romanesque interior with its nave and two aisles, divided by columns with fine decorative capitals, contains a number of interesting **works of art★**. The triptych of the Annunciation (*first chapel on the right*) is by Bicci di Lorenzo (1414). There is a superb glazed terracotta tabernacle (*chapel to the right of the chancel*) by the della Robbias and a 14C wooden Crucifix (*centre of the apse*). The Madonna and Child (*chapel to the left of the chancel*) is by Andrea della Robbia and the Madonna and Child with two Angels (*over the altar*) is by the Master of Varlungo. The early 15C painting of the Assumption (*above the altar in the north aisle*) is by the Master of Borgo alla Collina.

The ancient **castle** (*Palagio Fiorentino, northeast of the village*), which belonged to the Guidi, has been totally restored in the neo-Gothic style popular in the late 19C. The **Museo d'Arte Contemporanea** (*second floor;* ◷*Open by appointment,* ✆*0575 50 38 85*) displays collections ranging from Futurism (1916) to contemporary art. The common characteristic of the artists represented is their love of Tuscany.

Romena★

Romena lies within the administrative district of Pratovecchio Stia (*2km/1mi north*), the neighbouring village that was the birthplace of Paolo Uccello, the artist who specialised in portraying volume and almost abstract compositions.

Pieve di San Pietro★

The road from Pratovecchio provides a view of the delightful **chevet of the church** and its two rows of decorative arcading. This is a particularly fine example of early 12C Romanesque architecture. The church lost its first two bays and its original façade in the 17C as the result of a landslide. The interior has columns carved out of single blocks of stone and crowned with attractive carved capitals. The central apse has attractive half-barrel vaulting.

▶ A few yards to the left on the road back to Pratovecchio is a tarmac path leading to the castle.

Castello★

◷*Opening time varies.* ▥€3. ✆*335 62 44 440. www.castellodiromena.it.*
The impressive ruins of **Romena Castle** stand on a hilltop overlooking the Casentino countryside. Built for Count Guidi and his descendants in the 11C, the castle now has only three of the original 14 towers – the keep, postern and prison. This was the setting for an episode narrated by Dante in his *Inferno* (Canto XXX, Verses 46–90). A man named Master Adam minted counterfeit florins here (21 carats instead of 24) at the request of the Guidi. His crime was discovered and he was arrested

and burnt at the stake in Florence in 1281, the statutory punishment for all counterfeiters.

There is a magnificent **view★★** of the picturesque ruins of the castle and its avenue of cypress trees from a point several hundred metres along the Poppi to Consuma road (SP70).

ADDRESSES

▨STAY

▱ **Foresteria del Monastero di Camaldoli** – *Via Camaldoli.* ✆*0575 55 60 13. www.camaldoli.it.* ▱. *Benedictine monks offer hospitality for those spending time on a personal retreat or enrolled in their courses.*

▱▱ **Albergo Ristorante La Torricella** – *Località Torricella 14, Ponte a Poppi, 4km/2.4mi N of Poppi.* ✆*0575 52 70 45. www.latorricella.com. 21 rooms. Restaurant.* ▣. *On a hill facing Poppi castle are comfortable rooms. The restaurant has a panoramic view.*

▱▱▱ **Borgo I Tre Baroni** – *Via di Camaldoli 52, Moggiona, 5km/3mi SW of Camaldoli.* ✆*0575 55 62 04. www.itrebaroni. it. 24 rooms. 5 suites. Restaurant.* Two Baroni sons are in the kitchen (▨*See restaurant Mater below*); a third serves good wines. New, with charm and elegance.

▨/EAT

▱▱ **Il Cedro** – *Via di Camaldoli 20, Moggiona, 5km/3mi SW of Camaldoli.* ✆*0575 55 60 80. www.ristoranteilcedro. com. Open lunchtime Wed–Sun; Fri and Sat dinnertime by reservation only.* This excellent provincial restaurant, simply furnished and family-run supplements their cuisine with mushrooms and truffles in season.

▱▱ **Mater** – *Via di Camaldoli 52, Moggiona, 5km/3mi SW of Camaldoli.* ✆*366 50 35 127. www.ristorantemater.it. Closed Wed.* Seasonal cuisine made from locally sourced ingredients. Choose from the *à la carte* or opt for one of three tasting menus – the "territorio" menu evokes traditional flavours and recipes from Arezzo and the Casentino area.

SHOPPING

Panno casentino is special wool famous to this area since the Middle Ages.

INDEX

INDEX

INDEX

INDEX

INDEX

🏨 STAY

INDEX

MAPS AND PLANS

MAP LEGEND

	Sight	Seaside resort	Winter sports resort	Spa
Worth a special journey	★★★	��	✹✹✹	‡‡‡
Worth a detour	★★	� ☆	✹✹	‡‡
Interesting	★	☆	✹	‡

Tourism

◉ ➡	Sightseeing route with departure point indicated	AZ B	Map co-ordinates locating sights
⌂ ♦ ⌂ ♦	Ecclesiastical building	🛈	Tourist information
🕍 ☪	Synagogue – Mosque	⚔ ∴	Historic house, castle – Ruins
⌂	Building (with main entrance)	⌣ ☼	Dam – Factory or power station
■	Statue, small building	☆ ⌒	Fort – Cave
✝	Wayside cross	⛏	Prehistoric site
◎	Fountain	▾ Ψ	Viewing table – View
━●━━►━	Fortified walls – Tower – Gate	▲	Miscellaneous sight

Recreation

🏇	Racecourse	🏃	Waymarked footpath
⛸	Skating rink	◈	Outdoor leisure park/centre
≋ 🏊	Outdoor, indoor swimming pool	🎿	Theme/Amusement park
⚓	Marina, moorings	⚘	Wildlife/Safari park, zoo
⛺	Mountain refuge hut	✿	Gardens, park, arboretum
▫▪▪▪▫	Overhead cable-car	🐦	Aviary, bird sanctuary
🚂	Tourist or steam railway		

Additional symbols

═══ ═══	Motorway (unclassified)	✉ ☎	Post office – Telephone centre
❶ ❶	Junction: complete, limited	⌧	Covered market
⊏══⊐ ═══	Pedestrian street	•╳•	Barracks
ɪ═════ɪ	Unsuitable for traffic, street subject to restrictions	△	Swing bridge
▭▭▭▭	Steps – Footpath	⌣ ╳	Quarry – Mine
🚆 🚍	Railway – Coach station	B F	Ferry (river and lake crossings)
▫┼┼┼┼┼▫	Funicular – Rack-railway	🚢	Ferry services: Passengers and cars
━━ ◉	Tram – Metro, underground	⛴	Foot passengers only
Bert (R.)...	Main shopping street	③	Access route number common to MICHELIN maps and town plans

Abbreviations and special symbols

A	Agricultural office (Chambre d'agriculture)	P	Local authority offices (Préfecture, sous-préfecture)
C	Chamber of commerce (Chambre de commerce)	POL.	Police station (Police)
H	Town hall (Hôtel de ville)	🛡	Police station (Gendarmerie)
J	Law courts (Palais de justice)	T	Theatre (Théâtre)
M	Museum (Musée)	U	University (Université)
		⌂	Hotel
		🅿	Park and Ride
		⛱	Beach

COMPANION PUBLICATIONS

travelguide.michelin.com
www.viamichelin.com

MAPS OF ITALY

Michelin map 563 Italia Centro
A map of central Italy on a scale of
1:400 000 with an index of place names
and town plans of Florence and Rome

Atlas Italia
A practical, spiral-bound atlas on a
scale of 1:300 000 with an index of
place names and maps of 70 cities
and conurbations

Michelin map 735 Italia
A practical road map on a scale of
1:1 000 000 which provides an overall
view of the Italian road network.

ROUTE PLANNING

Michelin is pleased to offer a
route planning service at
www.viamichelin.com.

Personalised route plans, comprehensive
maps, addresses of hotels and
restaurants featured in *The Red Guides*
and practical and tourist information.

**YOUR OPINION IS ESSENTIAL
TO IMPROVING OUR PRODUCTS**

*Help us by answering the
questionnaire on our website:*
satisfaction.michelin.com

NOTES

Michelin Travel Partner

Société par actions simplifiées au capital de 15 044 940 EUR
27 cours de l'Ile Seguin - 92100 Boulogne Billancourt (France)
R.C.S. Nanterre 433 677 721

© Michelin Travel Partner
ISBN 978-2-067242-49-4
Printed: July 2020
Printed and bound in France : Imprimerie CHIRAT, 42540 Saint-Just-la-Pendue - N° 202003.0190

Although the information in this guide was believed by the authors and publisher to be accurate
and current at the time of publication, they cannot accept responsibility for any inconvenience,
loss, or injury sustained by any person relying on information or advice contained in this guide.
Things change over time and travellers should take steps to verify and confirm information,
especially time-sensitive information related to prices, hours of operation, and availability.